THE SIXTEEN-TRILLION-DOLLAR MISTAKE

THE SIXTEEN-TRILLION-DOLLAR MISTAKE

How the U.S. Bungled Its National Priorities
from the New Deal to the Present

Bruce S. Jansson

COLUMBIA UNIVERSITY PRESS   NEW YORK

Columbia University Press
Publishers Since 1893
New York   Chichester, West Sussex

Library of Congress Cataloging-in-Publication Data
Jansson, Bruce S.
The sixteen-trillion-dollar mistake : how the U.S. bungled
its national priorities from the New Deal to the present /
Bruce S. Jansson.
p. cm.
Includes bibliographical references and index.
ISBN 0–231–11432–X (cloth)
ISBN 0–231–11433–8 (paper)
1. Human services—United States—Finance.
2. Government spending policy—United States.
3. United States—Appropriations and expenditures.
4. United States—Politics and government—20th century.
I. Title.
HV95 .J355 2001
361.973—dc21   00–060323

Casebound editions of Columbia University Press books
are printed on permanent and durable acid-free paper.

Printed in the United States of America
c 10 9 8 7 6 5 4 3 2
p 10 9 8 7 6 5 4 3 2

To the staff and director of the Center on Budget and Policy Priorities, who courageously reform national priorities on a day-to-day basis

CONTENTS

PREFACE

I first became interested in national priorities in the wake of Desert Storm when the press was filled with stories about a potential peace dividend. My initial research on the politics of peace dividends soon expanded into a critical analysis of federal spending priorities from the presidency of Franklin Delano Roosevelt (when the United States first institutionalized a large federal budget) through the presidency of Bill Clinton.

I soon encountered major challenges. To analyze federal spending priorities, I had to engage in multidisciplinary research that spanned military and foreign policy, social policy, tax policy, and budget policy—topics usually examined separately from one another. I had to analyze the politics of spending from the perspectives of both the White House and Congress, because presidents propose budgets while Congress actually crafts budget and tax legislation. I had to analyze historical budget data maintained by the Office of Management and Budget and the Congressional Budget Office to estimate the magnitude of spending and tax mistakes. And I had to cover the budget politics of eleven presidencies.

Thus began a nearly ten-year project that took me to five presidential libraries and extended research visits to the Library of Congress. Three grants helped finance this project: the Lyndon Baines Johnson Foundation, the John Randolph Haynes and Dora Haynes Foundation, and the Zumberge Faculty Research Innovation Fund of the University of Southern California. The Lucy and Henry Moses Distinguished Visiting Research Professorship at the School of Social Work of Hunter College allowed me to devote an entire year to archival research at the beginning of this project.

I am indebted to many people. I gained many insights from interviewing Paul Warnke, Robert Jervis, Lawrence Korb, Steven Kosiak, Iris Lav, Wendall Primus, Seymour Melman, Martha Phillips, Robert Reischauer, Isabel Sawhill, and Robert Greenstein, as well as from a telephone interview of Robert McNamara. Three anonymous reviewers saved me from many errors of fact and interpretation.

The archivists at the Franklin Roosevelt, Harry Truman, Dwight Eisenhower, and Lyndon Johnson presidential libraries, as well as the Richard Nixon Presidential Materials, helped me navigate their archives. (I am particularly indebted to Dennis Bilger of the Truman Library and David Humphreys, formerly of the Johnson Library.) Bruce Martin, director of research facilities at the Library of Congress, helped me secure a research office at the library on two occasions and facilitated my work in many other ways. I secured many ideas for this project while working in the Millikan Library at the California Institute of Technology, where the staff was always helpful to me.

Sarah-Jane Dodd performed numerous computer runs of historical budget data that led to the figures I use at the end of many chapters and throughout chapter 15. Without her inspired assistance I could not have made an estimate of the magnitude of budget mistakes since 1933. Jeanette Cambra and Martin Munguia provided indispensable help in photocopying and summarizing hundreds of articles in the mass media on specific budget controversies during the seven decades this book considers.

Rino Patti and Marilyn Flynn, deans at the School of Social Work at the University of Southern California, facilitated leaves to do archival research and writing and gave me funding for research assistance at pivotal points.

John Michel, acquisitions editor for Columbia University Press, encouraged me to proceed with this project and provided helpful guidance along the way. Anne McCoy, Columbia's managing editor, expertly shepherded this book through the production process. Polly Kummel skillfully copyedited the text, immeasurably improving its flow and accuracy.

Lee Hood, the noted biologist, encouraged me to undertake the project at its outset. Harlan and Martha Rosacker allowed me to stay with them in Washington, D.C., for an extended period and lent sympathetic ears as I discussed my central arguments. Barbara Kraft and Kathy Malone, friends and historians, repeatedly urged me onward and provided me with many insights. Ruth Britton, librarian at the University of Southern California, routed relevant material to me on numerous occasions. Dona Munker provided invaluable editorial advice to me in the early stages of the writing process, helping me to establish a writing style for the book that would make it accessible both to a scholarly and broader audience.

Betty Ann, my long-suffering spouse, put up with my scholarly debris and my numerous absences for many years. Without her support I could never have completed this book.

All errors of omission or commission are mine alone.

THE SIXTEEN-TRILLION-DOLLAR MISTAKE

CHAPTER

1

Failed National Priorities
from FDR to Clinton

Every nation must decide how much to tax its private
wealth and how to spend the resulting revenues. Public
servants probably make no choices that are more
important—choices that singly and in tandem determine a nation's priorities. From 1931 through 2004 the
federal government will have spent roughly $56 trillion
in constant 1992 dollars—and that's not even counting
more than $12.8 trillion just since 1968 in indirect
spending through so-called tax expenditures, the tax
concessions to individuals and corporations that
deplete federal tax revenues.[1]

My interest in this subject was piqued in the early
1990s when considerable pressure for a "peace dividend"
surfaced as the cold war ended. When I found no
extended critical analysis of U.S. national priorities in
recent American history, I decided to write one, beginning in the early 1930s when the federal government first
developed a large ongoing budget. (Large budgets during
the Civil War and World War I returned to peacetime
levels once those wars were over.) This analysis of the fed-

eral budget extends through eleven presidencies and encompasses government budget projections through 2004.

Curiously, presidential scholars, historians, and political scientists have not written extensively about national priorities, whether the tension between guns and butter, battles between liberals and conservatives about budgets, or the economy of scarcity that has often bedeviled the domestic agenda in a low-tax nation with high military spending. Indeed, indexes of presidential biographies by such noted scholars as Stephen Ambrose and Robert Dallek do not even list *budgets*—a remarkable omission in light of the prevalence of budget controversies during the Johnson and Nixon presidencies.[2] Yet choices about budget priorities are arguably the most important made by the federal government, profoundly shaping the well-being of citizens, the nation's security, and the national economy.

I began this research with the suspicion that Americans had made numerous errors in their national priorities from the presidencies of Franklin Roosevelt through Bill Clinton. I knew, for example, that Americans devoted smaller resources to their domestic agendas in recent decades than most European nations—and that the United States had spent larger sums than these European nations on military forces when measured as a percentage of gross domestic product (GDP).[3] I knew that certain resources had been wasted on tax expenditures (or loopholes) for affluent Americans, corporate subsidies (or corporate welfare), and pork-barrel spending. I knew that excessive deregulation had sometimes required large federal outlays, as in the case of the savings and loan debacle of the 1980s and 1990s. And I suspected that the nation had spent excessively on interest payments on the national debt at certain points in recent history.

I was surprised, however, to find that Americans had, conservatively, made fiscal and tax errors totaling roughly $16 trillion from 1931 through 2004. That's $16 trillion in constant 1992 dollars, which is how the Office of Management and Budget states budget figures in its *Budget of the U.S. Government, FY 2000, Historical Tables* (1999), the source of much of my data. (In fact, if we were to convert that enormous figure to account for inflation in the remainder of the decade, it would be $18.46 trillion.) Many Americans underestimate the magnitude of mistaken budgetary and tax choices because they associate them only with specific instances of fraud or corruption—such as a specific defense contractor's overbilling of the government or a specific welfare recipient's fraud. Or voters associate these errors with "government bureaucracy." Such instances of waste ought not be dismissed and should be rigorously investigated, but they amount to pennies on the dollar when compared with failed national priorities. Failed priorities stem from misguided assumptions, such as overestimating the amount of weaponry or the numbers of troops needed to provide national security. Or they occur when the nation undertakes an ill-advised military engagement such as the Vietnam War. Or when public officials fail to foresee the negative consequences of their budgetary choices, such as the sheer size of interest payments from deficit spending that will take significant percentages of future budgets. Or when lobbyists obtain funding for projects or tax concessions that do not serve the public interest, such as for a weapons system that is not needed or by convincing legislators to write into the nation's tax code specific concessions that deplete the treasury for many decades. Or when presidents and Congress establish tax rates at excessively low levels, thereby depleting the resources available for military or domestic programs.

Such fiscal and tax errors have often had negative consequences for the domestic agenda. With a substantial portion of the federal budget already preempted for military allocations and veterans' benefits, as well as interest payments on the national debt, scant resources have been available for critical domestic programs when tax and fiscal errors also depleted the treasury. The so-called discretionary budget, which is determined annually in the push-and-pull of budgetary politics, has been especially devastated since the early 1930s in such pivotal periods as the New Deal, the Fair Deal, the Great Society, and the Clinton administration. (Entitlements such as Social Security, Medicare, and Medicaid are more immune to annual budget battles because they are automatically funded to the level of benefits claimed during a specific year.)

Liberals, who favor an expanded domestic agenda and usually are unable to secure tax increases, should have been militant in seeking cuts in mistaken allocations and tax loopholes since the 1930s. Curiously, however, they often let conservatives pose as the advocates of responsible finance, even when conservatives favored ill-advised tax loopholes and corporate welfare, excessive military spending, pork, or deregulation that would ultimately require mammoth federal expenditures.[4] Indeed, conservatives often sent liberals to their political graves by calling them "tax-and-spend liberals," a phrase attributed to Harry Hopkins, Franklin Roosevelt's top domestic aide, before the congressional elections of 1938. Although Hopkins denied that he had said that Democrats would "tax and tax, and spend and spend, and elect and elect" if they prevailed in those elections, Republicans seized on the phrase and have used it to tar liberals ever since.[5]

Had the $16 trillion in squandered resources been diverted to the domestic agenda, American society would have been dramatically transformed. For roughly $2.15 trillion (in 1992 dollars), for example, the United States could have funded, from 1945 to 1996, free child care for women with the smallest annual incomes, substantially subsidized child care for women in the next two income quintiles, and funded one thousand primary-care health clinics to serve twenty-five million Americans in medically understaffed urban and rural areas.[6] It could have increased funding for entitlements—such as food stamps, Supplemental Security Income, Medicaid, and the earned income tax credit—designed to assist (mostly working) people in the two lowest quintiles of annual income. The United States could have increased funding for social investment programs, here defined as certain education, social service, employment, and training programs, mostly funded by the discretionary budget. (These programs averaged less than 1 percent of the federal budget from 1944 to 1966, 3.7 percent in the 1970s, and 2.7 percent from 1980 to 1994.[7]) It could have lowered taxes of low- and moderate-income people or granted them major tax concessions to help them buy houses, set up businesses, and further their education. Or it could have vastly increased the amounts spent on public transportation, environmental cleanup and protection, and programs to repair the nation's fraying infrastructure. The squandered resources would have provided $15.78 trillion—more than sixty times the entire domestic discretionary budget of 2000—to more than double the U.S. discretionary budget each year since 1933. Or the United States could have substantially increased some of its entitlements, such as expanding Medicaid to cover everyone or almost everyone without health insurance, from 1965 through 2004.

Skeptics might contend that it is unfair to criticize fiscal errors with the advantage of hindsight. In fact, however, dissenters from both parties *did* criticize most of the fiscal and tax mistakes discussed in this book in each presidential era. Such dissent would include FDR's effort to use taxes to fund a larger portion of World War II, the insistence of Sen. Claude Pepper, D-Fla., that civilian agencies take control of military procurement in World War II and the cold war, the determined behind-the-scenes opposition of Sen. Mike Mansfield, D-Mont., to the Vietnam War, and the opposition of Sen. John McCain, R-Ariz., to pork-barrel spending in the late 1990s. Citizens and think tanks that have questioned failed priorities would include William Kaufmann and his estimates of necessary U.S. military spending after the cold war.[8]

This book is an interdisciplinary and critical analysis of American national priorities from 1933 through 2004. It melds military, tax, budget, and social policies—subjects usually discussed in isolation from one another—into a discussion of the fiscal and tax choices by successive presidents and Congresses. It draws heavily on archives in the Franklin Roosevelt, Harry Truman, Dwight Eisenhower, and Lyndon Johnson presidential libraries, as well as in the Nixon Presidential Materials. (Congress placed Nixon's papers in a special archive, now located at the University of Maryland, because it feared he might destroy some of them.) It both explores the hypothesis that Americans could have greatly enriched their domestic agenda had they pruned excessive expenditures by the military, for corporate subsidies, and for pork and estimates the magnitude of the failed priorities. Chapters 2 through 14 provide a blow-by-blow description of priorities of presidents and Congresses from FDR to Clinton, placing them in their political context. Chapter 15 provides the data that support my contention that the United States has squandered nearly $16 trillion.

A brief technical note: although specific chapters describe budget data in terms of the dollar's value at the time, summary data at the ends of chapters, as well as in chapter 15, are presented in constant 1992 dollars. (Overview data rely heavily on the historical tables issued annually by the Office of Management and Budget as part of its review of the federal budget.) Total federal receipts, outlays, surpluses, and deficits include the receipts and outlays of all government programs, including those that, like Social Security, have been placed "off budget" at specific points in time. In each chapter I present an overview of fiscal and tax errors and estimate their magnitude in chapter 15. Estimates of projected expenditures and revenues for fiscal years 1999 through 2004 come from the Office of Management and Budget, *Budget of the U.S. Government, FY 2000, Historical Tables*.

2

Roosevelt as Magician

Considering that federal government spending today is equal to roughly 20 percent of the gross domestic product, government spending into the 1930s was relatively low—roughly 10 percent of the GDP. Moreover, roughly one third of these resources were devoted to military spending and veterans' benefits, reducing expenditures on the New Deal to less than 50 percent of these small government budgets. I contend that the United States developed such a small domestic agenda during the largest economic catastrophe in the nation's history partly because the federal government lacked sufficient revenues. Even with the diminished national economy during the Great Depression, the United States could have collected nearly $1 trillion (in constant 1992 dollars) without imposing undue hardship on those taxpayers who were gainfully employed.

Roosevelt's Grim Options

Franklin Delano Roosevelt knew he faced a grim situation in the summer of 1932 as he began his campaign against Herbert Hoover for the presidency. He knew that the Great Depression had cut federal tax revenues in half—to a little more than $2 billion—and that economic activity was at a standstill. He knew that Hoover had markedly increased taxes in 1932 to try to contain the growing deficits, but Roosevelt also knew that revenues would still be insufficient to pay the regular costs of government, much less emergency programs to help destitute Americans. He was familiar with the fiscal realities that he would likely confront as president if the depression did not lift—he had seen its consequences as governor of New York State, where state and local finances, which hinged on property and sales taxes, had been devastated. If the federal government did *not* bail out states and localities, perhaps on the order of billions of dollars, many would be unable to foot the cost of feeding and housing millions of unemployed people—unemployment insurance, federal welfare programs, and food stamps did not yet exist. (Roosevelt knew that private agencies could not address the enormity of the population's needs; he had seen about a third of the agencies go bankrupt in New York City between 1929 and 1939 as private donations ceased.)[1] And he knew that if the federal government failed to provide substantial subsidies to unemployed people, mass starvation would ensue unless the Great Depression miraculously ended.

Yet Roosevelt also knew that he risked political suicide if he openly disclosed any plans to bail out state and local governments. No precedent existed for large peacetime spending by the federal government; the federal outlays totaled only $4.2 billion in 1933, or 8 percent of the gross domestic product (it was 19.7 percent of the GDP in 1998). Conservatives, who believed that the Constitution did not even vest the federal government with relief responsibilities, much less the power to spend on other social programs, would have lambasted him as violating the Constitution. Nor would Americans have been likely to elect a president who openly discussed massive increases in federal spending because they had a puritan fetish about balancing the budget *and* eliminating the debt that had accumulated in World War I.

Roosevelt was in an impossible situation. If he did not acknowledge that he might have to spend considerable sums to avert mass starvation, his foes might accuse him of not leveling with voters during the campaign. If he *did* advocate increased spending, Republicans could portray him as a big spender. He resolved this dilemma by a mixture of allusion and artifice—a combination that not only got him elected but protected him from political attack.

The allusion was a vaguely worded statement that he might resort to greater spending; in a campaign speech he made an analogy between the nation's economy and a family's finances. A family must live within its means or it will go bankrupt, he argued, but it may live beyond its means for "a year or two" if it encounters an economic emergency, by financing this emergency with credit if it lacks sufficient savings. He coupled this veiled reference to temporary deficits with an equally subtle promise to relieve "starvation and dire suffering," no matter the cost, and to make doing so a higher priority than balancing the budget. He provided no detailed spending proposals and expressed his fervent hope that the depression would suddenly end.

His artifice was the political sleight-of-hand for funding for the New Deal. On the one hand, he promised to cut government spending by 25 percent so he could balance the federal budget—well aware that he would probably have to increase spending to avert mass starvation. Roosevelt followed the suggestion of Henry Morgenthau, his secretary of the treasury and economic adviser, to segregate his "emergency spending" from the "regular," or ordinary budget, of the government.[2] The emergency budget would consist of those programs directed at relieving economic suffering, much as presidents establish wartime budgets to finance emergency military needs. He proposed to finance this still-undisclosed emergency budget by borrowing; tax revenues would fund the ongoing "regular" costs of government agencies and the military. It was a brilliant solution that allowed Roosevelt to simultaneously to balance his (regular) budgets while seeking billions of "off-budget" spending increases in the emergency budget. To defuse Republican attacks that this accounting device was a ruse to obscure actual government deficits, Roosevelt countered that Hoover had used the same technique when he had placed the spending of one of his agencies (the Reconstruction Finance Corp.) outside the regular budget—just as corporations sometimes fund permanent capital improvements from accounts separate from those that finance their regular operating expenses.

Roosevelt would not have had to use this device if he had increased taxes substantially in 1933, but he knew that trying to raise taxes would be politically impossible. Congress had raised taxes significantly in 1932, because Hoover wanted to cut the nation's growing deficits, and would be ill disposed to raise them again. He knew that citizens and corporations would object to—and probably be unable to pay—tax increases during a period of economic catastrophe. Southern Democrats, in particular those who chaired the powerful Senate Finance and House Ways and Means committees, would oppose tax increases, as would conservatives. Working-class and middle-class Americans—many of whom had voted Democratic for the first time in 1932—were not accustomed to paying income taxes and might abandon the party in future elections if Roosevelt tried to broaden the income tax to include them; even employed Americans were financially insecure and resistive to new taxes.[3] Roosevelt also knew that a grassroots tax revolt against local property taxes had commenced in many localities in the wake of the Great Depression; the revolt could easily spread to the federal level if Congress agreed to impose new taxes.[4]

Even at this early point, however, Roosevelt should have realized that his domestic agenda would be imperiled if he failed to increase federal tax revenues during his term in office. The problem lay in the federal income tax, which had been enacted in 1913. Rather than taxing the population broadly, the tax law applied to only 1.7 million American families in 1932; fewer than 300,000 families accounted for more than 90 percent of the revenue it brought in. While as many as 30 percent of Americans were unemployed during the Great Depression, 70 percent of taxpayers (or more) were gainfully employed—and considerable numbers could have paid taxes to varying degrees. In fact, fewer than 5 percent of families and individuals paid any federal income tax in 1933.[5] Federal income taxes amounted to only 0.7 percent of the GDP in 1934, compared to 5.8 percent in 1950, 7.9 percent in 1960, and 9 percent in 1970. (Corporate income was barely taxed either, with corporate income taxes equal to only 0.6 percent of the GDP in 1934, compared to 3.8 percent in 1950, 4.1 percent in 1960, and 3.3 percent in 1970.)[6] In short, although the GDP had plummeted in 1929, it amounted to $61.1 billion in 1934 and rose considerably during the remainder of the 1930s—but was virtually untaxed by the standards of succeeding decades. The arithmetic was simple: if Roosevelt failed to increase federal income taxes markedly during the New Deal, his programs would require huge deficits, which would, in turn, make Congress reluctant to allocate funds sufficient to address the malaise of the unemployed. Moreover, the lack of a funding base for the New Deal would contribute to the notion that its programs were temporary because they lacked ongoing funding sources.

Roosevelt's plan to segregate the regular and the emergency budgets reached the press on February 19, 1933. But few Americans paid attention to this obscure accounting change. Noting that Roosevelt was imitating corporate accounting procedures, the *New York Times* dryly observed that this technique would make the official budget deficit shrink if Roosevelt cut the spending of government departments.[7]

As the economist Paul Samuelson noted years later, the distinction between regular and emergency budgets made no sense from an accounting perspective. Roosevelt developed a huge emergency budget without obtaining tax increases to pay for it, which meant he would run a government deficit even if his two-budget approach obscured it. Roosevelt was not interested in the niceties of formal accounting, however, but in developing a political means for reconciling his pledge to balance the budget with his pledge to avert starvation. It was brilliant strategy even if it stretched the truth.

Roosevelt as Penny Pincher

Roosevelt could have remained silent until his inauguration in March but chose to lobby Congress on January 7 for legislation that would allow him to fulfill his promise to cut the regular budget by 25 percent. Accused of seeking "dictatorial powers" because the Constitution reserves to Congress the power of appropriation, Roosevelt proposed legislation that would grant the president the power to impound appropriations, including as much as $1.06 billion set aside for the Veterans' Bureau.[8] He planned to make drastic cuts in government, in part by ordering mass dismissals of government employees.[9] On February 10, House Democratic leaders granted Roosevelt unprecedented powers over the federal economy by approving legislation that allowed him to abolish bureaus, cut salaries, reduce or suspend a range of government programs, and impound spending for two years with minimal congressional participation. These powers were so sweeping that even Senate Democrats were stunned by what their House counterparts had done.[10]

Stung by charges that he sought dictatorial powers, Roosevelt proffered a compromise the next day but still sought unprecedented presidential powers to reorganize the government. As Democratic leaders in Congress were discussing FDR's proposal to cut the regular budget, the cabinet secretaries, including the secretary of defense, contended that doing so would require the dismissal of twenty-five thousand employees, the retirement of part of the fleet, abandonment of the border patrol, and withdrawal of diplomats from many nations.[11] Faced with these pressures, Congress decided on February 20 not to grant Roosevelt powers of impoundment and to give him only limited powers to reorganize the government.

Arguing that "too often in recent history liberal governments have been wrecked on the rocks of loose fiscal policy," Roosevelt resumed his budget-cutting offensive immediately after his inauguration on March 4. His first targets were veterans' benefits and the salaries of federal employees, from which he hoped to realize savings of $500 million.[12] Veteran's benefits originally were limited to those who had been injured during conflict or who had served in wars, but in the 1920s and early 1930s Congress had expanded eligibility to include veterans injured during peacetime and awarded pensions for brief service, as well as widows whose husbands did not die of war injuries. Payments for disabilities, moreover, did not fully distinguish between major disabilities and lesser ones, so veterans with minor injuries often received large payments. Roosevelt sought to restore the original intent for veterans' benefits: compensation for injuries sustained in combat and pensions for wartime service. He proposed to cut $400 million from the roughly $1 billion appropriation. He started by eliminating the $200 million paid annually to veterans of the Spanish-American War who had not incurred battlefield injuries. Because constituent pressure would mean that Congress would oppose these cuts, Roosevelt wanted the power to cut these benefits unilaterally. He also wanted to cut the salaries of federal employees by 15 percent in 1933 and 1934, which would provide savings of $150 million, coupled with savings of $500 million more from his reorganization of the federal bureaucracy. These various cuts and savings would, Roosevelt contended, allow him to make good on his campaign pledge to cut the regular budget by 25 percent.

In mid-March a bipartisan majority in Congress approved the Economy Act, which that granted Roosevelt powers to reorganize the federal government. On March 21 he announced cuts in veterans' benefits that totaled $508 million—he reduced Spanish-American War pensions by $95 million, slashed disability payments, and suspended all admissions to veterans' homes and hospitals except for emergency care.[13] In late March he proposed regulations that would cut $250 million from the budget by eliminating agencies and reorganizing government, $75 million by cutting federal employees' salaries by 15 percent, and $75 million by cutting the post office. He announced that as many as 406,000 veterans would lose their pensions and another 1.4 million pensions would be reduced by April 2. By April 7 Roosevelt had established committees in each government department to reduce its operating costs by 31 percent. He also proposed to reduce the military budgets, with reductions of $365 million rumored for the army alone. He even floated a proposal to raise another $500 million in revenue by levying special taxes on beverages and sugar.[14]

These proposals were met with ferocious protest. Defenders of the War Department's budget suggested that pacifists had persuaded Roosevelt to seek wrongheaded economies. Veterans' organizations convinced thousands of veterans to send letters to members of Congress; one veteran complained that his pension had been cut from $120 to $80 even though he had lost a leg and had shrapnel fragments lodged in his spine. Claiming they were already underpaid, government workers demanded that their pay cuts be less severe and limited to a single year.[15]

Ultimately, they forced Roosevelt to retreat on several fronts; for example, he established a ceiling of 25 percent on reductions in veterans' disability payments. He held his ground on other cuts, however, and asserted that he would meet his goal of reducing government spending by 25 percent on June 1. But by June Congress had fully entered the fray against Roosevelt. The Senate imperiled $170 million in savings by encouraging a "pro-vet stampede," proposing to restore benefits for 150,000 veterans of World War I who had not enlisted until after the armistice.[16] Because he needed the goodwill of Congress to enact his New Deal legislation and because he still wanted to cut the budget, Roosevelt backed down on some of his recommended cuts while threatening to veto excessive benefits.

Roosevelt had succeeded in establishing his credentials as a frugal president. Summarizing his cutting of $1 billion from the budget he inherited from Hoover, the *New York Times* lauded him for "the greatest government retrenchment in [American] history."[17] Roosevelt vowed to bring the regular budget, which was still running a small deficit, into balance with his next budget.

The depression had not lifted by early 1933, and Roosevelt knew that his vague promise to place no limits on spending to avert suffering could cost billions of dollars and set a precedent. He wanted to show that he meant to balance the regular budget *before* he initiated the emergency one, thus diminishing the political risks when Republicans attacked his spending increases. He also wanted to preserve his credibility with the southern

Democrats who chaired virtually every committee in Congress, including the pivotal appropriations committees, and on whose support he would depend for the funding of his relief and work-relief programs.

Gingerly Seeking Resources for the New Deal

Within weeks of assuming office, Roosevelt began a fiscal revolution that quintupled domestic spending by 1934. He initiated his bold program of "emergency" spending with a message to Congress on March 31, 1933, that advocated making grants to the states for relief and initiating "a broad public works labor-creating program."[18] But Roosevelt chose to minimize the fiscal effects of these measures because he did not want to jeopardize his new reputation for frugality. He noted during a press conference on April 7, for example, that the Civilian Conservation Corps would cost only $250 million and direct relief to the states only $500 million—sums more than offset by the nearly $1 billion in cuts in the regular budget.[19] True to his word, Roosevelt sought only $500 million for the Federal Emergency Relief Administration (FERA); Congress approved the enabling legislation on May 12, 1933, for the agency that would oversee relief expenditures. In a message to Congress on May 17, Roosevelt finally hinted at the revolutionary course on which he was embarked. "A careful survey convinces me that approximately $3 billion can be invested in useful and necessary public construction," while putting to work the largest number of people possible, he said. The money was to come not from general tax revenues but from borrowing to be financed by "a form or forms of new taxation" totaling $220 million per year.[20] But he focused on the frugality of his program, saying the federal government would assist states with their relief costs *only* when localities, states, and private charities have done "everything that they could possibly do within reason."[21] All told, he sought roughly $3.75 billion from Congress and promptly received it.

Although he had decided to segregate his emergency spending from his regular budget, he artfully camouflaged this intention in the spring of 1933 by implying that tax increases and spending cuts would offset his new spending. He continued his attack on the regular budget by, for example, issuing a June 6 statement on cuts in veterans' allowances and a June 10 announcement of an executive order that abolished many government agencies.[22] As if to underscore his frugality, Roosevelt spent the emergency allocation so slowly that the *New Republic* angrily complained that he was not helping poverty-stricken people and even had diverted some emergency money to augment spending in the regular budget that he had just slashed.[23]

Roosevelt's aides established administrative guidelines in 1933 for his largest work and work-relief programs (the FERA, CCC, and Public Works Administration) that emphasized their frugality. Grants were to go only to those states, for example, that could show they lacked the ability to meet the relief needs of their population. Wages in the work programs were set at subsistence levels, especially for workers in unskilled or semi-skilled jobs. Federal officials urged states and localities to contribute resources and supplies whenever possible. Expensive public works projects, such as dams and airports, were screened so rigorously that getting to the construction phase took years. When Roosevelt initiated a huge public works program in November 1933—the Civilian Works Administration (CWA)—but he chose not to seek additional funding for it, preferring to divert money from the Public Works Administration.[24]

Roosevelt did not tip his hand about the magnitude of the spending revolution that became the hallmark of the New Deal until January 1934, when he released a budget so large that the *New York Times* described it as "the most extraordinary budget in the history of the United States."[25] It proposed spending $10.6 billion on relief and work-relief programs and another $4 billion to cover costs of the national debt and the new borrowing required to finance the emergency budget. British commentators were amazed at the "staggering deficits." Members of Congress, who thought Roosevelt would stick to his cautious funding of relief and work-relief programs in 1933, were caught off guard by the size of Roosevelt's budget.

Roosevelt had carefully done his political spadework before seeking these monster appropriations. He had sought far smaller amounts in 1933, his first year in office, so that he could construct a national bipartisan constituency for his emergency expenditures if the depression did not lift by 1934. During his first year he focused on developing an administrative apparatus for relief and work-relief programs, establishing rules for distributing relief money to the states and building a regional network of federal officials who could work closely with state officials. The PWA and the CWA, working closely with state and local officials as well as with members of Congress, developed a national wish list of public works projects. With thousands of projects identified and the apparatus in place to implement them, Roosevelt had made it virtually impossible for conservative political opponents to succeed. Because the work-relief programs were carefully distributed among the constituencies of *all* politicians, even Republicans from affluent districts dared not vote against the appropriations. By setting wages at low levels, Roosevelt deflected charges of waste. By giving local officials a large role in devising work projects and by letting states establish their own standards of relief, he minimized the political fallout from the charge that federal authorities were usurping the roles of state and local governments.[26]

To obtain even greater support Roosevelt compared the nation's struggle with the Great Depression to a war. Noting that when hostilities cease, wartime spending ends, he insisted emergency spending to avert starvation would cease when the depression lifted. He did not seek to build a lasting edifice, he insisted, but merely temporary programs to get the nation through the emergency.[27] He used the war analogy again on January 5, 1934, to demonstrate his frugality, predicting the New Deal would cost only $15 billion whereas the country had spent $25 billion on World War I.[28] The outlays for the New Deal would prove, he also argued, more cost effective than wartime expenses: the nation would emerge from the depression with roads, bridges, dams, reforestation, airports, and myriad other improvements that would contribute to its economic growth, whereas the tangible legacy of World War I was only nonproductive goods such as artillery and ammunition.

Keeping Conservatives at Bay

Roosevelt and Harry Hopkins, his chief domestic aide, also realized that asking aid recipients to work for their benefits was more palatable to many Americans than welfare. They initiated the PWA and the CCC, both for altruistic reasons and to increase political support for the New Deal. They vastly increased their work-relief programs in the fall of 1933 when they created the CWA, which put sixteen million Americans to work on 190,000 projects between November 1933 and January 1934. Whereas the PWA envisioned enrolling relatively small numbers of workers to build dams, bridges, and other complex structures, the CWA sought to put millions of Americans to work on projects that could be completed quickly.[29] The PWA emphasized skilled workers; the CWA focused on unskilled workers—those who could, for example, haul dirt in wheelbarrows to build roads. The press and radio news were full of reports of Americans working on an array of projects, locally as well as nationally. By underscoring the desire of unemployed people to work, the work-relief programs undercut the assertion that they corrupted the unemployed.

To de-emphasize the cost of these projects, Roosevelt stressed the "self-liquidating" nature of those projects that generated revenue or were partially financed with revolving loans. He continued to fund the Reconstruction Finance Corp.'s loans to local governments and to business. Although the government had to provide start-up funds for such projects as the Tennessee Valley Authority (TVA), it eventually received some income from them, such as by selling the electricity and fertilizer produced by the TVA.[30]

Even as early as 1933 Roosevelt used another tactic to defuse congressional opposition to his emergency spending. When seeking money from Congress, presidents usually "cost out" specific items, such as a dam or a section of highway. After reviewing these estimates, Congress approves (or rejects) the request in its appropriations. Had Roosevelt chosen this traditional method, his aides would have sought money from Congress only *after* they had defined the work-relief projects in detail, such as a specific bridge at a specific cost. Roosevelt asked Congress to appropriate lump sums for his relief and work-relief programs before any specific projects were planned.[31] He argued that projects could be initiated more rapidly if the money was available immediately.

He also favored lump-sum financing because it gave him greater flexibility in a period of economic uncertainty. The traditional approach would have given conservatives time for endless objections to specific projects: their cost, advisability, or administration. Confronted with requests for lump sums, however, they could only vote the appropriation up or down—a choice that usually forced them to vote for the entire sum, lest they be cast as obstructionists to the entire relief enterprise.

Roosevelt used another tactic to keep conservatives at bay. He surrounded himself with both those who approved of such massive spending—such as Harry Hopkins and Harold Ickes, the head of the PWA—and those who were against it, such as Morgenthau, the treasury secretary, and Lewis Douglas, the budget director. Thus both factions could claim they had the president's ear on the worth of maintaining such programs as the CWA. By encouraging rumors in the fall of 1934 that he might close the agency, Roosevelt promoted grassroots pressure on its behalf. He then closed the agency, received tens of thousands of letters urging him to reconsider, and quickly replaced the CWA with the Works Progress Administration (WPA).[32]

Populism Over Revenues

Roosevelt desperately needed new tax revenues so he could run on a balanced budget platform in 1936; tax revenues were insufficient to balance even the regular budget, which ran large deficits in 1933 and 1934. Liberals, such as Robert La Follette, then a Republican senator from Wisconsin, urged him to expand the income tax to include the middle class and even the working class, whose incomes were the largest untapped source. Concerned about budget deficits, some conservatives urged Roosevelt to enact a national sales tax.[33]

Roosevelt needed new tax revenues for several other reasons as well. He wanted to expand the New Deal; his work-relief programs reached only a third of unemployed and able-bodied Americans. And if he were going to institutionalize major federal expenditures for social policy, he had to find a significant source of money for the New Deal. Otherwise, people would assume that federal domestic spending that went beyond the minimal programs of the 1920s would incur huge deficits. He also wanted to jolt the economy out of the depression and needed to be able to spend to do that. With more revenue coming in, he could fund a larger New Deal and still incur deficits until the depression eased.

Although large increases in income taxes would have been politically difficult to obtain, they were feasible despite the widespread unemployment and suffering of the depression. The GDP, which had bottomed out at $57.4 billion in 1933, had risen to $69.5 billion in 1935 and would reach $96.5 billion in 1940.[34] It is true: many families had scant resources; 38 percent of U.S. families earned less than $1,000 in the early 1930s and 74 percent earned less than $2,000 when welfare departments contended that a family of four needed about $1,000 a year to meet "bare subsistence." Yet 26 percent of the population earned more than $2,000, 5 percent earned more than $4,000, and 1 percent earned more than $10,000.[35] But the tax law provided generous exemptions that equaled or exceeded annual incomes: $1,000 for single people and $2,500 for married couples earning more than $2,000 a year—plus exemptions of $400 for each dependent. A couple with two children paid no income taxes, then, at least until they earned more than $3,300—and not until they earned even more if they took various deductions, such as for home mortgages. (When placed in the context of 1982 wage scales, most people who earned less than $60,000 would have paid no federal income taxes.) These high exemptions meant that only 2.5 to 5 percent of the population paid income taxes from 1933 to 1939—and the thirteen thousand tax returns of people earning more than $50,000 accounted for 50 percent of all tax revenues from 1933 through 1939 when so many paid no income taxes at all.[36] Indeed, the government collected 1 percent of total personal income in the 1930s, compared to about 12 percent in 1982.[37]

Numerous critics of Roosevelt scored his reluctance to broaden the federal income tax in the mid-1930s. One hundred and one economists had urged the president soon after he took office to broaden the federal income tax to give the government more substantial resources.[38] La Follette wanted to cut exemptions for couples to $2,000 and for individuals to $800 to bring to one million the number of people who paid income taxes; in 1935 only 600,000 single people and families filed tax returns.[39] The Peoples' Lobby, led by the philosopher John Dewey, economist Paul Douglas, and theologian Reinhold Niebuhr, contended that the New Deal was unresponsive to the needs of many people because it was underfunded.[40] In addition, the United States was out of synch with European nations in regard to taxation and spending policies. Although the United States did not tax families with a net annual income of $2,000, the British, French, and Germans taxed them at 5.6 percent, 8.5 percent, and 15.8 percent, respectively. Whereas the United States taxed families with a net annual income of $5,000 at 2 percent, the British, French, and Germans taxed them at 14.2 percent, 17.2 percent, and 21.6 percent, respectively. (Similar discrepancies could be found in other net income categories.) Taxes on estates in these three nations were three to four times as great as in the United States up to levels of $2 million, above which they exceeded American rates by a ratio of 2 to 1.[41]

Roosevelt demurred from seeking major taxes for the same reasons he had not proposed them in 1933: he feared the middle class would bolt the Democratic Party and that conservatives demand spending cuts if he broached tax increases. He encountered a critic in 1934, however, who made taxes a central feature of his attack on Roosevelt. As part of his bid for national power, Sen. Huey Long, the Louisiana Democrat, proposed a "Share Our Wealth" program that included sharp tax increases for the wealthy and a sweeping tax on inheritances. Long, who announced in August 1935 that he would run for president, chided Roosevelt for emphasizing regressive excise, beer, food-processing, and liquor taxes, not to mention the large payroll taxes enacted that month as part of the Social Security Act.[42]

Roosevelt knew that Long's scheme was symbolic rather than revenue producing because the 5 percent of Americans with the most wealth already paid relatively high taxes—the highest marginal rates approached 70 percent. He decided, however, to outbid Long's Share the Wealth Plan by proposing to raise $250 million in new revenues by increasing the taxes on the wealthy. Roosevelt's proposal also allowed him portray the Republicans as insensitive to the needs of working people because the GOP had periodically sought regressive taxes, such as a national sales tax and additional excise taxes to balance the budget.

As the historian Mark Leff has noted, Roosevelt's decision not to seek large tax increases meant that he would have to continue to amass large deficits to fund his work-relief programs, which gave them a weak fiscal foundation.[43] His New Deal remained starved for resources. Other than closing some loopholes used by wealthy Americans and increasing corporate taxes somewhat, Roosevelt was unwilling to address an antiquated federal tax system that provided insufficient resources to address the needs of the population during a depression—or to institutionalize a welfare state in a nation that lagged behind European nations in funding an array of social programs.

Inventing Negative Images

Republicans were dealing with a president who by 1934 had built an intricate network of programs that assisted millions of Americans who might otherwise have experienced intolerable hunger, homelessness, and poverty. The GOP could not oppose these relief and work-relief programs without appearing to oppose the humanitarian principles on which they rested or the needs of their own constituents. The president insisted, moreover, that his vast spending from the off-budget emergency accounts did not preclude balancing the regular budget, which he continued to cut. Roosevelt was a master tactician—a politician who simply outdid Republicans on their budget-balancing and anti-spending policies while quintupling the domestic budget by 1934. He was an elusive target: just when he seemed vulnerable to charges that he was a big spender, he returned to budget balancing and frugality and even attacked Congress on numerous occasions for its budget-busting appropriations.

Republicans attacked Roosevelt's division of the budget into regular and emergency segments as a gimmick to disguise his deficits in 1933 and 1934. They attacked his use of lump-sum appropriations to fund work-relief and relief programs as a technique for avoiding congressional scrutiny. They attacked the administration of the New Deal programs, arguing that they were riddled with waste, graft, and patronage jobs. Nor did these attacks cease when Hopkins opened the books of local projects or when Roosevelt insisted that applicants for assistance not be asked about their party affiliation. Republicans charged that relief programs sapped the work ethic of recipients and that work-relief programs merely provided make-work or competed with private industry. They argued that Roosevelt should turn these programs over to the states or municipalities.[44]

Republicans had treated Roosevelt gingerly in 1933 but launched aggressive personal attacks on him in 1934 and thereafter. They argued that he sought to create permanent programs to build a political dynasty, akin to the urban machines of cities like Chicago and New York. They compared him to Stalin and subsequently to Hitler, contending that Roosevelt cynically manipulated an insecure public to follow him blindly. He wanted to usurp congressional powers, they argued, by proposing myriad programs, whereas previous presidents often had been content to let Congress fashion the domestic agenda.

Conservatives adroitly attacked the New Deal in a manner that was both clever and disingenuous. On the one hand, they castigated relief programs as sapping initiative—an argument that appeared to favor work-relief programs like the CWA, CCC, and PWA. On the other hand, they balked at funding the additional costs of work-relief programs, which had to pay not just the salaries of recipients but the costs of materials and supervision. (Work-relief programs cost roughly a third more than a program that merely provided welfare.[45]) Arguing that work relief competed unfairly with the private sector, Republicans failed to note that the private sector did not provide sufficient jobs to ease unemployment.

Conservatives flooded the nation with negative images, evoking large bureaucracies, wasted resources, patronage, graft, dampening of initiative, left-leaning officials, dynastic ambitions, and centralization. The public ignored the negative images in 1934 or even 1936, but they sowed seeds that might flower if Americans tired of the New Deal or if Roosevelt's popularity plummeted.[46]

To their delight, conservatives found some Democrats ready to join their vitriolic attacks. Members of the northern conservative wing of the Democratic Party, such as Al Smith, had mistrusted Roosevelt from the outset, but their dislike magnified as he aggressively used the powers of his office and the federal government to attack economic and social problems. Some significant defections had occurred by mid-1934, such as Lewis Douglas's resignation from the Bureau of the Budget on the ground that Roosevelt spent too much money. Some southern Democrats, whose ideology was closer to the Republicans' than the Roosevelt Democrats', worried that FDR might use the expanded powers of the government to attack racial policies in the South and would perhaps go so far as to support anti-lynching legislation. Some progressive Republicans like George Norris, the Republican senator from Nebraska who supported Roosevelt's work-relief projects and wanted the TVA extended to other river basins, also feared Roosevelt's expansion of the federal government. But Republicans had made only marginal progress by late 1935 in melding these disparate forces into a coherent entity that would oppose Roosevelt's policies, much less present a threat to his electoral base. But Republicans *had* fashioned a series of arguments that they might eventually be able to use to form a broad, conservative opposition to Roosevelt.[47]

Tilting at Windmills

Roosevelt hugely increased domestic spending on employment, training, education, and social services during his first four years (see "social investments" in fig. 2.1), a marked departure from tradition. Indeed, the New Deal was the *only* period in American history when such spending dominated the federal budget. Although the New Deal was a remarkable achievement, its scope was relatively small in light of the magnitude of the Great Depression and its effect on the populace: aggregate federal spending was roughly equal to 10 percent of the GDP, whereas it reached about 20 percent after 1950.

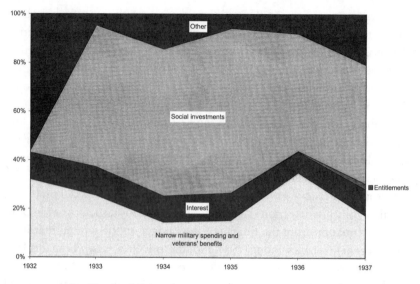

FIGURE 2.1 Five Types of Expenditures as Percentages of Total Federal Outlays, 1932–1937

Source: U.S. Bureau of the Budget, *Budgets of the U.S. Government, FYs 1933 Through 1939* (Ann Arbor, MI: University Microfilms, 1968).

Despite the widespread economic devastation wrought by the depression, which cast tens of millions of Americans into unemployment and poverty, Roosevelt had to use a complex strategy to fund the New Deal. He was like a magician, who entertains the audience with one hand, which diverts their attention from what the other hand is doing. Desperate to obtain resources for his domestic agenda, Roosevelt's tactics sometimes came back to haunt him. It was politically advantageous for him to contend that he sought only *emergency* spending that would be rescinded once the depression ended, but this tactic undermined the concept of an ongoing domestic budget that would address the various needs of the population—for economic assistance, housing, medical attention, education, employment, or job training. By defining much of the New Deal as emergency spending, Roosevelt gave conservatives a reason to rescind it as soon as the Great Depression lifted—a rationale they would readily use at the first opportunity. He might have framed the New Deal as an ongoing set of programs that also provided jobs for unemployed Americans. Public health, child welfare, and education programs could have hired tens of thousands of people—and served enduring functions even when the Great Depression ended.

Roosevelt made a single exception to his dictum that most social spending should cease when the depression ended: the programs of the Social Security Act. He defined these reforms as permanent, including the so-called social insurances (Social Security pensions and unemployment insurance), welfare programs (aid to dependent children, old age assistance, or aid to the blind), and small federal subsidies to the states for public health and child welfare programs. Unlike ordinary social programs, the social insurances had their own source of funds—payroll taxes—which immunized them from conservatives' attacks during the annual appropriations process. (Because they did not not rely on general tax revenues, they did not have to compete with the military or other programs.) Although they were minuscule by contemporary standards, the welfare programs of the Social Security Act also had immunity. They were dependent on general revenues for their funding, but the law defined them as "entitlements," to be automatically funded each year to the level of benefits claimed by those eligible. Thus the social insurance and welfare programs survived the end of the depression. Entitlements are necessary in a humane society, but so too are social programs that increase education, prevent illness, provide job training, pay for child care, or provide services to vulnerable populations.

Historians often portray the New Deal as mammoth, but it had relatively few resources. Because most of its expenditures were channeled to relief and work relief, it did not attempt to provide social programs. Some people received surplus food from distribution centers, but many others went hungry and were malnourished. When Eleanor Roosevelt commissioned her friend Lorena Hickok to send her daily reports as the reporter roamed the country investigating social conditions by car, the first lady was shocked to learn of the extent of human deprivation. A middle-class man lamented to Hickok that he could do nothing about his wife's rotting teeth because he lacked the money to pay for dental care.[48] Nor were the New Deal's expenditures sufficient to end the Great Depression.

The paltry size of the New Deal derived partly from inadequate tax revenues. Faced with unprecedented domestic needs during the Great Depression, the U.S. president and most members of Congress were unwilling to raise federal income taxes, as well as corporate income taxes, sufficiently to allow the government to fund its new responsibilities. It would be simplistic to blame Roosevelt, although he failed throughout the 1930s to assume a leadership role in expanding the federal income tax. Other politicians also failed to take leadership positions. Only a few, like La Follette, spoke out. Most Americans opposed broadening the income tax to include the middle and upper-middle classes, preferring that only those in the top 5 percent of annual income pay income taxes—and most preferred relatively low rates even for those in the top 5 percent. Politicians from both parties used the tax issue to partisan advantage, claiming the other party was a pro-tax party. While Roosevelt bragged in the presidential campaign of 1936 that he had *lowered* income taxes for 99 percent of taxpaying heads of household during his first term, for example, Republicans claimed he had increased taxes by $2 billion.[49] The failure to raise taxes in the New Deal, like many of the fiscal and tax errors discussed in this book, was a bipartisan affair in a nation that had not yet become accustomed to either a large federal government or the taxes needed to fund it. As chapter 3 details, low federal taxes not only crimped the New Deal but contributed to a paltry military force. Even if the United States had had the political will to contest Hitler's course of aggression, it lacked a tax base sufficient to fund a military force equipped to address global threats.

3

Roosevelt's Dilemma

The late 1930s and early 1940s provide a preview of the tension between guns and butter that would arise again on numerous occasions in the future. Could Roosevelt, the master tactician, preserve both, or would one prevail? With minimal tax revenues would Roosevelt be forced to choose between his New Deal and his desire to counter Hitler's flagrant aggression?

Roosevelt as Warrior-in-Waiting

Because they equated Roosevelt with the New Deal, few Americans realized that he had long been obsessed with military strategy. When asked later in his life what position he would have wanted had he not chosen politics, he answered, unhesitatingly, "An admiral."[1] Roosevelt had developed a love for the sea as a child and that led to an obsession with the navy as an adult. As a young man, he revered his uncle Theodore Roosevelt, admiring his assertive, gunslinging diplomacy in the Far East and in

Latin America. Unlike those progressives who opposed U.S. rearmament before World War I, FDR militantly supported his uncle's advocacy of preparedness and his desire to expand the U.S. Navy. Franklin Roosevelt became assistant secretary of the navy in 1913 and joined "militant admirals" in seeking a massive ship and troop buildup in the prewar years, but President Woodrow Wilson rejected it as provocative.[2] Like his uncle, FDR wanted U.S. military power to extend to the Philippines "and over the sea wherever [American] commerce may be."

He was in open conflict with American pacifists as well as the secretary of the navy, Josephus Daniels, whose reluctance to rearm Franklin Roosevelt sarcastically denounced. He attacked the administration's disinclination to rearm in favor of forming a council of national defense in 1915 to orchestrate rearmament; he also wanted the United States to enter the war nearly six months before it actually did, in April 1917.[3] He became a skillful propagandist for rearmament, telling hushed audiences about German designs on the Caribbean while entreating Wilson to enter the war in behind-the-scenes meetings.

Franklin Roosevelt believed Germany to be the only viable competitor of the United States, and he viewed Germans as a savage people with aggressive tendencies, which led the historian Robert Herzstein to call FDR a Teutonophobe.[4] Roosevelt predicted soon after the United States entered World War I that the country might need to lead a coalition to restrain Germany—and Adolf Hitler had decided by the early 1930s that "he would one day have to confront the United States."[5]

Roosevelt's views did not change in the decade after the First World War. He opposed reducing U.S. forces after the war and even favored universal military training for all youth until he realized that these views were politically unacceptable in a postwar nation that had reverted to isolationism. He advocated an ongoing French, U.S., and British alliance as the best way to counter renewed German expansionism. Roosevelt regarded Hitler as sinister even in 1933 and wrote in his edition of *Mein Kampf* that "this translation is so expurgated as to give a wholly false view of what Hitler says."[6]

Roosevelt gave few indications during his first term as president that he feared the Germans or that he retained his interest in military strategy. Yet Frances Perkins, Roosevelt's secretary of labor, wondered retrospectively in her autobiography whether Roosevelt had developed the vast work-relief programs of the New Deal to prepare the nation for war. She wrote in

1946: "I don't think he consciously said to himself that these reforms at home would make us a more united people if we had war. Yet . . . he was getting us ready for graver tests."[7] The thesis of Perkins's ruminations seems more plausible when we realize that Roosevelt frequently received diplomatic dispatches in the mid- and late 1930s that documented Hitler's and Mussolini's use of huge public works, both to revive their economies and to develop infrastructure that would increase their war-making abilities.[8] Moreover, a significant portion of the New Deal's work-relief programs focused on projects with military implications, such as airports, military installations, and ship building. Roosevelt appeared to cut nearly half (or six thousand) of the army's officers in his economy drive in 1933—only to rehire all of them to supervise the Civilian Conservation Corps's camps.[9] (The CCC was jointly administered by the War Department and the Department of the Interior.) Roosevelt got $247 million for naval construction from the public works section of the National Recovery Act in June 1933—a huge sum when the combined budgets of the War Department and the navy came to $500 million.[10] The navy received $145 million of an emergency allotment of $275 million to build thirty-two ships in 1934—with the remaining funds to be disbursed to the navy in the next two years.[11] A huge percentage of the expenditures of the Civilian Works Administration and the WPA went to projects with military uses, such as airports and barracks.[12] Such military leaders as George Marshall, who later served as the army's chief of staff, supervised CCC camps. This use of New Deal funds so angered isolationists such as Sen. William Borah, R-Idaho, that they got an amendment passed in 1935 that banned the use of New Deal money for "munitions, warships, or military or naval materiel"—a stricture that Roosevelt ignored when he used New Deal money later in the 1930s and in the months preceding Pearl Harbor to subsidize an array of military projects.[13]

Rhetorical Warnings but Few Dollars

Roosevelt was acutely aware even before his landslide victory in November 1936 that world peace was unlikely to last. Hitler had increased the size of his army fivefold to thirty-six divisions, violating the terms of the Versailles Treaty that the Allies had negotiated with Germany at the end of World War I. With his military and economic mobilization fully underway, and with his dictatorial powers established, Hitler committed his first aggression in March 1936 when he reoccupied the Rhineland, where no German troops had set foot since 1918. Nor was Germany the only aggressor: Japan had invaded Manchuria in 1931 and Mussolini had invaded Ethiopia in 1935.

Had Roosevelt proposed rearming the United States before the elections of 1936, he would have encountered overwhelming political opposition from isolationists in both parties. Most U.S. military experts believed the British fleet and the French army could deter German aggression—and the public did not believe that Germany or Japan threatened the United States.[14]

Roosevelt chose a low-profile, low-risk strategy that emphasized rhetorical warnings to the American people. Even before Germany's invasion of the Rhineland, he said in his annual message to Congress in January 1936 that "the [international] situation has in it many of the elements that lead to the tragedy of general war."[15] In the summer of 1936, in his acceptance speech to the Democratic convention, he obliquely warned that fascism was increasing the danger of war: "It [the New Deal] is not alone a war against want and destitution and economic demoralization. . . . It is a war for the survival of democracy . . . [to] save a great and precious form of government for ourselves and for the world."[16] Three events in 1936 and 1937 increased his belief that war was likely: Germany's pact with Japan against the Soviet Union, Japan's invasion of China, and Mussolini's pact with Germany against the Soviet Union.

Roosevelt continued his rhetorical campaign, using Japan's invasion of China on July 7, 1937, to describe a global military threat that encompassed the Pacific and the Atlantic oceans. Over the objections of key advisers, who feared he would set back rearmament by frightening the public, Roosevelt gave his famous quarantine speech in the fall of 1937, likening Japanese aggression to an epidemic that could be contained only by a navy that barred aggressors from international trade. (He sought additional money for the navy that December.)

By the time of his State of the Union Address on January 3, 1938, Roosevelt cleverly supported rearmament only for self-defense, thus countering isolationists' contention that rearmament would foster foreign entanglements. Roosevelt called his message to Congress on January 28, 1938, a "defense message," and itemized specific categories of defensive weapons that the military would need: antiaircraft materiel, ammunition, ships, and an enlisted army reserve. He sought no allocations for offensive weapons or a standing army.[17] He asked Congress to appropriate $8.8 billion for antiaircraft and other weapons; Germany's invasion of Austria in March 1938 secured congressional approval. The general public came to favor "defensive" military spending in 1938 and thereafter, even as it opposed U.S. entry into World War II.

Military spending was attractive to many Americans during the Great Depression for other reasons. In late 1937 the *New York Times* came out in favor of military spending to stimulate the nation's economy.[18] But many legislators were unlikely to embrace military spending when the nation's budget was unbalanced and when competing priorities, such as New Deal programs, existed. Roosevelt knew that his proposals to increase defense spending even further would encounter the nearly united opposition of the Republican Party as well as opposition from many isolationist Democrats.

Rearmament and the New Deal

Rearmament coexisted with the New Deal in 1938 and 1939, even though some New Dealers, like John L. Lewis, the fiery leader of the United Mine Workers, feared that new military spending would displace the New Deal. Both because unemployment remained high and because he had to solidify his New Deal coalition as the congressional elections of 1938 approached, Roosevelt sought dramatic increases in New Deal spending even as he continued to seek rearmament. He desperately needed the support of trade unionists, who had become his largest campaign contributors, and he feared that Lewis might even start a third party.

Roosevelt did not yet see a contradiction between rearmament and the New Deal. He understood that if the economy remained paralyzed, the nation could not retool and augment its factories to produce armaments. Therefore, he wanted to quickly raise the GDP from $68 billion to nearly $100 billion and to use New Deal appropriations to prime the pump. The large social spending increases of 1938 also funded public projects with strategic value such as dams, power plants, roads, and airports.[19] He proposed and received a $5 billion increase in funding for work-relief programs in April 1938.[20]

In the seven months between his request for spending increases for the

New Deal and the election of 1938, Roosevelt continued to couple the New Deal and preparedness. He intensified his educational campaign, actually predicting a world war and its eventual course in a press conference on April 20: "Well, of course, if [we] have one enemy, we are all right. But suppose you have two enemies in two different places, then you have to be a bit shifty on your feet, you have to lick one of them first and then bring them around and then lick the other. That is about the only chance."[21]

Secretly Preparing for Vast Rearmament

The Munich crisis of September 1938 dramatically transformed military strategy within the White House. Intent upon taking the Sudetenland portion of Czechoslovakia, with its large German-speaking population, Hitler forced a showdown with the French and the British, leading to the infamous decision by Neville Chamberlain to concede the Sudetenland to Hitler if he agreed to leave the rest of Czechoslovakia alone. Unlike most Americans, who believed Chamberlain had fashioned a reasonable settlement, Roosevelt was horrified, convinced that it would encourage Hitler to escalate his predatory behavior. Roosevelt's alarm further increased when he received a telegram from William Bullitt, the U.S. ambassador to France, warning that the Germans could bomb Paris at will, because the French had only seventeen modern airplanes to defend the city.

Roosevelt, who had been relatively restrained in his quest to rearm the United States, secretly moved into high gear. Before Munich, U.S. military planners had devised a war plan only against Japan. Now they devised a series of five plans (called the Rainbow Plans) that assumed the United States would be at war in both the Atlantic and the Pacific.[22] Plan 1, the worst-case scenario, assumed that Germany had conquered Great Britain and France (or they had sued for peace) and that the United States had to take the offensive in both oceans instead of focusing on a single front. Few Americans and virtually none of the top military believed this scenario was likely because they assumed that the British navy would control the Atlantic and that France could repel a German invasion. Although the precise timing and nature of his decision is shrouded in mystery because he never discussed it, Roosevelt selected plan 1 in the fall of 1938 to provide the rationale for expanding the U.S. Navy.[23]

Desperate to stall Germany's aggression, Roosevelt seized on airpower as the answer. The military had relegated the Army Air Corps to a secondary position since the 1920s. Most military brass saw it only as aerial artillery that would provide protection for advancing infantry. Three people became its chief advocates. Gen. Hap Arnold became the head of the Army Air Corps after Munich and quickly became its leading theorist, aided by technological advances of the late 1930s that allowed the development of long-range bombers with sophisticated guidance systems and engine improvements that allowed them to fly at higher speeds and altitudes, as well as to carry more bombs. The B-17, which rolled out of the hangar in the fall of 1938, embodied these technological breakthroughs. Arnold believed that B-17s could soon become the central feature of the U.S. military, because their offensive capabilities would deter foes, who would fear the mass destruction of their cities and industry. Arnold also believed bombers would protect Asian nations, such as the Philippines, from Japanese invasion and that bombers might even supplant standing armies because of their ruthless efficiency.[24]

Arnold found allies in Robert Lovett and Harry Hopkins. Lovett had left Yale during World War I to pilot primitive biplanes on the European front, later became a banker, and readily joined the Army Air Corps to orchestrate the production of bombers through the fledgling commercial aircraft industry in California. Both Arnold and Lovett got access to Roosevelt through Hopkins, who was already a convert to airpower. Thus it is not surprising that Roosevelt saw airpower as the answer when he lacked the money to build a large army. Surely, he reasoned, the Germans would pause if they realized their industrial centers would be attacked if they continued their aggression. Roosevelt vented his fascination with airpower at a November 14 meeting, declaring he wanted ten thousand planes immediately and annual production of twenty-four thousand aircraft. He realized that these goals would require huge increases in military funding, such as a $500 million emergency appropriation.[25] Because he needed a government official who could get private airplane manufacturers to produce huge numbers of planes, Roosevelt transferred Hopkins from his New Deal post to serve as secretary of commerce in December 1938.

But Roosevelt's fascination with airpower was not fully shared by other military advisers, such as George Marshall (now the army's deputy chief of staff), who was convinced that the United States needed "balanced forces"—an infantry, navy, and air force—to deter the Germans. Marshall convinced Hopkins that Roosevelt's intention to use the emergency appro-

priation exclusively for airpower was misdirected in a nation with a minimal army. Marshall argued that the United States needed awesome power
to match Germany's massive tank forces, mobile and vast infantry divisions, supportive aircraft, and bombers. Besides, he asked, how could
Americans build a massive air force when the nation lacked sufficient airfields, pilots, and trainers? At a pivotal meeting in late December proponents of balanced forces convinced Roosevelt, who agreed to use only $180
million of a $552 million emergency appropriation for airplanes and to
devote most of the money to the army and navy.[26]

Nor was Hitler unaware that Roosevelt had made a basic commitment
to rearmament. After November 1938 Hitler believed that Roosevelt
"methodically and consciously" sought to avert any future appeasement of
German aggression.[27] (Undeterred, he took the rest of Czechoslovakia in
March 1939.)

Preparedness in an Economy of Scarcity

Roosevelt had to know at this juncture that the New Deal might soon take
a backseat to preparedness—he did not seek major tax increases in 1939.
Absent an infusion of new resources, Congress would inevitably demand
cuts in domestic spending to offset the large increases in military spending
that the president now planned. When he transferred Hopkins from the
New Deal to Commerce and charged him with stimulating airplane production, Roosevelt also knew that he was transferring his most powerful
New Dealer to the preparedness effort. Working from an agency ideally
suited to facilitate a partnership between the government and industry for
war preparedness, Hopkins, an avid foe of fascism, devoted himself to rearmament with the same zeal that he had brought to the New Deal.[28] Nor
did Hopkins have inhibitions about diverting "relief money" to rearmament in 1938, even before he moved to the Department of Commerce,
according to Gen. Arthur Wilson:

> It was evident that a sleepy War Department plus an overzealous atti-
> tude on the part of many WPA officials [led to] . . . spending millions
> on useless [work-relief] projects and letting the national defense starve.
> . . . Harry Hopkins shared my views and was very critical of the lack of
> plans of the War Department for sharing in the "relief money" (they

were going after it with pitchforks when they should have been using shovels). . . . Several millions of dollars of WPA funds were transferred [secretly] to start making machine tools for the manufacture of small arms ammunition.[29]

Because isolationists and Republicans opposed marked increases in military spending, Roosevelt sought only $210 million in additional appropriations in January 1939. When he later increased this sum to $309 million, for a total military budget of $1.3 billion, the *New York Times* marveled at Roosevelt's audacity and called it the largest peacetime military budget in U.S. history. Roosevelt was so intent on beginning rearmament at once that he decided to operate at the edges of legality. Although the Neutrality Act forbade sales of U.S. military aircraft to foreign nations, Roosevelt secretly shipped planes to the French. The crash of an American airplane in France in 1939 blew his cover, forcing him to hold off on further arms sales to allies until he could persuade Congress to amend the Neutrality Act.

Roosevelt introduced legislation to authorize the production of six thousand airplanes in April 1939, declaring war with Germany to be preferable to appeasement. Correctly predicting that a contemptuous response from Hitler and Mussolini would inflame American opinion, he sent them a letter on April 14 that publicly asked them to promise not to attack thirty-one specific nations. After his case was bolstered by Hitler's seizure of the rest of Czechoslovakia early in 1939, Roosevelt openly discussed the possibility that the United States might eventually increase its army by seven times.

The president fully understood the grim possibilities facing the nation. If the Germans conquered the Continent, they might soon defeat Britain, leaving the Americans to face the Germans alone. The appropriations that he was receiving from Congress could not provide weapons instantly, because it took two (or more) years from the development of production facilities to the actual delivery of weapons. In the summer of 1939 the U.S. Army remained undersized and ill equipped with its 140,000 troops distributed among 130 U.S. posts and still carrying 1903 Springfields. (Supplemental appropriations would allow this force to increase to only 210,000 troops, whereas the German army numbered two million.) Although Congress had authorized the production of fifty-five hundred planes, hardly any had been built. Meanwhile the Luftwaffe was expanding rapidly. The inadequacy of U.S. forces was grimly illustrated by Germany's demonstration of its blitzkrieg of Poland in September 1939 when its panzer divisions, Luftwaffe, and infantry combined to conquer the country with startling speed.

Nor could Roosevelt wrest more funds from Congress in the fall and winter of 1939 or in the spring of 1940. In the fall of 1939 he halved his military requests in order to court the support of congressional isolationists for amendments to the Neutrality Act that would allow the United States to sell munitions to foreign nations. The so-called phony war in the eight months after the fall of Poland, when Germany desisted from further aggression, lulled Congress into such complacency that it actually trimmed by 10 percent Roosevelt's request for $800 million for the military.

Convinced that the United States had to speed up its rearmament, Roosevelt agreed with Adm. Harold Stark's recommendation for a $4 billion increase in the navy's budget to allow the U.S. fleet to equal the British fleet in size and to surpass the Japanese fleet, which already equaled the U.S. fleet.[30] But the president encountered the nearly unanimous opposition of Republicans to major increases in defense spending, which forced him to whittle his request to $1.3 billion for ninety-five ships, three thousand naval airplanes, and an array of support ships and submarines—a budget sufficient only to boost U.S. naval forces in the Pacific. The Americans would have to rely on the British fleet to protect the Atlantic Ocean. Despite objections from many Republicans and isolationists, Congress supported this increase.

Even with this success in hand, Roosevelt remained noncommittal in December 1939 about the size of his military requests in his forthcoming budget. As memories of the invasion of Poland dimmed, Congress and the American public went into denial. When he finally presented his budget in early 1940, he sought only $1.8 billion for the military, a small increase over the 1938 budget.

Because he could not spur military production with government appropriations, Roosevelt developed an ingenious and low-cost substitute: the United States would sell arms to France and Britain. These markets, he hoped, would entice U.S. manufacturers to increase production of armaments even if the federal government could not buy them. Americans shipped vast amounts of arms to England and France after the neutrality legislation was amended in the fall of 1939.

The Noose Tightens on the New Deal

Roosevelt decisively cut his commitments to domestic reform in 1939 by supporting the New Deal verbally while placing it on the budgetary back burner. In his annual message to Congress in January 1939 he eulogized the New Deal's role in building the nation's morale and unity, summarizing its accomplishments in the past tense. He even said that "events abroad have made it increasingly clear to the American people that dangers within are less to be feared than dangers from without."[31] Even more pointedly than before, he referred to the New Deal as an aid to national preparedness rather than (as before) a set of programs with its own objectives. He sought budget increases of more than $300 million for rearmament in January while proposing cuts in domestic programs of nearly $1 billion—a move that liberals widely attacked. Roosevelt's growing disinterest in funding the New Deal was reflected, moreover, in his decision not to offset defense spending increases with tax increases. In these circumstances a balanced budget, which most legislators wanted soon, could be achieved only with cuts in domestic spending.

A liberal coterie within the administration, composed of Harold Smith, the budget director; Marriner Eccles, the Federal Reserve chairman; Laughlin Currie, an assistant to Eccles; and Alvin Hansen, a Harvard economist, advocated a "third New Deal" to restore its momentum.[32] Influenced by the theories of the English economist John Maynard Keynes, these liberal advisers believed that the U.S. economy would remain stagnant without permanent infusions of capital from the federal government through an array of housing, social service, public works, and health care programs. (They strenuously opposed substituting military spending for this pump priming.) Eager to convert Roosevelt to their cause, they included Henry Morgenthau, the treasury secretary, in their meetings in spring 1939, but they found him to be unreceptive at a meeting on June 6; indeed, Roosevelt had already signaled his intentions to Harold Smith, his budget director, to not exacerbate the budget deficit. Rather than side with Eccles, who wanted billions of dollars in additional domestic spending, Roosevelt asked Smith at the end of the June 6 meeting to mediate between Eccles and Morgenthau, who wanted the federal government only to make off-budget loans to private business and local governments to promote public works.[33] Morgenthau prevailed, and Roosevelt approved of only $800 million in loans for housing projects despite a strong letter of dissent from Eccles.[34] Roosevelt also instructed Smith on May 12 to inform Ickes that he opposed making the PWA permanent because he needed more money in the budget for defense spending.[35] As if to add an exclamation point to Roosevelt's retreat from the New Deal, Congress summarily rejected even these loans in the summer of 1939, claiming they were an off-budget ruse to make the deficit look artificially small.

Roosevelt's priorities had shifted decisively by the summer of 1939 because of the situation in Europe. Hitler's army stood at two million strong, many European nations had mobilized and moved their troops to their borders, and the French were holding gas-mask drills in Paris. The U.S. ambassador to Belgium told Roosevelt that war was imminent. Morgenthau later acknowledged that neither he nor Roosevelt focused on domestic matters that summer.[36]

Domestic political forces also made social reform less attractive to Roosevelt. Interpreting their gains in the 1938 elections as a popular mandate to cut domestic spending, Republicans joined forces with conservative and moderate Democrats to attack the New Deal. They cut the WPA's funding from $875 million to $725 million—and Joe Martin of Massachusetts, the minority leader in the House, led a Republican crusade for 10 percent across-the-board cuts in all government spending.[37] Roosevelt needed broad support from Congress to gain the revisions in the Neutrality Act and increases in military spending and realized he might alienate Congress if he resisted cuts in domestic spending. He was, moreover, acting from a position of weakness because of the Republican gains as well as a series of defeats on the domestic scene, including his court-packing plan, since 1937. Roosevelt increasingly invested his scarce political capital in foreign policy and military matters rather than the domestic agenda, even as he sought more than $2 billion for the WPA in 1939.[38]

Roosevelt told Smith, his budget director, in mid-October that he wanted to terminate all new public works projects and implied that he would soon phase out all work-relief spending.[39] He ruled out any new programs, even "laudable ones" like expanded health care.[40] He decided to hold the deficit in his forthcoming budget to $2 billion by making deep cuts in domestic spending.[41] When Eccles protested cuts of $500 million in work relief in December when more than eight million people remained unemployed, Roosevelt told him,

You are absolutely right. But with the war in Europe likely to spread, we simply must get an increase in the military budget from last year's $1 billion to $1.5 billion [for] the coming year. To do this . . . the budget for relief is the only place from which I can transfer additional funds that are needed for the military. . . . But even so, Marriner, despite the immediate decrease in relief appropriations, it is going to be extremely difficult to get Congress to pass the military budget.[42]

The Explosive Growth of Military Spending

Everything changed with the end of the phony war as Germany conquered first Denmark in April and then Luxembourg, Belgium, and the Netherlands in May 1940. With eight nations conquered and Germany poised to take France, U.S. military planners grimly concluded that the United States could only hope for a stalemate in a battle against Germany, Italy, and Japan if Britain and France fell. Named the army's chief of staff in April 1939, Marshall had fought a losing battle with Congress and within the administration to secure more money for the army; he found even Roosevelt to be excessively timid and still preoccupied with airpower. In desperation Marshall turned to Henry Morgenthau on May 11 and told him that the nation had but 300,000 infantry equipped with modern weapons even though the army's official plans called for four times that number. Marshall insisted that the nation needed $650 million for its army (twice what Roosevelt had sought) but found that politicians widely believed that the military would spend new funds wastefully and that it would even use the emergency as a pretext to build a military empire. Contending that Roosevelt had not been more assertive in seeking military appropriations because he had not been seen the "whole picture," Morgenthau encouraged Marshall to convey his thoughts to the president[43] Still enamored with aircraft rather than balanced forces, Roosevelt said he would seek funding for fifty thousand aircraft at a May 13 meeting, only to encounter an impassioned three-minute outburst from Marshall, who argued that U.S. forces were about as big as they had been eighteen months before the nation entered World War I and that the country had barely begun to convert its industry to the production of armaments, lacked sufficient weapons of all kinds, had failed to divert strategic materials such as steel from civilian to military uses, and had no national rearmament policy. Attacking once more Roosevelt's advocacy of airpower, Marshal argued that the United States needed an infantry sufficient to match Germany's.

Stunned by Marshall's impassioned speech, Roosevelt asked him to return the next day to discuss a $657 million supplemental appropriation. In fact, Roosevelt decided to seek $896 million at once as a prelude to a request for $11 billion over several years. On May 16 he sent a proposal to Congress to increase aircraft production by fifty thousand per year and to vastly increase production of tanks, artillery, and other armaments. As Germany swept toward victory in France, Roosevelt asked for additional military funds on May 31 and signed legislation that gave the navy an 11 percent increase; it had been in the works since earlier in the spring. Repeatedly emphasizing that the military increases were meant only to provide the United States with defensive capabilities, and portraying his spending proposals as "moderate and sensible," Roosevelt got Congress to approve $1.5 billion in new money in May and $1.7 billion more in June. Hitler's invasion of France lent additional credence to the need to expand the navy, because the Nazis were about to seize the French fleet and might soon take control of the British fleet. Admiral Stark developed a proposal for a 70 percent increase for the navy to allow a true, two-ocean navy—a proposal that key members of Congress promptly supported.

The events of the spring and summer of 1940 had transformed the politics of rearmament. Even before the fall of France, Roosevelt's rhetoric had made opponents of preparedness nervous because he had implied that they might ultimately be blamed for Nazi aggression or even the eventual invasion of the United States. With the elections of 1940 looming, Republicans realized that they could suffer catastrophic political losses if Roosevelt portrayed them as helping Hitler, now that France had fallen. Many became converts to preparedness, allowing total appropriations to top $17 billion by July, nine times the military appropriations of 1939. Cleverly seeking a united front against the Nazis, Roosevelt named two prominent Republicans to head the War Department (Henry Stimson) and the navy (Frank Knox). Both were militant internationalists and big spenders compared to their predecessors. But U.S. preparedness would have rung hollow without conscription. Cagily refusing to endorse conscription until bipartisan support emerged in Congress, Roosevelt finally got a draft law enacted in the summer of 1940, although the legislation limited conscription to 900,000 inductees per year and they would serve for only one year.

Roosevelt's energies were now completely consumed by war preparations and the battle for public opinion. He had to build an offensive fighting force to hold the Atlantic as soon as possible. He had to develop joint military strategy with the British in secret agreements long before Pearl Harbor. He had to get weapons into the hands of Britain to help the British survive the Nazis' onslaught.[44] He devoted his State of the Union Message in January 1941 to America's role as supplier of weapons to allies, soon proposing that 62 percent of the federal budget be devoted to military spending.[45] Members of the House were startled by these huge amounts. Republicans' whistling echoed through the chamber when the budget was announced, requiring the Speaker to stop the reading of the proposal twice to get order restored.

In a poll taken in late March 1941 barely half of Americans wanted the United States to produce arms more rapidly, even as Germany continued its relentless aggression, resuming air attacks on Britain in the spring; conquering Yugoslavia, Greece, and Crete; and beginning initiatives in North Africa.[46] Germany invaded the Soviet Union in June with 3 million troops, 1,800 airplanes, and 3,580 tanks, soon killing 5 million Russians and destroying 2,000 aircraft while absorbing only 30,000 casualties. Roughly 11 million Germans were under arms by July. Many U.S. leaders doubted that Britain could hold out for long—and Marshall was so convinced the Russian cause was hopeless that he advised Stalin to withdraw his entire army from battle to avert its utter destruction.

The true measure of Roosevelt's rearmament intentions were reflected in secret planning in the fall of 1941. Many U.S. manufacturers still refused to convert their plants from civilian to military production, and American armaments were stretched thin with allocations to the British, the Russians, the Atlantic front, and the Pacific front. Led by Robert Nathan, an economist in the Office of Production Management, economic planners analyzed how many weapons the U.S. economy could produce in a relatively brief period. While pessimists, including many top military advisers, believed that Roosevelt had often been unduly optimistic about the numbers of airplanes and other weapons that the United States could produce, Nathan doubled their estimates of U.S. capabilities, arguing that the country could spend $120 billion to maintain a standing army of 8.5 million men and to produce 60,000 aircraft, 45,000 tanks, and 6 million tons of ships in 1942 alone. He doubled those figures in 1943 to allow the nation to take the offensive in the war with Hitler by that July, rather than later dates that some advisers had suggested. Armed with this optimistic data, Roosevelt asked Stimson, Marshall, Hopkins, and Knox to prepare a victory plan with precise numbers of troops and armaments needed to prevail over the Axis powers.[47] Secretly discussed with a congressional committee, the Victory Plan (which recommended mobilizing 13.5 million men and manufacturing 63,467 planes) was leaked to the press only two days before Pearl Harbor by someone who wanted to discredit the huge expenditures that Roosevelt envisioned.[48] Spending $120 million for arms seemed reckless to many Americans. Even Sam Rayburn, the powerful Speaker of the House, thought that American war costs would total only $35 billion.[49]

Everything changed, of course, with the Japanese bombing of Pearl Harbor on December 7, 1941. The Victory Plan became the blueprint for a massive mobilization in which the United States became the arsenal of the Allied nations, providing huge amounts of materiel to the Allies as well as to U.S. troops. This frenzied war production also provided, as we shall see, the pretext for demolishing domestic programs.

The Noose Tightens Further

Congressional opposition to New Deal spending had intensified in 1940 as the presidential election approached, even as a new threat to the program emerged that spring—a decline in unemployment. Because Roosevelt had promised to end work-relief programs once the depression ended, conservatives demanded that he make good. They insisted that unemployment had been halved even as New Dealers contended that nine to eleven million Americans remained unemployed. With preparedness stimulating the economy, conservatives sensed that time was on their side.[50]

Congress mounted another economy drive when it assaulted Roosevelt's domestic spending in the spring of 1940, using the pejorative term "tax-and-spend Democrats."[51] Caught between conservatives, and liberal defenders of the New Deal such as the Congress of Industrial Organizations, which wanted to retain high levels of funding for the WPA, Roosevelt tried to defend his New Deal programs in his presidential campaign. He attacked "certain political influences pledged to reaction in domestic affairs and to appeasement in foreign affairs."[52] He emphasized the WPA's production of war goods, noting at a shipyard, for example, that nearly half its ships were being built with WPA funds.[53] (Administrators of virtually all domestic programs, even the U.S. Fish and Wildlife Service, were forced to emphasize their military functions to retain their funding.) Roosevelt argued that the New Deal contributed to preparedness by enhancing the nation's morale. Even Eleanor Roosevelt used a military analogy to defend domestic spending, calling the New Deal "defense at home." (In 1941 the president proposed an endless array of social programs within the rearmament effort, including establishing a committee on fair employment, housing for armament workers, and an office of health and welfare services.[54]) He appointed Col. Francis Harrington to serve as director of the WPA to underscore its uses for preparedness and sought $1 billion for it. He let Harold Ickes craft legislation to establish a Columbia River Valley Authority in the Pacific Northwest that would be similar to the TVA.[55] To underscore his allegiance to the New Deal, Roosevelt recommended that the Democratic Convention nominate the liberal Henry Wallace to succeed the conservative John Garner as his running mate.

As he was defending the New Deal, however, Roosevelt also undermined it when he declared in May 1940 that he did not care how rearmament was financed, whether from borrowing or from taxes. He made this strategic retreat on the issue of taxes just two days before he announced his request for large increases in military appropriations; he knew that conservatives would demand domestic cuts to offset increases in the military budget as the budget deficit increased.

Roosevelt now had to contend, moreover, with a militant opponent of domestic spending, Sen. Harry Byrd, the Virginia Democrat who had opposed New Deal spending for years and who intended to force Roosevelt to offset his increases in military spending with domestic spending cuts. Byrd wanted Roosevelt to impound 10 percent of each nonmilitary appropriation and gained support from legislators who were furious that Roosevelt had vetoed $300 million in pork for highway construction. Because Byrd's proposal resonated with many legislators, Roosevelt and budget director Smith began to impound funds to demonstrate their frugality.[56] Nor was Roosevelt's heart with the New Deal at this point: an aide was astonished to hear him say that he was "getting sick and tired of having to listen to complaints from these goddamn New Dealers."[57]

Conservatives' power to force cuts in domestic spending was augmented in 1940 and in succeeding years by their ability to hold preparedness legislation hostage to cuts in domestic spending. Aware that Roosevelt needed revenue increases to fund the growing military budget, they stonewalled tax legislation until he promised to cut social spending. They held increases in the national debt ceiling hostage to spending cuts. They sometimes hinged support of conscription and the Lend-Lease program to spending cuts in domestic programs. When Roosevelt's budget message proposed a deficit of $9.2 billion along with $10.8 billion in military spending in January 1941, conservatives declared Roosevelt's cuts of $600 million from the 1940 domestic budget to be insufficient. When Morgenthau said that the nation needed $3.5 billion in new taxes, conservatives insisted they could be averted if Roosevelt gutted his domestic program.

Roosevelt tried to appease conservatives by slashing the WPA budget by more than 25 percent and by impounding nearly a third of the money earmarked for the National Youth Administration (NYA) and nearly half the CCC's funds. But these actions merely whetted the appetites of Senate conservatives, who created the Joint Committee on Reduction of Nonessential Federal Expenditures in September 1941 under Byrd's leadership. The committee then asked Smith to produce three alternative plans for decreases of $1 billion, $1.5 billion, and $2 billion in domestic spending. (The $2 billion cut would have slashed funding of work-relief programs by nearly three-fourths, the NYA by 95 percent, and food programs like free lunches by half.)

Although it served only in an advisory capacity to congressional appropriations committees, the Byrd Committee provided a public forum for budget-cutting conservatives. With its membership dominated by conservatives (only Robert La Follette defended domestic spending), the committee was utterly disdainful of New Deal programs in its public hearings, accusing the CCC of coddling lazy young people, declaring the WPA and NYA to be obsolete, and calling NYA and WPA enrollees deadbeats.[58] When the Byrd Committee issued its report seventeen days after Pearl Harbor, it recommended terminating the CCC and NYA, making rapid cuts in the WPA, and enacting no new reforms.

Flawed Priorities During the New Deal

What was unique about the New Deal was the importance it placed on domestic discretionary spending for training, work, social programs, and employment for an extended period ("social investments" in fig. 3.1). As figure 3.1 shows, Roosevelt succeeded in prolonging his New Deal spend-

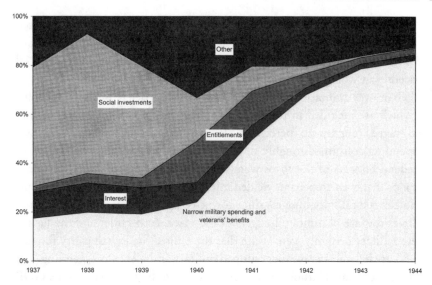

FIGURE 3.1 Five Types of Expenditures as Percentages of Total Federal Outlays, 1937–1944

Source: U.S. Bureau of the Budget, *Budgets of the U.S. Government, FYs 1933 Through 1939* (Ann Arbor, MI: University Microfilms, 1968).

ing through 1939. Whereas narrow military spending (outlays for armaments, personnel, and operations, not including interest payments on debt or outlays with indirect military uses, such as scientific research, technology, and foreign aid) and spending on veterans' benefits absorbed roughly 35 percent of the federal budget from 1933 to 1940, these allocations were eclipsed by spending on work and welfare programs, which received almost 50 percent of budget resources from 1933 to 1939. During no other period in contemporary U.S. history has domestic discretionary spending for social programs so dominated the federal budget; indeed, later chapters will show that federal spending on education, training, employment, and social service programs never again rose above 4.5 percent of the federal budget during the twentieth century.

Although they comprised a large percentage of Roosevelt's budgets, New Deal expenditures were relatively small by contemporary standards because his budgets were so small (see fig. 3.2). Roosevelt's New Deal was not sufficiently large to address Americans' needs during the Great Depression or to bring the economy out of its doldrums. To do nothing more than provide work for the unemployed, Roosevelt's work programs should have been three times their actual size. And because it concentrated on the needs of the unemployed, the New Deal failed to address a host of other needs, such as health insurance, education, or myriad other social needs that would have to await the Great Society of the 1960s.

Nor was military spending adequate. If we delete veterans' benefits (which are included in the military budget in fig. 3.1), military spending averaged roughly 20 percent of Roosevelt's budgets, whereas military spending consumed roughly 10 percent of budgets of the late 1990s—but federal budgets of the 1930s were so much smaller than they were in the 1990s that even 20 percent yielded minuscule military budgets. In constant dollars the military budgets since 1950 (see fig. 15.3) have been at least ten times the size of military budgets of the 1930s. And Hitler and the Japanese military certainly were aware that the United States had paltry forces.

Tiny federal tax revenues crimped military and New Deal spending. On the eve of Pearl Harbor, the nation collected only 7.7 percent of its GDP in taxes, compared to roughly 20 percent since the early 1950s. Even to fund his inadequate New Deal and military, Roosevelt had to incur large

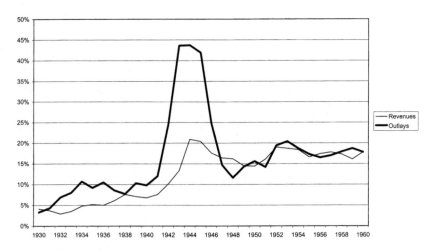

FIGURE 3.2 Federal Outlays and Federal Tax Revenues as Percentages of Gross Domestic Product, 1930–1960

Source: Office of Management and Budget, *Budget of the U.S. Government, FY 2000, Historical Tables* (Washington, D.C.: U.S. Government Printing Office, 1999), table 1.2, pp. 19–20.

deficits (see fig. 3.2) that in turn stimulated further political opposition to his inadequate spending. Roosevelt's inability or unwillingness to increase these tax revenues contributed to his plight on both domestic and military fronts, because fiscal conservatives could rightly contend that spending increases of any kind would exacerbate the deficit. (Roosevelt's ruse of two budgets, an emergency and regular budget, was no longer believable by the late 1930s—and the New Deal was on the ropes even before World War II because Roosevelt could not fund both his New Deal and rearmament.)

As we review Roosevelt's strategy during the 1930s, we can ask whether he ought to have broached tax increases more forcefully. Instead of using his two-budget strategy, perhaps he should have contended that the nation, as in major wars, had to raise taxes to fund its domestic agenda and its military—even if it ran deficits—to jolt the nation from the Great Depression. He might even have vetoed some social legislation until Congress enacted some tax increases, thus linking tax legislation and the New Deal. (Had Congress balked, he could then blame its members for not enacting social legislation during a period of dire suffering.) And when Republicans coined the term "tax-and-spend Democrats" in 1938, he should have countered with slogans such as "no tax-and-starve-'em-out Republicans." These strategies might have failed in light of bipartisan opposition to tax increases, but he made virtually no effort to raise taxes other than regressive taxes (like the beer and liquor levies) or the symbolic tax-the-rich rhetoric of the mid-1930s.

How much money did Americans sacrifice by not increasing tax revenues during the New Deal? The federal government taxed roughly 6.37 percent of the GDP in the 1930s, compared to 16 percent in the late 1940s, so Americans ought to have taxed at least 15 percent of the GDP during a national catastrophe like the Great Depression. Had they done so, they could have increased New Deal revenues from 1933 through 1941 from $660 billion to $1.6 trillion in constant 1992 dollars. Had Roosevelt sustained deficits similar in size to those he actually ran during the New Deal in order to jolt the economy out of the Great Depression, he could have increased New Deal spending from a mere $340 billion to roughly $1 trillion—and military spending from 1933 through 1941 from $64.8 billion to almost $190 billion while still leaving sufficient resources for other government programs.

CHAPTER

4

The Conservatives' Revenge

Because the United States was mobilizing a military of more than twelve million people that was supplied by an armaments industry of unprecedented size, Congress had to decide whether to fund all, most, or some of this gigantic undertaking with tax revenue. If elected officials decided not to use taxes, they would vastly increase the overall cost of the war by making successive generations pay the interest on a huge wartime debt. Other dangers lurked. Eager to mobilize after Pearl Harbor, the nation risked wasting resources through ill-advised procurement policies that granted major corporations excessive profits, just as rivalry and duplication between the services might waste additional resources. With its fiscal resources scarce or depleted, the nation might be tempted to eliminate the federal role in social policy, which would mean that reformers would have to start from scratch at the end of the war.

Expending Untold Treasure

As the first truly global war, World War II was destined to be extraordinarily costly. In the Axis the United States faced not only three formidable enemies but also their combined forces around the world. While it was fighting these nations in the Pacific and Atlantic and on numerous continents, the United States could not focus on any specific area, lest its opponents gain insurmountable advantages in neglected areas. With Western European nations overrun or devastated by air attacks, the United States had to expend huge resources to prop up the Allies with materiel and weapons. It sent vast quantities of armaments and munitions to the Allies throughout the war.

Although some people hoped that technological innovations, such as long-distance bombers, would shorten the war markedly, technology was itself extraordinarily costly, whether bombers, tanks, fighters, submarines, aircraft carriers, or an endless array of new armaments. Because Germany, Italy, and Japan possessed advanced weapons, the United States had to counter with unceasing innovation.

Tactical errors by the Allies also may have increased the sheer cost of the war. Both Gen. George Marshall (the army's chief of staff) and Brig. Gen. Alfred Wedemeyer (the architect of the Victory Plan and a top wartime planner) were convinced that strategy would determine the war's duration. Choose the right strategy, they believed, and Germany could be defeated in 1944—but select a flawed strategy and Germany might survive well into 1945 or beyond.[1] They knew that the duration would also determine the overall cost, because each month would require the expenditure of billions of dollars.

Marshall and Wedemeyer realized that the Allies could not invade France until they had accumulated massive fighting forces in the key staging area, Britain—hundreds of thousands of soldiers as well as huge numbers of landing craft, naval support vessels, and airplanes. Nor would these massive forces be easy to mass because the United States had begun to mobilize so late. On the eve of Pearl Harbor, the United States had only 1,100 combat-worthy planes and 1.3 million uniformed troops, whereas the German army was at least six times that size. (The most advanced fighter the U.S. Army Air Forces had was the P-40 Marauder, which army pilots called "the Murderer" because it was so dangerous to fly. The air force had only 159 four-engine bombers.) It would take two years for the U.S. Army to achieve parity with European armies because of the logistics of inducting, training, and transporting these troops, as well as manufacturing the weapons, transport vessels, cargo planes, and landing craft that they would need, all of which had to be transported across the Atlantic, which German U-boats patrolled with devastating effectiveness. Yet Marshall and Wedemeyer calculated that the Americans and British could assemble an awesome force in Britain sufficient to support a cross-channel invasion by the spring or summer of 1943 (Operation Bolero)—*if* they did not excessively divert their forces elsewhere.[2]

Marshall and Wedemeyer soon confronted an articulate and determined opponent of their strategy, Winston Churchill.

Because England had suffered massive casualties in the trench warfare of World War I, Churchill and most British military leaders were ill disposed to head-to-head battles with the Germans in France. Churchill, who privately confessed to frequent nightmares about the carnage of World War I, was determined to find a strategy that would gradually deplete Germany's military forces, industrial base, and citizen morale in order to spare the Allies a frontal assault on an enemy at full strength. Why not, he argued, engage Germany on its southern flank in North Africa or its northern flank in Norway as a prelude to moving gradually toward Berlin in extended campaigns? The Allies could weaken Germany over a number of years if Hitler were forced to fight the Russians in the East and a succession of battles on his periphery while enduring saturation bombing at home, Churchill reasoned. Moreover, the strategy would preserve British colonies in Egypt, North Africa, and India.[3]

To the dismay of Marshall and Wedemeyer, Churchill succeeded in shaping the Allies' strategy as they fought their way from North Africa and up through Italy in 1942, 1943, and early 1944. Marshall's desire to mass troops in Britain for Operation Bolero was frustrated as well by a diversion of resources to the Pacific. Immediately after Pearl Harbor the Allies had decided to take defensive positions in the Pacific to enable them to concentrate their forces against Germany; they planned to defeat Japan only after they had conquered its military. They supplied two separate and uncoordinated campaigns, commanded by Gen. Douglas MacArthur, and by admirals Chester Nimitz and Ernest King. MacArthur was contemptuous of the navy and wanted the army to assume the central role in defeating Japan. He demanded huge numbers of troops and armaments for a southern thrust from Australia north through New Guinea toward the Philippines, which he had already pledged to retake as a prelude to invading Japan itself. Nimitz and King were equally contemptuous of the army and favored an "island-hopping" strategy from east to west to retake scores of islands, whether in the Solomon, Caroline, Marianna, or Marshall islands. They planned to make heavy use of amphibious forces and carriers to confront entrenched Japanese forces on these various islands before conquering islands near Japan (like Okinawa) that could serve as bases for bombing raids on Japanese targets.

Roosevelt and Marshall acceded to King and Nimitz *and* to MacArthur in 1942 and much of 1943, sending nearly half of all U.S. troops and huge quantities of aircraft, transport vessels, and landing craft to the Pacific. Nimitz commenced a costly and bloody island-hopping campaign in 1942 and 1943. Loathe to give the army control of navy carriers or other vessels, Nimitz and King hoarded them jealously, even when this strategy endangered MacArthur's effort to hold New Guinea. In turn, MacArthur incessantly demanded naval forces that would allow him not just to hold New Guinea but to launch other initiatives. Like Churchill's peripheral strategy, this Pacific strategy depleted forces that could have been used to invade France in 1943.[4]

We shall never know whether Marshall and Wedemeyer's strategy would have shortened the war or prevented even greater casualties than the Allies endured using Churchill's peripheral strategy. (A frontal attack on the Germans earlier in the war would have incurred massive casualties, though the peripheral strategy also cost Americans hundreds of thousands of lives.) Perhaps partly because of Churchill's peripheral strategy, the war became unbelievably costly to the United States, which fought the war for nearly four years and mobilized virtually the entire economy to do so.

Demolition Derby

While the administration was preoccupied with the war, Republicans and conservatives were demolishing the New Deal at home. The GOP, which had attacked deficits during the New Deal, now blamed the minuscule domestic spending for the wartime deficits, not the *real* culprits: huge military spending and relatively low federal taxes. Using the term "nonessential spending" to portray domestic spending, they mercilessly cut and closed New Deal programs; by 1944 the nation's spending on education, training, employment, and social services had dwindled to 0.2 percent of the federal budget, or only $160 million.[5]

In January 1942 Roosevelt predicted that the nation would have deficits of $35 billion in 1942 and $60 billion in 1943; that April he publicly advocated higher income taxes. The Republicans promptly targeted six New Deal programs: the CCC, WPA, the National Youth Administration (NYA), Farm Security Administration (FSA), Office of Civil Defense (OCD), and National Resources Planning Board (NRPB). Because the CCC focused on conservation rather than training workers for war plants, it was an easy target. Aware of its vulnerability and eager to retain at least a skeletal CCC for the postwar period, the agency's allies and administrators frantically tried to change the CCC's mission to a social service program that would help African Americans, Native Americans, and young teenagers by providing vocational training, preparing youth for work in war plants, fighting forest fires, and building roads in army camps.[6] Congress countered that these changes were merely a ploy to preserve a program that had outlived its time and terminated the agency's funding in the summer of 1942.

Roosevelt had established the OCD by executive order in May 1941 to coordinate civil defense. At first he wanted it to focus narrowly on civil defense but relented when Eleanor Roosevelt insisted that it serve social purposes as well. She had seen how British civilians had established communal feeding stations, child care, health programs, and other social activities to help maintain the social fabric during the Battle of Britain, and— assuming that the United States would soon face similar pressure—she wanted the OCD to mobilize hundreds of thousands of volunteers and develop an array of community programs. She became assistant director of the Office of Civil Defense in September 1941 and recruited many social activists, whom she encouraged to promote street theater and grassroots community organizing. She soon learned that Americans, who had no bombs raining down on them, saw "community organizing" as superfluous, and conservatives charged that the agency was a liberal plot to sustain the New Deal in the guise of civil defense. Conservatives threatened to kill its funding, forced Eleanor Roosevelt to resign in February 1942, and required the agency to limit its activities to traditional civil defense.[7]

Franklin Roosevelt, who was determined to preserve a united front against the Axis powers, refused to be drawn into partisan conflicts over domestic issues. He needed conservatives' votes for tax and military spending and feared he would lose his political effectiveness if he answered each attack. Irked by Roosevelt's passivity, cabinet member Harold Ickes warned the president (to no avail) that "your leaders in Congress sit tongue-tied, while vicious attacks are made upon various of your policies which, if successful, will weaken you and expose you to more direct attacks as the enemy grows bolder with success."[8]

Democrats suffered devastating losses in the 1942 congressional elections. With unemployment virtually ended, the president preoccupied with the war, and many party regulars staying home instead of voting, the party barely retained a majority in the House. And, given that many southern Democrats regularly defected to the Republicans on domestic issues, this new Congress was, for all intents, a Republican Congress.

The Democratic losses strengthened Roosevelt's determination to remain aloof from domestic battles. He was convinced that he would lose prestige if he campaigned for a Democratic Congress, much as Woodrow Wilson had been rebuked by the electorate when he sought a Democratic victory in 1918.[9] Aside from a speech to Congress in January in which he advocated a "cradle to grave" set of social and economic protections in the postwar era, Roosevelt provided little opposition to Republicans' assault on domestic spending in late 1942 and 1943.[10] He unilaterally eliminated the Works Progress Administration in December 1942. He pledged to cooperate with Republicans in cutting nonessential spending in early January 1943 while noting, "we are fast approaching the subsistence level of government."[11] He failed to counter wild statements by Republicans, such as the assertion by John "Meataxe" Taber of New York that "we all know that nondefense appropriations have run absolutely wild."[12] Roosevelt did not defend the NYA, which was terminated in the summer.[13] He hardly contested the demise of the Farm Security Administration in 1943—the agency was anathema to corporate agricultural interests, which loathed its advocacy on behalf of tenant farmers and sharecroppers.

With the CCC, WPA, NYA, and FSA ended, conservatives turned to the National Resources Planning Board. Roosevelt had created it in 1939 because he needed research on the long-range development of natural and human resources. After Pearl Harbor he asked the agency to prepare plans and programs for the postwar era. With a staff dominated by liberal economists who subscribed to the countercyclical theories of John Maynard Keynes, the resources board issued a number of reports that recommended increases in federal spending. In 1939 it supported the right of citizens to work, have access to health care, and obtain an education. In a 1941 report it warned of a postwar depression unless the nation embarked on large-scale domestic spending and enacted a redistributive income tax. But it saved its major salvos for 1942, when it issued three reports that urged huge postwar spending on public works, national health care, schools, and Social Security.

Conservatives were furious at the audacity of the resources board, which they believed was staffed by radicals who sought to dictate a postwar agenda. The powerful Army Corps of Engineers, which oversaw the public works programs so popular with Congress, opposed the board for intruding on its turf, just as established agencies of government believed the resources board interfered with their postwar planning. Rather than endorse these various reports, Roosevelt merely sent them to Congress and made little effort to publicize them or to discuss their merits. Congress killed the resource board by deleting its funding from the budget in the summer of 1943 and promptly established Senate and House Special Committees on Postwar Economic Policy and Planning, with the Senate committee chaired by Walter George, an arch conservative from Georgia who advocated tax reduction rather than domestic spending as the best way to stimulate economic growth in the postwar period.[14] House Republicans, who were determined to sabotage postwar reforms by cutting taxes severely, demanded a 50 percent cut in federal taxes at the war's end.[15] Roosevelt countered with his own planning body, the Office of War Mobilization, but decided that the United States ought to avoid *any* postwar planning until it had defeated Germany, both to avoid partisan conflict and to avoid distracting Americans from the war effort.

As conservatives ran amok during the war, Democrats were fragmented. Some, like Harry Hopkins, wanted to concentrate on the battle against fascism, while others pushed Roosevelt to articulate social reforms. If some fought to protect the rights of labor, others disassociated themselves from labor on the ground that its strikes and collective bargaining were unpatriotic. If Democrats from rural areas wanted to keep agricultural prices high, even in the face of wartime price controls, Democrats from urban areas wanted to keep them low to protect consumers. If southern Democrats were maddened by Roosevelt's establishment of the Fair Employment Practices Commission early in the war to diminish racial discrimination in the hiring practices of corporations with government contracts, northern liberals favored it.

At a press conference in December 1943, Roosevelt let it be known that the press should abandon the term *New Deal,* for the program no longer was necessary. In fact, "Dr. Win the War" had taken over for his partner, "Dr. New Deal," said the president, who only vaguely hinted at a postwar reform program. In a rousing speech in early 1944 he advocated an "economic bill of rights" that would entitle every American to work, food, clothing, recreation, a decent home, medical care, and education. By equating postwar social reforms with patriotism and international security, Roosevelt both called social reformers to arms and challenged conservatives: "America's own rightful place in the world depends in large part upon how fully these and similar rights have been carried into practice for our citizens, for unless there is security at home there cannot be lasting peace in the world . . . [and] we shall have conquered our enemies on the battlefield abroad . . . [but] yielded to the spirit of fascism here at home."[16] But he failed to propose any specific policies—and resumed his silence on domestic matters for the war's duration. So ill that he could not hold a tea cup without spilling its contents, he lacked both the energy and the will to focus on domestic issues in late 1944 and in early 1945.

Although Roosevelt's desire to focus all attention on winning the war is understandable, his silence on social reform was a boon to Republicans. They enunciated their postwar intentions on numerous occasions, uniting behind a platform to restore the minimalist government and taxes of the 1920s. With their leader silent, liberals lacked a guide for the postwar period or as well as a means to articulate counterpositions to the GOP.

Funding the War with Deficits and Debt

After Pearl Harbor, Roosevelt had to decide whether to adopt a pay-as-you-go tax policy or rely heavily on government borrowing through the sale of war bonds. If he sought pay-as-you-go taxes, he might avert the accumulation of a huge national debt, the interest on which could absorb as much as one fourth of postwar budgets. But he knew it would be difficult to raise taxes markedly in a Congress dominated by conservatives, who also chaired the committees charged with tax policy.[17]

Roosevelt tipped his hand in his first budget message after Pearl Harbor when he predicted a huge deficit of $45.4 billion for 1942, based on federal spending of $56 billion and federal revenues of only $18 billion. Rather than seek taxes that would fund most of the war's cost, he requested only $9 billion in additional taxes—an amount so small that it would hardly dent the impending deficit.[18]

A debate quickly developed, however, about the size of tax increases needed to stem the double-digit inflation of early 1942.

Some of Roosevelt's advisers wanted high taxes to "sop up" consumers' purchasing power, but others believed that rationing, wage controls, and price controls could suffice.[19] Another debate emerged about who should pay taxes; liberals emphasized removal of tax loopholes for rich people and corporate levies, whereas conservatives wanted a national sales tax that would mostly fall on the working class.[20] In an election year, however, most members of Congress were nervous about imposing large taxes of any kind.

Roosevelt vacillated and finally developed a proposal that would placate everyone.[21] In a package designed to spread the tax burden among members of all income groups, he proposed collecting the $9 billion in equal measure from working- and middle-class people, corporations, and affluent people by taxing their incomes and inheritances. Corporate officials counterattacked with their own proposals, advocating a general sales tax that would raise only $5 billion in new taxes, borne primarily by the working class.[22]

Roosevelt retreated; in mid-April he proposed to cover only one third of the war's costs from taxes.[23] Within weeks he became more militant, saying he wanted "drastic increases" in taxes on people and corporations, as well as wage-and-price controls and more rationing as part of a seven-point anti-inflation program.[24] Congress balked; the House Ways and Means Committee planned to add only $5.1 billion in new taxes.[25] The House approved a $6.2 billion tax bill in a "stormy session" on July 20, which led the administration to place its hopes on the more generous Senate version.[26] But when the Senate Finance Committee reported out its version in mid-August, it was only slightly larger than the House bill.

Congress's animus toward taxes was further revealed when it stipulated that additional tax increases could not be enacted before March 15, 1943—or more than fifteen months after the United States had entered the most costly war in its history. To make certain that taxes would not target affluent people, Congress required that any new tax must take the form of a sales tax or a withholding tax, well aware these stipulations would sabotage tax increases for the foreseeable future.[27] Liberals would not abide a national sales tax because it hurt working-class Americans. And it would be difficult to institute a withholding tax at a time when all Americans paid their income taxes in full in the spring, *after* a tax year had ended. The problem was simple: in the year of transition taxpayers would have to pay both their withholding taxes and their taxes for the preceding year. In short, they would have to pay two sets of taxes at once.

Congress considered numerous ways to ease this burden. Some legislators favored a plan that would forgive taxes for the preceding year, so people could pay their withholding taxes for the current year. Others proposed this lenient option only for those taxpayers who lacked the means to pay both sets of taxes simultaneously. Still others were reluctant to let any taxpayers off the hook, because doing so would further enlarge the deficit. It took Congress until the summer of 1943 to enact a scheme that forgave some income taxes in return for partial withholding. As Congress dilly-dallied, the national debt rose from $ 41.1 billion in 1939 to $136.7 in 1943, en route to $270 billion in 1946.[28]

Relying on an ambitious and effective public relations campaign by Henry Morgenthau, the treasury secretary, to get citizens and investors to purchase war bonds, the federal government resorted to huge sales of these bonds to finance much of the war's costs. Many people bought them as a patriotic duty and because they had little else to spend their money on— consumption was constricted by rationing and the unavailability of consumer goods. To a nation hostile to federal taxes, the voluntary purchase of war bonds was far preferable to higher taxes, though few Americans realized that they and their children would foot the bill for these bonds for years to come.[29]

Still faced with the threat of inflation and a budget that was accumulating extraordinary deficits, Congress and the president resumed their tax deliberations in 1944. Roosevelt wanted to remove $16 billion from consumers' purchasing power. A fierce debate developed within the administration between Morgenthau, who favored making only general recommendations to Congress on tax revenues, and tax hard-liners, like Harold Smith, who wanted to make explicit recommendations to Congress as well as seek a compulsory savings plan. A wild cabinet meeting ensued in which Roosevelt was forced to declare, "I am the boss."[30] He chose Morgenthau's plan and sought tax increases of only $10.4 billion, mostly from increasing the income tax. Congress responded coldly even to this modest proposal. Robert Doughton, the North Carolina Democrat who chaired the House

Ways and Means Committee, called the increase "utterly indefensible" and sponsored legislation that called for only a $2 billion increase, mostly from excise taxes. (It also expanded many loopholes for affluent Americans.) When Congress finally enacted legislation in February 1944, it proposed to raise only a fifth of the amount Roosevelt sought.[31]

Calling the legislation "not a tax bill but a tax relief bill, providing relief not for the needy but the greedy," Roosevelt vetoed the bill—the first time in American history that a president had vetoed a tax bill.[32] Congress, furious at Roosevelt for his unprecedented action and for his insistence on higher taxes in an election year, easily overrode his veto. Even Democratic leaders castigated the president; Alben Barkley, the Kentucky Democrat, resigned as Senate majority leader to protest Roosevelt's derogatory comments about the tax legislation. (In sympathy, Senate Democrats resoundingly voted Barkley back into office.) Chastened by this bipartisan rebellion and aware that Republicans would portray him as a tax-and-spend liberal in the 1944 presidential elections, Roosevelt apologized to Barkley for his intemperate remarks about the tax legislation. But the tax issue did not die. Fifteen state legislatures approved a resolution favoring repeal of the Sixteenth Amendment, which had granted the government authority to levy income taxes in the first instance, and proposing a constitutional amendment to limit income and inheritance tax rates to 25 percent of income or assets except in national emergencies—a policy that would have vastly decreased the tax bills of affluent Americans.[33] Congress made no further tax increases during the war, and many legislators and corporate executives vowed to seek drastic tax cuts once the war ended.[34]

Even so, Congress had revolutionized the federal income tax. In 1940 income taxes were paid mostly by Americans in the top 5 percent income bracket; in 1944, 74 percent of the working population paid income taxes.[35] Still, Americans' taxes were extremely low in comparison to Europeans'—and Americans' timidity in raising taxes during the war left a huge debt for succeeding generations to pay.[36]

Toward a Double Standard

As Congress savaged the domestic budget on grounds that it was wasteful, ineffective, and not essential, it rubber-stamped extraordinary military spending, rarely even inquiring about its details. House members and senators viewed even muted criticism of military budgets as unpatriotic—and scarcely required briefings by military officials, lest the practice lead to leaks to the enemy. Thus the United States spent several hundred billion dollars with minimal oversight.

The government established a procurement system that made large amounts of waste inevitable. Once he had decided that the United States would be the producer of awesome amounts of armaments for itself and its allies, Roosevelt engaged in an elaborate seduction of his old enemies, U.S. corporations. To persuade them to shift from civilian to wartime production, he (essentially) bought their support by various inducements, particularly when it became clear that many would not otherwise cooperate with his preparedness program. He placed in high positions within the military various corporate leaders, the dollar-a-year men (so called because their companies still paid their salaries), and vested them with the duty to place armaments contracts with their former employers. The terms gave corporations extraordinary profits. Military officials dispensed with competitive bids because they wanted production to proceed rapidly, and they often resorted to "cost-plus" contracts that gave companies the right to estimate their costs while guaranteeing them high profits. (Needless to say, most corporations chose to estimate their costs generously by taking every imaginable contingency into account.) Military officials often made generous loans to companies to build new facilities and to purchase machines—or actually built factories for them and allowed them to estimate their production costs as though the company had to finance or build these facilities itself. The government also made lucrative tax concessions on depreciation, often allowing corporations to write depreciation off over five years instead of the usual sixteen to twenty years.[37]

Desperate to induce civilian manufacturers to convert to military production, Roosevelt knew that many armament manufacturers would realize runaway profits under these cost-plus contracts. Take, for example, an airplane manufacturer that had produced 1,000 planes a year but that began to produce 10,000 planes each year under the lucrative government contracts. With its expanded manufacturing facilities financed by government loans and grants and with huge profits from government purchases, this corporation would find its profits increased many times in a brief period. One alternative would have been to set fixed limits on profits, such as limiting profits on contracts to 8 percent of cost—but when Congress chose this approach, manufacturers refused to accept contracts. Faced with a virtual strike by U.S. business, Roosevelt and the military backed off and persuaded Congress to enact an excess-profits tax that taxed only the corporation's increased profits over a base period before it accepted government contracts.[38] This tax was so lenient that corporations barely felt it.

The initial costs of rearming were vastly increased, moreover, by runaway inflation in 1941 and 1942, a result of Roosevelt's tardiness in establishing an industrial mobilization plan. As military production increased, manufacturers had to compete for raw materials and labor. Roosevelt could have moved rapidly to reserve some portion of raw materials and labor for military production, but he chose not to. Nor did he restrain consumer purchasing by seeking higher taxes, so mounting consumer demand, itself fueled by the prosperity brought by rearmament, further heightened civilian demand for raw materials and labor. As inflation escalated to double-digit levels by early 1942, the government's procurement costs increased commensurately. Only considerably later did Roosevelt implement effective means of diverting raw materials and labor to the armament manufacturers.[39]

In 1942 Harry Hopkins had advised that the federal government establish civilian oversight boards and give them some muscle; civilian agencies in England handled procurement by negotiating with corporations and trade unions. Instead, the U.S. government gave military officials exclusive responsibility for procuring weapons, as well as for deciding what share of raw materials would be diverted from civilian to military production.[40] Gen. George Marshall insisted that only the military had the expertise to make these decisions, and he put most military procurement under Gen. Brehon Somervell, the abrasive chief of the military agency charged with most army procurement, and under James Forrestal, the undersecretary of the navy who handled procurement. Congress asked virtually no questions and funded whatever the military sought—and congressional largesse was so extraordinary that the U.S. military had $55 billion in unspent military appropriations on V-J day.[41]

Enormous waste was inevitable. The United States had only begun to prepare for war when the Japanese attacked Pearl Harbor; a frenzy of war production ensued as Americans tried to supply the British and Russians, as well as their own forces. Somervell's aim was to produce whatever was needed, as fast as possible, and at whatever cost the manufacturers charged. With his office as well as procurement offices in the U.S. Army, Air Force, and Navy loaded with dollar-a-year men, sweetheart deals and favoritism occurred on a grand scale.

Only Harry Truman, then a senator from Missouri, provided some degree of external scrutiny of this emerging military-industrial complex. Truman was a tightfisted person who prided himself on careful scrutiny of budgets. He launched a personal investigation of military waste before Pearl Harbor when he began a thirty-thousand-mile trip in his dilapidated Dodge to inspect military spending on bases and in corporations with government contracts. As he visited installations, he said, "Boy, they are really wasting manpower and materiel and everything else."[42] (He also believed that U.S. business and the Republican Party had embraced a double standard: "Every 10 cents that was spent for those relief projects . . . was looked into . . . but the minute we started spending all that defense money, the sky was the limit and no questions were asked."[43]) Truman found considerable waste and established the Special Committee to Investigate the National Defense Program, soon nicknamed the Truman Committee. But the Truman Committee had few resources with which to track military spending. He started with only $15,000 and one staff member and eventually obtained funding for ten staffers—whereas military budgets came to exceed $80 billion.[44] Marshall deserves credit for cooperating with the Truman Committee when it sought specific information, but even his assistance could hardly compensate for the small size of the committee's staff.

The profits of the large corporations that received the bulk of government contracts tell the full story. Take the case of the aircraft industry, where the combined profits of the six largest aircraft companies rose 144 percent (i.e., from $21.4 million to $52.3 million) from 1939 to 1944. Most of the aircraft industry's expansion in these years was financed by the federal government, which invested $3.7 billion, while the industry kicked in only $293 million. (Much of the production occurred in government-owned plants that were sold to the companies after the war, often for 30 cents on the dollar.)[45]

Marshall implied the extent of the waste when he estimated that the Truman Committee had saved the nation $15 billion (or about $100 billion today).[46] If this minuscule operation saved that much money by catching some sweetheart deals, padding of contracts, and outright corruption, much greater waste clearly went undetected. Only after the war did congressional hearings reveal even a portion of this waste.

Nor did Roosevelt exercise much surveillance of the military's extraordinary budgets. He wanted the United States to be an arsenal for democracy and demanded rapid production of weapons, no matter their cost. He spent vast amounts of time strategizing in the White House War Room and in meetings with military figures and more or less gave the military carte blanche to buy weapons and supplies.

The national security state of the cold war era took root during World War II. The resources used by New Deal agencies in the domestic economy were transferred to the War Department and the navy during World War II but multiplied exponentially in the process. Accustomed to massive resources that it could spend with minimal oversight, and responsible for vastly expanding such huge industries as airplane manufacturing, military officials re-created World War II's military-industrial complex during the cold war—and continued to receive vast resources for the four decades of the cold war and on into the new millennium. Advocates of civilian control of military procurement during World War II, like Claude Pepper of Florida, were dismayed that the cold war military spent its huge resources with wild abandon for a dizzying array of nuclear weapons and overkill capabilities.[47]

A War Within a War

The war's cost to the United States was also increased by inefficiencies in the military establishment. A chasm existed between the War Department (with its infantry and air force) and the navy (with its carriers, destroyers, submarines, and Marine Corps). Admirals believed that Japan and Germany could be defeated primarily by blockading them and by bludgeoning them with air attacks from carriers. Generals believed that the infantry would prove decisive. Both the War Department and the navy, moreover, were split into subfiefdoms. The fledgling air force was buried in the army and forced to report to generals who favored the infantry. But the air force believed that long-distance bombers could almost single-handedly defeat Japan and Germany. But many generals viewed the air force with disdain, believing it to be (merely) a kind of aerial artillery unit that would provide protection to advancing troops. The navy tended to be critical both of infantry and airpower. Even on the eve of Pearl Harbor, many in the navy brass believed the nation needed an army of only 1.3 million troops. Most naval officers did not appreciate the usefulness of airpower and favored destroyers over aircraft carriers, which they viewed as vulnerable and of little useful purpose. Submariners were relegated to the lowest rung within the navy, despite the obvious success of German U-boats in sinking British supply vessels in 1940 and 1941. Submarine duty was so unpopular that only those officers who could not find assignments elsewhere became submariners. Nor did most naval officers vigorously support antisubmarine activities, focusing instead on battles between surface ships.[48]

These rivalries hugely increased the ultimate cost of the war. The services often saw themselves as engaging in parallel rather than coordinated missions, which gave them an incentive to maximize their forces to enhance their missions. They were prone to overorder for themselves and to hoard resources and weapons, even if this meant depriving other services. This go-it-alone mentality had tragic consequences in numerous battles in World War II, such as lack of air protection for infantry landing in Sicily. This vastly increased the casualties and slowed the advance against entrenched German and Italian forces.[49] The lone-wolf behavior also delayed an effective defense against U-boats until 1943.

Inefficiencies were coupled, moreover, with an extraordinary lack of tactical foresight. It was clear by 1940 that this war would be a global one, unlike World War I, which was confined to specific areas of Europe. The Allies would have to wage war in the Pacific and Atlantic, not to mention the Middle East, Africa, and India. George Marshall quickly perceived that logistics would profoundly shape the war's outcome as both Allies and Axis powers strove to deliver personnel and materiel to far-flung places. Such logistics, in turn, required huge numbers of transport planes, transport ships, and landing craft—a fact lost on most military brass, who had little patience for the more prosaic aspects of war. Had the nation prioritized these logistical elements even during its preparedness phase, the strategists would have had more options during the war, which probably would have ended sooner.[50]

Nor did American planners understand the importance of tanks, submarines, and antisubmarine weapons. U.S. military officers should have learned from Germany's blitzkrieg against Poland that a new kind of warfare had emerged. It called for mobility and firepower and depended on the combined efforts of tank troops, infantry, and tactical air support. American tanks were undersized, slow, poorly armored, and poorly designed. Originally designed to fight guerrillas in the sugar-cane fields of the Philippines, the leading American tank had a high turret so personnel could see over the cane. In the desert and on the plains, the high turret made the tank an easy target for enemy gunners.

The lack of foresight among military officials had tragic consequences during the war, in lives lost and resources wasted. Huge amounts of Lend-Lease materiel and other supplies bound for the Allies were lost to U-boats. The tank problem meant that Americans had to delay or refrain from specific offensive tactics. Logistical realities often dictated Allied strategy: insufficient landing craft were a major cause for delaying the D-Day invasion of Normandy until well into 1944.[51]

Defining Postwar Reforms in Military Terms

With Roosevelt silent and Republicans intent on preventing a resurgence of the New Deal after the war, few people even discussed a reform agenda for the postwar world. Yet Americans chose the central portion of that postwar agenda in 1944 when Congress enacted the GI Bill. It was inevitable that leg-islators would propose benefits for veterans, both because of their rightful needs and for political reasons. Legislators knew that voters were sympa-thetic to veterans of a war that brought more than one million U.S. casual-ties. And Congress was lobbied strenuously by such groups as the American Legion, which had secured bonus payments (special one-time payments to veterans) in the 1930s.[52] Indeed, an advocate of bonus legislation for World War II veterans wanted payments of $7,800 (or roughly $85,000 today). Congress focused initially on mustering-out pay (a lump sum at point of dis-charge) rather than huge bonus payments and enacted a modest measure in early 1944. Perhaps sensing that far more expensive legislation would soon emerge, Roosevelt chose in late 1943 to propose education benefits, hospital care, vocational rehabilitation, and reemployment rights for veterans, but he gave no price tag. Sen. Elbert Thomas, D-Texas, an ally of Roosevelt's, intro-duced a modest measure that limited education opportunities to a single year; the only exception was for an elite group of "exceptionally skilled or able veterans." This modest proposal was soon vastly increased in an election year when many Americans wanted to help the millions of veterans. Avid New Dealers like Pepper wanted no limits on education benefits, but the American Legion favored a more modest approach in its "Bill of Rights for G.I. Joe and G.I. Jane," such as a year's subsidy for education, home and farm loans, unemployment allowances, and fifty-two weeks of "readjust-ment subsidies" to help veterans make the transition to civilian life. After the Senate approved the measure unanimously, Rep. John Rankin, a conservative Democrat from Mississippi, pruned the House version; he saw it as a liberal plot to place veterans under the evil influence of academic sociologists.[53] He narrowed education benefits to veterans whose education had been interrupted by the war—and limited readjustment subsidies to twenty-six weeks. Rankin soon found, however, that many House members wanted more expansive legislation, and they forced him to rewrite it to make it similar to the Senate version. Soon after the House unanimously approved it, Roosevelt signed the GI Bill in July.

The GI Bill became *the* postwar domestic agenda because little domestic legislation was enacted during the war. It gave education or training benefits to 7.8 million veterans (about half the war's veterans) and readjustment subsidies and home-loan guarantees to nearly ten million veterans by 1955, as well as vocational training and health benefits to millions.[54]

While the GI Bill was invaluable for millions of veterans, it was a poor substitute for a broader domestic agenda that would provide health, child care, education, job training, and other benefits to an array of citizens—as European nations and Canada did after the war. After the war, Americans returned to the minuscule domestic budget of the 1920s.[55]

Failed Priorities in World War II

The Roosevelt presidency was a fiscal roller-coaster. Franklin Roosevelt inherited the minimalist federal budget of the 1920s that funded neither a domestic nor a military agenda and quintupled the domestic budget within two years of his election in 1932. He maintained this huge (by American standards) domestic budget until 1940. This fiscal feat proved to be temporary, however, as Congress cut deeply into the domestic outlays of the New Deal in 1940 and slashed it nearly to nothing during World War II. It was a demolition derby: domestic discretionary spending, which had often exceeded $5 billion a year during the New Deal, was reduced to a mere $160 million by 1944; that year the total budget exceeded $45 billion.

The U.S. domestic budget was fragile in the best of circumstances in a nation that hardly charged a federal income tax. Conservatives attacked the domestic budget roundly, even during the economic devastation of the Great Depression, when tens of millions of Americans from all social classes became destitute. But the domestic budget was particularly fragile when it had to compete with military spending, particularly from 1940 on. Because Americans were unwilling to adopt a pay-as-you-go policy, military spending blew U.S. deficits up to unprecedented levels, which gave added force to conservatives' arguments that the country should eliminate nonessential spending. Conservatives realized that the war was fully absorbing the president's energies and required a united front, and they opportunistically used the war to assault the domestic agenda, to devastating effect. Aside from programs mandated by the Social Security Act, the New Deal had virtually vanished by 1943. Figure 4.1 shows the marked decline in spending on employment, education, social services, and train-

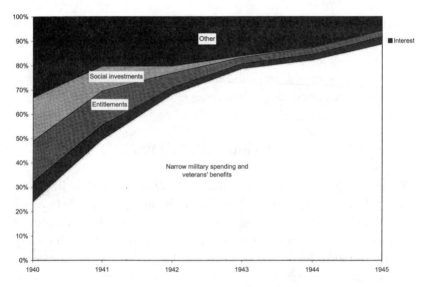

FIGURE 4.1 Five Types of Expenditures as Percentages of Total Federal Outlays, 1940–1945

Note: I calculated spending on social investment programs by totaling annual expenditures for "education, training, employment, and social programs"—and then adding to that sum public health expenditures by totaling annual expenditures for "health," as provided in the OMB's *Historical Tables*, table 3.1, p. 42. Entitlements are primarily the social insurances and welfare programs of the Social Security Act. Military expenditures are the totals for "national defense" and "veterans' expenditures."

Source: Office of Management and Budget, *Budget of the U.S. Government, FY 2000, Historical Tables* (Washington, D.C.: GPO, 1999), table 3.1, p. 42.

ing—called "social investments" in figure 4.1—as well as entitlements from 1940 to 1943.

Roosevelt invented big government twice, once for domestic reform and once to establish a warfare state, and he used similar tactics to achieve both revolutions. The tragedy was that his second revolution supplanted his first one—and that he had little choice but to be a collaborator (primarily through inaction) in its demise. On V-J Day in August 1945, the United States had virtually no domestic programs, save those mandated by the Social Security Act. Social reformers must have felt like Roosevelt did in early 1933, when he had to build a domestic agenda from scratch. Unlike Roosevelt, however, they did not have the urgency of the Great Depression—tens of millions of unemployed and desperate citizens on the verge of starvation. If Republicans were on the defensive in 1933 because the Great Depression had begun on their watch, they were a confident resurgent group in 1945, fresh from annihilating the domestic agenda during the war and determined to prevent a resurgence of social reform.

World War II would have been hugely expensive no matter how penurious and perspicacious its planners were. (Military spending, minus interest payments on the debt, rose to nearly $800 billion per year by 1945 in constant 1992 dollars—or nearly three times the cold war budgets of the early 1990s.) The country was, quite simply, deeply indifferent to the cost of fighting the war. As a result, the military developed a vast empire of contractors, mostly large corporations, that dealt directly with military procurement officials and had virtually no civilian oversight. Many of these industries, such as aircraft manufacturers, came to view federal largesse as integral to their survival, even when military spending was sharply reduced after the war. Meanwhile, southern Democrats had come to dominate the congressional committees and subcommittees on the military and appropriations, and senior legislators became cozy with military contractors who held contracts disproportionately placed in the South, Southwest, and California—a pattern that would be repeated in the five decades after 1950.[56]

Legislators contributed to budgetary tightness after the war by funding the war largely through borrowing. In constant 1992 dollars, interest payments on the federal debt rose from a mere $8.8 billion in 1940 to $29.8 billion in 1946—or nearly a fourth of Truman's postwar budgets. We argue in the concluding chapter that the United States would have saved $193 billion in constant 1992 dollars had it doubled its wartime taxes—and tens of billions in additional funds by altering its procurement procedures (this does not even include savings that could have been realized by cutting duplication and competition between the Navy and Army or revising wartime strategies in ways favored by Generals Marshall and Wedemeyer).

5

Truman's Nightmare

A frugal man who wanted to balance the budget, Harry Truman came to the presidency in the spring of 1945 when the budget was in chaos. It was laden with an array of postwar costs, such as occupying and assisting an array of nations in Asia and Europe, funding benefits and services for millions of veterans, and financing a national debt that had increased from $51 billion to $260 billion during the war. As Truman tried to balance the budget from the spring of 1945 through 1948, he battled with Congress over tax and spending policies each year, culminating in Congress's overriding of three vetoes in 1947 and 1948 to hand voters a large tax cut. Legislators slashed taxes to an average of 16 percent of gross domestic product (GDP) from the much higher levels of 1944 and 1945 when taxes had averaged more than 21 percent of GDP. The budget now had to fund a military that had grown twentyfold since the 1930s and was carrying myriad costs associated with the war. Could Truman establish a domestic agenda under these circumstances? I argue in chapter 15 that Truman and Congress sacrificed $1.17 trillion in constant 1992 dollars by failing to collect sufficient taxes from 1946 through 1952, tolerating waste in the military budget, and using a mistaken strategy in the Korean War.

Truman's Quandary

Truman was frugal in both his public and his personal life. (The National Park Service was astonished to find that the Trumans had saved hundreds of empty peanut jars in the basement of his home in Independence, Missouri, to be used for canning—and he had used roofing nails to mend tears in the kitchen linoleum, with neat double rows clearly visible to visiting dignitaries who toured the house.)

He also liked to follow relatively fixed rules. He was the first U.S. president to develop a budget arranged in broad categories like "defense," "ordinary costs of government," and "debt payments." He hoped to allocate (roughly) fixed percentages of the budget to each category: 20 percent to 30 percent for the military and the remainder to be split equally to pay for the ordinary costs of government, debt reduction, and interest on the national debt.[1] These guidelines meant that Truman did not have to determine priorities de novo during each budget cycle, and they helped him to resist the demands of lobbyists who favored greater spending for specific programs.

Truman entered the postwar world uncertain about the parameters of the nation's budget.[2] He knew that the country would have to pay the millions of U.S. troops occupying war-torn nations and help the starving citizens of those nations. He also knew that millions of refugees needed to be relocated and that the United States would have to help European nations restore their economies through loans or grants. He had to fund mustering-out pay, disability payments, and unemployment benefits for military personnel whose tours were up and pay for their benefits under the GI Bill. He realized that payments on the huge debt accumulated during the war would consume nearly a fourth of the budget. Because he did not know how long U.S. troops would have to remain in Europe and Japan, he could not predict the exact size of these various expenditures, nor could he know whether interest rates would vastly increase borrowing costs, or how many veterans would use their benefits.

Nor did Truman know whether tax revenues would be sufficient to cover these costs, much less provide a surplus he could use to reduce the national debt. Because he had experienced poverty and bankruptcy in his youth and during the 1920s, Truman believed that nations, like families, risk economic ruin when they fail to balance their budget. Although tax revenues had quadrupled during the war to roughly $43 billion annually, most of the money came from hikes in the federal income tax, and Republicans had promised huge tax cuts after the war.[3]

A tax-cutting frenzy began even before the war ended. In late June 1945, two months after Truman became president, Fred Vinson, his secretary of the treasury, warned that taxes would be "the number one problem" of the postwar period because Congress would make excessive cuts.[4] Joined by Walter George, the conservative Georgia Democrat who chaired the Senate Finance Committee, Republicans vowed in late July and early August 1945 that they would cut federal taxes in half and bring the federal budget in well under $26 billion. Encouraged by business executives and corporate allies within the Truman administration, such as Navy Secretary James Forrestal and John Snyder, director of the Office of War Mobilization and Reconversion, the Republicans, joined by many Democrats, began by slashing $5.5 billion in corporate taxes even before V-J Day to stimulate conversion from armaments to civilian goods.[5] Faced with a runaway Congress, in early September Truman urged that members cut merely the excess profits tax and leave the income, excise, and general corporate tax rates intact. As he was to do on scores of occasions during the next three years, Truman contended that he could not cut spending dramatically because most of the federal budget was fixed by prior obligations, such as the costs of veterans' programs, payments on the federal debt, and the unavoidable occupation costs. The conservative chairs of the congressional appropriations committees, led by Democrat Robert Doughton of North Carolina in the House Ways and Means Committee and George, were nevertheless determined to proceed with tax cuts—and were joined by Joseph Martin, the Republican House minority leader from Massachusetts, who demanded cuts of 20 percent in *all* federal taxes. He was then outbid by George, who was eager to start cutting taxes so he could ultimately make good on his pledge to chop income taxes in half.[6]

Vinson recognized that tax cuts were inevitable in 1945 and sought to limit them by proposing cuts of only $5 billion that year. He suggested that Congress defer other tax cuts until 1946 or later and warned that further cuts in 1945 or 1946 could trigger inflation and cause the deficit to top $30 billion.[7] Truman easily prevailed during this period of budget uncertainty but only because Republicans, sensing a campaign issue, chose to put the issue off until the congressional elections of 1946. (The tax-cut legislation, which Truman signed on November 9, cut taxes by only about $5 billion.) But this was merely the opening skirmish in a protracted battle.[8] Congress had cut federal taxes by nearly a fourth even before it was clear what post-war occupation, veterans' benefits, and other costs would be. And both Republicans and conservative Democrats were predicting far deeper tax cuts in the coming year. Relatively few voices were raised against them.

Searching for Hitler's Reincarnation

As he faced a polarized domestic situation with limited funds, Truman had to decide what his priorities were. Truth be known, he was primarily interested in foreign affairs—not the domestic agenda—when he inherited the presidency.[9] Before World War I, Truman had been intrigued by military history and often read dusty tomes on epic campaigns and battles from ancient history and the Civil War in a local public library. His personal heroes were military figures, such as Stonewall Jackson, Andrew Jackson, and (most important) Robert E. Lee.[10] Truman, who prided himself on his patriotism and courage, had used guile to convince military officers to allow him to enlist during World War I, although his eyesight and age (thirty-three) should have disqualified him. His wartime experiences, the high point of his prepresidential years, allowed him to develop leadership skills as a captain of an artillery unit.[11] An associate of Truman's during the White House years later recalled how Truman told his fascinated guests one evening about the fourteen most important military battles in world history "starting at the time of Hannibal" and using silverware and dishes to demonstrate the positions of contending armies.[12]

After serving in various posts in Missouri, Truman became a senator in 1934, and his interest in military affairs was rekindled. His reading of *Mein Kampf* convinced him that Hitler posed a threat to the Western democracies.[13] Truman became a zealous supporter of Roosevelt's campaign for preparedness from 1938 on and even jeopardized long-term relationships with isolationist senators to do so. Like many members of his generation, Truman was haunted by the memory of Neville Chamberlain's appeasement of Hitler at Munich.[14] They had watched the capitulation of Western democracies to Hitler, believed that it had led to the most destructive war in world history, and determined never to repeat this mistake.

Truman signaled his personal interest in military matters as soon as he moved into the Oval Office. Roosevelt had festooned his Hyde Park home and the White House with scores of pictures of naval battles. Truman replaced many of them with pictures of military aircraft. He spent endless hours in the White House Map Room, where he personally orchestrated the end-game strategies for Germany and Japan in the spring and summer of 1945.[15]

He was determined to place foreign policy at the heart of his presidency.[16] He wanted strong presidential oversight of the military because he resented the elitism of West Point, the U.S. Naval Academy, and the officer corps. To avert duplication and waste, he wanted to meld the War and Navy Departments into a single entity whose secretary would report directly to the president. He envisioned a people's military dominated by a nonprofessional reserve corps and an officer corps drawn from the ranks rather than from the military academies.[17]

Understandably paranoid because of the appeasement at Munich and World War II, Truman and Marshall nervously scanned the horizon even during the war as they tried to guess where a reincarnation of Hitler might reappear. Their eyes gravitated naturally to Stalin, though their suspicion of him was initially muted by the wartime alliance with the Soviet Union. Indeed, Marshall was favorably impressed by Stalin at Yalta, partly because Stalin helped him prevail over the British by insisting on a firm deadline for the D-Day invasion of France. Marshall, and subsequently Truman, believed the United States could do business with Stalin if U.S. leaders spoke bluntly.

It was inevitable, however, that Truman and many of his advisers would soon view Stalin as Hitler's reincarnation. As his purges and efforts to starve Ukrainians suggested, Stalin was, above all, a ruthless dictator—and he possessed a large armaments industry, albeit in a war-devastated economy. Stalin's actions in 1945 and 1946 in Eastern Europe, as well as his provocative language, cemented Truman's intrinsic dislike of the Soviets, though Truman was somewhat misled by his own moralistic and parochial perceptions. Unlike the diplomat George Kennan, who tried to view Stalin's actions through the prism of Russian history, Truman took the Soviet leader's words literally and personally. After all, Stalin had pledged at Potsdam to honor democratic elections in Poland—and don't honorable men keep their agreements? Do reasonable men make blustering and threatening statements?

Stalin was an evil man, but he also had legitimate interests as well as grievances. He knew that his country had carried the brunt of the war from the summer of 1941 through the spring of 1944. Nearly twenty million Russians had died, whereas U.S. fatalities totaled about 405,000. Because Russia had been invaded twice from the west, Stalin wanted a buffer zone under his control and believed that his country deserved territorial concessions. After all, the Allies had betrayed him on numerous occasions during the war by waiting so long to invade France, an action that the Russians needed so that Germany would divert some of its troops from Russia to the West. (Stalin believed that many Russian deaths were caused by the Allies' adherence to Churchill's peripheral strategy.) Nor did Stalin want democratic countries within his buffer zone—he wanted to be sure that those nations could not be seduced or coerced into becoming allies of would-be invaders. He intended to control Eastern European nations through puppet regimes, which he intended to install as soon as possible. (Writing to State Department officials from the U.S. embassies in Lisbon and Moscow during the war, Kennan brilliantly predicted precisely these developments—and wanted U.S. leaders to tell the American public in blunt terms that the Soviets would assert hegemony over Eastern Europe through puppet and dictatorial regimes so Americans would not be disillusioned when it occurred.)

Stalin also believed that he had reached an informal understanding with Roosevelt and Churchill: in return for bearing the brunt of the fighting on the eastern front at a cost of twenty million lives and devastated cities, the Soviets would gain their buffer zone of Eastern European nations in the Soviet orbit. This agreement could not be stated in actual words, because it would have induced Eastern Europeans to fight the Soviets as they chased the Germans westward after Stalingrad and millions of American immigrants from Eastern Europe would have protested loudly. So it was an unspoken and implied agreement—one that the actions of the Allies during the war seemed to confirm, moreover. At one point Churchill had secretly offered to trade portions of Eastern Europe with Russia, an arrangement promptly rejected by the Americans. By waiting until June 1944 to invade France, moreover, the Allies gave Stalin reason to assume they had invited him to take control of Eastern Europe, because both

Stalin and the Allies knew that delaying Operation Overlord meant Soviet troops would reach Eastern Europe in advance of Allied troops.

Stalin would doubtless have liked to control Western Europe as well. Indeed, as the historian John Gaddis notes, Stalin always held the romantic notion that the intrinsic shortcomings of capitalism would become clear to Western Europeans, who would then turn leftist and willingly become close allies of the Soviets. Nor would Stalin have had moral reservations about actually invading Europe if he believed he would encounter minimal resistance. But Stalin was also a pragmatist, aware that the United States could virtually destroy the Soviet Union by using the atomic bomb on Moscow, the nerve center of his sprawling empire. He knew that the Soviets' primitive economy, still reeling from World War II, could not survive an extended land war. And he knew that his nuclear technology, while developing far faster than Westerners imagined, was inadequate for a counteroffensive, much less a first strike. He recognized that the United States had succeeded through diplomacy and the Marshall Plan in pulling together a formidable coalition, even an "empire," that would provide devastating resistance to any Soviet invasion of Europe. (Far from welcoming the Soviet Union, many people in Western Europe were appalled by the installation of puppet regimes in Eastern Europe, even as they often supported leftist parties in their own countries.) So Stalin backed off in Iraq and other places whenever he met U.S. or British opposition and limited his aggression to the eastern European zone ceded to him during and after the war.[18]

But Harry Truman never fully understood Stalin's beliefs, resentments, and traditions. He failed to place Stalin's actions in Eastern Europe in the context of wartime events and Russian history and saw Stalin as a miscreant who had violated solemn agreements. Nor was the American public forewarned as Kennan had advised, so U.S. voters, like their president, often regarded Stalin's installation of puppet regimes as conquests similar to Hitler's in the prewar years. If Stalin was Hitler reincarnated, Truman would have to mobilize against him or become a latter-day Neville Chamberlain.

A Reluctant—and Partial—Demobilization

The newly sworn-in Truman was inclined to seek greatly reduced appropriations for the military—and for the same reasons as Marshall, whom he deeply admired. (Both knew the country would have would have limited money for military appropriations because of the costs of veterans' programs, debt repayment, and the occupation.) Both wanted a substantial military force but were critical of the military's wasteful ways during the war and angered by the services' intramural battles for money and power.

Both realized that military spending during a period of demobilization would have scant congressional or public support. Within days of V-J Day, Truman had decided his goal for a post-transition military budget would be $5 billion to $6 billion and told the Joint Chiefs of Staff to plan for a military budget of 20 percent to 25 percent of the national budget of $25 billion, as well as funds sufficient to conduct postwar occupation and to fund those troops not yet demobilized.[19] Truman used a "remainder method" to compute this budget. He predicted a federal budget of roughly $26 billion based on likely postwar revenues and arrived at his military total after reckoning that veterans' programs, interest on the national debt, payments on the wartime debt, and the regular domestic costs of government would each total roughly $5 billion, for a grand total of $20 billion. The projections of postwar budgets by five leading economists and planning groups tended in a similar direction.[20]

Although they were resigned to a modest military budget, Truman and Marshall feared excessive cuts in the armed forces because both already feared the Russians, despite the wartime alliance. Both knew, however, they had the luxury of time because Russia was economically prostrate and did not possess the atomic bomb. Because they realized that the United States might have to rearm itself, they aimed in the meantime to reorganize the military and to educate the public so that the nation could take the lead in countering Stalin.

Their reading of the voters' mood was confirmed by a demobilization frenzy after V-J Day under the banner "Bring the Boys Home." Still resentful of the cursory wartime briefings by the military, as well as its vast appetite for dollars, many members of Congress demanded vast cuts in military spending.[21] (Congress had spent money on the military with such abandon during the war that the treasury held $55 billion in unspent military appropriations on V-J Day.[22]) Rivalry between the navy and the War Department further tarnished the military's image; their wasteful competition in the Pacific soured many Americans. Then, after the war, the War Department, the navy, and the army air force began competing for funding and specific weapons systems. Furious that its share of the military budget had declined from 61 percent in 1935 to 29 percent in 1943, the navy was determined to reverse this trend by enlarging its carrier fleet and its aerial role. In turn, the army air force wanted to become an independent branch with a budget equal to or exceeding that of the army or the navy— and attacked the navy's plans to increase its airborne capabilities.[23] But while the services were seeking more money, Congress was getting ready to cut their budgets. Some Republicans still subscribed to the "fortress America" doctrine, as the isolationist position was known, in the belief that the nation could rely on its atomic weapons and stateside forces to repel hostile nations. Meanwhile, just as many Democrats placed their postwar hopes in the newly created United Nations, eager to see nations not only disarm but place fissionable materials under international control.

After he encountered public demand to demobilize far faster than he had thought would be necessary, Truman planned in November 1945 to reduce U.S. forces in Europe from 3.5 million to 370,000 by July 1, 1946, and then used every available ship and plane to bring these troops home in late 1945.[24] He reconverted about 90 percent of munitions plants to civilian use by late 1945.[25] He planned a military budget of $15 billion for 1946, only to be greeted by a chorus of protests from the military brass, who feared their budgets would be inadequate to pay for occupation or to maintain troop levels. Dwight Eisenhower, who had replaced Marshall as the army chief of staff in November 1945, became their articulate spokesman. He sought seventy air groups, far larger ground forces, and rejection of the premise that the United States could take a full year to remobilize if threatened by another nation.[26] Truman too harbored growing doubts about the speed of demobilization, telling military leaders in November 1945: "The only language those people [the Russians] understand is the language of force. At the rate we are demobilizing troops . . . we are heading directly for a third world war."[27]

When Truman announced a slowdown in demobilization, however, the public was livid, and troops mutinied at many bases around the world. Taxpayers also were angered by widespread reports that military leaders were jealously seeking to protect their wartime budgets and had secretly stockpiled materials and weapons for the postwar period. Determined to force Truman to make greater cuts in the military budget, Congress in 1946 and in the three years that followed went over the military budget line by line.[28] Congress would not even approve routine wage increases for the navy.[29] Nor did the pressure to reduce military spending abate during 1946. Truman demanded cuts of nearly $2 billion in military spending in early 1946, only to be outbid by Republican senator Robert A. Taft of Ohio and other Republicans who demanded a cut of $5 billion. In an era when the military-industrial complex had not yet become accustomed to demanding higher military spending, corporate leaders joined Republicans in supporting cuts in the military budget.[30]

The Phantom Military with Awesome Power

This rapid demobilization ought not suggest that the United States lacked awesome power at all points in the postwar era. The nation had spent only $500 million on the military per year for much of the 1930s, whereas it averaged $19.4 billion a year from 1946 through 1949 for military personnel and weapons. When veterans' spending, interest payments on wartime debt, and foreign aid are coupled with military spending, the United States spent an average of $33.8 billion a year from 1946 through 1949—or roughly 85 percent of federal spending—on direct or indirect security measures or international programs. This left scant resources for a domestic agenda.

Budgetary expenditures represented, however, only a fraction of the nation's true military strength because Truman and Marshall had devised an ingenious way to keep U.S. power intact at minimal cost. Determined to maintain the nation's monopoly on the atomic bomb, Truman never seriously considered placing fissionable material under international control. (Truman's advisers did not believe the Russians would develop an atomic bomb before the mid-1950s.)[31] Truman and Marshall also maintained the industrial base that had built almost half of all munitions used in World War II. Although the government terminated its wartime contracts, and large numbers of wartime plants were converted to civilian use, the government retained control of 131 war plants worth more than $3.5 billion and stockpiled almost fifty thousand machine tools.[32] The military mothballed vast numbers of aircraft, ships, tanks, and other equipment. While Truman knew that some of this equipment would eventually be rendered obsolete by rapidly technological developments, he realized that it would provide an effective deterrent for years to come, particularly because other world powers were so devastated economically that they could not produce large amounts of munitions.[33] Truman took many steps to sustain U.S. investments in technological advances in aircraft, jet engines, atomic bombs, and many other areas.

Truman and Marshall also were determined not to lose the global network of military installations and alliances that had defeated the Axis powers, whether 170 active airfields in overseas locations or far-flung naval bases, and an intricate network of treaties with scores of nations.[34] They also kept 750,000 troops in Europe and Asia as late as mid-1947—troops that helped to feed, clothe, and house millions of people and deterred aggressors from risking war with the United States.[35] Truman also knew that the United States possessed millions of battle-hardened veterans who could be rapidly mobilized in an emergency—to be supplemented, Truman hoped, with universal military training to produce an armed force of two to three million men by requiring all men aged seventeen to twenty to attend one year of training spread over four years. (If Congress would not go along with the plan for universal military training, Truman hoped to continue a compulsory draft, which lapsed only briefly in the postwar period.) In the postwar world the United States remained the preeminent military power with a large military budget as well as the camouflaged power of the phantom (mothballed) military; the United States had no major competitor in a postwar world where major powers had been nearly reduced to rubble. Truman's ace-in-the-hole was the atomic bomb—and the monopoly on it that he he believed the country would retain until the mid-1950s.

The Assault on Domestic Spending

Truman was not an advocate of big spending in the mold of the prewar Harry Hopkins. Truman's personal brush with rural poverty and personal bankruptcy had sensitized him to the economic desperation of unemployed Americans.[36] He was a loyal supporter of Roosevelt's domestic policies, having directed Missouri's Reemployment Agency, which administered work-relief programs. Ater he was elected to the Senate in 1934, he supported the large public works and work-relief programs of the New Deal. But he was not a "radical liberal" (a term he used) in the mold of Sen. Robert Wagner of New York. Truman was so angered by Roosevelt's efforts to pack the Supreme Court in 1937 that he moved from "left of center" to "right of center."[37] Nor was Truman an avid supporter of federal aid to education, partly because he believed that citizens should be self-taught (like him and his heroes Abe Lincoln and Stonewall Jackson).[38]

Truman did support civil rights and health insurance, but these reforms conveniently required few expenditures from the general revenues. Truman did not possess the deep-seated racism of many southern Democrats, even if such advocates of civil rights as Sen. Paul Douglas, D-Ill., viewed him as a reluctant supporter of civil rights.[39] Truman understood both the incongruity between discrimination and religious teaching, and the political uses of civil rights when the votes of African Americans in Kansas City and St. Louis gave him the winning margins in several close elections. In his first term in the Senate he strongly supported federal legislation that prohibited lynchings and the use of poll taxes at a time when such measures were considered daring.[40] Truman's life experiences also had sensitized him to the need for national health reforms—he had experienced the trauma of caring for an aunt and a mother with chronic health problems and as a local elected official had helped fund a mental hospital.[41] His personal commitment to health insurance was eloquently reflected in the best speech of his uphill campaign for the presidency in 1948.[42] His version of health insurance required no funds from general revenues because it was financed by payroll deductions and segregated from the regular budget like Social Security.

Truman was ill equipped to lead a crusade for major social reforms, even had he desired them. As an administrator who excelled in budgeting and details, he was an awkward public speaker who was given to staccato phrases and had a high-pitched voice. Although he believed that presidents should assume leadership in foreign affairs, he thought they should merely articulate broad goals in domestic affairs and leave the development of specific legislation to Congress.[43]

Thus Truman did not seek large domestic expenditures in late August 1945; he wanted merely to consolidate social legislation left by the New Deal, not launch bold new reforms.[44] Nor did he want to antagonize the southern Democrats who had vowed to help Republicans abort a postwar resurgence of the New Deal.

Yet Truman also wanted to placate liberals, who viewed him with suspicion because he came from a border state. Searching for a way to do that short of committing himself to a major spending program, Truman quickly came out in favor of national health insurance, only to find it stalled in the Senate Finance Committee by Senator George. Truman also supported an array of social reforms that he had inherited from Roosevelt; on September 6, in a speech carefully tailored to appease liberals as well as his conservative advisers (such as John Snyder, Matthew Connelly, and Jake Vardaman), Truman laid out a twenty-one–point manifesto. These points seemed breathtakingly liberal because no president (before or since) has ever compressed into a single message so many reforms, including federal aid to education, national health insurance, federalizing unemployment insurance, civil rights, and full-employment legislation. John Snyder had advised Truman not to issue the twenty-one points and wept when Truman rejected his advice; Republicans and some Democratic conservatives decided to go to war against a president who had clearly sided with New Deal liberals.[45]

Truman's points were not as liberal as they first seemed, however, because they did not commit Truman to any specific legislation or new federal expenditures. A disgruntled Harold Smith, the budget director, complained that Truman, by stating so many reform interests, had committed himself to nothing specifically—and Smith was convinced that Snyder and Vinson, two of Truman's most trusted advisers, would block any reform or spending initiatives that might emerge.[46]

Truman's decision not to seek specific appropriations for domestic reforms became clearer as 1945 progressed. On October 11 he appointed the conservative Snyder as his coordinator of domestic legislation, a move that liberal aides deeply resented.[47] He devoted virtually no time to federal aid to education.[48] Veterans protested Truman's inaction with respect to housing legislation to help ease the shortages that they confronted. Nor was organized labor happy with Truman: Philip Murray of the Congress of Industrial Organizations accused him of cowardice for supporting anti-strike measures.[49]

Truman's middle course on domestic matters not only failed to satisfy liberals but maddened conservatives. The House Ways and Means Committee stalled a measure on unemployment compensation. Although Truman favored keeping the U.S. Employment Service (USES) federalized so that it could help displaced war-production workers and veterans find jobs, Congress turned it over to the states. Conservatives launched a furious assault on appropriations for various social programs in late 1945, seeking to gut a small school lunch program, threatening appropriations for the Fair Employment Practices Commission, attacking the Office of Price

Administration, cutting funding for the Children's Bureau (which conducted surveys of children's needs), and cutting the appropriation for the National Labor Relations Board.[50]

Truman as Symbolic Reformer

Nowhere was Truman's frugality more evident than with respect to the full-employment legislation. Recall that Roosevelt had established the National Resources Planning Board (NRPB) before the war to develop a postwar agenda for domestic reforms, but conservatives, angered by its support of a cradle-to-grave welfare state, had terminated its funding in 1943. Partly at the insistence of liberals who feared conservatives would dominate the postwar era, Roosevelt affirmed his support of full employment in an "economic bill of rights" in January 1944—followed by a vow in late October to create sixty million jobs at the end of the war.

At the behest of Democratic senator James Murray of Montana, a group of liberal civil servants and congressional aides set to work on a full-employment bill in late 1944, using this term because it attracted bipartisan support in a nation that vividly remembered the Great Depression. Influenced by Keynes, Murray and these civil servants were convinced that the United States could avert a postwar recession or depression only if the nation massively increased domestic spending, which had nearly been eliminated during the war.[51] The National Farmers Union, an ultra-liberal lobbying group, developed a wartime proposal to seek $40 billion in annual domestic spending—a huge amount that would have dwarfed even the New Deal's budgets.[52]

Searching for a way to head off conservative opposition, the Murray group invented a procedure that would automatically trigger public spending in the event of a recession or depression. The president would submit a "full-employment budget" at the start of each year after his economic advisers had calculated the amount of federal spending needed to promote full employment. A joint congressional committee on the budget would implement the president's recommendations by recommending sufficient spending to avert a recession or depression. It seemed an ingenious strategy because this procedure, the group believed, would force the incumbent president, Congress, and conservative heads of key committees to support major spending. With memories of the Great

Depression still fresh, the liberals hoped Congress would enact the legislation. To make it even more palatable to conservatives, Murray downplayed public spending when he introduced the legislation in the Senate on January 22, 1945, saying the government would not have to "step into the breach with a spending program except in the most dire emergencies."[53] Nor, Murray said, would greater spending lead to budget deficits, because Congress could raise the money through taxes rather than by borrowing.

Preoccupied with ending the war and weakened by heart disease, Roosevelt had not committed himself to the legislation when he died. Liberal senators, including Wagner and Murray, feared that Truman would not support "advanced social legislation." They were delighted when he included the full-employment legislation in his twenty-one points in August.

The liberals' hopes of securing conservative support were somewhat dashed, however, when a minority report of a Senate committee headed by Taft declared that the legislation reflected "the compensatory spending theory" of Keynes and labeled its guarantee of full employment totalitarianism, akin to the policies of Hitler and Stalin. A conservative coalition headed by the U.S. Chamber of Commerce and the National Association of Manufacturers intoned that guarantees of full employment represented government paternalism and eroded business confidence.[54] Nonetheless, the Senate approved the full-employment legislation in late September.

The House Rules Committee ominously referred the legislation to the unfriendly House Committee on Expenditure of Executive Departments, which was chaired by the conservative Carter Manasco, a Democrat from Alabama. Although Rep. Wright Patman, D-Texas, had secured sixty-five cosponsors, conservatives opposed the legislation and stalled it in Manasco's committee. Urged by liberals to intercede, Truman called Manasco, who reluctantly agreed to support the legislation on the condition that he not be bound to the original bill or even the words "full employment."[55]

Although he had interceded, Truman signaled that he did not favor an expensive version by assigning Snyder, his conservative adviser, to track the full-employment legislation in Congress. Snyder conveyed his intent to hold down social spending when the House committee asked him whether the legislation would stimulate federal spending, and he replied that he "would look into that." After castigating the House committee in late October for delaying the legislation, Truman exerted no further pressure on the House, despite a subcommittee's decision to excise the measure's commitment to full employment and to limit its authority to preparing for the president an annual and (merely) advisory economic report by a council of economic advisers.[56] Although even this diluted version proved too strong for the four conservatives on the full committee, whose minority report opposed the bill, the House approved the legislation in December.

Liberal hopes for the stronger Senate version were dimmed by runaway postwar economic growth and inflation—hardly the postwar depression predicted by many liberals. The public was largely unaware of the full-employment legislation.[57] The House-Senate conference committee made various semantic changes to appease the House in early 1946, such as changing "full" to "maximum" employment and deleting explicit references to social spending. The Senate version had sought "such volume of federal investment and expenditure as may be needed . . . to achieve . . . full employment"; the revised version merely urged "the federal government to use all practicable means . . . to coordinate and utilize all its plans, functions, and resources." The original legislation had required the president to submit a national budget that described social spending needed to bring full employment; the final legislation merely asked a joint (congressional) committee to study the annual economic report "as a guide to the several committees of the Congress dealing with legislation relating to the Economic Report."[58]

The saga of the full-employment legislation reflects the postwar anti-spending climate that gripped Congress, as well as Truman's reluctance to champion measures that required major federal spending. It also revealed a political naïveté on the part of those liberals who thought they could invent a procedural gimmick to require the president and Congress to expand spending. Even if the original legislation had been enacted, congressional committees would not have approved social programs or appropriated resources for them because their conservative chairmen were pledged to cut postwar spending.

Unable to get Congress to approve postwar reforms during the war, some liberals took solace in the enactment of the GI Bill, as well as other veterans' programs. These programs became the domestic agenda in the postwar years. The United States spent only $797 million in federal monies on social, educational, training, and employment programs from 1946 to 1950, whereas it spent $30.7 billion on veterans' benefits and services. Indeed, veterans' programs became a kind of welfare state within the military establishment and far outshined the meager civilian benefits offered under the Social Security Act. Instead of helping all citizens or impoverished citizens by instituting educational and health programs, the United States extended its largesse only to veterans.

Nervously Plotting Rearmament

Truman eyed the Russians nervously. He intended to devote 1946 to close scrutiny of the Soviets to determine their actual threat and was bombarded by a succession of theoretical statements that underscored the Russian threat to Western democracies. Kennan argued in his "Long Telegram" to the State Department from Moscow in February that negotiating with the Russians would be fruitless, because their insecurity was the result of centuries of isolation and could not be overcome by reason. However, the Soviets were not risk takers and would retreat when faced with determined resistance by foreign powers. Although Kennan implied that Western nations ought to pursue a confrontational strategy, he made no specific recommendations about military forces.[59] Churchill, although out of office, used his influence to further this agenda. In his famous speech in Fulton, Missouri, in March 1946 Churchill contended that "from Stettin in the Baltic to Trieste in the Adriatic, an iron curtain has descended across the continent" that endangers "Christian civilization."[60]

At first Truman openly endorsed Churchill's speech, then publicly backtracked when he discovered that it was widely perceived as exaggerating the Russian menace. He ordered Clark Clifford, his legal counsel, to undertake an analysis of Russian intentions. When Clifford issued his confidential report in September, it was even more paranoid about the Soviets than the Long Telegram or Churchill. Truman suppressed it by placing it in a White House safe, fearful the report (and he) would be attacked by internationalists in the Democratic Party, such as Henry Wallace, his secretary of commerce.[61] But Truman moved swiftly to change his foreign policy advisers. He fired Wallace in September 1946 for a speech excessively conciliatory to Russia—and replaced the accommodationist James F. Byrnes, the secretary of state, with George Marshall in January 1947—

moves that also neutralized Republicans' charges that Democrats were coddling communists in trade unions and the State Department.

Truman faced a political dilemma in 1946. While his response to Churchill's speech and Clifford's report strongly suggested that he believed the Soviets had expansionist intentions, he could not embark on a militant course for fear of antagonizing those Democrats who wanted conciliatory policies. Nor did he have resources in his spartan budget to fund a larger military, which most Republicans also would have opposed. If he wanted the United States to spend significant resources on international or military strategies to counter communism, he had to educate the public about the Russian menace (as Kennan had suggested), much as Roosevelt had gradually convinced Americans to rearm themselves to counter Hitler. And he had to find a way to counter this Russian threat that was politically acceptable to conciliatory and hard-liner politicians from both parties.

Truman's task was simpler than Roosevelt's, however, on several counts. He did not have to contend with widespread isolationism, which had been discredited by Hitler's aggression.[62] If Americans before the war had believed themselves immune to foreign conquest, technological advances in weaponry, such as the development of long-range bombers and the atomic bomb, made them more aware of their vulnerability to distant foes. Polls on March 31, 1941, and June 7, 1946 revealed considerable anti-Soviet sentiment. In the first poll 71 percent of respondents disapproved of the "policy Russia is following in world affairs," compared to only 7 percent who approved. In the second poll 58 percent of respondents believed the Soviet Union was " 'building herself up to be the ruling power of the world," compared to 29 percent who thought the USSR was "just building up protection against being attacked in another war."[63] Yet Truman still faced a formidable challenge in rallying public support for measures to counter the Soviets because the country had insisted on rapid demobilization and would not have supported massive increases in military spending in 1946 or 1947.

The Elusive Peace Dividend

The postwar period, while prosperous compared to the 1930s, brought many social problems and considerable domestic squalor. Because of the depression and the war, local and state governments had been unable to invest in local improvements for more than fifteen years, and public schools showed the effects of years of neglect.[64] Teachers, who were poorly paid, lacked prestige, and often lacked credentials, vented their frustrations in an epidemic of strikes. Teacher shortages led to the closure of six thousand schools across the nation; 1 in 6 children either had no school to attend or could attend only part time.[65] When discussing schools in New York City, a minister said, "Here in New York we know all about crowded conditions, ancient buildings, and poor equipment."[66] Major cities harbored huge blighted slums that had been home to two (or more) generations of low-income residents. Then came the great migration to the North of African Americans in search of jobs during the Great Depression and then World War II. These black migrants from the rural South were greeted with profound discrimination in employment and housing, and Chicago saw a major riot in July 1947.[67] Five thousand whites had marched on an emergency veterans' housing project in a white area where two blacks had been given leases, and Chicago "swayed on the brink of a city-wide riot."[68] Poor areas of cities swelled from coast to coast, but only 165,000 homes were built for low-income urbanites in the postwar years.[69] Americans were headed toward an even more highly segregated society: the rapidly growing suburban areas used zoning to "standardize wide areas within narrow income limits," made wide use of restrictive convenants in housing titles, and used discriminatory tenant selection policies.[70] (These suburban bastions would oppose social investment programs for urban populations in coming decades.[71])

Many Americans faced economic uncertainty. With their wages controlled during the war, industrial workers emerged from the war to find food prices had jumped 32 percent in one year. A family that earned $5,000 a year (or $368 a month after taxes) found itself with only $5 in monthly savings after paying for food, rent, clothing, cars, insurance, incidentals, and taxes.[72] Census data painted a somber picture of the condition of U.S. housing; 52 percent of American homes had no central heating, 35 percent had no private tub or shower, and 21 percent had no running water. Most new housing, whether for sale or lease, was priced beyond the means of the poor.[73]

Nor were social programs adequate. Unable to obtain wage increases for their members during the war, unions had to settle for negotiating fringe benefits, such as health insurance, with their employers. Few Americans understood how a medical system funded by private insurance would exclude many from coverage, including the 69 percent of Americans who were uninsured in 1947—and the many others with health plans that did not provide a range of benefits they needed.[74] (Uncovered Americans did not get health care or went to poorly funded municipal and county hospitals that depended on physician volunteers.) Unemployment insurance met less than half the subsistence needs of recipients.[75] Federal and state welfare programs, such as Aid to Dependent Children and Old Age Assistance, paid near-starvation benefits in most states. Millions of women, who had joined the industrial labor force for the first time in World War II, assumed they would return to housewifery when the war ended. Instead, they found they had to continue to work to make ends meet, but rampant discrimination restricted them to low-wage positions, and lack of subsidized child care depleted their paychecks.

Most European nations faced even more onerous social conditions because of the devastation of World War II. They embarked on bold domestic reforms such as the so-called Beveridge Plan in Great Britain, which instituted national health insurance, expanded social services, and provided housing programs. But the United States, with Congress controlled by conservatives and with Truman's attention increasingly diverted abroad, chose a meager federal budget based on minimal tax revenues. With entitlements still small and growing slowly—and with domestic discretionary social spending actually declining—Truman's budgets were dominated by military and related spending to a remarkable degree—narrow military spending and veterans' programs absorbed roughly 58 percent of his budgets.

In other words, the United States made no effort to convert guns to butter; it merely reduced military spending from its wartime levels and added little domestic spending. Federal spending on education, training, employment, and social services (the "social investments" in fig. 5.1) decreased from $3 billion in 1944 to merely $1.9 billion in 1947, though entitlements rose from $9.7 billion to $17.7 billion (all figures in 1992 dollars)—and amounted to only 5 percent of the federal budget in 1947 (see fig. 5.1).

Conservatives had momentum on their side, having abolished most New Deal programs during the war and increased their numbers in successive elections. Franklin Roosevelt, the liberals' icon, was succeeded by a man with little ability to coalesce liberals into a cohesive political force. After fifteen years of war and depression, the American people wanted to

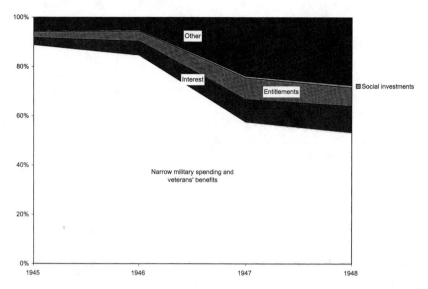

FIGURE 5.1 Five Types of Expenditures as Percentages of Total Federal Outlays, 1945–1948

Source: Office of Management and Budget, *Budget of the U.S. Government, FY 2000, Historical Tables* (Washington, D.C.: GPO, 1999), table 3.1, p. 42.

return to normalcy. They did not want to embrace social reform. They wanted to spend their wartime savings on consumer goods, not debate social reform. Unaccustomed to a large central government, although it had grown considerably during the New Deal and the war, many Americans were sympathetic to Republicans' call to cut spending and reduce taxes. Even Roosevelt's first limited New Deal budget for 1933 seemed huge compared to the domestic agenda Truman set at the end of the war.

6

Truman's Bombshells

After Republicans gained control of both houses of Congress in a smashing victory in November 1946, both parties girded for the presidential election of 1948. Republicans were certain that they would prevail by slashing taxes, savaging domestic spending, cutting military spending, and balancing the budget. Truman's intentions were still unclear: would he try to rekindle domestic reform or, armed with Kennan's theoretical statements of 1946, push the nation to give first priority to military spending? As I discuss in chapter 15, his efforts to fund social reforms were frustrated by tight budgets, the result of tax and other fiscal mistakes totaling roughly $1.17 trillion in constant 1992 dollars.

The Republicans' Time Capsule

Republicans fired their opening salvos the day after the election, with Rep. Harold Knutson, R-Minn., now chair of the Ways and Means Committee, pledging a 20 percent cut in all federal taxes, with "quickie legislation" to be enacted by April 1947 and retroactive to January 1.[1] He pledged to work with the new Republican chair of the House Appropriations Committee, John "Meataxe" Taber, the New York Republican who had earned his nickname with his long crusade to cut federal spending. The Republicans counted on Ohio's Robert Taft, who chaired the Senate Finance Committee and was Senate majority leader, to spearhead tax and spending cuts in that body. The Democrats' only hope of averting the GOP's plans was a slight fissure in the Republicans ranks; Knutson wanted 20 percent cuts in all federal taxes, but the Republican senators who worried about balancing the budget wanted to make smaller changes. They seemed to reach a compromise when the House Republican Steering Committee approved a 20 percent cut only for federal income taxes, at a cost of about $3 billion in revenue.[2]

Convinced they had received a mandate from the voters for tax and budget cuts, the Republicans introduced HR 1 on January 1; it called for a 20 percent cut in federal income taxes, which would put rates for middle-class voters below 12 percent. To offset the charge that they risked a deficit by proceeding on tax cuts before they had established any spending objectives, the Republicans demanded that 500,000 federal civilian employees be laid off. To avoid political flak they did not name the programs that would be cut.[3]

Truman was unequivocally opposed to any tax cuts, contending that domestic spending had already been cut to the bone—the number of federal civilian employees already was down 40 percent from its wartime peak. He charged that the Republican plan to cut taxes would throw his 1947–1948 budget out of balance—and it was the first presidential budget to be balanced since 1930. (Truman could aspire to this balanced budget because he slashed military spending by $3.4 billion to a total of $11.3 billion and anticipated higher revenues from economic growth and bracket creep as double-digit inflation sent taxpayers into into higher brackets.) When Republicans attacked his budget as excessive because it was four times the size of the prewar budget, Truman countered by citing the population growth in the intervening years, as well as the costs over which he had no control: veterans' benefits, international obligations, and debt financing. He hinted he might even consider a tax increase in July to combat inflation, arguing that deep tax cuts would only exacerbate it.[4] Nor was Truman inhibited about using some budget deception to achieve his ends.

He deliberately understated the nation's anticipated revenues for 1947 and moved some expenditures from later years to 1947 to make the budget look even more off kilter, in the hope of forestalling a tax cut.[5]

Truman's opposition to tax cuts and to dismissals of federal employees seemed to guarantee that Republicans would take over the White House in the 1948 election. After all, the Republicans had gained control of Congress in 1947 by insisting on spending and tax cuts. Truman's strategy was based on a slender reed: that Americans would buy his argument that if Congress slashed taxes, a balanced budget would be impossible—and so would be any hope of reducing inflation.[6] He used his tax and budget positions, moreover, to cement his liberal coalition—the Republicans' tax cuts would have devastated the federal civil service.

Republicans soon found that it was easier to make sweeping promises to cut spending and taxes than to implement them. Because much of the budget consisted of uncontrollable costs like debt payments and veterans' programs, because domestic spending had already been slashed during and after the war, and because Truman had already cut military spending, they could find little more to cut. And while Knutson wanted across-the-board cuts in everyone's rates, other Republicans wanted cuts that would benefit less affluent taxpayers to offset the Democrats' charge that they were the party of the rich. Some Republicans wanted to delay tax cuts until they had decided where the spending cuts would come, while others wanted tax and spending cuts to proceed simultaneously. Some wanted a 20 percent cut in military spending; others preferred 10 percent. Taber wanted to cut one million federal civilian employees at once, whereas others feared these cuts were too draconian.[7] These conflicts spilled onto the House floor in late January 1947, to the delight of Democrats. House Republicans finally settled on a resolution to cut Truman's budget by $6 billion by the end of February, but Senate Republicans supported only $4.5 billion in cuts on the ground that the House cuts would force excessive cuts in military spending.[8]

Truman's First Bombshell

Following the logic of the Kennan's and Clifford's theories, Truman's attention was drawn to Greece where an unstable regime faced a left-wing insurgency in 1946. In February 1947 Dean Acheson, the undersecretary of state, told the president that Britain lacked the resources to continue its economic and military support of the Greek regime beyond March 31. Truman feared that Greece would fall to communism, only to be followed by Turkey, which had its own unstable regime. Were communists to prevail in these two nations, Truman believed, "we are faced with the first crisis of a [possible] series which might extend Soviet domination to Europe, the Middle East, and Asia."[9] Working with Acheson and Marshall, he coupled a request for $400 million in military assistance to help Greece and Turkey with his so-called Truman Doctrine in a speech to Congress on March 17. The Truman Doctrine pledged global leadership against communist aggression, whether that aggression took the form of outright invasion or subversion of democratic regimes from within. By comparing Greece to Munich, Truman found a way to mobilize public opinion against communism.

Truman had not only changed the subject but had done so in a manner that placed Republicans on the defensive. With the memories of Hitler's aggression still vivid, few politicians would risk opposing Truman's proposal, lest they be branded as isolationists or as communist sympathizers even as Republicans were claiming that the State Department housed left-leaning officials. Republicans feared that if they opposed Truman, and Greece fell to communist insurgents, the GOP would be blamed—although they also realized that the $400 million might be only the first installment and it could well derail their tax-cutting crusade.[10] Some Republicans charged that Truman had issued the "Greek thunderbolt" to embarrass them.[11]

By establishing an open-ended doctrine that pledged U.S. opposition to communism around the world, Truman was, in effect, rejecting the Republicans' desire to return to the minimalist government of the 1920s, even if he initially sought only $400 million in foreign aid. If the United States helped Greece, why not France or Italy or *any* nation where democratic regimes were threatened either by invading communist armies or by insurgent communist parties within their boundaries? The likelihood of major American expenditures on anticommunist projects was magnified, moreover, by Truman's failure to place any limitations on U.S. involvement. Would Americans intervene when foreign or domestic intelligence sources believed an invasion might occur? when communist parties won an election in a particular nation? or when "left-leaning" governments or parties—or even "neutral" ones—took charge? Would the United States intervene in civil wars? Would it side with dictators against leftist movements?

Truman's boldness in intervening in Greece signaled a tendency to assume that the Soviets were behind turmoil in other nations. As many critics pointed out, Truman used a loose standard of proof in the case of Greece, where there was no sign of invading communist forces and where opposition to the regime emanated from popular discontent with its dictatorial bent rather than from a communist insurgency.[12]

The open-ended Truman Doctrine was certain to lead to multibillion-dollar expenditures in the political turbulence of the postwar years. Because local communist and left-wing parties had led the Resistance to occupying Nazi forces during World War II, they were popular in many European nations—not because of their connections to Moscow but because of their antifascism. Left-leaning and communist parties also were popular because they advocated sharp increases in domestic spending, which were supported by many Europeans who faced poverty, homelessness, and malnutrition at war's end. Anticolonialism also had spawned left-leaning parties in some developing nations. U.S. officials viewed both left-leaning and communist parties as sinister—and even disliked governments that favored neutrality; the Americans seemed to be on the verge of supporting foreign intervention on a grand scale. This would likely require substantial resources at the very time that Republicans' tax cuts had depleted revenues that might have been applied to the domestic agenda.

The Republicans resolved their predicament by proceeding with their tax and spending cuts anyway, as well as their pledge to balance the budget, noting that this could be the last chance for sweeping tax cuts before Americans "take up the world burden."[13] To attract southern Democrats to their side, House Republicans fashioned a tax-cut measure that allowed somewhat heavier (30 percent) cuts for people with low incomes while still giving 20 percent cuts to middle-income people and 10 percent cuts to people in the upper-income brackets. House Democrats waged a fierce battle against these cuts, but the measure passed on March 27, 273–137, with 40 Democratic defections. (The measure proposed to reduce taxes by $4.2 billion.) Republican leaders in the Senate soon jumped on the bandwagon, ratifying most of the House tax-cut provisions by early May, and producing passage of the Senate tax-cutting measure in early June. Republicans were far less successful on the spending side, because they were able to cut spending by only $2.5 billion in House appropriations bills—this was far less than the $6 billion in cuts that the House Republicans had voted to achieve. Democrats, as well as the *New York Times*, contended that the

Republicans had managed even these minimal cuts only by slashing military spending by $400 million even as the Soviet menace was growing.[14] Truman vetoed the tax cuts and was sustained by a 2-vote margin in the House, which Democrats hardly found reassuring.

Truman's Second Bombshell

With Republicans still forcing Truman on the defensive with their tax and spending cuts, the president loosed a second bombshell in early summer. During the war some Americans had anticipated the need for massive economic assistance to European nations; now this idea appealed to Truman's top advisers in early 1947 as a kind of nonmilitary extension of the Truman Doctrine. Convinced that the Russians wanted to use the hunger and poverty of Europeans to destabilize democratic nations, Marshall and Acheson increasingly believed that economic assistance to Europe was a prudent means of checking communist subversion. Marshall, who became Truman's secretary of state in January 1947, persuaded Acheson to remain undersecretary of state for six months—and named George Kennan to direct a newly created policy planning staff to conduct long-range planning. Marshall spent March and April 1947 in Moscow at a conference on developing a plan for reunifying Germany. When he encountered Russian intransigence, Marshall became convinced that the Soviet Union wanted merely to exacerbate Europe's economic chaos to foster the rise of communist governments. He asked Kennan on April 29 to develop a plan for reviving Europe; Marshall's only instruction was to avoid trivia. Drawing on diverse ideas that had already been floated by people in the State Department, Kennan developed a rationale for massive U.S. assistance to Europe: attack the economic problems of Europe to diminish the appeal of communism.

The Marshall Plan made sense, of course, on purely economic and humanitarian grounds—and Kennan and Marshall realized this. Even if the Soviet threat had not existed, helping to revive the European economy and to bolster the Federal Republic of Germany was sound policy; fascism might again have resurfaced had the Allies acted as bad winners—as they had after World War I.[15]

While Kennan's project partly sought to stem communism, its planners underplayed this aspect for political reasons. They understood that the Russians would probably attack any large-scale U.S. assistance to Europe as imperialistic and that the Soviets would oppose any assistance to Eastern European nations. U.S. officials couched their emerging plans as exclusively humanitarian in nature. They also decided to charge European nations with developing the plan's particulars, both to underscore the U.S. role and to entice some Eastern European nations to participate in the planning process, thus splitting the Soviet bloc. In late May, Marshall met with Acheson and other top aides to rework the plan and even decided to let the Soviets participate to further undermine whatever criticisms they might raise. (He assumed that the Soviet Union would decide not to participate.) Truman discussed the emerging plan with Marshall; the president hoped that its association with a war hero would increase its popularity on both sides of the aisle.[16]

Marshall was at Harvard to receive an honorary degree on June 5, 1947, and gave a low-key speech in which he revealed the plan to help Europe. The Marshall Plan was instantly acclaimed. No one knew its precise size, which would be determined only after participating European nations had devised lists of projects, but it was widely assumed to be a multibillion-dollar and multiyear initiative that would dwarf aid to Greece. Its political chances appeared to be excellent because it fused humanitarian concerns (which Democratic internationalists favored) and anticommunism (which appealed to many Republicans, conservatives, and Democratic hard-liners). Marshall cleverly diminished Republican opposition by recruiting Sen. Arthur Vandenberg of Michigan, the leading Republican foreign policy expert, to head up the fight for the Marshall Plan in Congress. The Soviets' decision not to participate in the development of the plan further enhanced its political prospects because many legislators would have opposed assistance to Russia.

The European planning conference proceeded in the fall of 1947; how much the Marshall Plan would cost was still not known. Truman carefully chose not to disclose his estimates because the major opposition was coming from the House Appropriations Committee, where Taber fretted that it would unbalance the budget.[17] When Vandenberg read an article in the *New York Times* that guessed the plan might cost as much as $7 billion, he telephoned a journalist to say that Congress would never approve such a large amount.[18] Truman then briefed Sam Rayburn, D-Texas, the House minority leader, on the costs; Rayburn came away believing the plan would bankrupt the United States. Truman finally announced the operational plan on December 19 and sought $6.8 billion for its first fifteen months.

Truman viewed the Marshall Plan as a low-cost alternative to a massive national security state as well as a humanitarian plan. A democratic and nonleftist Europe would weaken the Soviets by denying them trading privileges. By strengthening its alliances with European nations and encouraging their economic recovery, the United States would gain a buffer against Soviet expansionism. To rally support for the plan, Truman and others offered a bleak alternative: a massive national security state that would require higher taxes and regimentation of the economy akin to that in World War II. The Marshall Plan was, in effect, pennies on the dollar compared to a national security state—a preventative measure that might allow the United States to avoid a large standing army.[19]

While Truman issued the plan partly to avert the spread of communism in Europe, he realized that it also hobbled the Republicans' tax-cutting strategy. If they cut taxes excessively, how could the United States fund the Marshall Plan without encountering huge deficits that both parties were pledged to avoid? Republicans still believed they could wrest the presidency from Truman by fulfilling their pledge to cut taxes and spending while balancing the budget—and wanted to get the legislation enacted before Congress approved the Marshall Plan. Therefore, Representative Knutson resubmitted the tax bill but changed its effective date to January 1948 to entice more Democrats to vote for it. Many Democrats sensed they were fighting a losing battle and that voting against the tax cuts would hurt them in the elections of 1948; they considered proposing their own tax-cut legislation that would remove low-income people from the tax rolls, but the House approved the new Republican version overwhelmingly in early July with sufficient votes to override a veto. The Senate followed suit, 60–32. Truman once again vetoed the legislation in mid-July but with a significant change in his rationale. He had opposed the tax cut in his first veto because it would exacerbate inflation and curtail payments on the national debt. He now emphasized the imprudence of cutting taxes in light of "foreign risks," citing the Soviets' refusal to take part in the Paris conference to develop implementation of the Marshall Plan.[20] By emphasizing the adverse effects on national security of cutting taxes, Truman was putting the Republicans in a public relations dilemma. Once again Congress was narrowly unable to overturn Truman's veto.

Truman's opposition to tax cuts seemed even more warranted as the European nations struggled to determine how to implement the Marshall Plan in Paris in the summer and fall. The European Planning Committee issued a

report in mid-September that sought $17 billion over four years, to be used by
sixteen nations and the Western-occupied zones in Germany. Truman called
Congress into special session in November 1947, and he and Marshall presented legislation appropriating $6.8 billion during the first fifteen months of
a plan that called for $15 billion to $18 billion over four-plus years.

Indeed, the Marshall Plan revealed several traits of Truman that were
not widely recognized. Although he was a frugal budgeter with a fetish for
balanced budgets, he was willing to make daring new expenditures when
it came to international affairs, whether to counter communism or to provide humanitarian assistance abroad. With the military budget already at
roughly $11 billion, the Marshall Plan represented a huge addition to the
nation's budget.

Frequently blunt to a fault, Truman offered no guarantees that the Marshall Plan would work. Just as he had stated when he had obtained funds
to aid Greece in 1947, he sternly warned in early 1948 that he would not
hesitate to seek greater military spending if the Marshall Plan failed to neutralize a Soviet threat in Europe or if the Soviets posed a serious threat to
U.S. interests in other parts of the world.[21]

Determined to stick to their plan to take the presidency from Truman
by emphasizing tax cuts, the Republicans resumed their tax-cutting strategy and still hoped to enact it before the Marshall Plan, which they knew
would probably destroy any chance of balancing the budget. They enacted
a new version of their tax-cut legislation in early 1948 after making small
changes to obtain support of more southern Democrats. Truman quickly
vetoed the legislation for the third time, only to have his veto finally overridden by Congress—it was now an election year and politicians were
loath to resist tax cuts. Once again Truman lambasted the tax cut as fiscally
irresponsible in an era of increasing international and military obligations.

Demonizing the Russians

The Truman Doctrine had already begun a process of demonizing the
Russians by implying they meant to—and could—subvert democracies
around the world, even if Greece was the immediate concern. In fact, the
Russians had not invaded any Western European nations, had not urged
communist parties in Western Europe to engage in violent actions,
encouraged communist parties to accept minority status in parliamentary

governments, and had not massed troops at the frontiers of Western European nations. The Soviets had not spearheaded political turmoil in Greece despite Truman's allegations. U.S. intelligence reports, moreover, continued to declare that the Soviet Union was not an imminent or near-term military threat to Western Europe.[22] Indeed, the Soviet Union would wrestle with the economic devastation of World War II for (at least) the next decade—and, even then, would emerge with an economy a mere fraction of the size of the U.S. economy. Moreover, though few Americans realized it, the Soviet people and leaders might talk big, but they were not about to risk another war, especially one that could too easily turn nuclear. The horrors of World War II were too fresh in their minds for that.

Influenced by the theories of Kennan, Clifford, and Churchill, however, Truman viewed the world through the prism of his anticommunism, as well as his belief that Stalin was the reincarnation of Hitler. Truman realized too that his electoral chances in 1948 hinged partly on his ability to mobilize voters against the communists—advice given to him in a confidential memo forwarded to him by Clifford. (It was written by James Rowe, a former adviser to Roosevelt, but Clifford sent it to Truman under his own name after adding some refinements.) As if on cue, the Russians played into Truman's hand as sponsors of the communist coup that toppled the democratic regime in Czechoslovakia in February 1948. Truman renewed the analogy to Munich, even though this coup was a logical extension of the Russians' decision to dominate Eastern Europe and no surprise to many foreign policy experts. Truman delivered a bellicose speech to Congress on March 17, luridly warning of Soviet worldwide aggression. The navy intentionally issued a false report that enemy submarines had been seen off the U.S. coast.[23] Administration officials also falsely declared that the Soviets had embarked on a crash program to develop long-range bombers. When the Russians put pressure on Finland to sign a nonaggression pact in the spring and summer of 1946, U.S. officials falsely portrayed it as an effort to make Finland a puppet state. In March 1948 Gen. Lucius Clay, the commander of U.S. military forces in Europe, sent a telegram to the director of army intelligence warning that war with Russia was imminent. High-level intelligence reports denied that this was so, but the telegram circulated widely in the upper reaches of government.[24] Top U.S. officials repeatedly compared Stalin with Hitler, implying that the Soviet leader intended to invade Western Europe.

The Russians' protest of the Allied occupation forces' decision in March

1948 to unite their Berlin zones in a single economic unit began in the spring and by June 24 had escalated to a total blockade that cut Berlin off from the West. This seemed to confirm the administration's characterization of Soviet intentions. The Berlin blockade was a frightening episode—and Stalin, like Khrushchev during the Cuban missile crisis less than fifteen years later, was clearly not averse to testing the waters. Western occupation of portions of Berlin—a kind of Western beachhead in East German territory—was embarrassing to the Soviets and posed substantial problems to them as East Germans sought refuge in the Western zone. Truman responded assertively by stationing in Britain bombers that were capable of delivering atomic bombs. The United States and England also began to airlift food and other supplies to Berlin. But by not moving against West Germany and by not interfering with the airlift, which continued until May 1949, Stalin signaled that he did not want to risk war with the United States.[25]

Although Truman was able to push the Marshall Plan through Congress on April 2, 1948, he encountered serious reservations from such Republicans as Robert Taft and from the columnist Walter Lippmann.[26] By not distinguishing between "peripheral" and "vital" interests, for example, wasn't the president risking a commitment of his administration, as well as future ones, to unlimited involvement in countering the Soviets abroad? Did not demonizing the Russians impede rational discussion of their actual intentions? Kennan, who had drafted key documents that had seemed to support militant opposition to the Russians and an early version of the Marshall Plan, had reservations about Truman's policies by 1949 and 1950. He liked the principles behind containment, aid to Greece, and the Marshall Plan, but he increasingly agreed with Lippmann's criticisms of the administration's foreign policy. Kennan preferred a rational discussion of options to a call to action or a demonizing of the Russians. Although Kennan remained the director of the Policy Planning Staff, he became isolated as hard-liners became more prominent in the State Department and in Truman's inner circle.[27]

Truman as Symbolic Reformer

Truman knew that he was painting himself into a corner with respect to domestic spending when he supported the Marshall Plan. It was simple arithmetic: Congress had cut taxes, and the budget included certain fixed costs of government as well as international spending. Enactment of the multibillion-dollar Marshall Plan meant no resources existed for social reform initiatives in the United States for the foreseeable future, unless Truman was willing to run a deficit.

Facing a Congress dominated by Republicans and southern Democrats, lacking the money for new initiatives, and giving first priority to international affairs, Truman became a symbolic reformer during 1947 and 1948. Although he supported pending measures for housing and aid to education in both years, he did not foster his own legislative measures or actively lobby Congress for either bill in 1947.[28] He assumed a passive role with respect to education, housing, and health measures but took daring risks with respect to international affairs in 1947, not only issuing his Truman Doctrine to a surprised Congress but working closely with Acheson, Vandenberg, Marshall, and Clifford to secure enactment of the Marshall Plan. He hardly communicated with congressional leaders about social legislation, but he orchestrated a bipartisan coalition to secure aid to Greece and the Marshall Plan. And he assertively vetoed tax cuts, more from a concern that they would imperil funding of international programs than because he was worried about any adverse effects from curtailing domestic ones.

Truman did campaign vigorously in 1948 as a liberal advocate of national health insurance, federal aid to education, and government-funded housing, but these public positions rested on political calculations. His electoral strategy followed the script outlined in the Clifford-Rowe political memo: demonize the Russians but rhetorically support health, education, and housing initiatives to cement the liberal base of the Democratic Party; and understand that securing actual domestic legislation from the Republican Congress would be impossible.[29] Truman penciled only $415 million in domestic reforms into his proposed budget for 1948, which suggests he doubted anything would pass.[30]

Truman did invest his political energies domestically for policies that required little expenditure of funds. He called Congress into special session in both 1947 and 1948 to deal with inflation, and he lambasted Republicans for exacerbating it by cutting taxes and rejecting certain price controls. Truman continued to support civil rights policies.

His frugality on the domestic front was matched by the Republicans' continuing assault on the meager domestic budget in 1948, where they managed several billion dollars in cuts. When they proposed cuts in public works, several Republicans defected. The GOP even abandoned two initiatives that Taft, their widely respected leader in the Senate, had initiated with bipartisan support in 1947: federal aid to education and federal housing legislation. (Because he wanted conservatives to support his quest for the Republican nomination in 1948, Taft stopped pressuring his colleagues to vote for the housing and education proposals, which languished in committee in 1948; these would be the last major social reforms proposed by Republicans for nearly twenty-five years, aside from incremental increases in such programs as Social Security and the National Defense Education Act of 1958.)[31] Preoccupied with foreign affairs, Truman provided virtually no presidential leadership for the housing and education legislation during critical periods in 1947 and early 1948, though the Republicans in Congress as well as some southern Democrats viewed the Truman's national health insurance plan as a left-wing measure and probably had the votes to kill any major health legislation Truman might have proposed.[32]

Truman earned his famous upset victory in 1948 over Republican Thomas E. Dewey with rhetorical support for social reforms, the popularity of the Marshall Plan, aggressive verbal attacks on the Soviet Union, refusal to capitulate to the Soviets in Berlin, and principled defense of balanced budgets by vetoing congressional tax cuts. His inaugural address was devoted exclusively to foreign policy and much of it focused on the dangers that communism posed for democracies. This signaled that foreign policy, not domestic policy, would absorb the bulk of Truman's attention in his coming term.

Institutionalizing Military Duplication

The prewar and wartime conflict between the War Department, the navy, and the army air force subsided with D-Day as the services cooperated to achieve victory over Germany under the leadership of Gen. Dwight Eisenhower. Even Douglas MacArthur and Chester Nimitz increasingly coordinated their efforts in the Pacific.

But such amity disappeared with the end of the war. With military budgets rapidly declining as the nation demobilized, the top brass in each service, afraid another service would gobble its budget, not only touted their service's merits but aggressively attacked the utility of other services.[33] Top air force officials, eager to gain independence from the army, and convinced that the future lay with them, argued that long-range bombers and the atomic bomb would provide the nation's security in coming decades. After all, Hiroshima and Nagasaki had demonstrated these weapons' awesome power—and the United States, they were certain, would maintain its atomic monopoly until the mid-1950s. Air force officers insisted that the navy's carriers were "sitting ducks" for enemy bombers. And air force boosters, such as Sen. Stuart Symington, D-Mo., rallied Congress in 1948 to provide $3 billion to build more long-range bombers over Truman's objections.

The navy, in turn, left the war with an inferiority complex, believing that its pivotal role in the Pacific had been underreported and that both the army and air force had conspired to reduce the navy's resources. The admirals feared too that all planes would be given to the air force, including aircraft based on carriers and used in antisubmarine activities—and that the army would insist that all land-based troops be placed under its control, including the U.S. Marine Corps. The navy, of course, wanted to retain its carriers, antisubmarine, and amphibious troops—and feared it would be reduced to a kind of taxi service that transported troops and materiel for the other services. The admirals contended that long-range bombers could easily be shot down, particularly when laden with atomic bombs, which then weighed as much as ten tons. Besides, the admirals asked, weren't atomic bombs, which destroyed civilian populations, immoral?

The army feared its infantry was vulnerable to drastic cuts during the demobilization frenzy because it lacked the glamour of planes or carriers. Citing the army's pivotal role in the months after D-Day, the generals insisted that infantry remained the most important military force.

This competition between the services was further exacerbated by Marshall and Truman's determination to consolidate the services into a single organization. Marshall had chafed at interservice rivalry and duplication during World War II and wanted a single chief of staff of an integrated military establishment to replace the Joint Chiefs of Staff, whose members incessantly bickered about the services' budgets and prerogatives. (The secretaries of war and navy both sat in the cabinet, moreover, where they aggressively represented their needs to the president and to the separate congressional committees that authorized and appropriated funds for their departments.) Truman shared Marshall's vision of an integrated military establishment, with a single civilian secretary, and a military chief of staff who would preside over naval, air, and infantry forces—and with a single budget fashioned by the secretary in consultation with the president. In Marshall and Truman's scenario the services would become components of a Department of Defense rather than free-standing agencies, and the joint chiefs would be supplanted by a single chief of staff.[34]

Truman and Marshall realized that Congress and the services would protest bitterly if they sought legislation that truly merged the three services. In the antimilitary tenor of the postwar period many legislators also feared a centralized military establishment, likening it to Germany's wartime military—and they wanted to retain the specialized congressional committees that established appropriations for the separate services and whose members received military contracts for their districts. Truman blinked, deciding (merely) to support a federation of the services under a loosely organized national military establishment that would retain the Joint Chiefs of Staff.[35] The congressional discussion of unification that followed focused less on unification and more on the development of policies to coordinate the separate services. A single secretary was established but with virtually no staff—not even control of the services' budgets—and largely ceremonial functions. Under the National Security Act of 1947 each service (including the now-independent air force) retained its own chief of staff and civilian secretary and controlled its own budget, which was presented to congressional committees specializing in naval, air, and infantry matters. Although the legislation established the National Security Council (NSC), the Central Intelligence Agency (CIA), and the National Security Resources Board, these entities had little power—and Truman even refused to attend the NSC on ground that it infringed on his prerogatives as commander in chief.

Unable to convince Robert Patterson, the secretary of war, to become the secretary of defense because he had wanted true unification, Truman chose James Forrestal, the secretary of the navy. Forrestal's tenure was a disaster. With the three services engaged in vicious and public conflict, the public image of the military plummeted as its budget declined to $11 billion. Despite temporary truces between the three services at key conferences in 1948 held to define their respective missions, they remained embroiled in conflict, leading Truman and Forrestal to push for amendments to the National Security Act to bolster the power of the secretary of defense. Once again, however, Truman blinked as he faced the awesome power of the services and their congressional allies and the near impossibility of fundamental reform: rather than seek true unification, he settled for incremental changes, such as giving the secretary of defense greater power over the services' budgets, increasing the secretary's staff, and reducing the three services to (merely) military departments within the Department of Defense so that only the secretary of defense sat in the cabinet.[36]

But duplication and rivalry persisted. Both the army and the navy retained huge air forces, for example, insisting on separate procurement and design processes rather than seeking common aircraft. Because the Department of Defense did not have centralized control of weapons, the Pentagon became a giant procurement machine, with different sets of designers and procurement officials in each of the three services—and with a growing army of contractors linked to these officials.[37] Each service jealously expanded its role in the emerging technology, determined to get access to atomic weapons—the navy sought supercarriers sufficiently large to accommodate bombers carrying atomic bombs. When the tightfisted Louis Johnson (appointed to succeed Forrestal in March 1949) decided not to fund supercarriers, a veritable "revolt of the admirals" occurred, not merely to protest his policy but to accuse army generals of corruption in procurement of the B-36 bomber. Truman fired Adm. Louis Denfeld and quieted the services by giving them roughly equal shares of the pie.

This highly public conflict between the services probably contributed to cuts in the military in the postwar era because their self-serving statements and public disagreements angered the public and the president, but it also frustrated efforts to integrate the armed forces into a coherent structure. That failure would eventually cost the nation hundreds of billions of dollars in unnecessary expenditures as the services duplicated weapons and missions on a grand scale during and after the cold war.[38]

The Missing Debate

Americans ought to have discussed the inherent conflict between domestic and military policy at the dawn of the nuclear age. With federal taxes hovering around 16 percent of GDP in the postwar years and large expenses for veterans, interest payments on the war debt, and the Marshall Plan, the nation lacked resources to address even rudimentary domestic needs. The Truman Doctrine promised global battle against communism, both to avert actual military invasion and the internal subversion of democratic institutions. But the doctrine was a one-sided—and open-ended—

statement of threats that the nation faced, and it ignored domestic threats such as the rapidly growing slums of northern cities, racial animosity, rural poverty, dilapidated schools, and lack of access to medical care.

Americans also needed to discuss how they could address external threats in a way that also allowed them to address domestic ones. Perhaps the United States ought to have been content with providing nuclear deterrence against a military invasion of Europe and economic assistance to war-destroyed economies in Europe and Asia and dispensed with the charade of preserving or securing democracies throughout the world. Perhaps the United States should have insisted that Western European democracies fund their own conventional defenses with some time-limited assistance from the United States. Or maybe the United States should have encouraged the United Nations to manage some local conflicts—or even oversee some economic assistance functions of the Marshall Plan. If U.S. intelligence reports were accurate, no national emergency existed in the postwar period because the Russians did not pose an imminent military threat to European nations, so the United States had time to discuss such questions. Perhaps the United States should have publicly drawn lines in the sand in those areas of the world where Americans were determined to prevent invasion, such as on the Korean peninsula where communist and noncommunist regimes coexisted uneasily, while ruling out U.S. involvement in civil wars or parts of the world where the United States lacked a vital interest. (No other nation presumed to police the entire world.)

Truman could have muted some of his rhetoric about the Soviet Union, because the United States was the only nuclear power. Indeed, as Paul Warnke, an assistant secretary of defense in the Johnson administration, sagely observed many decades later, the Soviet Union lacked multiple centers of finance and industry, which rendered the country vulnerable to even a few well-placed bombing raids by the United States. Truman also could have noted that Soviet expansion into third-world nations would run into many barriers, such as nationalism and factionalism, as well as logistical problems, because of their distance from Moscow. Indeed, he might even have suggested a positive U.S. policy, akin to the Marshall Plan, for helping third-world nations—and contrasted this policy to ones that relied on negative approaches, such as military assistance and subversion.

But Truman and his advisers did not promote or initiate rational discussion. They conducted their work against the backdrop of increasing hysteria at home about communism, whipped up by politicians who branded many Democrats and civil servants as communists or as communist sympathizers. Even the virulent anticommunist Dean Acheson was blamed for letting China fall to Mao Tse-tung.

It would be a mistake, however, to attribute Truman's exaggerations solely to public opinion. Truman, Acheson, and Marshall believed that hyperbole was necessary in a democratic nation to rally citizens behind meritorious military and foreign policy goals. Vividly remembering Roosevelt's difficulties in mobilizing the nation against Hitler, they decided in 1947 and 1948 to demonize the Russians, to argue that a crisis existed, and to imply that Armageddon would ensue if the nation failed to recognize its peril. Imbued with the idea that they could not secure their programs unless they resorted to hyperbole, they deliberately created and magnified a paranoia about the Soviets.[39] In simplifying and polarizing the world on the international front, Truman established a mind-set supportive of huge military forces at some future point, even if the military received only moderate funds as late as the summer of 1950.

Some dissenters emerged, such as George Kennan, who wanted a rational foreign policy. In the late 1940s other people, including Senator Taft, Henry Wallace, and the editors of such liberal magazines as the *Nation* and the *New Republic*, feared the emergence of an institutionalized national security state. The cost of a worldwide military capability might approach, some feared, $20 billion annually, thus requiring vast tax revenues that would deplete the nation of investment capital, slow economic growth, curtail the spending power of civilians, divert raw materials from civilian to military uses, and force resumption of wartime measures such as rationing and controls. Some people feared a permanent national security state might precipitate a breakdown of democratic institutions because voters, frustrated by regimentation and a lower standard of living, would turn to demagogues like the late Huey Long.[40] While many praised the Truman Doctrine, legislators like Taft and liberals like Wallace were less certain about it. Taft feared that Truman would make the United States the policeman of the world by committing it to fight the Soviets wherever they threatened democracies around the world. Wallace feared that the Marshall Plan would provoke the Soviets into massive rearmament that would require ever-larger military expenditures by both nations.

But these reservations and doubts were increasingly not heeded by Truman or his top officials, including Dean Acheson, who replaced George

Marshall as secretary of state in early 1949, and Paul Nitze, who replaced Kennan as director of the Policy Planning Staff that fall. The viewpoints of Acheson, Nitze, and Truman were crystallized in a remarkable and top-secret document. Drafted by Nitze and the Policy Planning Staff and bearing an arcane title of the foreign policy bureaucracy, NSC-68 essentially restated the Truman Doctrine. It declared that the Soviets were driven by a "new fanatic faith, antithetical to our own," that the Soviets wished to impose their "absolute authority over the rest of the world . . . [including] domination of the Eurasian land mass," and that "any further extension of the area under the domination of the Kremlin would raise the possibility that no coalition adequate to confront the Kremlin with greater strength could ever be assembled."[41] It did not merely state U.S. policy in defensive terms but sought to revive nationalist aspirations among the Soviet Republics and to dislodge the Soviets from Eastern Europe—feats to be accomplished through covert operations and psychological warfare. In a strikingly new development NSC-68 advocated vast new resources for the military, to be obtained from new taxes and curtailment of social and welfare programs. (Nitze wanted to triple military spending, even if NSC-68 remained silent on precise costs.) It warned that the Soviet Union would become bolder in its designs as it increased its atomic arsenal. Saying that containing the Russians was insufficient, NSC-68 called for "superior aggregate military strength, in being and readily mobilizeable" to counter the Russians.[42] As the historian Melvyn Leffler notes, "In the worldview of NSC 68, there was no room for neutrality; diplomacy was a zero-sum game."[43] Indeed, NSC-68, like the Truman Doctrine, created a tautology. Asserting a worldwide Soviet threat, it encouraged onlookers to attribute to the Soviet Union almost every major disruption, coup, left-wing government, or communist government. In the world as it actually existed, these phenomena usually arose from indigenous factors, whether communism in China, Ho Chi Minh's growing popularity in Vietnam, left-wing parties in Europe, or unrest in some third-world nations.

Truman's Simultaneous Declaration of Two Wars

Truman and Congress fashioned a military budget of $14.4 billion in the spring and summer of 1949. Behind the scenes, however, a critical debate took place within the administration. The military, always after more funds than the frugal Truman was willing to grant, sought as much as $23 billion to allow it to defend Europe—and even sought forty-five European divisions and three hundred to five hundred bombers laden with atomic bombs and scattered across myriad foreign bases.[44] In light of the Soviet threat, the services asked, why not markedly increase military spending and partly fund it by cutting domestic programs, including the $790 million that Truman had included for new social programs?[45] They argued that the U.S. economy, now much larger than in the immediate postwar years, could afford a military that absorbed as much as half of the GDP. Truman demurred for several reasons. He was worried about creating a large deficit, lest postwar inflation return. He continued to fear that the Soviets wanted to bankrupt the United States by goading the country into spending excessively on its military. Like Marshall, he hoped the establishment of the North Atlantic Treaty Organization (NATO) and providing $1 billion in U.S. military aid would push the Europeans to rearm and thus lessen the American burden. He remained confident the Soviets would not develop an atomic bomb, meaning that the United States could deter aggression even with modest conventional forces. Truman was uncomfortable, moreover, with a large central government. He, like many of his contemporaries, had reached adulthood before the New Deal and feared a "garrison state" if military spending increased too much.[46] Truman never envisioned large increases in domestic spending but nonetheless feared that massive military spending would foreclose even a modest domestic program.

But Truman was on guard—and ominous developments quickly raised his alarm. The Soviets exploded an atomic bomb in September 1949. The Chinese signed a pact of solidarity with the Soviets in early 1950, which suggested sinister global intentions akin to Hitler's alliance with the Japanese. Truman's budgetary inhibitions about high military spending eased somewhat as the economy rapidly grew and inflation ebbed. And he received NSC-68 that spring.

Now he inherited Roosevelt's prewar political dilemma. With the Republicans led by quasi-isolationist Robert Taft and with most legislators fixated on producing balanced budgets, Truman could not easily have secured a large military budget from Congress. Moreover, the three services were engaged in such fratricidal conflict that they would have bickered publicly over which service got what resources.[47]

Truman made key decisions that suggested even in 1949 that he would veer toward higher military spending. When he replaced Marshall as secretary of state, he named Acheson, a hawk who wanted to increase military spending. Acheson, in turn, promptly replaced Kennan, who had recanted his earlier hard-line views, with the hawkish Paul Nitze, who chaired the planning committee that issued NSC-68. Nitze wanted military spending to increase from roughly $14 billion to as much as $50 billion to allow the United States to mobilize to counter an expected "maximum threat" from the Soviets in 1954 when they might have three hundred to five hundred atomic bombs.[48] Truman approved NSC-68 "in principle" in April 1950 but withheld his final approval until the various departments submitted actual budget estimates.[49] Truman's frugal secretary of defense, Louis Johnson, suddenly became a big spender and strongly suggested that his forthcoming military budget might rise to $50 billion.[50]

Truman's speeches hinted at more military spending yet. Citing communist threats in Western Europe, Korea, the Philippines, Iran, and "countries in the general area of China," Truman said, "we have not fully determined the size and the nature of the forces . . . necessary to insure ourselves against future aggression directed toward the North Atlantic area."[51] He worried that European nations had not significantly rearmed, even with the $1 billion in U.S. military assistance. Within minutes of receiving a phone call from Acheson informing him of the invasion of South Korea by North Korean troops, Truman told his daughter, Margaret, "that he feared this was the opening of World War III."[52] On July 6 he denied he would seek additional military funding for anything other than Korea. Less than two weeks later Truman sought to link the Korean attack to broader communist aggression when he said, "The attack upon the Republic of Korea makes it plain beyond all doubt that the international communist movement is prepared to use armed invasion to conquer independent nations. We must therefore recognize the possibility that armed aggression may take place in other areas."[53] He urged an increase in U.S. military power "not only to deal with the aggression in Korea but to increase our common defense." At first he sought only $10 billion in additional military funds, but by early September he was asking Congress to authorize $30 billion more and implied these costs would continue "for years to come."[54] Although Truman wondered whether the United States could afford more than $200 billion in military spending spread over five years, as Nitze now recommended, he decided to proceed after U.S. troops had suffered a defeat in the early stages of the Korean War.[55]

Truman's military buildup in the opening months of the Korean conflict exceeded even the mobilization in the early days of World War II. He
increased the number of troops from 1.5 million to 3.2 million, of army
divisions from 10 to 18, of air force wings from 42 to 72, and the number
of ships from 618 to 1,000, including fourteen carrier groups—in the first
year of the Korean War. Congress allocated $50 billion to do the job, and
Truman sought $62.2 billion for the next year—and still had to ward off
the Joint Chiefs of Staff, who wanted more than $100 billion.[56] Only
about 25 percent of these huge sums was meant for the Korean War—most
of the money was earmarked for the global struggle against communism.[57]
But the Korean War proved useful in securing these resources for "general
mobilization" because relatively few legislators even understood (despite
Truman's public statements) that only a small share was intended for
Korea.[58] (Marshall even feared support might evaporate if the war ended
quickly.)[59]

What is remarkable is that few legislators, save for some isolationists,
disputed Truman's massive military increases, much less questioned their
likely effects on the domestic agenda. In the House report on the 1952
authorization, only two paragraphs in 158 pages discussed the legislation's
objectives.[60] Almost no public debates took place about the long-term
implications of the Truman buildup.[61] Only one legislator—Sen. Paul
Douglas, D.-Ill.—questioned the efficiency of Truman's buildup, which
led to noncompetitive awards of billions of dollars in contracts and
remarkable duplications between the services for airplanes, missiles, and
conventional forces.[62] As with respect to Greece and Turkey earlier, Truman's assumptions lacked a factual basis. While he assumed that the Soviets had instigated the invasion of South Korea, he had no proof of this con-
nection—and many historians believe that Stalin, although he approved
the invasion, had no role in instigating it. Nor did any evidence suggest
that the Soviets viewed the Korean invasion as the first stage of a worldwide pattern of aggression.

Overreaching in Korea

Truman wasted huge resources on the Korean conflict by making a major
tactical mistake. By taking advantage of a Soviet boycott of the United
Nations Security Council, Truman cleverly persuaded it to support a

"police action" to oust the North Koreans, thus providing the United States with cover as it funded 90 percent of the war, the bulk of its troops, and its military leadership. Truman placed the flamboyant Douglas MacArthur in command. During World War II, MacArthur had masterminded the brilliant counterattack that combined air strikes with amphibious invasions as his forces pushed the Japanese from Pacific islands from Australia to the Philippines. But he often ignored commands from his superiors—a propensity he was even more likely to display in Korea where his rabid anticommunism would tempt him to reunify Korea and to attack China if China dared enter the conflict. He assumed, moreover, that airpower was a cure-all, which lulled him into complacency when his foes had virtually no planes.[63] Buoyed by his early success in pushing the North Koreans back over the 38th parallel within three months of the invasion, MacArthur decided to go for the jugular by pursuing them toward the Chinese border. He left his overextended troops in a death trap near the Chinese border where large numbers of well-trained Chinese soldiers, adept at night-time attack, routed the Americans, who took nearly five months to retreat back to the 38th parallel.

It is tempting to dismiss the tactical decision to seek total victory in Korea as a meritorious gamble. In fact, Truman and MacArthur meant to upset an agreement that had been devised years earlier—and accepted by the United States—to divide Korea into communist and noncommunist sections. To say the least, their decision to try to unify Korea was a highly provocative and destabilizing strategy when placed in the broader context of the cold war. Without such overreaching, the fighting phase of the Korean War would have ended about three months after the initial invasion instead of continuing for another five months—at a savings of tens of thousands of lives and billions of dollars. In fact, they might have saved as much as 40 percent of the war's ultimate cost—or $504 billion in constant 1992 dollars, when narrow military and veterans' expenditures are considered.[64]

As in World War II, conservative Republicans and many southern Democrats were determined to offset military increases with cuts in the domestic budget and quickly defeated Truman's proposed $1 billion increase in domestic spending in early 1951. By the time Congress was done, the domestic budget was 9 percent smaller, and social, education, employment, and training programs amounted to less than 1 percent of the federal budget. Were the cold war to last for decades, as Truman implied, the domestic agenda might be crimped indefinitely, with conservatives incessantly able to attack it as not affordable or as diverting resources from the military.

Liberals bought the argument that external threats trump domestic ones and offered no resistance. Even such liberals as Douglas attacked domestic spending as "nonessential" for the duration of the war.[65] Hubert Humphrey (perhaps the most liberal senator) and Adlai Stevenson, the erudite Democratic candidate for the presidency in 1952, urged greater military spending.[66] So did organized labor throughout the 1950s, partly because corporations with military contracts proved a fertile ground for organizing.[67] Liberals were placed on the defensive, moreover, by a red scare whipped to a frenzy by Joseph McCarthy, R-Wis., that assumed that many, even most, "left-leaning people" were communist sympathizers or members of the Communist Party—an astonishing conceptual leap in a nation that had recently enacted the New Deal.[68] Even moderate Republicans, who recognized that McCarthyism was helping their party at the polls, remained silent as thousands of citizens were fired from government jobs on hearsay evidence. Not even Eisenhower, who privately despised McCarthy, dared criticize him, lest he antagonize Old Guard Republicans.[69]

Failed Priorities in the Truman Era

When viewed from a fiscal perspective, Truman's major accomplishments were in foreign policy and military matters, because he markedly increased spending in these areas when measured in constant 1992 dollars (see fig. 6.1). After reaching a low point in 1948, military spending rose in 1949 and early 1950—and then took off in the summer of 1950 with the outbreak of the Korean War. But entitlements and domestic spending on education, training, employment, and social services, when aggregated, hardly rose in constant dollars, making the so-called Fair Deal—a term that Truman coined for his domestic program in early 1949—a shallow and empty era of reform.

Given the U.S. government's huge postwar costs, as well as an array of important domestic problems that needed attention, Americans ought to have levied taxes that averaged at least 20 percent of GDP from the end of the war in August 1945 to the beginning of the Korean War in the summer of 1950. (These rates would have been roughly equivalent to the rates from

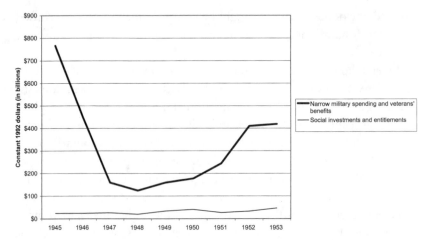

FIGURE 6.1 Narrow Military Spending and Cost of Veterans' Benefits Versus Aggregate Social Spending, 1945–1953

Source: Office of Management and Budget, *Budget of the U.S. Government, FY 2000, Historical Tables* (Washington, D.C.: U.S. Government Printing Office, 1999), table 3.1, pp. 42–43.

1950 on.) Had they done this, they would have had the money to pay for guns, butter, and the Marshall Plan. (See fig. 6.2, where the huge growth in spending on international affairs between 1942 and 1952 largely reflects the Marshall Plan.)

Figure 6.2 shows the extent to which narrow military spending and veterans' programs dominated the federal discretionary budget. (So-called mandatory spending, such as for entitlements and interest payments, is not included in the discretionary budget, which funds virtually the entire military budget.) Although the military's share of the discretionary budget declined markedly in 1947 as discretionary spending rose with the funding of the Marshall Plan, the Korean War and the end of the Marshall Plan in 1950 again pushed the military share to nearly 90 percent of the discretionary budget by 1952. It is surprising that Truman caught so much flak for cutting the military excessively in the postwar years from some hawks who assumed that the deep cuts meant that the United States was in jeopardy after 1946. With other nations, including the Soviet Union, devastated by the war, the United States faced no serious threat. In fact, by 1948–1949 Truman had both a growing economy and huge mothballed forces, intricate treaties with nations around the world, scores of overseas bases that encir-

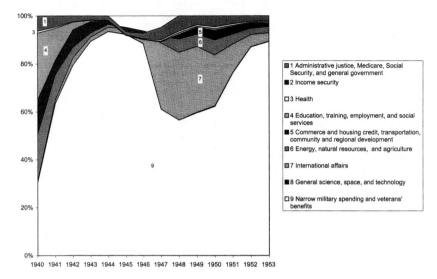

FIGURE 6.2 Competition for Discretionary Spending: Military Versus Domestic Spending as Percentages of Total Outlays, 1940–1953

Numbers 2 and 8 are not shown on the graph because discretionary spending was so small for the former that it does not "appear" prior to 1960 and because a negligible amount was spent on the latter.

Source: Office of Management and Budget, *Budget of the U.S. Government, FY 2000, Historical Tables* (Washington, D.C.: GPO, 1999), table 3.1, pp. 42–43.

cled the Soviet Union, and strong alliances with European powers that he cemented with the Marshall Plan and the formation of NATO.

To the extent that Truman had a domestic agenda, it consisted of veterans' spending, which was 20.5 times the size of all federal aid to states and local governments—and many times the size of other entitlements and domestic social programs combined.[70] Congress, in turn, was more interested in pork-barrel spending than funding such domestic programs as federal aid to education. When preparing estimates for Truman's 1950 budget, for example, the director of the Bureau of the Budget informed the president that he estimated expenditures of $6.7 billion on an array of public works projects, with a huge backlog of other items that might, an aide feared, raise it by another $2 billion.[71] While such programs often had merit, they absorbed a large share of the minimal domestic budget, crowding out other domestic programs.

7

Eisenhower's Ambivalence and Kennedy's Obsession

Federal social spending during the 1950s and early 1960s was so meager as a percentage of GDP that a federal presence in social policy hardly existed. This outcome was partly the result of a dearth of resources as the United States funded a cold war military budget while setting taxes at extraordinarily low levels. I argue here and chapter 15 that, had the United States raised taxes somewhat and pruned considerable waste from the military budget, it would have had more than $1 trillion to spend on its depleted domestic agenda from 1953 through 1963 without endangering national security.

Eisenhower: Hawk or Dove?

Paradoxically, no president has been more conflicted about the nation's military than Dwight Eisenhower, a distinguished general who commanded D-Day forces and NATO forces. On the one hand, he often fretted about the sheer size of the U.S. military during his presidency, even as he oversaw eight years of cold war budgets. Because Eisenhower was acutely aware of the destructive power of nuclear weapons, he had opposed Truman's decision to drop atomic bombs on Japan.[1] Having witnessed firsthand the savagery of World War II, as president he was determined not to lead the nation into a new war. Although he feared the Soviets' imperial ambitions, he was convinced they would not engage in nuclear conflict with the United States because World War II's carnage was such a fresh memory for them.[2]

Eisenhower also worried that excessive military spending would bring economic ruin. A healthy economy was as important, he believed, as military power in protecting the security of the United States. He feared inflation most of all, because it erodes economic growth by diverting investment funds into bonds and real estate, impedes exports, and substantially increases interest payments on the national debt. Like Truman, Eisenhower revered balanced budgets—but, unlike Truman, he wanted to cut federal taxes markedly to free up money for private investment. Under these circumstances the only way to balance the budget was to contain military spending, which comprised the bulk of Eisenhower's budgets.[3]

Eisenhower's skepticism about military spending derived too from his deep knowledge of the military. He knew each service hoped to increase its share of the pie each year. He knew that military culture emphasizes preparing for worst-case scenarios, but he also knew that these scenarios often led to unrealistic spending recommendations.[4] Rather than prepare for every possible contingency, he argued, the United States had to take some risks, particularly in remote areas not connected to its vital interests.[5] He was skeptical whenever someone alleged that a "crisis" existed (such as a bomber or missile gap); he understood that politicians and the services often allege crises as a ploy to obtain greater resources or political advantage. He was acutely aware, moreover, that the primitive Soviet economy impeded the Russians' efforts to produce planes or arms as rapidly as the United States.[6]

Eisenhower found a zealous budget-cutting ally in George Humphrey, his secretary of the treasury. Humphrey was among those who were convinced that the Soviets were planning to bankrupt the United States by enticing the country to overspend on its military. (During meetings of the National Security Council, Humphrey repeatedly opposed military spending increases, against the wishes of military chiefs and the Dulles brothers.)[7] Often unwilling to cut the military budget to the extent that

Humphrey wanted, Eisenhower used him to parry the Joint Chiefs' spending recommendations, then would suggest compromise figures. To force some restraint in military spending, Eisenhower (like Truman) often imposed ceilings on military spending, using a remainder method after he had subtracted the nonmilitary expenditures from estimated tax revenues.[8] The Joint Chiefs frequently chafed at this approach, demanding whatever money they thought they needed. In turn, Eisenhower constantly pushed Charles Wilson, his secretary of defense, to silence their protests. Eisenhower told Adm. Arthur Radford, who had replaced Omar Bradley as the chairman of the Joint Chiefs in the summer of 1953, to abandon his navy identity, to champion all the services, and to be governed by "the single criterion of what is best for the United States."[9]

Eisenhower's determination to restrain military spending was matched by his resolve not to let military incidents escalate into nuclear conflict, and he never came close to using nuclear weapons. Whether off Formosa as the Chinese shelled the small islands of Quemoy and Matsu, in the Middle East where Arab nations fought Israel, in Eastern Europe as revolts against the Soviets occurred in such places as Hungary, or in Indochina where communists fought with the French, Eisenhower skillfully avoided military conflict. Sometimes he rattled his sabers loud enough to imply that he might use nuclear force. Sometimes he mobilized ships and troops, holding them ready for action. But he always moved with caution and successfully avoided armed conflict. Nor was Eisenhower inclined to participate in regional conflicts in faraway places or to get caught in quagmires. He toyed with sending troops to help the French as they battled Ho Chi Minh in 1954 but backtracked when Gen. Matthew Ridgeway warned that the United States would have to commit hundreds of thousands of troops for an extended period and would have scant chance of prevailing.[10] Eisenhower also was determined to persuade the Western European nations to increase their own military forces to enable the United States to withdraw troops from Europe; over the objections of the British and the French, he supported the rearming of West Germany.

Yet Eisenhower's dovish tendencies were counterbalanced by hawkish ones. He agreed with the Truman Doctrine and NSC-68.[11] He believed the Soviets *did* intend to conquer the world, although he tended to believe they would try to do it by subverting governments rather than direct invasion.[12] That was why he used the Central Intelligence Agency to overthrow left-leaning governments in Iraq and Guatemala and to plan covert actions against Fidel Castro in Cuba.[13] Eisenhower also believed the Soviets acted in tandem with the Chinese communists to try to gain supremacy in Europe, Asia, Central America, and Africa.[14] He subscribed to the domino theory, warning in 1954 that "you have a row of dominoes set up; you knock over the first one, and what will happen to the last one is the certainty that it will go over very quickly."[15]

Although Eisenhower wanted the Europeans to assume larger roles in their self-defense, he worried that premature withdrawal of U.S. forces would be demoralizing. Europeans leaders sensed his unwillingness to force the issue and balked at increasing their military budgets. Nor would they agree to the rearming of West Germany, which would have allowed a pullback of some American forces.[16]

Eisenhower usually wanted to maintain a vast superiority over the Soviets in nuclear forces.[17] He reasoned that the Soviets would be less likely to invade Europe or the Middle East if they knew that the United States could destroy them many times over. If the atomic superiority of the United States after World War II had deterred the Soviets from moving beyond Eastern Europe, why not continue this superiority by funding a vast bomber fleet as well as an endless array of other weapons? Nor was Eisenhower inclined to limit extravagant duplication between the services in missiles and weapons, because he believed a free-for-all competition would yield superior technology.

The Soviets: Paper or Real Tiger? (Part 1)

While U.S. spending on general purpose forces increased more than fourfold from 1950 to 1952, spending on strategic nuclear forces increased nearly fivefold in a procurement frenzy of bombers, atomic bombs, and tactical nuclear weapons.

The crown jewel of this rearmament was the Strategic Air Command (SAC) commanded by Curtis LeMay, an aggressive anticommunist who even favored a first strike against the Soviets. In the early and mid-1950s SAC had built 2,041 B-47 Stratojets and wanted an even more potent bomber—and got the massive B-52 into full production by 1955. By 1962 the United States had a fleet of 744 B-52s, supplemented by B-66 Destroyers. That gave the United States a fleet of roughly 1,600 bombers (B-47s, B-52s, and B-66s), each of which could deliver atomic or hydrogen bombs.[18] (After Truman decided to develop a hydrogen bomb in early 1950, the United States exploded one in early 1953 that had eight hundred times the power of the atomic bombs used against Japan.)

This upsurge in weaponry occurred in an atmosphere of widespread fear that the Soviets would secure superiority in nuclear arms. Had they not exploded an atomic bomb far ahead of Western predictions in 1949— and might they even best the United States in the competition to build a hydrogen bomb? (The Soviets developed a weaker version by August 1953, or just eight months after the first American explosion.) These fears continued once Eisenhower took office. Relying on their missile genius, Sergei Korolev, the Soviets produced the R-7 rocket by 1955 and even displayed an M-4 Bison jet bomber in May 1954.

Americans often believed the Soviets were real tigers but overlooked abundant evidence that they were paper tigers. Mesmerized by nuclear weapons and the means to deliver them, whether bombs, missiles, or planes, Americans measured military power unidimensionally, mistakenly focusing merely on numbers and capabilities of weapons and bombs while ignoring the Soviets' primitive economy.[19] Given the state of their economy and that Moscow was the nerve center of their empire, the Soviets would suffer extraordinary damage with even a few well-placed nuclear devices. The Soviets had been able to evade the Nazis by relocating much of their industry east of the Ural Mountains during World War II, but long-distance bombers now foreclosed this option. Meanwhile, the United States was producing seven thousand nuclear devices each year, to be delivered by sixteen hundred SAC bombers.[20]

U.S. foreign-policy experts as Dean Acheson and Paul Nitze feared that the Soviets would invade Europe but failed to recognize the difficulties they would have encountered. The Soviets would have needed long supply lines to sustain their advancing troops, which would have been devastated by U.S. bombers. The Soviets could not count on cooperation from conquered East European nations to allow passage of troops and supplies to the western front. They did not know whether Warsaw Pact troops would be loyal during a war.

Nor could the Soviets have *held* Western Europe. One lesson dictators learned from World War II was the peril of overreaching. Hitler *was* defeated, after all, in a relatively brief period, even if this defeat caused untold suffering and cost to other nations. Guerrilla movements, not to mention Allied bombing strikes, severely contested his occupation of Western Europe. Now that they knew how effective the underground had been against Hitler, European nations would immediately develop effective campaigns against occupying Soviet troops.

The Soviets were equally realistic about the threat of nuclear annihilation. It was one thing to blockade Berlin, as they did in the late 1940s and the early 1960s—a limited action focused on a single city. But a frontal invasion of Western Europe was another matter: the United States had demonstrated its allegiance to Western Europe in World War II, had developed the Marshall Plan, had joined NATO, and conducted a flourishing trade with Western Europe. Truman, Eisenhower, and John Foster Dulles had made clear on numerous occasions, moreover, that the United States would defend Europe.

Thus the United States was engaged in an arms race against itself during the 1950s. The Soviets had virtually *no* long-range nuclear-capable bombers until 1956—and these bombers, lacking the range to reach the United States, were targeted at Europe.[21] (See fig. 7.1.) Moreover, the United States had about 2,200 strategic warheads, whereas the Soviets had about 300 in 1959.[22] The Soviets were capable of hurling a 184-pound object into space by the time they launched *Sputnik* in 1957, but for most of the 1950s they lacked missiles that could deliver nuclear weapons to the United States or sophisticated bombers. Neither side possessed reliable intercontinental ballistic missiles (ICBMs) in the 1950s, so the U.S. superiority in long-range bombers and nuclear warheads gave Americans a strategic advantage.

Acutely aware of their marked inferiority in nuclear forces, Stalin and Khrushchev engaged in a strategy of bluffing and secrecy to make an American first-strike less likely and to highlight the Soviets' superiority in conventional weaponry.[23] Stalin shut access roads to Berlin in 1948, partly to demonstrate that U.S. atomic weapons were of little use in such situations and partly to threaten that he might use his conventional forces if the Americans sought to force a reopening of access routes. Khrushchev flamboyantly promised that the Soviets would bury Western capitalism as he issued glowing Five-Year Plans and displayed early versions of weapons that vastly overstated the power of the Soviet economy and weaponry. Stalin and Khrushchev prevented Westerners from deciphering the extent of Soviet economic and nuclear inferiority by declining to participate in

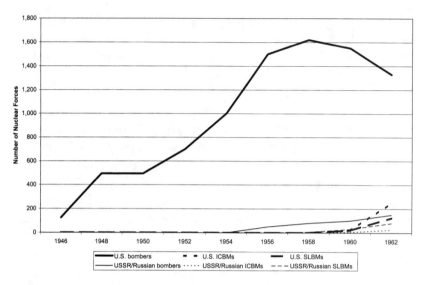

FIGURE 7.1 U.S. and Soviet/Russian Strategic Offensive Nuclear Forces, 1945–1962
    Source: Stephen Schwartz, ed., *Atomic Audit: The Costs and Consequences of U.S. Nuclear Weapons Since 1940* (Washington, D.C.: Brookings Institution, 1998), 187.

the Marshall Plan, Eisenhower's Open Skies arms-control proposal, and arms inspections. In 1955 the Soviets even flew a small number of Bisons past a reviewing stand *twice* to give the impression of larger numbers of planes in their air force.[24]

Unable to get a spy network established in the Soviet Union and lacking other data until U-2 spy plane flights began in late 1956, Allen Dulles repeatedly overestimated Soviet strength. For example, he wrongly assumed that Soviet bombers and missiles were trained on the United States, when they were aimed at Europe—partly because they could not reliably reach U.S. targets.[25]

Nikita Khrushchev recognized that the United States had jumped out of the nuclear gate with breathtaking speed and at huge expense and set in motion planning and research designed to bring his nation to parity. But the Soviets found this difficult to achieve, despite enormous expenditures, because U.S. leaders were equally determined to retain their superiority. The United States possessed more than six thousand nuclear warheads in 1970, for example, as compared to fewer than twenty-five hundred for the Soviets.[26]

Eisenhower's Failed Crusade

Eisenhower wanted desperately to contain military spending in the 1950s and frequently berated military leaders, the Dulles brothers, and others who favored sharp increases in military spending during meetings of the National Security Council.[27] Yet the United States embarked on military spending so prodigious that Eisenhower often blanched. At times, Eisenhower's hawkish tendencies overrode his dovish ones. He also was ill disposed to educate the American public about the limits of military power as well as the primitiveness of the Soviet economy and military forces. Primarily, however, his good intentions fell victim to a political context that promoted runaway military spending.

Two groups were Eisenhower's political nemeses: Old Guard Republicans and Democratic hawks. The Old Guard Republicans, including senators Joe McCarthy of Wisconsin, William Jenner of Indiana, Barry Goldwater of Arizona, and Henry S. Bridges of New Hampshire, were cold warriors with an emphasis not so much on increasing military spending as on hard-line diplomacy. They wanted to use the atomic bomb in Indochina, reunify Korea rather than accept its division, and liberate Eastern Europe by military means if necessary. Some favored a first strike against the Soviets to prevent them from developing nuclear forces. They wanted Eisenhower to support a resolution that condemned the Yalta agreements because they were convinced that Stalin had tricked Roosevelt and Churchill into ceding Eastern Europe. In 1953 and 1954 they demanded that Eisenhower support the Bricker Amendment, which would have given treaty-making powers exclusively to Congress in order to avoid future Yaltas—and some even wanted to cede to the states the power to approve treaties. The Old Guard strongly backed Joseph McCarthy and opposed *any* negotiations with the Soviets. Eisenhower used the aging but genteel conservative Robert Taft to mollify the Old Guard even as the president ignored their edicts, but Taft's death in 1953 left Eisenhower to face the Old Guard alone.[28] (Eisenhower often fantasized about starting a third party so he would not have to contend with them.)

The Democratic hawks were Eisenhower's other nemeses: senators Lyndon Johnson of Texas, John Kennedy of Massachusetts, and Stuart Symington of Missouri. Although Democratic presidents had presided over U.S. entry into World War II and the Korean War, issued the Truman

Doctrine, approved NSC-68, and instigated the huge military budgets of the cold war, Republicans widely portrayed Democrats as soft on communism. Had not China been "lost" during Truman's administration because the United States did not intervene to help Chiang Kai-shek defeat Mao Tse-tung? Had not the North Koreans invaded South Korea because Acheson had declared Korea to be outside America's defense perimeter in 1949? Were not large numbers of Democratic social reformers and trade-union leaders communist sympathizers? The Democratic hawks, then, were out to show the Republicans and the country that the Democrats were not soft on communism, and they were buoyed in their efforts by public opinion polls that showed voters favored high military spending throughout the 1950s.[29]

Hoping to find middle ground that would satisfy both his dovish and hawkish tendencies, in the fall of 1953 Eisenhower developed the "New Look," a military posture that funded large numbers of troops even after the Korean armistice had been signed but that cut the military budget enough to allow a tax cut and a balanced budget in 1954. Eisenhower did this by proposing to rely heavily on nuclear deterrence. He cut the army and navy somewhat, reducing the army, for example, from 1.55 million to 1.4 million men. He also wanted to save money by helping European and other nations build their own military forces; his budget included $6 billion in military assistance.

Both the Old Guard and the Democrats attacked Eisenhower's New Look. Tired of the costly Marshall Plan, Republicans demanded cuts in foreign aid. Led by Johnson, Symington, and Kennedy, the Democrats repeatedly attacked Eisenhower's military budgets as inadequate throughout the decade, with Truman often seconding their demands from retirement. Democrats voted for increases in military spending far more frequently than Republicans in the 1950s.[30]

The military too repeatedly pressured Eisenhower to increase military spending. Flush with vast resources in the final Truman budgets, the three services entered the arms race with gusto as they embraced the emerging electronics, missile, and nuclear technologies. Whereas procurement in World War II had focused on producing massive numbers of guns, tanks, and planes for combat, procurement in the cold war emphasized a "baroque arsenal for weapons never put to the ultimate test."[31] Major contractors produced different "platforms" to fire nuclear weapons, whether planes, submarines, ships, or land-based missiles, and subcontracted subsystems like guidance systems and firing mechanisms. Because these weapons were not actually used in warfare during the cold war, a kind of internal competition evolved between contractors on performance criteria like speed, lethality, versatility, and immunity from attack.[32] As a specific contractor produced an aircraft, for example, other contractors would soon claim they could surpass it in several performance criteria, leading to a non-stop process of acquisitions by the Pentagon as contractors developed successive innovations. Between 1957 and 1959, for example, contractors produced twenty-three kinds of combat aircraft, seventeen makes of helicopters, and twenty-one types of antisubmarine aircraft. In this spiralling competition between weapons systems, few officials or legislators even asked whether the military needed the increasingly exotic weapons, whether their price tags were excessive, or whether the costs of operating and maintaining these systems, as well as training personnel to use them, were too high. And hardly anyone asked whether they would actually work under battle conditions. No one asked whether the Soviets had comparable weapons—U.S. leaders simply assumed that the Soviets did or soon would.

Meanwhile, missile production had simply exploded in the mid-1950s in the aftermath of the production of hydrogen bombs, whose relatively light weight and destructiveness meant they could be carried by IRBMs (intermediate-range ballistic missiles) and ICBMs. But the United States still did not have missiles that worked. Eisenhower established the Air Research and Development Command of the Western Development Division (WDD) at Inglewood, California, to develop ballistic missiles. He gave WDD a higher priority in 1955 than the Manhattan Project had in World War II.[33] Instead of seeking a relatively small variety of workable missiles, the WDD and the Pentagon funded a dizzying array of projects, including the Atlas, Titan, and Jupiter ICBMs; the Polaris, Thor, and Redstone IRBMs; the supersonic Terrier and Tartar surface-to-air guided missile; the LaCrosse surface-to-surface guided missile; the Vanguard three-stage rocket to put an earth satellite into orbit; the X-7 supersonic ramjet missile; the X-17 ballistic rocket; the Snark surface-to-surface intercontinental guided missile; the navy's Talos missile; the GAM-63 Rascal air-to-ground strategic missile; the ramjet-powered SM-64 Navaho cruise-type missile; and many others. Missile procurement had constituted a small fraction of military spending in the early 1950s. By 1958 it consumed 49 percent of the army's procurement budget and sizable portions of the navy's and the air force's.[34]

All three services scrambled frantically to secure their share of ICBMs, IRBMs, and tactical nuclear weapons. The navy wanted long-range and short-range missiles to be fired from aircraft, ships, and submarines, just as the army wanted land-based ICBMs and IRBMs, not to mention tactical (or short-range) missiles as well as artillery or hand-held launchers that could fire nuclear shells. The air force wanted SAC to have the lead role in delivering nuclear weapons—and even got a monopoly over land-based missiles because the service developed key links to the electronics industry and missile contractors.

Missile production required new plants because aircraft plants could not be used to make them. Vast new armaments centers arose in the United States. The Thor, Jupiter, and Titan missiles required, for example, sixteen principle contractors in nineteen locations supported by more than two hundred major subcontractors. Huge corporations received extraordinary revenues from missile production in 1957—Lockheed got $53 million, Martin got $405 million, and McDonnell received $34 million, for example.[35] The U.S. military-industrial complex, then, had evolved in several stages. It began with the myriad weapons of World War II, concentrated on the aerospace industry with the construction of the SAC fleet in the early and mid-1950s, and added the missile-producing industry in the mid- and late 1950s—all of which was closely linked to the emerging electronics industry.[36]

As with Truman's and Eisenhower's advocacy of strategic airpower, which was assumed to be far less expensive than conventional forces, advocates of missiles assumed they would save the nation countless billions by supplanting long-range bombers.[37] But these hopes for an inexpensive deterrent proved as elusive as the earlier hopes for airpower. The air force staunchly resisted cuts in its bomber fleet and constantly sought new and more expensive versions, not just to deliver nuclear weapons but to launch air-to-ground missiles. Surely, the generals contended, a nuclear arsenal that relied only on sea-based and land-based missiles was excessively vulnerable. The new missiles were, in turn, quickly replaced by countless new versions on the basis of their lethality, range, and power—with each missile requiring extensive training of personnel and a budget for operation and maintenance. By the late 1960s military planners would want multiple warheads on ICBMs—which increased exponentially the number of nuclear devices aimed at the Soviets—but multiple warheads would require, in turn, more powerful rockets. Each service would want *its* arsenal of IRBMs and ICBMs and resisted consolidation of missiles in a single service.

Nor did the missiles displace conventional forces any more than the SAC bombers had. The army tenaciously maintained myriad divisions for the defense of Europe as well as for regional wars. The army outfitted its divisions, moreover, with tactical nuclear weapons, such as atomic shells fired from artillery and short-range missiles. These tactical weapons had dubious value because they would kill U.S. troops and nearby civilian populations. Such weapons also required extensive training. Although the army did not really know whether or how to use them, it nonetheless incorporated tactical weapons into conventional forces to a remarkable degree.[38]

Southern and California Democrats chaired virtually all the major congressional committees that authorized and appropriated money for military expenditures. As a result, they had secured a disproportionate number of military contracts for their areas during World War II and the postwar period.[39] They continued this pattern in the 1950s as missiles, electronics, and aerospace firms in the South and in California received a huge share of military contracts. But the Pentagon and Democratic hawks were careful too to locate contracts and subcontracts in the districts of politicians from both parties and in all regions, with New England and the Northwest, for example, receiving key submarine, shipping, and aerospace contracts. Although corporations had been indifferent to the growth of military spending in the late 1940s when relatively few firms received military contracts, they were key lobbyists by the mid- and late 1950s, working with the Pentagon to put awesome pressure on Congress.[40] Now the red scare teamed up with constituency politics to fuel the arms race.

American overkill was reflected in the development of the annual Single Integrated Operation Plans (SIOPs), which established industrial, military, and other targets in the Soviet Union, Eastern Europe, China, and North Korea. The United States aimed more than two thousand nuclear warheads at more than two thousand targets in the Soviet Union and China; that kind of firepower could kill 285 million people in 1960.[41] Although their enemy could not even hit their country with nuclear weapons through much of the 1950s, Americans seemed to act as if World War II were still in progress, "as if a phantom German army continued to design and develop weapons."[42]

Although Eisenhower wanted the Europeans to rearm, they continued to resist. They de-emphasized military spending during the 1950s, choosing instead to create huge welfare states and to repair the infrastructure destroyed by the war. Where Eisenhower had hoped they would contribute forty divisions to NATO, they contributed only six to eight. Eisenhower was unwilling to force the issue, lest European nations become neutral in the cold war, and kept six American divisions (or about 400,000 troops) in NATO throughout his term, augmenting them with tactical nuclear weapons.[43]

Qualms About Candor and Conflict

Had Eisenhower *really* wanted to control military spending, he would have had to educate voters about nuclear warfare and the Soviet threat; public opinion polls throughout the decade showed that the public favored the massive military budgets.[44] As a distinguished former general, he would have been less vulnerable than other politicians to questions about his patriotism. He could have shared ideas that he held, such as when he said: "If you are in the military and you know more about these terrible destructive weapons, it tends to make you more pacifistic. . . . [The Soviets are] not ready for war and they know it. They also know if they go to war, they're going to end up losing everything they have."[45]

Eisenhower had an opportunity to begin this educational process early in his administration, when Robert Oppenheimer, the physicist who oversaw the Manhattan Project, chaired a panel that suggested that Eisenhower discuss nuclear weapons and the Soviet threat with the American people in candid terms. Comparing the United States and Soviet Union to "two scorpions in a bottle" that would destroy one another, Oppenheimer believed the government could not make rational policy unless it periodically informed the public about the status of the arms race. How else could voters decide whether their country needed more or fewer weapons or whether defense against nuclear attack was even possible? Eisenhower accepted this advice and launched Operation Candor, which the president would kick off with a speech to the American people.[46] But the draft produced by an aide presented a grim (if realistic) picture, informing the public that H-bombs dropped on New York City and Washington would kill most citizens within one hundred miles of the epicenter. It even noted that people within New York City's vast subway system would be incinerated.

But word of the speech got out to people like Lewis Strauss, head of the Atomic Energy Commission, and they mounted a vigorous counteroffensive. They argued that sharing information with the public would jeopardize classified information and that the public would either become hysterical when told of the sheer power of hydrogen bombs (and demand even higher military spending and vast shelter systems) or so depressed as to surrender to the Soviets. A public smear campaign against Oppenheimer implied that Operation Candor reflected the naïveté of a man who had opposed development of the hydrogen bomb.

Eisenhower eventually yielded to the opponents of candor and decided not to tell the public about the power of nuclear weapons or his belief that bomb shelters were useless. He decided instead to preserve the fiction of survivability and abandoned the speech altogether. He gave a speech that proposed that the superpowers share fissionable material with the United Nations.[47] We do not know what effect Eisenhower's speech and the other elements of Operation Candor would have had upon the American people. In the absence of a decision to discuss nuclear warfare and the Soviet threat in realistic terms, widespread popular ignorance created a rich opportunity for politicians to demand even greater military spending.

Led by Symington, the Democrats alleged a "bomber gap" in 1955 and 1956, partly because they had been fooled by Khrushchev and partly because they wanted to make political gains at Eisenhower's expense. The Soviet leader had decided his best chance of avoiding a first strike by the Americans was to convince them that his country possessed the means to hit the United States with nuclear weapons. Symington and other Democrats, eager to shed the GOP accusation that they were soft on communism, contended that the Soviets might soon surpass the huge SAC fleet (soon to be augmented by hundreds of B-52s). The Democrats scored heavily with the public and forced Eisenhower to increase his request for the air force.[48]

With an eye to the congressional campaigns of 1958, the Democrats seized upon the Soviets' successful launch of *Sputnik* in 1957 as proof of a missile gap. They predicted that the Soviets soon would train hundreds, even thousands, of ICBMs on a defenseless United States. Eisenhower viewed the Democrats' assertions as baseless. He knew that the ability to hurl a small object into space hardly meant the Soviets could hit the United States with warheads on ICBMs. He had known since 1956, thanks to the U-2 spy planes, that the Soviets lacked operational ICBMs and had only a small number of bombers. His long-standing disinclination to present Americans with factual evidence that might have defused the arms race was now supplemented by fear that he would jeopardize these surreptitious flights if he divulged what he knew. In fact, the Soviets already knew about the U-2 flights, which they had identified on their radar and even vainly tried to shoot down. But they had maintained their own silence because they did not want Westerners to know they could not shoot down the U-2. By saying little, Eisenhower again lost an opportunity to educate the public and legislators about the actual Soviet threat, as well as the awesome power of the U.S. nuclear arsenal. Indeed, the United States *tripled* its strategic arsenal in Eisenhower's second term through more bombers and bombs, just as it supplemented its bomber lead with liquid-fueled Atlases and Titans, as well as solid-fuel Minuteman ICBMs, plus the Thor, Jupiter, and Polaris IRBMs—yielding a huge lead over the Soviets despite *Sputnik*.[49]

Eisenhower fought a lonely battle from 1957 through 1960 against the efforts of the Democrats and the Joint Chiefs to force large increases in military spending. As Stephen Ambrose suggests, Eisenhower saved the nation untold billions as he curtailed military spending toward the end of his administration.[50]

Eisenhower was the only president from 1950 through 2000 who openly discussed tradeoffs between military and domestic spending, saying in his valedictory speech in early 1961 that "an immense military establishment" had arisen with "unwarranted influence" that threatened to crucify the domestic agenda on an "iron cross." Coming so late in his presidency, however, this speech had little effect on an electorate that was surprised by what he said. Indeed, Eisenhower may have had John Kennedy in mind when he made the speech, because he often told aides that he worried that succeeding presidents, who lacked his military knowledge and would be unable to resist lobbying pressures from the military-industrial complex, would seek even larger military budgets.

Eisenhower's Quid pro Quo

Eisenhower fashioned an informal agreement with Sam Rayburn, the Democratic Speaker of the House, and with Lyndon Johnson, the Senate majority leader, from 1954 on.[51] Eisenhower agreed not to cut the remnants of the New Deal—and to accede to occasional increases in Social Security—but made clear that he would oppose virtually *any* increases in other domestic programs or the establishment of new ones. Rayburn and Johnson, in turn, agreed to support Eisenhower's foreign policy, albeit with the right to urge increases in military spending and to propose modest increases in spending for existing programs.

The results of this deal were predictable. The Democrats mostly sought what a *New York Times* reporter called "an unspectacular" extension of existing programs.[52] Domestic federal spending remained flat during the 1950s, even as the gross national product grew markedly.[53] Without increases in federal spending, the only way to address the burgeoning needs of the white population, which had spilled over into countless new suburban communities, was to increase state and local spending dramatically—from 7 percent to 9.4 percent of the GNP between 1950 and 1960, an incredible jump given the growth of the GNP.[54] Indeed, cumulative state and local spending—$47.3 billion—exceeded total federal domestic spending of $30.2 billion, meaning that state and local governments presided over U.S. social policy.[55] With the New Deal long dead and with federal entitlements still in their infancy, the U.S. welfare state was primarily a state and local one.

National policy makers were oblivious to the major new domestic needs that led to the social turmoil of the 1960s.[56] With their attention focused on racial injustice in the South, they ignored the effects of the massive migration of African Americans to northern cities, where they occupied tenements and houses vacated by whites as they fled for the suburbs. In Chicago the African-American population grew by 77 percent in the 1940s and another 65 percent in the 1950s, from 278,000 to 813,000 people in these two decades. At the peak of the migration in the 1950s, twenty-two hundred African Americans moved to Chicago each week.[57] With attention diverted to the cold war and no money for domestic programs in the federal budget, little effort was made to help these new arrivals, most of whom were illiterate and unskilled. Billions of military dollars should have been diverted to the education, housing, job training, and social needs of these people, whose poverty so clearly stemmed from the deprivations they had faced in the South and from the dehumanizing conditions they faced in urban ghettos.

Only the Social Security program expanded markedly. With its own source of revenues from payroll taxes, it did not have to compete with the military for general revenues, as most social programs did. And because its expenditures were not even counted in the federal administrative budget, the Social Security program could not be blamed for deficits. Although some conservative Republicans wanted to do away with Social Security, it drew support from both sides of the aisle as an earned benefit, unlike the less popular welfare programs.

The growth of Social Security was not automatic, however. Many legislators viewed the program as a small one in the 1940s. They believed that the economic well-being of older people hinged on Old Age Assistance, a federal welfare program. But Social Security was supported by a tax of only 1 percent on payrolls of employers and on the first $3,000 of a worker's wages; it lacked the resources to pay more than minimal benefits. Indeed, no major changes in Social Security were enacted in the 1940s.[58]

A small group of Social Security advocates was determined to make it a massive program that would outstrip and supplant Old Age Assistance. This group included Arthur Altemeyer, chairman of the Social Security Board; Wilbur Cohen, legislative liaison for the Social Security Board; Robert Ball, staff director of the Advisory Council to the Social Security Board; and Elizabeth Wickenden, a representative of the American Public Welfare Association, an organization of the directors of state and local public welfare agencies. Cohen wanted Social Security to use payroll taxes to fund health insurance, disability insurance for workers, and pensions sufficiently large that Old Age Assistance would be unnecessary for most senior citizens. He wanted it to extend, moreover, to millions of people excluded from the program, such as farmers and self-employed people. To achieve these goals, he and his allies needed to convince Congress to raise the payroll tax and enact new and higher benefits. With considerable help from organized labor, they convinced Truman to support Social Security reforms in 1950; they got a modest increase in the payroll tax and benefits but failed to secure disability insurance.[59]

But little by little they racked up a string of policy successes, spread over many years, that would transform Social Security from a residual program for individual retirees to a family program and an antipoverty measure. It would eventually provide disability insurance to younger people; help widows; assist dependents of the deceased such as by helping their children pay for college; and sharply reduce poverty among older people.[60] It would finance these benefits through increases in payroll taxes, which rose from 1.5 percent in 1950 to 5.85 percent in 1973.[61]

Their success in increasing benefits was linked, of course, to legislators' discovery that they could woo voters by supporting Social Security increases in election years, even in 1952 when the nation was involved in the Korean War.[62] More success came in 1954, with Eisenhower's blessing. Determined to broaden the base of the Republican Party by not reflexively opposing *all* social legislation, Eisenhower seized on Social Security as a strategy for advancing "Modern Republicanism," which he contrasted with the views of the Old Guard. He supported legislation to give coverage to farmers and other groups, to expand benefits somewhat, and to raise the tax base from the first $3,600 of a person's wages to the first $4,200. (The tax base was raised from $3,000 to $3,600 in 1950.) This legislation, which added ten million people to the program, marked an historic shift in the politics of Social Security: a Republican president and Republican Congress had endorsed major Social Security legislation for the first time, confirming its bipartisan support and decisively rejecting those few conservatives who wanted to eliminate it.[63] Another major success occurred when the Democratic Congress enacted disability insurance against the initial wishes of Eisenhower in 1956.

With Social Security now institutionalized, Cohen set his sights even higher: why not incorporate hospital insurance for the elderly into Social Security by raising the payroll tax markedly in a proposal that Sen. John Kennedy found appealing? No one could have predicted at this point that Cohen would achieve this policy in 1965 or that entitlements would become the bulwark of the American welfare state by the mid-1970s, surpassing even military spending.

Getting Butter Through Guns

It is fitting that much of U.S. domestic policy was an adjunct to national security in the 1950s when the federal budget was dominated by military spending. Spending on veterans remained a large part of the domestic budget, with the GI Bill now extended to veterans of the Korean War. In 1954, for example, the federal government spent $3.9 billion on veterans' programs as compared to $1.6 billion for the combined programs of the newly established Department of Health, Education, and Welfare.[64]

Eisenhower opposed virtually all new domestic programs, save for those related to national security.[65] His largest domestic initiative, a massive program to build an interstate highway system, was stimulated by his observation of Hitler's impressive highway system during World War II. The nation would need a similar system if it became immersed in another war, he decided. Although he often confided to aides that the nation could not survive a nuclear war, he wanted a federal highway system that would facilitate evacuation of major cities if it happened.[66]

America's infatuation with the automobile had begun decades earlier as successive administrations from Woodrow Wilson on contributed major sums to local and state governments for road construction. The purchase of automobiles comprised one sixth of the GNP in the 1950s, but Americans had to navigate a patchwork of small roads when they went long distances. Construction of freeways began inauspiciously with a six-mile highway from Pasadena to downtown Los Angeles in 1940; the Pennsylvania Turnpike soon followed as many planners wondered whether "super-highways" should be built across the nation.

Eisenhower was intent on building an interstate system and convened an advisory committee headed by retired general Lucius Clay, who also was familiar with Hitler's freeway system. Disagreements emerged: some on the panel wanted the system to be financed by tolls, while others wanted complete federal financing. At a time when no spare money existed for the domestic agenda, many people wondered how resources could be found.

Seizing the initiative, Eisenhower proposed forty-one thousand miles of freeways, including seven thousand miles within metropolitan areas, in a scheme that made Roosevelt's New Deal pale by comparison. In early 1955, in a special message on a proposed highway program, Eisenhower said the federal government would foot 90 percent of the costs (with the balance contributed by states). Uncle Sam would issue revenue bonds, which would be retired by federal taxes on lubricating oils and gasoline, as well as excise taxes on buses and trucks. Like Social Security, this massive program would be off-budget, funded by its own source of tax revenues collected in the Highway Trust Fund and would not even be counted in the annual administrative budget.

Not surprisingly, the so-called highway lobby, a loose association of highway officials, automobile clubs, trucking associations, automobile manufacturers, highway contractors, producers of cement and other building materials, and oil companies—perhaps the most important economic and political bloc in the nation in the 1950s—mobilized huge pressure on behalf of the legislation.[67] Congress approved the measure with virtually no dissenting votes in 1956—and with no discussion of such basic questions as whether it would displace many urban neighborhoods and what would happen to urban public transportation systems as thousands of miles of freeways were constructed in cities. Nor was there discussion of whether reliance on automobiles would create pollution in urban areas.

Prompted by the launching of *Sputnik,* Eisenhower's other dramatic initiative was the National Defense Education Act of 1958. The legislation, which supported science education in colleges, drew bipartisan support because many Americans feared the Soviets' victory in launching an object into orbit. But funding for the legislation was minuscule, providing only several hundred million dollars at a time when the federal government gave virtually no money to public education. (Both Eisenhower and Congress rejected proposals for large-scale funding of public schools, such as that by Michigan governor Mennen Williams, who wanted $16.6 billion over five years, and Adlai Stevenson, who proposed $5 billion to $10 billion a year for ten years.)[68]

Kennedy's Obsession

John F. Kennedy, scion of one of the wealthiest families in the United States and taken with foreign policy, was less interested in domestic policy. When asked what position in government he would have wanted had he not been president, he answered without hesitation: "secretary of state." He believed New Deal liberalism was outmoded, but he had no alternative approach, aside from notions that poverty was caused by some combination of structural and cultural factors.[69] In the early presidential primary campaigns in 1960 he hardly discussed domestic policy but then reversed course when he found that his Democratic opponent, Hubert Humphrey, was besting him in the West Virginia primary partly because he discussed strategies for helping unemployed miners. This shift, coming as it did during the middle of the primary season, was more tactical than a reflection of the candidate's commitment to domestic policy.[70] Nor did Kennedy emphasize domestic policy during his brief presidency. In his first State of the Union address he touched on "unfinished and neglected tasks" on the domestic front, including "cities engulfed in squalor," but then said that "all these problems pale when placed beside those which confront us around the world."[71] He championed an array of legislation but got little of it enacted, because of the intransigence of congressional conservatives, because he invested relatively little political capital in it, and because he failed to use the bully pulpit.[72] A task force that he commissioned to address poverty had barely begun its work—mostly, it had assembled a laundry list of small measures that Congress had failed to enact—when he was killed.[73]

Kennedy's domestic strategy was handicapped by budget realities. Government revenues were growing sluggishly, and he hoped to stimulate the economy by initiating greater domestic spending, as recommended by the economist John Kenneth Galbraith. He believed that the United States underinvested in its public needs, and he proposed increasing domestic spending by $3.2 billion for various small programs in early 1961 while increasing deficits to combat unemployment. (The AFL-CIO wanted increases of $20 billion to $40 billion.)[74] Even Kennedy's small program was attacked by Republicans and southern Democrats as a "resurrection of the New Deal." Richard Nixon demanded domestic spending be cut to allow for large increases in military spending.[75] With its major committees chaired by conservative southern Democrats, Congress would not act on Kennedy's proposals, stubbornly resisting deficit spending and harboring ideological reservations about public spending. Kennedy made a strategic retreat at this pivotal moment and accepted the advice of an array of "New Economists," who contended that economic growth could also be stimulated by huge tax cuts. These New Economists were convinced that "fiscal drag" retarded economic growth—that the federal government pumped too few resources into the economy in comparison to the monies it took from the economy in taxes. They differed from traditional Keynesians by placing equal emphasis on tax cuts and federal spending to stimulate economic growth.[76] Rebuffed by Congress with respect to spending, Kennedy sought large cuts in corporate taxes in 1962—and then supported a proposal to cut income tax rates by as much as 20 percent in the biggest tax cut since the end of World War II. It is true that such tax cuts might eventually enhance tax revenues by stimulating economic growth, but tax cuts would discourage domestic spending in the short term by creating deficits.

Nor did Kennedy's military budgets leave much for domestic spending. After alleging a missile gap during his presidential campaign, as president Kennedy soon learned from satellite data that the Soviets had only about the same number of ICBMs as the United States—and that no signs of a

Soviet crash program existed.[77] But he was committed to greater spending on missiles, so Kennedy greatly increased spending on ICBMs anyway.

Kennedy, who long had been fascinated with communist subversion of third-world nations, became riveted on South Vietnam. He believed that Ho Chi Minh, the diminutive leader of North Vietnam who had bested the French, had collaborated with China and the Soviet Union to reunify Vietnam under communist leadership. Kennedy also subscribed to Eisenhower's domino theory and feared the fall of South Vietnam would trigger other communist victories in Southeast Asia and the Philippines.[78] He was equally worried about dominoes in the Caribbean and Central America: Fidel Castro, who had allied himself with the Soviet Union soon after overthrowing Fulgencio Batista, might mastermind similar communist takeovers in the Caribbean and Central America.[79] Kennedy developed the Green Berets, specialists in guerrilla and covert warfare, and supplemented them with large transport planes, amphibious craft, and helicopters. He sent "advisers" to South Vietnam and used the CIA to mastermind the overthrow of Ngo Dinh Diem with the intent of installing Gen. Duong Van Minh.

Kennedy's propensity for increasing military spending markedly was also related to his embrace and that of his secretary of defense, Robert McNamara, of the so-called game theorists, who had assumed prominent roles in shaping nuclear strategy. Advocates of massive deterrence, such as Gen. Curtis LeMay and Eisenhower, adhered to simple tactics: if the Soviets invaded Western Europe or other areas where the United States had vital interests, they should be repulsed with nuclear weapons aimed at their military and industrial centers. Massive retaliation was brute force openly declared, with no soft edges—and its advocates realized that it would lead to two-way destruction once the Soviet Union had its own nuclear arsenal.

But a number of theorists were troubled by massive retaliation. They were centered at the Rand Institution, a think tank heavily subsidized by the air force. People like Bernard Brodie conceptualized nuclear strategy as a "two-way affair" and drew heavily on game theory, which had been pioneered by the mathematician John von Neumann.[80] Von Neumann contended that players in games search for moves that advance their interests and do so within the context of the moves their opponents are likely to make. Thus they seek an optimal solution, one that allows them to avoid catastrophic losses while realizing (at least) modest gains.[81]

When used to analyze nuclear strategy, game theory implied that each side would consider an array of moves at the outset. Perhaps one side would strike first in the hope it could destroy enough of the opponent's nuclear arsenal to avoid utter destruction. Or perhaps one side would initiate conflict with lesser tactical nuclear weapons, hoping that the other side would refuse to escalate the nuclear match, lest it be annihilated. In this scenario, for example, the Soviets might fire tactical weapons into Europe as a prelude to invading with conventional forces. Game theorists also contended that protagonists would calculate their moves *during* extended nuclear conflict. If the Soviets attacked SAC bombers, Americans might destroy a single Soviet city in hope of forestalling all-out nuclear conflict, only to escalate their strategy if the Soviets made further aggressive moves.

Whereas Truman and Eisenhower viewed nuclear warheads primarily as deterrents rather than as weapons to be actually used during wars, game theorists viewed them as resources to be used, whether to initiate conflict (as in first strikes) or during nuclear exchanges in a kind of lethal chess. A protagonist might strike a foe's pawn with nuclear arms in retaliation for a modest indiscretion. If the foe persisted or launched a larger move, the protagonist might take a castle while sternly warning the foe that a queen or even the king might be next.

Kennedy gave game theorists top posts in his campaign and his administration. In the late 1950s Rand theorists had evolved a doctrine known as "counterforce," which contended that the United States would hit key Soviet military and industrial targets in a planned sequence if the Soviets used nuclear weapons or invaded Europe. (Counterforce was taken to its ultimate expression by Herman Kahn, who identified "44 rungs of escalation," dispassionately noting, for example, that one rung would kill "only" two million people.)[82] McNamara developed his own version, which he called "flexible response"; he wanted to expand the U.S. arsenal of existing conventional, tactical, strategic, and guerrilla forces and weapons that could be used to counter aggression.[83]

As proponents of game theory, Kennedy and McNamara proposed and obtained major increases in military spending in the early 1960s. An array of new weapons with varying degrees of lethality had to be produced and placed into the field, in contrast to relatively fewer weapons in the Eisenhower era.

Many people in the early 1960s believed flexible response to be a flawed theory. Eisenhower opposed it. Several of Kennedy's aides criticized it as promoting excessive military spending because it required the United States to develop an array of capabilities.[84] Such Europeans as French premier Charles de Gaulle rejected it on the ground that all-out nuclear war was likely once any protagonist resorted to nuclear weapons.[85]

To add an exclamation point to their military buildup, Kennedy and McNamara also contended that the United States ought to be able to fight 2.5 wars *at the same time*, in other words, two major wars and one regional war. (They assumed the major wars would be with the Republic of China and the Soviet Union—and that the "half war" would occur against a communist insurgency in a third-world nation like South Vietnam.) For each of these wars, the United States would have and perhaps use a full range of competencies, extending from full-fledged conventional war to all-out nuclear war. Kennedy and McNamara also were sharply critical of Eisenhower's use of ceilings on military spending, contending that the military should receive whatever resources it needed to defend the nation.

Kennedy inherited military and related spending of $305 billion (in constant 1992 dollars) and increased it to $333 billion by the time of his death. In the same period he increased domestic spending—both entitlements and discretionary spending—from $103 billion to only $114 billion. And Kennedy had planted the seeds for an all-out commitment of U.S. forces when he put the advisers into South Vietnam.

What is remarkable is that military spending did not rise even more rapidly in the Kennedy years, given his expansionary foreign policy and military doctrine. The credit belongs partly to McNamara, who was determined to cut costs by using the aggressive management skills that he had honed at Ford Motor Co. He developed a new budgeting system for the Pentagon to curb interservice duplication, such as identifying all weapons and programs that contributed to various objectives, like strategic nuclear power, tactical nuclear power, and limited (conventional wars).[86] He used this budgeting system to prune weapons and troops from specific services when he believed they were not necessary, causing howls of protest from the Joint Chiefs and other top brass. He tried to develop weapons that two or more services could use, such as an aircraft suitable for both the navy and the army.[87] He sought many economies, such as closing scores of unneeded military bases to the outrage of legislators in whose districts they lay. But McNamara was tilting at windmills. Used to corporate settings where CEOs could achieve efficiencies merely by ordering changes,

McNamara discovered that economies were elusive in the Department of Defense as legislators and the services objected to most cuts. McNamara was surrounded by corporate lobbyists, Congress, and the Joint Chiefs, and by late 1962 an array of enemies had vowed to seek his ouster.

Pork, Corporate Welfare, and Tax Waste

I have focused on waste in the military budget, as well as flawed tax policies that fostered excessive debt or failed to raise sufficient revenues to support a domestic agenda. A careful appraisal of the federal budget in 1951 by Sen. Paul Douglas, D.-Ill., a respected economist and a liberal who did not reflexively oppose government spending, suggests that many other kinds of waste existed.[88]

Douglas contended, for example, that Congress could cut $310 million (in 1951 dollars) from the agriculture budget by excising bonus payments to farmers for carrying out approved farming practices that most would use anyway; consolidating federal, county, and field offices to cut administrative costs; and reducing price supports during periods when farmers saw rising (not falling) prices. He proposed cutting $400 million from the $2 billion spent on public works for rivers, harbors, irrigation, flood control, airports, and highways by curtailing those clearly designed to reward lobbyists and contractors, enacting some user fees, requiring states and localities to contribute some resources, or requiring some projects to contribute a portion of their revenues. He favored cutting $425 million from veterans' programs by reducing overhead costs and personnel and by eliminating abuses in the GI education program. The country could save another $100 million, he argued, by rescinding corporate subsidies to silver producers, airlines for carrying the mail, and to the shipping industry. Improving efficiency in the post office would save $400 million more. He contended that cutting interest payments on refunds to taxpayers and on funds borrowed by the government from trust funds would save $165 million.

On top of these savings, Douglas proposed saving $4 billion from the military budget by curtailing excessive overcharges in procurement and by eliminating other inefficiencies, like "hazard pay" for pilots, given that reinstituting a compulsory draft would mean such incentives would not be necessary. Douglas further contended that the United States could save another $2.4 billion by replacing "depletion allowances" for oil and gas producers with direct subsidies, by increasing the capital gains tax, by increasing estate and gift taxes, and by enacting withholding taxes on dividends and corporate bond interest payments.

Douglas's total recommended savings from all these sources came to $8.2 billion in a federal budget of $71 billion—an extraordinary sum.[89] These savings suggested that conservatives were wrong: waste in government derived primarily from a mixture of inefficiencies in military spending, pork-barrel spending, tax subsidies, and corporate welfare rather than the minuscule social programs of that period. (His estimate of $4 billion in inefficiency in the military budget exceeded the combined funding of all discretionary social programs, which totaled only $3 billion in 1952.)

Eliminating such waste would prove difficult, however. Powerful lobbyists and legislators supported each source of savings, and they usually secured bipartisan support. These items were often slipped into legislation with scant public attention, and voters rarely were even aware they existed.[90] Decades later many of Douglas's wasteful items remained in the budget, supplemented by others.

Missed Tradeoffs and Failed Priorities

Estimates of enemy intentions and forces, as well as what is needed to deter them, are intrinsically difficult to make, but considerable evidence suggests that the U.S. military consistently made inflated estimates between 1950 and 1963. The Joint Chiefs frequently wanted far greater resources than they received and would cite the possibility that the Soviets would invade Western Europe or that they would take over myriad third-world nations. The chiefs' estimates were wrong, of course, and the Soviet threat never became a reality, even with much less military spending than the Joint Chiefs desired. Democratic leaders were wrong when they believed a bomber gap existed in the mid-1950s or a missile gap a few years later. Kennedy was incorrect in assuming that the reunification of Vietnam under Ho Chi Minh would cause the fall of other nations in Asia, because no domino effect occurred when Vietnam was reunified under communist rule in the mid-1970s.

Although we have the advantage of hindsight when identifying these errors by the Joint Chiefs, presidents, and legislators, some people did identify them during the 1950s. Eisenhower contended that the Democrats were wrong about bomber and missile gaps. Gen. Maxwell Taylor argued that the United States had many more nuclear weapons than it needed in the late 1950s and even contended that 150 to 200 nuclear warheads (whether on missiles or in bombers) would suffice.[91] Such magazines as the *Nation* and the *New Republic* were filled with articles that criticized Kennedy's strategy in South Vietnam, using words like *quagmire* to describe what probably would happen. George Kennan believed that U.S. leaders excessively demonized Soviet leaders. Robert Oppenheimer wanted the president to be candid with the American people about the Soviet threat and nuclear weapons. Sen. Robert Taft asked why the United States needed a large land army in Europe when no one believed a land war would occur there—or why Congress should view as credible such generals as Omar Bradley when they wanted more than $50 billion in 1951 after insisting one year earlier that the military needed only $13.5 billion.[92] Some legislators wanted to peg the numbers of U.S. troops that would serve with NATO to specific troop commitments by European nations.[93]

But Congress mostly abdicated to the executive branch its constitutional powers of raising armies. It failed to cut a major weapons system from 1945 to 1961, with the single exception of a second nuclear carrier, and instead pushed to spend even more money on the military or to place military contracts with vendors in specific legislative districts.[94] On those rare occasions when a legislator did raise basic questions, such as when Sen. George McGovern, D-S.D., proposed a 5 percent cut in military spending in the early 1960s, congressional leaders prevented substantive discussion of their merits.[95] Debates about military spending also were stifled by excessive secrecy by the executive branch and the withholding of key information from the public.[96]

U.S. leaders were not inclined to analyze tradeoffs between military spending and the domestic agenda. The National Security Council and the Joint Chiefs became the key arenas for making military choices "with no executive committees of comparable importance in domestic areas."[97] Though military spending precluded domestic spending to a degree unmatched during any period in American history when the nation was not in a shooting war, virtually no one asked whether military spending could be pruned to allow greater domestic spending. The term *guns and butter,* used before World War II to describe the tension between production of armaments and civilian goods like automobiles, was not used in the

1950s to discuss the tension between military and domestic spending. (Not until 1961 did the term appear in the mass media, when John Bailey, chair of the Democratic National Committee, contended that United States could "have both guns and butter," a position bitterly and belatedly contested later in the 1960s and early 1970s by some liberals.)[98] Ironically, it was Eisenhower—not liberals—who made the most eloquent statement about tradeoffs between military spending and domestic needs, even if he saved it for his valedictory speech.

As figure 7.2 shows, military and related spending dominated Eisenhower's budgets. Narrow military spending and veterans' programs averaged 68 percent of the federal budget from 1954 through 1961. When interest payments (mostly on World War II debt) are also included, roughly 73.6 percent of the federal budget was accounted for, leaving Congress and the president room to decided how to allocate the money remaining in the treasury. (Federal spending on social services, education, training, employment, and entitlements, called "social investments" in fig. 7.2, averaged only 1.8 percent of the budget in this period.)[99]

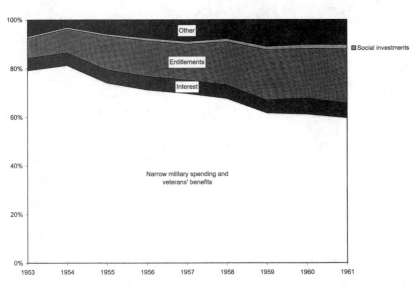

FIGURE 7.2 Five Types of Expenditures as Percentages of Total Federal Outlays, 1953–1961

Source: Office of Management and Budget, Budget of the U.S. Government, FY 2000, Historical Tables (Washington, D.C.: GPO, 1999), table 3.1, pp. 43–44.

These percentages understate the extent to which military spending dominated federal spending. As figure 7.3 shows, considerably more than 85 percent of the money that Congress "controls" each year in the discretionary budget (the budget minus mandatory spending and entitlements) went to military spending from 1951 to 1963, leaving far less than 15 percent of discretionary funds for nonmilitary purposes.

Although Eisenhower saved the nation tens of billions of dollars by opposing the Joint Chiefs and the Democrats on numerous occasions, he also institutionalized cold war military spending at levels that exceeded the actual threat faced by the United States. (When military spending peaks in the Korean War, the Vietnam War, and the military buildup of President Ronald Reagan are not considered, the United States spent roughly $250 billion per year on its military from 1950 through 1991. In subsequent chapters I refer to this spending as the *cold war base*.) Far from being restrained, this cold war budget was laden with excessive nuclear weapons and forces as well as chronic inefficiencies that precluded a domestic

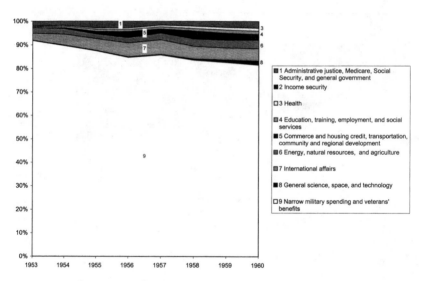

FIGURE 7.3 Competition for Discretionary Spending: Military Versus Domestic Spending as Percentages of Total Outlays, 1953–1960

Number 2 is not shown on the graph because discretionary spending was so small for this item that it does not "appear" prior to 1960.

Source: Office of Management and Budget, *Budget of the U.S. Government, FY 2000, Historical Tables* (Washington, D.C.: GPO, 1999), table 3.1, pp. 43–44.

agenda other than off-budget programs like Social Security and the interstate highway system. Far from diminishing these excesses, John Kennedy continued them and actually increased military spending markedly during his brief tenure. Narrow military expenditures totaled roughly $2.3 trillion during Eisenhower's tenure (1954–1961) and roughly $529 billion during Kennedy's tenure (1962–1963), for a grand total of $2.8 trillion for the two presidencies in constant 1992 dollars. These presidents and Congress established the cold war budget at unnecessarily high levels and presided over a military that wasted vast resources in its procurement and operations.

Nor did the United States collect sufficient taxes from 1953 through 1963 to fund its huge military and a sufficient domestic agenda. Tax revenues averaged only 17.6 percent of GDP from 1953 through 1963, yielding revenues of $4.9 trillion, as opposed to somewhat higher rates of taxation in succeeding decades.[100] Had the United States taxed 20 percent of GDP during these years, it would have gained $633 billion that it could have used to fund a domestic agenda or to lighten the tax burden for people in the lowest two economic quintiles. I argue in chapter 15 that the nation made fiscal and tax errors that exceeded $1 trillion (in constant 1992 dollars) during the Eisenhower and Kennedy administrations—and that figure does not even count excessive corporate welfare, excessive tax concessions to affluent Americans, or pork-barrel spending.

8

Johnson's Policy Gluttony

Lyndon Johnson wanted to be the first president in
American history to couple an ambitious military program with far-reaching domestic reforms while slashing
taxes and maintaining balanced budgets. Would his
Great Society dramatically change the priorities of a
nation that spent a majority of its budget on military and
veterans' programs but only 1.3 percent for education,
social, training, and employment programs? His efforts
to fund his domestic agenda would be frustrated by fiscal
and tax errors exceeding $1.55 trillion from 1964 through
1969 (in constant 1992 dollars).

Cutting Taxes—and His Throat?

Faced with an unemployment rate higher than 6 percent,
President John Kennedy tried to stimulate the economy
with modest social spending. But congressional conservatives opposed the creation of budget deficits when
Kennedy was increasing military spending. Walter Heller,

who chaired the Council of Economic Advisers, recognized that Congress would not grant the spending increases JFK sought. Heller recommended that to stimulate the economy Kennedy should seek massive cuts—roughly $12 billion, or more than 10 percent of total federal tax revenues—in individual and corporate income-tax rates in early 1962. Kennedy found ready support in the House, which finally approved the tax cuts in September 1963. When Kennedy was assassinated, the cuts were still before the Senate. Heller briefed Johnson about them and found, to his delight, that the new president immediately endorsed them.[1] Johnson had proposed large tax cuts in 1954 and was profoundly aware of their political popularity during an election year.[2] He realized too that the Republican presidential candidate in 1964 would make tax cuts a campaign issue. Johnson hoped to fund his domestic agenda, as well as any foreign interventions, from the added revenues these tax cuts would stimulate and confidently predicted the treasury would see revenues of $90 billion even in the first year, although revenues before the cuts totaled only $89 billion.[3]

Johnson encountered a formidable opponent, however, in Harry Byrd, the Virginia independent who chaired the Senate Finance Committee—the same Harry Byrd who had led repeated crusades against domestic spending since the New Deal. Byrd was not buying the New Economists' promise that short-term deficits would quickly be erased, but he agreed not to oppose the tax cuts on two conditions: Johnson had to hold spending below $100 billion (at least until tax revenues returned to their pre-cut levels) and he had to allow the Senate Finance Committee to review his budget proposal before he made it public. Johnson toyed with using a parliamentary maneuver to bypass Byrd, but friends convinced the wily Texan that this tactic would antagonize both Byrd and Wilbur Mills, the powerful chair of the House Ways and Means Committee.[4] Capitulating to Byrd and outmaneuvering Senator Albert Gore Sr., who feared the tax cuts would deplete funds needed for the domestic agenda, Johnson got Congress to enact the tax quickly and signed it on February 27. The election-year bonanza cut personal income taxes by 20 percent and made sizable cuts in corporate income taxes. When Barry Goldwater, the GOP's presidential candidate, subsequently demanded an additional cut of 25 percent in federal income taxes in the summer of 1964, he was widely perceived as fiscally irresponsible and a johnny-come-lately.[5] Johnson, leaving nothing to chance, promised to cut excise taxes within a year.

Neither Heller or Johnson had anticipated an array of likely events. Federal taxes in the early 1960s were not extraordinarily high, consuming about 18.2 percent of the GDP—or roughly the same share as in the 1950s and 1970s. By slashing them markedly, Johnson put severe limits on his budget just as he began his complex juggling act of domestic reforms and a possible escalation in Vietnam. If he failed to keep his budget request under $100 billion until tax revenues rebounded, he would encounter short-term deficits and draw the ire of congressional conservatives. It is always easier, moreover, to cut taxes than to increase them. Johnson would soon find that Congress would balk at tax increases even in the face of deficits.

Keeping Military Waste Intact

Once he had opted for huge tax cuts, Johnson had to cut military and related spending to make room for his domestic reforms, because the military consumed roughly half the federal budget (about $50 billion) just for personnel, weapons, and intelligence—never mind the space program, veterans' programs, or interest on wartime debt.

But Lyndon Johnson was not inclined to question cold war assumptions. Eager to make his mark, he came to the presidency with well-formed beliefs about foreign policy. He was deeply influenced by southern military lore, such as the surprise attack by Americans (including LBJ's great-great uncle) under Gen. Sam Houston that devastated the Mexican fortification in the Battle of San Jacinto in 1836; his grandmother's brush with death as she hid in a cellar during an Indian raid; and a relative who had battled Mexicans, Indians, and bandits as a member of the Texas Rangers. Johnson prided himself on casting a pivotal vote to extend the draft in 1941. After he was appointed to the House Naval Committee, he became close to its chair, Carl Vinson, the Georgia Democrat, and even aspired to become secretary of the navy in 1944. Although Johnson after World War II toyed with the idea of world government and sharing nuclear materials with the United Nations, he soon veered toward a virulent anticommunism. He supported the Joint Chiefs of Staff when they battled Harry Truman for a seventy-group air force and saw the Marshall Plan as a way to keep "Stalin from overrunning the world."[6] Using red-baiting language like Joe McCarthy's, Johnson accused his opponent in his 1948 Senate campaign of sympathizing with communists and in 1949 attacked Truman's nominee for the Federal Power Commission as a communist. Johnson favored total mobilization of U.S. power even before the Korean War, supported sending aid to save Vietnam from communism, wanted to send even more assistance to Chiang Kai-shek, and advocated quadrupling U.S. military spending in the early 1950s. When he served on the Senate Armed Services Committee, he became extraordinarily close to its powerful chairman, Democrat Richard Russell of Georgia. Johnson formed and chaired a Special Committee on Preparedness soon after the Korean War began. Arguing that small wars between the Russians and Americans would occur in such places as Korea, Indochina, Iran, or Yugoslavia, he predicted a direct showdown with the Soviets in which the United States would "crush this tyrant once and for all."[7] By February 1952 Johnson was demanding a nuclear attack on the Soviet Union, saying "*any* act of aggression, *any*where, by *any* communist forces, will be regarded as an act of aggression by the Soviet Union . . .[requiring the United States to] unleash all the power at our command upon the vitals of the Soviet Union."[8] He regularly sought increases in military spending in the 1950s and led the Democrats' "missile gap" attack on Eisenhower—the gap that later turned out not to exist. Johnson's interest in military policy also stemmed from more mundane motives—his rise to power was financed largely by oil money and donations from such military contractors as Brown and Root.[9]

Beginning the Frugal Society

Because he had removed barely a nickel from the military's budget and had gotten Congress to enact huge tax cuts, Johnson had to develop a frugal domestic policy that would not undermine his promise to Senator Byrd about keeping a lid on spending until revenues rebounded. Yet Johnson was not content with modest reforms; he wanted to best Franklin Roosevelt's New Deal and motivate liberal Democrats to work for his election in November.

Johnson was a genuine reformer, even if he does not warrant the adjective *revolutionary*, which Joseph Califano has applied to him.[10] LBJ had heard his grandfather, Samuel Johnson, discuss the plight of tenant farmers. LBJ's father had supported legislation that outlawed the wearing of sheets by the Ku Klux Klan at a time when such a proposal was not only daring but personally dangerous. Lyndon Johnson had seen poverty first-hand while Texas director of the National Youth Administration. He ran for Congress as a Roosevelt supporter in 1938, and the young representative often breakfasted with the president. Johnson avidly sought WPA, public housing, and rural electrification funds for his constituents.[11] As a senator he killed bills by southern Democrats that attacked the Supreme Court's landmark decision in *Brown v. Board of Education* (1954) and assumed a critical role in enacting modest civil rights legislation in 1957. He voted for increases in Social Security benefits as well as myriad smaller programs and supported major increases in domestic spending to redress the recession of 1957. Johnson often collaborated with legendary Speaker Sam Rayburn and helped Eisenhower expand existing social programs while resisting efforts to terminate New Deal or Fair Deal programs.[12]

Yet Johnson was hardly a wild-eyed reformer. He believed that his grandfather and his father had failed in politics because they had been unwilling to compromise, and Lyndon Johnson was determined not to be known as a tax-and-spend liberal.[13] He turned his back on social reform and the New Deal when he began his senatorial career in 1948, saying, "Frankly . . . I'm for nearly everything the big oil boys want because they hold the whip hand and I represent 'em. Yeah, I represent farmers and working men . . . [but] the New Deal spirit's gone from Texas and I'm limited in what I can do."[14] He refused to take stands on civil rights measures during and after World War II or during his early years as senator. He opposed domestic reforms during the Korean War, warning that "we must not permit the tax money which could go for defense to be depleted by unjustified demands for government programs."[15] He disliked welfare programs and welfare recipients; he frequently used pejorative terms to refer to them during his presidency, and he wanted to take the word *welfare* out of the title of the Department of Health, Education, and Welfare.[16]

Just as Roosevelt had established his frugality at the outset of his presidency, Johnson began his presidency by cutting domestic programs in the "greatest economy drive in American history." He boasted in late December 1963 that he had granted domestic agencies only $3.5 billion in increases when they had sought $10 billion.[17] He found billions of dollars of additional cuts, mostly in the Department of Agriculture, veterans' programs, and the Department of Commerce—and used various budget gimmicks to appease Byrd, such as deferring expenditures and selling $2.5 billion worth of government assets.[18] He defied those liberals who wanted his 1964 budget to exceed $100 billion by cutting it to $97.9 billion and vowed to extend McNamara's efficiency techniques to domestic agencies.

He selected two initiatives to champion in 1964 that were both inexpensive and dramatic: civil rights and antipoverty legislation. The Kennedy brothers had watched the growing violence in the South in 1961 and 1962 with trepidation but had relied on southern police to keep the peace. The Kennedys also had relied on the naive theory that the South could be gradually transformed through voter registration, a political philosophy that also placated powerful southern legislators. But the Kennedys' hand was forced by escalating violence that horrified northern voters and forced the administration to use federal marshals to enforce federal law in the South. (By late 1963 public opinion polls were showing that Americans ranked the deprivation of civil rights as a problem as serious as communism.) Fearing northern liberals would upstage him, Kennedy finally assented to civil rights legislation in the summer of 1963.[19]

As president, Johnson, who knew northerners viewed the civil rights legislation as a litmus test, supported Kennedy's proposal and refused to weaken its provisions; LBJ was confident he could count on southern support in the 1964 elections because he hailed from the South. From a budgetary perspective, the Civil Rights Act of 1964, enacted in July, was a godsend to Johnson. By augmenting the Justice Department's enforcement budget only slightly, he could establish his social reform credentials instantly and inexpensively.

He seized on antipoverty legislation as another means of expanding his domestic agenda dramatically and frugally.[20] In the fall of 1963 Kennedy had commissioned an executive task force, led by Heller, to brainstorm a federal antipoverty program, but it had barely begun its work when JFK was assassinated. Some task force members wanted to fund a laundry list of programs that the conservative Congress had refused to enact: job training, legal aid, and public health measures. Meanwhile, officials from the Bureau of the Budget wanted (merely) to coordinate existing federal, state, and local programs by establishing local nongovernment agencies (citizen action agencies, or CAAs).[21] Partly because it required little money to implement, Johnson endorsed the Budget Bureau's concept, saying on December 29 that "the fight on poverty" would "involve a realignment of federal, state, and local government welfare programs . . . to eliminate duplication, thus getting greater value for each dollar spent on helping the poor."[22] He intended the poverty program merely to be "glue money" to coordinate existing programs rather than establish new ones.[23]

But Johnson knew that a program limited to coordination would not appeal to many liberals, who had secured few reforms during the previous twenty-five years and whose appetites had been whetted by the civil rights movement. When someone suggested the title "War on Poverty," Johnson concurred and used this term in his State of the Union message on January 8, although he earmarked only $300 million for it in his budget proposal. By selecting Sargent Shriver, Kennedy's brother-in-law, to head it in late January 1964, Johnson further elevated the program's visibility. A dynamic and idealistic go-getter who was not content merely to head a coordinating effort, Shriver sought to create a comprehensive, multibillion-dollar program to attack poverty. He quickly supported the Job Corps, the Neighborhood Youth Administration, Legal Aid, and public health programs, as well as the CAAs favored by the Bureau of the Budget. Shriver failed to recognize that community activists would use the phrase "maximum feasible participation of the poor" as an organizing tool and agreed to insert it in the legislation that established the CAAs.[24]

Even at the War on Poverty's inception, Johnson reined in those people who wanted it to encompass a large and expensive public works program.[25] He would frequently boast of the War on Poverty's efficiency in serving hundreds of thousands of citizens with scant appropriations. His hyperbole and his minimal allocations (it never received more than $2 billion) had unfortunate consequences. Once the civil rights legislation was enacted, many black activists broadened their concerns to the economic and social plight of urban African Americans. Misled by Johnson's boasting, they felt betrayed when they realized that the war was merely a skirmish—a potpourri of small programs loosely linked to CAAs. (The CAAs were quickly overpowered by local political interests when activists used them to mobilize pressure against local policies.)

A War by Any Other Name . . .

Johnson knew many conservatives would attack his domestic agenda if his budget exceeded $100 billion, yet this realization did not deter him from planning an aggressive strategy in Vietnam even before the presidential elections. He believed that Eisenhower had committed the United States to aid South Vietnam in a letter he had written to its president, Ngo Dinh Diem—and was aware that Eisenhower had warned Kennedy that the United States must intervene even if its allies demurred.[26] Johnson told the National Security Council in his first days as president: "Hell, Vietnam is just like the Alamo. Hell, it's just like if you were down at that gate and you were surrounded . . . and I thank the Lord that I've got men who want to go with me, from McNamara right on down to the littlest private who's carrying a gun."[27] He was acutely aware that the Republicans might accuse him of being soft on North Vietnam in the 1964 elections and even feared that Henry Cabot Lodge, the U.S. ambassador to South Vietnam, might join the Republican ticket as vice president to make this charge.[28]

Johnson implied that the United States would become more involved in Vietnam even in his first budget message in January 1964 when he said, "The less-developed nations are engaged in a critical struggle for political independence [with] this struggle [taking] many forms, from combating armed aggression and subversion in Vietnam to advancing national efforts to reduce poverty." He added that he would seek prompt action from Congress to provide "additional funds to meet emerging requirements. . . [against] threats to the free world."[29] As Johnson and his top military advisers met during early and mid-1964, they discussed the option of large-scale escalation from the relatively small cadre of "advisers" that Kennedy had sent. Johnson and the brass believed that Ho Chi Minh had master-minded political unrest as part of a global communist crusade. They regarded Vietnam as similar to Korea in 1950 and minimized the indigenous conflict between local insurgents and a despotic corrupt regime in South Vietnam. In fact, a civil war was underway there, and North Vietnam had chosen to help one side by sending it troops and supplies. Partly because the analogy to Korea was wrong—the primary dynamic in Korea *was* an invasion—Johnson and his men often assumed that the United States could quickly prevail by cutting the flow of invading troops—but that remedy did not address the conflict in South Vietnam itself. The analogy to Korea also underplayed the difficulty of the terrain in South Vietnam; it contained vast jungles and bordered other nations. Yet Johnson and his advisers adhered to the domino theory and believed that the United States had to act quickly, lest the fall of South Vietnam precipitate a communist takeover of other nations in Southeast Asia.[30]

Johnson knew that a costly escalation in 1964 would doom his domestic legislation in light of his promise to Byrd. As a witness to the attacks on "nonessential spending" during World War II and Korea, he also knew that if Congress declared war on North Vietnam, conservatives would attack the Great Society. Johnson needed a way to engage the nation in conflict without an official declaration of war—and only after Congress had approved most of his Great Society. His probable Republican opponent in 1964 was a hawk, Barry Goldwater, who held extremist views on foreign policy; Johnson knew he would lose his advantage as a peace candidate if he escalated the U.S. presence in Vietnam before the 1964 elections. He might, of course, have abandoned South Vietnam, but his cold war instincts, as well as his determination not to give conservatives the ability to "out-hawk" him in the 1964 elections, made him reject this option.[31]

Johnson became convinced in the summer of 1964 that he needed to get congressional support for an escalation of American military activity in Vietnam before adverse public opinion and acrimonious public debate developed; he had seen early signs of opposition even to Kennedy's low-scale involvement. Johnson's advisers mulled the options for getting "something binding." The State Department even drafted alternative resolutions. Some advisers wanted a public campaign to secure a congressional resolution that permitted selective use of force, whereas others advocated caution, lest the effort precipitate a public debate. Johnson demurred in light of low public support for escalation.[32]

It was in this context that Johnson and his military advisers chose provocative tactics: they provided U.S. assistance to covert South Vietnamese hit-and-run attacks on the North Vietnam coast, including landing sabotage teams. North Vietnamese boats chased the *Maddox*, a U.S. destroyer engaged in such assistance on August 2, apparently after receiving unauthorized orders to do so—and the *Maddox* seriously damaged one of the North Vietnamese boats.[33] The United States seemed to want to provoke an incident when it approved more covert attacks. On the morning of August 4, the crew of the *Maddox* believed it had been attacked. By noon Johnson had seized on the incident as an "opportunity for something he had perceived as desirable for a long time"—a congressional resolution that would empower him to "take all necessary steps, including the use of armed force . . . to assist any member or protocol state of the Southeast Asia Collective Defense Treaty requesting assistance in defense of its freedom."[34] In fact, Johnson acted precipitously because the ship's captain had raised doubts by 2 p.m. that *any* attack had occurred—and pilots from the

U.S. aircraft carrier *Ticonderoga*, which had provided air cover for the *Maddox*, reported they had seen no hostile boats. (By 6:45 p.m. Johnson had told congressional leaders that nine torpedoes had been fired at the *Maddox*.) Moreover, McNamara lied to Congress to make the "attack" seem even more provocative, such as by saying the *Maddox* was merely on routine patrol and contending that the U.S. Navy had no knowledge of offensive actions by the South Vietnamese.[35] With virtually no dissent and hardly any discussion, Congress approved the Gulf of Tonkin Resolution on August 7. A declaration of war would have required Johnson to escalate at once and at high cost; the resolution allowed him decide when to begin and at what pace. It was a brilliant tactic, and it allowed Johnson to keep his Great Society, pose as the peace candidate, and prevent the just-nominated Goldwater from attacking him as too easy on Vietnam—even if the maneuver would boomerang in coming years because liberals deeply resented his manipulation of Congress.[36]

Juggling Three Pins in 1965

Johnson wanted desperately to keep juggling his tax cut and domestic and military goals but feared even after his landslide victory over Goldwater that his complicated act might collapse. He remembered how Franklin Roosevelt had squandered his popularity by trying to pack the Supreme Court and purge the Democratic Party after his landslide victory in 1936.[37] Might the military pin knock the domestic pin from his hand? Would the combined cost of his domestic and military pins require him to raise taxes, which would lead conservatives to demand cuts in domestic spending in return? Everything depended on robust economic growth to produce annual increases in tax revenues of $7 billion to $9 billion—revenues Johnson needed to reduce deficits as he funded his complex agenda.

Johnson decided to launch a barrage of social programs in 1965 because he now possessed overwhelming Democratic majorities in both chambers of Congress. Yet he still encountered a dearth of budget resources because of the huge tax cut in 1964 and growing military commitments to South Vietnam. He could increase domestic spending by only $3.6 billion in his budget request for 1965—a paltry sum in light of the extraordinary domestic agenda that he had unveiled in January: health insurance for the elderly, an Older Americans Act, federal aid to education, and legislation to establish a department of housing and urban development, as well as many smaller bills and greater funding for the War on Poverty.

Johnson boasted that he had won enactment of fifty pieces of domestic legislation in 1964; he vowed in June that Congress would enact eighty-nine pieces in 1965—and the month before, he had established fourteen task forces to plan a new round of domestic legislation for 1966.[38] With his parliamentary skills, huge congressional majorities, and high standing in the polls, Johnson seized the legislative initiative and got virtually all his domestic legislation enacted by August.

He could keep his domestic agenda lean because most of his programs were new ones that required a year's planning before they could be implemented and because he sought only minimal funds for the War on Poverty. He obscured the meager funding by proclaiming that his budget request would fund three hundred CAAs and participation by 330,000 youths in the Job Corps and Neighborhood Youth Corps. When he promised a military budget of $49 billion on January 19, 1965, he also promised a military budget cut of $400 million in 1965—and a "leveling off" of military spending after that.[39] Meanwhile, in secret meetings with his top advisers in the spring and early summer, Johnson moved methodically toward a large-scale commitment of troops to Vietnam. (He later divulged to Dean Rusk, his secretary of state, that he had decided in December to escalate the U.S. presence in Vietnam.)[40] Johnson established some initial enclaves of U.S. forces and ordered the air force to strafe the demilitarized zone. When the Vietcong attacked Pleiku in early February, Johnson ordered a brief bombing of North Vietnam and introduced U.S. ground forces. Aware that he would need congressional support to fund the escalation, Johnson convened congressional leaders several times, beginning in February, to discuss specific actions and found that most approved of what he was doing. When Undersecretary of State George Ball, like Senate Majority Leader Mike Mansfield, expressed fear that Vietnam would become a quagmire that would mean extraordinary costs and perhaps cause China to enter the conflict, McNamara impatiently used elaborate statistics to prove that the United States would prevail.[41] When the first debate on the unfolding Vietnam policy occurred in the Senate in February, the few dissenters were isolated, feared reprisal from Johnson, and realized that the Gulf of Tonkin Resolution gave Johnson a free hand. Johnson had already commenced a pattern he would follow in succeeding years: issue no policy reports and confine discussion of policy options to a small cadre of already committed advisers while not consulting Congress on key deci-sions.[42] He increased the bombing of North Vietnam in March with Operation Rolling Thunder while raising the troop ceiling from twenty thousand in January to eighty-two thousand in April. He ratcheted his escalation upward in early May when he sought $700 million to fund actions in the Dominican Republic and South Vietnam, using militant cold war language to justify it and equating his policies with patriotism in his personal meetings with 32 senators and 108 representatives. Rumors circulated in Washington that the $700 million was merely the first install-ment for huge military increases that eventually would mean 500,000 troops in Vietnam.[43]

Guns Versus Butter

Johnson viewed his presidency as a kind of Texas barbecue with something for everyone: conservatives liked his anticommunist policies, tax cuts, and frugal budgets, and liberals liked his Great Society. Johnson could preside over the party, granting concessions to liberals (who wanted sufficient but-ter) and to conservatives (who wanted frugal domestic spending and hawkishness abroad). But the success of the party required that both lib-erals and conservatives trust Johnson to protect their interests even as he granted concessions to others.[44]

In a nation that had only a bare-bones domestic agenda in 1963, liber-als would normally have been delighted with Johnson's Great Society, which brought numerous reforms as early as the spring of 1965. But the mid-1960s were not ordinary times—the nation had been convulsed by civil rights protests for years. The socialist Michael Harrington had believed that his book, *The Other America*, which showed the relationship between increasing wealth and increasing poverty, would sell only a few copies and found himself with a best-seller in 1963 as the public increas-ingly embraced social reform.[45] In April 1965 Sen. J. William Fulbright contended that cold war expenditures precluded a sufficient domestic agenda, and Mansfield pointedly asked Johnson that spring to divulge the likely cost of escalation in Vietnam.[46] By the fall of 1965 liberals such as Robert Kennedy and Sargent Shriver were pushing for a negative income tax and massive public works, as well as a $4 billion budget for the War on Poverty.[47] Liberals in fact became increasingly critical of the scant funding increases Johnson sought for his Great Society. The president's program, which proposed major reforms, seemed increasingly timid to many Americans.

Johnson carefully waited until he had gotten his domestic legislation through Congress to put his military pin into his juggling act. He announced on July 28 that he intended to lift the troop ceiling from 82,000 to 125,000 in Vietnam, "with additional forces later"; this meant that the draft would be stepped up and that he would seek increased military appropriations from Congress. Buried in a news conference, this announcement might have been viewed as just another incremental escalation, but it took place amid rumors that Johnson meant to commit hundreds of thousands of U.S. troops and tens of billions of dollars to the Vietnam conflict. An editorial in the *Nation* contended that Johnson had already decided to send 330,000 troops "over the next year or so."[48] Some liberals saw the ghost of Munich, heard his warning of "additional forces later," and feared the worst.

Johnson's juggling act started to come undone as he escalated U.S. involvement in Vietnam.[49] Liberals' propensity to view this escalation as harming domestic policy heightened after the Watts riot in Los Angeles two weeks later, which was followed by riots in Chicago and other cities that continued for the remainder of Johnson's presidency. Conservatives viewed the riots as criminal behavior, but liberals saw them as the inevitable result of the detestable living conditions that poor Americans were forced to endure. Now the Great Society seemed even less adequate. Before the summer of 1965 federal resources were not a major issue in the civil rights struggle, but they became increasingly pivotal as liberals focused on urban problems. Some liberals became disenchanted when Johnson, who needed to curtail spending to hold the budget to $100 billion, launched a huge economy drive in the summer and fall of 1965.

House Republicans Gerald Ford of Michigan and Melvin Laird of Wisconsin believed that Johnson should cut his funding of the Great Society to finance his Vietnam escalation, and they demanded that he do so immediately. They had no faith in the economists who argued the nation could afford both guns and butter.[50] Throughout the fall of 1965 and the winter and spring of 1966, they attacked the "excesses" of the Great Society and even gleefully sided with Democratic mayors against the insurgent CAAs. (Because the most reform-minded CAAs were located in urban areas and most big-city mayors were Democrats, the CAAs split the Democratic

Party as many mayors urged Shriver to curtail the CAAs' activism.) Ford and Laird denounced the unprecedented expansion of the federal government's powers and made common cause with southern Democrats disaffected by Johnson's civil rights measures.

Robert Kennedy gradually became the liberals' point man on the domestic front and Vietnam. He had supported his brother's decision to send advisers to Vietnam, but he harbored growing misgivings; in July 1965 he had decided only at the last minute that he would not lead opposition to funding the Johnson escalation, but in December he attacked the war's diversion of funds from the domestic agenda.[51] Johnson resented Bobby Kennedy as an easterner, feared he meant to topple his administration, and believed that Kennedy and Shriver had conspired to demand greater spending for the War on Poverty.

Americans had begun to debate the relative merits of guns and butter for the first time since the cold war had begun. As early as August 14, the *New York Times* headlined a Tom Wicker story "Guns or Butter: Republicans Pressing the Issue."[52] Conflict between guns and butter was Johnson's worst nightmare because it polarized the happy diners at his Texas barbecue into ideological factions, with conservatives attacking the Great Society to fund the war and liberals attacking the war to fund the Great Society. Although both sides had initially trusted Johnson to protect their interests, each side increasingly saw him as beholden to the other. Johnson feared that the major casualty of this crossfire would be the Great Society itself, because Americans traditionally rallied to the flag during hostilities, when conservatives always demanded cuts in nonessential spending. He also feared that the military and its congressional supporters would demand an all-out war that would consume tens of billions in annual funding, devastate the Great Society programs, and bring China into the war, as had happened in Korea.

The Juggler as Illusionist

Given the fiscal realities, Johnson needed time. He wrote himself a note on August 20: "McNamara's got to find ways to drag his feet on defense expenditures."[53] Johnson was still counting on economic growth to bring $7 billion to $10 billion in new revenues to the treasury each year; he reckoned in July 1965 that he could have as much as $15 billion in additional

revenues by January 1967 to help fund Vietnam and other government
costs. There was just one problem: increasing U.S. troop levels above
300,000 would cost (at least) $20 billion, although McNamara and John-
son chose not to reveal this fact. Even if tax revenues grew by $15 billion
between July 1965 and January 1967, he would be short by about $5 bil-
lion—even if he sought no increases for any other items in the budget. He
might, of course, have followed McNamara's advice just before the July
1965 escalation: enact a tax to fund it. Saying McNamara "didn't know
anything about politics," Johnson angrily rejected this option, because he
knew that full disclosure of the war's cost, as well as enactment of a tax to
fund it, would embroil the nation in a debate about the merits of the war
and turn conservatives against the Great Society.[54] So Johnson faced a
Catch-22. If he did not raise taxes, Vietnam could cause deficits that would
impel conservatives to attack the Great Society. If he proposed new taxes,
conservatives would demand they be coupled with cuts in social spending
(as in 1964)—or that spending cuts precede a tax increase, perhaps making one unnecessary. Increased revenues from a tax increase might have
emboldened conservatives, moreover, to demand an escalation even
greater than Johnson wanted, by giving them the money to finance it.[55]

To retain the Great Society under these circumstances and to preclude
a need to seek tax increases, Johnson used an array of strategies to disguise
or understate the war's true cost, even as he increased troop ceilings from
125,000 in July to 200,000 by February 1966 to more than 250,000 by May
1966 and to more than 400,000 by July 1966. He sought only $1.7 billion
in additional funds to finance the war after his initial escalation, beginning
a pattern that he repeated for the next eighteen months: seek minimal
funds at the outset of a period to give the illusion that Vietnam would be
an inexpensive conflict; argue in ensuing months (when asked whether
additional funds were needed) that the war was too volatile to permit anyone to accurately gauge its costs; seek an additional sum about six months
later to fund accrued and immediate expenses; and start the process all
over again by asking for another small sum for next period. After seeking
only $1.7 billion in July 1965, he sought only $12.8 billion in January 1966
for the first half of the year and $10.3 billion for the fiscal year beginning
in July. This chronic pattern allowed Johnson and McNamara to avert a
donnybrook between advocates of guns and advocates of butter. Had
Johnson been honest and sought $15 billion (instead of $1.7 billion) in July
1965 and $25 billion in his budget message of January 1966 (instead of $10.3

billion), the truth would have been out: this was a costly war with grave implications for the funding of the Great Society.

Johnson resorted to other strategies to understate the military budget. He sold strategic materials, such as copper, that the government had stockpiled in the cold war, raising $1.1 billion in 1964 and anticipating sales of $4.7 billion in 1967.[56] McNamara gave virtually nonstop press conferences on cost reductions in the regular programs of the military, claiming extensive reductions in 1965, 1966, and 1967 while not divulging that these were partly achieved by deferring expenditures, transferring funds between military accounts, and diverting forces and weapons from Europe to Vietnam.

But Johnson was too clever by half. In the summer and fall of 1965 rumors circulated that he had grossly understated the war's cost. Republicans charged outright that he was lying. William McChesney Martin, the chairman of the Federal Reserve Board, realized that he could not rely on the president for accurate data, but he needed to know how much the nation was actually spending. Martin used figures generated by the Senate Armed Services Committee and enunciated by Sen. John Stennis, the powerful Mississippi Democrat who had predicted the war would cost $12 billion to $15 billion more than Johnson's estimate in 1965–1966.[57] (Even two years later, as Stennis continued to argue that Johnson's military funding requests were inadequate, the *New York Times* noted that he had provided the most reliable data.) As rumors circulated about Johnson's lack of candor, doves and liberals increasingly feared that Johnson was sacrificing the Great Society on Vietnam's altar. Conservatives feared that he was hiding the war's true cost to protect the Great Society. As both liberals and conservatives came to distrust Johnson's information, they also increasingly questioned his claims about the war's progress. Because they wanted Americans to believe the war was worthwhile and would soon end, Johnson and McNamara issued glowing assessments of battlefield successes in 1965 and early 1966, even as journalists reported quite different accounts. Doubts about Johnson's veracity, in turn, triggered growing conflict between hawks and doves. Johnson may have been overstating the war's gains, but hawks increasingly wanted to escalate far faster and to "bomb the hell out of" Vietnam, while doves feared the worst and wanted to cut American losses by negotiating with the North Vietnamese.

In light of the fiscal realities and his promise to conservatives to control spending, Johnson continued to minimize the size of the Great Society program. He launched many economy drives against older programs, such as cutting public works programs in the Commerce Department, slashing agricultural subsidies, and cutting the space program. He discussed how his funding for the Great Society grew only by 1.5 percent in the budget proposal he issued in January 1966. He allocated only $1.7 billion to the War on Poverty in 1966, even though its director wanted at least $3 billion. He sought funding of the Elementary and Secondary Education Act so far beneath the level authorized by Congress that school districts and such administration liberals as John Gardner, the secretary of HEW, howled in protest. Even in mid-1966 Johnson boasted that his budget, minus Vietnam, still was about $100 million.

He resorted to various strategies to appease liberals. He tried to fashion some cuts in domestic programs secretly.[58] He often boasted about how much his administration had increased domestic funding, failing to note that even small increases from a base of nearly zero look large. He often equated the quality of the Great Society plan not with its expenditures but with the sheer number of programs that he had devised, a sort of foot-in-the-door approach: enact scores of programs while it is politically feasible and hope that Congress will provide adequate funding for them after the war. (Many top administration officials were dismayed by the low funding of domestic programs, as illustrated by an irate memo that Charles Schultze, the budget director, sent to Johnson on November 7: "We are not able to fund adequately the new Great Society programs . . . [leading] to *frustration, loss of credibility . . . backlogs, queuing, and griping . . . only increasing the distance between legislative achievement and actual funding.*")[59] Johnson emphasized the sheer number of people his new programs served even with their minimal budgets.

The escalation in Vietnam was not the only factor pinching Johnson's funding for the Great Society. To win modest increased taxes from Congress in 1965 and 1966, he had promised conservatives further cuts in domestic spending. Early signs of inflation in 1966 made some conservatives demand further cuts in domestic spending.[60] When administration economists like Gardner Ackley pressured Johnson throughout 1966 to raise taxes to avert inflation, he both refused to raise them and suppressed public discussion by members of the administration, lest they incite conservatives to attack the Great Society.[61]

Johnson's ability to fund his Great Society also was severely jeopardized by a congressional revolt in 1966. By recommending cuts in many older and popular programs, such as milk subsidies, to free up resources for his Great Society, Johnson antagonized large numbers of legislators from both parties, who retaliated with billions of dollars in congressional "add-ons" to his domestic agenda, such as for so-called impacted schools near military bases and other pet projects. Congress used these add-ons to pressure Johnson to reduce his appropriations requests for such pending legislation as rent supplements and the Model Cities Program. Because he realized that vetoing these add-ons could alienate Congress even further, Johnson acceded to many of them, placing even more fiscal pressure on his Great Society.

As a result, many people wondered about the true size of a federal deficit that Johnson had predicted in January 1966 would be only $1.8 billion. Rumors surfaced that he would disclose its true size, and the actual cost of the war, only after the congressional elections in November. Rumors of Johnson's deceptions about the cost of the war and the size of the deficit, as well as fears of inflation, reached a crescendo just before the elections, when polls showed that voters thought that inflation rivaled Vietnam in importance—and both issues far outdistanced such social issues as poverty. Close friends like Sen. George Smathers, D-Fla., beseeched Johnson to declare a tax increase to avert inflation and reduce the deficit.[62] All of Johnson's economic advisers, as well as a number of cabinet members, implored Johnson to support whatever tax measures and budget increases were needed to cover the costs in South Vietnam.[63] Faced with this near rebellion, Johnson chose merely to seek the temporary suspension of a investment tax credit enacted in the Kennedy administration. Only after the election did he reveal that the deficit would be $10 billion—or four times his prediction nine months earlier.

This deficit would have been far higher had Johnson not resorted to sleight-of-hand tactics to fund the Great Society. With no money in the till he had resorted to an off-budget strategy in the summer of 1965 when he signed the Medicare and Medicaid legislation that would provide health benefits to millions of Americans. With hospital benefits (Part A) funded by payroll taxes and with half of doctors' fees (Part B) funded by monthly premiums paid by people sixty-five and older, Medicare tapped general revenues for only the other half of Part B. As the Vietnam War sucked money from his discretionary funds and deficits threatened, Medicare was a welcome sight to a beleaguered president. Medicaid got less public attention. States paid roughly half the tab, and its benefits went only to those eligible under means tests established by the states, so Medicaid was expected to require only modest federal appropriations. (In fact, both Medicare and Medicaid eventually required huge federal outlays.)

The elections of 1966 were an unmitigated disaster for Johnson, the Democrats, and the Great Society, nearly obliterating the huge majorities that the Democrats had won in 1964 in both houses of Congress. Irate Democratic governors demanded that Johnson rein in his reforms and reduce them to a "popular pace."[64] The War on Poverty lost forty-five supporters in the House, which left only 189 who supported the program, 211 who opposed it, and 35 who had their doubts about it.[65] The die was cast: Johnson would get few new programs enacted and would encounter constant pressure to cut spending for older ones.

The Struggle for Scarce Resources

Many people still assumed, nonetheless, that the nation could have both guns and butter, as Johnson continued to assert in his State of the Union and budget messages in January 1967, even as he projected the cost of the war in Vietnam at $22.4 billion in the coming year. Aside from a few budget experts, few people noticed a subtle shift in Johnson's budget message, where he switched from a discussion of an "administrative budget" to a "national accounts budget," which also included the receipts and expenditures for the Social Security and Medicare trust funds. While this shift had technical merit, Johnson was also attracted to it because it lowered the estimate of the probable deficit for fiscal 1968 because the trust funds' revenues exceeded their expenditures. (This budget gimmick reduced the deficit from $8.1 billion to $2.1 billion—and Johnson proposed a 6 percent temporary surcharge on corporate and individual taxes for two years to bring the budget into balance.)

As rumors continued to circulate that Johnson had again underestimated the true cost of the war and the size of the deficit, conservatives demanded radical cuts in the Great Society during the spring of 1967. Congress refused to enact appropriations bills in a timely fashion. In early August Johnson disclosed that the deficit for the administrative budget would rise to $23.6 billion—a staggering sum that resulted from the billions in additional spending on Vietnam, the failure of Congress to enact his surcharge, and declining revenues from a slowdown in the economy.

With all his economic advisers now concerned about inflation, Johnson asked Congress to enact a 10 percent surcharge immediately to raise $6.3 billion; he planned to cover 25 percent of the emerging deficits by cutting spending, 25 percent more by increasing taxes, including the surcharge, and the remaining 50 percent by borrowing more money by floating bonds—hardly a formula acceptable to conservatives, who favored deeper cuts. Although Johnson had repeatedly encouraged the belief that the country could pay for both guns and butter, it was now clear that these were competing needs, even if Congress enacted Johnson's surcharge.

Scarce resources were hardly the sole cause of national tension, of course. The nation was remarkably polarized in 1967 and 1968 because of the civil rights struggle and the Vietnam War. Johnson had hoped to divorce foreign policy from domestic policy and wanted all Americans to unite behind his Vietnam policy. Many liberals and civil rights leaders had maintained an uneasy silence on the war in 1965 and 1966 but were catalyzed against it by Martin Luther King's militant antiwar speech in the spring of 1967 and Robert Kennedy's growing opposition. Liberals increasingly saw the war as evil, not only on its own terms but because it diverted resources from the domestic agenda. Activists sometimes advocated domestic spending at levels many times higher than Johnson's commitments. Doves, domestic reformers, civil rights activists, students, and intellectuals emerged as a liberal phalanx that mobilized for antiwar protests.

This liberal phalanx was increasingly opposed by a conservative one that also drew upon disparate elements. The term *white backlash* had begun to appear in the press and in internal memoranda within the administration as early as 1964, when liberals feared Goldwater would benefit from white opposition to civil rights.[66] This white backlash, at first confined to the South and the West, extended to northern cities in the wake of riots (which continued at regular intervals for five years with 239 disturbances, 8,133 deaths, and 49,604 arrests) and after the administration declared its support for busing to desegregate northern schools. Johnson understood that the riots would inflame white backlash and often castigated "lawless elements," then angered some white citizens by making conciliatory speeches and supporting the findings of the Kerner Commission, which blamed the riots on oppressive conditions. The sheer number of new programs enacted by Johnson—and the perception that they unfairly favored African Americans—also stimulated white backlash.

White citizens disaffected by the domestic scene increasingly joined those who favored a militant course in Vietnam. Antiwar demonstrations repulsed many blue-collar voters, who viewed them as unpatriotic. If Martin Luther King and Robert Kennedy emerged as leaders of the doves and social reformers, George Wallace and Richard Nixon aspired to lead the hawks and opponents of the Great Society. Caught between these factions, Johnson found it increasingly difficult to fashion deals on foreign or domestic policy.

As the nation entered 1968, the stage was set for a game of chicken between conservatives and liberals. Inflation, which began with the infusion of tens of billions of dollars of spending on Vietnam into an economy already operating at full steam, now was a serious threat. With the United States still tied to the gold standard and many foreigners eager to discard their greenbacks, now weakened by inflation, deficits, and an adverse balance of payments, many economists predicted a run on gold that could deplete U.S. gold reserves.

Everyone agreed: the nation *had* to shrink its deficit to solve its economic crisis, but conservatives and liberals advocated divergent policies. Even in the fall of 1967, conservatives like Wilbur Mills insisted that cuts in the Great Society had to precede any tax increases; he feared the administration would use any added tax revenues to augment domestic programs rather than to cut the deficit. Liberals like Robert Kennedy, and the administration's economic advisers, wanted tax increases to to underwrite the domestic agenda and sought cuts in the military budget.

Furious at the rise in military spending, liberals not only wanted to constrict the Vietnam War but to cut the regular military budget by withdrawing troops from Europe and cutting U.S. subsidies to NATO. They also opposed funding for antiballistic missiles (ABMs), which conservatives strongly supported to counter the intercontinental ballistic missiles that China was developing. As this impasse continued, Johnson predicted in November that the deficit could be as large as $35 billion.

Although Johnson's earlier budget messages had brimmed with optimism that he could easily finance guns and butter, his budget message in 1968 began with grim words: "The Budget I send you today reflects a series of difficult choices." Intoning that the nation faced "a costly war abroad" and "urgent requirements at home," he outlined a bleak budget that focused on cuts, delays, and deferments, as well as ending programs. He repeated his demand that the 10 percent surcharge be enacted at once and predicted that without it, the country faced economic catastrophe. Even with the normal growth of tax revenues of $11.5 billion and revenues of $12.9 billion from his 10 percent surcharge (and several smaller taxes), the nation would still face a huge deficit. His proposed budget, which was $10.4 billion fatter than the previous year's, was not good news to advocates of butter: it provided no increases for Great Society programs, except for the entitlements, and relied on cuts in some programs to allow modest increases for others.[67]

With polls showing overwhelming opposition to tax increases and Mills demanding large budget cuts, Johnson revealed in early February that U.S. operations in South Vietnam would run $7 billion higher than expected, and inflation remained a concern. Mills and Johnson were still miles apart in late March, with Mills conditioning his support for tax increases on spending cuts of $9 billion to $10 billion. Johnson would concede cuts of only $3 billion to $4 billion.

During this budgetary morass U.S. commitments to the Vietnam War finally peaked. Facing enormous deficits and battlefield losses—and with Clark Clifford (who had replaced McNamara as defense secretary) and myriad foreign policy experts finally regarding the war as a quagmire, Johnson turned down Gen. William Westmoreland's request to increase troops from 400,000 to 600,000 after the Tet Offensive disaster. (Although U.S. troops achieved battlefield victories during the Tet Offensive by communist forces, the media widely portrayed Tet as a reflection of the vulnerability of U.S. forces.) Even Johnson finally seemed to realize that the United States could extricate itself from Vietnam only through negotiations.

Embarrassed by a surprisingly strong showing by the antiwar Eugene McCarthy in the New Hampshire Democratic primary, Johnson announced on March 31 that he would not seek nomination for another term. He hoped his removal from the presidential sweepstakes would foster solutions for both the budgetary crisis and Vietnam. A chastened Lyndon Johnson now questioned his huge 1964 tax cuts, even asking aides to calculate the size of revenues he could anticipate if he returned the nation to the tax levels of 1963. He also considered seeking a major new tax to fund a huge effort to improve the lives of urban slum dwellers before abandoning it: polls showed overwhelming opposition to tax increases.[68]

Congressional conferees finally approved Johnson's surcharge and $6 billion in spending cuts on May 9, but both the Left and Right attacked this budget. Liberal Democrats and many mayors demanded that Johnson veto it because its cuts exceeded $4 billion. HEW workers mobilized a phone blitz to muster congressional opposition. A growing group of liberals opposed the 10 percent surcharge, claiming it would fund the war in Vietnam. Many conservatives wanted even larger spending cuts and opposed the surcharge. With both conservatives and liberals eager to avoid economic catastrophe—and the blame for it—as the 1968 presidential season began, and with cities again in flames after King's assassination, Congress finally approved the tax increases and the $6 billion in spending cuts in late June.

The Soviets: Paper or Real Tiger? (Part 2)

Smarting from their strategic inferiority in the 1950s, the Soviets made striking movement toward nuclear parity in the 1960s. Unlike the United States, which emphasized the so-called triad of submarine-based, aircraft-based, and land-based missiles, the Soviets emphasized powerful land-based missiles in hardened silos. Unlike the smaller, solid-fuel Polaris and Minuteman missiles of the Americans, the Soviet SS-9 missiles were heavy, carried liquid fuel, and required rockets far more powerful than the Americans.' The SS-9s presented a truly frightening spectacle to U.S. military planners because they might have the ability to destroy Minutemen buried deep in silos. Although the Soviets possessed few ICBMs in 1962, they had built nearly fourteen hundred by 1968; the Americans had but one thousand Minutemen.[69]

The Soviets were equally determined to eliminate the U.S. lead in submarine-launched ballistic missiles (SLBMs). The United States, which had perfected the Polaris missile by the early 1960s, had about six hundred SLBMs by 1968; the Soviets had roughly one hundred SLBMs but had put in place a massive production system that would yield roughly one thousand SLBMs by 1978—or nearly a third more than the Americans had.[70]

Clearly, the Soviets would obtain nuclear parity or even superiority in coming decades. Both sides would possess massive overkill capabilities. The prospects for overkill became even more likely when both countries began developing so-called multiple independent targetable reentry vehicles (MIRVs) in the mid-1960s. The final missile stage of a MIRV is like a bus that releases its payload of missiles one at a time to different targets.

Thus, rather than construct more missiles, the superpowers could simply place multiple warheads on their ICBMs and SLBMs; this would also give them the ability to shower their foes with warheads.[71] The deterrent value of missiles increased exponentially; if even a few missiles escaped a first strike, the initiator of that strike could expect multiple hits from each of the surviving missiles, whether launched from land or sea.

What was needed at this critical juncture were arms talks to avoid an escalating arms race. But with a huge lead over the Soviets at the start of the decade, U.S. leaders would have had to accept negotiated parity with the Soviet Union. And negotiated parity ran counter to the instincts of the military, not to mention many members of Congress. Many wanted to maintain American superiority by accelerating research and development to produce new weapons, whether tactical or nuclear, never mind that pesky term *overkill*.

The U.S. also was disinclined to sacrifice its MIRVs because it had a distorted view of the capabilities of the Soviets' primitive antiballistic missile system around Moscow. Some wondered whether this system would allow the Soviets to destroy incoming U.S. missiles, thus eliminating their deterrent effect. Couldn't the powerful Soviet SS-9 rockets destroy Minutemen in their silos? Wouldn't the security of the ABM system and the power of the SS-9s tempt the Soviets to make a first nuclear strike against the United States?[72] Worse, China had exploded a low-yield nuclear weapon in 1964 and a thermonuclear bomb in 1967. Some of Johnson's advisers recommended that the United States bomb China's atomic plants to prevent its development of nuclear capability.[73]

Such paranoia was coupled, moreover, with the calculated self-interest of the different services. The air force wanted a new strategic bomber and an ICBM larger than the Minuteman. The navy wanted missile-firing ships, more nuclear submarines, and more nuclear carriers. The army wanted an ABM system for U.S. cities.[74] The Joint Chiefs became vocal advocates for these and other weapons, convinced that Johnson had diverted money, troops, and weapons from the regular military to Vietnam—and that, to avoid budget deficits and to fund his Great Society, he had kept many weapons systems "in the pipeline" rather than place them into production.[75]

The Joint Chiefs were furious, moreover, because they believed that Johnson had siphoned funds to the Great Society from the military while the nation was at war and the Soviets were striving for nuclear parity. In private memos to Johnson they demanded cuts in the Great Society.[76] With Johnson increasingly vulnerable politically from early 1967 on, the Joint Chiefs went directly to Congress to get funding for these weapons. Both they and legislators from the armed services committees and the military appropriations committees were furious at McNamara, moreover, because the central planning he had imposed on the Pentagon had limited the independence the services in planning weapons and overseeing procurement. Many members of Congress vowed to oust McNamara and planned to start by investigating his procurement policies.

All these fears were overblown. The Soviets had closed the nuclear gap with the United States, but they had not surmounted its sizable lead. Whereas the United States had roughly six thousand strategic warheads in 1970, for example, the Soviets had only about two thousand.[77] Soviet rockets had to be more powerful than American rockets because they used heavier fuel.[78] The Soviets' submarine technology was behind that of the Americans, who were soon to launch a new generation of Trident submarines.[79] U.S. fears of a Soviet invasion of Europe ought to have been eased not only by the crushing nuclear power of the United States but by U.S. placement of astonishing numbers of nuclear weapons in Europe— seventy-two hundred nuclear warheads had sprouted in Europe by 1966. (As McNamara confessed, "There was no military requirement for 7,000 of these weapons . . . or two thousand.")[80] None of the fears about China were realized; China did not develop a significant nuclear program in the 1960s or 1970s.[81] It is truly remarkable that many legislators, as well as Johnson himself, took the Soviet ABM seriously, because technology was not even remotely available to intercept incoming missiles—and any system, even one that worked, could be overwhelmed simply by increasing the numbers of strategic missiles.[82] (Even in 2000, the United States did not possess effective antimissile technology.) Although the Soviets still maintained a huge lead in conventional forces, their troops from the Warsaw Pact nations were no more reliable than they had been in the 1950s. Poland, Hungary, and Czechoslovakia all saw uprisings by the late 1960s. Moreover, these Warsaw Pact troops were poorly equipped and armed compared to U.S. and NATO troops, who also possessed a huge arsenal of tactical weapons.

The 1960s had offered a golden opportunity to end the arms race before it got out of control, but this would have required remarkable leadership from the Americans. The Soviets, after all, saw themselves—with some reason—as the aggrieved party because it was the United States that had developed huge nuclear superiority in the 1950s and early 1960s. The Soviets saw themselves as the nuclear underdog and feared the Americans might try to "lock in" their nuclear superiority with treaties just as the Russians were gaining ground.

The Vietnam War also poisoned the atmosphere for serious negotiations between the superpowers. Because he so firmly believed that the Soviets and Chinese were the prime sponsors of Ho Chi Minh, Johnson refrained from serious negotiations until late in his presidency. Preoccupied with prosecuting the war, he did not give sufficient attention to diplomacy or to the implementation of his myriad domestic reforms. The Soviets, meanwhile, were angry that Americans thought they were the prime instigators of the Vietnam War and that the Americans were moving troops and materiel into Indochina—the Soviets primarily sent armaments and money to North Vietnam. (Archival evidence in North Vietnam, the Soviet Union, and China strongly suggests that the North Vietnamese were not mere puppets of the Soviets and Chinese and frequently quarreled with them and dictated strategy: at several points the Soviets actually tried to persuade Ho Chi Minh to decrease his efforts in order not to poison Soviet-U.S. relations.)[83]

American leaders were ill prepared to provide leadership, however. The Pentagon wanted to retain nuclear superiority and therefore sanctioned only discussions that would freeze existing levels of missiles and not impede development of MIRVs. Key legislators insisted on developing an American ABM. Nor were the Soviets ready for full-fledged talks, contending that their primitive ABM system around Moscow should be exempted from discussion. They too did not fully comprehend the extent to which the development of MIRVs would escalate the arms race on both sides, realizing only late in the 1960s that they were involved in a spiraling arms race that seemingly had no end.[84] The two nations were cautiously poised to enter into Strategic Arms Limitation Talks (SALT) in late 1968 to consider some limits on both offensive and defensive weapons, but the talks were called off once the Soviets invaded Czechoslovakia.

With nothing to limit their development, nuclear weapons production took off in the 1970s and 1980s. As figure 8.1 shows, by 1966 both nations possessed an array of platforms from which to launch nuclear weapons. The United States had a sizable lead in strategic nuclear warheads even as late as 1980, but the Soviet Union had nearly achieved parity by 1985, as figure 8.2 shows. Both sides were extravagantly overarmed yet continued to produce an endless series of new weapons. Both spent extraordinary sums of money needlessly. With its sizable lead in strategic warheads, the United States could have cut its nuclear arsenal unilaterally without suffering loss of deterrence from 1959 on because it still had enough weapons to destroy the Soviet Union many times over.

Nor was excessive military spending confined to nuclear forces. Although the Soviets maintained massive forces in Eastern Europe, the nuclear capabilities of the United States and its allies precluded their use. The United States still had six divisions in Europe, devoted as much as 60 percent of the total U.S. military budget to the defense of Europe, and had plans to transport many divisions to Europe in the event of war. Indeed, in the 1970s the United States had about eleven active divisions at home, as well as nine reserve duty divisions, and most active duty divisions specialized in Europe.[85] (France, West Germany, and Britain ignored pleas to ease the American burden and spent 4.8 percent, 3.6 percent, and 5.4 percent of their GNPs, respectively, on the military in 1968, whereas the

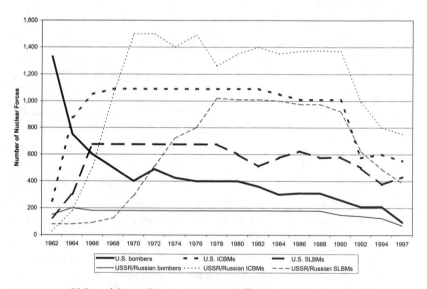

FIGURE 8.1 U.S. and Soviet/Russian Strategic Offensive Nuclear Forces, 1962–1997
Source: Stephen Schwartz, ed., Atomic Audit: The Costs and Consequences of U.S. Nuclear Weapons Since 1940 (Washington, D.C.: Brookings Institution, 1998), 187.

United States spent 9.3 percent of its GNP.[86]) Sen. Mike Mansfield proposed a resolution in 1966 to withdraw U.S. troops from Europe, only to meet determined opposition from Johnson.[87]

McNamara realized that MIRVs would lead to a massive increase in nuclear warheads on both sides during the next ten years while making neither superpower more secure. He urged Johnson to negotiate with the Soviets to curtail both ABMs and MIRVs.[88] But McNamara's political capital was low by 1967—he had belatedly realized the folly of the Vietnam War and fell out of favor with Johnson as the Joint Chiefs became outspoken critics of the defense chief's policies. Johnson's power too had eroded significantly; he no longer had the clout to obtain congressional approval of a far-reaching arms control treaty, had he he sought it. The Vietnam War had cost the nation more than fifty thousand casualties to date and untold sums, but it also sabotaged any meaningful way to halt the arms race. Still, it is an open question whether either Johnson or McNamara would have boldly sought arms reduction during the cold war even without Vietnam.

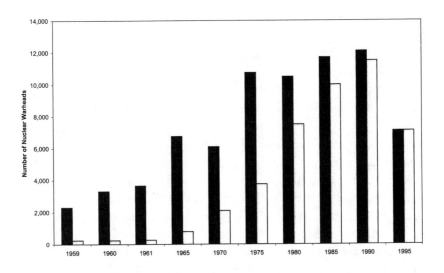

FIGURE 8.2 U.S. and Soviet/Russian Strategic Nuclear Warheads, 1959–1995.
    Source: Stephen Schwartz, ed., *Atomic Audit: The Costs and Consequences of U.S. Nuclear Weapons Since 1940* (Washington, D.C.: Brookings Institution, 1998), 206.

Failed Priorities in the Johnson Administration

Johnson believed his administration was a success; he never declared his Vietnam policy to be misdirected and believed he had achieved most of his domestic agenda, despite meager funding. His major regret was the tax cut of 1964. He confided to Joseph Califano, his domestic policy adviser, that "my advice to my successor will be: never lower taxes."[89] Johnson believed he had outfoxed conservatives in the final two years by making only superficial cuts in domestic programs in return for enactment of a tax increase.[90]

It is true: federal spending on education, training, employment, and social programs (called "social investments in figs. 8.3 and 8.4) increased dramatically during Johnson's tenure when measured in percentages. Such federal spending increased more than 200 percent from 1964 to 1969, or from $10.2 billion to $33.5 billion. (See fig. 8.3; all data are in constant 1992 dollars.) Johnson frequently boasted about these increases, particularly when liberals questioned the adequacy of the Great Society program. These percentage increases are less impressive, however, when we remember that even a small increase appears gigantic when measured in percentage terms from a small base. (Were public officials to increase spending on a specific project from $1 to $3, for example, they would accomplish a 200 percent increase but would have increased spending by only $2.) Although Johnson often did outfox conservatives by preventing them from cutting his Great Society program, he often allayed their opposition by asking for minimal appropriations in the first instance, whether for the War on Poverty, the Elementary and Secondary Education Act, or many other programs.

His increases in spending for these programs appear modest against the huge increases in military spending. Military and veterans spending rose from $289 billion in 1964 to $376 billion in 1968, a hefty increase of $87 billion; meanwhile, spending on education, training, employment, and social services rose only $23.3 billion—and social spending rose only $79.3 billion when entitlements are included—or $7.7 billion less than military and veterans spending during a major reform period. Johnson did not markedly alter the cold war military budgets that he had inherited from presidents Truman, Eisenhower, and Kennedy, despite his constant proclamation of McNamara's success in cutting Pentagon waste. If we add interest payments on the debt to military and veterans expenditures, such

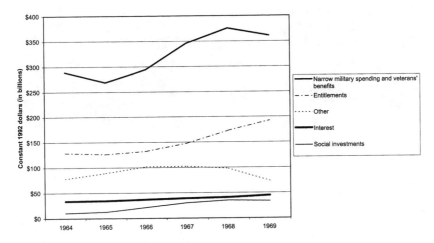

FIGURE 8.3 Five Types of Federal Expenditures, 1964–1969
    Source: Office of Management and Budget, *Budget of the U.S. Government, FY 2000, Historical Tables* (Washington, D.C.: GPO, 1999), table 3.1, pp. 44–45.

spending averaged 58 percent of the budget from 1964 through 1969, while the aggregate of entitlements and social investments averaged 28 percent. (See fig. 8.4.) Narrow military spending and veterans programs continued to take the lion's share of discretionary spending—or almost 80 percent during the Johnson years. (See fig. 8.5.)

While Johnson deserves credit for developing his Great Society and for averting deep cuts in its funding, he had to be tactically ingenious to protect the Great Society, partly because he had created an inhospitable environment for it in the first instance, whether by his tax cuts, his Vietnam policy, or his retention of the cold war base.

Johnson's last two years in office were excruciatingly difficult. He saw no new initiatives passed or funded. His War on Poverty was under constant siege, facing dismemberment and loss of funds. He barely managed to hold on to the funding for his domestic programs after 1966. Unable to fund education, training, employment, and social programs from his depleted treasury, Johnson increasingly favored programs that had their own source of funds—Social Security and Medicare. Because they were financed by payroll taxes rather than appropriations, Johnson did not need the approval of the appropriations committees to increase benefits. Nor were Medicare and Social Security endangered by the complex bargaining

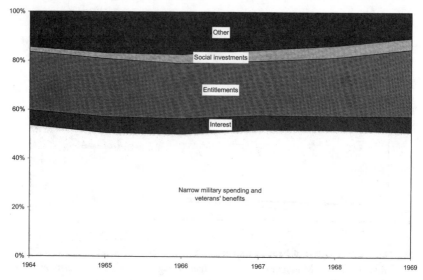

FIGURE 8.4 Five Types of Expenditures as Percentages of Total Federal Outlays, 1964–1969

Source: Office of Management and Budget, *Budget of the U.S. Government, FY 2000, Historical Tables* (Washington, D.C.: GPO, 1999), table 3.1, pp. 44–45.

games of 1967 and 1968 when advocates of guns frequently attacked programs funded from general revenues. Entitlements were politically secure when compared to such controversial programs as the War on Poverty, rent supplements, and Model Cities because a huge share of the entitlements' benefits went to the middle and upper classes.

Johnson made a fatal miscalculation when he assumed that the peace dividend after the war would impel Congress to fully fund myriad reforms.[91] He bequeathed to his successors a nation that was deeply polarized into conservative and liberal factions. Johnson does not deserve all the blame for this polarization because conservatives would have been against the Great Society no matter what he did about taxes and Vietnam, particularly because he lacked a mandate for social reform. (A Gallup Poll in December 1964 found that only 23 percent of the public wanted him to "go more to the left."[92]) And it was his civil rights legislation that pushed many southern Democrats into the arms of Republicans. Yet his simultaneous pursuit of guns, butter, and tax cuts polarized the country much more than would otherwise have occurred. His war policy and his systematic underfunding of domestic reforms goaded liberals to take

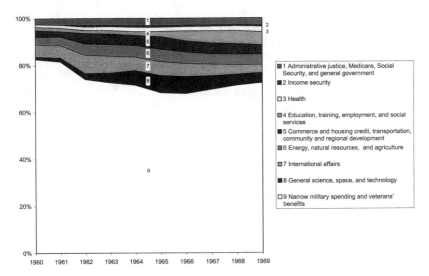

FIGURE 8.5 Competition for Discretionary Spending: Military Versus Domestic Spending as Percentages of Total Outlays, 1960–1969
   Source: Office of Management and Budget, *Budget of the U.S. Government, FY 2000, Historical Tables* (Washington, D.C.: GPO, 1999), table 3.1, pp. 44–45, and table 8.8, p. 136.

positions and actions (such as demonstrations and teach-ins) that stimulated a counterreaction from conservatives. His tax cuts, combined with his military and domestic programs, created deficits and inflation that provoked conservatives to oppose the Great Society. As liberals and conservatives took divergent positions on the war and on domestic policy, polarization accelerated in a dynamic process, with antiwar demonstrations and efforts to cut military spending stimulating prowar demonstrations and attacks on social spending. Johnson's policies powerfully contributed to this accelerating polarization, which continued after he left office, imperiling the future funding of discretionary social programs that he had created.

   The Johnson administration wasted huge resources that might otherwise have been used for the domestic agenda. The waste lay in the prosecution of the Vietnam War, excessive funding for noncombat military appropriations, and the failure to fundamentally reform the nation's procurement processes. With tax revenues that averaged only 17.9 percent of GDP from 1964 through 1969 while the nation fought a major war, supported huge cold war military forces, and developed many new domestic programs that were often poorly funded, Johnson and Congress ought to have kept taxes at 20 percent of GDP—a strategy that would have added $410 billion in revenues. I contend in chapter 15 that Johnson wasted more than $1.5 trillion in constant 1992 dollars.

9

Nixon's Megalomania

Now that liberals had seen the first substantial increases in spending for domestic nonentitlement programs since the New Deal, they were eager to spend the peace dividend at the end of the Vietnam War. If the nation were not spending so much on the military, couldn't it pump money into the Great Society programs? The decision would be powerfully influenced by Richard Nixon but in ways that few commentators could have guessed at the outset of his presidency. Some domestic programs grew substantially during the 1970s, but others languished and many needed reforms were not enacted. I argue here and in chapter 15 that Congress and presidents Nixon, Ford, and Carter made fiscal and tax mistakes in excess of $1 trillion in constant 1992 dollars.

Nixon's Tactical Complexity

John Ehrlichman, arguably Nixon's most powerful aide on domestic affairs, contended that no one understood

Nixon, probably not even his wife, Pat.[1] He remains the most complex president in contemporary history. Liberals encountered in Nixon, moreover, a wily foe who was convinced that neither a purely conservative nor liberal course would serve his political interests at home or abroad. He agreed with Ehrlichman when he characterized his policies as "zig zags," with concessions alternating between different political factions in a complex pattern.[2]

Nixon's complex tactics derived from his persona and the turbulent political currents of the late 1960s and early 1970s. His intense ambition, coupled with his insecurity, often led to his having paranoid fears of his opponents. Nixon, the son of a small businessman whose enterprises rarely succeeded, grew up poor in southern California during the Great Depression. The family sometimes had to eat oranges from local groves to survive. He was raised by a stern Quaker mother, who often withheld praise and affection from her children when they failed to meet her stringent moral codes. He went to a small local liberal arts college (Whittier), where his academic prowess got him into law school at Duke University.

Nixon emerged from this childhood with a determination to succeed in life. He saw himself as an underdog who could excel only by outwitting and outworking people with greater advantages in life, such as graduates of Ivy League schools, the eastern Republican establishment, and well-connected liberals. He also believed that others conspired to foil him.

After graduating from law school in 1937, he returned to southern California, where he became a small-town attorney, then joined the navy in World War II. Discharged as a lieutenant commander in 1946, he quickly decided to reach for the national political stage. He won elections for the House and the Senate with unusual speed (1946 and 1950, respectively)—and reached the national scene when Eisenhower, who wanted to cement relations with the conservative wing of the Republican Party, chose Nixon to be his running mate in 1952.

In these early races and during the Eisenhower presidency, Nixon demonstrated his conservative side as well as a remarkable skill in using negative tactics to conquer political opponents. In the rabid anticommunism of the late 1940s and early 1950s, he excelled at questioning opponents' patriotism by implying they were communist sympathizers. Eisenhower used him repeatedly to do the dirty work, whether by attacking the patriotism of Adlai Stevenson in 1952 and 1956 or by lambasting "tax-and-spend Democrats." Nixon demonstrated a remarkable facility for smearing his opponents through innuendo.

Nixon's tendency to view himself as an underdog was accentuated in the late 1940s and the 1950s by virulent attacks against him by Democrats, liberals, and (even) Eisenhower. Many Democrats simply despised Nixon. Not only had he called their patriotism into question but he had overreached in his investigation of Alger Hiss, a State Department official who had been accused of espionage by Whittaker Chambers, a former member of the Communist Party. Republican leaders frequently rebuffed Nixon as well, with Eisenhower nearly dumping him from the ticket when he was accused of misusing campaign funds in 1952. (Eisenhower backed off after Nixon made his famous Checkers Speech in which he reframed the charges as an unfair attack on him and his family.) But Eisenhower did not trust him and never admitted Nixon to the inner sanctum of his presidency.[3] Nixon believed, moreover, that the eastern wing of the Republican Party was determined to shut him out of national politics.

He was determined both to become president and to make good Eisenhower's ambition to broaden the base of the Republican Party to include working-class citizens, who mainly voted Democratic. Because of his own humble origins, Nixon believed he could identify with the hopes and fears of blue-collar voters.

The term *megalomania* aptly describes Nixon's obsession with power, as reflected in hundreds of annotations on countless memos and newspaper stories as well as comments in the famous taped conversations with his aides. All presidents want and seek power, but Nixon was more obsessed than most of them with achieving political supremacy. He meant to best his political opponents and was prepared to use an extraordinary range of tactics. Sometimes he would co-opt their issues. Sometimes he would throw them off balance by springing new policies. Sometimes he would outflank them by resorting to so-called wedge issues to divide their ranks, such as using busing and affirmative action to gain the support of those white Democratic ethnic voters who resented the economic and legal gains made by African Americans. Nixon invested extraordinary resources in obtaining political intelligence about his adversaries—planting spies, tapping telephones, and even sanctioning the theft of sensitive documents. Nor was he content merely to best Democrats, for he saw civil servants, the State Department, and government bureaucracy as adversaries to be outwitted and outmaneuvered. Republicans were hardly immune to this paranoia and maneuvering. He detested such liberal Republicans as Sen. Charles Percy of Illinois, and he used his aide Pat Buchanan to provide nonstop intelligence about conservative Republicans.[4]

As president, Nixon's diplomatic ambitions took priority over domestic policies.[5] He had been obsessed with foreign relations from the beginning of his political career and often traveled abroad to meet and cement relations with scores of promising and rising figures in the 1950s and 1960s.[6] His ambitions were not modest: like a twentieth-century Metternich, he aimed (with foreign affairs adviser Henry Kissinger) to construct a new balance of power in the world—a new world order that would arise from ceaseless secret negotiations, covert activities, and an array of treaties. This new balance of power, with détente with the Soviets as its centerpiece, would advance the interests of the United States, serving its need for exports and national security, as well as to secure an end to the Vietnam War, which Nixon was convinced would continue so long as the Soviet Union and China provided materiel and funds to Ho Chi Minh.[7] Like other cold war presidents, Nixon intended to best the Soviet Union, but he would do so through a curious combination of détente, triangulation, hard-line rhetoric, and covert activity.

Although Nixon gave priority to foreign policy, he saw domestic policy as integrally related to it. He knew that he had to outwit the Democrats at home to stay in office, for he needed two terms to complete his reshaping of international relations. He also knew that he had to play a complex game to get sufficient support from legislators and the public to pursue his international diplomacy. Because the Vietnam War had catalyzed widespread opposition to military spending, Nixon had to build alliances with key Democrats in order to maintain high budgets for the military during the cold war—alliances that partly depended on acceding to some Democratic wishes on domestic policies. (Nixon's election had in fact increased Democrats' inclination to attack military spending and Vietnam policy, because the strong hand of Lyndon Johnson had muzzled these instincts.)[8] Dependent on a Democratic Congress not only for military spending but for money to implement his Vietnam policy, Nixon had to fashion a Vietnam strategy that was appealing enough to doves and moderates that they would not cut off funding for the war. Nixon also had to convince moderates and doves that he was not merely a reflexive cold warrior, such as by opening initiatives to China, pursuing negotiations with the Soviet Union, or promising to end the Vietnam War even as he extended it for many years.

Because Congress was controlled by Democrats who were determined to expand funding for the Great Society and obtain a peace dividend, Nixon knew that he would be barraged with social reform initiatives. If he blocked these with a string of vetoes, the Democratic Congress would often override them with the help of moderate Republicans—and then would cite the vetoes as proof that Republicans were insensitive to the domestic agenda. A purely conservative strategy was not acceptable to Nixon, either, because he wanted to best Democratic moderates and liberals by preempting a portion of their social reform agenda. They had "owned" the domestic agenda since the New Deal; many Republicans had even opposed such popular measures as Medicare and civil rights legislation. Nixon, convinced that his best defense was offense, determined to promulgate bold domestic measures that would surprise and disorient the Democrats.

Nixon also knew that some white ethnics and southern white Protestants favored domestic reforms. Many were long-time members of the Democratic Party and trade unions and had supported liberal domestic policies—and they would benefit personally from expanded entitlements. Nixon worried that the Democrats' presidential candidate in 1972 would retain the loyalties of these Democrats by pushing a positive message, much as Robert Kennedy had done before his assassination in 1968. Convinced that his defeat in 1960 was the result of voter discontent with Eisenhower's passive economic policy in the recession of 1957, Nixon was determined not to repeat the mistake.[9] Nixon had no doctrinaire commitment to laissez-faire economics and willingly embraced Keynesian economics, eventually using even wage-and-price controls and large deficits to attack stagflation, the mixture of unemployment and inflation that bedeviled the economy during much of his presidency.[10] If he were too conservative at home, Nixon feared, he would encourage liberals and moderates to oppose funding of the Vietnam War—and to champion butter over guns as a strategy for retaking the presidency in 1972.

Yet a mainly liberal course on domestic issues posed its own risks. It might alienate the traditional base of the Republican Party, which included remnants of the Old Guard that had frustrated Eisenhower and championed Goldwater in 1964.[11] It also would not help him lure to the Republican Party those white southern Protestants and northern Catholics who were disenchanted with the Great Society and with civil rights. Nixon considered two other factors as he contemplated his strategy for 1972:

George Wallace's surprising success in presidential primaries in 1964 and 1968, and a campaign demographer's prediction that Republicans could become a majority party by enlisting northern white ethnics and southern white Protestants. These factors bolstered Nixon's resolve to use race-coded terms such as "the silent majority of law-abiding citizens"; to attack busing; to support anticrime, antidrug, and antipornography measures; and to pledge vigorous prosecution of the war in Vietnam.[12]

Nixon's conservative side also reflected the darker side of his persona, which prompted him to appeal to voters' fears and resentments. Just as he had used anticommunism earlier in his career to defeat opponents, he used race-coded language, appeals to patriotism, and wedge issues like affirmative action to appeal to the fears of white ethnics and southern Protestants. He read polls compulsively, skillfully detecting resentments and fears in those portions of the Democratic base that he wanted to lure into the Republican Party. He cynically baited war opponents with his Vietnam policies—using the resulting antiwar demonstrations to rally "patriotic Americans."[13]

This mixture of liberal and conservative policies was advantageous in such a volatile political environment. By developing both conservative and liberal policies, he could allow himself to move to the left or the right in the presidential election of 1972, depending on political circumstances and the positions of the Democratic candidate. If public opinion moved to the right and Democrats nominated a far left candidate, for example, Nixon could move to the right without fear of losing the center. If public opinion moved to the center and the Democrats nominated a centrist candidate, like Scoop Jackson of Washington or Edmund Muskie of Maine, Nixon could move to the center by touting his moderate or liberal policies.

Nowhere was Nixon's tactical complexity more obvious than in foreign policy. On the one hand, he was a quintessential cold warrior—he believed the Soviets intended to gain world domination and nuclear superiority, whether to blackmail the United States or to attempt a first strike.[14] He believed that the Soviets had incited Ho Chi Minh's invasion of South Vietnam, and he subscribed to the domino theory: the war could be ended only if the United States could coax or coerce the Soviets to influence Ho Chi Minh to withdraw his forces from South Vietnam.[15] Nixon resorted to what he called "madman tactics" in South Vietnam to induce Ho Chi Minh to withdraw, such as by expanding the war to Cambodia and Laos without congressional consent, bombing Vietnam with an intensity unprecedented in world history, and mining Haiphong harbor even at risk of sinking Soviet ships. He endorsed covert activities in developing nations to avert communist takeovers. He wanted the United States to have nuclear forces not only to discourage the Soviets from a first strike but to use as a bargaining chip in arms-control and Vietnam negotiations.

Yet Nixon was willing to rethink some cold war maxims. He regarded the communist world as multicentered with the emergence of China as a great power and wondered whether the United States could play the Chinese against the Soviets in a strategy that might allow some cuts in U.S. military forces and make simultaneous wars with the Soviets and Chinese less likely.[16] He sometimes sought nuclear parity with the Soviets rather than superiority as he observed their huge nuclear forces.[17] He decided the United States should avoid involvements in the civil wars of third-world nations in coming years, even issuing the Nixon Doctrine, which downsized U.S. military commitments to developing countries.[18] He decided that the United States should be able to fight only 1.5 wars simultaneously (a war against a major power and a regional war) rather than the 2.5 wars that Kennedy had advocated, even if Nixon did not cut military forces to reflect this doctrine. Although he was instinctively a hard-liner who wanted to best Ho Chi Minh, Nixon also saw political reasons to withdraw from South Vietnam; he remembered well how Harry Truman's popularity had plummeted during the Korean War.[19]

The Odd Couple

Unlike most presidents, who accord their secretaries of defense and state substantial roles in foreign policy, Nixon decided from the outset to centralize foreign policy in the White House and the National Security Council.[20] He named Henry Kissinger to be his national security adviser, partly as a reward for having secretly given him sensitive information about the Johnson administration's negotiations with the North Vietnamese in Paris on the eve of the 1968 elections. Nixon met his match in Kissinger, who shared his passion for secrecy, back-channel negotiations, détente, intrigue, deceptions, and realpolitik.

Nixon and Kissinger almost single-handedly fashioned the administration's foreign policy. Nixon often ceded back-channel discussions with the Soviets, Chinese, and North Vietnamese to Kissinger and both relied on him and feared he would usurp presidential powers by making concessions that had not been cleared or by claiming personal credit for break-throughs. In turn, Kissinger often believed that Nixon was setting him up for failure and that he would be fired after the 1972 election. In this bizarre relationship Nixon bugged Kissinger's phone just as Kissinger often taped his phone conversations with Nixon.[21]

When the Soviets made an early overture to resume the SALT negotia-tions that had been cut off in 1968, Nixon decided not to cooperate, hop-ing to pressure the Soviets to force Ho Chi Minh to withdraw from South Vietnam.[22] (He also thought that he could get a better deal from the Sovi-ets if he made them bide their time.) Nixon's decision was flawed. He wrongly assumed the Soviets had the power to oust Ho Chi Minh from North Vietnam. In fact, Ho Chi Minh, confident he could wait out the Americans after the Tet Offensive in 1968, was hardly a puppet for either the Soviets or Chinese.[23] (While Ho Chi Minh had suffered severe losses in the Tet Offensive, he gained a psychological victory by demonstrating that the United States would remain bogged down in Vietnam indefi-nitely.) By not moving assertively on SALT, moreover, Nixon increased the possibility that MIRVs would not be outlawed—a policy favored by the military brass, who believed the United States had a strong technological lead. (Nixon was unmoved by frantic efforts by Sen. Edward Brooke, D-Mass., to end the testing of MIRVs, even when he got forty senators to pass a resolution urging the United States and Soviet Union to suspend their tests.)[24]

SALT talks commenced in late 1969 in Helsinki and continued for the next thirty months before an agreement was reached. By not changing their minds on MIRVs in 1970, Nixon and Kissinger compounded their initial error in not seeking to abolish the use of multiple warheads; they did not fully understand that the Soviets would soon match the United States MIRV for MIRV, just as they had matched many other U.S. nuclear capabilities in the 1960s.

Nixon and Kissinger had little to show for their diplomatic efforts by late 1970. The Soviets declined Nixon's invitation to resume SALT negoti-ations because Nixon had dismissed their early overtures. The North Viet-namese made it clear they would not tolerate Premier Nguyen Van Thieu's remaining in office, even if the Americans unilaterally withdrew. The new world order that Nixon had hoped to establish, much less the prospects for arms control or peace in Vietnam, had not emerged.

The Liberals' Pent-up Frustration

Unable to secure major domestic reforms for nearly twenty-five years after the New Deal, liberals were finally rewarded with the Great Society, but it was a severely underfunded Great Society that limped into the late 1960s. Lyndon Johnson, who harbored some guilt about his tax and military policies, which had taken resources from the Great Society, established task forces to plan a transition from war to peace, but he could not openly champion a peace dividend for fear of energizing advocates of butter to attack his Vietnam policy even more aggressively.[25] To quiet liberals' demands for greater domestic resources, Johnson ordered drafters of the report for the Kerner Commission—established by Johnson to discuss the causes of the 1967 riots—to delete a request for major resources for domestic programs.

Johnson could not prevent other people from discussing a peace dividend, however. Within both Congress and the civil rights movement many people explicitly linked the war to the underfunding of the Great Society. Although Vice President Hubert Humphrey warily refused to question Johnson's Vietnam policy during his 1968 presidential campaign, he promised a huge peace dividend at the end of the war. Few people defined what they meant by a "peace dividend," but the rhetoric of the time implied several variations. A minimalist version merely wanted money used for the Vietnam War to be applied to domestic spending—about $25 billion a year plus the roughly $8 billion per year from the annual growth in tax revenues as the economy expanded.[26] A more radical version wanted $40 billion (or more) transferred to the domestic agenda by also cutting the military appropriations from their pre-Vietnam levels and by closing tax loopholes.[27]

The Democrats, who controlled Congress, were emboldened to demand changes in national priorities from the new Nixon administration. Why not systematically increase domestic appropriations above Nixon's requests and cut military appropriations? Why not delay approval of key appropriations bills until 1970 to force Nixon to veto them as the nation approached congressional elections, even though this tactic would force the government to operate on continuing resolutions? Why not cut taxes by taking millions of low-income Americans off the tax rolls and closing tax loopholes while supporting a spending ceiling to combat inflation—policies that would force Nixon to cut the military, lest he be blamed for breaching the spending ceiling as the elections neared.[28] Some Democrats informed Nixon they would not support his foreign policy strategy if he failed to support more resources for the domestic agenda.[29]

Increasing the entitlements proved particularly enticing to congressional Democrats at this juncture.[30] Although they wanted to increase funding for the scores of Great Society programs funded by the discretionary budget, they knew that these programs did not elicit bipartisan support. By contrast, Social Security and Medicare enjoyed bipartisan support because they assisted people from all social classes and from the districts of all politicians. Even Wilbur Mills, the powerful Democratic chair of the House Ways and Means Committee, had endorsed a large increase in Social Security in 1968 as he was seeking cuts in discretionary programs of the Great Society.

Aware that Nixon meant to entice many white voters from their party, Democrats viewed entitlements, and tax cuts for moderate- and low-income Americans, as a way to retain their support. By supporting entitlements, tax cuts, and a spending freeze, then, liberals could force Nixon to cut military spending and to get out of Vietnam faster than he had wished.

Democrats put their many-sided strategy into effect in 1969 with remarkable skill. They attacked Nixon's military budget. They introduced amendments to force a rapid end to the Vietnam War. They introduced amendments to force cuts in U.S. forces in Europe. They achieved tax cuts of $10.6 billion in fiscal 1970 and $12 billion in fiscal 1971 and coupled them with a spending freeze. They supported marked increases in Social Security, Medicare, and food stamps. They refused until early 1970 to enact most appropriations bills for the fiscal year that had started in July 1969. They emphasized increases in entitlements over discretionary social programs. Surely, they reasoned, Nixon would either be forced to cut military spending when faced with these policies or he would have to oppose popular increases in entitlements.

Evading the Democrats' Trap on the Domestic Front

Nixon seemed bewildered by the Democrats' strategy in early 1969. He did not even announce a domestic agenda until mid-April, but he soon decided to beat the Democrats at their own game by proclaiming entitlements as distinctively Republican initiatives that provided tangible (or "hard") benefits to citizens as opposed to the "soft" and "ineffective" programs of the Great Society.[31] Nor did he have to search far for proposals to expand entitlements or to find policy alternatives to the Great Society. Walter Heller, who had chaired the Council of Economic Advisers in the Kennedy years, had pestered Johnson with a nonstop series of memos beseeching him to support revenue sharing, a proposal to give money to the states with few strings attacked.[32] The staff of the War on Poverty, including Sargent Shriver, had frequently implored Johnson to fund huge increases in food stamps, institute a negative income tax, augment Social Security benefits, and begin a program of public service jobs. (Shriver urged Johnson in October 1965, for example, to commit to spending $4.7 billion for a negative income tax, $5.3 billion for an increase in Social Security, and $2.5 billion for an increase in the War on Poverty to raise its funding to $4 billion.)[33] Only by supporting such initiatives, they had argued, could poverty be redressed in the United States. While Johnson had appointed a commission on income maintenance, which issued recommendations for overhauling the welfare system in the late 1960s, he was so preoccupied with the Vietnam War and discretionary programs of the Great Society that he took no action on any of these policy initiatives.

So Nixon co-opted these Democratic ideas and contrasted them with the "failed" social service, job training, and poverty programs of the Great Society. In memos to one another such presidential aides as Daniel Patrick Moynihan and Arthur Burns frequently cited research that impugned the effectiveness of Great Society programs: the Coleman report, studies of the Job Corps, and the Westinghouse study.[34] Funded by HEW, James Coleman set out to determine whether spending on education improved student performance. His report, published in 1966, shattered the prevalent belief that spending mattered; he found no correlation between spending and student performance in a large number of school districts. Various evaluations found the Job Corps—the most intensive job-training program of the Great Society—to be ineffective. The Westinghouse study contended that Head Start, the most popular innovation of the Great Society, did not improve enrollees' performance on cognitive tests as compared to children not enrolled in the program.

Virtually no one in the Nixon administration asked whether the findings of these various studies were accurate. Nixon himself believed "money can be found for the solution of technical problems [but] few [solutions] can be found for human problems."[35] They might have asked whether Coleman had examined intradistrict variations in facilities and student-teacher ratios to see whether they influenced educational performance, as subsequent reanalyses of the data would suggest.[36] They might have questioned the outcome measures of the Westinghouse study, which relied on culturally biased measures. They might have asked whether negative evaluations suggest that a program should be reformed rather than terminated, because the performance of the Job Corps and Head Start might have been enhanced by different approaches. They might have asked whether social service programs sometimes "fail" because so many factors negatively influence the lives of low-income people, making it difficult for any single remedy to show dramatic results unless enrollees receive assistance from a battery of programs. Rather than cite a need for entitlements *and* service and educational programs, Nixon pitted them against one another and vowed to expand the former and cut the latter.

Because many Democrats had also decided to emphasize entitlements, a peculiar dance ensued. Usually, the Democrats took the lead, initiating increases in food stamps, Social Security, and Medicare, with Nixon usually endorsing increases after securing concessions even when he privately feared what the increases would do to the budget. Sometimes Nixon took the lead, such as with the Family Assistance Plan that he proposed in August 1969 to the astonishment of liberals and conservatives. This entitlement would have established a floor of $1,600 beneath every family of four—given each family $1,600—whether the family was intact or headed by a single adult and whether the parents were employed or not. This mechanism was similar to a negative income tax, except that it proposed a work requirement and was limited to families; it would have replaced Aid to Families with Dependent Children with a program for which millions of the working poor would have been eligible. (In such poor states as Mississippi, nearly 30 percent of the population would have been eligible for family assistance.)

But Nixon was not content merely to dance with the Democrats around entitlements, fearing this strategy would help the Democrats more than him. Wouldn't most voters automatically credit Democrats for expanding entitlements because they usually were the champions of such measures in the past? Searching for programs that would be distinctively Republican and acceptable to the conservative wing of his party, Nixon latched onto revenue sharing in an effort to downsize the federal government while increasing the power of state and local governments. Co-opting Heller's plan, in August 1969 Nixon announced his intention to institute revenue sharing as part of a "New Federalism" that by mid-1975 would annually return $5 billion to the states with few strings attached. (He would markedly expand this proposal in coming years.)

The Democratic Congress, however, did not have a cordial welcome for revenue sharing. Well aware of how southern states had ignored African Americans, many liberals feared that the states would not implement social programs in an evenhanded manner. Moreover, some liberals wondered whether Nixon meant to fund general revenue sharing from resources currently devoted to existing social programs. A partisan battle over revenue sharing was averted in 1969, however, because Nixon, preoccupied with his Family Assistance Plan and lacking the money to implement his revenue-sharing idea, did not push it.

However, a fierce battle over the budget developed that presaged future budget conflicts during Nixon's tenure. When congressional Democrats secured tax cuts far greater than Nixon wanted in 1969, they began a protracted battle with the president over national priorities, with military spending and entitlements competing for scarce resources. (Nixon explored the possibility of a value-added tax to augment tax revenues but ultimately rejected it.)[37]

So Nixon evaded the Democrats' trap on the domestic front by openly endorsing entitlements and claiming some credit for expanding them. Yet he was also finding ways to distinguish himself from the Democrats, such as by attacking discretionary social programs that he equated with the Great Society and by supporting a restructuring of federal-state relations. Above all, he would be an activist president domestically and would not allow the Democrats to dominate domestic policy as they had since the New Deal.

The enactment of tax cuts in 1969, coupled with both parties' endorsement of increases in entitlements and the continuation of the war in Vietnam, meant that fierce budget battles were inevitable.[38]

Evading the Democrats' Trap on the Military Front

Nixon needed a strategy for averting deep military cuts: he faced a Democratic Congress intent on a peace dividend, and he wanted to delay any action until after the elections of 1970 and 1972, when he hoped Republican gains would allow him to actually increase military spending.[39] He used a combination of dovish and hawkish policies to keep the military budget intact. He bought the argument of Mel Laird, his secretary of defense, that the Vietnam War itself stimulated attacks on the military budget. As a result, Nixon implemented phased withdrawals and supported the eventual end of the draft. He assented to incremental cuts in military spending—$3 billion here, $4 billion there—as he withdrew troops from South Vietnam to assuage the doves, while he was careful that cuts did not extend to the cold war base that had preceded Vietnam. The incremental cuts were particularly necessary because of the growing unpopularity of the military.[40] It was in this climate that Sen. William Proxmire, the Wisconsin Democrat, devised the "Golden Fleece Award" to publicize cost overruns in the military, as well as such examples of waste as overpriced wrenches, toilets, and other components of military procurement. The Vietnam War, unpopular with large segments of the population, had eroded the military's reputation. For the first time since the cold war began, a majority of the public said that the United States overspent on the military. Sen. Mike Mansfield was determined to reintroduce his resolution to drastically cut U.S. forces in Europe.

To avert deeper cuts in the military, Nixon relied heavily on the histrionics of Laird, who frequently declared that military cuts would force the closure of scores of military bases and huge cuts in military and civilian personnel—claims that incited widespread opposition from Congress and from voters in districts laden with military contracts.[41] Nixon also relied heavily on two conservative Democrats in Congress: Henry (Scoop) Jackson in the Senate and George Mahon in the House, senior and respected members who repeatedly rallied key Democrats against military cuts, as well as against proposals to withdraw U.S. forces from Europe.[42]

Nixon also defused efforts to cut military spending by undermining the quest for a peace dividend. Some advisers had doubted that any peace dividend would materialize because of the rapid growth in entitlements, veterans' benefits, interest payments on the national debt, and military pay when the draft was ended, none of which could be controlled. (Draftees receive little pay, but recruiting and retaining enlistees requires substantial salaries.)

Nixon cleverly selected Daniel Patrick Moynihan, the neoconservative Democrat and Harvard professor then serving as a presidential adviser, to administer the coup de grace to talk of a peace dividend at a press conference in San Clemente in August 1969. Moynihan declared it to be "as evanescent as the clouds over San Clemente." Had Nixon selected someone from the military or foreign policy side to deliver this obituary, the statement would have aroused greater liberal opposition, but its delivery by Nixon's house "liberal" diminished this response.

Moynihan's statement implied a certain inevitability about the demise of a peace dividend, but it could have been realized if Nixon had made certain specific choices. He could have pulled U.S. forces out of Vietnam, which would have freed resources more rapidly. He could have declared that it was impossible to win the war given the corruption of the South Vietnamese regime and that the war was costing the United States too many lives and too much money.[43] He could have opposed funding for some expensive weapons, either because they overlapped other weapons or because they were unlikely to be effective. (High-level Pentagon officials informed the *Congressional Quarterly* that Congress could cut as much as $10.8 billion—by eliminating the antiballistic missile system, other unneeded weapons systems, and unnecessary personnel—without sacrificing national security.)[44] Nixon could have sought deep cuts in strategic weapons during the Salt I negotiations that began in the fall of 1969. Had Nixon ended the Vietnam commitment by mid-1970, cut regular military spending, and redressed tax loopholes, he would have had ample funds for major increases in the domestic budget, whether for discretionary social programs or entitlements. Indeed, Nixon could have upstaged doves and liberals and reaped political credit for a peace dividend.

Instead, Nixon coupled his concessions to doves with iron-fist strategies designed to maintain the coalition of hawks and conservatives that would oppose cuts in the military budget. He militantly supported an array of new weapons systems. He implemented his madman tactics in Vietnam. He attacked doves and demonstrators by questioning their patriotism. The coalition, joined by key Democrats such as Scoop Jackson, provided the bulwark of opposition to deep cuts in the military.

Nixon's determination to seek "peace with honor" in Vietnam was a prime example of his frantic efforts to gain support from both doves and hawks. He insisted he would leave Vietnam only under terms that safeguarded the integrity of South Vietnam's government, and he often emphasized that he would not agree to withdrawal of U.S. forces if North Vietnamese forces remained in the South. Yet the phased withdrawals, as well as the end to the draft, emphasized "peace," which allowed him to tell doves that the end of the war was near. Thus "peace with honor" allowed him to pursue dovish policies with an iron fist—a strategy that protected him from attacks from doves and from hawks while allowing him to move toward withdrawal from Vietnam. Just as Nixon's penchant for coupling conservative and liberal domestic policies served his political interests, so did his ambiguous foreign policy. Nixon's peculiar combination of tactics resonated with most Americans, who wanted to cut U.S. losses but not at the cost of capitulating to North Vietnam.

So Nixon outflanked the doves and liberals on military and Vietnam policy with a complicated strategy. Undermined by Nixon's coupling of phased withdrawals with aggressive pursuit of the war in the meantime, the peace movement crested in late 1969 and would never again have significant influence.[45] He succeeded in avoiding military cuts and the rapid withdrawal from Vietnam advocated by doves.

Nixon Contemplates Turning "Hard Right"

As 1969 neared an end, however, Nixon feared that Democrats were besting him. They were pressuring him to sign larger increases in Social Security than he had wanted, were eager to cut his military budget, and were threatening to greatly increase discretionary spending by boosting appropriations for the Department of Health, Education, and Welfare and the Department of Labor. Determined to distinguish his agenda from the Democrats', Nixon took a more aggressive posture in his State of the Union Address in 1970. He restricted new discretionary spending to water pollution and local law enforcement. He opposed expansion of Great Society programs, contending that "we have heard a great deal of overblown rhetoric during the 1960s in which the word 'war' has perhaps too often been used—the war on poverty, the war on misery, the war on disease, the war on hunger."[46] (He confined his use of *war* to an anti-crime proposal.) Declaring inflation to be the nation's major problem, he took a militant stand against new spending, pledging to balance the budget by keeping spending beneath $201 billion. He vetoed the appropriations bill for HEW and Labor on January 26. Mail had been running 34 to 1 against the veto before his televised speech; it ran 5 to 1 in favor of the veto after the speech.[47] He increasingly emphasized the punitive features in his Family Assistance Plan, such as its relatively small grants and its work requirement.[48]

To ease the pressure on his military budget, Nixon proclaimed that the country had already reordered its national priorities, contending that total domestic spending had eclipsed spending for military personnel and weapons for the first time. He failed to note that domestic spending was dominated by the fast-growing entitlements, whereas spending on discretionary social programs had reached a plateau.[49] To make clear that he intended to spend available resources on his programs, not Lyndon Johnson's Great Society, Nixon estimated that the country could increase spending for the Family Assistance Plan (if it passed) and revenue sharing from $3 billion in 1971 to $18 billion in 1975. Meanwhile, he proposed to save $2 billion by replacing fifty-seven government programs with general revenue sharing and block grants.[50]

Moynihan continued his role of diminishing domestic expectations with his now infamous memo to Nixon urging "benign neglect" of race relations. Moynihan proposed that the administration pay less attention to black militants than to "silent majority blacks" and counseled that the administration should emphasize research rather than initiate new programs.[51] Even Moynihan found himself imperiled as the administration moved to the right. Convinced that Moynihan had leaked the memo to draw attention to himself, conservative aides advised Nixon to move Moynihan's papers from his office to the central files. Moynihan resigned from the administration on October 15, ruefully noting that "the problem is that when someone like me is attacked, *no one* comes along to help."[52]

Nixon worked hard in 1970 to avert deep cuts in the military at a time when such notions were gaining respectability. Democratic senator George McGovern of South Dakota had proposed that the annual military budget of just over $70 billion be cut by $50 billion over three years. Nixon acceded to small cuts in military spending while privately acknowledging to Adm. Elmo Zumwalt, the chief of naval operations, that he planned to seek major increases in military spending if he won a landslide victory in 1972.[53] He continued phased withdrawals from Vietnam, reducing U.S. forces from 549,500 to 284,500 by early 1970, even as he bombed Cambodia and Laos. Administration officials blitzed the media with stories that they had already shifted national priorities to domestic spending.

Many liberals feared that Nixon was outwitting them. They noted, for example, that he counted as "cuts in military spending" the reduced expenditures in Vietnam realized from his phased withdrawals.[54] Liberals also alleged that the Defense Department was leaking stories about job losses from military cuts at a time when unemployment was rising. A story in *U.S. News and World Report* contended that 600,000 jobs would be lost in the next eighteen months and another 400,000 servicemen would be discharged into the job market in 1971.[55] Liberals charged that the Pentagon was designing a raft of new weapons systems that would cost tens of billions over the next few years. They noted that while Nixon said that the United States would need forces for only 1.5 wars instead of 2.5 wars, he had made no substantial revisions in actual forces.

The budget became even tighter as 1970 wore on. A sharp increase in unemployment reduced federal revenues and increased federal spending. A continuing rise in inflation increased federal interest payments on the national debt. Now suffering from a budgetary credibility problem like Lyndon Johnson's, Nixon pledged a balanced budget in the coming two budget years. Meanwhile, Wilbur Mills predicted in August 1970 that deficits would approach $20 billion for the coming fiscal year—a staggering number in light of Nixon's pledge to balance the budget. (Some Nixon aides secretly concurred with Mills's assessment, aware that federal spending would top $225 billion, whereas revenues would be only $200 billion.)

Nixon toyed with moving hard to the right as the 1970 elections neared. Had he not already sounded conservative themes in his State of Union message? Didn't mounting deficits suggest the need for deep cuts in discretionary programs? Shouldn't he appeal to white ethnics by focusing on social issues such as crime, busing, drugs, and pornography? Such aides as Pat Buchanan insisted that political realignment could be achieved only by turning hard right—and grimly told Nixon that many conservatives were increasingly frustrated by his liberal policies.[56] As Nixon's messages swung toward conservative themes, John Ehrlichman wrote a memo asking whether the president still supported some "liberal zigs" to accompany "conservative zags."[57] Nixon seemed poised to turn hard right despite his assurances to Ehrlichman that his strategy had not changed.

The Crunch on Discretionary Domestic Spending

Nixon increased his efforts to distinguish his domestic policy from the Democrats' in 1971 when he sought not just general revenue sharing but six "special revenue sharing" block grants that would consolidate 129 programs and represent about a third of the federal funds given to state and local governments. This proposal boldly attacked the structure of discretionary social programs that Democrats had constructed since the depression. Nixon obtained none of these programs in 1971—they aroused widespread opposition from Democrats, supporters of existing programs, and even some Republicans.[58]

Recall that Johnson had bequeathed the nation scores of poorly funded discretionary social programs, theorizing that constituency pressures would force future administrations to vastly increase their funding once the Vietnam War was over.[59] But Johnson was overly optimistic. His discretionary social programs were caught in a vise between entitlements and continued high spending on the military even as military costs diminished with Nixon's phased withdrawals from Vietnam. Nor had Johnson anticipated that members of both parties would embrace entitlements over social programs funded by the discretionary budget. And he could not have anticipated that his successor would regard domestic discretionary programs with hostility, attack them as ineffective, and seek to place them with block grants. The $16 billion in block grants for general revenue sharing, moreover, would necessitate further cut funds in discretionary programs.[60]

Nor had Johnson anticipated that his successor would impound funds for domestic discretionary programs. Beginning with Thomas Jefferson and including Franklin Roosevelt, Truman, and Johnson, many presidents, faced with deficits, had impounded funds appropriated by Congress. Nixon had impounded some funds in 1969 and 1970 and dramatically increased the amount he impounded in 1971 as he faced ballooning deficits, unemployment exceeding 6 percent, and rising inflation. He did not want to veto entitlements, rescind prior increases in them, or cut the cold war base, so he portrayed himself as frugal by impounding discretionary spending while contrasting his programs (entitlements, revenue sharing, and block grants) with "failed" Democratic discretionary programs.

Impounding appealed to Nixon, moreover, as a tactic for freeing up resources for his embattled military budget. Never mind that domestic discretionary spending comprised only a small share of the budget in 1970. Worried that the growth in entitlements and huge increases in military pay when the draft ended would necessitate substantial cuts in other military spending, Nixon saw only two options: increase taxes or cut domestic discretionary spending. He tipped his hand in 1970 when he asked a committee of the National Security Council that had only two participants from nonmilitary agencies to pit military spending against "a range of new or expanded domestic programs of varying priorities" over the next five years to expose "various trade-offs between defense and domestic programs."[61]

Impounding also appealed to Nixon's adversarial approach to liberals, the Democrats, and Congress. Although Congress had tolerated modest impounding from previous administrations, and even had asked some presidents, including Franklin Roosevelt and Lyndon Johnson, to impound funds for brief periods to staunch deficits, many legislators viewed Nixon's impounding as sinister because it was unsolicited, secretive, and substantial. Sen. Sam Ervin, the South Carolina Democrat and expert on constitutional law, believed that impounding violated the power of the purse, which the Constitution gave to Congress. When in mid-April 1971 some Democrats charged that Nixon had impounded $12.8 billion, Ervin threatened to sue the president.[62] And because Nixon impounded mostly domestic funds, doves believed he used impounding to frustrate a reordering of national priorities. Many Democrats especially resented impounding after Nixon coupled it to his all-out crusade for revenue sharing in 1971, which threatened to divert funds from existing programs or to fold them into block grants.

If the peace dividend was evanescent in 1969, it had disappeared by late 1971 in the wake of tax cuts, continued high military spending, and soaring costs of entitlements. As both parties anticipated the 1972 presidential elections, they tried to outbid one another for large tax cuts, despite the large deficits, and eventually approved tax cuts totaling $100 billion over ten years. (Such liberals as Charles Schultze, LBJ's budget director, vainly opposed these huge tax cuts, noting how they would constrict resources for the domestic discretionary budget.) Only the administration's failure to gain congressional approval for the Family Assistance Plan, still stalled by the polarization of liberals and conservatives, slowed the continuing rise in entitlements.

Nor did the budgetary future look promising. Further cuts in military spending would prove difficult because the U.S. presence in South Vietnam was already severely reduced by late 1971. (Opposition to further cuts in the military budget grew markedly in 1971 as Congress decisively defeated efforts to markedly reduce U.S. forces in Europe. Congress also rejected an effort to impose a $68 billion ceiling on military spending [Nixon's military budget for fiscal 1972 had been $77 billion and for fiscal 1973 it was $83.4 billion].) With the draft likely to end with the war, military costs would rise extraordinarily to pay competitive salaries to enlistees—whereas draftees were relatively inexpensive.[63] The costs of new or expanded entitlements would also rise rapidly in coming years.

In this environment of budgetary scarcity, the outlook for domestic discretionary programs was bleak, with two important exceptions. As unemployment soared, many liberals wanted the federal government to subsidize jobs in the public and nonprofit sectors with a public service employment program reminiscent of the New Deal. Because he feared he could be portrayed as unsympathetic to the unemployed, and because he regarded job programs as providing tangible benefits like entitlements, Nixon signed the Comprehensive Employment and Training Act (CETA) in 1973, a special revenue-sharing block grant. It was deeply flawed legislation. Rather than provide extensive training to millions of workers who were becoming displaced from manufacturing jobs in steel, automobile, and other industries as U.S. corporations moved plants abroad and as Japan and Europe increased their exports to the United States, CETA mostly provided temporary jobs to the unemployed. Nixon also got general revenue sharing enacted in 1972, providing billions of dollars to local and state governments to use as they wished.

Nixon Turns Hard Right

With the exodus of such relative liberals as Moynihan and Robert H. Finch, the HEW secretary, by late 1971 the Nixon administration was moving in a conservative direction. Much depended, however, on who the Democrats nominated for the presidency. Afraid that Edmund Muskie would be the Democratic contender and that George Wallace would run on a third-party ticket, Nixon was running scared in early 1972—Muskie would appeal to white northern Catholics and Wallace to white southern Protestants. Nixon unleashed party operatives on the Muskie campaign, spreading vicious personal gossip that came to involve Jane Muskie and that reduced her husband to tears at a rally.[64] Relieved when Muskie withdrew from the race, Nixon also benefited politically from the disabling of

Wallace by an assassin's bullet, because Nixon no longer had to fear that Wallace would siphon conservative votes from him.

With Nixon now convinced that the Democrats would nominate George McGovern, the dynamics of the race changed completely. McGovern's positions on myriad issues made it easy for Nixon to portray him as an "ultra-liberal," "radical," and "ideologue" on military and social policy issues. If he could keep McGovern pinned on the far left of the political spectrum, Nixon could secure the votes of moderate and conservative voters of both parties while positioning himself considerably further to the right than if Muskie had been his opponent. This posture would solidify Nixon's position with voters who liked Wallace's politics and with Republican conservatives, who had been angered by Nixon's huge deficits, the marked rise in entitlement spending, the Family Assistance Plan, his phased withdrawals from Vietnam, his use of wage-and-price controls to control inflation, and some cuts in military spending.[65] So eager was Nixon to see the Democrats nominate McGovern, he ordered his aides not to attack McGovern, lest they undermine his nomination.[66]

After the Democratic Convention Nixon commenced an assault on McGovern that is unprecedented in contemporary campaign history. Realizing that McGovern would score points if stagflation became an issue, Nixon meant to make his opponent's character, not the economy, the campaign's central issue. Although many people viewed McGovern as a political outsider, Nixon hoped to make them see the Democrat as a insider stand-in for Ted Kennedy. McGovern was widely viewed as a responsible reformer, but Nixon wanted to portray him as an extremist who would bankrupt the nation with tens of billions of dollars in new spending. Further, Nixon wanted to portray McGovern as an irresponsible advocate of unilateral disarmament and of relinquishing South Vietnam to the communists, although the South Dakotan was regarded as a principled opponent of the Vietnam War and excessive military spending. Nixon also wanted to portray the Democratic Congress as an extension of McGovern in regard to its "excessive spending," cuts in military spending, and its opposition to legislation that would have curbed pornography and busing. He also wanted to induce McGovern to modify his positions on key issues so Nixon could portray him as vacillating and dishonest.[67]

Nixon accomplished these feats through a carefully orchestrated campaign of accusations, largely delivered through intermediaries like Vice

President Spiro T. Agnew, allies like former labor secretary George Shultz, and various campaign officials who kept McGovern constantly on the defensive. Nixon charged that McGovern would raise national deficits by $144 billion, requiring $90 billion in tax increases.[68] Caspar Weinberger, the Nixon reelection campaign official who would become HEW secretary after the election, alleged that McGovern's new spending would exceed available revenues by $99.4 billion.[69] Nixon aides charged that McGovern had once advocated a 100 percent tax on inheritances as well as a $1,000 payment (called a demogrant) to all citizens that would effectively place the entire nation on welfare.

While they painted McGovern as a wild spender at home, they portrayed him as unpatriotic and derelict in his foreign and military policy. Above all, the president's men wanted to "scare the hell out of the public" and to show that McGovern's military budget would be "an invitation to disaster in Europe, the Mideast, and the World," as Buchanan put it.[70] They argued that the senator's $28.6 billion in cuts in military spending would invite the Soviets to take over Europe. They charged that McGovern, if elected, intended to withdraw *all* U.S. aid from Vietnam in the first ninety days of his administration and warned that he would undo Nixon's quest for peace with honor. Nixon's cronies also suggested that McGovern had provided office space for war protesters, that a McGovern presidency would trigger the spread of communism around the world, and that his military cuts would devastate the U.S. economy, which was already in the throes of stagflation. To drive his point home Nixon ordered the Pentagon to tell him how many military-related jobs each congressional district had—and to estimate how many of these jobs would be lost if McGovern were elected. After Bill Baroody, assistant to Defense Secretary Laird, predicted that McGovern's election would cost 1.8 million jobs, including 264,00 military and civilian positions in California alone, Nixon's campaign used these data in local campaigns with great success.[71]

Nixon's aides distorted McGovern's domestic proposals. They failed to note, for example, that the bulk of McGovern's proposed increases in domestic spending ($60 billion) derived from his proposal for national health insurance—legislation that was unlikely even to be enacted in light of certain opposition from conservatives, the American Medical Association, health insurance companies, and drug companies. (Had it passed, it would largely have been financed by payroll and other taxes.) They failed to note that much of McGovern's new spending would be financed by military cuts and the closing of some tax loopholes. Nor did they note that he proposed modest increases in domestic nonentitlement spending, including relatively small increases for education and job training.

Nixon's aides also distorted McGovern's military and foreign policy proposals. Offering the first rethinking of military policies by a presidential candidate since the cold war's inception, McGovern began with the premise that the United States ought not seek superiority over the Soviet Union but merely "credible deterrence."[72] He accepted Nixon's dictum that the United States needed the capability to fight only 1.5 wars but argued that Nixon had (in fact) retained the capabilities for 2.5 wars that Kennedy had favored. The Democrat contended, moreover, that the "base military budget" (i.e., minus forces for Vietnam) had remained remarkably intact, even as the firepower and capabilities of U.S. forces had vastly increased since the late 1950s. Why not, he asked, eliminate many bombers and many land-based missiles and rely heavily on submarines for nuclear deterrence? Why not cut military personnel from the 2.35 million on active duty to 1.73 million? Why not evaluate new weapons systems on their merits rather than as as bargaining chips with the Soviets? Why not keep most U.S. forces in Europe and Japan but vastly increase Europe's and Japan's fiscal contributions to their own defense and to the cost of the U.S. troops stationed on their land?

Nixon charged that McGovern meant to abandon South Vietnam, but he failed to tell the voters that Henry Kissinger had secretly proposed to the North Vietnamese that the United States would unilaterally withdraw all its forces from South Vietnam in the fall of 1972. Nixon and his aides greatly overstated the effects of McGovern's proposed military cuts on the economy. Many economists had documented that domestic expenditures prompt greater economic growth than military expenditures because consumer purchases are associated with a higher multiplier—they create more jobs. Because McGovern had proposed to channel military dollars into civilian expenditures, his program would create more jobs than would the existing military appropriations.

George McGovern hurt his cause by making many tactical errors. While trying to distinguish himself from other moderate Democratic contenders for the nomination in 1972, such as Muskie, Humphrey, and Scoop Jackson, McGovern had developed proposals that were quite liberal. Although this tactic allowed him to secure the nomination in a party convention whose rule changes had vastly increased the voting power of liberal delegates, it came back to haunt him. He should have made certain that the figures for his various proposals *did* add up, so Humphrey and Muskie could not contend that his arithmetic was faulty and make it easy for Nixon to charge that McGovern was fiscally imprudent. McGovern should not have supported the $1,000 demogrant for some families because conservatives could attack it as runaway welfare in a nation that had long opposed "handouts." He should have left national health insurance off the table during the election—or he should have said he would decide on its exact form after the election so that Nixon could not claim that it would cost $60 billion in new revenues when the nation was already running large deficits. McGovern probably should not have issued a detailed plan for cutting the military while the cold war was still in high gear and as he faced an opponent whose career had been built by questioning the patriotism of his opponents. McGovern gave Nixon too much ammunition by offering so many detailed military and domestic proposals.

The tragedy of McGovern's landslide loss was that it discouraged for decades to come any open discussion of national priorities because liberals feared that advocating cuts in military spending would expose them to the same kind of withering attacks that McGovern had experienced. (McGovern's resounding defeat had much to do with Democrats' surprising unwillingness to question Ronald Reagan's huge military increases in 1981, not to mention Bill Clinton's timidity in slashing military spending at the end of the cold war.) McGovern's defeat also intimidated liberals on the domestic front, because they feared any major initiatives could be attacked as fiscally irresponsible. Nixon's success in demonizing McGovern as a radical facilitated the Republicans' effort to coax moderate and conservative Democrats to vote Republican for the next two decades, thus setting up Reagan's landslide victories of 1980 and 1984.

Nixon's shift to the right in 1972 profoundly affected the nation's politics for the next thirty years. By luring millions of white ethnics and southern white Protestants to the Republican Party and by capturing many southern states, Nixon paved the way for the electoral successes of Reagan and George Bush during the 1980s and early 1990s. Except for the one-term presidency of Jimmy Carter, Republicans would control the presidency for the next twenty years and one or both chambers of Congress for twelve of the next twenty-eight.

A Hawk Poses as a Dove

A quintessential cold warrior who had secured the votes of hawks and conservatives by painting McGovern as soft on communism, Nixon also
wanted the votes of the many moderates who were disturbed by continuing tensions between the superpowers and by the Vietnam War. Nixon
ensured his landslide victory in 1972 when he was able not only to out-
hawk McGovern but to out-dove him by making the first presidential visit
to China, consummating the SALT talks, and raising hopes that he could
fashion a treaty to end the Vietnam War—and he did all three before the
1972 election.

Because he wanted to fracture the communist bloc and secure Chinese help in restraining Ho Chi Minh, Nixon was determined to visit
China before the 1972 election. This would also preempt the doves and
such Democratic senators as Ted Kennedy and Muskie, who had already
applied for visas to China.[73] Turning the secret negotiations over to
Kissinger, Nixon offered the Chinese incentives to approve his visit,
including continuing the phased withdrawals from South Vietnam, providing less support for Taiwan, and reducing the prominence of the Sev-
enth Fleet in waters near China. (In turn, Kissinger got the Chinese to
promise to intervene with Ho Chi Minh to curb his efforts to claim
South Vietnam.) In a public relations tour de force Nixon visited China
in early 1972. That he obtained only modest policy concessions scarcely
mattered.

With the SALT talks grinding along in 1971, to speed their course
Nixon offered to send massive amounts of grain to the Soviet Union and
to allow unionized longshoremen to load the grain into Soviet ships.[74]
Kissinger, meanwhile, aware that the United States could deter any Soviet
nuclear move, stood by while the Soviets continued their rapid increases
in submarine-launched and intercontinental ballistic missiles (SLBMs and
ICBMs) to offset U.S. forces and bombers in Europe. Given the huge U.S.
arsenal, Kissinger and Nixon knew that the United States was risking
nothing by agreeing during the SALT talks to cut some of its troops in
Europe and to freeze the numbers of ICBM and SLBM launchers.

Although Kissinger portrayed SALT I as a giant breakthrough, it was in
fact a porous treaty that had little effect on the arms race. Because the Pentagon did not want to give up its MIRVs, and Kissinger and Nixon were

unwilling to challenge the military on this point, both the United States and the Soviet Union rapidly increased their nuclear forces in the 1970s by MIRVing their ICBMs and SLBMs. (From 1972 to 1980 the U.S. arsenal grew from 9,000 to 14,000 warheads and the Soviets' from 7,000 to 12,000.)[75] Nor did SALT constrain the Soviets' development of heavier missiles. Restrictions placed on silo diameters meant the Soviets were not supposed to build heavier missiles, but Kissinger failed to understand that they could deploy these missiles merely by deepening the silos.[76] Nor did the treaty prohibit the United States from planning a new class of submarine for the late 1970s known as the Trident; its missiles would project farther into Soviet territory and possess more destructive power. Nor did the treaty limit research and development, constrain the development of cruise missiles, or curtail conventional forces.

Under the rubric of SALT I, then, the United States and Soviet Union forged two agreements: an antiballistic missile treaty (ABM) that limited each side to two ABM installations (later reduced to one by mutual agreement), and an interim agreement on strategic offensive arms that froze or set limits on ICBM and SLBM launchers for a five-year period, to be renegotiated in the late 1970s.

Nixon had strengthened his dovish credentials with the China visit and the SALT agreements, but he desperately wanted to show progress on Vietnam before the presidential election. This was his dilemma: he wanted to end the war before the election in a master stroke against the Democrats, yet he feared a peace treaty might hurt him at the polls if the United States seemed to be abandoning South Vietnam on terms that guaranteed the eventual defeat of Diem Bien Thieu by communist insurgents. Nixon played it both ways, publicly maintaining a hard line while secretly trying to move negotiations so that the United States could exit South Vietnam before the election. In the meantime he implemented phased withdrawals with drumbeat regularity, reducing U.S. ground strength in Vietnam to roughly fifty thousand troops by the spring of 1971.[77]

Kissinger made key concessions to the North Vietnamese in back-channel negotiations, telling them for the first time that they could keep troops in South Vietnam even after a negotiated settlement and after U.S. troops had left Vietnam. He also said the United States would agree that the provisional revolutionary government (the communist insurgency) could share power with Thieu. By continuing to withdraw U.S. troops even during a large North Vietnamese offensive in the spring, Kissinger implied that the United States would withdraw its forces unilaterally, no matter the course of conflict.

As the election loomed, North Vietnam finally made some key concessions. Now conceding that Thieu could remain in power, the North Vietnamese agreed to negotiate peace if U.S. troops withdrew and North Vietnamese troops were allowed to remain in the South. To secure Thieu's agreement for an arrangement that would pit his regime against insurgents with scant U.S. assistance, Kissinger made key concessions, such as agreeing to leave him with huge stockpiles of equipment. Working frantically to secure the treaty before the election, a frustrated Kissinger was chagrined to learn that Nixon would not pressure Thieu to stop objecting to the treaty—a pollster had warned Nixon he might lose the election if the United States announced a unilateral withdrawal and allowed the North Vietnamese to remain in the South. Leaving Kissinger in limbo, Nixon decided to wait until after the election to effect a complete U.S. withdrawal.

Still, Nixon had decided he had to get out of Vietnam, both for political reasons and because Congress was about to cut off the war's money supply. (Moreover, Democrats were pushing to end the draft by early 1973.) After bombing North Vietnam heavily after the election, Nixon forced Thieu to sign the treaty by threatening to sign a separate peace with the North Vietnamese. Nixon promised, moreover, that the United States would continue to bomb insurgents from offshore bases once the United States had withdrawn its forces.[78] A treaty was finally signed in early 1973, and the end of the draft soon followed.

Although it is tempting to contend that the visit to China, the SALT agreement, and withdrawal from Vietnam gave Nixon and Kissinger the right to call themselves peace makers, these initiatives merely disguised their hawkishness. China and SALT were symbolic changes that hardly diminished Nixon and Kissinger's desire to maintain U.S. forces at full strength and to oppose real reductions in nuclear power. Withdrawal from Vietnam had taken nearly four years to achieve—under terms that guaranteed that Vietnam would be reunified under communist rule in the near term. It is difficult to see "honor" in this end game. Unlike Robert McNamara, moreover, neither Nixon or Kissinger acknowledged his error in continuing this tragic conflict for four years at enormous fiscal and human cost. Once the United States did withdraw, it was just a matter of time before the corrupt South Vietnamese regime fell, which occurred in 1975.

Nixon's Disinformation

Buoyed by the 19.5 million Americans who had voted for him for the first time, Nixon bristled at newspaper accounts that attributed his victory not to his own popularity but to widespread animus toward McGovern. Nixon believed he had a mandate for conservative policies and was determined to prevail over liberal Democrats. He wanted to increase military spending by (at least) $4 billion annually, not just in his forthcoming budget but for years to come. Given the substantial deficits the treasury was incurring, the only way to fund an increase in military spending was to cut domestic discretionary spending to meet Nixon's spending ceiling of $250 billion.

Despite the deficits, congressional liberals and doves still hungered for a peace dividend that would increase domestic nonentitlement spending markedly. The Brookings Institution estimated that liberals could realize $24 billion from "moderate" military cuts and by closing loopholes—and $40 billion with even more drastic military cuts by fiscal 1976.[79]

Nixon skillfully framed his case to put liberals on the defensive. He correctly noted, for example, that military spending had declined as a percentage of the GNP from 1964 to 1972 and that its share of the federal budget had declined too, but he failed to note that the military percentage of the budget, when examined in constant dollars, had merely returned to the pre-Vietnam levels of 1964. When he argued that military spending had declined more than 33 percent in constant dollars, he chose 1968 as the base year because it was the height of the Vietnam War—an artifice that obscured the derivation of much of the recent military cuts in the phased withdrawal of troops from South Vietnam rather than from cuts in the cold war base that had preceded Vietnam.

Nixon similarly skewed data to portray "runaway domestic spending." He correctly noted that aggregate social spending has risen dramatically from 1964 to 1972—and that its share of the federal budget and the GNP had also risen—but he failed to note that even small increases brought large percentage increases because social spending was so much less than military spending. The nation spent $289 billion on its military in 1964 but only $119 billion for its combined entitlement and discretionary social programs in constant 1992 dollars. Nixon did not distinguish between entitlements and discretionary spending and failed to note that the bulk of domestic spending increases came from entitlements, primarily from the burgeoning Medicare, Medicaid, and Social Security programs.

Nixon continued to attack domestic discretionary programs. In his message on human resources in March 1973, he equated domestic programs with "special interests" and with "sweeping . . . almost utopian commitments" of the Great Society, charging that "results in case after case amounted to dismal failure."[80] Nixon failed to note the minuscule funding of the Great Society and contended that its framers assumed "that even the most complex problems could be quickly solved by throwing enough federal dollars at them." He did not note that evaluative research was in a primitive state and had not yielded definitive findings for virtually any programs. Nixon continued to associate domestic discretionary spending with budget imbalances and inflation while not implicating military or entitlement spending.

Shootout at the OK Corral

Nixon and his aides put into place an antispending crusade in 1973 that they called the "Battle of the Budget" in numerous confidential memos. They planned to cut domestic discretionary spending by $6.5 billion in the present fiscal year, $17 billion in fiscal 1974, and $22 billion in fiscal 1975 to offset increased military spending and $10 billion in entitlement increases while holding overall spending to $250 billion to battle inflation. Nixon proposed deep cuts in War on Poverty, Model Cities, educational, and many other programs and decided to replace seventy domestic programs with four special revenue-sharing programs at a cost of $6.9 billion. He already had impounded about $15 billion in the current fiscal year and threatened to continue his impounding crusade if Congress exceeded his recommendations for domestic spending.

The core of Nixon's support derived from two hundred legislators in both chambers who had supported budget-cutting measures in the past. Using the White House Office of Communications as the focal point, Nixon's aides barraged the media with stories about liberals' extravagant spending, which had (they argued) caused the nation's growing inflation, now more than 8 percent. Convinced that the Democrats would enact domestic spending measures that exceeded his wishes, Nixon planned as many as a dozen vetoes that would blame his political opponents for the nation's inflation. As the Democrats attacked impoundments with lawsuits or legislation, Nixon steadfastly defended impounding as necessary to combat the inflation he blamed on the Democratic Congress.

Nixon began his vetoes in late March with the Vocational Rehabilitation Act and continued to veto throughout the summer while impounding various funds. Congress fought back. It wrote legislation that required Nixon to return impounded funds to Congress, held hearings on impoundments affecting rural and agricultural programs, and threatened to cut appropriations for the twelve departments that Nixon had ordered to impound funds.[81] When Nixon ordered some cabinet officials not to appear before congressional committees, Sam Ervin, chairman of the Senate Government Operations Committee, threatened to subpoena them. Sen. J. William Fulbright, the Arkansas Democrat who chaired the Senate Foreign Relations Committee, threatened to cut off foreign aid until Nixon released impounded funds. As these initiatives went forward, so also did litigation. Though a federal court had thrown out an earlier challenge to impounding, a succession of court federal rulings went against Nixon in mid- and late 1973. Defiant even in the wake of these rulings, Nixon continued to impound funds on the ground that Congress would breech his spending ceiling if he failed to act.

As Nixon impounded funds and vetoed specific measures, many mayors declared that he had betrayed them when he had insisted in 1972 that general revenue sharing would be funded from new resources rather than by cutting existing social programs. This promise had secured their support for revenue sharing, yet Nixon proceeded to impound and freeze spending, as well as to demand cuts in specific programs. Such cities as Gary, Indiana, saw federal grants drop by 30 percent because of Nixon's actions—sure, Gary was getting general revenue-sharing money, but it came from cuts in other programs, such as Title XX, job training, equal opportunity, education, and Model Cities programs, and by the time it arrived in Gary, the pot was 30 percent smaller.[82]

The Battle of the Budget also attacked liberals' efforts to cut spending for such military weapons as the B-1 bomber, AWACS (the long-range mobile air defense system), and the Trident submarine, weapons that even the conservative American Enterprise Institute declared unnecessary or redundant.[83] Nixon planned a lobbying effort that dwarfed even his earlier efforts to staunch cuts in military spending; he established a command office run by the Pentagon to provide statistics, rallied corporations that made these various weapons, and continued to rely on senators Scoop Jackson and John Tower of Texas, who met nearly daily with White House lobbyists to develop strategy.[84] Nixon repeatedly maintained, moreover, that failure to produce these weapons would reduce the United States to "the second most powerful nation in the world."[85]

Still reeling from McGovern's defeat, liberals tried to mount a counteroffensive, hoping to cut Nixon's military budget by $2.7 billion and add $1.1 billion to his domestic agenda. Arms experts such as Paul Warnke contended that Nixon's planned military increases represented the first time a U.S. president had sought increased military spending after a war.[86] (A group of former national security officials contended that Congress could safely cut $14 billion from the fiscal 1974 budget to capture savings from the SALT agreement and from the cease-fire in South Vietnam—and the Brookings Institution believed tax reforms and modest military cuts could free $24 billion immediately.[87]) When the Democrats realized they lacked the votes in the subcommittees for deep military cuts, they attacked appropriations for specific weapons on the Senate floor. The battle between many Democrats and Nixon reached a climax in September when Democrats initiated a series of amendments on the Senate floor to cut military authorizations, such as proposals by Sen. Walter Mondale of Minnesota to cut military civilian personnel by 7 percent, by Sen. Thomas Eagleton of Missouri to stop funding of AWACS, by Republican senator Clifford McIntyre of Maine to cut Trident funds, and by Mike Mansfield to phase down U.S. participation in NATO forces over three years. Again relying on senators Jackson and Tower, unleashing a host of lobbyists, and retaining Pentagon researchers and technicians in their command post on Capitol Hill, Nixon beat back these amendments.[88] With even Democrats supporting a spending ceiling of $268 billion to battle inflation, the only way to free money for the domestic agenda was to cut the military. Liberals lost key votes by large margins because many Democrats, fearing attacks from military contractors in their districts and remembering the sheer size of McGovern's defeat, balked at cutting military spending.

It is difficult to overstate the extent that impounding triggered bipartisan congressional resentment of Nixon. The House Judiciary Committee even briefly considered it to be an impeachable offense because Nixon engaged in impounding more openly and provocatively than had his predecessors.[89] Nixon reverted to a more moderate course, stopped impounding funds, and softened his rhetoric in a vain attempt to head off the congressional move to impeach him over Watergate in 1974.

After Nixon resigned, Gerald Ford served the remainder of his term, then was defeated by Jimmy Carter in 1976. Neither president broke new ground with respect to national priorities, but, as I discuss in chapter 10, considerable sentiment had built by the late 1970s for large increases in military spending.

Failed National Priorities in the Nixon Administration

Richard Nixon came into office determined to place his stamp on the nation's priorities. He wanted to maintain military spending at (at least) the level of the cold war base, curtail additional funding for Great Society discretionary programs, and increase spending for domestic entitlement programs. Moreover, he wanted to keep enough money in the military budget so he could maintain an American presence in Vietnam for an extended period. It is extraordinary that, facing a Democratic Congress and significant numbers of doves from both parties who opposed some of these objectives, Nixon largely succeeded. Indeed, Congress approved policies during Nixon's terms that revolutionized domestic spending; entitlements grew at extraordinary rates throughout the 1970s to become the dominant portion of the federal budget.

Determined to maintain military spending at the same level even after ending the war in Vietnam, Nixon squelched doves' efforts to cut military spending significantly below the cold war base that had preceded Vietnam. In 1964, on the eve of U.S. involvement in Vietnam, narrow military and veterans' spending had totaled $289 billion; by fiscal 1974, when Vietnam expenditures had nearly ended, narrow military and veterans' spending came to $266 billion (all data from this point are in constant 1992 dollars). In other words, as figure 9.1 shows, Nixon was able to contain military cuts to slightly more than the cost of waging the Vietnam War, thus protecting nearly the entire cold war base that preceded it. Nixon's achievement in the face of widespread disenchantment with the military and a cadre of doves from both parties was a major victory for advocates of military spending. During the presidencies of Ford and Carter in the mid- and late 1970s, military spending remained at roughly the same level as in 1974.

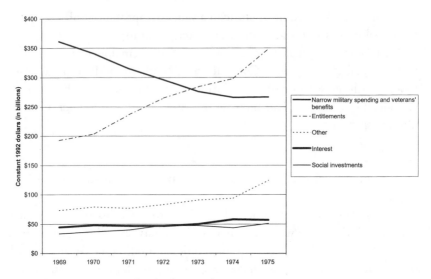

FIGURE 9.1 Five Types of Federal Expenditures, 1969–1975

Source: Office of Management and Budget, *Budget of the U.S. Government, FY 2000, Historical Tables* (Washington, D.C.: GPO, 1999), table 8.6, pp. 126–30.

The growth in entitlements was so extraordinary in the 1970s that these expenditures equalled narrow military and veterans' spending by 1973 (see table 9.1). When we break out the figures for specific entitlements, the breathtaking growth of those wholly or partially funded by payroll taxes is particularly remarkable, though even means-tested entitlements also grew markedly.

These entitlements, which rose from merely $146.6 billion to $358.8 billion in eleven years, singly and as a group created a safety net for the first time in U.S. history. Whereas some programs, such as food stamps, provided the sole boost that a family or individual needed, others were used in combination, such as by the disabled elderly who took advantage of their eligibility for Medicare, Social Security, and Supplemental Security Income (SSI). Some people used one or more programs for brief periods, such as food stamps during a period of unemployment; others used them for extended periods, such Medicaid and SSI during periods of chronic illness. Congress enacted a new entitlement in 1975 after Nixon left office—the earned income tax credit, which allowed working families that fell beneath specific minimum income levels to get a tax rebate (or credit). The program would become a major weapon against poverty

TABLE 9.1   Expenditures for Entitlements, 1969–1997
(in billions of constant 1992 dollars)

	1969	1980	1997
UNIVERSAL ENTITLEMENTS			
1. Social Security	96.1	203.6	319.0
2. Medicare	19.2	54.0	165.3
3. Unemployment Insurance	8.2	29.4	18.1
4. Subtotals	123.5	287.0	502.4
MEANS-TESTED ENTITLEMENTS			
1. Medicaid	8.2	24.3	84.1
2. Food Stamps	1.9	22.8	27.9
3. Supplementary Security	—	9.9	23.5
4. AFDC	13.0	12.7	14.5
5. Earned Income Tax Credit	—	2.2	19.2
5. Subtotals	23.1	71.9	169.2
TOTALS	146.6	358.9	671.6

among working Americans when the income levels and credit were raised in succeeding decades.

Considering that Lyndon Johnson had created scores of new social programs funded by the discretionary budget and that he had funded them poorly, it is remarkable that their funding increased only modestly in the Nixon and Ford administrations. In 1969 social, educational, job training, employment, and public health programs (called "social investments" in figs. 9.1. and 9.2) received $33.5 billion; in 1975 they received $51 billion.[90] It was a kind of stalemate: Democrats and liberals often rallied to defend these programs even as Nixon orchestrated a nonstop campaign against them. Spending on these discretionary programs was also limited by budgetary scarcity in the 1970s stemming from the sheer growth of entitlements, two major tax cuts, and doves' failure to secure deeper cuts in military spending.

As figure 9.2 shows, important shifts in budget allocations were made during Nixon's tenure. Spending on the military and veterans' benefits, which accounted for 48 percent of the budget in 1970, declined to 31 percent of the budget in 1975, while entitlements rose from roughly 29 percent to 41 percent of the budget. Social investment programs, 5.2 percent of the budget in 1969, had grown to only 6 percent of the budget by 1975.

Budgetary data disprove Nixon's assertion that military spending, having declined as a percentage of the budget and GDP, no longer constrained domestic spending. Recall that most military spending, unlike entitlements, derives from the discretionary, or controllable, portion of annual budgets. Military and veterans' discretionary spending still absorbed more than 60 percent of total discretionary spending during the 1970s, which squeezed domestic discretionary spending (see fig. 9.3).

Although national priorities shifted markedly during Nixon's tenure, he squandered an opportunity to make significant cuts in the military by not getting out of Vietnam in 1969 or 1970. (To offset some of the political animosity from hawks, he could have stressed that Vietnam diverted the United States from other national security concerns, a belief widely held even by the Joint Chiefs of Staff.) He should have taken bolder positions in the SALT negotiations, such as outlawing MIRVs and placing even greater restrictions on ICBM and SLBM launchers on both sides. He should have educated the American public about the sizable lead of

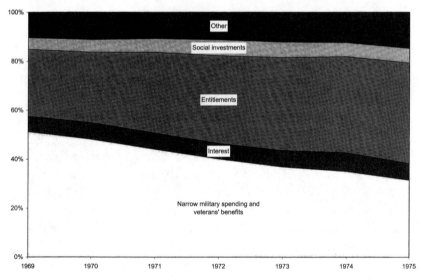

FIGURE 9.2 Five Types of Expenditures as Percentages of Total Federal Outlays, 1969–1975

Source: Office of Management and Budget, *Budget of the U.S. Government, FY 2000, Historical Tables* (Washington, D.C.: GPO, 1999), table 3.1, pp. 45–46.

the United States in nuclear forces in the late 1960s to assuage fears that limiting U.S. nuclear forces jeopardized national security. (See figs. 8.1 and 8.2.)

Neither Nixon or his two successors, Gerald Ford and Jimmy Carter, sufficiently questioned the size of cold war military spending. The United States possessed, for example, nuclear megatonnage that far exceeded what the country actually needed to deter the Soviet Union. The United States retained excessive forces dedicated to the defense of Western Europe when the Soviet Union would not have dared invade because of the power of U.S. and European nuclear forces. Not one of these three presidents attempted far-reaching reforms of the military's procurement practices.

Although Nixon deserves credit for expanding entitlements, his role should not be exaggerated. The Democrats were frequently the initiators of proposals to augment entitlements—and would likely have secured veto overrides had he tried to kill many of them. (Even the concept of the Family Assistance Plan came from Democrats, and its demise became virtually certain when Nixon failed to work for its passage in

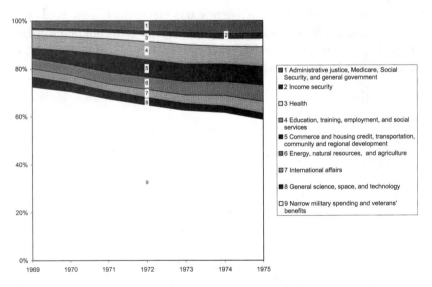

FIGURE 9.3 Competition for Discretionary Spending: Military Versus Domestic Spending as Percentages of Total Outlays, 1969–1975

Source: Office of Management and Budget, *Budget of the U.S. Government, FY 2000, Historical Tables* (Washington, D.C.: GPO, 1999), table 8.8, pp. 136–37.

1970. A revised version was introduced during the next session of Congress but went nowhere and was defeated in 1972.)[91] Nixon can be faulted, moreover, for creating a false dichotomy between entitlements and discretionary social programs. Meeting the income, food, and health needs of citizens is important, but so is addressing their educational, training, employment, and social needs. Nixon launched these attacks, moreover, during a decade when millions of Americans were losing well-paid manufacturing jobs and were thrown into unemployment or forced into lower-paying service jobs. Automobile, steel, and other industries were relocating their plants abroad, and foreign corporations were competing with U.S. firms more effectively than they ever had. Indeed, the United States ought to have launched huge remedial education and job-training programs during the 1970s for both the unemployed and welfare recipients. Nixon also seemed oblivious to the millions of Americans who suffer debilitating social problems, such as mental illness, substance abuse, and abusive relationships. Although social problems have no magical cures, and some programs are wholly ineffective, Nixon attacked such programs as useless when the ability to evaluate these programs was still primitive or nonexistent.

I argue in chapter 15 that Congress and presidents Nixon, Ford, and Carter wasted $1 trillion—and that figure does not even count pork-barrel spending, corporate welfare, excessive deregulation, or excessive tax concessions for affluent Americans.

10

Reagan's Fantasies

Ronald Reagan came into office intending to reduce taxes by 30 percent, vastly increase military spending, *and* balance the budget. With a Democratic House as well as a number of Republicans who prized balanced budgets, could he accomplish this fiscal revolution, or would it founder on its internal contradictions? Would he savage the domestic programs established by his predecessors in order to achieve his goals? Would he cut government waste, as he promised in his campaign, or would he contribute to it? I argue in chapter 15 that the Reagan administration and Congress made fiscal and tax errors exceeding $3.4 trillion from 1982 through 1989 in constant 1992 dollars.

Past as Prologue

Reagan, a man untroubled by the complexities of life, held four specific goals with remarkable constancy for at least thirty-five years: to cut federal taxes, rescind federal regulations, slash federal spending, and pursue hawkish policies toward the Soviet Union.[1] (His four-cornered philosophy had already surfaced in the New Deal, although he did not switch his party affiliation from Democratic to Republican until 1962.) Reagan believed that before the emergence of big government in the New Deal, the United States was a utopia—a land of hardworking citizens who rarely used federal programs and voluntarily took care of those who genuinely needed assistance. Thus he ignored such realities of history as the depression of 1894, slavery, the brutal treatment of Native Americans, and the hardships of immigrants in sweatshops.[2] He disliked the New Deal's welfare relief programs, claiming they so sapped recipients' work ethic that they shunned its work relief programs; he failed to realize that many people had to stay on relief because the New Deal's work programs were so poorly funded that they could handle only a third of those who needed work.[3] Unaware that Roosevelt meant to revive social reform after World War II, Reagan believed that Roosevelt was a closet conservative who would have eliminated federal bureaucracy after the war. Reagan regarded the growth of federal bureaucracy and federal taxes during World War II with disdain. He was oblivious to the need for a massive bureaucracy and many regulations to superintend the nation's economy during a global war. He also believed that the fiercely partisan Harry Truman was a closet conservative and even wondered why Truman had not switched parties.[4] Reagan's conservative inclinations were strengthened by his personal experiences after World War II—the heavy taxation of his newfound wealth from movie acting; his fight, as president of the Screen Actors' Guild, against communist infiltration in the guild; and his financial losses when the Department of Justice ruled that movie studios had to give up ownership of movie theaters because they were in violation of antitrust laws.[5]

Reagan's disdain for government programs comes through clearly in his autobiography. At no place does he suggest that *any* federal program, save military ones, had any virtue, contending they discouraged work, were wasteful, or undermined citizens' liberty. He lampooned the federal bureaucracy, alleging, for example, that "$2 was often spent on overhead for every $1 that went to needy people" and even suggesting that "there probably isn't any undertaking on earth short of national security that can't be handled more efficiently by the forces of private enterprise than by the federal government."[6] Nor does Reagan identify a single federal regulation that he thought worthwhile, dismissing them all as interfering with private

markets or as attacking citizens' freedom. He had opposed the Civil Rights
Act of 1964 on the ground that states should enforce civil rights. He saw
himself as heroically saving American society from liberals when he delivered hundreds of speeches sponsored by General Electric in the 1950s. He
always reiterated his four-cornered philosophy in speeches that were virtually identical to ones that he gave in the 1970s and 1980s.[7]

His political career was born during the Great Society in a remarkable
victory in 1966 over two-term California governor Edmund "Pat" Brown
Sr. (Brown epitomized the tax-and-spend policies that Reagan had come
to despise. Brown used state funds to construct California's highway and
water systems, its system of higher education, and a social welfare system
that was widely regarded as the best in the nation.) But during his two own
terms as governor, Reagan was saddled with a Democratic legislature that
frustrated his efforts to effect major cuts. As a result, state spending went
from $4.6 billion to $10.2 billion during his tenure—which allowed Jerry
Ford to claim in the 1976 Republican presidential primary campaigns that
Reagan was "the biggest taxer and spender" in California history.[8] Although
overall state spending rose dramatically, however, Reagan had aggressively
sought cuts in programs used by stigmatized and poor people—he slashed
funding for mental health, child welfare, and welfare. He also displayed a
curious contradiction between his words and deeds that would resurface
during his presidency. Although he favored balanced budgets, he cut taxes
for corporations and affluent Californians so deeply that he had to restore
some taxes when deficits zoomed out of control.

It was a country club governorship in which Reagan surrounded himself with advisers and associates who came from the large banks, defense
contractors, agribusiness, road contractors, and building contractors that
had thrived in California during the 1950s and 1960s. (Of the $4 million
he raised for his 1966 campaign, $3 million came in sums of $5,000 or
more—and in 1970 he spent 2.5 times what his Democratic candidate
could afford in the gubernatorial campaign.)[9] Reagan appointed virtually
no women or people of color to his inner circle, his cabinet, or myriad
commissions and boards. He collaborated with California's congressional
delegation, moreover, to maintain the state's position as the leading recip-
ient of federal military contracts.

Because his major complaints since the late 1940s lay not with state governments but with the federal government, Reagan hungered to become
president even in the late 1960s when he was first encouraged to run. Bear-

ing animus toward California's social programs for poor people, he was even more hostile to federal ones. He believed that federal social programs fostered centralization of power and made poor people less inclined to work. He even opposed the enactment of Medicare and Medicaid in the belief that charity medicine by private doctors was sufficient. Roosevelt (and Johnson) had built big government. Reagan wanted to dismantle it. Roosevelt had presided over the growth in federal income taxes in World War II. Reagan wanted to equal or surpass Johnson's tax cuts of 1964. Richard Nixon, Jerry Ford, and Jimmy Carter had presided over cuts in military spending at a time when the Soviets were rearming. Reagan wanted to build the military to levels far exceeding the cold war base.

Supply-side theorists, such as Arthur Laffer, gave theoretical legitimacy in the early and mid-1970s to proposals to slash the taxes of corporate and affluent elites. Laffer contended that tax cuts for the affluent would cure both the inflation and stagnation that afflicted the economy in the mid- and late 1970s in an approach remarkably similar to the trickle-down economics of Reagan's personal hero, Calvin Coolidge, who had used a similar rationale to cut federal taxes in half.[10] According to Reagan and Laffer, lower taxes on the rich would mean they could invest in job-creating enterprises and plant modernization that would redress inflation by enhancing productivity. Laffer stated, moreover, that the tax cuts would stimulate economic growth, which would boost tax revenues and thereby diminish the deficits created by huge tax cuts.

Although supply-siders were primarily interested in tax cuts for affluent citizens, a populist disdain for all taxes in the late 1970s provided a favorable climate for tax cuts.[11] The double-digit inflation of the 1970s had catapulted many resentful citizens into higher tax brackets, although their inflation-adjusted income had not increased. The success of the referendum on Proposition 13 in California in 1979, which slashed property taxes, galvanized tax cutters to broaden their scope to federal income taxes. It is small wonder that Rep. Jack Kemp, R-N.Y., and Sen. William Roth, R-Del., took Laffer's theories a step further by proposing to slash everyone's taxes by a whopping 30 percent over three years, and make deep cuts in corporate rates, in legislation they introduced in early 1975.[12] (They also came to favor indexing brackets for inflation, a policy that would greatly cut the automatic rise in tax revenues.) Kemp and Roth quickly generated support from both sides of the aisle. When Jimmy Carter and leading Democrats opposed the Kemp-Roth legislation on the ground that it would exacerbate deficits, they created an opening for Reagan to use the tax issue to seek the presidency.

Mobilizing for "War" in Peacetime

Reagan's ambition to become president was fueled not only by his conservatism and nostalgic view of the country but by his desire to slay international communism. Here too an array of theorists had developed military and foreign policy prescriptions in the 1970s that dovetailed with his beliefs. Since the end of World War II, the Joint Chiefs of Staff had often sought far greater resources than presidents or Congresses had given them. But their restlessness had increased since the mid-1960s because the brass believed that Lyndon Johnson had diverted materiel and troops from the defense of Europe to South Vietnam and kept important weapons systems in the pipeline instead of moving them into production. They also believed that Nixon had rejected Zumwalt's plea for a six-hundred-ship navy, given the Soviet Union unnecessary concessions in SALT I, and ceded nuclear superiority to the Soviets.

Two hawks teamed up to campaign for dramatic increases in military spending in the 1970s.[13] William Van Cleave, a professor of international relations at the University of Southern California, contended that the Soviets intended to unleash a first strike because of their numerical superiority in ICBMs and SLBMs, as well as the sheer power of their rockets, which would enable them to destroy even U.S. ICBMs in protective silos. (He argued that U.S. SLBMs and Minuteman ICBMs lacked sufficient power or accuracy to destroy Soviet land-based ICBMs.) Paul Nitze, who had served as director of the State Department's Policy Planning Staff, the Office of International Security Affairs, and secretary of the navy hypothesized that only 3 percent to 4 percent of the Soviet population would be killed, even with two thousand U.S. nuclear warheads hitting Soviet targets, because of the sophisticated Soviet civil defense network.[14] Van Cleave contended that with most of their population safe from U.S. counterattacks and most U.S. land-based missiles destroyed, the Soviets would be able to convince Americans to not even counterstrike and to accept whatever peace terms the Soviets wished to impose, such as a Soviet takeover of Western Europe.[15]

Nitze and Van Cleave reserved particular animus for Jimmy Carter, who had come into his presidency asking the Joint Chiefs whether the United States could destroy 90 percent of its nuclear warheads. Carter, who was against increases in military spending, also opposed the B-1 bomber in favor of maintaining the aging fleet of B-52s until a Stealth bomber was built. Nor did Nitze and Van Cleave favor Carter's approach to arms talks. Recall that the porous SALT I's interim agreement had to be renegotiated after only five years. Hawks like Nitze had been furious that Nixon had forfeited the U.S. ability to develop an antiballistic missile system when he signed SALT I's ABM treaty, as well as SALT I's limits on U.S. ICBM and SLBM launchers. Because Nitze believed that SALT I had already given the Soviets an advantage, he was furious when Carter signed SALT II in June 1979; although the Senate never approved the treaty, it allowed the Soviets to retain a numerical lead in ICBMs and to build new bombers while preventing the United States from augmenting its ICBMs, even though the treaty froze the number of warheads on existing ballistic missile launchers, limited the number of reentry vehicles allowed for new ICBMs, and probably prevented the Soviets from deploying three thousand additional missiles. Nitze was not appeased by the fact that SALT II allowed the United States to implement a large force of mobile and powerful mobile ICBMs, proceed with Trident submarines, develop Cruise missiles, continue its large research-and-development programs, retain its current conventional forces, and deploy submarines near Soviet coastlines.[16] He was angry, moreover, that the United States took few actions to improve its bomber fleet other than modernizing the B-52.

Nor was Nitze's anger at Carter assuaged by the president's conversion to increases in strategic power late in his term when he and Harold Brown, his defense secretary, endorsed policies that had long been favored by game theorists, such as developing U.S. capabilities to survive an extended nuclear war. (This was a return to lethal chess as advocated by game theorists, who dismissed the theories of massive retaliation and mutual assured destruction, which contended that use of nuclear weapons by either side would bring a nuclear holocaust.)[17] Nor was he appeased by Carter's marked increases in military spending in his last two years or his proposal to increase military spending by 7 percent annually, over and above the rate of inflation, for the next five years.

Many critics dismissed the theories of Van Cleave and Nitze.[18] They doubted the Soviet ICBMs had sufficient accuracy to destroy U.S. ICBMs from a distance of six thousand miles. They contended that U.S. SLBMs, which could devastate Soviet cities and industry, provided sufficient deterrence even without ICBMs. These critics noted the awesome power of U.S. forces in Europe, not to mention the nuclear capabilities of NATO allies such as France and Britain. The critics doubted that Warsaw Pact forces possessed the fighting capabilities or the morale of NATO forces, making a Soviet invasion of Europe as problematic as it had been for decades. They cited the awesome power of U.S. nuclear forces and their relative invulnerability because they were based on land and in the sea and air, unlike the Soviets' heavier reliance on vulnerable land-based missiles. Van Cleave and Nitze believed the superior "throw weight" of Soviet missiles made them more potent than U.S. ICBMs, but critics contended that Soviet missiles needed to be more powerful because their rockets used liquid fuels, which were heavier than the solid fuels that powered U.S. rockets and because the Soviets lacked the technology to miniaturize their rockets' components. Critics argued that the Trident was evidence the United States led the Soviets in submarine technology and had a significant technological lead in communications and command structures.[19] Some also doubted that the Soviets spent a lot more money on their military than the United States, contending the Central Intelligence Agency's estimates of Soviet expenditures were wrong because the agency had based its calculations on what the United States would spend for comparable troops rather than factoring in the lower pay scales in the Soviet Union. Critics also argued that roughly 35 percent of Soviet military spending was allocated to troops and weapons at the Chinese border. Giving due consideration to these factors, the International Institute for Strategic Studies in London—a widely respected source of military data not connected to either superpower—estimated that U.S. military spending surpassed the Soviets' military spending by a wide margin throughout the 1970s—by as much as 44 percent in 1977 alone.[20]

Critics contended, moreover, that the CIA overestimated the effectiveness of Soviet forces. The agency wrongly assumed that the gross weight of the top stage of a missile predicted its destructive power. (While the MX's top stage weighed only thirty-five pounds more than the Minuteman's, for example, it was twice as destructive.) True, the Soviet navy had 1,764 ships, whereas the U.S. Navy had 462, but 1,045 of their ships were assigned to patrol, laying mines, or serving in auxiliary roles. Meanwhile, their 269 major ships lacked the firepower and technology of their 178 U.S. counterparts. The Soviets possessed only 50 nuclear attack submarines; the

United States had 75. The Soviets had only 2 aircraft carriers; the Americans had 13. The Soviets had 870 naval combat aircraft; the United States had 1,820.[21] Critics doubted the Soviets had an advantage even with respect to conventional forces. U.S. troops may have numbered only 774,000, but 800,000 of the 1.8 million Soviet troops were committed to the 5,813-mile Chinese border and only 600,000 to the Warsaw Pact. Nor had the Soviets markedly increased their Warsaw Pact commitment, having added only four divisions since 1967. With NATO's standing forces at 2.8 million troops and the Warsaw Pact's at 2.6 million, virtual parity existed in central Europe if we make the dubious assumption that the Warsaw Pact forces possessed the same fighting abilities as NATO forces.[22]

Critics also dismissed Van Cleave's belief that the United States would stand idly by once the Soviets had launched a first strike. With about twelve thousand nuclear warheads at his disposal, a U.S. president would know that he could destroy most of Soviet society and industry, as well as the Soviets' eight thousand armaments, even if a Soviet first strike destroyed some American assets.[23] Nitze's critics also contended that he exaggerated the global significance of the Soviet invasion of Afghanistan in 1979. Nitze contended that it presaged a Soviet invasion of the Middle East, whereas these critics contended that the move was designed to put down an Islamic regime at the Soviet border, lest other Islamic peoples seek power in several Soviet republics.[24]

Nitze found George Bush and Ronald Reagan, the two Republican front-runners for the presidential nomination in early 1980, to be preferable to Carter. As director of the CIA during portions of the Nixon presidency and during Jerry Ford's tenure, Bush had burnished his hard-line credentials in a curious exercise in 1976. Angry that the CIA had decided that the Soviets did not pose a first-strike danger, Nitze and Van Cleave had pressured Bush to revise the agency's estimates. So Bush commissioned an exercise in which "Team A" (CIA officials) and "Team B" (alarmists like Van Cleave, Nitze, Richard Perle, and Richard Pipes) separately examined CIA classified intelligence to gauge the Soviet threat. When both teams failed to change the result of their analyses, Bush decided that Team B's views would become official CIA doctrine, thus legitimizing the alarmist position.[25]

Although Reagan had no foreign policy experience, no one could doubt his hawkishness. In 1976 he readily joined the Committee on the Present Danger, which was formed to campaign for a U.S. military buildup. The committee counted among its members many people who would become part of Reagan's administration, among them Perle, a former Senate aide who became an assistant secretary of defense; Fred Ikle, a former Nixon White House aide who became undersecretary of defense, and John Lehman, who became secretary of the navy.[26] The committee membership also included an array of military analysts, military contractors, former military officers, and conservatives who subscribed to alarmist views. Although the committee began as a nonpartisan venture, it became intensely committed to electing a Republican president in 1980 after Carter proved unresponsive to its views.[27]

Alarmists were further bolstered by shifts in public opinion. Still smarting from the Vietnam debacle and concerned about the Soviets' invasion of Afghanistan, many Americans favored a significant military buildup— and the amount of buildup they thought necessary was mounting. Early in 1979 most military analysts spoke of a 1 to 3 percent annual increase in real dollars but widely discussed a buildup of (at least) 15 percent after Afghanistan.

Reagan manifested a curious contradiction in his beliefs. While he was a hawk who wanted to increase military spending hugely, he was also a romantic when it came to nuclear arms. He was morally opposed to their use and wanted to rid the world of them. He had no coherent theory about how to fashion this miracle as he entered his presidency, however. This anomalous quality of Reagan's appeared at several points during his presidency, to the surprise and dismay of some of his advisers.[28]

Estimating the Counterrevolution's Cost

President-elect Reagan appointed Van Cleave to chair a transition force that would cost out a military budget. Van Cleave worked closely with Benjamin Plymale, an executive with Boeing and former Pentagon official, from an office building in Virginia and was given complete access to classified information about the current procurement plans of the armed services, as well as permission to use many Pentagon staffers who estimated the cost of weapons systems. Nor were Van Cleave and Plymale timid. They proposed an immediate supplemental military budget of $20 billion and large annual increases, but they wanted Reagan to avoid specific numbers for fear that "premature numbers might act as a ceiling."[29]

But Van Cleave and Plymale, unable to secure high-level appointments in the Reagan administration, failed to leave behind a military budget proposal, according to Lawrence Korb, who was brought in by Caspar Weinberger to help fashion a military budget.[30] But Van Cleave and Plymale did give Reagan a fifty-five-page report in late March 1981—and large portions of it ended up in various forms in Reagan's budget and defense policy directives. The centerpiece of Reagan's buildup would be the funding of a six-hundred-ship navy. This recommendation was based on top-secret naval planning undertaken during the previous three years by Adm. Thomas Hayward. His recommendations were so warmly received by Sam Nunn, the powerful Georgia Democrat who chaired the Senate Armed Services Committee, that he was promoted to chief of naval operations in 1978. Hayward contended that the Soviet navy had shifted from a defensive orientation, with its submarines and ships dedicated to protecting the homeland, to an offensive strategy that aimed to destroy the U.S. Navy in both Atlantic and Pacific theaters in coordinated and daring maneuvers.[31] He agreed with Zumwalt, that the navy needed 138 new vessels and a massive augmentation of the Pacific Fleet, which was considerably smaller than the Atlantic Fleet because the defense of Europe had priority. Hayward wanted U.S. ships lurking in protective Norwegian fjords to be able to fire missiles at Soviet ships in the Barents Sea, 1,250 miles away on the Soviet Union's northern border. He wanted to immunize the U.S. Navy from a Soviet strike by dispersing it to scores of new and smaller ports on both coasts. And he wanted three new nuclear carriers and an armada of destroyers, submarines, and support vessels, as well as hundreds of aircraft, to accompany them.

Critics doubted that the naval buildup was warranted. Classified naval intelligence maintained that the Soviets kept a vast portion of their ships and submarines near their coasts and in a defensive mode to protect the homeland from nuclear and conventional strikes. They were in no position to initiate offensive strikes against the United States or NATO.[32] Large numbers of Soviet submarines were still powered by diesel rather than nuclear fuel and were vulnerable to missile and bomber attacks because they were stationed near Soviet coastlines. When Soviet naval vessels visited foreign ports, some people observed that many were severely corroded.

Critics asked other questions about the planned naval buildup. Wouldn't U.S. carriers be vulnerable to Soviet missile and bomber strikes? Would the country have the money to maintain and operate a six-hundred-ship navy once it was been built—and would such a commitment prove to be a drain on the army and the air force?[33] Wouldn't some of the navy's new aircraft and missiles duplicate those held by the other services?

Other portions of candidate Reagan's agenda quickly fell into position. Worried that Kemp could divert enough votes in Republican primaries to give George Bush the nomination in 1980, Reagan got Kemp to withdraw from the race by agreeing to support the Kemp-Roth tax legislation—the measure that proposed to slash taxes by 30 percent over three years and to index brackets.[34] During the campaign Reagan was circumspect about stating his desire to cut domestic programs, then signaled his desire for large cuts by selecting Rep. David Stockman, R-Mich., to direct the Office of Management and Budget. Stockman had developed a counterbudget in the spring of 1980 that proposed cutting $38 billion in government spending, mostly from the domestic budget.[35]

Even before Reagan's inauguration, then, a policy blueprint for his administration had emerged in regard to military appropriations, tax cuts, and the domestic budget, even if he had not formulated a precise military budget. However, the emerging budget numbers did not add up. If Reagan were to cut taxes severely and boost military spending, deficits would ensue even with deep cuts in the domestic discretionary budget. Only deep cuts in entitlements could yield a balanced budget because they comprised almost 50 percent of the budget in 1980, but Reagan had already learned that he risked his political future if he even hinted that he would cut entitlements. During the Republican primaries in 1976 Reagan had proposed cutting Social Security and Medicare, to the delight of Jerry Ford, who made Reagan pay dearly for this mistake.[36] Determined not to repeat this error, Reagan did not discuss entitlements in the 1980 campaign and officially placed them off the table scarcely a month after his inauguration, save for some cuts in means-tested entitlements like Aid to Families with Dependent Children (AFDC) and food stamps.

How, then, could Reagan repeatedly promise a balanced budget during his campaign? Partly, he did not understand the budget, mistakenly believing that sufficient savings could be found in domestic discretionary spending or in such means-tested entitlements as AFDC. (A frustrated Stockman could never get Reagan to realize that these items were too small to offset the huge tax cuts and military increases he was touting.)[37] Partly, Reagan simply ignored harsh realities. Lou Cannon, Reagan's most able biographer, speculates that Reagan, the child of an alcoholic, sometimes took flight into the fantasy world that children of alcoholics use to escape the harsh realities they confront.[38] Supply-siders made it even less likely that he would grapple with deficits because they provided a kind of secular religion that tax cuts would be followed by a surge in revenues from the economic growth that they stimulated. As Martin Anderson, Reagan's domestic adviser, has convincingly argued, many supply-siders did not predict that all revenues sacrificed by tax cuts would soon be recouped—indeed, Alan Greenspan predicted that the treasury would regain only half the lost revenues in the first years after the cut—but Reagan (and Edwin Meese, later his attorney general) *inferred* this erroneous conclusion, as their autobiographies clearly reveal.[39] As I discuss subsequently, moreover, Reagan may have tolerated deficits because they placed downward pressure on domestic discretionary spending.

Disguising His Intentions

Reagan obtained the Republican nomination for the presidency in the summer of 1980 by defeating Bush in a campaign largely funded by corporate contributions and wealthy investors and guided by a forty-seven-member, all-male "executive advisory committee."[40] All but two members of Reagan's cabinet appointees were millionaires or near millionaires, and his cabinet members and many other appointees had long-standing ties to large corporations, from military contractors to oil companies. It is hardly surprising that much of the energy of his presidency was directed toward massive deregulation, attacks on the Environmental Protection Agency and the Occupational Safety and Health Administration, opening of offshore lands to drilling, and numerous concessions to timber and mining interests.

It is well known that Reagan came into office dedicated to cutting welfare programs, having invented the term *welfare queen* in 1976.[41] It is less known that Reagan and such aides as Anderson disliked programs that helped the working poor as much as they disliked welfare programs.[42] Reagan did not see government assistance to the working poor as a way to help them better their condition when their wages failed to bring them above the poverty line. Instead, he saw such aid as blunting their work initiative by offering them perverse incentives—even when their wages failed to bring them above the poverty line. So it is no surprise that Reagan targeted means-tested entitlements such as food stamps for cuts, hoping to change their eligibility rules so that working poor people would be made ineligible.

But Reagan knew that he would face an uphill battle. He knew that the Democratic Congress would oppose many of his measures and that the Republicans needed to win control of the Senate so that they could pressure the Democratic House to enact his tax, spending, and military package. He also needed a landslide victory to claim a mandate for his policies and to make conservative southern Democrats fear reprisal in upcoming primaries if they failed to support his policies. (These Boll Weevil Democrats became a pivotal part of Reagan's governing coalition in 1981.)

Remembering Goldwater's defeat vividly, Reagan realized that he had to keep his policies ill defined during the campaign to avoid giving Democrats ammunition. He mentioned *no* specific domestic program that he intended to eliminate, vaguely referred to a military buildup, rarely mentioned his intention to cut income taxes by 30 percent, and frequently promised balanced budgets. Indeed, Reagan's campaign staffers succeeded in presenting Reagan to the voting public as a moderate because they believed that "anyone who is far-right cannot be elected as President of the United States."[43] With the help of public relations expert Mike Deaver, Reagan was carefully scripted in his campaign appearances, which were elegantly staged in surroundings not unlike movie sets. He exuded optimism that the nation's economic woes could be corrected, whereas Carter preferred technical discussion of issues and often urged Americans to make difficult tradeoffs between economic growth and preserving national resources like oil reserves. As Mark Shields astutely observed, Reagan "put a smile on the face of conservatism."[44]

Reagan's cause was greatly aided by mass mailings from an array of conservative groups. The New Religious Political Right (NRPR), which had ninety affiliates by 1980 and huge volunteer and financial resources, set out to wrest the Senate from the Democrats by targeting liberal Democratic senators through TV ads, direct mail, and door-to-door pamphleting, carefully disguising its work as "educational campaigns," lest someone challenge its tax-exempt status.[45] Unprepared for this onslaught, such Democratic senators as Birch Bayh of Indiana and Frank Church of Idaho were ousted by conservative Republicans sympathetic to Reagan's impending counterrevolution. Many southern Democratic legislators also lost their seats because constituent groups of the NRPR, such as Jerry Falwell's Moral Majority, were heavily concentrated in the South.

Finding a Quarterback

Reagan needed a quarterback who would get his legislation through Congress's complex budget process. The budget reforms of 1974 required Congress to develop an annual budget resolution each spring that stated overall tax and spending plans to reach a specific budget goal (such as a specific surplus or deficit) during the coming fiscal year. The work of scores of congressional committees had to be coordinated so that their authorizing and spending totals equalled the totals in the budget resolution. Moreover, tax and entitlement statutes had to be revised in a "reconciliation bill" so they would dovetail with the budget resolution. In this complex process, goals in budget resolutions were vulnerable to sabotage at numerous points, while interest groups and cabinet secretaries could lobby for the restoration of appropriations that had been cut. Presidents Ford and Carter had let Congress develop budget resolutions without much direction from the White House, but Reagan's top aides realized that his sweeping reforms required central direction if they were to be enacted, particularly because Democrats controlled the House of Representatives.

So Reagan centralized budget power in the White House, choosing the brash Stockman to lead the charge.[46] Stockman was eminently qualified for this role because he possessed encyclopedic knowledge of the budget and was familiar with the congressional budget process from his tenure in the House. Moreover, Stockman was an antigovernment ideologue who wanted to downsize the federal government even beyond Reagan's intentions. With Stockman taking the lead, Reagan's first budget proposed to take income, in-kind benefits, or public service jobs from roughly twenty to twenty-five million Americans just above the poverty line—and to make aggregate cuts in the programs for low-income people 2.5 times the size of aggregate cuts in other social programs. Food stamps were be be cut 11 percent, child nutrition programs 28 percent, AFDC 13 percent (mostly by making working poor people ineligible), student financial aid 25 percent, and fuel assistance to the poor 28 percent.[47] Carter's last budget had proposed $100 billion in spending for the poor, but Reagan planned to reduce this to $62 billion. Congress only cut spending for the poor to $82 billion, but 660,000 children lost their Medicaid benefits, one million people became ineligible for food stamps, twenty million received fewer food stamps, 365,000 families with dependent children lost AFDC coverage, 260,000 families had AFDC checks reduced, 3.2 million children no longer participated in school lunch programs, and 500,000 children were dropped from summer meals programs.[48]

Nor were Reagan and his aides unaware of the effects of their policies. Anderson and Meese, hardly liberals, were astonished at Stockman's aggressiveness in targeting these programs, though they took no action to soften his decisions.[49] Nor was the smiling Reagan unaware of his actions, telling Stockman just before his first budget was presented to Congress, "We won't leave you out there alone, Dave. We'll all come to the hanging."[50]

Stockman faced formidable challenges. He needed to get cabinet secretaries to support the spending and tax policies of the administration by overcoming their likely defense of departmental programs. He had to demonstrate that Reagan's tax, military, and spending policies would lead to a balanced budget, as Reagan had promised. He had to battle the Democratic Party and committee leaders, to whom he referred as the "Politburo of the Welfare State," particularly Democratic leaders and chairs of pivotal authorizing and appropriating committees.[51] He had to get Reagan's budget through Congress quickly, before the opposition could mobilize, and he had to convince conservatives that Reagan's proposals would bring balanced budgets soon.

Signals from the Sideline

Unlike supply-siders, Stockman worried about budget deficits, fearing they would exacerbate inflation and slow economic growth by diverting private money from job-producing investments and by sending that money into government bonds. But he soon convinced himself that Reagan could achieve a balanced budget by 1984 by making deep cuts in discretionary spending and some cuts in entitlements. As the designated quarterback, Stockman assumed he would be able to recommend cuts that would restore the budget to balance. He also assumed that he would have considerable authority to modify Reagan's spending and tax recommendations in order to avert huge deficits if economic forecasts became less rosy or if Congress insisted on making changes in Reagan's package.

What Stockman did not realize, however, was that he would be a quarterback who lacked the authority to call signals. Wedded to his tax, military, entitlement, and spending policies, Reagan was determined not to modify them, no matter the course of economic events, much less cede to Stockman the power to make modifications. Only Stockman's ego and naïvêté prevented him from understanding by mid-February that he would not be calling the signals. Meese took Social Security, Medicare, and veterans' benefits off the table in mid-February at Reagan's behest. When Stockman tried to tinker with Social Security by ending the so-called minimum benefit for retirees with little work experience, the public outcry forced Reagan to backtrack.[52]

Nor would Stockman have any power over military spending. When he met with Frank Carlucci, Weinberger's assistant at the Defense Department, to write an estimate in February, Stockman penciled into the budget a 7 percent increase (after inflation) over five years and inadvertently added these increases to Carter's proposed military budget, which already contained a 5 percent annual increase over five years. This yielded a 12 percent annual increase in military spending on top of annual rates of inflation; Stockman's error led to military spending that would rise from $142 billion in 1980 to $368 billion in 1986, for a staggering increase of $226 billion—or a 160 percent rise that was double what Reagan had promised during his campaign.[53] When Reagan announced his proposed military spending increase in his State of the Union message on February 18, along with his tax cuts and his intention to cut large amounts from domestic discretionary spending while balancing the budget by 1984, Stockman naively assumed he was responsible for this huge military budget because of his computational mistake. He did not realize that Reagan and Weinberger, whose modus operandi was to ask for "200 percent, hoping to get 160 percent," probably would have sought comparable increases anyway.[54] (Had Weinberger and Reagan been willing to settle for mere 7 percent annual increases, they would have asked Stockman to correct his error soon after it surfaced—or Carlucci, who had long budgeting experience, would have corrected it on the spot.)

Nor would Stockman have the power to change the size of the huge tax cuts. Reagan decided at numerous points during 1981 that he would push these cuts even when presented with evidence that deficits would exceed $200 billion a year in coming years. Neither he or Don Regan, his treasury secretary, would agree to Democrats' suggestions in 1981 and later that the tax cut be reduced. Indeed, such White House aides as Meese and Anderson viewed Stockman as a traitor even for suggesting modest tax increases in subsequent years.[55]

Stockman was spared from having to make immediate adjustments in Reagan's package because he relied on rosy economic projections in early 1981 that predicted that tax revenues would rise rapidly, but he had a sinking feeling even in February that huge deficits loomed—and some economists already were warning that Reagan's counterrevolution would cost far more than the nation's revenues could support.[56] Stockman later blamed himself for not trying to abort the whole effort even in February. Had he not followed Reagan's script on military, tax, and entitlement fronts, however, he would have been quickly replaced or overridden by Reagan. Had he tried to cut military spending less than Reagan wanted, Weinberger would have gone over Stockman's head to Reagan, as Weinberger did on numerous subsequent occasions.

So the game plan was set by mid-February: an all-or-nothing approach to secure enactment of Reagan's tax and spending cuts and his increases in military spending while claiming the budget would balance by 1984. Reagan would claim his landslide victory as a mandate for these sweeping changes, even if he did not discuss them in fiscal terms during the campaign of 1980 and gave the misleading impression he would obtain balanced budgets.

Manipulating the Budget Process

By framing his proposal as an economic package designed to end stagflation and not as a collection of separate initiatives, Reagan hoped to create an atmosphere that would make the plan's enactment appear urgent.[57] If Congress balked, he threatened to blame its members for the economic situation during the congressional election campaigns of 1982—when voters were already traumatized by soaring gas prices and the double-digit inflation that crested above 20 percent in 1980. Perhaps Reagan's greatest challenge, however, was to convince legislators that his economic package would lead to balanced budgets, because he knew his package would not be viewed as a compelling anti-inflation measure otherwise. He realized too that many conservative legislators in both parties revered balanced budgets, including the Republican chair of the Senate Budget Committee, Pete Domenici of New Mexico. Reagan feared that Democrats might counterattack in the House with a budget proposal with smaller tax increases and smaller military increases, which would allow them to argue their's was more fiscally responsible than his. So Reagan's strategists made a tactical decision to give the impression the budget would balance by 1984 by focusing on spending cuts while downplaying both the tax cuts and the military increases.[58]

To focus on spending cuts rather than the probable deficits that the complete Reagan package would incur, Stockman and James A. Baker, White House chief of staff, cleverly manipulated the budget process. Budget reforms enacted in 1974 required Congress to enact a budget resolution that established a target deficit (or surplus) and aggregate spending and tax approaches to achieve it before proceeding to specific cuts. Stockman and Baker decided to write a budget proposal that detailed myriad domestic spending cuts and did not even mention the military increases or tax cuts in it. If this so-called legislation, which they called an "omnibus reconciliation bill," was enacted first, it would give the misleading impression that Reagan's package focused on spending cuts rather than on huge military increases and tax cuts, thus suggesting that Reagan's entire package would quickly lead to a balanced budget by 1984.[59]

Moreover, they disguised the extent to which the tax cuts and military spending would add to deficits by spreading them over several years. The Reagan plan would cut income taxes by 10 percent in each of the next three years. Military spending would increase in yearly increments, from $142 billion in 1980 to $368 billion in 1986, as weapons were placed in production. With most of the costs of the tax cuts and military increases thus deferred, Reagan could claim that his 1982 budget would incur only a modest deficit. Few people understood the budget well enough to discern what would happen as tax cuts and military increases were put into place in later years.

Stockman, who did not trust Congress's resolve to cut spending, identified scores of spending cuts for hundreds of specific programs in a black book that he locked in a White House safe and even cabinet secretaries could not see.[60] When the projected cuts were finally revealed to them, Stockman denied the secretaries their traditional right to appeal specific cuts to the president and forced them to go instead through a White House budget committee staffed by people from Stockman's office.

Stockman and Baker realized that they had to begin Reagan's revolution in the Senate, where Republicans had won a majority in the 1980 elections. To succeed in the Senate, however, they had to work closely with Domenici, who was convinced that the Reagan revolution would bring huge deficits and who did not want to leave as his legacy a contribution to deficits. Domenici coyly agreed to support Stockman's measure to cut spending, which bundled hundreds of cuts in domestic discretionary programs, because Domenici was convinced that even these cuts were insufficient to offset Reagan's large tax cut. So the senator also insisted that the legislation freeze cost-of-living adjustments (COLAs) for Social Security for a year.[61]

Domenici's proposed limit on COLAs was alarming to Stockman and Baker for two reasons. If they conceded this change, Domenici might later insist on other changes in Reagan's package to avert deficits, which might leave the entire package in tatters and give House Democrats ammunition. And cutting the COLA could alienate those Republican legislators who feared Democrats would attack them in 1982 for cutting Social Security. So Baker persuaded Reagan to make a trip to the Hill to persuade Domenici to abandon COLAs. Reagan told Domenici, "We just can't get suckered into [touching Social Security]. . . . The other side's waiting to pounce."[62] After the Senate Budget Committee rubber-stamped Stockman's cuts in the domestic discretionary budget, Stockman had to overcome another major hurdle: a Republican-sponsored amendment on the Senate floor to restore $1 billion for education, heating fuel and weatherization funds for the poor, community and mental health services, and mass transit—increases that, if enacted, would have opened the door for restoration of other domestic measures. Baker and Domenici persuaded sixteen Democrats (mostly from the South) to oppose the amendment. When it was defeated 59–41, Stockman believed for the first time that Reagan's package had a chance to pass Congress.

Once the full Senate approved these spending cuts, Stockman pressed senators to enact a budget resolution that encompassed not just Reagan's spending cuts but his tax cuts and military increases, as well as his promise of balanced budgets by 1984. Once again Stockman had to outmaneuver a reluctant Domenici, who remained convinced that even $74 billion in cuts from domestic spending would not allow a balanced budget by 1984—views shared by such deficit hawks as Republican senators Bill Armstrong of Colorado and Charles Grassley of Iowa. Republican senators were so worried that the package would cause deficits that most of them voted *against* it in the Senate Budget Committee, where Armstrong asked whether such huge military increases would bust the budget. So the measure was defeated 12–8 in committee as Democrats and Republicans alike threatened to expose the counterrevolution as a deficit-exacerbating program that would result in a $60 billion deficit in 1984.[63]

As prominent Republicans declared the "fundamental architecture" of the Reagan budget package to be flawed, Stockman feared that the Reagan counterrevolution was over. When Domenici announced he would demand that Reagan make smaller tax cuts, Stockman played hardball, leaking a story to the *Wall Street Journal* that "John Maynard Domenici" was a closet Keynesian rather than a believer in supply-side economics—a charge in Republican circles tantamount to being called an atheist in a Fundamentalist congregation.[64] Domenici caved in under a barrage of phone calls from Reagan, whose popularity had soared after the assassination attempt on March 30, 1981. Because they did not want to be accused of sabotaging the counterrevolution, Domenici and the other Republican senators now supported a budget resolution that rubber-stamped the entire Reagan package, even if it retained what Stockman termed a "magic asterisk" that referred to undesignated cuts that supposedly would bring the package into balance by 1984.

Reagan and his aides used other tactics to disguise the extent to which his package would cause deficits. He underestimated increases in entitlements. He made excessively rosy economic forecasts to exaggerate tax revenues for the next five years. He manipulated internal economic projections to overstate revenues and rejected the less optimistic economic forecasts from the Congressional Budget Office. Mesmerized by soothing administration predictions for more than six months, most legislators and the public remained in the dark until the next year, when deficits commenced that would range from $200 billion to $300 billion for the next thirteen years.

What made Reagan's proposals so terrifying to many Democratic legislators was their demagogic value. Given his landslide victory and his awesome communication skills, might Reagan further inflame public opinion into a frenzied desire for tax and spending cuts, not to mention increased military spending? Could he realign American politics by using these themes to convert the Republican Party into a majority party for decades to come? Many Democrats had voted for a Republican president for the first time in 1980. Both the tax-and-spend and soft-on-communism epithets had particular force in conservative districts of the South where Republicans had made heavy inroads in the 1970s and where Reagan had run particularly strongly. Many Boll Weevils feared they would be targeted by Republicans or conservative Democrats if they opposed Reagan's program.

Democrats' fears were further heightened by the assassination attempt. Reagan's popularity had been sagging and his counterrevolution stalled before John Hinckley took aim. Afterward, Reagan's popularity surged, and it seemed almost unpatriotic to deny the Gipper his legislative package.

Divide and Conquer

Faced with a multifaceted package from a popular president who aimed to stampede Congress, Democrats were bewildered about how to proceed. Most decided not to contest Reagan's military increases, raising few objections in the spring or summer and stifling their reservations about the simplistic assumptions that undergirded them, such as the Soviets' supposed offensive intentions or their military superiority. Indeed, some Democrats urged additions to the Reagan buildup, such as large increases in conventional forces. Scoop Jackson, the Washington State Democrat who had helped Nixon frustrate doves' attempts to cut military spending, worked closely with John Tower of Texas to push Reagan's proposals through the Senate. Meanwhile, key military specialists on the staffs of Democratic legislators supported Reagan's huge military requests, delighted that their patrons had dodged the charge of being soft on communism.

The next decision for Democrats was whether to oppose spending cuts, tax cuts, or both. Stockman was astonished in early meetings with such Democratic House leaders as Tip O'Neill, Jim Wright of Texas, and Dan Rostenkowski of Illinois that they did not militantly oppose many of the domestic spending cuts that he proposed; apparently, they had decided that if they opposed the cuts, they would be vulnerable to the charge that they had contributed to inflation.[65] Aware that Stockman would try to divide them by appealing to Boll Weevils who favored large spending cuts, Democratic leaders realized they might be outvoted by a coalition of Democrats and Republicans.

Democrats made a first major mistake when both Wright and O'Neill naively believed that, if they acquiesced in the cuts, voters would blame Republicans in 1982 and 1984 after finding services had been slashed.[66] This might have happened if entitlements had been the focus of Reagan's cuts, but only low- and moderate-income people would feel the cuts in eligibility for means-tested entitlements—people who often failed to vote.

House Democrats still presented a problem for Stockman. Jim Jones of Oklahoma, the Democratic chair of the House Budget Committee, let Stockman know that he wanted to limit the tax cuts to 10 percent and that he wanted Stockman to restore funds for such programs as child nutrition. Fearing once more that the entire package might unravel, Stockman and Baker decided to take matters into their own hands by trying to engineer a vote on the House floor on a budget resolution that was similar to the Senate's, thus bypassing the House Democratic leadership. Now Jones and his associate, Leon Panetta of California, were in a difficult position, trying to appease Boll Weevils while trying to hold such Democratic liberals as Ron Dellums of California in the Democratic coalition. The House Democratic leadership added scores of concessions to conservatives and liberals in the proposed budget resolution—including new spending cuts to show that their version would bring lower deficits than Reagan's while overriding some of Stockman's cuts to appease liberals. When the Democrats used budget gimmicks, Stockman countered with his own gimmicks and his own concessions to Boll Weevils—and both sides claimed *their* version would not aggravate the deficit.[67]

Now well into recovering from his bullet wounds, Reagan used television appearances and personal contacts to persuade Boll Weevils to defect. O'Neill realized that a coalition of Republicans and Boll Weevils probably would prevail and allowed floor votes on the budget resolutions offered by Jones and Reagan. Meanwhile, Democrat Phil Gramm of Texas was convincing other Boll Weevils to defect to Reagan's package. When the House approved the budget resolution on May 8, complete with the 30 percent tax cuts, huge military increases, and large spending cuts, the Reagan counterrevolution had begun.

Democrats made another critical mistake at this juncture. Reasoning that Reagan would be able to starve social programs for years to come if the Kemp-Roth tax cut was enacted, many Democrats decided to make a last stand on taxes. Rostenkowski, chair of the House Ways and Means Committee, tried, for example, to direct the tax cuts to people with modest incomes while proposing that the tax cuts be limited to 10 percent for a single year. Rather than demand that the tax cuts in the second and third years be pegged to the deficit so they could be canceled or diminished if deficits soared, Rostenkowski tried to condition them on whether they raised inflation—a relatively abstract notion that did not gain widespread support.[68] In courting the Boll Weevils, Reagan threw many sweeteners into the tax legislation, finally agreeing to limit the three-year tax cut to 25 percent. The events of the summer of 1981 were anticlimactic as Congress approved Reagan's entire package.

As clever as Stockman and Baker may have been at numerous points, their political skills ought not be exaggerated—the essence of much of Reagan's program was pork. As American history has frequently demonstrated, few politicians can resist the lure of tax decreases or increases in military spending that play to the worldly concerns of constituents and special interests.

Although he achieved astonishing success in his first year in office, many wondered whether Reagan's revolution had staying power. It remained to be seen, moreover, whether his impending deficits, as well as the bloated military budget, would ultimately deprive the treasury of several trillion dollars that might have been put to more constructive use.

11

Reagan's Gordian Knot

In 1981 Reagan tied an intricate knot with four strands —military spending, tax cuts, retention of entitlements, and cuts in domestic discretionary spending— that remained unbreakable during his presidency even though it was clear by early 1982 that it would cause extraordinary deficits for years to come. Republican senators like Pete Domenici of New Mexico and Bob Dole of Kansas tried to untie the knot in the 1980s because it created huge deficits; they sometimes were joined in fragile coalition by such Democratic House chieftains as Tip O'Neill, Jim Wright, and Dan Rostenkowski. But they labored in vain. Why did Reagan's Gordian knot prove so durable for the next seven years and even into the presidencies of George Bush and Bill Clinton? What effects did the knot have on national priorities and domestic spending? I argue here and in chapter 15 that Reagan's combined spending and tax policies yielded $3.4 trillion in waste that could have been used for more constructive purposes.

From an Ordinary Knot to a Gordian Knot

Even in late 1981, when Stockman fully understood that Reagan's economic plan would create huge deficits, Reagan made clear that he would
abide no fundamental modifications in it. Desperately looking for ways to
slow the deficit's growth, Stockman suggested that Reagan consider light
brakes on the rate of increases in military spending. At a meeting in the
Oval Office with Reagan and Weinberger to discuss whether to make such
small cuts, Stockman noticed that Reagan sat bolt upright as Weinberger
made his case against cuts by displaying both a Soviet tank superimposed
over the Capitol and a chart with two GI Joes. One GI Joe was bespecta-
cled, wimpy, and held a handgun; he symbolized Stockman's cuts. The
muscular macho toy soldier held an assault weapon and symbolized the
full-fledged buildup. Stockman realized that he had lost the "debate" when
he presented his more conventional charts and Reagan's eyes glazed over.[1]

In January 1982 Reagan ruled out any tax increases as well as any cuts in
his military budget, even though Stockman had secretly notified the president that the deficit would approach $100 billion. (Reagan said, "Raising
taxes won't balance the budget. It will encourage more government spending and less private investment.")[2] Despite numerous lectures from Stockman that his policies had created a chronic imbalance between revenues
and spending, Reagan refused to accept blame for the emerging deficit and
made clear that his "solution" would rely exclusively on drastic cuts in discretionary domestic spending. Reagan stuck by his solution, even though
Stockman told him repeatedly that these domestic cuts would hardly dent
the epic deficit. Many Democrats, already remorseful that they had
acceded to Reagan's spending cuts in 1981, militantly opposed further cuts
in domestic spending in 1982 as a major recession drew attention to the
plight of poor people whose social programs had been cut.

Paul Volcker, head of the Federal Reserve, warned of economic disaster
if the deficits were not dealt with. Stockman informed Reagan in mid-February that his budget was in deep trouble. But the Gipper dug in, not even
listening to Republican leaders who warned of the impending deficit.[3]
Domenici declared Reagan's budget dead in late February and proposed an
alternative budget with new taxes, cuts in military spending, freezes in federal pay, limits on increases in Medicare and Medicaid, a freeze on cost-of-
living adjustments (COLAs), and a freeze on domestic discretionary

spending for three years. Sen. Fritz Hollings of South Carolina proposed an alternative Democratic budget that would trim the deficit by freezing military spending at 1982 levels, halving the 1983 tax cut, and freezing certain federal benefits.[4] Unable to decide whether to let Reagan take the blame for the deficit or to join efforts to secure an alternative congressional budget, the House Democratic leadership remained silent, finally deciding to await a Republican Senate initiative to be certain that Reagan and the Republicans would support such controversial measures as freezing COLAs before lending Democratic support.[5]

It became clear that no deal could emerge without negotiations between Reagan and congressional leaders, particularly in an election year. Legislators feared retaliation by voters if taxes were raised or entitlements cut. Reagan demanded deeper domestic cuts, opposed large tax increases, and opposed military cuts—and accused Democrats of wanting a "bargain basement military." He rejected a deal worked out by White House staff and congressional negotiators that proposed a $30 billion tax increase, a rollback in Reagan's military increases, a 4 percent surcharge on incomes higher than $35,000, and a three-year freeze on domestic discretionary spending.[6] (A bipartisan group of seventeen legislative leaders had developed this package in exhaustive talks.) Democrats disengaged from these talks too, afraid that Reagan meant to set them up on the tax issue in the 1982 elections and with second thoughts about the three-year freeze on domestic spending. As the talks fell apart, the Office of Management and Budget startled the nation by predicting a deficit of $180 billion in the coming fiscal year with no end in sight—the largest deficit since World War II. Reagan himself feared Republican losses in these elections as the nation slid into a deep recession. He and GOP leaders finally agreed on a budget fashioned by Domenici that cut the forthcoming deficit to $105 billion by increasing corporate taxes and closing some loopholes; cutting domestic discretionary spending by $39 billion; and cutting Social Security by $40 billion by freezing its benefits. But this budget went nowhere because Democrats attacked its cuts in Social Security. Moderate Republicans released their own budget, which focused on trimming the military buildup while rescuing Social Security and domestic spending; they feared Democrats would use these proposed cuts against them in the 1982 elections. Reagan too feared losses in the 1982 congressional elections and backed off on the entitlement cuts. Senate Republicans reconfigured their budget by rescinding entitlement cuts, but the House of Representatives was stalemated, so divided ideologically that it could approve no budget proposal. The House finally approved a Republican budget resolution by one vote, which led to a compromise with the Senate's version that Democrats grudgingly accepted as the best they could get. (Reagan supported this budget resolution only because he was convinced that Democrats had agreed to cut three dollars in domestic spending for every dollar in tax increases.) This budget barely modified Reagan's 1981 policies, hardly slowed his military buildup, backed off entitlements cuts, and made token cuts in discretionary spending—and reduced the deficit in the coming year only to $208 billion.

Both parties emerged from these budget deliberations even more wary of each other. The Democrats used Republicans' early toying with entitlement cuts against them in the elections—a tactic partly responsible for cutting the Republicans' majority in the House. Reagan believed that Democrats had reneged on their promise to cut domestic spending when they put together the appropriations bills, forcing him to sign spending legislation that he disliked on election eve. Democrats were furious that Reagan rigidly refused to cut military spending, rescind some of the huge tax cuts of 1981, or restore some of the spending cuts of 1981. Senate Democrats would not even vote for the tax increases that Reagan endorsed, convinced that Republicans would try to pin the tax increases on them in the 1982 elections. Leaders of both political parties, including such Republican conservatives as Domenici and Dole, were horrified by the extraordinary deficits that Reagan's policies had created. Nor were many liberals content with Reagan's policies, which redistributed resources from low- and moderate-income citizens to the affluent and corporate elites.

The politics of 1982 reveal why Reagan's Gordian knot endured for the remainder of his presidency. Above all, Reagan exerted no leadership to undo the Gordian knot, conceding no miscalculations in his budgets, even as Stockman repeatedly told him he had vastly overestimated future revenues and that he faced structural deficits stemming from a chronic gap between revenues and expenditures.[7] Reagan dared Congress to unravel his masterpiece, vowing to use the full power of his office, including vetoes, to stymie them. Nor were Reagan and his top aides charitable to people like Stockman, who repeatedly warned them of impending deficits or sought corrective action, such as tax increases. Indeed, Meese called Stockman a "tax-hiking mole in a tax-cutting government."[8]

Congress, in turn, labored under mighty handicaps when confronted with presidential hostility, because Reagan framed budget deficits in ideo-logical and partisan terms when he declared that they were caused by tax-and-spend Democrats. If Democrats proposed tax increases, they could count on many Republicans to attack them in partisan terms. Nor could Democrats consistently present a united front because the Boll Weevils were less willing than liberal Democrats to support military cuts or tax increases. Republicans who wanted to untie Reagan's Gordian knot labored under their own hardships. Because they were less willing to abide cuts in military spending or tax increases than liberal Democrats, they had to endorse cuts in entitlements—such as freezing COLAs in Social Secu-rity and other benefit programs—if they wished to curtail deficits. When-ever Republicans proposed these remedies, however, Democrats lambasted them as indifferent to senior citizens.[9] As Republican leaders discovered in 1982 and ensuing years, moreover, Reagan was not afraid to attack them as vehemently as he attacked Democrats if Republicans proposed major revi-sions in his policies. Aware that Reagan had transformed the Republican Party from a minority to a majority party and that his landslide victory had allowed them to win control of the Senate for the first time since 1947–1949, few Republicans wanted a public confrontation with him.

Any serious effort to untie the Gordian knot also required that each side be willing to concede certain points that ran against its beliefs or political interests in order to get concessions. The challenge was to get some mix of tax increases, military cuts, and entitlement cuts. Haggling over the budget is always a difficult process. Republicans usually want domestic spending cuts before they will concede tax increases; Democrats want tax increases before they concede domestic spending cuts. Military spending proved to be an especially controversial item in these budget debates, with Democrats proposing military cuts that the Boll Weevils and many Republicans opposed.

Nor did leaders of either party trust one another during these delibera-tions. Republicans feared the Democrats would pin entitlement cuts on them, and Democrats feared Republicans would accuse them of seeking tax increases. Virtually all House Republicans refused to vote for major tax increases through the balance of Reagan's term, because they knew their opponents could use the issue effectively in the next election. With lead-ers of both parties recognizing their vulnerability if they proposed initia-tives that their opponents could use against them, they mostly refrained from major deficit-reduction initiatives.

And neither side of the aisle trusted the president and his top aides. Would the president undo months of negotiations by vetoing a budget package? Would his aides leak key concessions that a party leader had proposed, exposing the legislator to the wrath of party members and even electoral defeat?[10]

Party leaders nonetheless initiated proposals to untie the Gordian knot during the 1980s because they feared voter retaliation for the huge Reagan deficits. Then they would sit in frustrating "budget summits" with the president, where fundamental changes were usually defeated.

It is remarkable that political leaders invested as much energy in deficit reduction as they did in light of the public's indifference. Politicians of both parties discovered in the elections of 1982 that voters cared more about policies affecting their personal lives than the federal deficit.[11] Polls consistently suggested that most voters were leery of raising taxes and opposed cutting entitlements, even if huge deficits ensued. While many voters favored a reduction in the size of the military buildup, legislators of both parties were reluctant to staunch the flow of military dollars into their districts. So the voters too favored mañana, preferring to abide deficits rather than the personal sacrifices needed to untie the Gordian knot.[12]

In this polarized atmosphere coupled with public apathy and no presidential leadership, periodic budget settlements cut budget deficits only marginally, although the various deficit-cutting deals together substantially reduced what the deficit would have been had Reagan's fiscal policies of 1981 continued unchecked. The budget deficit for fiscal 1983 was $208 billion and remained at similar levels for most of the next fifteen years in what a disenchanted Stockman called "a willful act of ignorance and grotesque irresponsibility. . . . In the entire 20th century fiscal history of the nation, there has been nothing to rival it."[13]

The Gordian Knot Binds the Domestic Agenda

Reagan flailed at the pathetically small domestic discretionary programs and means-tested entitlements like a boxer who, having bloodied his opponent, wants to drive him to the canvas. Having cut social services by nearly a quarter in 1981 and tightened AFDC eligibility, Reagan pushed ahead with a second round of "New Federalism" in 1982 that proposed to shift food stamps, AFDC, and forty-three other grant programs to the states in return for the federal government's taking sole funding responsibility for Medicaid. (Reagan saw this 1982 transfer as merely the first phase of a broader transfer over ten years that would involve forty programs costing $47 billion and that would cede virtually all social programs to the states, save Medicare, Medicaid, and Social Security.) Although Reagan's aides told the governors they would come out even financially, other analysts contended the states would be big losers.[14] Moynihan, now a Democratic senator from New York, contended that the states would have to raise taxes by 8.8 percent or cut welfare and food stamps by nearly a third in the coming year to fund the added costs of the transfer, even though Reagan promised to give the states $28 billion a year by placing certain excise taxes in a "grass roots trust fund."[15] Governors quickly realized that the deal disguised further cuts in domestic spending, because the trust fund would be given only $28 billion to cover the forty programs funded at $47 billion.[16] Still smarting from the federal budget cuts of the previous year that had drastically cut federal resources for scores of social programs, the governors forced the administration to abandon the swap by early April. Nor did Congress accept some other cuts that Reagan proposed, signaling that it would not accept large spending cuts in coming years.

Reagan introduced new rounds of cuts in early 1983, as well as a broad freeze in the growth of domestic spending programs. He used the deficit, which he threatened would soon rise to $300 billion, as a club to make Congress cut spending.[17] Nor was Reagan inclined to make any cuts in the military buildup—he wanted real increases of 11 percent for the military in fiscal 1984 to supplement the real increase of 12 percent he had pushed through in the previous two years. Also, like clockwork, the Democrats fought to avert cuts and freezes in domestic programs. Now that the country was in a deep recession, most Boll Weevils abandoned Reagan. With the Democrats successfully portraying Reagan as excessively harsh on the poor, his cutting mania abated somewhat in 1984 as the presidential election loomed. He proposed few cuts and ran a "feel-good" campaign from the Rose Garden that emphasized the nation's prosperity.

In this hostile environment liberals dramatically downsized their policy goals from the 1960s and 1970s. Placed on the defensive, they mainly sought to avert further cuts in domestic programs rather than seek to increase their funding. Sometimes they insisted they would not support

Reagan's military increases if he did not compromise on social spending. Sometimes they presented him with modest increases in social spending, daring him to veto appropriations bills during a deep recession. But they were poorly positioned to augment the domestic agenda because Reagan accused them of exacerbating the very deficits that he had created whenever they sought increases in social programs. Moreover, public opinion was hardly in the liberals' corner. Although only 13 percent of voters believed that the federal government spent too much on domestic programs, only 28 percent believed the federal government should "do all possible to help the poor"—down from 38 percent in 1973.[18] In other words, the widespread cynicism about government that had grown since Vietnam and Watergate focused primarily on the federal government's responsibility for helping poor people.

Reagan's Hubris

Although the Reagan knot severely circumscribed domestic discretionary spending, such was not the case with respect to military spending. Reagan claimed the buildup, which he predicated on such flawed premises as inflated estimates of Soviet capabilities and intentions, would speed peace by bankrupting the Soviet Union as it tried to match increases in U.S. military spending. (In effect, Reagan inverted Truman's and Eisenhower's argument that the Soviet Union meant to bankrupt the United States by manipulating it to spend excessively on its military.)

Reagan's theory contained a kernel of truth: the Soviet economy could ill afford its military expenditures and the cost of an empire that included propping up Cuba and financing insurgencies in Africa and Eastern Europe and adventurism in Afghanistan. Even incremental increases in military spending would harm the fragile Soviet economy. But Reagan's belief that he held the key to the Soviets' demise was simplistic. The Soviets had already vastly increased their military spending before the 1980s, achieving strategic parity by vastly increasing their ICBMs and SLBMs in the 1970s. Subsequent analysis of Soviet military spending provides no evidence that the Soviets significantly escalated their military spending in the 1980s in response to Reagan's military buildup. (The 3 percent rise in Soviet military spending from 1985 to 1988, for example, was initiated before Reagan took office.)[19]

Lacking knowledge of the intricacies of Soviet history, Reagan also failed to consider the possibility that a U.S. military buildup might slow the course of reform within the Soviet Union. Reform had tenuously existed in Russia since the nineteenth century as an array of dissidents had tried to convince high-level officials to allow more freedoms, to tolerate some holding of private property, or to decentralize the economy. Savagely repressed by Stalin, the reform impulse had reemerged during the regime of Nikita Khrushchev, who himself succumbed to a repressive order presided over by Leonid Brezhnev. As Stephen Cohen astutely observes, dissidents were most vulnerable in Soviet history when East-West relations soured, such as before and after World War II and in the mid- and late 1960s when Soviet hard-liners could persuasively contend that the country had to have a powerful military to protect its interests.[20]

Make no mistake: the Soviets viewed Reagan as a serious threat to their existence. The KGB advised "its stations in Western capitals that the U.S. was preparing to attack the Soviet Union," John Newhouse has reported, and told them to try to find out when the attack might occur. (The KGB did not rescind this order until 1983.)[21] Reagan's buildup was so provocative to the Soviets that Reagan observed during a 1985 summit that after a 1984 NATO exercise that simulated the firing of nuclear weapons at the Soviet Union (ABLE ARCHER), the Kremlin feared that the United States intended a first nuclear strike.[22]

Reagan's theory that he could decisively change the course of Soviet history by spending a trillion additional dollars on his military reeks of hubris. Political systems rise and fall primarily from internal developments, not from the actions of outsiders—as even the United States has had to admit when it has sought, in vain, to advance human rights in China and elsewhere. The Soviet Union was ripe for upheaval and dissolution even before Reagan commenced his buildup. Brezhnev's conservative allies were hard-pressed to defend a Soviet system that could barely feed its people and failed to invest in its consumer-based industries, its agriculture, or its health-care system. Party leaders and bureaucrats managed the Soviet economy from Moscow in a corrupt and inefficient way, repressed such ideas as decentralization and limited private markets, and lacked any strategy for reforming the economy. Severe tensions and conflicts, including rebellions in Eastern Europe and escalating defections and escapes over guarded borders and the Berlin Wall, had already eroded the Soviet empire before Reagan took office. Moynihan predicted as early as

1975 that the Soviet Union would ultimately succumb to ethnic conflict.[23] Moreover, as I discuss in more detail in chapter 12, Mikhail Gorbachev made a series of tactical mistakes that speeded the Soviet Union's dissolution.[24]

The Naval Juggernaut

Over the objections of some of his closest aides, Reagan appointed John Lehman, a brash proponent of naval power, to be secretary of navy in early 1981. Alarmed by the precipitous decline in the fleet, from 1,000 ships in 1968 to roughly 480 ships by 1981 and from 33 carriers in 1963 to 13 by 1976, Lehman accepted Adm. Elmo Zumwalt's call in the mid-1970s to rebuild the navy to 600 ships as well as Jimmy Carter's requests for new carriers. To bolster the naval budget Lehman launched a campaign that was unprecedented in its ferocity. He wanted $1 trillion for the navy, to enlarge its personnel and operations as well as to purchase, among other items, three new carrier groups ($54 billion), 27 Aegis cruisers ($27 billion), 40 new Trident submarines ($40 billion), and additional aircraft ($128 billion). Aware that the success of his campaign required that he make alarmist assessments of the Soviet navy, Lehman set out to convince the president, top military officials, and navy boosters in Congress that the Soviet navy was designed to be an offensive force and was capable of delivering a devastating blow to the United States in a first-strike offensive.

After he learned that naval intelligence had recently found that the Soviet navy was not designed to be an offensive force and was inferior to the existing U.S. Navy, Lehman fabricated data or gave misleading information. He suppressed a 1982 study that showed the navy could afford only a 450 to 500–ship fleet, even with its $1 trillion.[25] He fired intelligence officers who might leak accurate data and replaced them with people who would supply supportive data.[26] He built a wall around naval intelligence within the Pentagon so that outside analysts could not question the data that he released. Counting everything in the water, including patrol boats, he claimed the Soviets possessed seventeen hundred ships.

Many critics within the navy and the Defense Department contended that the United States could not maintain a six-hundred-ship fleet because the maintenance and operating costs would be staggering, as would the costs of recruiting and maintaining of tens of thousands of sailors. When Lawrence Korb, on the defense secretary's staff, confronted Lehman in 1982 about the impossibility of sustaining a six-hundred-ship navy, Lehman angrily replied, "Who cares, we're not going to be here."[27]

Lehman was also skilled at enlisting Ronald Reagan's support. When Paul Thayer was appointed deputy secretary of defense in 1983, for example, he became so incensed that the navy was receiving the lion's share of military resources that he decided to cancel two of its carriers with Weinberger's consent. Before he could issue his order, however, Lehman asked Reagan to name the two carriers, thus making their construction inevitable.[28] Because Reagan had loved military adventures since his movie career, Lehman conducted flamboyant and unnecessary naval maneuvers.

Lehman built an elaborate political and public relations apparatus to sustain naval expansion. He made nonstop media appearances. He publicized the incessant launching of new vessels. He orchestrated the careful placement of contracts and facilities in the districts of legislators on the armed services committees and the defense appropriations subcommittees. He scattered scores of new "home ports" along U.S. coastlines on the dubious assumption that dispersing the fleet among small ports would make it less vulnerable to Soviet attack.[29] He used home ports to reward legislators who supported the navy's expansion and to punish those who did not, telling Democratic senator Claiborne Pell that Rhode Island would have none of the home ports after he had the temerity to call them pork. So successful was Lehman that the navy received $81 billion in 1983, whereas the air force and army had to make do with $74 billion and $57 billion, respectively.)[30]

Lehman developed procurement procedures that made its purchases even more costly as the navy rushed to spend its windfall.[31] Career naval procurement officers had managed procurement before Lehman took office; now he placed it directly under his personal control so that he could decide in whose districts the contracts were placed, use corporations that particular legislators favored, and avert external monitoring by higher-level Pentagon authorities and the General Accounting Office. Both of the latter increasingly complained that they lacked even rudimentary cost data about specific weapons and believed that Lehman deliberately understated the cost of aircraft.[32] Many contracts were were awarded to corporations based merely on an assessment that they were best able to do the job. Without competitive bids and a requirement that the companies build prototypes first, the military often found itself, years later, with huge cost overruns and malfunctioning weapons.

Legislators on key committees were often at the center of the procurement process. Corporate officials and consultants literally streamed through the offices of such legislators as Rep. William Chappell, the Florida Democrat who chaired the House Defense Appropriations Subcommittee and who often authorized and funded weapons systems and technology that the Pentagon had rejected. (Chappell once boasted that he often saw one hundred corporate officials a day in his congressional offices.)[33] In return, corporations would donate generously to the campaigns of legislators, give them honoraria, and allow them to use corporate jets.

Consultants, corporate officials, legislative staffers, and Pentagon officials freely associated with one another at social events organized by associations whose membership was secret to anyone but other members.[34] At lavish social events in exotic places these people exchanged classified information and made key contacts in a kind of seamless web that crossed organizational boundaries and that invited conflicts of interest. Thousands of so-called military consultants—who often were former employees of the Pentagon or of military contractors—acted as middlemen between the Pentagon and the corporations, informing corporations of forthcoming contracts or weapons that Pentagon officials contemplated and helping Pentagon officials locate firms that possessed the technical competence to fulfill specific contracts. These consultants often engaged in unethical practices, such as obtaining classified planning documents from the Pentagon that they conveyed to client corporations to give them an inside track on contracts or illicitly obtaining confidential bids on specific contracts so their clients could underbid their competition.

Already subject to abuse, military procurement became a sieve when unscrupulous people teamed up within and outside the Pentagon. Lehman appointed Melvyn Paisley as assistant secretary of the navy in charge of research and engineering, for example, even though Paisley had been censured for illegally obtaining classified military documents while working for Boeing Aircraft.[35] With Lehman's knowledge, Paisley worked closely with Bill Galvin, a military consultant with a poor reputation. Galvin bribed Pentagon officials to obtain contracts for clients and helped steer campaign contributions from his clients to key legislators to secure funding of their projects.[36] Paisley received kickbacks for the awarding of contracts and gave contracts to a firm that he had secretly formed with

Galvin. Paisley impeded outside monitoring of key contracts so that non-performance and malfeasance would not be discovered.

Such illegal behavior might have gone undetected had not "Mr. X," a still-anonymous individual who was a defense company executive, called the U.S. attorney in Virginia to report that a consultant named John Marlowe had solicited Mr. X for a bribe on the promise that Marlowe would get the defense executive a military contract. Confronted by government investigators, Marlowe agreed to let the FBI tap his phones in return for immunity from prosecution—he was hoping to escape prosecution for bribery and to decrease jail time for a child-molestation conviction.[37] The prosecutors, who dubbed their investigation Operation Illwind, worked their way up into the Pentagon's hierarchy as they immunized scores of additional consultants to secure information about bribes and other illegal activities. They raided offices of corporate officials and military consultants in forty-four locations in a final blitz that led to many indictments and guilty pleas. Prosecutors collected fines of $190 million and sent many people to jail, including Paisley and Galvin. Those convicted probably would have included members of Congress if high-level officials in the Justice Department not declared Congress off limits and if Chappell had not died before prosecutors could act.

Even when Lehman attempted to reform military procurement, corporations and consultants often out-witted the Pentagon.[38] When Lehman shifted from sole-source to competitive bids, corporations often presented artificially low estimates, figuring they could use their political clout to get the contract revised after work had commenced. When Lehman tried to get different firms to produce the same weapon so that he could select the least-expensive product, the companies often colluded to produce the weapon at precisely the same cost so that they could share the contract.

While the primary source of military waste in the Reagan administration stemmed from the erroneous foreign policy and strategic premises of the buildup, procurement inefficiencies added tens of billions of dollars of waste and produced defective weapons. During the Persian Gulf War in 1991 the Pentagon had to rely on air force and army planes because it could not rely on many navy planes produced during the Reagan buildup.

Both Caspar Weinberger and Reagan were oblivious to military waste. Weinberger was focused on public and congressional relations, and on outmaneuvering Stockman and even Nancy Reagan (who believed the runaway military spending meant programs serving children were poorly funded), and was inattentive to operational details.[39] Weinberger eventually fired Lehman because he tired of the navy secretary's arrogance and increasing insubordination, but Weinberger never tried to reform navy procurement. As James Baker, Reagan's chief of staff and treasury secretary, revealed to a Reagan biographer, the president never emphasized ethics and was content to give department secretaries a free hand in running their agencies.[40] (Neatly compartmentalizing the military from other government agencies, Reagan equated "waste" with civil servants in domestic programs and "fraud" with welfare recipients.[41]) If Reagan and Congress had been serious about reforms, they would have banned campaign contributions from corporations with military contracts, made it illegal for former Pentagon officials to advise corporations about military contracts, forbidden the Pentagon to employ anyone who had worked for a military contractor, and established technical boards independent of the Pentagon and military contractors to award and rescind contracts solely on performance and cost data.

Freezing Social Investments

After his landslide victory over Walter Mondale, Reagan again sought deep cuts in domestic discretionary spending in early 1985. He wanted an "aggregate freeze" and then a "modified freeze" on a large block of domestic spending. Reagan's penurious bent in regard to domestic programs was encouraged by Don Regan, his new chief of staff, who had risen from modest origins to vast wealth on Wall Street and who empathized only with affluent Americans. Thus Reagan developed ever more grandiose plans for cutting programs for the poor and for the working poor.

But Reagan had less power to effect his plans in 1985 than in 1982. He had lost credibility on budget issues by submitting numerous dead-on-arrival budgets that always favored domestic spending cuts, increases in military spending, and no tax increases—and made no dent the nation's huge deficits. Senators Domenici and Dole introduced the most ambitious deficit-cutting legislation in U.S. history. They proposed to limit COLAs for one year, to cut domestic spending severely, and to freeze military spending, not even raising it to compensate for inflation. (Many legislators finally concurred that Reagan's military buildup had been extravagant.)[42] But Democrats on the House Budget Committee rebelled against the large domestic spending cuts, opposed the COLA freeze, and wanted deeper military cuts. Worse yet, Reagan went behind Domenici's back and cut a deal with Tip O'Neill—Reagan would not seek cuts in entitlements if the Democrats would limit their cuts in the military budget. Domenici and Dole were livid that Reagan had sabotaged any prospect for a budget deal; they had proposed unpopular cuts in entitlements in an attempt to cut the deficit and thereby save Reagan from himself, and they resolved not to do so again during the Reagan administration.[43] (Ironically, George Bush bested Dole in the 1988 Republican presidential primaries partly by alluding to Dole's efforts to raise taxes to diminish the deficits that Reagan had created.)

With no budget in the offing by the early fall of 1985, however, both parties realized that voters might blame incumbents seeking reelection in 1986. Phil Gramm, the Texas Democrat who had defected to the Republican Party and won election to the Senate, initiated a clever proposal that came to be known as Gramm-Rudman-Hollings and relied on a procedural gimmick to solve annual budget stalemates. (Senators Warren Rudman, R-N.H., and Fritz Hollings, D-S.C., were cosponsors.) Why not, Gramm asked, establish annual deficit targets so the deficit would drop incrementally to zero between 1986 and 1991? Why not mandate automatic across-the-board cuts (called sequestration) to meet these targets if Congress could not bring itself to make the cuts? With entitlements and a few popular programs like Head Start protected from draconian measures, sequestration would fall in equal measure on two areas in the discretionary budget: military and domestic spending. Moreover, no new programs could be established unless they were funded by cuts in existing ones.[44]

The proposal was both daring and one that allowed Congress to avoid hard decisions. Gramm-Rudman-Hollings impeded the development of any new programs or increases in spending, but it gave Congress a big out: it could amend the targets in Gramm-Rudman-Hollings by extending the schedule for balancing the budget. Weinberger urged Reagan not to support the legislation. The defense secretary feared that Congress might deliberately fail to meet the targets to force huge cuts in the military through sequestration. In turn, some Democrats feared sequestration could devastate domestic discretionary spending. But Reagan and leaders of both parties, desperate to resolve their impasse on the budget, gave Gramm-Rudman-Hollings their support.[45]

Reagan thought Gramm-Rudman-Hollings was similar to a line-item veto and a constitutional amendment to balance the budget—measures that he had long supported.[46] As the measure gathered bipartisan support in Congress, Reagan feared that if he vetoed or did not support it, he would give Democrats an issue in the 1988 elections. Hawks insisted that Gramm-Rudman-Hollings be amended to establish a so-called fire wall between military and domestic discretionary spending so that cuts in the military budget could not be transferred to domestic accounts.

Gramm-Rudman-Hollings created annual negotiations between the two parties, the two chambers, and between Congress and the president. To meet the deficit targets Democrats would demand some tax increases and military cuts, while Republicans would seek some cuts in domestic spending. Reagan would demand all the cuts come from domestic spending and until the last minute would resist any military cuts or tax increases. If a stalemate occurred—and it did in 1987—Congress would simply extend the year when the balanced budget was due, thus requiring fewer hard choices.

Gramm-Rudman-Hollings created an environment that was devastating for domestic discretionary programs because it exempted Social Security, veterans' benefits, Medicaid, and food stamps and made only small cuts in Medicare.[47] Because Congress could meet the deficit targets only with great difficulty, and because most entitlements were immune to cutting, Congress was under pressure to cut domestic discretionary spending—and any proposal to increase domestic spending raised the problem of triggering sequestration, a cumbersome procedure that would dock most existing discretionary programs with across-the-board cuts to meet the deficit-reduction target. When Rep. Thomas Downey, D-N.Y., wanted to add $6 billion to fund child care and job training to get welfare recipients off the rolls under the Family Support Act of 1986, he was overruled by such liberals as House Majority Leader Jim Wright, D-Texas, who feared sequestration and who also feared that this spending increase would cause Reagan to oppose modest tax increases.[48] (Partly because it was so poorly funded, the Family Support Act failed to decrease the welfare rolls markedly, which opened the door for Republicans' punitive versions of welfare reform in 1995 and 1996.) So aggregate funding of discretionary social, education, employment, and training programs remained stagnant in Reagan's second term. As a percentage of the budget and in constant dollars, the funding for these programs was less than in the last year of the Carter administration—by 20 percent or more. By contrast, military spending was roughly 133 percent higher in 1988 than in 1980, although Reagan's military budgets had peaked in 1985.

We can speculate that Reagan supported Gramm-Rudman-Hollings partly because he knew sequestration would not harm his buildup because the military had already bought many of the weapons and forces he had sought in 1981. Reagan also knew that liberals would be extraordinarily fearful of sequestration because means-tested entitlements and domestic discretionary spending, already severely cut, would be hard hit by sequestration. With the firewall in place, moreover, Reagan did not have to fear that liberals would transfer military resources to the domestic sector.

Stockman's "Revelation"

Curiously, it was not until 1985 that a plot within a plot became widely publicized when Moynihan charged that Stockman had confessed to him in 1981 that Reagan had deliberately sought to deplete funds for domestic spending by slashing taxes.[49] What is remarkable is that Moynihan's statement caused a stir at all: Reagan and Republicans in Congress had openly discussed "linkage" in 1981, meaning that he intended that tax cuts would stimulate spending cuts to compensate for the losses in revenue.[50] Still sensitive to the charge that Reagan was insensitive to the poor, Meese hotly denied the existence of a plot but conceded that what Moynihan had said "contained a grain of truth," apparently unaware that Reagan had publicly discussed linkage in 1981 and that he had often made clear during his political career that he favored tax cuts to deplete revenues that liberals and civil servants might use to increase domestic spending.[51] Indeed, this "plot" makes more understandable why Reagan was not perturbed by the unprecedented deficits that he created. Deficits, after all, squeezed domestic discretionary spending because they promoted cuts in spending in the many budget deals aimed at reducing deficits.

Although Reagan said he wanted to cut domestic spending in general, he focused his energies on programs used by poor people. He cut spending on social, employment, training, and education programs from $61 billion in 1981 to only $48 billion in 1989. These mostly means-tested programs comprised less than 4 percent of the federal budget when Reagan commenced his administration, but he reduced them to less than 3 percent of the budget.

While Reagan increased overall spending on entitlements, he implemented policies that discriminated against means-tested entitlements, such as seeking lower eligibility levels and cuts in benefit levels. It is instructive to contrast the fate of universal entitlements (Social Security and Medicare), which benefit members of all social classes, with such means-tested entitlements as food stamps, Supplemental Security Income (SSI), the earned income tax credit (EITC), and AFDC, which are used by low-income people (see table 11.1). Reagan managed to hold the funding of the means-tested entitlements during his first term to a 5 percent increase, whereas universal entitlements increased 28 percent. For his full two terms, the means-tested entitlements rose by only 26 percent while universal entitlements grew 38 percent. Most increases in the means-tested programs occurred, moreover, in a single program, Medicaid, which had powerful defenders in the medical establishment and among state and local officials. Not counting Medicaid, means-tested entitlements increased only 8 percent during Reagan's two terms. (Sensitive to the charge that Reagan treated poor people harshly, his defenders often refer to the overall growth in domestic spending, which obscures the static funding for means-tested programs.)[52]

The hostility of the Reagan administration to low-income people is even clearer, moreover, when we place these cuts in discretionary social

TABLE 11.1 Means-Tested and Universal Entitlements in
Constant 1992 Dollars, 1980–1989

	1980	1985	1989
MEANS-TESTED			
Food Stamps	$22.8	20.9	21.3
Supplemental Security	9.9	11.4	13.0
Earned-Income Tax Credit	2.2	1.5	4.5
AFDC	12.7	12.1	12.7
Medicaid	24.3	29.9	39.2
SUBTOTALS	71.9	75.8	90.7
UNIVERSAL			
Medicare	54.0	84.8	94.0
Social Security	203.6	246.2	261.3
SUBTOTALS	257.6	331.0	355.3

Source:. Office of Management and Budget, *Budget of the U.S. Government, FY 2000, Historical Tables* (Washington, D.C.: Government Printing Office, 1999), table 8.6.

programs and the static funding of means-tested entitlements in a broader context. They occurred during and after a deep recession in the early 1980s that was devastating to many in the lowest economic quintile. It also occurred in the midst of the shift from a manufacturing to a service economy, which meant that incomes of many in the lower economic strata had declined as they moved from high-paying manufacturing to low-paying service jobs. These changes occurred, moreover, as the Reagan administration initiated tax policies that significantly exacerbated economic inequality. One way to see this is to compare the effects of income-tax and Social Security tax changes from 1980 to 1984 for the lowest and highest income brackets, as in table 11.2.

Shifting income to people in the higher tax brackets continued, moreover. When we examine the effects of the Tax Reform Act of 1986 on various income groups, we find that people earning less than $30,000 showed hardly any tax savings on their average returns, whereas people earning $75,000 to $100,000 gained $7,203 a year, and people with incomes from $100,000 to $200,000 gained $24,603 a year. (People earning $500,000 to $1 million gained $86,040.)[53] If we add the cumulative effects of the 1981 and 1986 changes in the tax code to changes in the Social Security payroll tax, we find that people earning $10,000 to $20,000 a year broke even, whereas those earning $100,000 to $200,000 gained $26,872, and people earning more than $200,000 gained $50,000 or more.

TABLE 11.2 Shifts in Income and Social Security Tax Burden, Factoring in Inflation, 1980–1984

INCOME	Tax Increases from Social Security and Inflation	Net Tax Reduction from Tax Bills of 1981–82	Net (+) Gain or (-) Loss
Less than $9,999	$153	$58	$-95
$10,000–19,999	573	387	-186
$20,000–29,999	1,020	882	-138
$75,000–99,999	4,855	5,258	+403
$100,000–199,999	5,979	8,248	+2,269
More than $200,000	7,579	24,982	+17,403

Source: Thomas Edsall, The New Politics of Inequality (New York: Norton, 1984), 205.

Failed Priorities in the Reagan Administration

Reagan markedly transformed national priorities during his tenure, principally with respect to military spending and interest on the national debt (see fig. 11.1). While spending on military and veterans' programs increased from $278 billion to $372 billion per year from 1981 to 1989, interest payments on the national debt increased from roughly $106 billion to almost $189 billion. (All data are stated in constant 1992 dollars.)

Reagan can be indicted for extraordinary waste in these two areas. The only major external review of Reagan's military buildup, a classified eight-volume report completed by the General Accounting Office (GAO) in June 1993, casts serious doubt on its advisability. It concluded that the Pentagon understated the cost of many weapons, deliberately overstated the radar-evading capabilities of the Stealth bombers, exaggerated the threat posed by Soviet weapons and defenses, created an overblown image of U.S. vulnerability, overstated the necessity of the buildup, relied on "unconvincing rationales" for developing nuclear arms in the first place, understated the probable performance of existing mature weapons sys-

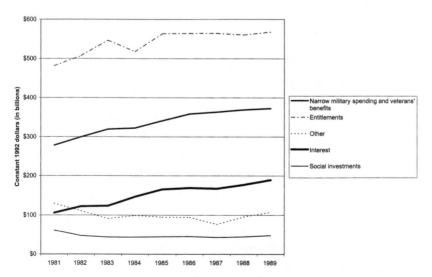

FIGURE 11.1 Five Types of Federal Expenditures, 1981–1989
  Source: Office of Management and Budget, *Budget of the U.S. Government, FY 2000, Historical Tables* (Washington, D.C.: GPO, 1999), table 3.1, pp. 47–48.

tems, overstated the expected performance and costs of proposed upgrades, and devised insufficient tests for weapons that came off the assembly line.[54] In other words, many arguments made by critics (such as Tom Gervasi and Fred Kaplan) just before and after the Reagan military buildup had merit.

The Soviets did have a numerical superiority in strategic offensive nuclear forces in 1978 on the eve of Reagan's military buildup if we count ICBMs, SLBMs, and bombers (see fig. 8.1). The United States had enough missiles and bombers to deter any Soviet first strike and had more strategic warheads than the USSR if we count the American IRBMs, MIRVs, and other warheads (see fig. 8.2). Moreover, the United States, France, and Great Britain had numerous nuclear forces in Europe that could easily hit Soviet targets, whereas the Soviets lacked a comparable capability.

Reagan can also be faulted for his failure to secure major treaties to cut nuclear arms and conventional forces on both sides. Curiously, his idealistic desire to eliminate nuclear arsenals may have been his undoing, because he resorted to panaceas like Star Wars rather than engage in a laborious negotiating process. (He promised the Soviets he would give them Star Wars technology once it was perfected, which would immunize both nations from nuclear attack by each other.) Reagan simply failed to focus on nuclear arms talks during most of his first term and during the first portion of his second term as the Iran-contra scandal unfolded. He failed to cut nuclear and conventional arsenals, moreover, even when a reform-minded leader with new proposals (Gorbachev) had finally appeared in the Soviet Union.

Thus we can estimate a portion of the wasted expenditures in the Reagan administration by contrasting the cost of Reagan's narrow military spending with the cost of such spending had Reagan merely continued, in fiscal years 1982 through 1992, Carter's level of military spending in fiscal year 1981. (These wasted expenditures roughly equal the shaded area in fig. 11.2 beneath the line depicting narrow military expenditures—or $714 billion.) In addition to the waste created by its military buildup, the Reagan administration overspent on maintaining the cold war base as well as on procurement, operations, and personnel (see chapter 15).

Similarly, we can estimate wasted expenditures on interest on the debt from 1982 through 2004 by comparing actual interest payments with what the interest payments would have been if Reagan had kept interest rates in constant dollars at the same level as in Carter's last budget, fiscal year 1981. (It is fair to charge excess interest payments to the Reagan administration

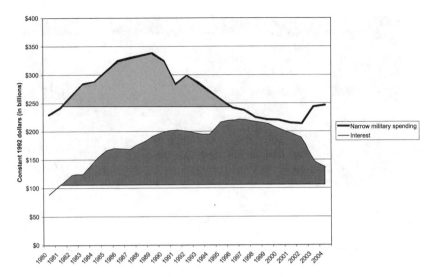

FIGURE 11.2 Excess Expenditures on Narrow Military Spending and Interest on the Debt, 1980–2004

Source: Office of Management and Budget, *Budget of the U.S. Government, FY 2000, Historical Tables* (Washington, D.C.: GPO, 1999), table 3.1, pp. 47–48.

for 1990 through 2004 because his White House successors could not easily reduce interest payments, given the sheer amount of debt that the Reagan administration had created. Indeed, interest payments on the debt will approach levels of 1981 only by 2004.) The Reagan administration will have wasted $1.4 trillion on excess interest payments from 1982 through 2004.

In addition to this waste, the Reagan administration presided over deep cuts in corporate income taxes. Although the nation had collected corporate income taxes at a rate of 2.6 percent of GDP in 1979, it taxed corporate income at only 1.9 percent of GDP in 1989. If the United States had taxed corporate taxes at 2.6 percent of GDP from 1982 through 1989, it would had $366 billion more in the treasury.[55]

Reagan aides liked to note that military spending did not rise markedly as a percentage of the budget even though it increased in constant dollars, and they often denied that the large increases in military spending affected domestic spending. It is true that military spending did not increase markedly as a percentage of the budget, as figure 11.3 shows.

However, narrow military and veterans' spending, which absorbed slightly more than 50 percent of the discretionary budget in 1980, accounted

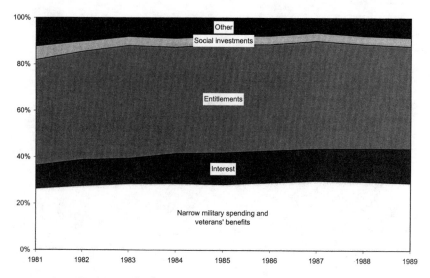

FIGURE 11.3 Five Types of Expenditures as Percentages of Federal Outlays, 1981–1989
   Source: Office of Management and Budget, *Budget of the U.S. Government, FY 2000, Historical Tables* (Washington, D.C.: GPO, 1999), table 8.8, pp. 138–39.

for more than 60 percent of the discretionary budget when Reagan left office. (Recall that most military spending, unlike entitlements and interest payments on the debt, derives from the annual discretionary budget and therefore competes with domestic discretionary programs in the annual appropriations process.) So Reagan's military expenditures placed strong downward pressure on domestic discretionary spending.

In 1981 Reagan managed to frame the policy agenda for the next seven years, as well as for the presidencies of George Bush and Bill Clinton. His huge deficits trapped Congress in endless debates about how to diminish them that dominated the entire session in such years as 1985, 1990, 1993, and 1995. These huge deficits, in turn, placed advocates of domestic reform on the defensive for the next sixteen years until a budget surplus finally surfaced in the late 1990s. No other president has so decisively influenced the course of budgetary and political events for such an extended period. And no other president has wasted more than $3 trillion, as I demonstrate in chapter 15.

12

Bush's Myopia

With the Soviet Union in the throes of dissolution, George Bush had an opportunity that no president had seen since the beginning of the cold war: to reform U.S. priorities. With military spending in constant dollars far above levels seen at the height of the cold war in 1980, would Bush cut military spending as the Soviet threat diminished, perhaps redirecting some of these resources to the domestic agenda? Would he seize the moment to become a transformational leader, or would he fight, instead, to preserve the status quo? I contend here that the Bush administration and Congress made fiscal and tax errors in excess of $642 billion.

A Dinghy in Reagan's Wake?

Compared to his predecessor, George Bush came to the presidency with modest goals. He wanted primarily to preserve Reagan's legacy, whether by continuing his military buildup or by holding the line against major new domestic initiatives. Instinctively a cautious man, his overriding motto was "Do no harm."[1]

Bush had long been a cold warrior. He was the last U.S. president to have fought in World War II (when he was eighteen, he volunteered for the navy), and he was determined to avoid appeasement of the Soviets. He had fervently endorsed Barry Goldwater, as well as Johnson's Vietnam policy, in 1964. Bush served two terms in the House in the 1960s and failed twice to win a Senate seat, the last time in 1970. Invited by Nixon to head the U.S. Liaison Office in China, Bush served briefly as ambassador to the United Nations and as CIA director, where he strongly endorsed Paul Nitze's alarmist views about the Soviet Union in the mid- and late 1970s.

As Reagan's vice president, Bush focused on foreign and military policy. He strongly backed Reagan's military buildup. He personally orchestrated the invasion of Grenada. He was a key player in the illegal diversion of funds to the right-wing contras in Nicaragua despite denials to congressional investigators. (Only in 1995 did he acknowledge that he had been "in the loop.") He unabashedly attacked Michael Dukakis, the Democratic presidential candidate in 1988, on military and foreign policy grounds—one Bush ad featured a sarcastic picture of a helmeted Dukakis riding in a tank. At no point do Reagan aides remember Bush challenging any of Reagan's policies or viewpoints, even in numerous behind-the-scenes policy meetings.

Yet Bush was also somewhat more moderate than Reagan on several fronts. One biography has described Bush as a "conservative moderate" as opposed to a "moderate conservative."[2] Bush told Gorbachev at a reception in 1987 that he had had to hew to a harsh anticommunist line as Reagan's vice president but that, if he were elected president, he would be willing to negotiate with Gorbachev. (Were he to move faster toward negotiations, Bush said he feared Reagan's "intellectual thugs" would accuse him of being a closet liberal.)[3] Bush initially was suspicious of Gorbachev in 1989, but he soon decided that his central mission was to preserve Gorbachev as leader of the Soviet Union by softening the U.S. rhetoric, offering Gorbachev some trade concessions, and engaging in some arms-reduction talks. Indeed, Bush came to fear "instability" in the Soviet Union sufficiently that he related awkwardly or with hostility to dissidents such as Lech Walesa in Poland or Boris Yeltsin in Russia.[4] Bush's overriding interest in preserving the Soviet Union and Gorbachev's power—as opposed to an ascension to power of such dissidents as Yeltsin or Walesa—conformed with Bush's inherent dislike of social change. This made Bush, in the words of coauthors of a Bush biography, a "militant fighter for the *status quo*" (emphasis added).[5]

Bush's cautious persona, when combined with his cold war views, lent credence to the charge that he lacked "vision." Bush had served as a faithful foot soldier for Reagan for years and lacked distinctive views at home or abroad. He failed to develop a mandate during his 1988 campaign, securing his victory not from an overarching mission but from mostly trivial or scurrilous charges against Dukakis, such as the charge that as Massachusetts governor he had released a black sex offender, Willie Horton, as part of a prison furlough program. (Horton terrorized a white couple.) Bush's go-slow inclinations were abetted by his appointees. When the Senate refused to confirm the hawkish John Tower as secretary of defense, Bush responded by nominating Dick Cheney, who fought to preserve the cold war military base during the rest of Bush's tenure. Brent Scowcroft, Bush's national security adviser, had opposed the Intermediate-Range Nuclear Forces (INF) Treaty on the ground that it did not reduce Soviet conventional forces. James Baker, his secretary of state, was widely viewed as a savvy negotiator and political operative with no overriding foreign policy perspective.[6] All these advisers, as well as Bush, entered 1989 profoundly skeptical of Gorbachev's sincerity.

Although Bush was intent on preserving the status quo, he also revered such presidents as Lincoln, Eisenhower, and Teddy Roosevelt, all of whom had presided during a war or had advocated strong interventionist policies abroad. Bush strongly believed presidents became national heroes only if tested in battle, which implied early in his presidency that he would prove no exception, even if it was not clear what nation would emerge as an adversary as the Soviet Union unraveled.[7]

Throwing in the Towel?

Gorbachev had worked diligently to reform his nation and fully intended the union of republics would remain intact and he would remain as the leader of a reformed Communist Party. But by late 1988 he had encountered devastating realities. Under the rubrics of perestroika and glasnost he had introduced reforms that would have been politically unthinkable even several years earlier and that led to a gradual transformation of the Soviet

Union and its eastern European satellites. Meanwhile, he retained his power as president of the Soviet Union and general secretary of the Soviet Communist Party. By late 1988 he realized that he was in a race with time to revitalize the moribund Soviet economy. He wanted to spend massive new resources on industry and agriculture and to secure Western capital to purchase technology and resources from capitalist countries.[8] To secure these resources Gorbachev realized that he had to cut the huge Soviet military, which consumed as much as a fourth of the Soviet gross national product. (SALT I, SALT II, and the INF treaties had hardly dented the military forces of either nation.) Even before Bush took office, Gorbachev had also decided to cut Soviet forces in Afghanistan, as well as to moderate the Soviet role in Eastern Europe, where signs of dissent had begun to appear even before 1988.[9]

During a remarkable speech at the United Nations in December 1988, Gorbachev announced that he would unilaterally cut 500,000 troops and 10,000 tanks and followed this dramatic move by announcing in May 1989 that he would cut 500 tactical warheads from Eastern Europe. He also proposed that both sides make huge cuts in conventional forces. (These initiatives led Moynihan to say that U.S. leaders ought to have realized that "the Soviets could see they were beaten" by late 1988.)[10] With their minds still in the cold war, American leaders and intelligence analysts failed to grasp that the Soviet Union's hold on Eastern European states was weakening and that internal dissent was vastly increasing—and that Gorbachev's initiatives reflected these realities and his desperate effort to maintain power while increasingly caught between Soviet hard-liners and Soviet reformers.

Any doubts about what would happen in the Soviet Union ought to have been erased when breathtaking changes occurred in Eastern Europe in 1989. Polish voters ousted the Communists, leading Gorbachev to support the Solidarity coalition government in August, just a month after he had publicly pledged to the Warsaw Pact that he would not contest liberal changes in their nations. The Hungarian government opened its border with Austria, which allowed people to flee Eastern Europe—and it rejected Leninism in October. The Lithuanian Communist Party declared its independence from the Soviet Communist Party. Communist regimes in Bulgaria and Czechoslovakia toppled.

Most important, the linchpin of the Warsaw Pact, East Germany, became engulfed in turmoil. Thousands of East Germans fled their nation by crossing into other Eastern European nations and often sought refuge in West German embassies. With East Germany afraid to close its borders with Hungary for fear of causing further turmoil, many East Germans crossed into Hungary en route to Austria and West Germany. When East Germany again closed its borders, street protests forced the East German dictator Erich Honecker and his successor to resign. When a party reformer was finally appointed as prime minister in November, he reopened the borders but forgot to exclude the border between East and West Berlin, only to have the wall breached and partly demolished by throngs of East and West Berliners.

Nor was turmoil confined to Eastern Europe as various Soviet republics moved toward independence. Georgia declared its independence in September, noting that it could reject any federal law that did not advance its interests. A Ukrainian popular front endorsed perestroika. Azerbaijan declared independence, followed by Armenia, even though Gorbachev outlawed secession.

Of course, no one could predict with certainty where these tumultuous events would lead. As the year progressed, however, it should have become increasingly clear that the reform genie could not be placed back in the bottle. The Soviets formerly had simply put down insurrections in single nations. Now they had to deal with attacks from dissidents throughout Eastern Europe and in myriad Soviet republics if they wished to retain the old order even as the Soviet economy was deteriorating. Already desperately in need of resources for agriculture and industry, Gorbachev could not possibly underwrite military actions throughout Eastern Europe and in many Soviet republics. Nor could he secure trustworthy troops for military operations in myriad locations when the republics and regimes that supplied them were in such turmoil. If he tried to repress reform, he might have to deal with guerrilla warfare on several fronts. And even if he did, wouldn't dissent simply gather momentum elsewhere?

Nor was Gorbachev well suited to the job of quashing dissidents. He had publicly pledged to Warsaw Pact nations in July that he would not contest their liberalizations. His unilateral cuts in troops and tanks, as well as his concurrence in the INF Treaty, suggested that he genuinely wanted cuts in military forces. If he embarked on a course of repression, it would put the lie to his efforts to achieve perestroika and glasnost and ruin his credibility as a reformer. He had promised immediate cuts in short-range nuclear forces in July if NATO entered into negotiations with him. And he had already suggested that he would be willing to make massive cuts in conventional forces in a pending European treaty that would slash Soviet forces by 50 percent. Further, he had publicly renounced the use of force in Eastern Europe, thus abrogating the Brezhnev Doctrine, which gave the Soviet government the right to prevent any attempt to leave the communist camp.

As turmoil gathered momentum, some Bush aides such as Scowcroft observed from time to time that restoration of the ancien régime seemed impossible.[11] Yet he and Bush constantly feared that a virulent right-wing movement would arise in specific nations or in the Soviet Union and quell reform.[12] As they surveyed the turmoil in Poland and East Germany, they doubted that the Soviet Union would tolerate efforts to overthrow its domination. Although Bush's fears were understandable when viewed in the context of twentieth-century history, they made little sense in the changed world of late 1989, when older institutions were under sharp attack in many locations. Indeed, it was the pervasiveness and depth of reform and dissent that marked the changing world.

Reformers in East Germany and Hungary watched and were inspired by developments in Poland, just as Polish dissidents were buoyed by dissent in other nations. Reformers in specific Soviet republics were similarly aware of the successes of counterparts in other republics, bringing a synergy and momentum that made a counterrevolution unlikely. If Gorbachev were supplanted by a right-wing communist dictator, this dictator would encounter a dike with many holes and would be unable to maintain the loyalty of troops or to find the resources to do so. A right-wing dictator would fear that a civil war in the Soviet Union would unleash forces not seen since the Russian Revolution.

Bush was disinclined to view Gorbachev as a genuine reformer during most of 1989. When Gorbachev issued unilateral concessions, for example, Bush believed the Soviet leader wanted to divide NATO by proposing cuts in short-range missiles that he knew were popular in certain nations but not in others.[13] Or, Bush thought Gorbachev's promises to cut his arsenal were as a trick to lull NATO nations into complacency so they would cut their arms or military budgets, only to find that Gorbachev had reneged.[14]

Although Bush portrays himself as more trusting of Gorbachev than were U.S. military advisers, Cheney, or Robert Gates, his deputy national security adviser, Bush was disinclined to overrule them at numerous points in 1989 when they balked at U.S. concessions. When Adm. William

Crowe, who preceded Colin Powell as chair of the Joint Chiefs of Staff, opposed Bush's idea of cutting European-based forces by 25 percent, Bush backpedaled to a mere 10 percent, recalling in his memoir, "I was determined not to bulldoze the military into silence or drag them into agreement."[15] He capitulated to Margaret Thatcher, the hawkish prime minister of Great Britain, on numerous occasions when she opposed negotiations, arms reductions, or cuts in military spending.[16]

If Bush and Scowcroft feared the rise of a right-wing movement in the Soviet Union and in Eastern Europe, they surely ought to have realized that genuine concessions on their part, and cuts in military spending, would have helped to prevent it. As Bush frequently surmised, Gorbachev needed to demonstrate that he had obtained concessions from Western powers so that Soviet hard-liners would understand that he was not making undue concessions.[17] To their credit, Bush and his top aides softened their rhetoric in 1989 and 1990, mostly forswearing militant anticommunist language in the hope of not undermining the course of reform. (Bush bit his tongue in late 1989, for example, in refusing to gloat over the sundering of the Berlin Wall.) But softened rhetoric was hardly a substitute for hard concessions and bold initiatives at a time when Soviet military power was clearly eroding.[18]

Nor was Bush lacking for concessions he might have granted Gorbachev in 1989. Bush could have offered large unilateral military cuts without even breaching the cold war base that Reagan had inherited from Carter in 1980. Instead of nominating for secretary of defense someone willing to rethink the military budget, he nominated Tower, who had spearheaded congressional support for Reagan's military buildup. When Tower's nomination foundered, Bush turned to Cheney, who opposed any significant cuts in military spending. When Richard Darman, the budget director, asked Bush to reject real increases in military spending for the next three years so that the deficit could be reduced, he countered with a proposal to seek real increases of 1 or 2 percent in each of the next three years.[19] He failed to contest Powell's disinclination to cut military forces after Powell became chairman of the Joint Chiefs in September.

While budget agreements and deficits meant that Bush could obtain aid for the Soviet Union and eastern European nations only with difficulty, he could have sought legislation to redirect some military appropriations to these nations. When Polish leaders sought $500 million to redress their deficit and $1 billion for currency reforms, Bush provided only $100 million and $200 million for these requests, respectively—even as George Mitchell of Maine, the Senate majority leader, favored $1.2 billion spread over three years, to be funded from the military's research and development budget. (Bob Dole favored $10 billion.)[20] No money was provided to Hungary—and virtually no resources to Gorbachev. What Bush did provide early in 1989 was a version of Eisenhower's "Open Skies" proposal of the 1950s that even Scowcroft dismissed as "gimmickry . . . wrongly giving the impression that we did not have the brain power to think of something innovative [forcing us] to reach back 30 years for an idea."[21] Bush refused even to consider deep cuts in U.S. conventional forces in Europe—or any cuts in U.S. military spending. He adopted an overall strategy, moreover, to prompt Gorbachev to make major concessions, with the United States venturing little until the Soviets had implemented their changes.[22]

Much like Nixon when he made his famous trip to China, Bush was uniquely equipped to seize the moment. As a war hero and hard-liner, Bush could have matched Gorbachev's concessions without being viewed as militarily soft, even if some conservatives objected initially. He could have sought historic arms reductions and gone into history as the U.S. president who negotiated an end to the cold war. He could have untied Reagan's Gordian knot and used military savings, and modest cuts in universal entitlements, to reduce the deficit with only small increases in taxes, thus (basically) remaining true to his campaign pledge not to raise taxes.

Kinder and Gentler?

Even more than many of his cold war predecessors, Bush was utterly bored by domestic policies. He even said during his campaign that he would focus most of his attention on international and military issues.[23] He was, according to Thomas Mann of the Brookings Institution, an "in-box president . . . when it came to domestic policy . . . reacting to what fell into his lap."[24] He lacked an ability, moreover, to empathize with key groups of voters whose support would be critical to his reelection bid, such as Reagan Democrats whose economic condition had often deteriorated as many unionized jobs continued to disappear or to be relocated to other nations. As an establishment figure who had been born with a "silver spoon in his mouth"—a jibe made by Texas governor Ann Richards at the Democratic

National Convention in 1988—Bush lacked Reagan's ability to communicate with northern white ethnic voters or southern white Protestants—groups that had propelled Nixon and Reagan to power and had been instrumental in Bush's victory over Dukakis.[25] Such sage commentators as Kevin Phillips, who had predicted the flight of blue-collar whites from the Democratic Party in the Nixon administration, warned Republicans they might lose support of these Reagan Democrats in the 1992 elections if they failed to advance social and economic measures to help them.[26] (Once the Soviet threat diminished, merely impugning Democrats' patriotism could no longer lure many of these Reagan Democrats to the Republican Party.)

Polls told Bush, moreover, that white suburban independent voters—a key group that had rallied to him in 1988—wanted the federal government to support such social programs as child care, job training, and education.[27] (They had become increasingly restive with the negative messages of Republicans that focused on spending and tax cuts.) Bush wanted to woo these voters and had some personal misgivings about the harshness of Reagan's nonstop attacks on domestic discretionary spending. Thus Bush promised a "kinder and gentler" presidency during his campaign, although he offered no specifics and only vague promises to improve the environment and education. Many of these suburban independents became dismayed when Bush did not fulfill his campaign promises by offering concrete proposals.

Bush's domestic policy was, of course, constrained by the huge deficits he had inherited from Reagan, by stipulations of the budget deal of 1987 that required spending cuts to move the nation toward balanced budgets, and by his decision to take tax increases and entitlement cuts off the table during his campaign. Recognizing Bush's fiscal dilemma, Darman devised a scheme to make Bush appear to be expanding social spending while not actually increasing the domestic budget. Bush proposed modest increases in selected programs for education, the homeless, the environment, and combating poverty, while he forced Congress to offset these with unpopular cuts in discretionary spending to meet the Gramm-Rudman-Hollings deficit-reduction targets. (Recall that Gramm-Rudman-Hollings legislation required yearly progress toward eliminating deficits.)[28] Bush's proposed increases were so modest that they would not even compensate for inflation.

Neither party wanted to develop a major deficit-reduction package in 1989. Preoccupied with foreign affairs, Bush wanted to wait another year.

Convinced the president had the most to lose by not meeting Gramm-Rudman-Hollings deadlines, Democrats were in no hurry to develop a budget deal. In addition, George Mitchell was furious at Bush for tarring Dukakis with a pro-tax image and wanted to lay a trap for Bush in 1990 that would force him to break his no-tax pledge to comply with Gramm-Rudman-Hollings.[29] So both parties accepted a status quo budget in 1989 that relied on gimmicks to comply with Gramm-Rudman-Hollings, such as moving to the fiscal 1989 budget from the fiscal 1990 budget some federal subsidy payments to farmers.

Bush made a decision in early 1989, however, that profoundly shaped the rest of his presidency. Because he wanted to preserve his political capital for foreign policy issues, feared Democrats would outbid him on the domestic front, and had no domestic policy imagination, Bush had decided by early 1989 not to propose any major domestic initiatives for the remainder of his first term. He would let Democrats propose domestic initiatives, demand specific revisions to avoid a veto (such as significant cuts in their size), make frequent use of vetoes when the Democrats failed to heel, and mobilize congressional coalitions to block Democratic efforts to override his vetoes.[30] To assuage Republican conservatives and the Moral Majority, he also decided to veto any measures that funded abortions.

Bush's reactive domestic strategy carried huge risks, however. It could make him vulnerable to the charge that he neglected domestic needs, both by not initiating measures and by vetoing many Democratic proposals. (He eventually vetoed nearly thirty domestic measures.) It could add weight to the long-standing charge that he lacked vision. He risked allowing the Democrats to monopolize discourse on policy reforms and alienating those suburban independents who had supported him because he had promised a kinder and gentler America. Little did Bush realize, moreover, that many voters would refocus on domestic matters when the Soviet threat diminished and when a recession occurred.

Two kinds of domestic proposals did intrigue Bush, partly because they cost little money. He favored civil rights legislation for the disabled, although he had opposed the landmark Civil Rights Acts of 1964 and 1965 to curry favor with southern conservatives. He supported "volunteerism" and private philanthropy (which he called a "thousand points of light") because both approaches placed the onus on the private sector rather than on government to address the nation's ills. But he left his two most assertive appointees on the domestic scene (Jack Kemp at the Department of Housing and Urban Development and William Bennett, his drug czar) in limbo by failing to provide them with resources or strong support.[31]

Holding Gorbachev's Feet to the Fire

The Soviet hold over eastern Europe had weakened markedly in 1989 and essentially ended in 1990, save primarily for the Baltic states. A mass exodus from East Germany continued in early 1990 as tens of thousands of citizens sought residence in West Germany. Elections in March brought a coalition government and reformist premier to power in East Germany, which now favored reunification of East and West Germany. So-called four-plus-two talks commenced as diplomats from the United States, the Soviet Union, France, and Great Britain (the big four) joined leaders from the two Germanys to discuss reunification.[32] Gorbachev initially wanted confederation rather than reunification and resisted membership of a reunified Germany in NATO but eventually realized that he could prevent neither and conceded these points in July in talks with Helmut Kohl, West Germany's chancellor. Gorbachev's concession came after West Germany had agreed to make substantial payments to the Soviet Union and after Bush had offered key assurances to the Soviets such as limitations on the size of German conventional forces and that it would possess no nuclear forces at all. (Because West Germany was already a member of NATO, it had every reason to claim that a reunified Germany was entitled to remain a member of NATO, though NATO promised, at least implicitly, that East Germany's admission would be the extent of any NATO movement to the East.) Talks between the two Germanys led to a reunification treaty by September, with formal reunification taking place in October and the Soviets agreeing to remove their troops from the former East Germany by the end of 1994. (In 1989 François Mitterrand, the French president, had predicted the Soviets would not accept a reunified Germany for five to ten years.)[33] Scowcroft astutely dates the end of the cold war as the point in July when the Soviets accepted reunification and the entry of a reunified Germany into NATO.

Although Gorbachev had acceded to reunification of Germany and did not intervene in other eastern European states, he was less inclined to tolerate independence of the Baltic states, partly because they would establish a precedent for other republics if they secured independence. (Unlike eastern European nations, they had been incorporated into the Soviet Union itself.) Tension rose during the winter and spring of 1990 as Gorbachev put an embargo into place to force Lithuania to repudiate its declaration of independence, but he refrained from invading and lifted his embargo during the summer when Lithuania suspended its declaration of independence.[34] Events moved quickly in other Soviet republics too. The Supreme Soviet of Russia declared its independence from the Soviet Union in June after Boris Yeltsin was elected president of the Russian Federation in late May. Uzbekistan and other republics declared their independence, suggesting that the Soviet Union itself might disintegrate unless Gorbachev, scrambling to retain power at the center, could negotiate new arrangements with leaders of the different republics.

Whereas Bush and his top foreign policy aides had been suspicious of Gorbachev for much of 1989 because he remained a communist, in 1990 and much of 1991 they mostly wanted him to retain power. Partly they continued to fear a right-wing coup would displace Gorbachev, not merely to abort perestroika and glasnost but to reassert Soviet power in Eastern Europe.[35] If the Soviet Union disintegrated, they feared a factionalized military with uncertain safeguards and controls. Bush maintained a wary relationship with Yeltsin because Bush feared he meant to topple Gorbachev.

Although he wanted to keep Gorbachev in power, Bush was only marginally more charitable toward him in 1990 than in 1991. He signed a conventional forces treaty with the Soviets in late 1990 and made the Strategic Arms Reduction Treaty (START) negotiations a priority, but he also proposed real increases in his military budget in early 1990, prompting the *New York Times* to attack him for "far-fetched rationalizations for a huge military budget."[36] Nor did Bush consider giving major economic assistance to the Soviet Union, although Eduard Shevardnadze, Gorbachev's foreign minister, warned Bush that Gorbachev might not survive without it.[37]

Bush's dismissal of Gorbachev's pleas for economic assistance were grounded in his belief that any major assistance would be wasted unless the Soviets first reformed their economic system. But Bush, like many free-market advocates, did not understand the challenges of converting from a socialist to a market-driven economy. Bush told Gorbachev that economic reforms, like being pregnant, cannot be done halfway and believed that Soviet leaders had to sweep away all vestiges of government control at once. Gorbachev was closer to the mark when he retorted that women can't have the baby in the first month.[38] Surely, the Russian federation needed an extended transition period, as citizens experienced the insecurities inherent in market-driven economies. Although Bush was correct in noting that massive infusions of foreign capital were no panacea and could easily be misused, he was also miserly, providing virtually no funds, not even humanitarian aid, to the Soviets or the eastern European nations. (At various points, Scowcroft lamented the failure of the United States to provide foreign aid, even wondering whether the Bush administration would be held accountable if reform was stymied by popular discontent stemming from economic chaos.)[39] If the United States could develop the Marshall Plan at a point when it was burdened with postwar costs, the GI Bill, and huge interest payments on World War II debt, why could it not contemplate modest foreign aid at another pivotal juncture in world history when other nations faced dire economic conditions?

Save primarily for the conventional forces treaty in late 1990—even here, the Soviets made far larger cuts in their forces than NATO or the United States—Gorbachev could boast no major concessions from the United States nearly two years after Bush had taken office. Gorbachev faced Soviet hard-liners who believed they had made major concessions with little in return—and who were furious that Gorbachev had not contested German reunification and the country's imminent entry into NATO.[40]

Bush's decision to support expansion of NATO to include eastern European nations had some merit, but NATO expansion was also threatening and ominous to the Russian Federation, because it removed the buffer that Moscow had long desired on the western frontier. With the United States in desperate need of cooperation from the Soviets and the Russians on environmental problems, nuclear arms containment, and global financial and diplomatic issues, why was it necessary to expand NATO rapidly?[41]

Quest for a Peace Dividend (Part 1)

Buoyed by polls that suggested many U.S. voters favored some reductions in military spending as Soviet power diminished, some liberal Democrats revived the hopes of a peace dividend that had been dormant since the Vietnam War. (If even a third of the military budget were cut, $100 billion would become available for the domestic agenda.) Democrats' determination was strengthened by Bush's perceived political weakness compared to Ronald Reagan, whose personal popularity had frustrated Democrats' attempts to cut military spending. A coalition of antipoverty, education, civil rights, labor, and environmental groups demanded a peace dividend in the spring of 1989, just as the Urban Coalition and the Congressional Black Caucus demanded an "urban Marshall Plan."

An avalanche of peace-dividend proposals continued throughout the winter, spring, and summer of 1990. William Kaufmann, one of the nation's most respected military analysts, supported immediate cuts of 13 percent in the military budget and nearly halving military spending by the end of the decade if current trends continued in Eastern Europe and the Soviet Union—a recommendation that greatly exceeded even George McGovern's proposed cuts in military spending in 1972.[42] In December Sen. Sam Nunn of Georgia, the Democrats' military expert who had mostly supported Reagan's buildup, came out in support of pocketing a peace dividend of $8 to $15 billion. The *New York Times* advocated escalating military cuts so that the treasury would realize $20 billion in 1991 and $150 billion by the end of the decade.[43] Sen. Ted Kennedy, D-Mass., insisted that immediate cuts in military spending be devoted to a peace dividend rather than used to reduce the deficit, as some legislators urged. House liberals rallied behind a proposal by Rep. Barney Frank, D-Mass., to cut $18 billion in fiscal 1991, $30 billion in fiscal 1992, and $40 billion in fiscal 1993 by terminating the B-2 bomber, cutting back on the Star Wars program, and reducing the number of U.S. troops stationed abroad.[44] A poll in January showed that 75 percent of Americans favored cuts in the military in light of changes in the Soviet Union and that a large percentage wanted a peace dividend.[45]

When he encountered this significant challenge to his military budget, Bush initiated a determined offensive against a peace dividend. He insisted in early January that he would not fund domestic programs from money taken from his proposed $307 billion military budget, even as he promised to "restructure American defenses" and agreed to a modest 2 percent cut in military spending.[46] He took a page from Melvyn Laird's strategy book in the Nixon administration and asked Cheney to issue a long list of military bases to be scaled back or closed—in addition to the eighty-six closed or scaled back in 1989—well aware that this list would deter many legislators from supporting deep military cuts, lest they face the ire of their constituents.[47] Cheney hoped he could staunch the demand for short-term cuts by agreeing to long-term ones and promised to cut military expenditures by 25 percent over ten years, even though he knew that Bush proposed huge increases for development and production of new weapons that would reduce this to a mere 10 percent cut.

Even as Cheney held out an olive branch to advocates of a peace dividend, however, he and Bush tried to diminish pressure for a peace dividend. Bush attended a Mojave Desert military exercise against simulated Soviet tanks, which implied that the danger of a Soviet invasion of Europe had not diminished.[48] Cheney insisted that the United States needed to spend massively on research and development to keep the United States ahead of the Soviets.

Nor could advocates of a peace dividend count on strong support from many Democrats, who were often disinclined to push it strongly because the military-industrial complex reached its tentacles into every congressional district. It was particularly strong in voter-rich districts in the South and in California, where the term *conversion* (of military bases to civilian purposes) put chills into legislators from both parties. Trade unions, often supportive of liberal causes, usually opposed military cuts that would mean fewer jobs for their members. In April 1989 many House Democrats joined Republicans to defeat a modest proposal to take $1 billion from the military to fund social programs; that fall they approved Bush's $305 billion military budget. Their timidity increased in late 1990 and again in 1991 and 1992, when a deep recession made voters fearful of losing defense-related jobs. (The recession was particularly severe in California.) The other problem for Democrats was that they had to surmount the Gramm-Rudman-Hollings provision that prohibited transfers of funds cut from the military budget to the domestic discretionary budget. House Democrats supported a cut of $24 billion in Bush's requested military budget, while their Senate counterparts supported $18 billion in cuts. These cuts amounted to less than 8 percent of the existing budget authority when the major premise for military spending, the cold war, was rapidly receding and when budget analysts found $43 billion in usable military budget authority left over from the Reagan administration.[49]

As he watched the momentous changes in Eastern Europe and the Soviet Union, Bush might have contemplated major cuts in military spending, but he already was searching for ways to justify existing U.S. military power in an emerging "new world order." Analogizing those who wanted deep cuts in military spending to isolationists in the years preceding World War II, Bush would soon advocate a new world order that looked remarkably similar to the old one when viewed from the vantage point of the military budget.

The Gordian Knot Becomes a Hangman's Noose

Because he wanted to ingratiate himself with conservatives who often viewed him as lacking backbone, Bush had delivered his famous no-new-taxes pledge at the Republican National Convention: "Read my lips: No new taxes." Penned by speechwriter Peggy Noonan and enunciated in Bush's sharp-edged voice, these six words set the stage for the pillorying of Michael Dukakis as a tax-and-spend Democrat from "Taxachusetts."[50] While conservative Republicans loved the pledge, such advisers as Darman had opposed it on the ground that Bush probably would have to increase taxes to meet the Gramm-Rudman-Hollings targets.[51] (Even Reagan had raised taxes incrementally on many occasions after 1981.) By locking himself in to no new taxes, moreover, Bush infuriated such Democrats as Mitchell, who took umbrance at Bush's labeling of Democratic leaders as fiscally irresponsible when it was Reagan who had created the huge deficits in the first place and when such Republican senators as Dole and Domenici had often demanded tax increases in various deficit-reduction bills in the 1980s. To assuage Mitchell, Darman privately told him that Bush hadn't really meant the pledge—but to retain his credibility with conservatives, he would need a year's leeway before breaking it.[52]

Deciding to make Bush pay a political price for this pledge, Mitchell developed a strategy that rested on his knowledge that the Gramm-Rudman-Hollings targets could not be met without tax increases once Bush had taken entitlements and military spending off the table.[53] If Bush included no new taxes in his forthcoming budget in early 1990, Democrats could accuse him of issuing a phony budget and grab the political high ground by proposing their own budget. If he did recommend new taxes, Democrats would watch from the sidelines as conservatives savaged Bush for breaking his pledge. Either course of action, they decided, would damage Bush when he sought a second term in 1992.

Following his game plan, Mitchell attacked Bush's budget as phony in early 1990 when it contained only minor tax increases. Mitchell, meanwhile, was working with Democrats that spring to write their own budget resolutions, with some cuts in military spending and higher taxes on wealthy Americans. Bush decided he had to negotiate with Democratic leaders to develop a budget deal because at this pivotal juncture, the deficit ballooned to $160 billion, just as the Congressional Budget Office had said it would. Revenues dried up as the economic slowdown got worse and as Bush feared huge deficits would further harm the economy by raising interest rates even above their current level of 11.5 percent. He still wanted to preserve his military budget, moreover, and still feared across-the-board cuts in military spending if Gramm-Rudman-Hollings triggered sequestration.[54] (Bush also feared he might lose the 1992 elections if he allowed deficits to rise even higher than their levels when he took office.)

When Bush approached Democratic leaders about participating in negotiations, Mitchell cagily insisted that he verbally agree to "no preconditions," meaning Bush could not take taxes off the table. When Bush agreed to this proviso and talks began in May, howls of protest erupted from many Republicans, who were furious that Bush even agreed to place new taxes on the table in light of his campaign pledge. But the talks quickly bogged down as they had on many occasions in the Reagan years; Democrats wanted higher taxes on wealthy citizens, while Bush, responding to conservatives' angst, clarified that he did not necessarily approve of increases in income taxes, though he might favor increases in other kinds of taxes.[55] (Republicans also wanted Democrats to concede larger cuts in entitlements like Medicare while avoiding cuts in military spending.)

Having persuaded Bush to agree verbally to no preconditions and believing he was desperate to reach an agreement, Democratic leaders now insisted that he place in writing a pledge that tax increases would be part of the budget deal. Again, to the chagrin of such House Republicans as Newt Gingrich, who vainly tried to pass a nonbinding House resolution to prohibit tax increases in any budget deal, Bush agreed to this demand, meaning that the question no longer was whether taxes would be raised but whose taxes would be increased. (Bush and Darman favored regressive taxes on gas and cigarettes, while many Democrats supported a surtax on millionaires and increases in the top marginal rates of affluent citizens.)

Bush's concession did not allay partisan conflict, however. Mitchell convinced other Democrats to play a waiting game, offering few concessions and forcing Bush to concede major tax increases in a game of chicken right up to October 1, when sequestration would be required if Congress failed to meet the Gramm-Rudman-Hollings targets. Even more desperate for a budget agreement by late September because he could ill afford sequestration and deep military cuts on the eve of a major military offensive against Saddam Hussein, Bush conceded large, though regressive, tax increases.

In a development that was ominous for advocates of a peace dividend, however, cuts in military spending were not central to the negotiations between Bush and the Democrats. When House Democrats had earlier voted for $24 billion in cuts in military budget authority from Bush's budget recommendations, they were staunchly resisted by the hawkish Democratic chairs of the House Armed Services Committee and the Appropriations Subcommittee on Defense—chairs who were appeased only when reassured by House Speaker Thomas Foley that the Senate Budget Committee would ensure that the military saw no deep cuts.[56]

Using Desert Storm to Preserve the Military Budget

During these contentious budget talks in late July 1990, the U.S. ambassador to Iraq, April Glaspie, was summoned to the office of Saddam Hussein, Iraq's dictator, where they discussed tensions between Kuwait and Iraq. U.S. officials had long known that Saddam had many grievances against Kuwaiti leaders—he contended they took oil illegally from some of his wells by slant drilling across his border; depleted his revenues by driving down oil prices by selling oil in excess of quotas set by the Organization of Petroleum-Exporting Countries (OPEC); and undermined his national economy by refusing to give Iraq loans after its ruinous war with Iran.[57] Bush contends that Glaspie's statement to Saddam in this meeting—"we don't take a stand on territorial disputes"—was not encouragement to invade Kuwait but merely a pat phrase used by the State Department to tell nations that the United States takes no position on the merits of disputes but expects them to resolve their differences peacefully.[58] Bush also contends that Glaspie and the State Department had warned Saddam for a long time not to invade Kuwait or any other nation. (Other scholars and journalists believe that Glaspie did signify tacit acceptance of Saddam's intention to take from Kuwait disputed border oil fields and two tiny offshore islands, Warba and Bubiyan, that he believed belonged to Iraq.)[59] Within days of Glaspie's meeting, Saddam's troops invaded and conquered the adjacent state of Kuwait.

Once Iraq had invaded Kuwait, Bush contends, he gradually moved (over a period of weeks) toward the position that the United States had to forcibly evict Iraq if it did not withdraw from Kuwait. Partly, he feared Saddam's controlling a major portion of the world's known oil reserves if Kuwait's reserves were added to Iraq's. Partly, he feared that Saddam was positioning himself to assault Saudi Arabia in a move that would place a majority of the world's oil reserves under his control. As the last president who remembered the appeasement of Hitler, Bush saw parallels with the situation in Munich and feared that failure to turn back Saddam's invasions would encourage both Hussein and other dictators to invade other nations.[60] Other commentators suggest, however, that Bush took action because he had developed a deep personal animus toward Saddam and believed the Iraqi had betrayed a tacit agreement to limit his invasion to the offshore islands and the oil field.[61]

Other critics see Bush as reflexively defending the interests of large oil companies.[62] Some journalists speculate that the Iraqi invasion gave Bush an opportunity to fulfill his ambition to demonstrate "greatness" as president by leading the nation to battle in a war larger than the smaller invasion of Panama.[63]

With attention focused on the causes of the war, less attention has been given to Bush's broader use of the war to preserve the military budget. Coming as it did when pressures had built for a peace dividend, the timing of Saddam's invasion of Kuwait could not have been more fortuitous for Bush. Already fearful that the United States would revert to isolationism, Bush saw Iraq's invasion as the first post–cold war test of the U.S. resolve to counter aggression. Bush wanted the United States not only to take action against Saddam but to use this action as a kind of public relations exercise to demonstrate how Americans could rapidly repel a dictator. He wanted, moreover, a dramatic display of U.S. technology on the battlefield, and a demonstration of the prowess of U.S. ground troops—a display that would strengthen the case for the continuing development of new weapons and a massive military. Partly because he doubted it would work but also because it would not provide a dramatic display of U.S. military might, Bush quickly rejected reliance on an extended economic embargo to force Saddam to leave Kuwait, as some Democrats urged. (An economic embargo was put into place in the fall with the help of a resolution from the U.N. Security Council.) Bush also rejected the insistence of Colin Powell and Jordan's King Hussein that Arab nations take the lead in ousting Saddam Hussein from Kuwait and defending Saudi Arabia.

Bush also wanted to couple military prowess with a framing of the impending conflict as good versus evil. It was not difficult to portray Saddam as evil because he was evil, but Bush decided early to demonize him by frequently comparing him to Adolf Hitler. It was more difficult, however, to portray the Kuwaiti regime, itself dictatorial and ridden with corruption, as the paragon of virtue. Indeed, Moynihan, who was opposed to military action against Saddam, concluded in the aftermath of the Persian Gulf War, "All that's happened is that one nasty little country invaded a little but just as nasty country."[64] Bush's quest to demonize the Iraqis and to sanitize the Kuwaitis was fostered by charges that the Iraqis had brutalized patients in a hospital in Kuwait, a charge later found to have been fabricated by the Kuwaiti royal family.

Bush early realized that a quagmire similar to Vietnam would be counterproductive and would even make many Americans turn against the military. Such fears were eased, however, by military planners who confidentially told Bush and the National Security Council that the prognosis for rapid victory was excellent.[65] While Iraq had formidable military forces, it had not had to develop and defend long supply lines in its border conflict with Iran. Nor did Iraq have combat experience against a formidable airpower that, aided by satellite data, could devastate its communications system, airfields and aircraft, depots, fuel storage tanks, and tanks. Indeed, military planners predicted that Iraq could be largely vanquished in a thirty-day air campaign. Armed with this military intelligence, Bush dismissed the opinions of people like Robert McNamara, who predicted as many as thirty thousand American casualties.[66]

Although some Arab states at first wanted to take the initiative in repelling Saddam, they quickly supported the U.S.-led coalition, whether because they feared Saddam or succumbed to U.S. inducements (in the case of Egypt), such as a renegotiation of debt or other concessions. With Eastern Europe asserting its independence from the Soviet Union by late 1990, with many Soviet republics stirring with dissent, and with Gorbachev eager for economic aid from Western powers, the Soviet leader was in a poor position to oppose U.S.-led intervention, though he frequently tried to mediate the dispute. Without the Soviets exercising their veto in the Security Council that fall, the United States was able to secure supportive resolutions at key points that set in place an economic embargo of

Iraq and that laid down an ultimatum to exit Kuwait by mid-January or suffer dire consequences. Nor would the war be costly to the United States because Bush and Baker cleverly persuaded the gulf states and Japan to finance most of it.

The expulsion of Iraq from Kuwait was more than an "ordinary" conflict in Bush's eyes, then. With a dramatic and rapid victory over Saddam with broad support from allies, Middle Eastern nations, and the Soviets, the United States would place itself at the center of a new world order that relied on U.S. military power to restrain dictators of rogue nations. Lawrence Eagleburger, then deputy secretary of state, stated this doctrine succinctly at a National Security Council meeting: "This is the first test of the postwar system. As the bipolar world is relaxed, it permits this, giving people more flexibility because they are not worried about the involvement of the superpowers . . . if [Saddam Hussein] succeeds, others may try the same thing."[67]

A Status Quo Budget Deal

As international tensions rose in August and September 1990, budget negotiators frantically tried to reach a deal in secret negotiations as the Gramm-Rudman-Hollings deadline neared. Congressional liberals were furious at rumors that it would trigger deep cuts in Medicare and force Congress to enact regressive taxes. Some liberals feared that, because of Iraq's invasion of Kuwait, budget negotiators would not make deep cuts in the military. Republican conservatives were furious that they were discussing any tax increases, though Gingrich (now House minority whip) implied he would assent to tax increases even if he verbally assailed them before a deal was reached.[68] With partisan conflict running high and no agreement in sight, to put further pressure on Democrats to accede to a deal Bush refused to sign legislation to delay the effective date of sequestration in late September. Negotiators finally hammered out a deal that many liberals detested because nearly half of its significant tax increases came from regressive gasoline and cigarette taxes and big cuts in Medicare by imposing higher copayments on consumers.[69] When Dick Gephardt, the House majority leader, demanded more military cuts at the last minute, Darman silenced him by saying that such cuts would kill the deal—mere hours remained before sequestration would take effect.[70]

But Bush and Darman faced an irate Gingrich, who had decided to backtrack on his informal agreement. Why not, he decided, use the proposed tax increases as an issue to mobilize conservatives in Congress and nationally into a powerful movement that would gain control of the House in 1992 or 1994, which would allow him to become Speaker? Gingrich did not like Bush, whom he viewed as excessively moderate—why not urge House Republicans to repudiate the deal, even if this action could cause serious harm to Bush?[71] Most House Republicans voted against the budget deal and attacked Bush for violating his tax pledge; the House defeated the budget deal in a crushing defeat for Bush, who refused even to speak with Gingrich afterward.

When House liberals realized that most House Republicans would vote against the budget deal, liberals no longer believed they needed to support it, even if such Democratic leaders as Foley implored them to do so. Well aware that Bush needed a deal before the impending elections and to avoid sequestration on the eve of a war with Iraq, Democrats wrote a budget deal more to their liking, replacing regressive taxes with tax levies on affluent Americans and diminishing proposed cuts in Medicare. Feeling he had no choice, Bush signed the budget deal on November 8 in a huge victory for the Democratic negotiators.[72] (Had Gingrich not sabotaged the earlier deal, Bush would have been less vilified by his party because those tax increases fell mostly on low- and moderate-income people.)

The Democrats secured a budget deal more to their liking, but they again blinked with respect to military spending. With the Gulf conflict imminent, they chose merely to cap military spending for three years at $298 billion in 1991, $296 billion in 1992, and $293 billion in 1993, cutting military spending only modestly in 1991 and pledging not to make deep cuts in military spending for (at least) three years.[73] While Bush might ordinarily have viewed a freeze on military spending to be a defeat, it was actually a major victory at a time when many experts wanted huge cuts in military spending as the Soviet threat eased.

Even more astonishingly, Democrats did not contest Bush's placing of caps on domestic discretionary spending, allowing them to rise from only $198 billion in 1991 to only $222 billion in 1993. While some conservatives were furious that 1991 expenditures were higher than 1990 expenditures, this increase was relatively modest, considering that domestic discretionary spending had been frozen under the Gramm-Rudman-Hollings legislation for years. The Democrats also conceded a provision that sabotaged a peace dividend for three years when they agreed that any cuts in the military spending beyond the caps established in the deal had to be used for deficit reduction rather than for increased domestic spending.[74]

A Show-Biz War

As commander in chief, Bush decided that he had constitutional authority to wage war with Iraq without securing approval of the Senate, an assertion disputed by some constitutional theorists and some Democrats. He decided to seek supportive resolutions from both chambers to rally the nation behind the conflict. (He later confessed he would have launched Desert Storm even without congressional approval.)[75] Although the House approved a resolution by a wide margin, the Senate vote was narrow—52–42, with such Democratic leaders as Mitchell, Kennedy, and Nunn opposing it on the ground that an economic quarantine of Iraq would be sufficient to induce it to withdraw from Kuwait. (On January 14, 1991, Congress voted to support a resolution backing the U.N. Security Council decision to approve the use of force against Iraq.) Before and during these congressional deliberations, Bush and Baker continued to organize a coalition of nations against Saddam; to send huge quantities of weapons, supplies, and troops to the Middle East in a prolonged buildup; and to convince the United Nations to give Saddam an ultimatum to leave Kuwait by mid-January.

Bush launched Desert Storm on January 17, 1991, with about seven weeks of bombing, followed by an invasion of Iraq and Kuwait on February 24 that lasted only one hundred hours before fighting ended on February 27. It may have been the most one-sided war in military history. Coalition forces, dominated by U.S. military personnel, suffered only 148 casualties compared with 100,000 deaths and 300,000 injuries by Iraqi forces.[76] (In a matter of weeks the Iraqis incurred roughly twice the deaths of U.S. forces in Vietnam—and would have suffered even more deaths had Saddam not removed a significant portion of his troops from battle.) Against a desert nation whose air force was immediately destroyed or removed from action, and in possession of satellite data regarding Iraqi military installations and troop movements, coalition bombers pummeled Iraq's forces, installations, and communications using laser-guided weapons and cruise missiles. (In less than two months the United States dropped on Iraq 5 percent of the number of bombs used in World War II.)

Bush and the Pentagon produced a public relations extravaganza. Save primarily for reports of a single CNN correspondent in Baghdad, the American public saw only what the Pentagon wanted it to see, including videos of laser-guided missiles and bombs destroying specific installations with pinpoint accuracy, sophisticated aircraft returning from sorties, and cruise missiles being launched from naval destroyers. When the Iraqis fired some Scud missiles at Israel, the public was informed that Patriot missiles, fired from Israeli soil, had destroyed many of them. With the United States festooned with yellow plastic on many doors and street lamps, Bush's popularity rose to record levels, even approaching 90 percent approval at one point. Because the war ended only twenty months before the presidential election, Bush's reelection seemed so assured that many leading Democrats, such as Dick Gephardt, decided not to run against him in 1992.

A sober analysis of Desert Storm would have to await the war's end. Only in succeeding months and years did legislators and reporters determine that only 15 percent of the laser-guided bombs had actually hit their targets and that virtually none of the Patriot missiles had destroyed slow-moving Scud missiles.[77] Many naval aircraft produced during the Reagan buildup were so ineffective that they were not used at all or were hurriedly withdrawn from battle; the air campaign relied heavily on older fighters like the F-15s.

Nor did Desert Storm necessarily suggest that the United States needed massive military forces in the aftermath of the cold war. The one-sided affair strongly suggested that lesser forces would have sufficed against a third-world nation with a population of eighteen million people that faced a coalition of nations that had 1.8 billion citizens and 90 percent of the world's industrial capacity.

In light of the dramatic victory that cost the United States virtually no lives or resources, few people asked searching questions about it. Should the United States have borne such a large share of the weapons and troops used by Desert Storm?[78] Could Arab nations have spearheaded the war against Saddam, as Colin Powell and King Hussein had urged? Was Desert Storm a precedent for other third-world wars in which the United States would take the lead militarily and its partners would mostly watch from the sidelines? Did the United States possess an "army for hire," to be freely used in an array of conflicts around the world? Did the United States need a military as large as its cold war forces to contain dictators like Saddam? Did the air campaign cause excessive civilian casualties?

Bush hailed the war as vindication of his claim that the United States, with its huge military still intact, should become the primary force on the international scene after the cold war. In reflecting on the war years later, Bush and Scowcroft concluded:

> The war's impact on international relations went beyond breaking the diplomatic logjam in the United Nations. The United States had recognized and shouldered its peculiar responsibility for leadership in tackling international challenges, and won wide acceptance for this role around the globe. American political credibility and influence had sky-rocketed. We stood almost alone on the world stage. . . . Our military reputation grew as well . . . whereas Soviet weapons, with which the Iraqis were largely equipped, did not reflect well on their maker.[79]

Such military leaders as Powell became national heroes during and after a war that also allowed the military to rehabilitate its reputation following the procurement and sex scandals that had bedeviled it during Reagan's second term. The impending conflict had silenced demands for cuts in military spending during the budget negotiations of 1990, making it more difficult to seek military cuts in 1991 and 1992 as the Soviet Union disintegrated into a disparate set of republics.

The Quest for a Peace Dividend (Part 2)

Whereas Desert Storm had diminished pressure to cut military spending in late 1990 and early 1991, the continuing disintegration of the Soviet Union in 1991 revived pressure for a peace dividend after the Gulf War. Gorbachev's efforts to retain central control in Moscow and to keep the Soviet Communist Party intact proved increasingly futile. As a referendum on a New Union Treaty neared, six republics said they would boycott it. (Nine other republics approved it.) Yeltsin signed a security pact between Russia and the three Baltic states, thus undercutting Gorbachev. Meeting with officials from the nine republics that had approved the New Union Treaty, Gorbachev agreed to revise it to include the right of secession. With his economy in tatters Gorbachev pleaded with the

G-7 nations for $100 billion in aid, only to receive a cold shoulder. Rumors circulated in early summer that top military brass, seething at the fragmenting of power in regard to the republics and deep cuts in military spending, soon would initiate a right-wing coup against Gorbachev. Shortly after Gorbachev headed for vacation in the Crimea in August, a cadre of military and right-wing politicians tried just that, only to be rebuffed by a crowd in the streets and a defiant Yeltsin, who addressed the throng from atop a tank before taking refuge in the Supreme Soviet and Parliament Building. Gorbachev was officially restored to power when the Russian Supreme Soviet declared the attempted coup to be illegal, but he had been eclipsed by Yeltsin and discredited by the coup. Now the Baltic states, the Ukraine, and Byelorussia declared independence. Virtually all the republics had declared independence by the fall of 1991; the denouement occurred in November when Yeltsin dissolved all Russian ties with the central Soviet government and the Ukraine ratified independence by a 90 percent vote in a referendum. Bypassing Gorbachev altogether, Yeltsin spearheaded a separate confederation of Soviet republics, the Commonwealth of Independent States, which four republics with 90 percent of the Soviet GDP quickly joined. Feeling betrayed by Yeltsin, Gorbachev resigned on Christmas Day and soon transferred the authority to use nuclear weapons to Yeltsin as the Soviet military, Gorbachev's last hold on power, rapidly fragmented into military forces of the former republics. (Yevgeny Shaposhnikov, Gorbachev's new head of the Soviet Armed Forces, had announced cuts of 80 percent of the Soviet officer corps by fall 1991.)[80]

In the United States after the Gulf War, Democrats scrambled to shift national attention to the domestic agenda as the travails of the Soviet Union gathered momentum. Mitchell and Foley, among others, urged Congress to reopen the 1990 budget deal so that Congress could shift military resources to the domestic agenda, but Bush and Cheney adamantly refused to renegotiate it or to let Democrats backtrack on their promise not to make deep cuts in military spending for at least three years.[81] Nor were many Democrats willing to take the offensive against military spending in the wake of a popular war. They were afraid that Bush would remind the public that many Democrats had opposed the Gulf War by voting against congressional resolutions supporting it. Why not wait, some asked, until after the presidential elections of 1992 when memory of the war had faded?

Not content merely to launch a renewed offensive against a peace dividend, Bush used other strategies to maintain military spending. Anticipating that Democrats might attack military spending, he had already sought high military budget authorizations for fiscal years 1991, 1992, and 1993, hoping that Democrats could not cut hundreds of new military contracts for fear of causing layoffs in their districts—a tactic that Reagan had used in 1981 and 1982.[82] Bush employed another clever strategy in the fall of 1991. He appeared to be making deep cuts in military spending when he issued a unilateral concession to Gorbachev that pledged to eliminate multiple warhead systems, abandon the newest mobile ICBM, and sharply reduce arsenals. But these concessions cut only $500 million from the $291 billion military budget because they dismantled systems already built and paid for—they did not cut new systems.[83] (Bush betrayed his reluctance to make even these concessions by announcing them in a dry, technical television address scheduled when few people would be watching.)

Bush's unilateral cuts nonetheless emboldened Democrats to demand further military cuts, but they quarreled among themselves about the size of the cuts, as well as parliamentary strategy to undo the 1990 budget provisions that forbade transferring military savings to the domestic agenda.[84] Ted Kennedy wanted cuts of $210 billion over seven years, but James Sasser of Texas wanted cuts of $120 billion over four years. The Democrats' military expert in the House, Les Aspin of Wisconsin, confused matters further by developing four alternative military budgets with appropriations of $231 billion, $246 billion, $270 billion, and $295 billion by fiscal 1997 whereas Bush was recommending $291 billion.[85] (The budgets differed in the number and size of regional wars that the United States could wage at the same time.) To further complicate matters, Gramm proposed a 5 percent cut in military spending to fund a tax cut for middle-class families rather than to expand domestic spending. Meanwhile, other Republicans demanded that any military cuts be devoted to deficit reduction.

The disagreement in both parties about the size of military cuts and how they might be spent gave Bush a tactical advantage. He proposed small military cuts (or $66 billion by fiscal 1997) to avert larger cuts, prompting Sasser to label the president's plan as "indecisive when it should seize the historical opportunity to convert peace to domestic gain."[86] The Pentagon developed seven war scenarios that included

Iraq's invading Kuwait and Saudi Arabia, North Korea's attacking South Korea, Russia's attacking Lithuania through Poland, and the rise of a new "expansionist superpower."[87] To meet these threats, both singly and in tandem, the Pentagon contended that the United States needed "robust" military spending well into the next century, including 150,000 troops in Europe, a base force of 1.6 million, twelve carrier fleets, and military spending of $281 billion in fiscal 1993. Bush charged that the Democrats had threatened to "cripple national defense" as they opened a bidding war to see who could cut the military most rapidly.[88] When the Pentagon issued a document in early March that rejected any "collective internationalism" on the ground that United States alone was the ultimate protector of the world order, even senior White House and State Department officials called it a "dumb report"—the administration preferred to use the United Nations and regional alliances in certain circumstances. (This was a rare retreat by an administration mostly interested in retaining U.S. military forces even as its former enemy lay prostrate.)[89] In yet another tactic to avert a peace dividend, Bush and Cheney contended that large military cuts would exacerbate the recession—particularly in hard-struck California, a state vital to the political interests of both parties.[90]

During this political confusion, Lt. Gen. James Clapper, director of the Defense Intelligence Agency, stunned many legislators during public hearings when he said that Russia had cut military procurement by 80 percent and research and development by 30 percent—and that no offensive threat existed.[91] When Congress failed to exceed Bush's proposed cuts of $7.4 billion in the military budget for fiscal 1993, a *New York Times* editorial charged that "War Democrats" had blinked and had agreed to $1.5 trillion in military spending over six years.[92] (The Senate rejected a Democratic proposal to cut military spending more deeply and divert some money to domestic spending.) The Democrats capitulated in late spring, ratifying Bush's military request and even supporting major funding for the B-2 bomber, antimissile defense, and the Seawolf attack submarine—and Bush had not even sought funding for the Seawolf.

Perhaps Moynihan was correct when he asked Bush to declare a formal end to the cold war, complete with a ticker tape parade on Wall Street, as a prelude to deep military cuts and substantial enhancements of the domestic agenda. The United States had completed, and perhaps won, the most costly conflict in its history—at a cost of *more than $12.2 trillion*, from the summer of 1950 through 1993.[93]

Although the Bush administration needlessly kept the military budget intact, it deserves credit for signing the Conventional Forces in Europe Treaty in late 1990, START I in 1991, and START II in early 1993, just before Bush left office. After signing START I in July, which eliminated several thousand missiles, Bush announced a unilateral de-escalation in September that included taking all bombers off alert, destroying nuclear artillery shells, removing tactical nuclear warheads from naval surface ships and submarines, and removing nuclear weapons from land-based naval aircraft. (Gorbachev reciprocated with similar concessions in October.) Both sides commenced talks, moreover, that eventually led to START II, which would ban multiple warheads from intercontinental ballistic missiles if both nations ratified it. (The Senate ratified START II, but it remained stalled in the Duma—and Congress mandated that reductions in nuclear forces cannot go below START I limits until Russia has ratified START II.) The U.S. stockpile of intercontinental and submarine-launched ballistic missiles (SLBMs) declined from roughly 1,600 to 1,050 missiles, while Soviet ICBM and SLBM forces declined from roughly 2,500 to 1,600 missiles—and each side destroyed roughly 4,000 strategic nuclear warheads from 1990 to 1995.[94] These figures need to be considered in light of four caveats, however. Both sides retained huge strategic capabilities, even with the end of the cold war. While Soviet military spending had declined markedly by late 1992, U.S. military spending had dropped only slightly. The number of nuclear warheads on each side in 1995 was not much lower than in 1980, at the height of the cold war.[95] Not only has START II not been implemented but actual START I reductions occurred largely after Bush left office. (If START II is implemented, the U.S. arsenal of ICBMs and SLBMs will drop from 1,672 to 836 and the Russians' from 1,230 to 800 missiles—and each side will have about eight thousand strategic warheads—or two thousand fewer than before.)

"Empowerment" on the Cheap

Persuaded by James Pinkerton, his domestic policy adviser, to emphasize a legislative package under the rubric of *empowerment*, Bush used the term in his State of Union address in 1991, sending to Congress a group of housing, education, enterprise-zone, and small-business programs designed to "empower citizens." It seemed an innovative approach, long sought by Jack Kemp at Department of Housing and Urban Development and many conservative theorists, who contrasted empowerment with traditional programs of the welfare state. The idea was to help public housing tenants to own their own homes; to give vouchers to low-income parents so they could choose the school their children would attend; and to use federal loans and grants to encourage businesses to relocate to inner-city enterprise zones, where they would employ many former welfare recipients and low-income residents.

Even some Democrats were intrigued by empowerment, wondering, for example, whether welfare could be converted to a jobs program. Michael Sherraden, a professor of social work, advocated federally subsidized savings accounts known as "individual development accounts."[96] Bill Clinton, the governor of Arkansas who was rumored to be pondering a run for president in 1992, strongly supported empowerment, as did the centrist Democratic Leadership Conference (DLC), which he cofounded.

Bush made only a tentative commitment to empowerment in early 1991, however. Most of his senior advisers did not strongly endorse this concept, often viewing Jack Kemp, an outspoken advocate of empowerment, as a loose cannon who veered in a liberal direction. Another top aide doubted empowerment programs "speak that powerfully to most Americans." Bush waited until the end of Desert Storm to decide whether to commit himself strongly to this theme and backed off soon after a speech on empowerment in the spring of 1991 received a tepid response.[97]

Nor did Bush push empowerment programs later in 1991. Absent federal commitments and presidential support, empowerment became a rhetorical device rather than a strong policy initiative. Stuart Butler, a conservative theorist at the Heritage Foundation, conceded that "unless hard budget choices eventually get made, empowerment is a boutique program."[98] (Bush's disinclination to fund empowerment programs was further increased by huge deficits and caps on discretionary spending in the 1990 budget deal.) He committed only $2 billion to empowerment programs in January 1992.[99]

Bush betrayed his lack of commitment to any major domestic initiatives, save for rights for the disabled, a small child-care measure developed by the Democrats, and programs to lessen air pollution, by placing Roger Porter in charge of domestic legislation. Porter was a process-oriented bureaucrat who lacked imagination and kept initiatives from Kemp and other staff bottled up in endless committee meetings. When Kemp sought support from Porter for specific initiatives, he often received polite hearings, but but his initiatives went nowhere. During his campaign Bush had promised to fund Head Start so that it reached all four-year-olds, but he sought only a $500 million increase for the program, which reached only 1 in 5 eligible preschoolers in 1991.[100]

From Eyes Abroad to Defeat at Home

Even in early 1990, it was obvious to such political professionals as Ed Rollins, Ronald Reagan's former campaign director, that Bush was in deep political trouble. Although his personal popularity was high, fewer than 30 percent of Americans believed the United States was "on the right track."[101] Euphoric after Desert Storm, Bush believed he could coast to victory on his foreign policy successes and failed to understand that the deep recession had elevated in voters' minds the importance of unemployment and the state of the economy. Even such conservatives as Gingrich warned Bush that he risked losing the 1992 election if he failed to make domestic issues a priority.[102] Democrats gained a growing public relations advantage in 1990 and 1991 as they replaced Bush's regressive taxes in the budget deal with ones that focused on affluent Americans. Democrats also sought more money to retrain workers laid off during the recession, attacked corporate downsizing and mergers, and sought pump-priming expenditures on roads and construction. Voters viewed military preparedness as less important with the demise of the Soviet Union, even if few Americans favored deep military cuts.

Bush's support from fellow Republicans also eroded after he broke his pledge of no new taxes in 1990. Some supported Pat Buchanan, a former Nixon aide, in the 1992 presidential primaries, which divided the Republican Party. Nor did Bush endear himself to Republican moderates when he continued to rebuff Kemp's empowerment agenda in the spring of 1991, and his meager domestic agenda did not impress suburban independents. Belatedly acknowledging that the nation was in a recession, Bush initiated no major measures to help unemployed people, while he continued to advocate a cut in the capital gains tax for affluent Americans. By ignoring domestic issues, Bush left an opening for Bill Clinton, who quickly vaulted over other Democratic contenders in the primaries of 1992 by focusing his attention on such domestic issues as national health-care reform, educational reforms, increased job training, and a family leave act that Bush had vetoed. With some of the tax increases from the 1990 budget deal due to expire in 1993, Clinton emphasized tax cuts for poor and moderate-income people to be financed by tax increases for affluent Americans.

With his mind still enmeshed in the cold war, Bush underestimated Bill Clinton. How could a war hero lose to a person widely alleged to have avoided the draft? Surmising that this issue would resonate with most Americans, Bush made it a major issue in the campaign. He failed to recognize that many Americans were more interested in domestic issues than attacks on the patriotism of a political opponent that were left over from the cold war.

Bush was vulnerable, moreover, to the third-party candidacy of Ross Perot, an eccentric billionaire who attacked Bush savagely while muting his criticisms of Clinton. Perot emphasized two issues: gridlock and deficits. Perot said that Bush had contributed to the inability of Congress to address important issues, such as the deficit, by emphasizing his veto power and that Bush had failed to significantly attack the deficit. Perot said that Bush ought to be developing policies to help workers who had been victimized by global economic competition.

Ultimately, however, Bush's worst enemy was himself. Both Clinton and Perot "were good at the 'vision thing,'" staking out specific issues and connecting with the lives of voters.[103] Bush had almost no ability to relate to the public on domestic issues, much less to develop a coherent agenda. The curtain went down on the Bush presidency when he received only 38 percent of the vote. Perot received 19 percent and Clinton 43 percent—the same percentage George McGovern received in his landslide loss in 1972.

Failed Priorities in the Bush Administration

The U.S. and Soviet stockpiles of strategic offensive nuclear weapons declined during the Bush administration for the first time since the cold war began, whether measured in the numbers of bombers, ICBMs, and SLBMs or the number of strategic warheads. This reduction was real, even if START II was never implemented and START I reductions occurred largely after Bush left office. As figure 12.1 suggests, however, military spending declined only slightly in constant dollars from 1989 to 1991 and actually increased from 1991 to 1992. Cold war spending remained intact even as the confrontation ended. Bush bequeathed to his successor, then, a full-blown military budget that remained far above its cold war levels of 1980, before the Reagan buildup. In addition, Bush sent into production numerous weapons systems that would make it difficult to reduce military spending during his successor's term.

Despite his budget deal of 1990, Bush had not severed Reagan's Gordian knot. Entitlements resumed their meteoric rise after growing more slowly during the 1980s. Military spending and interest payments on the national debt remained relatively constant. The megadeficits of the Reagan years remained largely intact, albeit with important reductions as a result of the 1990 budget deal.

Bush missed a remarkable opportunity to revise national priorities when the cold war ended. Although the reductions in tactical and strategic missiles were salutory, they merely redressed overkill capabilities that had existed in the United States for decades. Bush should have proposed major cuts in military spending at this pivotal juncture and spent those

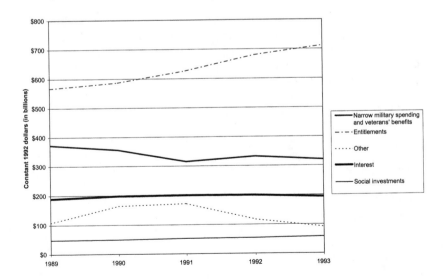

FIGURE 12.1 Five Types of Federal Expenditures, 1989–1993

Source: Office of Management and Budget, *Budget of the U.S. Government, FY 2000, Historical Tables* (Washington, D.C.: GPO, 1999), table 3.1, p. 48.

resources for some combination of aid to former communist nations, deficit reduction, and the domestic agenda.

With scant interest in the domestic agenda and a penchant for resorting to rhetoric like "kinder and gentler" or a "thousand points of light," Bush essentially continued the Reagan tradition of denying new resources to domestic spending, save for the automatic increases in entitlements mandated by statute (see fig. 12.1). A status quo president at home and abroad, Bush largely retained the budget configuration he had inherited from Reagan. It would remain for his successors to decide whether to seek basic changes in national priorities or continue a cold war configuration.

I argue in chapter 15 that Bush and Congress wasted $642 billion—not counting pork-barrel spending, most forms of corporate welfare, excessive tax concessions to affluent Americans, and excessive deregulation.

13

Clinton as Backpedaler
and Counterpuncher

Bill Clinton ran for the presidency on a relatively liberal platform. Coming to the presidency after his predecessors and Congress had repeatedly slashed and frozen the domestic budget, would he try to free money for domestic programs by cutting various kinds of waste, such as that in the military budget? In this and the next two chapters I contend that the Clinton administration and Congress made fiscal and tax errors exceeding $1.2 trillion.

The Liberals' Nixon?

Recall that Richard Nixon opportunistically moved in liberal directions when it suited his political needs, even if he was instinctively a conservative. As the governor of Arkansas during most of the 1980s and into the early 1990s, Clinton too had demonstrated tactical flexibility. Sometimes he supported such liberal reforms as expansion of the state's Medicaid program, major tax increases to fund road construction, school reforms, and lower utility rates. But he frequently retreated when he came under fire from the relatively conservative legislature, repudiating former allies like organized labor or school-teachers, refusing to support civil rights measures, seeking deep cuts in spending, or advocating tax cuts.

Clinton's shifting political views, likened to a kaleidoscope by aide George Stephanopoulos, partly stemmed from his early political career in the South, where, like Lyndon Johnson, he had confronted a strong populist tradition that coexisted uneasily with southern conservatism and fundamentalism.[1] On the one hand, Arkansas was a deeply conservative state, where any successful politician had to appeal to some conservatives and moderates to be elected. Even the liberal J. William Fulbright, the late senator from Arkansas, took deeply conservative positions on racial matters. Yet many successful Arkansas politicians, like Fulbright and Senator Dale Bumpers, supported progressive policies both at home and abroad.

Capable of going in liberal or conservative directions, Clinton was also adept at splitting the difference, as he revealed when he cofounded the Democratic Leadership Conference (DLC) in 1985. Clinton, who had witnessed the defeat of McGovern at firsthand, signaled his decision to ally himself with the moderate wing of the Democratic Party when he supported Jimmy Carter over Ted Kennedy in the presidential primaries of 1980.[2] Reagan's landslide victory over Carter further convinced Clinton that the Democrats had to find a "third way"—between conservative and liberal poles—if they wished to counter Reagan's attempt to lure white southerners and northern white ethnics to the Republican Party. Why not, Clinton asked, make major changes in Democrats' ideology under the rubric of "New Democrats"?[3] Whereas traditional Democrats had championed the needs of low-income Americans and those who suffered racial discrimination, New Democrats emphasized the economic needs of the middle class. Where traditional Democrats had favored the redistribution of resources to the poor, civil rights legislation, affirmative action, and tariffs to protect U.S. industries, New Democrats emphasized a narrower range of economic reforms—job training, national educational standards, free trade, and infrastructure improvements. Where traditional Democrats favored new spending on social programs, New Democrats favored balanced budgets. Where traditional Democrats wanted large cuts in military spending after the cold war, New Democrats favored only selective cuts. Where traditional Democrats emphasized entitlements, New Democrats emphasized the obligations of citizens to work, raise families, and obey laws. Nor were New Democrats supportive of traditional Democrats' lenience toward welfare recipients or criminals, favoring stiff work requirements, limits on benefits, tougher penalties for drug dealing and other crimes, and extending the death penalty to new crimes.

This DLC language failed, however, to capture Clinton's versatility. He sometimes occupied the DLC's middle ground but could veer left or right as circumstances dictated. Like Nixon, moreover, he was willing to occupy a lonely perch and let conservatives, liberals, and members of the DLC feel he betrayed them as he based his maneuvers in a turbulent political environment on polling data.

Clinton's Ambidexterity

Clinton decided to run for the presidency in the late summer of 1991. He faced an uphill battle because Bush's ratings had skyrocketed during Desert Storm. But Clinton already sensed the vulnerability of a president who had staked his future on foreign policy even as polls hinted that the public wanted domestic reforms. Clinton recognized too that Bush had divided his own party by breaking his no-tax pledge. With many top Democrats like Dick Gephardt refraining from joining the race because of Bush's high ratings, Clinton realized he had a good chance in a mediocre Democratic field.

Clinton's ambiguous positions served him well in the leaderless Democratic Party. Many Democrats were disposed to run a candidate from a southern state, well aware that Republicans had won five of the last six presidential races partly by wresting sections of the South from them. Yet Clinton appealed to many liberals by virtue of his work on McGovern's campaign, his liberal wife, his numerous liberal contacts and ease in addressing congregations in the African-American community, and his liberal reforms in Arkansas.

With the assistance of such liberal aides as Paul Begala, James Carville, and George Stephanapoulos, Clinton built his 1992 campaign on four themes: higher taxes for the wealthy, enhanced spending on social programs, national health insurance, and increasing economic growth by cutting the deficit and priming the pump. Decrying the growing inequality in the nation, and the tax breaks for affluent Americans in the Reagan years, Clinton demanded higher taxes for the affluent by saying that the two preceding administrations had excessively emphasized "greed." Clinton also supported enhanced "social investments." He was enamored with the theories of Robert Reich, a fellow Rhodes Scholar who contended in *The Wealth of Nations* (1991) that the United States could redress its economic inequalities only by upgrading the education and job training of relatively unskilled people.[4] (Reich wanted to spend as much as $100 billion annually to give millions of citizens free training and education for as long as two years.[5]) Troubled that nearly forty million Americans lacked health insurance, and observing that Pennsylvanians had just elected underdog Harrison Wofford to the Senate partly because he had advocated national health insurance, Clinton promised to make it a priority in his first year.

Clinton cleverly coupled these liberal measures with more conservative ones, such as promising to halve the deficit in four years, enact anticrime and antidrug measures, and "end welfare as we know it" by instituting two-year limits and stiffer work requirements. Even when he broached his populist themes, moreover, he emphasized their importance to the "forgotten middle class" rather than focusing on low-income people. (When Los Angeles became engulfed in the largest riots since the 1960s after a jury acquitted police officers who had brutally beaten Rodney King in 1993, Clinton made only a belated and brief visit to the city.)

Clinton's two-sided program appealed to many Americans. His spending increases for domestic programs appealed to suburban independents and liberals who had tired of Reagan's and Bush's disdain for the domestic agenda, and Clinton's pledge to raise taxes for the affluent appealed to liberals, who were alarmed by the growing economic inequality. Reagan Democrats liked his focus on the middle class and his pledge to halve federal deficits in four years.

Clinton's domestic package came together in June 1992 with the publication of "Putting People First," a sweeping manifesto that emphasized his liberal platform. But Clinton's program had a crucial shortcoming: its numbers did not add up. An aide hurriedly calculated its likely budgetary effects and found that Clinton's program would not allow him to halve the budget deficit within four years, as he had promised, because it coupled significant tax cuts with significant spending increases and offered no major spending cuts in domestic and military programs to make up the difference.[6]

Clinton won the election with only 43 percent of the vote, with Bush and Perot dividing the remaining votes. Arguably, Clinton became president because Bush lost the race, not because Clinton was wildly popular with the voters.[7] Thus he lacked a strong popular mandate for his programs.

Blinking on Military Spending

The military analyst William Kaufmann observed in 1992 that the military budget had declined by only 13 percent in real terms from 1985 to 1990— and that more than 80 percent of this reduction derived the completion of the Reagan buildup's huge acquisitions of weapons.[8] U.S. military spending seemed caught in a kind of time warp, while the former Soviet army consisted of fifteen national forces in different republics that were preoccupied with maintaining civil order, bickering over what what materiel and weapons they could retain from the old Soviet armed forces, and coping with massive reductions in resources. Nor did the republics' forces pose serious offensive threats. The Ukraine had to import 80 percent of its military components because it (like most of the republics) could not manufacture them. Moldova had thirty MiG fighter jets but no tanks.[9]

Kaufmann realized that the United States could not unilaterally disarm because it might have to intervene in one of the former Soviet republics or border states, for example, to defend Lithuania and Poland from invasion from Russia and Belarus. Desert Storm demonstrated that the United States needed sufficient military force to intervene when outright invasions took place. Moreover, the United States needed to be able to deter China if it enhanced its nuclear forces.

Although Bush intended to reduce military spending to $237.5 billion by 1997, this budget still struck Kaufmann as excessive in three major areas. The United States still spent nearly $40 billion on strategic nuclear forces when the nuclear threat from republics of the former Soviet Union had diminished. It spent $40.2 billion on army ground forces when the threat of invasion of Western Europe had receded to zero. It spent nearly $50 billion on nuclear carriers when missiles and land-based aircraft made them vulnerable to attack. Why not, he asked, consider cutting each of these expenditures in half while retaining full appropriations for reserve forces, amphibious Marine Corps units, land-based tactical air forces, special operations forces, intelligence, and communications? Why not, he proposed, cut the military in those areas that had been devoted to the cold war while retaining its ability to participate in regional conflicts and to sustain adequate deterrence in a post-Soviet world?[10]

Kaufmann's convictions that these cuts were feasible were reinforced by the results of a classified Pentagon planning exercise that were leaked to the press in 1992.[11] Looking at hypothetical conflicts, the Pentagon sought to gauge the ability of different levels of military forces: Current Base (existing forces at a cost of $237.5 billion), Force 2 (midlevel forces at a cost of $173.3 billion), and Force 3 (sharply reduced forces at a cost of $135 billion).[12] (See table 13.1.) Force 2 retains 18 Trident submarines, 1,752 nuclear warheads that could reliably demolish almost 90 percent of 1,060 targets, 7 active army divisions, and air power identical to that in Current Base. (Trident submarines could be outfitted with 3,456 warheads at no additional cost if more firepower were needed.)

TABLE 13.1 Annual Cost of Selected Force Options
(in billions of 1993 dollars in budget authority)

ITEM	Base Force	Force 2	Force 3
Strategic nuclear forces	39.3	20.5	11.2
Tactical nuclear forces	0.4	—	—
Ground forces			
Active duty	45.2	28.7	20.6
Reserve	4.4	4.4	4.4
Land-based tactical air forces			
Active duty	36.5	36.5	28.6
Reserve duty	4.9	4.9	4.9
NAVAL FORCES			
Carrier battle groups	49.8	24.9	24.9
Amphibious lift	6.8	4.5	2.3
Sea control	14.8	13.5	6.8
Special operations forces	1.8	1.8	1.8
AIRLIFT AND SEALIFT			
Airlift	11.1	11.1	11.1
Sealift	2.6	2.6	2.6
National intelligence and communications	19.9	19.9	19.9
TOTALS	237.5	173.3	135.0

Source: William Kaufmann, Assessing the Base Force: How Much Is Too Much? (Washington, D.C.: Brookings Institution, 1992), 74.

In the worst-case scenario of an attack on Poland and Lithuania by Russia, the Pentagon's simulations suggested that Current Base forces would win this hypothetical war in 9.5 days, whereas it would take Force 2 twelve days and Force 3 would require 16.5 days. Any of the three levels of force would prove adequate for the task, albeit requiring different amounts of time. (The Pentagon planners reached similar conclusions with respect to a hypothetical Persian Gulf War similar to Desert Storm and an invasion of South Korea by North Korea.)[13]

In light of changing world conditions and these Pentagon simulations, Kaufmann proposed a gradual downsizing of U.S. forces that could be interrupted if world conditions changed, for example, if a Soviet-style threat emerged elsewhere in the world. He proposed a gradual downsizing from Current Base to Force 2 by 1997 and from Force 2 to Force 3 by 2002 to give the United States time to forge closer alliances with NATO and the United Nations and develop less costly joint operations whenever possible. At the same time, the United States, NATO, and the U.N. would encourage preventative diplomacy, including efforts to limit proliferation of nuclear weapons and to secure further arms-reducing treaties with Russia.[14]

While major reductions in force would make it difficult to engage in several regional wars like Desert Storm simultaneously, the cold war had shown that the United States never had to fight multiple wars simultaneously in nearly fifty years, although troop levels were predicated on as many as 2.5 simultaneous wars. Because the United States itself was not threatened by regional conflicts or civil wars, it could decide which conflict was more important if simultaneous conflicts arose—or it could decide how to share the burden with NATO allies or U.N. peacekeeping forces. (Even Force 3 would amply protect the United States from nuclear attack.)

Kaufmann calculated that this gradual downsizing would lead to cumulative savings of $622.7 billion over ten years—or nearly two-thirds of a trillion dollars (in 1993 dollars).[15] Nor was Kaufmann alone. Also writing on the eve of Clinton's election, Leslie Gelb, the State Department correspondent for the *New York Times*, lampooned Bush's intention to spend $1.5 trillion on the military during the next five years—after all, Gelb observed, the Soviet Union no longer existed and no other nation "can marshal military power to threaten the U.S. for perhaps a generation." He urged the next president to cut military spending by one third over the five years so that $500 billion could be diverted to domestic expenditures, noting with hope that "Bill Clinton seems to be saying interesting things, including about cutting defense spending."[16] (Clinton had once proposed military cuts of 33 percent to free up funds for his domestic programs.[17])

Once Clinton won the Democratic nomination, however, he faced off against George Bush, a war hero whose major preoccupation was foreign affairs and who proposed cumulative cuts in military spending of only $47.5 billion during the next five years. Bush placed his opponent on the defensive when he made Clinton's draft avoidance during the Vietnam War a central issue of the campaign. Perhaps Clinton took a lesson from Nixon's successful campaign against McGovern that criticized McGovern's proposed military cuts; certainly, Clinton was aware that cuts would make him vulnerable in voter-rich California with its huge military contracts and a deep recession. Clinton deftly backtracked on military spending, promising to cut merely $60 billion over five years—or only $12.5 billion more than Bush.[18] (The extent to which Clinton backtracked on military cuts is revealed by Paul Nitze's endorsement of him in the summer of 1992—the same Nitze who had favored the huge military buildup of the Reagan administration.)

Clinton again toyed with military cuts after the election when he realized that the deficit for fiscal 1993 would be considerably higher than Bush had predicted before the election—and that Bush had also underestimated future procurement costs by roughly $60 billion. Clinton raised planned military cuts to $14 billion. Now, however, he faced a defiant military brass deeply resentful of his draft avoidance, unhappy about his support for gays in the military, and opposed to his selection of Les Aspin as secretary of defense because Aspin had been an outspoken congressional critic of military spending for years. Colin Powell, the chairman of the Joint Chiefs of Staff who had achieved legendary status as the overseer of Desert Storm, publicly attacked Clinton's proposal to cut military spending by a $2 billion more than Bush had proposed.[19] Clinton learned that Congress would not abide deep military cuts when John Murtha, the Pennsylvania Democrat who chaired the House Defense Appropriations Subcommittee, staunchly resisted military cuts and demanded large military pay increases, as did Daniel Inouye of Hawaii, the Democratic chair of the Senate Defense Appropriations Subcommittee.[20] Legislators from both parties opposed cutting pork-barrel spending in military appropriations—Murtha insisted, for example, that a $65 million grant be funneled to a university in his district.

On the defensive and lacking the fortitude to take on Powell, who threatened, upon Clinton's election, to leave the Joint Chiefs two or three months ahead of schedule, Clinton scaled back his proposal to cut military spending to $10 billion in the coming fiscal year. He lobbied against cuts in the CIA's budget in March, moreover, even though the Congressional Budget Office, a nonpartisan research agency, advocated cuts of $18.8 billion in the CIA's $29 billion budget at a time when the agency received three times what the federal government allotted to education and the environment combined.[21]

When the dust had settled, the military budget was cut by a scant $12.6 billion. But Clinton's challenge in cutting the military budget had just begun. Because troop levels were left intact and because the research and development spending still totaled nearly $80 billion, the only way to reduce military spending was to cut the $76.6 billion operations and maintenance section of the military budget. Cuts in operations and maintenance could be achieved, in turn, only if Congress closed scores of the 481 domestic military bases and installations—a politically difficult trick to pull off because each base and installation provided jobs and an economic boost to legislators' constituents. Like McNamara and Bush before him, Clinton found political cover for base closures by gaining recommendations from an external nonpartisan presidential commission on base closures. Even before Aspin announced that 180 installations would be closed in early March, the news media was filled with stories of the hardships that these closures would exact on local areas—hardships only partly offset by modest "conversion funds" to ease the economic burdens on the affected communities.[22]

Base closures provided few immediate reductions in military spending, however, because closing bases cost the Pentagon hundreds of millions of dollars to address environmental cleanup and other termination costs. (The army estimated it would not realize savings from closing thirty bases until the year 2000.)[23] Immediate and deep cuts in military spending could come only from cutting troop levels and weapons systems, such as reducing active and reserve army divisions, deferring the production of new weapons, or eliminating new weapons altogether. For example, canceling the F-22 fighter-bomber, the army's Comanche helicopter, and the Follow-on Early Warning System would produce immediate savings of $18.6 billion. If the Pentagon also retired Minuteman III missiles, halved the fleet of B-52 bombers, and slowed the operations of missile-carrying subs, it would save $10.8 billion more.[24]

Top Pentagon officials contended in the summer of 1993 that the United States needed nearly a million troops to wage two regional wars at the same time, such as against Saddam Hussein and North Korea. Lawrence Korb, a military expert at the Brookings Institution, said that careful scrutiny of the military capabilities of Iran and North Korea had shown that the Pentagon's estimates were inflated—the United States would need no more than 200,000 troops in each location—or only 16 percent of the 2.5 million personnel on active duty and the reserves. Nor were such expenditures needed to ensure "readiness," Korb contended, because the quality of U.S. troops, and their morale, had markedly improved since 1968; the percentage of troops with high school diplomas had risen from 68 percent to 96 percent, and retention rates had also shown marked increases. Korb, who doubted that weapons and procurement programs were grossly underfunded, contended that the Pentagon could delay weapons or purchase smaller quantities if it encountered cost overruns or higher levels of inflation than had originally been estimated.[25]

Many critics also doubted that the military needed vast new weapons systems in the 1990s because many weapons produced by the Reagan buildup were still usable and superior to the weapons of other nations. Why not, for example, retain the nation's fleet of F-15 fighter-bombers rather than replace them with F-22s? The F-15s had proved remarkably effective in Desert Storm, had a "shelf life" of two or more decades, and were projected to exceed the capabilities of any other fighter-bomber until (at least) the year 2010.[26]

While the United States kept its military spending at cold war levels, the military threat posed by the former Soviet Union continued to recede throughout the 1990s. Although Russia retained six thousand nuclear warheads poised for long-distance delivery, many Russian ships, submarines, and weapons were corroded, and the country's conventional forces had been sharply reduced—the Russians lacked the resources to operate them or to dismantle them. Unable even to feed its sailors, the government at one point asked for voluntary donations of potatoes.[27] The nation ground to an economic halt as its population declined, its death rate soared, and the life expectancy of men dropped to sixty-one years—and as experts predicted that the Russian economy would decline from the world's thirteenth largest to the twentieth largest during the next twenty years.[28]

Losing Social Investments

Because he came from a state that prohibited deficits and where he had faced only weak opposition from Republicans in the state legislature, Clinton assumed he could reduce federal deficits relatively easily.[29] Surely, he thought, Democratic majorities in Congress would allow him to halve the deficits in four years as he had promised in the campaign, even though the debt had grown from $995 billion in 1981 to $4.4 trillion in 1992, with interest payments consuming nearly 15 percent of the federal budget. Nor was he aware during the campaign of the extent to which his proposed middle-class tax cut would exacerbate deficits when coupled with virtually no spending cuts and continuing growth of entitlements. In August 1992 the GAO had warned that deficits would be far more difficult to resolve than anticipated, but Clinton failed to heed.

But soon after his election he learned that by 1997 the deficit probably would be far higher than he had anticipated. Nor had he fully appreciated the extent to which the mood had shifted in Congress toward deficit reduction and away from liberal reforms, even though Tom Foley, the House majority leader, had informed him that many House Democrats had defied the party leadership to seek deep spending cuts in the summer before the 1992 election.[30] Ross Perot had further elevated the political salience of deficit reduction in the 1992 campaign when he equated the deficit with gridlock, making incoming Democratic moderates and liberals determined to resolve the issue, lest they lose their seats. In turn, Newt Gingrich and his cadre of conservative allies were determined to make elimination of the deficit their ticket to taking control of the House in 1994, albeit with no tax increases.[31]

Right after the 1992 election deficit hawks and deficit doves in the Clinton camp went into battle. Robert Rubin, the head of the National Economic Council; Leon Panetta, the budget director; Alice Rivlin, the assistant budget director; and Lloyd Bentsen, the nominee for secretary of the treasury, made deficit reduction a priority. But the political consultants (Begala, Carville, Gene Sperling, and Mandy Grunwald); Robert Reich, nominated for secretary of labor; Laura Tyson, Clinton's chief economist; and Donna Shalala, nominated for secretary of the Department of Health and Human Services, did not want to scuttle social investments and a middle-class tax cut even if these required more modest deficit reduction.[32] A fierce behind-the-scenes battle between these factions soon tipped in favor of the deficit cutters when Alan Greenspan, the chairman of the Federal Reserve, convinced Clinton, Bentsen, and Rubin that robust economic growth would be stymied if the deficit remained large. Indeed, Clinton came to fear that Greenspan might raise the prime rate if he failed to cut deficits sufficiently.[33]

By the time he was sworn in, Clinton was backpedaling. He dropped his promise to halve the deficit in four years, withdrew his middle-class tax cut, and cut the size of a stimulus package meant to invigorate the economy through a variety of (mostly) pork-barrel projects solicited from Democratic legislators. Having previously immunized entitlements from cuts, he now discussed "sacrifices" that middle-class and affluent Americans should consider, such as entitlement cuts and tax increases. He proposed an energy tax (called the BTU tax because its levies were based on British thermal units) to fall on heating and other fuels. Even Greenspan praised the first Clinton budget proposal, which called for roughly the same amount of deficit reduction as in the 1990 budget deal.

Despite his emphasis on deficit reduction, Clinton was perceived by many legislators as exacerbating deficits because his budget retained his proposal to increase spending on social investments by $250 billion over five years, his small stimulus package, and a large increase in the earned income tax credit (EITC) for low-income families with children. While Clinton offset these spending increases with his BTU tax and tax increases for affluent Americans, he was vulnerable to the charge of many moderates and conservatives that he relied excessively on tax increases rather than spending cuts to achieve deficit reduction. (Many conservatives and moderates wanted a budget with a 2-to-1 ratio of spending cuts to tax increases, rather than Clinton's 1-to-1 ratio, to be certain that revenues from tax increases would not be diverted to fund new social programs.)[34]

The impetus behind deficit reduction became even greater by mid-January when Republican strategists decided to oppose Clinton's economic package en masse, no matter its specific provisions.

Robert Dole, the Senate minority leader, already planned to run for president in 1996 and realized that he might be outgunned by Phil Gramm in the Republican presidential primaries if he supported tax increases to curtail the deficit, as Dole had in 1983, 1985, 1987, and 1990.[35] Citing Clinton's heavy reliance on tax increases, Dole and Gingrich led the charge against Clinton's deficit-reduction plan.

Clinton presented his budget to a joint session of Congress in February 1993 to wide acclaim. On April 1 he secured a budget resolution from Congress that embodied most of his package, with one important exception—his social investments. Unaware that in its 1990 budget deal Congress had established strict ceilings on discretionary spending that extended through 1994, Clinton belatedly discovered that his social investments breached them significantly, meaning he could fund them only if he proposed offsetting cuts in other discretionary programs or if he persuaded Congress to lift the caps. (Clinton was irate at Panetta and Rivlin for not informing him of the caps; Reich even wondered whether these deficit hawks had deliberately sabotaged the social investments by not informing the president about the caps.)[36] So Democrats on both the House and Senate budget committees cut Clinton's social investments by another $63 billion to conform to the caps—and the House Budget Committee imposed a "hard freeze" (no allowance even for inflation) on discretionary spending that extended to 1995. As a result, the House budget resolution contained only $1 billion in new investments in the coming year and $6 billion for the following year, whereas Clinton had recommended $231 billion in new investments over five years.[37] Stripped of its social investments, Clinton's economic plan, save only its large tax increases, could easily have been broached by a conservative, as Clinton lamented when he told aides, "We're losing our soul."[38] Clinton suffered another damaging defeat at this point. After the House enacted his $30 billion stimulus package, Dole led a Republican filibuster against it in the Senate, forcing Clinton to accept a final version that contained only $4 billion.

But Clinton's problems were only beginning as opposition to his BTU tax grew. He convinced the House to support the BTU tax only by saying he would agree to cuts in it in the Senate. With Democratic senators David Boren of Oklahoma and John Breaux of Louisiana rallying Democratic opposition in the Senate, the BTU tax was eliminated and replaced with a smaller gas tax and deeper cuts in Medicare. Even the smaller gas tax increase proved politically perilous for some Democrats, with Republicans chanting "Good-bye, Marjorie" when Rep. Marjorie Margolis of Pennsylvania was persuaded by the White House to support the revised legislation in the House to allow a 218–216 victory.[39] (She lost her seat two years later.) The Senate passed this legislation only when Vice President Gore broke a 50–50 tie vote.

The reconciliation bill killed Clinton's remaining increases in social investments later in the summer. Congress extended caps on discretionary spending through 1998 with no allowance for inflation. Clinton could now achieve increases in social investments only by cutting existing programs, which usually had strong defenders in Congress, or by cutting military spending. (The fire wall between military and domestic spending enacted in the 1990 budget deal, which had disallowed the use of military cuts for domestic programs, expired in 1993.)

It remained for the appropriations committees in summer and fall to execute the cuts in discretionary spending mandated by the budget resolution. Congress eventually gave Clinton a mere $13 billion in increases in social investments by cutting other domestic programs. While euphoric that he had appeased Greenspan with budget legislation that was projected nearly to halve the deficit to $200 billion by 1997, Clinton realized that his only major liberal achievements in the budget negotiations were tax increases for the affluent and the extension of tax credits to six million additional low-income citizens, making the EITC the largest means-tested antipoverty program in the government's arsenal.

Perhaps most important, however, Clinton lost the public relations war with Republicans in 1993. Although he advocated only modest spending increases and tax increases about the size of Reagan's in 1982, Republicans incessantly portrayed him as a tax-and-spend Democrat throughout 1993, obscuring the huge deficit reductions that he had achieved.[40]

The "Inexpensive" Rube Goldberg Machine

Bill Clinton wanted universal health insurance coverage to be the crowning achievement of his presidency, with Carville placing "Don't forget health insurance" alongside "It's the economy, stupid" on the door of Clinton's campaign headquarters in 1992. The U.S. health-care system was the most expensive system in the world when measured by its cost as a percentage of the gross national product, partly because of a pivotal decision made during World War II when the federal government, unwilling to cede wage increases to unions for fear of triggering runaway inflation, allowed them to negotiate health benefits with corporations.[41] Although Americans had once paid for their health care directly, or been forced to seek medical attention from public clinics and hospitals that relied heavily on the pro bono services of physicians, many now relied on the health insurance provided by their employers through a growing array of for-profit insurance carriers as well as Blue Cross and Blue Shield. (The government further reinforced this approach to health care in 1954 when it allowed corporations to deduct the cost of providing health insurance from corporate taxes.)[42] What seemed to be an ingenious method of financing health care with scant public expenditures soon evidenced negative features. Many employers chose not to provide the health care benefit, particularly those with nonunionized workforces and with small workforces. People outside the corporate workforce, such as the self-employed, the unemployed, and retired people, had no health coverage unless they purchased it themselves. Many employers' plans provided insufficient coverage of medical care and drugs, forcing many to subsidize their own care at pivotal points. Although most retirees were insured after Medicare was enacted in 1965, millions of retirees with long-standing or chronic conditions had to deplete their assets in order to qualify for the means-tested Medicaid program. (Medicare covered only brief bouts of illness.) Medicaid, also enacted in 1965, had its own problems. With states given the authority to set their own eligibility levels, California and New York State set such high levels that Congress stipulated that no states could establish levels higher than 133 percent of a state's standard for Aid to Families with Dependent Children.[43] When many states eventually decided to cover only welfare recipients with their Medicaid programs, tens of millions of Americans who did not have employer-paid health insurance or did not qualify for Medicare or Medicaid had no coverage. (After exhausting their personal savings, they had to rely on public clinics and hospitals; long waits and inconvenient locations made many avoid health care until their medical conditions had become serious or life threatening.)

If access was a problem, so was the cost of health care. Fees were unusually high because private insurance companies, and Medicare, chose to reimburse physicians and hospitals at "prevailing rates," not at rates set by the government, as in regulated systems. Nor did market competition work to curtail costs because people with insurance had no incentive to price shop or question the charges. Physicians and hospitals, in turn, had no incentive to pare their charges or the number of procedures they provided to patients because their income rose as they provided more services. In contrast, providers in many nationalized health systems are reimbursed on a per capita, or per patient, basis rather than for specific services. The cost of U.S. health care was reflected in the high premiums that many employers paid to insure their employees. In the 1990s, as business became increasingly international, U.S. companies were at a competitive disadvantage with firms in nations with nationalized health-care systems. While personal income taxes for individuals are far higher in Europe than in the United States, income taxes for European corporations are considerably lower. Their competitive advantage over U.S. firms is further increased because they do not fund health-care fringe benefits. (As much as 10 percent of the cost of U.S. automobiles stems from the cost of employees' fringe benefits, and Chrysler Corp. had to sell seventy thousand vehicles just to pay its health-care costs in 1984.[44])

Bill Clinton ought to have known that he was entering a policy area fraught with political risks when he promised to enact national health insurance during his 1992 campaign. Pharmaceutical and insurance companies, as well as the American Medical Association and the American Hospital Association, possessed extraordinary lobbying resources that they would use against any proposal that threatened their interests. Any proposal would have to navigate a congressional system that split responsibility for health-care legislation among myriad committees. People already covered by private health insurance would examine any proposal to see whether it cut their coverage or increased their costs. Any proposal to mandate coverage of employees by employers would arouse opposition from small businesses, whose owners often believed they could not afford the cost of premiums for their employees. When Congress focused on deficit reduction, it would, moreover, closely scrutinize the budgetary costs of any national health insurance proposal.

Realizing that his plan could not draw heavily on the public treasury because of the federal deficits, Clinton decided to require most employers to bear the brunt of the costs of expanding coverage by requiring them to provide insurance for their employees. (Had he moved to a system like that of most European nations, the government—not employers—would have borne the brunt of the cost.) Even with this cost-saving decision, Clinton still had to finance federal coverage for people not in the workforce, such as the unemployed, welfare recipients, and retirees, thus necessitating the continuation of Medicaid and Medicare.

To diminish the cost Clinton relied heavily on market competition. He favored establishing local boards that would require each health insurance company, health maintenance organization (HMO), or preferred provider organization (PPO) to advertise in local papers what it would charge for the federally mandated package of universal benefits. (Many corporations had already enrolled their employees in HMOs or PPOs.) If employers, the Medicare program, and the Medicaid program chose the least expensive plans, Clinton believed the nation would realize huge savings in health care—savings that would partly offset new outlays required to insure people who had no insurance.

An intense debate took place within the administration about the likely cost. Ira Magaziner, Clinton's early point man on national health insurance, was convinced in 1992 that it would require no new funds because of market competition and the reliance on corporations to fund health care for most employed Americans. But Rubin, Panetta, and Rivlin, drawing on the advice of such economists as Henry Aaron, did not share Magaziner's optimism. They doubted enhanced competition could avert the need for huge federal subsidies; some White House advisers even believed that national health insurance would cost more than $100 billion over four years.[45] Forced to concede that national health insurance might require substantial funds during the start-up period, administration planners increasingly gravitated toward sin taxes on cigarettes and some cuts in Medicare and Medicaid to help pay for it, even though powerful congressional leaders, such as Rep. Dan Rostenkowski, D-Ill., warned that Congress would not approve new taxes.

Republicans were eager to deny Clinton a major legislative success before the 1994 congressional elections; their resolve to sabotage national health insurance was further strengthened when Clinton chose Hillary Rodham Clinton to head its planning. (Gore turned down the assignment, saying it would be too time consuming.) Hillary Clinton created further political problems when she convened a working group of hundreds of experts and four hundred federal employees to explore more than eight hundred issues behind closed doors, thus excluding key stakeholders like insurance companies, drug companies, and the AMA from its deliberations. She ignored the advice of Gore and others who told her it was unrealistic to expect Congress to approve national health insurance in 1993 because of the size and complexity of the issue.[46] (By late April she had conceded that the plan might cost as much as $100 billion a year during its start-up phase at a time when Congress was trying to cut the deficit.[47]) She also ignored the advice of some pundits who urged the administration to develop a more modest version that could attract some support from moderate Republicans, thus splitting the Republican Party.[48] Bill Clinton created further problems for the legislation when he decided in August 1993 that he was willing to compromise all details of the legislation, save only the principle of universal coverage—a decision that would encourage myriad alternative proposals from both sides of the aisle.[49]

He initially promised his national health insurance proposal by early May, then delayed its issuance eighteen times, finally announcing it on September 22 before a joint session of Congress. When he released a detailed proposal in late 1993, many legislators were astonished to see its complexity—the plan was more than one thousand pages long and contained so many regulations, procedures, and boards that many health-care experts and some members of Clinton's cabinet could not understand it. In February 1994 the Congressional Budget Office (CBO) at a critical juncture questioned Clinton's claim that it would cost little new money. Polls were ominously suggesting that many middle-class Americans, safely covered by their employers, feared they would have to pay higher taxes to cover uninsured people or that their services might be rationed.

Fearing their roles would be eclipsed by HMOs, many private insurance companies launched a media blitz against the plan in 1994 that featured conversations between "Harry and Louise," a fictional couple who feared their taxes or health-care costs would increase. Angered by the proposal to regulate drug prices, pharmaceutical companies orchestrated a huge lobbying campaign to defeat it. The chairs of the two legislative committees most central to enactment of national health insurance offered scant assistance to Clinton; Rostenkowski, chair of the House Ways and Means Committee, left Congress amid charges he had misused House funds, and Moynihan, who chaired the Senate Finance Committee, did not believe a health insurance crisis even existed and was furious that Clinton had given this legislation priority over welfare reform. The suspicion that national health insurance would cost money and require new taxes created additional opposition from a Congress that had just enacted a deficit-reduction plan. Republicans contended that Clinton's deficit reduction in 1993 was grossly inadequate and had already decided to vote against Clinton's insurance plan in unison if it reached the floor of either chamber. They argued that national health insurance was a big-government scheme that would bankrupt the Republic and enmesh citizens in a system of socialized medicine that would entail rationing. Deliberations had ground to a halt by August 1994 when Clinton conceded defeat less than three months before the 1994 congressional elections.

The defeat was a stunning blow to Clinton. His and Hillary Rodham Clinton's tactical errors, the excessive complexity of the plan, its uncertain costs, federal deficits, relentless lobbying and advertising by insurance and drug companies, and unanimous Republican opposition had sealed its fate and had bolstered Republicans' contention that Clinton was a tax-and-spend Democrat.

Gingrich's Conquest

As the House minority whip, in line to soon succeed retiring Minority Leader Robert Michel, Newt Gingrich was perfectly situated to develop a bold program to become Speaker if the Republicans took control of the House in 1994. Nearly half of the House Republicans had been elected since 1988—and many had received assistance from GOPAC, a political action committee founded by Gingrich—so Gingrich had the allegiance of a cohesive base of conservative Republicans ready to follow his lead in repudiating older and more moderate Republican leaders like Michel and Dole. Conservative Republicans wanted drastic downsizing of the federal government far beyond Reagan's achievements, huge tax cuts, termination of deficits by relying on cuts in domestic spending, and sharp increases in military spending. They concentrated their monies, advertising, and efforts on congressional swing districts where marketing experts told Gingrich that Republicans could win in 1994. Drawing on donations from investment, banking, and others, GOPAC financed a "farm team" of candidates for these districts; about 80 percent of Republicans who won House seats received GOPAC aid. Republicans relentlessly attacked incumbents as tax-and-spend Democrats—often using their votes for Clinton's 1993 budget deal as incriminating evidence.[50] Ominously for Democrats, not only were many independent voters leaning toward Republican candidates but so were many Reagan Democrats who had voted for Clinton in 1992.

No one was prepared for what happened on November 8, 1994. Republicans gained not only a majority in both houses of Congress but a majority of the nation's governorships and control of seventeen additional state legislative chambers. (Not a single incumbent Republican governor or member of Congress was defeated.) Republicans were now particularly powerful in the House, where they had a large majority and a cadre of nearly eighty conservatives eager to help Gingrich wrest policy leadership from the White House.

Backpedaling and Counterpunching as Explicit Strategy

It is difficult to overstate the debilitating effect of the Republicans' landslide victory on Bill Clinton. Having come to Washington with a relatively liberal agenda, he finally realized the extent to which voters were swayed by antigovernment sentiment. Now he encountered a formidable Republican machine led by Gingrich that meant to steamroll him. Gingrich's power was enhanced by a detailed political agenda established in a manifesto known as the *Contract with America.*[51] Issued on the steps of the Capitol the preceding September by a band of House Republicans, it received little initial attention from the media. The contract contained ten conservative policies that Gingrich promised to enact in the House within one hundred days, including balancing the budget without tax increases, increasing military spending, cutting taxes for families and middle-class people, reforming welfare, and establishing term limits.

After regaining his equilibrium, Clinton developed a master strategy for repelling Gingrich's crusade. Consulting daily with Dick Morris, the pollster and political adviser he had used extensively in Arkansas, Clinton decided to use a backpedaling and counterpunching strategy known as triangulation.[52] He realized that the new Congress would be a combat zone of liberal and conservative forces, because the percentages of both groups in both parties had been bolstered in the 1994 elections after many moderates had lost their seats to conservatives. Clinton decided to float above the political fray and let the Republicans take the initiative on many fronts. This would encourage them to dissipate their energies by enacting the numerous policies in their *Contract with America.* He would use his veto at pivotal points, but only if he could attract sufficient moderate votes to prevent Congress from overriding his veto. He would also selectively co-opt conservative themes, such as by embracing welfare reform and proposing deep reductions in the deficit. He would limit his domestic agenda to a few reforms such as tax credits for education while nonetheless aggressively defending entitlements, principally Medicare and Medicaid, and a few small programs like Americorps, a domestic service program that he had initiated. Timing would be critical to Clinton's strategy, because he would need to decide when to backpedal and when to counterpunch over the next two years.

Clinton's strategy was ideally suited to the budget politics of 1995. Gingrich had pledged to cut deficits markedly and to enact huge tax cuts. Clinton knew that the final mile of deficit reduction could occur only through deep cuts in entitlements, which had largely been spared in the last twelve years.[53] The arithmetic was simple: if Republicans wanted huge tax cuts and increases in military spending, they could reduce the budget deficit within the foreseeable future only if they made large cuts in entitlements because domestic discretionary spending had already been deeply cut. But cutting entitlements had proved elusive since 1981 because most Americans were averse to making large cuts in Social Security, Medicare, and Medicaid. So Clinton hoped to sucker Gingrich into proposing massive entitlements cuts, which would allow Clinton to counterpunch by opposing the size of the cuts while supporting the objective of eliminating the federal deficit. At a suitable time Clinton could counterpunch with his own budget, which would propose smaller entitlements cuts because he would propose fewer (if any) tax cuts.

Clinton began the year, then, by offering a status quo budget that proposed spending cuts sufficient to allow $144 billion in deficit reduction over five years—and even included modest increases for social investments and modest tax cuts. With his trap set Clinton awaited Gingrich's budget as the Speaker and Rep. John Kasich of Ohio, the Republican chair of the House Budget Committee, argued in mid-February about Republicans' strategy.[54] Gingrich wanted Republicans to demand elimination of the deficit within five years, whereas Kasich wanted merely a "glide path" because he feared that Republicans, who also had a fondness for entitlements as well as for demanding huge tax cuts, would not be able to meet this goal. Gingrich easily won this debate as other Republican leaders rallied to the policy of eliminating the federal deficit within seven years. They had embarked, however, on a perilous course. As the only Republican leader well versed in the budget's arithmetic, Kasich realized that Republicans would need nearly $1 trillion in cuts over seven years because they wanted to cut taxes by $245 billion. Indeed, they would need more than $300 million in cuts from Medicare and Medicaid, whereas in 1993 Clinton had sought cuts of only $56 billion in Medicare over five years.

Already facing a Herculean task, Republicans made their budget-cutting job more difficult yet when they devoted precious time to enacting the myriad proposals in their *Contract with America* in February and March; this gave them less than six months to enact a budget by the start of the new fiscal year on October 1.[55] The onus of developing a budget resolution fell to Kasich, who proposed to cut, over seven years, $270 billion from Medicare, $182 billion from Medicaid, and $175 billion from remaining entitlements such as SSI and food stamps. Moreover, he proposed extending caps on discretionary spending to 2002 to achieve $190 billion in cuts in domestic discretionary spending while allowing increases of $58 billion in military spending.

Kasich's plan made Reagan's proposals appear timid, not just by cutting Medicare deeply but by making major cuts in means-tested entitlements. The latter included converting Medicaid and AFDC from entitlements to mere block grants; making major cuts in the EITC; capping the funding of Medicare, which depended on the risky bet that enrollment of seniors in HMOs would cut costs in the future; and extending caps on domestic discretionary spending into the next century. Republicans predicted a showdown with the president in the fall when Congress presented him with a reconciliation bill and appropriations bills that reflected the views of the Republican majority. They confidently assumed Clinton would accede to their wishes rather than risk a government shutdown. (Clinton's concessions in the 1993 budget battle had convinced Republicans that he lacked backbone.)[56]

Democrats now united against Gingrich's budget, just as Republicans had united against Clinton's budget in 1993. Democrats contended that Republicans had found 65 percent of their cuts in social programs for the poor, young, and elderly. But attacks on Republicans' "heartlessness" did not allow Democrats to prevail over solid Republican majorities in both chambers, even though Republican senators sought somewhat smaller spending and tax cuts than their counterparts in the House. Beating back alternative Democratic budgets, and proposals to delete tax cuts to allow smaller spending cuts, Republicans enacted a budget resolution and reconciliation bill in the spring and summer on party-line votes.

Clinton at first supported House Democrats in their battle against the Republican budget proposals, then infuriated them by supporting a proposal to end deficits within ten (rather than seven) years. He thus co-opted the Republicans' goal of ending the budget deficits while allowing the cuts in entitlements to be more gradual than what the Republicans had pushed. In no mood to accept Clinton's compromise Republicans insisted on a seven-year schedule and huge tax cuts. As polls showed in the late summer of 1995, the public was finally responding to the Democrats' charges that Republicans meant to eviscerate Medicare and other programs. Gingrich's popularity began a spectacular decline.

Had Republicans enacted appropriations bills by the beginning of the next fiscal year on October 1, they would have forced Clinton to sign them or to bear the blame for causing a government shutdown if Congress failed to pass a continuing resolution to keep the government running. Instead, Republicans dallied by inserting in their appropriation bills various riders on extraneous issues such as abortion, which forced them to seek a six-week continuing resolution to fund the government. The Democrats used this hiatus to convince the public that Gingrich and the Republicans were "mean and evil" and further shifted public opinion against the Republican proposals.[57] Still confident they would prevail, however, Republicans told Clinton in early November that they would propose another continuing resolution only if he agreed to most of their spending cuts in advance. To their astonishment Clinton vetoed their continuing resolution as Democrats charged that the Republicans were trying to blackmail him. The public saw the government shutdown as resulting from Republicans' intransigence and extreme views and blamed Gingrich—not Clinton—for the inconvenience of closed national facilities, parks, and museums.

Continuing his strategy of triangulation, however, Clinton made another major concession to conservatives at this juncture and accepted the Republicans' seven-year timetable for balancing the budget, as stipulated in a new continuing resolution. Republicans believed they had finally trapped Clinton and failed to note that the continuing resolution gave Clinton wiggle room. It stipulated, for example, that a budget proposal to end deficits within seven years "must protect future generations, ensure Medicare's solvency, reform welfare, and provide adequate funding for Medicaid, education, agricultural, national defense, veterans, and the environment."[58] As Gingrich's popularity continued to plummet, Clinton dragged out the negotiations with Republicans by forcing them to go over every point in the budget while Democratic negotiators sought smaller cuts in Medicare as well as smaller tax cuts.

Now Clinton counterpunched by offering a way to balance the budget in seven years. Because his proposal hardly cut taxes, he did not need to cut entitlements as deeply as Republicans, which again endeared him to liberals. As negotiations extended into early 1996, public opinion continued to strongly favor Democrats in the wake of another shutdown in late December. Forced to concede on January 2 that a "tactical retreat" was necessary, Gingrich ended the shutdown on the condition that Clinton produce a seven-year budget that used economic forecasts from the CBO rather than the Office of Management and Budget. (The CBO's revenue predictions were not as optimistic as the OMB's.) When Republicans meekly accepted Clinton's resulting budget, most political commentators declared that he had won a smashing victory that whittled the Republicans' bold plan for $1 trillion in spending cuts and $350 billion in tax cuts to merely $40 billion in spending cuts and $30 billion in tax cuts over seven years.

Yet even Clinton savaged domestic discretionary spending in his proposal. Intent on neutralizing Republicans' efforts to set him up for charges of being a tax-and-spend Democrat in the presidential elections of 1996, Clinton proposed deep cuts of $261 billion in domestic discretionary programs not on the White House's short list of favored programs, slashing them by 20 percent to 30 percent in coming years, to the chagrin of such advisers as Carville and Reich.[59] Clinton proposed some cuts in means-tested entitlements and cuts in the EITC—his prize achievement in 1993. As one commentator suggested, "Clinton's budget is . . . a remarkable manifesto for a Democrat—proof of how far the Republicans had moved Clinton and the budget debate since sweeping into control of the Congress."[60]

Social Reform on the Cheap

The need for expanded social investments was nowhere more obvious than with respect to beleaguered welfare recipients, who are mostly poorly educated and unskilled. Paid about the minimum wage, a woman with two children could survive only if she rented a home in a high-crime neighborhood and by depriving her family of bare essentials, such as adequate child care. These women needed a massive training and education program to obtain the credentials and skills that would allow them to improve their earnings after they had left welfare, whether by winning (at the least) high school diplomas or community college or college degrees. (Considerable research suggests that poorly educated women who receive only brief training remain below or near the poverty line after they leave welfare.)[61]

While Clinton had campaigned in 1992 to "end welfare as we know it" and to support lifetime limits of two years on the welfare rolls, he was vague about such details as whether he would boost appropriations for child care, training, remedial education, transportation, housing subsidies, and health care in order to help many former recipients survive on low wages. Nor did Clinton clarify whether he simply wanted recipients (and their children) to be stricken from the welfare rolls (as many Republicans like Reagan favored) or whether he also wanted to find ways to help them rise substantially above the poverty level.

Some warning signs suggested that welfare reform would not receive priority from Clinton. Lloyd Bentsen, the Texas Democrat and deficit hawk, successfully demanded that Clinton remove welfare reform from his budget proposal in 1993.[62] When Clinton finally assembled a plan in the spring of 1994, it was poorly funded because his planners ran into the 1993 caps on discretionary spending, which required them to find the resources for welfare reform by cutting other programs.[63] Clinton's 1994 plan proposed to move only a third of welfare recipients off the rolls during an initial phase that would provide them with some educational and training benefits as well as child care and establish the two-year time limit. Advocates of Clinton's plan were disappointed when it was sidetracked by health-care reform, and by the opposition of key liberal Democrats on the Ways and Means Committee. They objected to its two-year limits and feared that Congress would enact punitive legislation if welfare reform was considered during an election year.[64]

The failure of the administration to enact welfare reform in 1994 meant that it would be placed on the congressional agenda in 1995 after Republicans had gained control of Congress. While Gingrich and his allies had not focused on welfare reform in 1993 or most of 1994, they increasingly came under the influence of Charles Murray, a conservative theorist who demanded the abolition of welfare on the theory that any benefits provided "perverse incentives" that addicted recipients to welfare.[65] The *Contract with America*'s version of welfare reform had proposed giving the states the right to opt out of the AFDC program by converting their AFDC funds to a fixed annual block grant. So it was but a short step from the contract to the House version of welfare reform, which demanded termination of the AFDC program. (Ending the entitlement meant that the federal government could fund welfare at whatever level it wished instead of having to cover its share of the benefits claimed in a given year.) The House Republicans' version of welfare reform both gave the states considerable autonomy in shaping their programs and showered them with regulations—a two-year time limit for receiving welfare benefits at any given time, a lifetime limit of five years, disallowing welfare payments for children born within ten months of when a family first received welfare benefits, and disallowing benefits for children born out of wedlock to a woman younger than eighteen. The proposal subjected the welfare block grant to a hard freeze for five years, meaning that federal funding would decline by the level of inflation in those years. Declaring the House version to be "weak on work and tough on children" because it contained no new funds to accomplish its sweeping goals, Clinton and many Democrats pressured Republican senators to enact a more liberal version, but the Senate version was only modestly more generous. (Although the legislation also ended AFDC as an entitlement, it required states to spend at least 80 percent of what they had spent on welfare in 1994 and included some funds for child care and job training, saving $70 billion over seven years, compared to $102 billion for the House version.)

Many Democratic senators might have opposed the Senate version had Clinton given them political cover by saying he would veto it. But Clinton supported it on the ground it was the best he could get, and it easily passed the Senate on a vote of 87–12, even as Clinton warned he might veto a conference version if it resembled the House version. He then vetoed two versions in late 1995 and early 1996 before the Republicans took the offensive, airing commercials in the spring of 1996 that derided him for vetoing welfare reform without presenting his own plan.[66]

As he began his race for reelection, Clinton had to decide whether to accede to the Republicans' version or veto it—and a veto would make welfare a central issue in the presidential campaign. He could have used many arguments to support a veto in August 1996 when the legislation came to his desk, for example, that millions of children would be cast into poverty when removed from safety net programs. But Clinton returned to his strategy of triangulation and signed the legislation.

Clinton had not markedly changed national priorities in his first term. He was governing in Reagan's shadow, stymied by huge deficits and a conservative opposition that hoped to regain the political momentum that had flowed to Clinton in the budget battles of 1995 and 1996.[67] As he faced off against Bob Dole in the presidential election of 1996, the question was whether Clinton, in a second term, would establish his imprint on national priorities or primarily wage a defensive struggle against entrenched congressional Republicans.

14

Clinton Boxes with Reagan's Shadow

After easily besting Bob Dole in the presidential contest of 1996, would Clinton find a way to balance the budget after fifteen years of huge deficits? Could he also develop new initiatives at home and abroad, or would he become known primarily as the president who had finally untied Reagan's Gordian knot? Would he finally make substantial military cuts in the post–cold war era to free money for his domestic agenda?

Huge Military Forces for Regional Conflicts?

A major test of the thesis that the United States needed to retain huge military forces would occur in Yugoslavia, which at the end of World War II had been cobbled together at the Versailles Conference from an array of "decaying, dying, and defeated empires that contained six republics, two autonomous provinces, five languages, and three main religions."[1] The strong hand and negotiating skills of Josip Broz Tito, a communist leader, had kept this mix of ethnicities and nationalities intact until his death in 1980. With Tito gone the central presidency rotated annually among the six republics (Serbia, Slovenia, Croatia, Montenegro, Macedonia, and Bosnia-Herzegovina) and (for a while) a region of Serbia known as Kosovo. But the disintegration of Yugoslavia seemed imminent when Slovenia, the smallest of the republics, sought independence from the central government in late 1989 as the Berlin Wall came down. Chaos ensued by the summer of 1991 as four wars erupted between different ethnic groups and nationalities. The United States, which had just finished Desert Storm and did not understand the combustible nature of the situation, distanced itself from the problems in Yugoslavia, where thousands of people were killed and two million displaced in 1991 and 1992.

What happened during the next eight years can only be described as a descent into hell, partly because Slobodan Milosevic emerged as the leader of Serbia. Determined to keep the republics within a union to be dominated by Serbia from its capital in Belgrade, Milosevic also wanted Serbs to be the dominant ethnic group in most of the republics, even if this required military suppression and "ethnic cleansing" of Muslims, Croats, and Slovenes. He had no moral compunction about using brute force to accomplish his aims.

After a brief war with Slovenia, Milosevic reluctantly ceded its independence because few Serbs lived there. Croatia earned its partial independence through a savage war with Serbia that required 12,500 U.N. peacekeeping forces to maintain some semblance of order as Serbs continued to attack Croats even after fighting was over. After Bosnia-Herzegovina declared its independence in the spring of 1992, a civil war quickly developed as local Serbs, allied with and assisted by Milosevic, attacked Croats and Muslims.

Fearing a quagmire, the Bush administration took no action even as evidence of ethnic slaughter surfaced. Clinton had campaigned for a more active American presence in Bosnia as news of the atrocities spread, but he received conflicting advice from his aides. Les Aspin, Clinton's secretary of defense, wanted no involvement; Warren Christopher, the secretary of state, was undecided; Tony Lake, Clinton's national security adviser, Vice President Al Gore, and U.N. Ambassador Madeleine Albright wanted strong U.S. intervention against the Serbs. Clinton decided in February 1993 that the United States should take an active role in Bosnia, including airdrops of food to Muslims and participation in talks to subdivide Bosnia into districts in which different ethnic groups would live. Already, Clinton (through Christopher) was asserting that the United States had an interest in avoiding the spread of hostilities from Bosnia to adjoining nations; the fear was that Milosevic might trigger retaliation by Greece and Turkey if he invaded Macedonia. (Clinton also feared a destabilizing flood of refugees to adjoining nations.) Bosnia was, he held, a test of how the world "will address the concerns of ethnic and religious minorities in the post–Cold War world."[2] The United Nations established certain "safe areas" in Bosnia in 1993 in the hope of containing conflict with peacekeeping forces and enforced an economic embargo of Serbia.

The Clinton administration remained inactive in Bosnia, however, for the rest of 1993 as its top officials disagreed about tactics. Gore and Albright favored American bombing of Serbia to limit its aid to Bosnian Serbs, but Colin Powell, still chairman of the Joint Chiefs of Staff, wanted no military intervention. Little public support for unilateral action existed in the United States even as the reports of atrocities continued and as Gore pressured Clinton daily to intervene. Meanwhile, peace talks commenced between Milosevic and Bosnian leaders; by fall an agreement to divide Bosnia into Muslim and Serb sections appeared to be imminent. Although the administration decided it would lend up to twenty-five thousand ground troops to a NATO force to implement this agreement if it established a clear deadline, the administration soon found that many members of Congress were disinclined to support involvement because the United States had no exit strategy. But the peace talks disintegrated, leaving the Clinton administration frustrated once more and with no role to play.

European nations increasingly wanted to withdraw their troops from the U.N. peacekeeping force in Bosnia as violence escalated in 1995. Richard Holbrooke, assistant U.S. secretary of state for European and Canadian affairs, urged the use of American airpower against the Serbs, but European nations and the Pentagon rejected his advice, lest this move lead to retaliation against the peacekeeping troops. As the Bosnian city of Sarajevo was surrounded by Serb troops firing artillery shells into it, NATO decided to bomb Serb positions outside Sarajevo and elsewhere in the summer and fall of 1995. Meanwhile, a Croat-Muslim offensive took significant lands from the Bosnian Serbs. As Milosevic saw Serbian positions threatened by bombing and by the Croat-Muslim offensive, he finally assented to negotiations. Even before the negotiations began in Dayton, Ohio, in November, Holbrooke and administration aides worked hard to persuade Congress to commit ground forces in case it became necessary to send a NATO contingent to enforce a settlement. They argued that "the United States cannot come in and out of the alliance . . . when it's to our benefit."[3] To offset fear that the United States would become involved in a quagmire, they contended that the Bosnian Serbs were a spent military force unlikely to be aided by Milosevic. The White House tried to convince the Pentagon that involvement with NATO forces would not be a slippery slope akin to Vietnam or Somalia.[4]

By agreeing to host the negotiations in Dayton and to play a leading role in them, the Clinton administration had taken a high-stakes gamble. If the talks collapsed, the administration risked becoming associated with a high-profile diplomatic failure in a conflict that most Americans did not understand. (Roughly 70 percent of the American public feared an extended entanglement.) Little was achieved in the first nine days of the negotiations; Milosevic made no concessions, and the Croat, Muslim, and Serb members of the Bosnian delegation often screamed at one another.[5] By the fifteenth day the parties had finally made progress on how to partition the country into Serb, Muslim, and Croat sections, as well as how to define NATO's role in keeping the peace, only to have the pending agreement blow up four days later over territorial concessions. Only a key concession from Milosevic sealed the agreement on the twentieth day.

The parties soon learned, however, that the pact would be no panacea. Clinton had difficulties obtaining support from Congress and the public, which wanted (at most) brief commitments, for sending troops to join the NATO police force. (The 60,000 NATO troops had to be kept in Bosnia indefinitely for fear that ethnic violence would erupt the minute they left.) The Pentagon often balked at troop commitments. Some European leaders resented the way U.S. diplomats had assumed leadership of the negotiations, even if they also wanted the United States to take a leading role. Serbs required to vacate specific lands under the partition agreement often burned their houses rather than allow Muslims to occupy them. Recognizing the fragility of the settlement and the seething ethnic hatred that remained, Clinton decided in late 1997 to keep U.S. troops in Bosnia past the original June 1998 deadline, thus committing the United States to a long-term occupation of Bosnia.

After winning reelection in 1996, Clinton wanted to reinvigorate his foreign policy team, which had performed competently in his first term but had been widely criticized for not projecting a coherent strategy in a post–cold war world. He replaced Warren Christopher as secretary of state with Madeleine Albright, made William Cohen the secretary of defense, named Sandy Berger to replace Lake as national security adviser, and sent Bill Richardson to the United Nations to fill Albright's seat. (Clinton subsequently chose Holbrooke to be his U.N. ambassador, though the Senate did not approve his appointment until the early fall of 1998.) This new team was more assertive abroad than his first team, with Albright, Cohen, and Gore supporting assertive action in an emerging trouble spot, Kosovo.

Western powers had long realized that Kosovo might emerge as another site of ethnic slaughter. Milosevic had fueled his rise to power in Serbia by an inflammatory speech in Kosovo in 1989 that incited the minority Serbs (who constituted only 10 percent of Kosovo's population and believed they were treated as second-class citizens) to "fight" to preserve their historic homeland (Serbs had vanquished Muslim invaders centuries earlier).[6] Milosevic also rescinded the autonomy of Kosovo, bringing it under the tight control of Serbia. Both Bush and Clinton had warned Milosevic in late 1992 and early 1993 that they would not tolerate ethnic slaughter in Kosovo, where the minority Serb population uneasily coexisted with the dominant Albanian Muslim population. Bush even threatened unilateral American bombing.

Clinton and his aides devoted less attention to Kosovo, even as Milosevic was increasingly alarmed by the emergence of a militant force, the Kosovo Liberation Army (KLA), which sought total independence for Kosovo. After initial victories by the KLA, Serb forces brutally retaliated in the Drenica area in early 1998.[7]

Western diplomats ought to have realized even at this juncture that Milosevic might take a more militant course in Kosovo than in Bosnia. Bosnia was a republic with coequal status with Serbia, but Kosovo was a region of Serbia itself. Whereas Bosnia's Serb population was semiautonomous and sometimes given only weak aid by Milosevic during the Bosnian conflict, Kosovo contained a contingent of security forces from Serbia. Kosovo had symbolic importance to Serbia, moreover, because many Serbs viewed it as their homeland and regarded the dominant Albanian Muslim population as intruders who oppressed the Serb minority and illicitly sought independence from Serbia. Milosevic had a wounded ego by early 1998, moreover, having seen his dreams of a "Greater Serbia" dashed by developments in Slovenia, Croatia, and

Bosnia. He probably doubted too that Western powers would intrude in Kosovo, because they were fatigued by their interventions in Croatia and Bosnia.

When a Kosovo Albanian leader told Clinton and Gore in the Oval Office in May 1998 that, unless the United States intervened, Kosovo was headed toward civil war, Clinton merely said, "We will not allow another Bosnia to happen in Kosovo" but offered no other assistance. As NATO warned Milosevic in June it would not let another Bosnia occur and even drew up plans for military action, the ground war between Albanian Muslims and Serbs heated up. Rather than dispatch a diplomat with a relationship with Milosevic, the United States sent the confrontive Robert Gelbard, its envoy to the region, who promptly accused an infuriated Milosevic of being ruthless. Clinton, now absorbed by sex scandals, did not focus on Kosovo in 1998. One aide divulged, "I hardly remember Kosovo in political discussions. It was all impeachment, impeachment, impeachment."[8] The kinds of debates that had occurred early in the Bosnia episode resumed; if Albright wanted to use military force, Berger disagreed. U.S. planners concurred that they must act in concert with NATO, but member states were reluctant to use force in Kosovo, lest the Serbs attack NATO peacekeeping forces in Bosnia.

Hoping he could repeat his success at Dayton, Clinton dispatched Holbrooke to discuss the situation with Milosevic after Cohen, Albright, and Gore advocated NATO air strikes in late 1998. Holbrooke thought he had a deal in which Milosevic would withdraw his forces in return for NATO's rescinding its authority to launch air strikes. But Milosevic, infuriated that NATO agreed only to suspend its authority, sent additional Serbian forces into Kosovo. With ethnic killing in high gear by mid-January 1999, NATO upped the ante, now demanding that Milosevic withdraw his forces from Kosovo to avoid an air bombardment.[9] (Albright had championed this approach.) U.S. intelligence vainly tried to decipher his intentions: did Milosevic want war, or was he moving troops into Kosovo to secure a bargaining chip during any negotiations that might ensue?

A last chance for a settlement existed at Rambouillet, France, in a negotiating exercise that turned out to be an utter disaster for Albright in early 1999. Not only did Milosevic not attend but the Kosovo Liberation Army demanded complete independence for Kosovo. When the talks failed, Albanian Muslims signed a peace plan three weeks later that the Serbs failed to sign, paving the way for NATO air strikes that commenced in late March.

From the perspective of Kosovo's Albanian Muslims, the next two months were a disaster. NATO at first exempted many targets from bombing but by mid-May had (in effect) declared war on Serbia, attacking its factories, electrical plants, and bridges. As NATO bombed targets in Serbia and Kosovo with fourteen thousand bombs dropped during six thousand missions, the Serbs proceeded to slay Albanian Muslims with an efficiency that few people had anticipated. Roughly one million Muslims were displaced across Kosovo's borders. Just as the American public, initially supportive of the bombing, became less certain by late May—Clinton's popularity fell more than ten points to 53 percent—and as twenty-nine House Democrats signed a letter to the president seeking a cease-fire, in early June Milosevic assented to a peace agreement fashioned by a Russian envoy. (It stipulated that Serbian troops and security personnel had to vacate Kosovo to end the NATO bombing, to be replaced indefinitely by a NATO occupation force of fifty thousand troops.)

Even if we assume that U.S. intervention in Bosnia and Kosovo was meritorious, neither conflict suggested that the United States needed (essentially) cold war forces for emerging regional conflicts. Although the United States provided the bulk of the airpower for Bosnia and Kosovo, the roughly $4 billion cost of U.S. military action in Kosovo through the spring of 1999 was merely a fraction of the military budget. This suggests that savings elsewhere could have offset the cost of the Kosovo campaign. Neither Bosnia or Kosovo required massive numbers of U.S. ground forces. With 100,000 troops already stationed in Europe, existing troops could easily be transported to both areas. For example, NATO projected that it would ask the United States to contribute roughly 7,000 troops for a peacekeeping force of 50,000 troops in Kosovo once Serbian forces withdrew. Even if the United States and its allies had confronted a force of 40,000 Serbian troops in Kosovo, the U.S. share of ground forces—say, 15,000 troops—would have been relatively small when compared with the roughly 1.4 million active-duty uniformed U.S. military personnel in 1999. As the defense analyst William Kaufmann, military expert Lawrence Korb of the Brookings Institution, and Pentagon planners had established earlier in the decade, regional wars required far fewer forces than the United States routinely funded in the 1990s.[10]

Many critics contended, moreover, that the Pentagon wasted considerable resources by failing to reconfigure its forces for interventions in situations like Kosovo. The army was not structured to allow rapid deployments, having decided not to implement radical changes in the mid-1990s that would have supplanted huge divisions with "mobile combat groups" that could be rapidly transported to points of conflict and quickly moved across the landscape. (Even in Desert Storm, it took the army six months to mass its forces.)[11] Airpower was effective in Desert Storm, Bosnia, and Kosovo, so it was not clear that future aircraft like the F-22 were necessary when existing planes sufficed. Franklin Spinney, a Pentagon planner, contended that the Pentagon invested such extraordinary resources in expensive and difficult-to-maintain weapons that it shorted other forces. (The Pentagon expected to pay $35 billion for 339 F-22 fighter jets but had paid only $45 billion for the 1,094 older but effective F-15s.) [12] The technological superiority of the U.S. military posed other dangers too. High-tech hegemony might make U.S. officials assume that laser-guided bombs and cruise missiles could solve problems on the ground like ethnic conflicts when they really required complex negotiations and peacekeeping forces. (Some prescient individuals realized that bombing in Kosovo might speed the displacement of hundreds of thousands of Muslim refugees.)[13] High-tech gadgetry could prompt the United States, much like the British in the nineteenth century when they possessed naval superiority, to enter ill-advised conflicts. It could tempt allies to rely on the U.S. military as the weapon of first resort, thus diminishing their own roles. Nor could the United States easily develop joint military efforts with allies that possessed aircraft and weapons that were substantially less sophisticated.[14] Other analysts wondered whether a White House reliant on high-tech aircraft that exposed few Americans to danger on the ground would be tempted to enter conflicts that brought no or few American casualties but that killed many people in other nations. Former president Jimmy Carter raised ethical objections to the U.S. modus operandi in Cuba, the Sudan, Iraq, and Serbia, fearing that the United States has often chosen "to devise a solution that best suits its own purposes, recruit at least tacit support in whatever forum it can best influence, provide the dominant military force, present an ultimatum to recalcitrant parties, and then take punitive action against the entire nation to enforce compliance."[15] Carter contends that punitive action by the United States, such as embargoes or military action against entire nations, has led to extraordinary civilian suffering.[16] He has urged the United States to emphasize patient negotiations, using the Security Council wherever possible, as well as nongovernmental organizations to provide "second-track" opportunities for resolving conflicts.[17]

With the world awash in myriad ethnic and regional conflicts in the late 1990s, including the Sudan, Tibet, Rwanda, Angola, Somalia, Liberia, Indonesia, Algeria, Sri Lanka, Chechnya, Turkey, Nagorno-Karabakh, Kashmir, the Congo, Eritrea, Sierra Leone, Northern Ireland, and Haiti, some people suggested that the United States needed huge military forces to engage in myriad conflicts simultaneously.[18] The experience of Desert Storm, Somalia, Bosnia, and Kosovo strongly suggests the improbability of this scenario, however. As noted earlier, such conflicts are exhausting, frustrating, and extended undertakings, making it unlikely that the American public would tolerate multiple simultaneous interventions. Rather than participate freely in numerous military interventions, the United States should carefully decide what interventions to undertake and how to share the burden with other nations.

In the late 1990s many critics, such as retired general Lee Butler (former commander of the Strategic Air Command), Thomas Friedman (a columnist for the *New York Times*), and Stansfield Turner (head of the CIA in the Carter administration), wondered why the Clinton administration had failed to assume bold leadership in reducing nuclear warheads, given that the military threat posed by Russia had declined so markedly.[19] Clinton might also have made a greater effort to persuade the Duma to ratify SALT II, thus cutting nuclear totals on both sides in half.[20] (The Duma considered SALT II at several points, but Russian antagonism toward U.S. interventions in Yugoslavia and Iraq had created strong resistance.) He might have diminished Russian hard-liners' opposition to such reductions by forgiving some Russian debt while proposing a START III treaty to fashion even more reductions in nuclear warheads.[21] He might have cut U.S. nuclear arms unilaterally, as Sen. Bob Kerrey of Nebraska proposed, much as Bush had made unilateral cuts in late 1991 when he eliminated thousands of U.S. tactical nuclear weapons and deactivated 450 land-based ICBMs.[22] Clinton might have followed Turner's suggestion (offered in 1999) that both sides deactivate many nuclear warheads by placing them in storage facilities at least two hundred miles from missiles; either side would be permitted to reactivate them if a nuclear threat developed from other nations.[23] (The world stockpile of nuclear warheads totaled thirty-seven thousand in 1999.)

A ray of hope appeared in the spring of 2000 when the Duma finally ratified START II, but further progress was threatened by the insistence of many members of Congress that the United States implement the defensive missile system, the so-called Star Wars program, to which the Reagan administration had devoted vast resources. Although the U.S. defensive missile program is meant to diminish the threat of incoming missiles from rogue nations such as North Korea, many Russian and Chinese leaders regarded it as an effort to neutralize their ICBMs, thus giving the United States a first-strike capability. (Clinton decided in September 2000 to defer American action on a defensive missile system to the next administration in the wake of several failed attempts to shoot down missiles in trials of antimissile technology.)

Runaway Pigs

Excessive military forces drained funds from the domestic discretionary budget in Clinton's second term, but so did other sources of domestic waste, including pork-barrel spending and excessive deregulation. Road construction and repairs had been both necessary and a source of projects that served the parochial political interests of legislators; a prime example was the 1998 Transportation Equity Act for the Twenty-first Century. State and local governments were struggling to maintain 3.8 million miles of roads and tens of thousands of bridges, and the nation's infrastructure clearly needed sustained investment. Lawsuits against state and local officials for negligence mounted as bridges collapsed and motorists suffered accidents from faulty maintenance of roads. Gridlock bedeviled many small cities.[24] In the summer of 1998 Congress enacted the Transportation Equity Act for the Twenty-first Century, which would provide $217.9 billion over six years. It was the largest domestic initiative of the Clinton presidency and increased highway and mass transit spending by 40 percent.[25]

The transportation act emerged under the skilled tutelage of Bud Shuster, the Pennsylvania Republican who chaired the House Transportation and Infrastructure Committee. He had supported spending on highway construction so ardently that he had earned the nickname "Highway." After narrowly losing a House vote to increase transportation spending in 1997, he resumed his quest in 1998 after the Senate agreed 96–4 to commit 4.3 cents of the federal gasoline tax, which had been dedicated to deficit reduction, to transportation projects. This immediately freed up $25.8 billion as a downpayment on a $214.3 billion program that would allocate $173 billion for highways and $41.3 billion for mass transit to the states over six years.

To build broad-based support for the legislation, Shuster wanted individual legislators to be able to propose specific projects that would be funded from sources other than a state's gas-tax allocations. He therefore invited members to submit projects and implied that they would receive funding only if the member voted for the entire package. Legislators such as Republican senator John McCain of Arizona saw this as an open invitation to secure pork-barrel projects that rewarded contractors, universities, and other constituents despite scant data to demonstrate the technical merit of a project. Gingrich and Shuster also proposed to take the highway trust fund out of the budget, meaning that its spending would not be subject to spending caps—a policy opposed by Clinton on the ground that it would invite runaway spending.[26]

The legislation prompted a feeding frenzy by legislators of both parties, with strong backing from the construction industry, state officials, and specific institutions. For example, buried in the mammoth bill was a "crisis response center" for an "underground emergency transportation management center utilizing satellite communications" in the event of tornadoes.[27] Wondering how such a provision had made its way into a transportation bill, a diligent reporter decided to find out who had sponsored it and where it would be located—the legislation said only that it would be built at an elevation higher than thirteen hundred feet and within "reasonably close proximity to military, space and/or nuclear facilities to provide rapid response time." After twenty-seven phone calls—in the course of which he learned he would have to figure out which tornado-intensive states had mountains of this height and which of those mountains were near military facilities—Guy Gugliotta of the *Washington Post* remained in the dark until an aide to the House Appropriations Committee divulged that Republican senator Richard Shelby of Alabama, chairman of the Senate Appropriations Subcommittee on Transportation, had written the provision. Sure enough, the town of Arab, Alabama, had an elevation of thirteen hundred feet and was near a military facility—and the crisis response center was to be located in the basement of the Arab Fire Department.[28] (Shelby had obscured its precise location because he did not want Clinton to use his line-item veto to excise it.) The transportation bill included $9.3 billion in funding for more than 1,467 projects proposed by three hundred House members from both parties, including a $15 million special project in the district of the chair of an ethics subcommittee that was investigating Shuster.[29] (Shuster was accused of accepting improper favors from a lobbyist who represented transportations interests that benefited from legislation that Shuster had supported.) Even many conservative Republicans blanched at such flagrant pork-barrel spending. Congress had to cut $2.3 billion from social service block grants to offset a portion of the cost. Rather than veto this legislation, as Franklin Roosevelt had done in the mid-1930s when confronted with a transportation bill also loaded with pork, Clinton signed it into law, saying, "It does a lot more good than harm."[30]

Pork-barrel spending was rampant in many appropriations bills, such as a 1998 omnibus Senate bill that contained wool and mohair subsidies (which Congress had killed in 1996), a subsidy for an Illinois company to research caffeinated gum, monies for onion research in Georgia, and funds for manure handling and disposal in Starkville, Mississippi. (Only one copy of the bill existed, so few senators could even examine it.) To get around spending caps a conference committee decided that "emergency spending" did not count against the caps and promptly placed $20 billion in the omnibus spending bill. Perhaps the most egregious example of corporate subsidies was a 1997 provision to give a $50 billion tax credit to tobacco companies, surreptitiously placed in a bill reported out by a conference committee after the committee had completed its work.[31] (Once it was detected, popular outcry led to its removal.) Another example was the Telecommunications Act of 1996 and budget reconciliation legislation of 1997, which gave certain airwaves with a market value of $70 billion to mass media companies despite the objections of McCain and Dole.[32]

It appeared that Congress might finally address the problem of ill-advised corporate subsidies when an array of liberal and conservative think tanks developed lists of these subsidies in 1995 and 1996. In 1995 the liberal Citizens for Tax Justice issued *Hidden Entitlements*, which identified 122 "tax expenditures" over the next seven years, including tax breaks for multinational corporations that would cost $95 billion, business meals and entertainment write-offs that would cost $44 billion, accelerated depreciation that would cost $259 billion, tax breaks for insurance companies and their products that would cost $204 billion, and energy tax loopholes that would cost $21 billion.[33] In 1996 the liberal *Public Citizen* issued a list of "corporate welfare tax breaks" totaling $155 billion over five years. In 1995 the conservative Cato Institute challenged Congress to cut $85 billion in corporate welfare and cited 125 corporate welfare subsidy programs, just as the Ralph Nader group, Essential Information, identified 153 sources of subsidies and tax breaks costing $167 billion per year.[34] John Kasich, the conservative Republican chair of the House Budget Committee, announced his determination to slash corporate subsidies, although he sought only $25 billion in savings over seven years. He even wrote this provision into his House budget resolution in 1995.

But this bipartisan convergence yielded scant legislative success. Bill Archer, the Texas Republican who chaired the House Ways and Means Committee, contended at a Republican retreat in the spring of 1995 that removal of corporate subsidies would be tantamount to a corporate tax increase. When Republican senators Fred Thompson of Tennessee, Phil Gramm of Texas, and McCain, along with Democrats Ted Kennedy and John Kerry of Massachusetts and Bill Bradley of New Jersey, proposed a "dirty dozen" programs to be eliminated in November, their proposal was voted down, 74–25. Even such liberal senators as Barbara Boxer of California opposed the legislation because of subsidies for the Gallo and Wente Brothers wineries, a Sunkist orange cooperative, and almond growers.[35] Nor did Clinton support cuts in corporate welfare in early 1996 after showing initial interest, probably because he feared the loss of campaign contributions from such corporate donors as Archer-Daniels-Midland, which supported an ethanol tax subsidy that cost the treasury $3.6 billion over five years.[36] Nor could supporters of cuts in corporate welfare persuade Congress and the president to establish a bipartisan commission, similar to those used to recommend closure of military bases, to devise a list of corporate subsidies for an all-or-nothing vote by the full Congress after the president had approved the list.[37]

The Demonization of China?

Many commentators speculated at the end of the cold war that China might emerge as a new superpower and take the Soviet Union's place. It too was ruled by dictators with scant interest in human rights, as reflected by the crushing of dissent at Tiananmen Square in 1989. Communist dictators in China still adhered to Marxist doctrine, China had provocatively fired missiles into the ocean near Taiwan in 1995—and a Chinese general had suggested that any conflict with Taiwan would be nuclear.[38] China, moreover, might have to conquer other nations to find the raw materials and food required for rapid economic growth and to feed its huge population. Caspar Weinberger, Reagan's secretary of defense, was among those who projected frightening scenarios about China in books seeking to scare

Americans into retaining (and increasing) their huge military forces.[39] Some Americans feared China meant to shape the U.S. political process to its own ends, pointing to the illegal channeling of campaign contributions from China to the treasury of the Democratic National Committee in 1996.

Fears of China were raised another notch in 1999 with the publication of the Cox Report, named after Republican Christopher Cox of California, who chaired House hearings on alleged Chinese espionage in the United States since the 1970s. In hearings triggered by allegations that a Taiwan-born scientist at Los Alamos National Laboratory had disclosed nuclear secrets to the Chinese government, the Cox Committee (with five Republicans and four Democrats) claimed it had uncovered a long-term Chinese conspiracy to obtain U.S. nuclear technology. Desperately searching for issues to use against Democrats in 2000, some Republicans saw China as "a red-meat Republican issue" after audiences back home applauded their attacks on Clinton's China policy.[40]

Clinton was vulnerable to criticism on China because he, like Nixon and Bush before him, had worked hard to thaw relations with China, saying the United States had far more to lose than to gain from hostile relations.[41] A hostile China might, for example, export nuclear weapons to such nations as North Korea and Iran, attack Taiwan, engage in an arms race with Japan, deny the United States access to Chinese markets, and foment hostilities in Southeast Asia.

Clinton chose a strategy of conciliation, holding summits with Chinese president Jiang Zemin in October 1997 and June 1998. Considerable evidence suggests that Clinton's strategy of conciliation led to gains. China made some human rights concessions; canceled some exports of nuclear technology, and arms, to Iran, Korea, Pakistan, and Syria; and opened its markets to U.S. corporations. Clinton and Zemin held a joint press conference in which they openly discussed subjects like Tiananmen and Tibet, never before debated on Chinese television. Yet relations between the two nations took a nosedive in 1999. After the United States inadvertently bombed the Chinese embassy in Belgrade during the Kosovo conflict in the late spring of 1999, many Chinese students rioted outside U.S. embassies in China, and the government cut back various exchanges with the United States. At about the same time Clinton reneged on his endorsement of China's entry into the World Trade Organization. The Pentagon heightened tension by conducting more than twenty war games against

China in the mid- and late 1990s—or more than against any other nation.[42] China was alarmed, moreover, by the U.S. proposal to develop an antimissile defense system for the Asian theater; the Chinese feared it would provide a protective shield for Japan and Taiwan as they developed offensive missiles aimed at China.[43]

No compelling evidence suggests that the United States needed military forces of cold war proportions to contain China in the late 1990s, however. China possessed only a single submarine that leaked so badly that the Chinese were afraid to leave it in its home port, and only twenty liquid-fueled ICBMs, which took as long as twenty-four hours to activate before they could be launched to targets in United States.[44] The entire Chinese nuclear arsenal equaled "what the United States stuffs into one Trident submarine," and the country had no long-distance bombers or aircraft carriers, and spent fourteen cents for every dollar that the United States spends on defense.[45] Although China may have obtained nuclear secrets that could enable its scientists to put smaller nuclear warheads aboard more deadly rockets, Chinese leaders knew they faced nuclear annihilation if they used their nuclear arsenal offensively. Most military experts believed in the late 1990s that China would not fundamentally change its largely defensive nuclear strategy, even if it modernized its nuclear forces to gain prestige.

Budget Scarcity in an Era of Budget Surpluses?

After sixteen years of megadeficits, a balanced budget finally seemed achievable in 1997. Most of the money for shrinking the deficit in this budget deal (which sought to balance the federal budget by 2002, as stipulated by the 1996 budget deal) came from Medicare ($116 billion of the $127 billion over five years) as both parties consented to substantial cuts by requiring managed care options for enrollees, slashing fees for providers, putting severe limits on physical therapy, cutting nursing home fees, reducing payments for outpatient services such as diagnostic tests and treatments, and cutting home health-care payments.[46] These cuts in fees were so deep that some HMOs refused even to serve Medicare recipients, some nursing homes refused entry to elderly people with complex medical conditions, and large numbers of home health agencies closed. (In the summer of 1999 even Gail Wilensky, Bush's Medicare chief, urged that

Congress rescind some of these cuts because they had eroded the quality of care for some patients.)[47]

The 1997 plan to balance the budget partly came out of Medicare's hide, but it also severely constrained discretionary spending. Neither Clinton nor the Republicans wanted deep cuts in Social Security, and both parties were intent on securing a substantial tax cut (Clinton secured a $500-per-child tax credit) and some spending increases. They extended the caps on discretionary spending that were due to expire in 1998 (under the 1993 budget deal) to the year 2002—and made them so low that total discretionary spending would not even keep up with inflation during these years.[48] As table 14.1 shows, Congress set specific, separate amounts for military discretionary spending and domestic discretionary spending in fiscal years 1998 and 1999 while establishing a combined, or pooled, ceiling for the two kinds of spending in fiscal years 2000 through 2002. To gain cover, moreover, they did not specify which programs would be cut to keep discretionary spending under these ceilings, leaving that to future sessions of Congress. In addition to caps, other budget rules conspired to prevent increases in discretionary spending. Savings from Medicare or other entitlements could not be diverted to the domestic discretionary agenda. Revenues from new taxes could not be diverted to discretionary spending.[49] Savings from military spending could not be used for domestic programs until 2000.

But by early 1998 it looked like the unprecedented economic prosperity would soon finally produce budget surpluses. Clinton triumphantly predicted a $219 billion surplus over five years as he announced a balanced budget on February 2. (He predicted a surplus of $10 billion in fiscal 1999 that would rise to $258 billion by 2008.) To get around the caps on appropriations that he had accepted just six months earlier, Clinton offset pro-

TABLE 14.1 U.S. Discretionary Spending, 1998–2002

FISCAL YEAR	Category	Outlays
1998	Military	$269.8
	Domestic	$282.9
1999	Military	$266.5
	Domestic	$287.9
2000	Military and domestic	$558.7
2001	Military and domestic	$564.4
2002	Military and domestic	$560.8

posed spending that exceeded the caps by proposing to increase revenue estimates from the rapidly expanding surpluses, settlements or awards arising from federal lawsuits against tobacco companies, some program terminations, some tax increases, and some cuts in Medicare. He proposed that the caps simply be ignored to allow a modest increase of $150 billion in spending for child care, education, and Medicare. Moreover, Clinton proposed to use the rest of the surplus to "save" Social Security, although he provided few details. Clinton's budget was a preemptive strike against a Republican Party that wanted to use the tax cuts to increase its congressional majorities in the 1998 elections. Indeed, Clinton had Republicans in a dilemma: if they proposed huge tax cuts, Clinton could accuse them of opposing his "rescue" of Social Security. If they opposed seeking settlements or fines from tobacco companies involved in the lawsuits, he could argue they were in cahoots with Big Tobacco. Undeterred, Republican leaders immediately attacked Clinton's modest spending increases as big government run wild, funded by illusory revenues from a tobacco settlement. They accused Clinton of violating caps on discretionary spending. They sought a tax cut in the form of ending the "marriage penalty," which imposed higher taxes on some married couples than the partners would have paid before they were married, even though this proposal would have required offsetting cuts in existing programs under the terms of the 1997 budget deal.[50]

So the stage was set for another budget showdown and was widely seen as a precursor to partisan conflict about how to spend surpluses in coming years. As the partisan acrimony extended into the summer and the congressional elections neared, the relationship between Social Security and budget surpluses took center stage. Democrats and even some Senate Republicans contended that House Republicans' huge tax cuts of $700 billion over ten years threatened Social Security by depleting the budget surpluses. As the CBO doubled its estimate of the surplus over the next decade to $1.6 trillion, Republicans contended that the treasury could easily afford huge tax cuts and subsidies to the Social Security Trust Fund (where the funds from payroll deductions accumulated), but Clinton objected "to talking of spending hundreds of billions of dollars on a tax cut based on projected surpluses that . . . may not materialize before we have spent the first dollar to save Social Security."[51] Defying Clinton's veto threat, the House passed a tax cut of $80 billion spread over five years in late September. Democrats labeled it fiscally irresponsible. Then some

Republicans attached abortion-related riders to appropriations bills, and Clinton threatened a government shutdown if they failed to enact a budget by October 1.

Still wincing at how Clinton had defeated them over similar budget impasses in 1995 and 1996, Republicans relented when Clinton wielded his veto on an agricultural appropriations bill that had deleted aid to farmers—and they quickly restored home-heating grants for low-income people, summer jobs programs for youth, and money for child care.[52] Sensing he had Republicans on the run, Clinton negotiated a $500 billion deal on various appropriations bills in mid-October that included $1.1 billion to hire 100,000 new teachers and many smaller initiatives, while Republicans' tax cuts were slashed to merely $9.2 billion over ten years.[53]

The budget deal of 1998 also illustrated the continuing inability of Congress to contain pork-barrel spending. Although it had already enacted transportation legislation loaded with pork, this budget deal contained appropriations for numerous similar projects. (On June 25, 1998, the Supreme Court declared the line-item veto unconstitutional.)[54]

With military spending capped at $271.5 billion by the 1997 balanced budget law, relatively little controversy surrounded military appropriations in 1998. Pressure was building, however, for large military increases because Pentagon leaders had asked Clinton to increase future military budgets by as much as $10 billion to $15 billion per year. They claimed the services were suffering from a sharp decline in readiness, inadequate training, archaic equipment, and inadequate maintenance. They said that the purchasing power of basic pay had eroded. Had Clinton honored the Pentagon's requests, the military budget soon would have exceeded its level in 1980 during the cold war, which led some liberals and even the conservative Cato Institute to question this seeming anomaly.[55]

Tiptoeing Toward 2000

Partly because Clinton had cleverly claimed credit for balancing the federal budget, devising a plan to rescue Social Security and another to increase spending on education, the Republicans suffered a major setback in the 1998 election, losing some Senate seats and finding its House majority whittled to a 12-vote margin (if six Republicans defected, the Democrats voted in unison, and one independent abstained, the result would be a tie vote). The big loser was Gingrich, who had masterminded the Republicans' losing strategy, which had focused on the Clinton sex scandal rather than on substantive issues. With House conservatives furious at him for his turn toward the center after the 1996 elections and with moderates disinclined to back him because of his earlier conservative militancy, Gingrich realized he would be defeated if a candidate with stature opposed him for the speakership. He announced his forthcoming retirement from Congress within hours of the announcement on November 6 that Robert Livingston of Louisiana, chairman of the House Appropriations Committee, would seek to become Speaker and had pledged a pragmatic "nuts and bolts" approach to the job. Republicans diminished their standing with voters even further by impeaching Clinton in the House and orchestrating a trial in the Senate when polls showed that most Americans had tired of hearing about Clinton's affair with Monica Lewinsky.

The budget landscape had changed even more decisively by early 1999 when the administration predicted surpluses of $117 billion in the coming fiscal year and $4.47 *trillion* over the next fifteen years as tax revenues surged from the booming economy and stock market. Republicans were likely to intensify their campaign for huge tax cuts, and Clinton and his aides wanted to outmaneuver them. The White House developed a proposal that cleverly linked two objectives: reducing the national debt (which had ballooned to $5.6 trillion because of the deficit after 1981) and saving Social Security and Medicare. Persuaded by economists that nearly cutting the national debt in half over fifteen years to $3.5 trillion (or the lowest level as a percentage of GDP since 1917) would reduce inflationary pressure and increase economic growth, Clinton proposed to earmark most of the projected surpluses for debt reduction. (With the national debt greatly reduced, the treasury would have to float fewer bonds to finance it, thus freeing private capital for job-creating investments.)

Clinton coupled debt reduction with "rescuing" Social Security by turning the Social Security Trust Fund into a kind of bank that received, lent out, and then re-received surplus funds years later. Surplus monies from the budget would be given to the trust fund by the treasury each year for the next fifteen years—and the trust fund would then "lend" this money back to the treasury to be used to diminish the federal debt by retiring bonds issued to fund it. In return, the treasury would give the trust fund IOUs in the amount it had borrowed. (The treasury had already given the trust fund many IOUs in recent decades when it used trust fund surpluses to finance annual operating deficits.) From 2014 to 2032, when annual revenues from payroll taxes would be insufficient to pay for all the pensions that it owed to baby-boom retirees, it would simply redeem the first set of IOUs to make up the difference from 2014 to 2032. Without the Clinton infusion of surpluses, the trust fund would become insolvent in 2032 when it would run out of IOUs and would lack sufficient payroll taxes to fund pensions. *With* Clinton's infusion of IOUs from the surpluses, the trust fund could remain solvent past 2050. (The government would fund the redeeming of IOUs from 2014 to 2050 from general revenues.)

By coupling reduction of the national debt with rescuing Social Security, then, Clinton co-opted another Republican issue (repaying the debt) with a traditional Democratic issue (saving Social Security). His proposal was politically ingenious because it would allow Democrats to charge that Republicans' tax cuts represented attacks on debt reduction, Social Security, and Medicare by depleting surpluses.

In his budget message in early February 1999 Clinton proposed to devote 62 percent of the surplus to his debt reduction and rescue of Social Security and another 15 percent to prop up Medicare—or 77 percent of the surpluses for the next fifteen years. He proposed to spend another 12 percent on tax credits for the establishment of new retirement accounts, thus committing a whopping 89 percent of the surplus over fifteen years to older people. Although the caps on discretionary spending tied his hands for the rest of his presidency, he nonetheless proposed $213 billion in new discretionary spending over five years for providing child care, hiring new teachers, retraining workers, and funding adult literacy programs as well as tax credits for long-term health care, stay-at-home parents of young children, and child care and tax incentives for environmental initiatives and school construction. He proposed to fund these spending increases by raising $33.4 billion in new revenues in the next fiscal year by closing some corporate tax loopholes, increasing taxes on cigarettes, and requiring the states to share some of the money from their lawsuits against tobacco companies.[56]

In the first sustained increase in military spending since the fall of the Berlin Wall a decade earlier, Clinton proposed $112 billion in new military spending over the next six years. It was, *National Journal* reporter James Kitfield contended, the start of the Era of the Indispensable Nation, in which the United States would act as a global sheriff with a military many times larger than that of any other nation.[57] Although Clinton and people like House Minority Whip David Bonior of Michigan had been dovish liberals in the 1960s, they had become assertive internationalists by the late 1990s. During the 1990s liberal hawks had, as the writer Paul Starobin put it, "philosophically routed" the dovish wing of the Democratic Party (which had opposed Desert Storm in 1990).[58] Liberal hawkism was, in effect, a marrying of Jimmy Carter's emphasis on human rights with bullets, holding that "the civilized forces of the world have an obligation to enforce the values of human rights, at gunpoint if necessary."[59] Not wanting to be left behind, many Republican leaders proposed to fatten a $6 billion supplemental military appropriation bill that Clinton proposed to fund the Kosovo military operation. The Republicans planned to add to the Kosovo measure $4 billion to $23 billion to restock military resources that they believed had been depleted in recent years.[60] Congress in fact appropriated $4.5 billion more than Clinton wanted. Moreover, legislators appropriated $21 billion over the spending caps established in 1997 by using accounting gimmicks such as deferring some of these outlays until the beginning of the 2001 fiscal year.[61]

Republicans quickly attacked Clinton's budget even though he proposed to increase government spending by only 2.2 percent over the current fiscal year. They contended that his proposed new taxes to finance his new spending were politically dead, most having been rejected by earlier Congresses. Republicans argued that a large share of the impending surpluses should be returned to taxpayers through tax cuts. They favored privatizing Social Security by diverting payroll taxes to private retirement accounts so that many individuals could manage their own retirement resources—a proposal opposed by Clinton and most Democrats.[62]

Although they disliked Clinton's budget, Republicans were hardpressed to agree on a budget resolution as they divided over how big the tax cuts should be. Such conservatives as Kasich wanted a huge 10 percent across-the-board cut, while moderates feared they would be portrayed as anti–Social Security or fiscally irresponsible if they supported such a large tax cut. They also feared Clinton would veto any budget with large tax cuts. So they passed a budget resolution in April that phased tax cuts in over a period of years as budget surpluses grew while also placing Social Security surpluses in a "lockbox" so they could not be spent or taxed away in future years. (Not to be confused with the general budget surplus, the

Social Security surplus is money that accumulates in the trust fund when payroll-tax revenues exceed the cost of pensions in specific years—annual surpluses that have existed for decades and were projected to continue until 2014.)

In a seeming paradox, discretionary spending appeared to be an endangered species even as the budget experienced surpluses. It faced current, midterm, and long-term threats. The current threat was that from 1999 to 2002 the ceilings on discretionary spending in the 1997 budget deal would mean that the budget could not even keep up with inflation. Partly because Republicans wanted large increases in military spending and tax cuts, their budget resolution in the spring of 1999 proposed an 18 percent reduction in domestic discretionary spending by 2002 and almost 30 percent by 2009. By that time domestic discretionary spending would constitute only 2 percent of the GDP, compared to 5 percent in 1980.[63] (So severe were their proposed cuts for fiscal 2000 that even many Republicans threatened to rebel, lest deep cuts alienate constituents as the nation approached the presidential elections of 2000.) Nor was Clinton charitable to domestic discretionary spending, proposing to reduce it by 7 percent by 2002 and 13 percent by 2009, although his cuts were less than half of what the Republicans wanted.

Discretionary spending also faced a midterm threat. Recall that Clinton had devoted most of the surpluses for the next fifteen years to programs for senior citizens, whether Social Security, Medicare, or individual retirement accounts, and had reserved only 11 percent for discretionary spending. With much of the remaining surplus used by the military, discretionary domestic spending was unlikely to grow even as the population increased and as millions of Americans needed training, remedial (or improved) education, and social services.

Discretionary domestic spending also faced a long-term threat. Because of demographic trends such as the retirement of tens of millions of baby boomers, longer life expectancies, lower birth rates, and rising medical costs, Medicare, Social Security, and the portion of Medicaid that pays for nursing homes for the elderly would account for *two thirds* of the federal budget by 2030 (compared to one third in 2000), according to Eugene Steuerle of the Urban Institute.[64] If we also subtract from the budget the interest on the debt; military spending; other entitlements such as food stamps, unemployment insurance, and SSI; infrastructure costs; and the ordinary costs of running government, virtually nothing would remain for

investments in human capital such as education, training, and social services—unless taxes were substantially raised or retirement benefits cut.

Failed National Priorities in the Clinton Administration

Clinton made relatively few changes in national priorities. By 1998 military spending had finally dropped below the (pre-Reagan) level of 1980—
but was slated to resume an upward trajectory in 2002 (see fig. 14.1). Discretionary spending remained stagnant, save for a few programs such as
Americorps. Entitlements also continued to grow.

   Clinton in fact faced daunting political barriers. To a remarkable
and unappreciated degree, he lived in the shadow of Reagan, both fiscally and politically. He entered the presidency with no money in the
till, which impeded his efforts to enact new initiatives. Reagan's deficits
also had wrought a potent set of political forces that impeded sharp
shifts in national priorities. After years of dead-on-arrival budgets and
failed attempts to undo Reagan's deficits, by the time Clinton took
office the American public was demanding that the country deal with

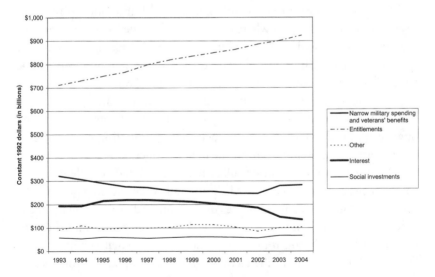

FIGURE 14.1 Five Types of Federal Expenditures, 1993–2004
   Source: Office of Management and Budget, *Budget of the U.S. Government, FY
2000, Historical Tables* (Washington, D.C.: GPO, 1999), table 3.1, pp. 48–49.

its deficit. That placed deficit reduction on the political front burner from 1993 through 1998.

Clinton was also bedeviled by a potent conservative movement partly spawned by Reagan's deficits. While Gingrich admired Reagan's conservative philosophy, he believed that Reagan's revolution had not succeeded in downsizing government radically, thus bringing the huge deficits. Gingrich was determined to complete Reagan's revolution by making huge cuts in domestic spending—an accomplishment that would also end the large deficits even as Gingrich planned to cut taxes and raise military spending.

Indeed, Gingrich used Reagan's deficits as an organizing tool for his conservative movement, pointing to them as symbols of excessive federal domestic spending and deriding any use of tax increases to redress them.

Clinton also was affected by the distrust of government that Reagan's deficits had created. As voters watched endless fruitless battles to eradicate these huge deficits from 1982 onward, they became disenchanted with gridlocked government. It was Clinton's misfortune to become president in the midst of this turmoil and distrust. Because he did not fully recognize the extent of public mistrust of government or the extent to which the public wanted the deficits to be resolved, Clinton broached traditional Democratic ideas like social investments and national health insurance in 1993 and 1994. But these could go nowhere in a period when the federal government was widely distrusted and when no money was available for domestic spending. Indeed, Clinton would have done better in 1993 and 1994 had he largely concentrated on deficit reduction and some modest initiatives, hoping to obtain greater successes after disposing of the deficit.[65]

The potent conservative insurgency that controlled Congress from 1994 onward meant that Clinton had to focus not on initiating new programs but on outwitting Republicans in the deficit-reduction game. Discerning that Republicans were willing (unlike Reagan) to attack entitlements, he let them propose huge cuts in Medicare and Medicaid in 1995 and the shutdown of government before he counterpunched with his own deficit-reduction plan that cut taxes and entitlements less severely. With the public behind him, Clinton routed Republicans in a pivotal victory in 1996 from which they had not fully recovered even in 1999. So Clinton became a defensive president to a remarkable degree, partly because his own tactical miscues in 1993 and 1994 may have allowed Republicans to take control of Congress but partly because he was boxing with Reagan's shadow.

Facing the iron triangle of interest groups, legislators, and the Pentagon, which had supported military spending throughout the cold war, and saddled with allegations of draft dodging, Clinton decided not to make deep cuts in the military budget. Indeed, he added military spending to the list of topics he co-opted from the conservatives' arsenal, such as welfare reform, deficit reduction, crime, and reducing the national debt. Curiously, his military and international approach became similar to Bush's as Clinton linked large cold war budgets to interventions in rogue nations, by 1999 even proposing to exceed the cold war budgets of the pre-Reagan era. At least in public venues, Clinton never asked basic questions about the military budget, such as whether such high levels of military spending were necessary to address regional conflicts.

Clinton deserves credit for incremental reforms in the harsh political environment that he faced. He used the tax code with considerable skill to secure reforms, whether the expansion of the EITC or targeted tax cuts for education and child care. He crafted clever phrases to secure support for domestic initiatives, like funding 100,000 police officers and 100,000 teachers. He not only ended Reagan's deficits but secured substantial surpluses. He also placed the Republicans on the defensive at many points in his presidency—but nowhere more emphatically than when he developed his plan for using the surpluses that preempted the Republicans' desire for huge tax cuts in 1999. And he secured an array of domestic reforms, including gun control, minimum wage legislation, making voter registration easier, and Americorps. What they had in common was that they were relatively inexpensive to implement. Perhaps his most substantial reform was expansion of the EITC, which grew from $8.5 billion in 1993 to $22.6 billion in 1999.

The question isn't whether Clinton ought to have backpedaled on occasion but whether he ought to have held his ground or taken the offensive more frequently—or obtained more concessions from Republicans at key points. As the columnist Molly Ivins astutely suggests, Clinton is tactically skilled but settles for a quarter loaf in certain situations when he might have obtained half a loaf.[66] Did he *have* to concede hard freezes on domestic discretionary spending in 1997, for example? Could he have initiated greater cuts in military spending at strategic points? Could he have sought more money for job training as part of welfare reform in 1996 when he had a strong lead over Dole in the polls—and might he also have retained welfare as a federal entitlement? Could he have proposed larger domestic discretionary spending as part of his plan for spending the surplus? Was he so absorbed with his tactical moves to co-opt and confuse conservatives that he often forgot his own moral principles?[67] Or did his preoccupation with co-opting conservative themes suggest he lacked a firm commitment to social justice?

Clinton failed to articulate a vision of revised federal priorities for the post–cold war era. He could have advocated a leaner military for regional conflicts and coupled this with a greater inclination to seek joint funding of military undertakings with the U.N. and NATO. Rather than settle for modest increases in discretionary spending and small targeted tax cuts, he could have continued the argument he made in 1993: that domestic discretionary spending needs to be substantially increased when education and training are the tickets to mobility for underskilled workers. Figure 14.1 shows how federal spending on education, training, employment, and social services ("social investments" in the figure) stagnated during Clinton's presidency. He might have sought greater tax increases so that the nation could afford its burgeoning entitlements and domestic discretionary spending, particularly if he was unwilling to make deeper cuts in military spending. He might have discussed the tensions between military spending and domestic discretionary spending by noting how military spending at near–cold war levels severely squeezes domestic discretionary spending even when it has receded as a percentage of the budget. (Fig. 14.2 shows that narrow military spending absorbed more than 50 percent of the discretionary budget during his tenure.)

Clinton might also have discussed tradeoffs between entitlements, domestic discretionary spending, and taxes. With entitlements consuming a steadily growing share of the federal budget (roughly 60 percent of the budget in 1999), the United States had scant resources for other social needs after paying for military spending and interest on the debt (see fig. 14.3). By proposing to devote most of the nation's surpluses to entitlements for fifteen years, Clinton was helping citizens in the years 2032 to 2050, when tens of millions of baby boomers would be using entitlements at a rate that would overwhelm the federal budget. But Clinton's proposal carried the risk that important discretionary needs would not be addressed from 2000 to 2015 because he had devoted such extraordinary resources to Social Security and Medicare. To ease the Social Security burden on taxpayers for the two decades after 2032 and to meet pressing educational, social, and training needs from 2000 to 2015, perhaps Clinton should have

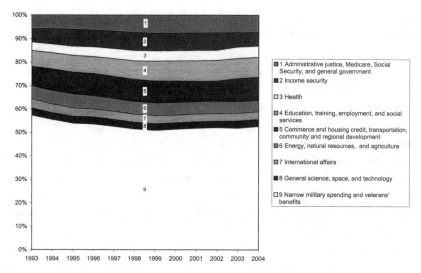

FIGURE 14.2 Competition for Discretionary Spending: Military Versus Domestic Spending as Percentages of Total Outlays, 1992–2004

Source: Office of Management and Budget, *Budget of the U.S. Government, FY 2000, Historical Tables* (Washington, D.C.: GPO, 1999), table 8.8, pp. 139–40.

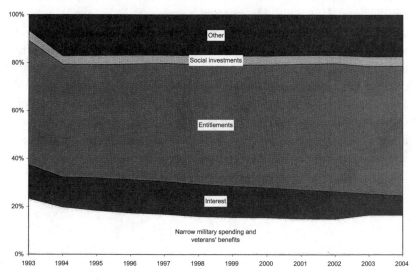

FIGURE 14.3 Five Types of Federal Expenditures as Percentages of Total Federal Outlays, 1993–2004

Source: Office of Management and Budget, *Budget of the U.S. Government, FY 2000, Historical Tables* (Washington, D.C.: GPO, 1999), table 3.1, pp. 48–49.

proposed tax increases and given some of that money to Social Security. Or perhaps some needs in 2000 to 2015 should trump some needs in 2032 to 2052.

Or perhaps the country should reduce its debt more gradually to meet some current needs of its citizens, particularly because domestic discretionary spending has been cut, frozen, and capped since 1981. (Although the Reagan deficits ballooned the federal debt to more than $5 trillion, it was still a smaller percentage of GDP than that of most other industrialized nations—and the size of the debt would shrink relative to the GDP if future presidents do not repeat Reagan's mistakes.)

A curiously unbalanced federal budget evolved as the nation entered the millennium—interest payments, military spending, and entitlements absorbed more than 80 percent of the federal budget, leaving scant resources for myriad other needs. Had Congress and the Clinton administration not wasted more than $1 trillion, the country would have had ample funds for an expanded domestic agenda or tax cuts for the poorest Americans. I discuss the magnitude of the waste in the next chapter.

Controversy over national priorities promised to be at the center of the nation's politics as the nation nervously awaited results from the contentious presidential election in 2000. George W. Bush, the Republican candidate, wanted to devote $1.32 trillion of a CBO-projected surplus of $2.17 trillion (over ten years) to new tax cuts, while devoting only $783 billion to new spending and debt reduction. Al Gore, the Democratic candidate, wanted to devote $1.55 trillion to new spending, while devoting only $575 billion to tax cuts. Both candidates promised major new military spending. Only time would tell whether public officials would make meritorious tax and spending[68] choices or merely revive older habits of waste in a nation possessing extraordinary economic inequality.

CHAPTER

15

On the Magnitude of
Failed National Priorities

BRUCE S. JANSSON AND
SARAH-JANE DODD

No one expects perfection in the spending of more than $56 trillion over seventy-three years (1931–2004)—and $12.8 trillion in tax expenditures just since 1968. (All data in this chapter are expressed in constant 1992 dollars.) Some resources will be spent on foolish or even fraudulent projects as scores of legislators and successive presidents—all mortals seeking reelection—allocate huge resources to specific projects in the push and pull of the political process. And members of Congress have often curried favor with voters by cutting taxes, even though they needed money to address domestic or international needs or to avert excessive federal deficits and federal debt.

Considerable evidence suggests, however, that public officials could have done much better. The United States will have squandered roughly $16 trillion from 1931 to 2004 that could have been used for such constructive purposes as social and educational programs, improving public transportation, cleaning up the environment, and lowering taxes for taxpayers in the lowest two economic quintiles. (And let us not forget that that's $16 trillion in constant 1992 dollars because those are the dollars used by the Office of Management and Budget; the more current equivalent is $18.46 trillion.)

Whereas the discussion thus far has focused on the military, tax policy, and pork-barrel spending, in this chapter the discussion broadens to include corporate welfare and excessive tax loopholes to arrive at an overall estimate of fiscal and tax errors.

Do Waste and Fiscal Errors "Matter"?

Does it matter that the United States squandered $16 trillion? Perhaps a nation with extraordinary wealth has the luxury of wasting extraordinary resources, much as affluent people can lavish their resources on things they don't need and frivolous activities. Wasted expenditures sometimes serve public purposes, moreover, as in the case of unnecessary military expenditures that provide jobs to military and civilian personnel and to residents of local communities. Politicians sometimes are able to push through meritorious legislation only by inserting pork-barrel provisions that entice reluctant legislators to support it.

Yet failed fiscal and tax decisions have many adverse consequences. They deplete the public treasury of resources it needs for constructive purposes. Roughly two thirds of the unemployed could not obtain public employment during the New Deal, for example, because excessively low federal income taxes—on only 5 percent of the population—meant the program could not be fully funded. Harry Truman could not fund many domestic reforms in the postwar period because he had to fund the Marshall Plan from a treasury depleted by excessive tax cuts. With military spending taking roughly 70 percent of the federal budget in the 1950s, the United States allowed its domestic agenda to languish while social and economic conditions in urban areas were deteriorating markedly. Lyndon Johnson's Great Society became a frugal society as excessive tax cuts and the Vietnam War again depleted the treasury. Federal domestic discretionary spending decreased from 1978 to 2004, whether measured as a percentage of the budget, a percentage of GDP, or in constant dollars. Meanwhile, public schools were providing education of questionable quality, urban problems festered, and economic inequality worsened.

When confronted with budget scarcity, presidents displayed remarkable ingenuity in securing funds for their domestic budgets. Roosevelt created two budgets so that he could claim to balance the regular budget while borrowing to fund the emergency budget, which financed the New Deal. Sometimes presidents took certain items out of the budget by providing them with their own source of funding, such as Roosevelt's Social Security Act or Eisenhower's Interstate Highway Program, the former funded by the payroll tax and the latter from federal gasoline and trucking taxes. They also resorted to tax expenditures that did not have to go through the appropriations committees, such as Clinton's funding of an array of tax credits for education. Presidents sometimes hid social spending in other programs, such as Robert McNamara's placing special services to low-income recruits in Johnson's military budget or Clinton's inserting social services in a huge crime bill. (McNamara justified these services as a strategy to recruit and retain low-income draftees and enlistees, whereas Clinton contended that recreation and social services for low-income youth would prevent crime.) Sometimes cost-free or inexpensive social initiatives—such as raising the minimum wage, enacting civil rights measures, or promulgating regulations constituted the entire social agenda of a president because he lacked the resources for other programs. With resources difficult to obtain many presidents enacted measures that had scant funding, such as the War on Poverty and a major federal education program, the Elementary and Secondary Education Act of 1965—or they enacted major reforms that were riddled with exemptions and loopholes to save money, such as a Medicare program in 1965 that failed to cover chronic conditions of and medications for the elderly, thus forcing hundreds of thousands to divest their assets to obtain coverage under the means-tested Medicaid program. When they encountered budget scarcity, presidents often slashed the funding of worthwhile domestic programs to obtain resources for new initiatives. But ingenious strategies to secure funding for some programs have hardly led to a robust domestic agenda. Lacking money in the public till, presidents were often loath to reduce taxes for low-income people even as economic inequality increased markedly from the 1970s on. Although many low-income taxpayers were removed from the rolls and the EITC helped improve the lot of other low-income people, the federal government did not reduce the inequitable Social Security payroll tax for low-income people, avoided sufficient expansion of eligibility for the EITC, and required too many low-income people to pay federal taxes.

Had the United States spent that $16 trillion wisely, it could have made remarkable additions to the nation's domestic agenda. In 2004, for example, when discretionary spending will total a mere $231 billion, not counting narrow military spending, $16 trillion could have paid for this discretionary budget sixty-nine times over, demonstrating that the United States could have more than doubled its total nonmilitary discretionary budget from 1933 through 2004 (see table 15.1).

The actual and projected cost of specific programs in recent American history give us some idea of what we could have achieved with the $16 trillion in squandered resources.[1] By spending merely $5 trillion, the United States could have tripled what it spent ($2.5 trillion) for all employment, training, education, and social programs from 1931 through 2004. The New Deal's employment and social programs could have been three times the size they were, and federal discretionary spending for education (which totaled only $800 billion from 1962 through 2004) could have been vastly increased. For a mere $1.9 trillion the United States could have greatly augmented its ground transportation program, such as by tripling federal expenditures from 1962 through 2004. For only $2.4 trillion it could have tripled spending of $792 billion on natural resources and the environment in the same period. Or it could have renovated its cities by quadrupling housing assistance from $527 billion to $2.1 trillion from 1962 through 2004.

The United States could have also have funded greatly augmented enti-

TABLE 15.1 Actual and Projected Federal Expenditures for Selected Social Programs in Trillions of Constant 1992 Dollars

	Total
1. Employment, training, education, and social programs, 1931–2004	$2.500
2. Housing assistance, 1962–2004	0.527
3. All entitlements, 1931–2004	22.400
4. Earned-Income Tax Credit, 1976–2004	0.274
5. Food and nutrition assistance, 1962–2004	0.659
6. Medicaid, 1965–2004	2.300
7. Medicare, 1965–2004	3.500
8. Social Security, 1962–2004	9.400
9. AFDC and welfare block grants, 1962–2004	0.620
10. Supplementary Security Income, 1972–2004	0.507
11. Community and regional development, 1962–2004	0.307
12. Ground transportation, 1962–2004	0.648
13. Natural resources and environment, 1962–2004	0.792

tlements. The nation will have spent $5.8 trillion on Medicare and Medicaid combined from 1965 through 2004 (see table 15.1). By doubling that sum the United States could have extended Medicaid's coverage to include many uninsured Americans, funded health care for many low-income children, and helped many elderly citizens with chronic health conditions rather than force them to divest their assets to gain eligibility for Medicaid. Similarly, by spending only $548 billion, the United States could have tripled the size of the EITC, from $274 billion to $822 billion.

Although some conservatives suggest that the United States has had a runaway welfare state, historical budget data present a different picture (see fig. 15.1). When measured in constant dollars, *only* domestic spending on big-ticket entitlements has increased markedly, whereas nonmedical means-tested entitlements, such as food stamps, SSI, and the EITC (called "other entitlements" in fig. 15.1), social investments (federal spending on education, training, employment, and social services), and domestic discretionary spending have remained relatively stagnant or have declined since the late 1970s. Nor does the picture change when we examine these four kinds of expenditures as percentages of GDP; only Medicare, Medicaid, and Social Security have increased appreciably since the late 1970s, whereas the other kinds of spending have declined (see fig. 15.2).

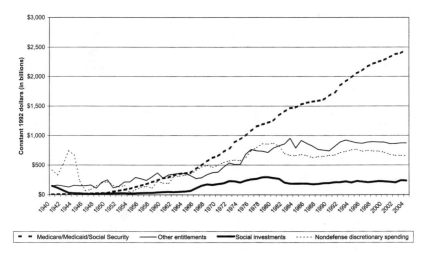

FIGURE 15.1 Four Kinds of Federal Expenditures, Per Capita, 1940–2004

Source: Office of Management and Budget, *Budget of the U.S. Government, FY 2000, Historical Tables* (Washington, D.C.: GPO, 1999), table 3.1, pp. 48–49.

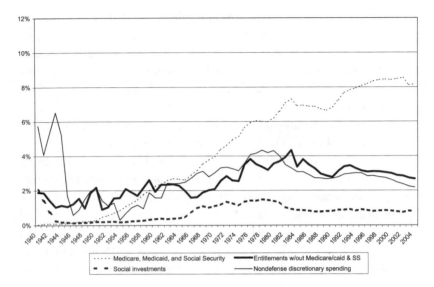

FIGURE 15.2 Four Kinds of Federal Expenditures as Percentages of GDP, 1940–2004
Source: Office of Management and Budget, *Budget of the U.S. Government,
FY 2000, Historical Tables* (Washington, D.C.: GPO, 1999), table 3.1, pp. 48–49.

Failed fiscal and tax errors fall into six categories: excessive military
spending, excessive interest payments on the national debt, undertaxation
of private wealth at pivotal points, excessive corporate welfare, excessive
tax concessions to affluent individuals, and excessive pork-barrel spending
(see table 15.2). I will discuss these six categories in the order in which they
appear in table 15.2.

EXCESSIVE MILITARY SPENDING

The United States has wasted roughly $5.47 trillion in its military
budget from 1941 through 2004. It could have cut the peaks above the
cold war base (see fig. 15.3) by abbreviating the combat phase of the
Korean War, staying out of Vietnam, and not consummating Reagan's
military buildup; cutting the cold war base from 1953 through 1992; cutting post–cold war spending from 1993 through 2004; and cutting
spending on procurement and operations from 1941 on. (I exclude military spending in the 1930s because it was significantly underfunded.)

TABLE 15.2 The Magnitude of Fiscal and Tax Mistakes, 1931 through 2004
(in trillions of constant 1992 dollars)

I. EXCESSIVE MILITARY SPENDING	*$5.470*
Peaks above the cold war base	
Inadvisable military tactics: Korea	0.504
Inadvisable military ventures: Vietnam	1.300
Reagan military buildup, 1981–1993	0.864
The cold war base, 1953–1992	
Nuclear forces	0.600
General purpose forces	0.670
Post–cold war spending, 1993–2004	0.769
Procurement, operations, and personnel, 1940–2004	
Procurement	0.410
Operations and maintenance	0.351
2. EXCESSIVE INTEREST PAYMENTS ON THE NATIONAL DEBT	1.500
3. UNDERTAXATION OF PRIVATE WEALTH	2.500
4. EXCESSIVE CORPORATE WELFARE	4.447
Corporate tax expenditures or concessions	0.950
Corporate subsidies	0.247
Corporate undertaxation	1.000
Undertaxation of harmful products and activities	1.500
Underregulation of certain corporations	0.750
5.EXCESSIVE TAX CONCESSIONS TO AFFLUENT INDIVIDUALS	1.500
6.EXCESSIVE PORKBARREL SPENDING	0.370
	$15.780

As figure 15.3 shows, military spending peaked above the cold war base three times: for the Korean War, the Vietnam War, and the Reagan military buildup. Each peak could have been smaller or eliminated altogether at a saving of hundreds of billions of dollars, not to mention lives.

Truman extended the fighting phase of the Korean War from three months (when U.S. and allied forces initially pushed the North Koreans back to the 38th parallel) to eight months in an ill-advised effort to conquer North Korea that was thwarted by entry of China into the war (see chapter 6). (By trying to conquer North Korea, Truman also violated an international agreement fashioned after World War II to divide Korea into

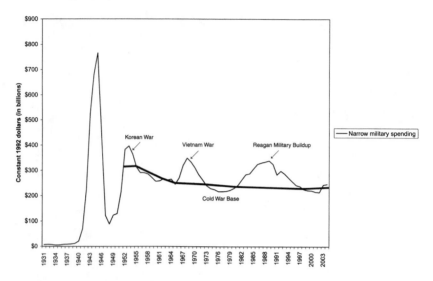

FIGURE 15.3 Narrow Military Spending and the Cold War Base, 1931–2004

Source: Office of Management and Budget, *Budget of the U.S. Government, FY 2000, Historical Tables* (Washington, D.C.: GPO, 1999), table 3.1, pp. 48–49.

northern and southern sections.) Had the United States stopped at the 38th parallel, the war, as well as the associated veterans' benefits, might have cost 40 percent less—or roughly $504 billion.[2]

Eisenhower chose not to place U.S. troops in Vietnam in the 1950s after Gen. Matthew Ridgeway warned him that he would trap the nation in a quagmire (see chapter 7). Many critics warned Kennedy and Johnson not to enter the Vietnam War (see chapter 8). Had the United States not fought the Vietnam War, it would have saved roughly $1.3 trillion when costs of prosecuting the war and veterans' benefits associated with it are considered.[3]

The Reagan military buildup was unnecessary. No credible evidence in the late 1970s and early 1980s suggested that the Soviet Union would invade Western Europe or launch a first strike against the United States (see chapters 10 and 11). Indeed, books by Fred Kaplan, Tom Gervasi, and Richard Stubbing persuasively contended that the United States possessed a considerable lead in military power in the late 1970s and early 1980s.[4] This was affirmed by an eight-volume (still classified) report from the General Accounting Office in 1993—the first analysis of Reagan's military buildup by an external nonmilitary agency—that contended that Reagan's military buildup had been unwarranted.[5] Had the United States merely continued narrow military spending through 1992 at the level inherited from President Jimmy Carter, it would have saved roughly $864 billion.[6]

The cold war base was the institutionalized level of narrow military spending (troops, armaments, and operations) from 1953 through 1992 and does not include the costs of the Korean War, Vietnam War, and the Reagan military buildup. Military spending dipped briefly beneath this base in the mid-1970s (see fig. 15.3).[7]

President Reagan's budget director, David Stockman, was astonished to learn that military budgets were not based on sophisticated simulations of U.S. forces fighting Soviet or other forces in specific situations but were put together by hundreds of clerks who calculated the cost of adding specific weapons and forces to existing ones. As Stockman relates,

> In fact, DOD [Department of Defense] arrived at the conclusion that it needed a quarter of a trillion dollars per year for defense by means of a subjective and approximate process. [In] theory . . . you started at the top by defining broad national security objectives . . . [and then] moved down the pyramid [as] you determined missions and capabilities [and then] structure, weapons, and resources. . . . The way it actually worked was rather different. The process really began at the bottom of the pyramid [as] clerks decided what they wanted; the colonels what they wanted; the generals what they wanted . . . and what ended up on the Secretary of Defense's desk was a wish list a mile long. "Need," therefore, was an unscientific melding of the wish list that rose up from the bottom and the policy guidance which came down from the top.[8]

The discussion in chapters 5 through 12 suggests that during the cold war the Pentagon, presidents, and congressional leaders frequently overestimated the capabilities of Soviet troops, the possibility of a Soviet invasion of Western Europe, the likelihood that the Soviets would initiate a first nuclear strike against the United States, and the ability of the Soviets to take control of developing nations. Likening military spending to private insurance, they wrongly argued too that the United States should err on the side of excessive spending when the nation's survival was at stake. When purchasing insurance, however, we do not forgo important essentials to protect ourselves against extremely unlikely dangers. We do not, for example, insure ourselves against hurricanes when we live in Kansas—nor do we insure ourselves against attacks by Martians. If we do foolishly purchase insurance for every contingency, we lack resources for essentials, much as various presidents found they had scant funds for the domestic agenda when the military sucked up most discretionary money during the cold war.[9]

Examining various components of the military budget raises suspicions about the size of the cold war base. Figure 15.4, for example, shows that spending on strategic forces—long-range and tactical nuclear weapons, as well as the missile, submarine, and bomber platforms that carried them— exceeded 40 percent of the total military budget in the late 1950s and early 1960s, whereas the percentage was much lower after that.[10] Yet the U.S. nuclear arsenal vastly exceeded the Soviet arsenal throughout the 1950s, 1960s, and 1970s (see chapters 7, 8, and 9). While the United States spent an annual average of $85 billion on strategic forces from 1954 through 1960, for example, the Soviets had virtually no long-range bombers or ICBMs capable of reaching U.S. targets. Thanks to the U-2 flights—and then satellites—American presidents and military planners were well aware of these Soviet weaknesses beginning in 1956.

Long-range strategic forces were excessive not only in the 1950s and 1960s but from 1970 through 1992 when the United States spent $42 bil-

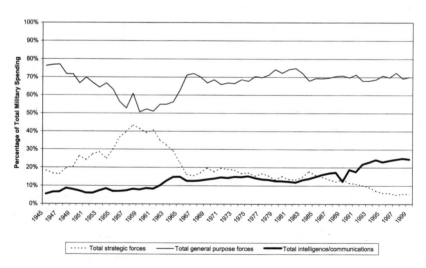

FIGURE 15.4 Three Types of Military Spending as Percentages of Total Spending, 1945–1999

Source: U.S. Department of Defense, Future Years Defense Program.

lion on strategic arms in an average year. Although the Soviets' nuclear arsenal had nearly caught up with the Americans' by the early 1980s, the United States already possessed sufficient numbers of warheads to deter a Soviet first strike.

Many military experts believed that the megatonnage of nuclear weapons actually required for deterrence was far less than the number of nuclear devices possessed by the United States. Adm. Arleigh Burke believed a force of forty-five Polaris submarines (with twenty-nine deployed at all times) would suffice "to destroy all of Russia."[11] Indeed, as Burke suggested, a persuasive case can be made that the United States could have relied on submarine-launched ballistic missiles (SLBMs). (Although not as powerful as ICBMs, they are potent weapons that are relatively invulnerable to countermeasures because destroying large numbers of submerged submarines is nearly impossible.) Gen. Maxwell Taylor contended in 1960 that "a few hundred reliable and accurate missiles" that were "mobile, concealed, and dispersed" and accompanied by a small number of bombs would be sufficient to badly damage the Soviet Union's war-making ability.[12] In 1964, when the air force wanted ten thousand Minuteman ICBMs, McNamara selected one thousand as a compromise figure when a Bureau of the Budget study suggested that a Minuteman force of 450 would suffice.[13] C. Paul Robinson, director of the Sandia National Laboratories, contended in 1997 that two thousand nuclear warheads were sufficient.[14]

With more than fourteen thousand strategic warheads that packed more than twenty thousand megatons of destructive energy from 1970 through 1990, the U.S. nuclear arsenal vastly exceeded the view of McNamara, Taylor, Burke, Jimmy Carter, and Harold Brown, Carter's secretary of defense, that less than four thousand megatons (or two thousand warheads or fewer) would suffice. (Even a 1995 National Security Council proposal, subsequently rejected by the Joint Chiefs of staff, sought to reduce the U.S. strategic arsenal to roughly five thousand weapons—or about one fourth of its size in 1996.)[15]

If the United States could have made substantial cuts in long-distance strategic forces, it could also have made drastic cuts in its short- and intermediate-distance nuclear forces, in other words, its tactical nuclear forces. Tactical nuclear forces were devised to attack targets with destructive power greater than conventional artillery or tactical bombing, whether to deter enemy forces from launching a preemptive strike or to destroy them in its aftermath. What seemed to make theoretical sense, however, made little operational sense. Many military officials doubted the usability of tactical nuclear weapons virtually from their inception because they would cause unacceptable damage to civilian populations behind enemy lines, such as in Eastern Europe.[16] Also, firing them would be likely to precipitate the launch of strategic nuclear weapons by the opposing side. Nor could a military commander in a specific location decide to launch tactical nuclear weapons because of the danger to civilian populations and to his own forces from radiation, as well as the fear of triggering counterstrikes of tactical (or strategic) nuclear weapons by opposing forces. Nor did the United States need tactical nuclear weapons to deter the Soviets because long-range nuclear weapons would do the job. Although even some military planners had misgivings, the Pentagon had supplied its general purpose forces with remarkably complete complement of tactical weapons even by the late 1950s, placing an array of short- and long-range missiles in Europe in the 1960s, 1970s, and 1980s, including nuclear artillery shells, mobile and fixed ground-launched short- and midrange missiles, and bomber-launched short- and midrange missiles.[17]

Had the United States cut its strategic arsenal in half from 1951 through 1992—a cut that would still have given it far more megatonnage in destructive power than it needed—it would have saved roughly $1.2 trillion from the $2.4 trillion it spent on strategic forces in that period. Had it cut its strategic arsenal by one fourth, it would have saved $600 billion. (I use this conservative option.)

As figure 15.5 suggests, the bulk of the U.S. military budget was devoted to general purpose forces during the cold war: troops, most naval vessels, helicopters, and the Marine Corps. In addition to the $2.4 trillion the United States spent on strategic forces in the cold war, it spent $7.8 trillion on general purpose forces from 1951 through 1992. The vast majority of these forces were dedicated to the defense of Europe; most were stationed in the United States for rapid deployment to Europe, but substantial numbers were based in Europe. (Forward bases in Europe had were supplied and armed so that European-based U.S. forces, joined by other U.S. and NATO forces, could rapidly mount a counteroffensive if the Soviet Union invaded Europe.)

Serious questions can be raised about the size of U.S. general purpose forces. The Soviets, faced with overwhelming U.S. nuclear power, were highly unlikely to risk a nuclear conflagration by invading Western Europe

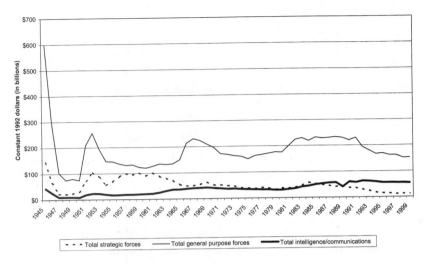

FIGURE 15.5 Three Types of Military Spending, 1945–1999
    Source: U.S. Department of Defense, Future Years Defense Program.

(see chapters 5 and 6). They were particularly unlikely to do so because they were up against a cohesive Western alliance, a nonisolationist United States, U.S. long-range bombers based around the world, U.S. tactical nuclear weapons that encircled the USSR, a fleet of nuclear-armed submarines and nuclear attack submarines, and massive combined military spending by the United States and its allies. Nor would Soviet leaders have believed they could hold Western Europe for an extended period even if they invaded it, because they would have encountered resistance movements, counterattacks by the United States on their long supply lines, and perhaps even defections from Warsaw Pact troops asked to repress Western Europeans—not to mention ongoing nuclear and conventional counterattacks on the Soviet Union. (The Soviets had witnessed the horrible destruction meted out to Germany in World War II when it had tried to hold Europe—destruction far less that the Soviets would experience in the nuclear age.) Soviet leaders regarded Eastern Europe as a buffer against a Western Europe that had invaded the Soviet Union on successive occasions. Would a country that remained traumatized by the twenty million civilian deaths in World War II risk losing one hundred million or more citizens in a nuclear war?[18]

If the Soviets had nonetheless invaded Western Europe, it was virtually inevitable that hostilities would escalate into nuclear warfare, thus rendering general purpose forces irrelevant. For starters, protracted battlefield confusion and uncertainty would prevail—as indeed they prevail among military experts in discussions of likely scenarios. Some military analysts believed that a "forward defense" could contain a Soviet invasion by immediately massing NATO conventional forces at the boundary separating East and West Germany.[19] These analysts believed that by raining conventional firepower on Soviet forces, NATO could win a war of attrition. Many other analysts, however, doubted this would work. Indeed, a 1979 army manual conceded that repelling a Soviet invasion would require chemical warfare and tactical nuclear weapons.[20] Still other analysts wanted to fortify the boundary between West and East Germany in the hope that NATO forces kept in reserve in West Germany could repulse Soviet and Warsaw Pact troops that penetrated the border. Yet another set of military analysts favored highly mobile forces that would launch surprise attacks against Soviet forces once they entered Western Europe.[21]

Such doctrinal confusion suggests that each side would nervously fear an all-out nuclear attack by the other. After a sustained period of nuclear nerves, one side or the other probably would resort to tactical or strategic missiles in an initial barrage that could only escalate. The United States needed a sizable force in Europe to make clear to the Soviets that if they invaded Western Europe, hostilities would only escalate. No U.S. president would tolerate the massacre of American troops. Even so, the United States did not need a standing force of two million active forces and large reserves during much of the cold war because a Soviet invasion was so improbable and because nuclear forces would have trumped conventional ones.

Had the United States cut the size of the three peaks above the cold war base, it could have saved roughly $1.1 trillion by cutting the cost of its general forces from $7.8 trillion to $6.7 trillion.[22] Had the United States cut the remaining general purpose forces by 15 percent from 1951 through 1992, it would have saved roughly $1 trillion more while retaining huge conventional U.S. forces in Europe, Japan, South Korea, and the United States. A reduction in force of only 10 percent would have saved the nation $670 billion. I use this more conservative option.

When the cold war ended at the stroke of midnight on December 31, 1991, the United States could have downsized its forces markedly. As discussed in chapter 13, William Kaufmann suggested two alternatives the next year: a "low option" and an even lower "cooperative security budget" (see fig. 15.6).[23] Kaufmann contended that either force would have allowed the United States to win a major regional war. His alternatives were prescient: the United States waged only regional wars from 1993 through 1999, whether in Somalia, Bosnia, or Kosovo. His alternative proposals provided sufficient deterrence against the downsized Russian nuclear forces as well as Chinese nuclear forces, which were so small that they were roughly equivalent to those contained in a single Trident submarine in 1999. The United States did not need troop levels of cold war size to wage regional wars in Somalia, Bosnia, or Kosovo (see chapter 14). Nor did it need cold war forces even when it faced simultaneous and overlapping conflicts, because the United States could share responsibilities with other nations and the U.N. Had the United States chosen Kaufmann's low option rather than (essentially) maintaining its base-line cold war forces, the country would have saved roughly $769 billion in budget authority from 1993 through 2004 while retaining huge strategic and general purpose forces.

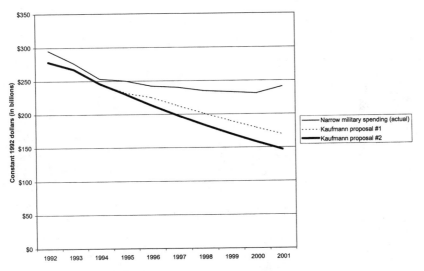

FIGURE 15.6 Actual Narrow Military Spending Versus Two Alternatives, 1991–2001
   Sources: William Kaufmann, *Assessing the Base Force: How Much Is Too Much?* (Washington, D.C.: Brookings Institution, 1992), 51–76; Office of Management and Budget, *Budget of the U.S. Government, FY 2000, Historical Tables* (Washington, D.C.: GPO, 1999), table 5.1, pp. 77–78.

Few people realize that most of the military budget goes to the mundane costs of operating a massive institution that had about three million civilian and military employees in 1985. From 1940 through 2004, for example, the nation spent $5.4 trillion on its little-known "operations and maintenance" needs and more than the $4.2 trillion to buy major and minor weapons.[24] (Figure 15.7 reveals the sheer size of this "soft underbelly," a term coined by Richard Stubbing.[25])

Writing fourteen years apart during the most expensive years of the cold war, Ernest Fitzgerald, who worked in the Pentagon's procurement programs, and Richard Stubbing, who worked for the section of the Office of Management and Budget charged with developing annual military budgets, agree that the military could have saved tens of billions of dollars annually by reforming its procurement, operations, and personnel systems—an opinion shared by many authors and government reports.[26]

The United States made a major mistake in World War II when it created a direct procurement partnership of the military and (mainly) giant corporations instead of developing an external body staffed by civil ser-

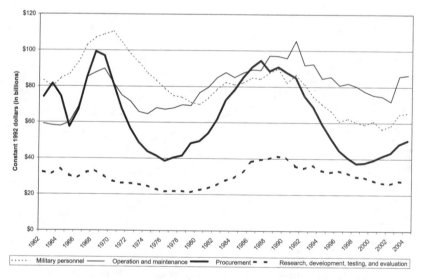

FIGURE 15.7 Military Spending for Personnel, Operations, Procurement, and Research, 1962–2004

Source: Office of Management and Budget, Budget of the U.S. Government, FY 2000, Historical Tables (Washington, D.C.: GPO, 1999), table 3.2, pp. 50–64.

vants to negotiate and monitor military contracts with private industry. (The British chose the latter course.)[27] Although this was a pragmatic choice by Roosevelt to speed war production, direct management of military contracts by the military vastly increased costs during World War II and thereafter. Given a lot of money but scant congressional oversight, the military had no incentive to seek competitive bids or to negotiate tough contracts with corporations.

As Fitzgerald persuasively contended, a pervasive culture of waste developed during the cold war.[28] The military had no reason to ride herd on corporations during the contracting process, because the services were beholden to corporations for lobbying Congress strenuously to authorize and appropriate money for various weapons systems. Nor did the brass want to publicize contract abuses, such as malfunctioning weapons or cost overruns, lest they jeopardize the size of military appropriations. (Many military officials, moreover, anticipated lucrative postretirement jobs with military contractors.) Nor did politicians want to jeopardize the flow of money to corporations in their districts and thus opposed the exposure of many contract abuses. The corporations, in turn, came to regard military contracts as different from their ordinary commercial business. Most contracts were noncompetitive, whether because only one firm made the weapon (or part) in question or because the company's lobbyists persuaded the Pentagon and Congress to send the contract its way. Because the Pentagon did not have many engineers, corporate negotiating teams could run circles around military brass in estimating the probable cost of a weapon—or in offering technical explanations for cost overruns.[29] Because corporations usually did not have to compete for contracts, they became adept at obtaining them on lucrative terms. Extraordinary leeway was usually built into the contracts from the outset for overhead costs, labor costs, and myriad contingencies. Aware that the Pentagon would not penalize the companies, they expected contract modifications rather than penalties for cost overruns or other errors. (When they did have to compete for contracts, corporations often lowballed their bids, because they knew they could get additional funding later on.) Unions joined this remunerative game, persuading the military and corporate contractors to pay aerospace and other unionized employees higher wages than regular union members.[30]

Myriad studies document the extraordinary inefficiencies of military contractors.[31] They hired excessive numbers of employees and paid wages and salaries far above what they needed to be competitive with commercial industry at all levels of production. Parts and spare parts—sometimes of inferior quality—regularly exceeded the cost of commercial products by a factor of two or more. Overhead costs were vastly higher than their commercial counterparts' as well, with military contractors often milking their Pentagon contracts for excessive contributions to the general costs of corporate overhead. Because the contracting process seldom was competitive, the contracts went to companies with the most skilled lobbyists, not the most efficient or innovative workforce.

Corporations not only trafficked in contracts initiated by the military but initiated contracts as their engineering staff proposed myriad modifications to existing weapons or developed new ones. Corporations lobbied the Pentagon to fund their proposals, sometimes even bribing Pentagon officials. Or corporations would lobby members of Congress to pressure the Pentagon to fund their innovations and often contributed heavily to politicians' campaign funds or allowed elected officials to use corporate jets or other corporate assets such as vacation condominiums.[32] Corporate officials, politicians, and Pentagon officials freely socialized and exchanged inside information in exclusive clubs at exotic locations.

Nor was the Pentagon inclined to closely monitor the work of military contractors. It suppressed internal reports that questioned its lack of surveillance, and it relied on historical cost data to gauge the accuracy of corporate estimates rather than obtain independent assessments based on actual studies of the effort and materials required to execute the contract.[33] It regarded close monitoring as "meddling" and socialized new employees to its culture of waste, by demoting or firing people who brought malfeasance to public attention.

Myriad reformers have tried to make procurement more efficient, with questionable success. They have changed the nature of contracts from cost plus a percentage for profit to fixed-price ones; replaced sole-source negotiated contracts with dual source ones, so that two corporations compete to produce the better product; used competitive bids; and asked corporations to produce prototypes so that the military can gauge quality and cost before moving to production. Although these innovations have achieved some efficiencies, the corporations have found ways to get around these controls, such as by providing a low-ball bid to secure a contract while counting on the Pentagon to provide additional money when they run over budget (see chapters 10 and 11).

Procurement remains riddled with waste because of the peculiar interlocking partnership of Congress, the Pentagon, and military contractors. What's needed is a radical restructuring of this incestuous arrangement. For example, the handling of contracts could be turned over to an institutional body with civil service technicians not beholden to the Pentagon or corporations. These government employees would provide technical advice to Congress and assign contracts based on the efficiency and quality of corporate contenders.

Such institutional reforms ought to have been coupled with establishing a truly integrated military rather than the fiefdoms known as the air force, navy, and army. As discussed in chapters 5 and 6, Truman and Marshall failed to persuade Congress to eliminate the three services in favor of a single department organized around missions and theaters. This approach would have eliminated duplication in such areas as intelligence, missiles, ground forces, and communications capabilities, as well as research and development. Instead of a crazy quilt of air force, army, and navy installations, the United States would have had fewer military bases with multiple capabilities around the world and at home.

In all, the United States spent $4.2 trillion on procurement from 1940 through 2004 (see fig. 15.7) and could therefore have achieved significant savings through major procurement reforms. Had the United States cut the three peaks above the cold war base and cut post–cold war spending as we have discussed, U.S. military spending would have been 35 percent lower— $11.46 trillion instead of $17.5 trillion—between 1940 and 2004.[34] Because procurement was a part of all these expenditures, it is reasonable to argue that procurement costs would also have declined by 35 percent, from $4.2 trillion to $2.73 trillion, even without any basic procurement reforms. If we assume that procurement reforms would have realized cost savings of 15 percent, the United States could have saved $410 billion by reforming procurement and developing a truly integrated Department of Defense from 1940 to 2004.

The United States spent $5.4 trillion on supplies, services, repairs, food, fuel, travel, maintenance of facilities, and other costs to operate the vast military apparatus 1940 through 2004 (see fig. 15.7). Here too gross inefficiencies have plagued the military services.[35] With four thousand military installations in the United States and with sixteen hundred around the world in 1985, the U.S. military unwisely retained many bases built during World War II, although it closed some during the Bush and Clinton administrations. These redundancies were coupled with extraordinary inefficiencies. In the mid-1980s each installation had several commissaries staffed by civilian personnel and given free rent and overhead—a wasteful practice in areas where military personnel could have used existing commercial facilities. The military often bought spare parts at exorbitant rather than commercial rates and often failed to use its purchasing clout to obtain discounts on fuel, clothing, food, and other commodities.

The military also could have realized huge savings by contracting with civilian firms for medical support and education, training, logistics inventory, certain facets of administration such as personnel and financial management, base maintenance and support, housing, and repair of equipment. Indeed, a report by the Defense Science Board in 1996 maintained that obtaining competitive bids for these services could have saved $30 billion annually.[36]

Opposition to such efficiencies often derived from Congress, veterans, corporations, and military personnel. Members of Congress usually opposed efforts to close military installations and actually nixed base closures after World War II, including those proposed in 1999 by Secretary of Defense Bill Cohen. Military personnel opposed President Ford's proposals to make commissaries more efficient.[37]

Had overall military spending had been reduced by 35 percent between 1940 and 2004—by cutting the three peaks above the cold war base, the cold war base itself, and post–cold war military spending—the cost of operations and maintenance would also have declined by 35 percent, from $5.4 trillion to $3.51 trillion, even without any reforms. If the military had realized savings of 10 percent by closing bases and instituting other economies, it would have saved $351 billion in the remaining operations and maintenance costs from 1940 through 2004.

As table 15.2 shows, the United States could have saved $5.47 trillion on its military from 1940 to 2004. To do so it would have had to reduce its strategic and tactical nuclear forces ($600 billion) and general purpose forces ($670 billion) during the cold war, cut post–cold war spending from 1993 through 2004 ($769 billion), stayed out of Vietnam ($1.3 trillion), cut the size of the Korean War ($504 billion), and not instituted a huge military buildup during the Reagan presidency ($864 billion). The nation could have saved $410 billion on procurement and $351 billion on operations and maintenance. The United States would still have had awesome military power, including strategic weapons sufficient to deter foes, a huge standing army, and an international network of military installations and binding treaties. The United States would have remained the preeminent military power in the world—and the extensive military assets of its allies would have further augmented U.S. power in the world during and after the cold war.

Some critics may retort, "But hasn't military spending served many constructive purposes, even if a considerable portion was not needed for narrowly military purposes?" The military has, for example, since 1964 provided job training for low-income (mostly minority) youth who would otherwise have languished in low-paid jobs; created and sustained jobs and subsidized local businesses in communities, regions, and states; and served a pump-priming function during recessions and depressions, even lifting the nation from the Great Depression. (Predictions of some economists, historians, and presidents that military spending would bring economic ruin to the United States proved erroneous.)[38]

In fact, the military is a poor substitute for civilian social and employment services. Skills obtained in the military are often not easily transferable to the civilian sector. Dollars spent directly on civilian projects, such as child-care centers, bring greater economic growth because they stimulate a wider range of direct and indirect economic benefits than does the production of armaments. Ethical questions can be raised about whether it is fair to entice low-income and minority youth to secure job training in the armed services by not providing it in the civilian sector— particularly when they are also required to risk their lives in military combat as part of the bargain. As Carl Rowan has contended, moreover, use of the military to achieve social objectives excessively militarizes U.S. society.[39]

Had military spending been cut even modestly, domestic spending would have been significantly increased, as figure 15.8 shows. While it is true that military spending became a progressively smaller percentage of the federal budget, which includes spending on entitlements, it took a huge portion of the discretionary budget, which is shaped each year in the push and pull of the budget process. Indeed, military spending will preempt more than 50 percent of the discretionary budget in 2004, having preempted far larger percentages in decades past.

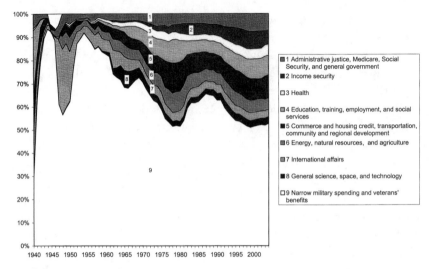

FIGURE 15.8 Competition for Discretionary Spending: Military Versus Domestic Spending as Percentages of Total Outlays, 1940–2004

Source: Office of Management and Budget, *Budget of the U.S. Government, FY 2000, Historical Tables* (Washington, D.C.: GPO, 1999), table 8.8, pp. 131–40.

EXCESSIVE INTEREST PAYMENTS ON THE NATIONAL DEBT

As discussed in chapters 2, 4, 10, and 11, the United States created large federal debt in three periods since 1930: the New Deal, World War II, and the Reagan presidency. (See fig. 15.9, which shows that imbalances in federal receipts and outlays were greatest from 1932 to 1941, 1942 to 1946, and 1982 to 1998.)

Deficits were needed in the Great Depression to stimulate the economy, but they had negative consequences during World War II and the Reagan period. They exacerbated inflation in World War II, contributed to postwar inflation when citizens redeemed billions of dollars in war bonds issued to finance the war, and caused high postwar interest payments that constricted resources for other programs. Had the United States more than doubled its wartime taxes to fund 75 percent, instead of 35 percent, of the war's costs, the debt at the end of the war would have been markedly smaller. This decision alone would have cut interest payments from 1946 through 1960 from $386 billion to $193 billion, for a savings of $193 billion.[40]

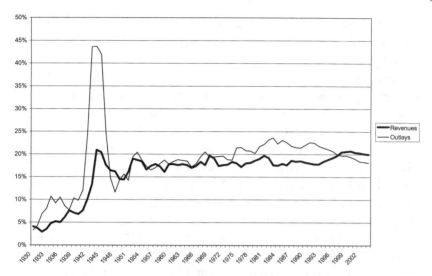

FIGURE 15.9 Outlays and Tax Revenues as Percentages of GDP, 1930–2004

Source: Office of Management and Budget, *Budget of the U.S. Government, FY 2000, Historical Tables* (Washington, D.C.: GPO, 1999), table 1.2, pp. 21–22.

Reagan's fiscal and tax policies in 1981 created huge annual deficits that were not erased until 1998—deficits that enlarged the federal debt from $710 billion in 1980 to $3.7 trillion by 1998. Annual interest payments to finance this debt burgeoned from $52.5 billion in 1980 to $243 billion in 1998.[41] (Interest payments rose from 8.9 percent of the federal budget in 1980 to 15.2 percent in 1998.) Had the nation kept interest payments through the 2004 at the same proportion of GDP as in 1980, the nation would have saved $1.4 trillion.

The nation wasted more than $1.5 trillion in excess interest payments when excess interest payments in World War II are added to those from 1981 through 2004.

UNDERTAXATION OF PRIVATE WEALTH

When a nation fails to tax private wealth sufficiently, it lacks resources to meet its foreign and domestic obligations. As chapters 2 and 3 and 5 through 8 discussed, revenue insufficiencies were particularly marked during Roosevelt's first two terms as well as during the Truman, Eisenhower,

Kennedy, and Johnson presidencies. (I discuss elsewhere the excessively low tax rates in World War II and the Reagan presidency.)

As figure 15.9 shows, tax revenues during the New Deal averaged only 5 percent of GDP, whereas they were closer to 20 percent after 1952. Placed on a precarious fiscal footing and given enough money to provide work-relief jobs to only a third the unemployed, the New Deal lacked sufficient resources to jolt the economy out of the Great Depression, to pay for humanitarian programs for the jobless, or to fund an adequate military. Had Roosevelt taxed 15 percent of the GDP from 1934 through 1941, he would have had $949 billion more to pay for his New Deal and the military—nearly triple the actual federal spending from 1934 through 1941.

Tax revenues also ought to have been raised during Truman's presidency, when they fell to 16 percent from their World War II peaks even as Truman faced huge interest payments on the wartime debt, occupation costs in Europe and Asia, and the costs of the GI Bill and the Marshall Plan (see fig. 15.9). With no resources for the domestic agenda, Truman's Fair Deal was an empty shell (see chapters 5 and 6), though he deserves credit for vetoing three congressional tax cuts and supporting federal aid to education, national health insurance, and expanded housing programs. Had taxes been set at 20 percent of GDP from 1946 through 1952, the federal government would have collected $511.3 billion in additional revenues for its domestic agenda.

While the United States had to increase its military spending during the 1950s in light of the Soviet threat, it starved its domestic agenda by devoting more than 60 percent of its total federal budget—and more than 80 percent of its discretionary budget—to narrow military spending. To tackle burgeoning social and development problems in its cities, it ought to have set taxes at 20 percent of GDP rather than an average of 17.6 percent from 1953 through 1960, thus obtaining an additional $482 billion for its domestic agenda.

Spurned by Congress when he sought to increase federal spending to stimulate the economy, President Kennedy turned to tax cuts. After enacting a small tax cut in 1961, he proposed a huge income tax cut that languished in Congress until Johnson got it enacted soon after he became president. As discussed in chapter 8, Johnson could not adequately fund his Great Society with taxes that averaged only 17.6 percent of GDP during his tenure (see fig. 15.9). Had the nation set taxes at 20 percent of GDP when military spending still dominated the federal budget, Kennedy and

Johnson would have had $592 billion in additional revenues to address the festering social and development problems of U.S. cities from 1961 through 1969.

By raising taxes during the New Deal, as well as during the Truman, Eisenhower, Kennedy, and Johnson presidencies, the United States would have had $2.5 trillion in additional resources for its domestic agenda from 1934 through 1968. (Of course, had the United States cut is military spending during this period, as I have advocated, it would have had massive resources for the domestic agenda, thus making tax increases unnecessary.)

EXCESSIVE CORPORATE WELFARE

U.S. corporations have been entangled with the federal government since the beginning of the Republic. In the nineteenth century, the federal government gave land grants to the railroads and used tariffs to protect fledgling industries from foreign competition; provided myriad tax incentives to mining, oil, and mineral interests; since the 1960s it has granted many tax concessions for corporate investment, research, and job-training activities; and since the New Deal it often has subsidized huge agricultural corporations through crop subsidies and tax write-offs. It also gave many contracts to defense and other industries, particularly in World War II and since; used tax incentives in the 1970s and succeeding decades to promote social policy goals, including job creation, job training, and economic development in inner cities; exempted certain industries from antimonopoly laws for brief or extended periods; and used tax incentives to induce corporations to provide health insurance, pensions, and life insurance to employees. The federal government's links to corporations included the vast regulatory system that oversees worker safety and environmental standards.

Americans have vacillated between positive and negative views of this federal-corporate relationship. If terms like *empowerment zones* and *public-private partnerships* reflect the positive view, *corporate welfare* reflects the view that the federal government unduly enriches certain corporations through specific tax concessions, subsidies, protections, or contracts. The robber barons of the late nineteenth century bribed legislators to raise tariffs to unreasonable levels, to secure subsidies for mining and other interests, and to block enforcement of the antitrust laws. The federal government provided excessively lucrative contracts to many military contractors, particularly since World War II. Nor has the federal government consistently enforced laws and regulations meant to protect the public interest, such as antitrust laws, environmental protections, and worker safety regulations. Such favoritism to corporations is often related, moreover, to powerful corporate lobbies that have contributed heavily to the campaign funds of legislators and the two parties.

Corporate welfare is multifaceted and includes the so-called tax expenditures (or tax concessions), corporate subsidies (or grants), contracts, and regulations that do not serve an overriding public interest (see table 15.2, which does not include corporate welfare in the military sector because it appears under waste in military procurement).

Records detailing the cumulative size of tax expenditures granted to corporations go back to 1975, when they totaled $33 billion. By 1982 they had risen to $47 billion and reached $67 billion in 1992 and $73 billion in 1998. They will amount to $63 billion in 2004 if Congress does not enact major new corporate tax expenditures.[42] Six of the biggest corporate tax expenditures in 2000 included deferral of income from controlled foreign corporations ($5.3 billion), the graduated corporate income tax rate ($4.6 billion), tax credits for corporations receiving income from doing business in U.S. possessions ($3.5 billion), accelerated depreciation of buildings other than rental housing ($2.9 billion), exclusion of income from foreign sales cooperatives ($2.1 billion), and the inventory property sales source rules exception ($941 million). Scores of these technical and relatively small items comprised the $65 billion in corporate tax expenditures in 2000. All told, the federal government will have lost $1.9 trillion in revenues from 1975 through 2004.

Because no one has thoroughly researched the actual effects of these corporate tax expenditures, it is difficult to determine which ought to be eliminated. In 1996 Public Citizen, an advocacy group founded by Ralph Nader, analyzed tax expenditures and estimated that the treasury could save $155 billion over five years—or about $30 billion per year (nearly 48 percent) of the roughly $63 billion in corporate tax expenditures in 1996.[43] (Public Citizen criticized such tax breaks as a provision allowing multinational corporations headquartered in the United States to use excess foreign-paid tax credits to reduce their tax liability for income produced in the United States; tax credits earned for corporate income earned in U.S. possessions; a loophole that gives large mutual life insurance companies a tax advantage over stock-owned life insurance companies; and an exemption of some income U.S. firms earn from exports.) If we assume that Congress ought to have eliminated 50 percent of corporate tax expenditures from 1975 through 2004, the federal government would have saved $950 billion in constant 1992 dollars.

We have even less data about the extended effects of corporate subsidies. A stern critic is, paradoxically, the probusiness Cato Institute, a conservative think tank that favors sharp cutbacks in such subsidies. Of the roughly $68 billion in subsidies that corporations enjoyed in 1996, Cato found thirty-five, or roughly 26 percent, to be "least defensible"—and they cost the treasury $17.7 billion.[44] The Cato list included some programs avidly defended by others, however, such as the Tennessee Valley Authority, road and trail construction by the U.S. Forest Service, and the Small Business Administration. If we cut Cato's estimate nearly in half, to a mere 14 percent, and if we assume that corporate subsidies roughly equaled federal corporate tax expenditures from 1975 through 2004 (as in 1996), the nation could have saved 13 percent of $1.9 trillion—or $247 billion.

Even more than corporate subsidies and tax entitlements, however, corporations have benefited from the low general rates of federal taxation of corporate income (see the third item under "Excessive Corporate Welfare" in table 15.2). After revenue from corporate income taxes peaked at 6.1 percent of GDP in 1952, it dropped to merely 1.1 percent of GDP in 1983 before rising to 2.3 percent of GDP in 2000 (see fig. 15.10). While this decline partly reflected a natural decline from the high corporate tax levels established in World War II to counter profiteering, it was also caused by sustained lobbying by such organizations as the U.S. Chamber of Commerce and the National Association of Manufacturers, which contend that excessive corporate taxation retards economic growth by depleting profits that would otherwise be invested in job-creating projects. They also contend that corporate taxation increases inflation because companies pass tax increases through to consumers in the form of higher prices.

Historical data do not support such contentions, however, as table 15.3 shows, because levels of corporate income taxation are not associated with levels of economic growth or with rates of inflation. Take, for example, the 1960s, when high rates of economic growth and low rates of inflation coexisted with relatively high rates of corporate taxation. Or the 1970s, when declining rates of corporate taxation coexisted with declining economic growth and sharp rates of inflation. Compared to the 1960s, economic growth was relatively modest in the 1980s, when corporate tax levels

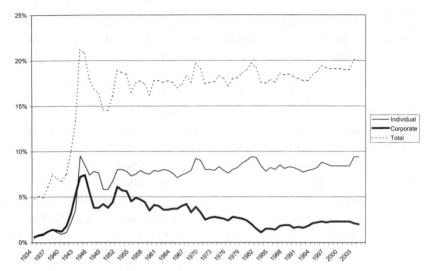

FIGURE 15.10 Total Federal Tax Receipts, Corporate Tax Receipts, and Individuals' Tax Receipts as Percentages of GDP, 1934–2004

Source: Office of Management and Budget, *Budget of the U.S. Government, FY 2000, Historical Tables* (Washington, D.C.: GPO, 1999), table 2.1, pp. 27–28, and table 2.3, pp. 31–32.

reached all-time lows, although inflation did decline in the 1980s after reaching astronomical levels in the 1970s. When corporate tax rates rose modestly in the 1990s, economic growth increased somewhat and inflation decreased markedly in comparison to the 1980s. While these historical data do not tell us what effects the high rates of corporate taxation of the 1950s and 1960s would have had on economic growth and inflation in the 1980s and 1990s, they undermine simplistic assumptions about relationships between these factors.

The federal government relinquished staggering resources by cutting corporate taxes so markedly when individuals' taxes remained relatively constant as a percentage of GDP (see fig. 15.10). Had it kept corporate taxes at the rate that prevailed in 1956 (4.9 percent of GDP) through 2004, for example, it would have had $5.8 trillion in additional resources. Had it kept corporate taxes at the rate that prevailed in 1967 (4.2 percent of GDP), it would have collected $4.1 trillion in additional resources. Had it kept corporate taxes at the rate that prevailed in 1979 (2.6 percent), it would have collected $1 trillion in additional revenues. Had the govern-

TABLE 15.3 Associations in Levels of Corporate Taxation,
Economic Growth, and Inflation, 1960–1999

	Average Level of Taxation as Percentage of GDP	Growth in GDP	Inflation Rate
1960–1969	3.81%	52.8%	28.2%
1970–1979	2.71%	38.4%	103.5%
1980–1989	1.70%	34.7%	64.4%
1990–1999	2.01%	36.6%	33.5%

Note. With respect to economic growth and inflation, the percentage change is measured from the last quarter of one decade to the last quarter of the next decade.

Source. Data on taxation as a percentage of GDP come from the Office of Management and Budget, *Budget of the U.S. Government, FY 2000, Historical Tables* (Washington, D.C.: Government Printing Office, 1999), table 1.2. Data on GDP and inflation come from Louis Uchitelle, "107 Months, and Counting: Expansion Redefines Economy's Limits," *New York Times*, January 30, 2000, sec. 3, pp. 1, 16.

ment recirculated these resources into the economy through increased spending or lower tax levies for people in the two lowest economic quintiles, it would have stimulated the economy and redressed inequality. (I use the low option, which would have provided $1 trillion in additional resources.)

Whereas the government has undertaxed corporations in general, it has also undertaxed (at least) four specific corporate goods or activities that harm the public interest, thus providing a kind of hidden subsidy to corporations that sell these products (see the fourth item under "Excessive Corporate Welfare" in table 15.2). Unlike other industrialized nations, the United States has undertaxed coal, oil, and natural gas, thus speeding their depletion and increasing the amount of pollution. Had the United States chosen any of three alternative taxes on these fuels in 1997, for example, it could have obtained $100 billion over five years.[45] Nor has the United States taxed petroleum products by the barrel or by the gallon as heavily as other nations, thus discouraging the production and sale of fuel-efficient automobiles and alternative forms of transportation. Even relatively modest levies in 1997 would have yielded revenues exceeding $80 billion over five years.[46] Nor has the federal government taxed cigarettes and liquor sufficiently: a combination of new federal taxes on these products in 1997 would have yielded $50 billion over five years.[47] Further, the United States focused on the use of regulations to clean the nation's air and water and failed to tax sufficiently various air pollutants expelled by industrial plants; had it enacted a package of such taxes in 1997, it would have given U.S. corporations an incentive to install antipollution equipment and obtained revenues of $290 billion over five years.[48]

If we combine the revenues that the federal government would have obtained in five years from these various taxes on goods or activities that harm the public interest, the United States would have collected $529 billion more from 1998 through 2002 alone. Had it imposed taxes like these, even at far lower amounts, the United States could easily have raised $1.5 trillion from World War II through 2004.

A final kind of corporate welfare deserves mention: excessive deregulation that leads to unnecessary government spending. Examples include the savings and loan debacle, environmental regulation, the telecommunications industry, and the tobacco industry. The Reagan administration should have liquidated failing S&Ls unlikely to become solvent and placed the remaining institutions under a regulatory regime that would have guided them into a competitive environment. By taking a hands-off approach, the Reagan White House invited the disaster that in the late 1980s and early 1990s cost the nation somewhere between $60 billion and $300 billion, depending on how calculations are made. (I use a middle figure of $180 billion.)[49]

With data showing even in the 1950s that tobacco products caused lethal health problems, the federal government ought to have placed them under the kind of regulatory regime that commenced only in the 1990s. Decades later and after spending billions in public money on tobacco-related illnesses under the Medicaid and Medicare programs, the federal government hoped to recoup losses that could partially have been averted. (I make no estimate because the federal government may recoup some of these losses from settlements between the tobacco industry and the states.)

When Congress gave certain airwaves to media companies in the budget reconciliation legislation of 1997 over the objections of Republican senators Bob Dole and John McCain, it gave away frequencies owned by the public. Had it sold these frequencies, the federal government would have realized roughly $70 billion.

The deregulatory environment of the 1940s, 1950s, and 1960s spawned environmental degradation by failing to regulate the emission of toxic wastes and air pollution. Nowhere was this more obvious than in the nation's facilities for producing nuclear weapons, such as Hanford and the

Savannah River Site. The cavalier attitude of military authorities fostered radioactive contamination, for example, by allowing nuclear wastes to be stored in leaky containers. As a result, 750,000 gallons of highly radioactive wastes seeped into the ground at Hanford alone during its first thirty years of operation. It will cost tens of billions of dollars just to remedy the disposal tanks at the Hanford Atomic Works in a project to continue until 2032—and the overall cost of cleanup will run $196 billion to $373 billion, with some experts predicting far higher costs.[50] Benign neglect also existed in the civilian sector, which saw widespread contamination of ground, soil, and air at urban as well as rural industrial sites. If we conservatively assume that civilian industrial pollution was three times that caused by the military, if we estimate military pollution as costing $250 billion, and if we assume that an earlier response would have averted half these costs, the nation would have saved more than $500 billion. If we combine the savings from earlier environmental regulation, a different approach to the savings and loan scandal, and selling rather than giving away frequencies to the mass media, the Unites States would have saved $750 billion by avoiding excessive deregulation alone.

Thus the nation sacrificed at least $4.44 trillion by providing excessive corporate concessions or deductions, providing excessive subsidies, not taxing corporate income sufficiently, not sufficiently taxing corporate products or activities that harm the public interest, or not sufficiently regulating corporations (see table 15.2). In my reckoning, waste from corporate welfare was exceeded only by excessive military spending. This estimate does not include the huge resources lost over decades because the Internal Revenue Service failed to monitor corporate tax returns sufficiently.[51] And some experts estimate that by using illegal corporate tax shelters, corporations annually evaded as much as $80 billion in taxes in the late 1990s.[52]

EXCESSIVE TAX CONCESSIONS TO AFFLUENT INDIVIDUALS

The extraordinary growth in tax loopholes from 1975 to 2004 took place not in corporate rates but in those for individuals. Although total corporate tax expenditures grew from $33 billion to $63 billion in this period (or nearly double), total tax expenditures for individuals grew from $163 billion to $569 billion (or more than triple).[53] All told, loopholes for individuals cost the federal government $10.9 trillion in lost tax revenues from

1975 through 2004—and these tax expenditures will amount to more than half the revenues from individuals' income taxes that the treasury will collect in 2004.

In general, loopholes for individuals provide a disproportionate amount of tax relief for people in the middle and higher tax brackets.[54] The value of deductions increases as one's income grows: someone whose top marginal tax rate is 39 percent, for example, gains $3,900 from a $10,000 deduction, while someone whose top marginal tax rate is 15 percent only gains $1,500 from the same deduction. (People too poor to pay any federal income taxes receive no benefit from tax expenditures.) Yet many individuals' tax expenditures are strongly or mildly redistributive such as the earned income tax credit, which helps people near or below the poverty line.

The range of loopholes for individuals is remarkable.[55]

Some, like the EITC, supplement the income of poor people. Some mean that government benefits are immune to taxation. Some help people with large medical expenses by allowing them some deduction. Others allow taxpayers to avoid double taxation by allowing them to deduct state and local taxes. Others provide special tax concessions to farmers and veterans. Others are surrogates for social programs, such as tax deductions and credits for child care, higher education, and adoption. Others encourage people to save for their retirement, by excluding from taxation contributions to pensions and the earnings of individual retirement accounts and Keogh plans. Others encourage corporations to provide pensions, insurance, and health-care benefits to employees by allowing them to deduct a portion of their share of these costs. Some encourage home ownership by allowing the deduction of mortgage interest. Some facilitate intergenerational transfers of wealth such as by exempting heirs from capital gains taxes on inherited assets. Some encourage charitable contributions by allowing deductions for them. Some assist retirees by allowing them to exempt all or a portion of their Social Security benefits from taxation. Some promote investment, such as the capital gains tax and the exclusion of interest on public purpose bonds, whereas others encourage taxpayers to purchase insurance, by exempting investment income earned by the policy.

A strong case can be made that some tax expenditures should be modified to diminish the extent to which they disproportionately assist the affluent. Take the deduction for the interest on home mortgages, which has grown markedly since 1968—from $7 billion to $53 billion projected for 2004, at a cost to the federal government of $1.2 trillion in revenues.[56] Middle- and upper-income taxpayers make the most use of this deduction. In 1988, for example, virtually no mortgage interest deductions ($658 million) were claimed by taxpayers who earned less than $20,000, whereas $9.8 billion went to people who earned more than $75,000—or roughly one third of all mortgage interest deductions, which totaled $27.7 billion.[57] The federal government could have used several methods to make distribution of these deductions more equitable.[58] It could have placed a ceiling of, say, $300,000, on the size of the mortgage eligible for interest rate deduction. It could have placed a ceiling on deductions, such as $12,000 per return (single) or $20,000 (double). It could have limited deductions on second homes to $100,000 mortgages. Had it taken such measures, it might have saved as much as a fourth of the $1.2 trillion in lost revenues from 1968 through 2000 (or $300 billion), while diminishing disproportionate use of the mortgage-interest deduction by affluent individuals.

The government could have applied similar remedies to some other tax expenditures that are severely inequitable in their effects, because they are rarely used by people earning less than $20,000 but heavily used by those earning more than $100,000. If the investment income from life insurance policies and annuities had been taxed, the federal government would have gained $98 billion from 1998 through 2002.[59] It would have gained $63.2 billion by imposing a 5 percent tax on the investment income from pension plans and individual retirement accounts; $56.2 billion by taxing capital gains in the last income-tax return of people who have died; and $25 billion by charging a 30 percent capital gains tax on the sale of houses.[60] Enacting these four policy initiatives would have brought $242 billion into federal coffers from 1998 to 2002, not counting any reductions in the home mortgage-interest deduction.

Even with relatively modest cuts in a range of tax deductions used by affluent Americans (including smaller cuts in the aforementioned loopholes) as well tying the mortgage-interest deduction tighter by $300 billion, the federal government could have realized $1.5 trillion from 1967 through 2004.

EXCESSIVE PORK-BARREL SPENDING

Considerable resources have been wasted through pork-barrel spending. Virtually any major piece of legislation contains provisions that fit the definition of pork, as the discussion of the 1998 transportation legislation in

382   On the Magnitude of Failed National Priorities

chapter 14 suggests. It is virtually impossible, however, to estimate the amount of pork-barrel spending, partly because it is irregular and secretive. Moreover, we lack data to determine whether pork-barrel spending is ineffective; indeed, some projects or contracts may be meritorious even if they are enacted as a result of pressure from special interests.

Yet pork-barrel spending does exist and constricts the resources available for meritorious programs. Perhaps the most complete discussion of pork-barrel spending from a conservative viewpoint is provided by David Stockman, Reagan's budget director, who wanted to cut the $29.4 billion appropriated for eleven programs to $17.4 billion in 1986.[61] (He proposed to cut non-nuclear energy subsidies, Amtrak subsidies, the postal subsidy, the entire budget of the Small Business Administration, assorted water projects, assorted highway programs, assorted mass transit subsidies, and assorted airport subsidies, while eliminating Urban Development Action Grants, the Economic Development Administration, and assorted loans and grants to stimulate economic growth in Appalachia.) Of course, many people would disagree with some of Stockman's items, and his definition of pork is more expansive than others.' If we halve the difference between Stockman's goal for 1986 of $17.4 billion and the actual spending on these projects in 1986 of $29.4 billion (or $7.45 billion in constant 1992 dollars), and if we assume that the nation spent similar sums on pork over a fifty-year period, a conservative estimate of pork-barrel spending is $373 billion.

Some readers may believe that an estimate of nearly $16 trillion in total waste from military spending, excess interest payments on the national debt, undertaxation of private wealth, excessive corporate welfare, excessive tax concessions to affluent individuals, and excessive pork-barrel spending from 1931 through 2004 is excessive. It is, in fact, a conservative estimate because it rests on low estimates of many errors. A significantly higher estimate would have resulted if I had chosen to use the higher estimates of military waste discussed in regard to procurement, strategic forces, and general forces. (Because data on tax losses derived from corporate and individual loopholes do not even exist for periods before the 1960s, I chose not to make estimates for the 1930s, 1940s, and 1950s.) The estimate of $16 trillion does not even consider losses to the treasury stemming from illegal corporate tax shelters or the inattention of the Internal Revenue Service that did not catch corporations illegally avoiding taxes. The estimate also is stated in 1992 dollars. Restated in terms of the dollar's value in the fiscal year 2000, it would roughly equal $18.46 trillion.

Mistaking Pennies for Dollars

Remarkably, many of the kinds of waste and tax mistakes that I have discussed in this book have not been discussed or debated in presidential campaigns or in budget deliberations by Congress. Military waste has been periodically or superficially discussed, such as after World War II, during and after the Vietnam War, following procurement scandals in the Reagan administration, and during a brief period in the Bush administration when a peace dividend seemed possible. Imbued with a strong antitax tradition, neither Democrats nor Republicans discussed at length tax revenue shortfalls in the New Deal or the Truman, Eisenhower, Kennedy, and Johnson presidencies. (Indeed, the political merits and relative size of tax *cuts* often assumed center stage.) Save primarily for Sen. John McCain's pledge to cut $150 billion in corporate welfare during the Republican presidential primaries in 2000, corporate welfare has rarely been discussed during campaigns or in congressional budget battles, despite a brief flurry of interest during Bill Clinton's second term. Nor has much discussion been given to modifying tax expenditures that disproportionately assist the affluent. This relative silence about failed national priorities is remarkable in light of the dearth of resources for many domestic programs.

Various factors have contributed to the relative silence about national priorities. Chapters 4 through 14 discussed the pressures placed on politicians and presidents to sustain and prime the network of military contractors and bases even when the appropriations were not related to national security. Because foreign threats are difficult to gauge, military technology is complex and fast changing, and much information is classified, most citizens and legislators tend to accept Pentagon and presidential estimates of the forces needed—at most questioning the need for specific weapons systems rather than seeking a far-reaching analysis of U.S. forces in a global context. Many taxpayers and legislators believe too that it is better to spend too much than too little on military security, even though I have demonstrated that since 1950 military spending has devastated domestic discretionary spending.

The history of peace dividends at the end of World War II, the Korean War, the Vietnam War, and the cold war illustrates the difficulties in sparking public debate about military spending. Sensitized to foreign dangers by these wars, Americans have been on the lookout for new threats, which enterprising politicians easily magnify to appeal to public malaise. I argued in chapters 5, 6, 7, 9, and 12 that presidents Truman and Bush, congressional Democrats in the 1950s, and high-level officials like Paul Nitze in the 1970s magnified the Soviet threat (or international threats before, during, and after the cold war) as a device for maintaining or markedly increasing military spending instead of developing peace dividends after World War II, the Vietnam War, and the cold war to increase domestic spending. The susceptibility of many Americans to the magnification of actual threats may be because Americans often believe they have not really won a specific war in a lasting sense. In the cases of the Korean and Vietnam wars, Americans disliked inconclusive endings or endings that left things merely in a stalemate. (Indeed, many Americans believed the United States lost the Vietnam War, thus making them eager to reassert national power.) In the case of the cold war, many Americans, used to a state of perpetual war readiness, seemed disinclined both to believe that they had prevailed over the Soviet Union and that no comparable threat existed. (In an almost desperate attempt to find new and equivalent threats, politicians and the military-industrial complex stumped for China, "regional conflicts," international terrorism, or drug cartels in the 1990s.) To the extent military forces were cut after World War II and the Vietnam War, deep tax cuts that eroded postwar resources either eliminated a peace dividend (post–Word War II) or diminished the size of a peace dividend (in the case of Vietnam). Huge budget deficits left by Reagan made for a meager a peace dividend after the cold war.

People who have contended (or do contend) that cuts in military spending will not jeopardize national security have been stigmatized and scapegoated since (at least) the start of the cold war. With extreme isolationism properly discredited by the appeasement of Hitler and the American lack of preparedness in the late 1930s, defenders of existing military budgets since have wrongly labeled critics of any military cuts as "isolationists" or as naive idealists—or, worse yet, as communistic or unpatriotic.

Failure to criticize the accumulation of excessive national debt in World War II and in the aftermath of Reagan's fiscal and tax policies in 1981 was linked to the American antitax tradition, as well as the political dexterity and budget manipulation of Reagan and his aides as the nation was emerging from the double-digit inflation and high unemployment of the mid- and late 1970s. This antitax tradition must be implicated as well for excessively low taxes during the New Deal, Truman, Eisenhower, Kennedy, and Johnson administrations when the nation could not address domestic needs because the treasury held scant funds; most of their budgets were preempted by military expenditures, interest payments on the debt, or various other nondomestic expenditures like the Marshall Plan. Perhaps unfortunately, a nation with an antitax tradition is more likely to heed economists who support tax cuts to stimulate economic growth (and who downplay the likelihood of major deficits) than those who favor increased government spending to stimulate the economy. Indeed, the recommendations of so-called New Economists in the Kennedy and Johnson administrations were similar to those of the supply-side economists of the Reagan administration—both groups favored sweeping tax cuts, minimized the danger of deficits, and minimized the need for immediate revenues for the domestic agenda.

The lack of attention to corporate welfare in contemporary U.S. history is particularly noteworthy in light of the sheer amount of waste in this area. Politicians are loath to criticize corporate welfare when they receive significant campaign contributions from these companies. Unlike the trust busting fervor of the progressive era and the New Deal, moreover, criticism of corporations has been relatively muted since World War II, when corporations were credited with winning the war by producing massive amounts of armaments and creating economic growth in succeeding decades. With legislators mostly silent about the extent of corporate welfare, most taxpayers know little about it and do not even realize, for example, that corporate taxes have declined markedly since the 1970s. Meanwhile, individuals' tax rates have remained relatively stable as a percentage of the GDP. The many different kinds of corporate welfare (see table 15.2) make it difficult for the public to see it as a huge raid on the treasury. Some economists also maintain that cuts in some kinds of corporate welfare will have dire economic consequences, even when they have scant evidence to support their argument.

A Challenge to Liberals and Conservatives

Thoughtful analysis of national priorities has been impeded by political pandering and misperceptions of both conservatives and liberals in the United States since the 1930s. Conservatives have frequently lambasted government waste, but they have rarely mounted an effective assault against it. Ronald Reagan was a prime example of the many conservatives who have looked for waste in the wrong places, such as the federal discretionary domestic budget, even though it constitutes a small fraction of the federal budget. (It comprised merely a third of the budget in the mid-1990s.) Or they have equated waste with welfare fraud or inefficiencies in the government, when such waste has constituted a pittance compared to procurement abuses in the military or corporate welfare. Posing as the party of fiscal stringency, Republicans have voted for countless measures that contributed to trillions of dollars in waste.

Because they were intent on accusing Democrats of being soft on communism in the 1950s, Republicans failed to subject the military budget to critical scrutiny, despite the leadership of Dwight Eisenhower in questioning the size of military spending in his valedictory speech. Surely, the isolationism of such party leaders as Sen. Robert Taft, who subjected military budgets of the late 1940s and early 1950s to withering criticism, could have evolved into a cautious internationalism grounded not in extreme isolationism but a realistic assessment of risks confronted by the United States during and after the cold war—and a determination to get involved in conflicts that were (and are) crucial to the nation's interest. Much like Eisenhower himself, Republicans ought to have viewed spending requests from the Pentagon with considerable skepticism, realizing they often rested on an insatiable appetite for funds. And in the 1980s, Republican members of Congress were so intent on supporting their Republican president that they failed to sufficiently criticize Reagan's military buildup.

Republicans, whose party has received a disproportionate share of corporate campaign contributions, have rarely criticized corporate welfare in its many forms. Reagan orchestrated, for example, the huge cuts in corporate income taxes of the 1980s that cost taxpayers roughly $1 trillion by 2004. Republicans supported myriad corporate tax concessions—and led the movement toward undertaxation of tobacco and deregulation that fostered additional waste in pollution, bankruptcies of savings and loan associations, and a giveaway of airwaves to mass media companies in 1997.

When resources can be saved by cutting ill-advised government spending, corporate welfare, and tax loopholes, Republicans are unlikely to channel the money to the people in American society who need it most: those in the lowest two economic quintiles. As Republicans have shown on numerous occasions since the 1930s, they more often favor tax cuts that disproportionately favor affluent Americans. Moreover, they have often opposed humane increases in domestic spending for job training, child care, public health, education, and housing programs and subsidies that people in the lower economic strata desperately need and cannot self-finance.

Nor have liberals acted prudently. After they were blamed for losing China to the communists in the late 1940s, and for causing the Korean War by withdrawing from the Korean peninsula in the early 1950s, they became intent on shedding an image of being soft on communism. Thus they regularly accused Eisenhower of depriving the military of resources in the 1950s, and failed to challenge Lyndon Johnson's ill-advised venture in Vietnam and Reagan's huge military buildup until it was too late. Bill Clinton blinked on military spending, deciding in 1992 to maintain military spending at levels that, when measured in constant dollars, approximated military spending at the height of the cold war in 1980. Although Clinton made some progress in developing multilateral interventions in such places as Bosnia and Kosovo, he failed to articulate a clear policy spelling out when the United States should intervene abroad and how it should coordinate its foreign policy with the United Nations and other nations. He failed, moreover, to state that the country did not need a military of cold war proportions in order to manage regional conflicts.

Although Democrats have sometimes attacked corporate waste, they have offered inconsistent leadership in closing corporate tax loopholes, raising corporate income tax rates, or levying heavier taxes on products that harm the public interest. Democrats too benefit from the largesse of corporate campaign contributions, and they have been reluctant to attack many forms of corporate waste in a concerted way. Clinton gave lip service to cutting corporate waste but failed to invest substantial political capital to do so.

Remarkably, Democrats often fail to link their stated interest in social justice with government waste. When they advocate excessive military spending, for example, they divert resources from programs that assist low- and moderate-income people. When they fail to redress corporate welfare, they limit the funding of myriad programs that they support in their campaign rhetoric. Indeed, liberals have often had to battle ferociously for crumbs in the federal budget process, partly because they have contributed to fiscal scarcity by not attacking budgetary and tax waste in the first instance. Liberals should develop annual programs that target specific kinds of government waste and that identify an array of projects and tax cuts that can channel these otherwise wasted resources to people of meager and moderate means.

Both liberals and conservatives need to rethink their priorities if the United States is to have more sensible national priorities. Conservatives need to move beyond rhetorical attacks on government waste to actual attacks on military, corporate, and other kinds of waste. The great failing of conservatives, however, is that they are likely to want to redirect wasted resources into tax cuts that disproportionately favor the affluent—a propensity they have displayed on countless occasions since the 1930s. Perhaps some of them should re-read the words of such founders of the Republic as Thomas Jefferson. Jefferson, an avid advocate of limited government, feared a division of the nation into haves and have-nots as opposed to a nation of yeoman farmers of similar social status. (He favored distribution of similarly sized plots of land to Americans to foster equality.) When Republicans insist upon diverting new or surplus resources to the affluent, they further exacerbate the tragic inequality that bedevils the United States and that leads some people to fear that the country resembles banana republics. Democrats need to move beyond advocating social justice rhetorically and inaugurate a campaign to find resources to fund social investments or tax cuts for taxpayers in the lower economic strata.[62]

The battle for campaign finance reform is intimately related to the battle for revised national priorities. The unwillingness of both parties to redress federal waste has been exacerbated by the ability of monied interests to subsidize campaigns extravagantly through various loopholes in campaign finance laws. Military contractors, multinational corporations, and affluent individuals have powerfully shaped public policy by purchasing the policy assistance of myriad legislators and presidents.

Recycling Aluminum Cans—And Trillions of Dollars

Wasted resources diminish attempts to build a just society by taking resources from the people who most need them and placing these assets in the hands of military contractors, the affluent, special interests, and corporations. If the past is a prologue to the future, massive waste of public resources is likely to continue beyond the millennium unless citizens appreciate its magnitude, breadth, and tenacity.

The debate about national priorities need not be monopolized by any particular party or ideology. Surely, liberals and conservatives can sometimes agree on the need to cut specific kinds of waste, even if they disagree about how to spend the resources recovered. Ferreting out waste in government programs has long been a part of conservatives' credo, even if they have targeted relatively small sources of waste such as social programs or government bureaucracy. Waste also runs counter to liberals' desire to construct a just society, because it preempts the funding of meritorious programs. Indeed, liberals can shed traditional images of themselves as tax-and-spend do-gooders if they link their quest for social justice with efforts to recycle wasted resources into humanitarian programs and tax cuts for the poorest of Americans.

Wasted budgetary resources are not unlike wasted environmental resources. As surely as municipalities collect aluminum cans and bottles for recycling to constructive uses, advocacy groups should collect each year an estimation of what wasted resources federal authorities could recycle in the form of tax cuts or social programs that benefit low- and moderate-income people. (Such estimates should not be confined merely to a single kind of waste but the many kinds of waste discussed here.) The federal budget procedures established in 1974 offer a wonderful opportunity. Each spring Congress must enact a budget resolution that states its overall spending and tax objectives for the coming fiscal year. Every winter advocacy groups should pressure legislators to earmark specific resources for recycling into constructive uses in the budget resolution, whether those wasted resources constitute corporate welfare, excessive military spending, or tax loopholes for affluent Americans. The organizations also should provide Congress with a menu of programs and tax cuts for low- and moderate-income people that these wasted resources could fund. Advocacy organizations should keep the heat on Congress after budget resolutions are enacted, to ensure that legislators actually accomplish recycling in the authorization, appropriation, and reconciliation bills enacted each summer and fall.

Advocacy groups should hold legislators accountable for their votes on recycling. They should publish lists of legislators who have excellent, fair, and poor voting records on budget recycling proposals. They should support those candidates who seek to recycle military, corporate, and other kinds of waste and oppose those who perpetuate the status quo. Instead of allowing voters to focus on national priorities only occasionally, such as in the aftermath of wars, advocates should develop annual recycling campaigns that match the persistence of the special interests that have captured trillions of dollars of wasted resources over the years through persistent and sophisticated political strategy.

The stakes are high: the pattern of waste institutionalized since the 1930s has harmed millions of people by depriving them of child care, education, housing, adequate public transportation, clean environments, and other basic amenities—deprivations that are likely to continue if the government continues to waste resources at an equivalent pace. Hard-hitting and persistent tactics by advocates may cause legislators to recycle sufficient waste that another author, seven decades hence, will not conclude that the United States has thrown additional trillions of dollars to the winds.

NOTES

1. FAILED NATIONAL PRIORITIES FROM FDR TO CLINTON

1. For further discussion of tax expenditures, see chap. 15.

2. Robert Dallek, *Flawed Giant: Lyndon Johnson and His Times* (New York: Oxford University Press, 1998), and Stephen Ambrose, *Nixon: The Triumph of a Politician, 1962–1972* (New York: Simon and Schuster, 1989).

3. See chart 1-2 in Office of Management and Budget, *U.S. Budget, FY 2000: A Citizens' Guide to the Federal Budget* (Washington, D.C.: Government Printing Office, 1999), 3.

4. Liberals who were exceptions include Sen. Paul Douglas, D-Ill., and William Proxmire, D-Wis.

5. Robert Sherwood, *Roosevelt and Hopkins: An Intimate History* (New York: Harper, 1948), 102–3.

6. Estimates of the cost of funding the clinics are based on data in Karen Davis and Cathy Schoen, *Health and the War on Poverty* (Washington, D.C.: Brookings Institution, 1978).

7. Data for education, training, social services, and employment are taken from table 3.1 (1940 through 1994) of Office of Management and Budget, *Budget of the U.S. Government, FY 2000, Historical Tables* (Washington, D.C.: U.S. Government Printing Office, 1999), 36–49.

8. William Kaufmann, *Assessing the Base Force: How Much Is Too Much?* (Washington, D.C.: Brookings Institution, 1992.)

2. ROOSEVELT AS MAGICIAN

1. William Bremer, *Depression Winters: New York Social Workers and the New Deal* (Philadelphia: Temple University Press, 1984), 88–100.

2. John Morton Blum, *From the Morgenthau Diaries* (Boston: Houghton Mifflin, 1959), 229.

3. Mark Leff, *The Limits of Symbolic Reform: The New Deal and Taxation, 1933–1939* (Cambridge: Cambridge University Press, 1984), 13, 71–73.

4. David Beito, *Taxpayers in Revolt* (Chapel Hill: University of North Carolina Press, 1989).

5. Leff, *Limits of Symbolic Reform*, 4.

6. Office of Management and Budget, *Budget of the U.S. Government, FY 2000, Historical Tables* (Washington, D.C.: U.S. Government Printing Office, 1999), 31.

7. Editorial, *New York Times*, February 19, 1933, pt. 4, p. 4.

8. Arthur Krock, "Plan Bold Moves for Federal Cuts: Details of Parlay Told," *New York Times*, January 7, 1933, p. 1.

9. James Hagerty, "Roosevelt Outlines Plan for Drastic Unifications Under Two New Bureaus," *New York Times*, January 27, 1933, p. 1.

10. "New Economy Plan Set as Compromise; 'Dictator' Opposed," *New York Times*, February 11, 1933, p. 1.

11. "Cabinet Protests a Flat Cut of 5% in Bureau Costs," *New York Times*, February 12, 1933, p. 1.

12. "House Passes Economy Bill, 266 to 138," *New York Times*, March 12, 1933, p. 1.

13. "Roosevelt Starts $500,000,000 Cuts," *New York Times*, March 21, 1933, p. 3.

14. See Arthur Krock, "President Speeds $900,000,000 Cuts in His First Month," *New York Times* March 29, 1933, p. 1; "Bureaus Wiped Out, 'Deadwood' Cut Off by Roosevelt Axe," *New York Times*, April 7, 1933, p. 1.

15. "Roosevelt Will Restudy Veterans' Cuts With a View to Making Some Less Severe," *New York Times*, May 11, 1933, p. 1.

16. "Roosevelt Urged to Veto Senate Veteran Increases to Save Economy Program," *New York Times*, June 4, 1933, p. 1.

17. "Economies Rushed; New Army Savings Put at $49,000,000," *New York Times*, June 18, 1933, p. 1.

18. Franklin D. Roosevelt, *The Public Papers and Addresses of Franklin Delano Roosevelt, 1933*, comp. Samuel Rosenman (New York: Random House, 1938–[ca. 1950]), 80–84.

19. Ibid., 120–21.

20. Ibid., 202–3.

21. Ibid., 239.

22. Ibid., 49–54, 219–20, 222–25.

23. "Curtain Call for Congress," editorial, *New Republic,* December 27, 1933, p. 181.

24. Henry Adams, *Harry Hopkins: A Biography* (New York: Putnam, 1977), 57–58, 82–88.

25. *New York Times,* January 5, 1934, p. 1.

26. See John Salmond, *A Southern Rebel: The Life and Times of Aubrey Willis Williams* (Chapel Hill: University of North Carolina Press, 1983), 45–59.

27. Robert Higgs, *Crisis and Leviathan: Critical Episodes in the Growth of American Government* (New York: Oxford University Press, 1987), 23.

28. *New York Times,* January 6, 1934, p. 8.

29. Salmond, *Southern Rebel,* 57–63.

30. For discussion of "self-liquidating projects," see *New York Times,* June 25, 1933, pt. 2, p. 1.

31. For an excellent discussion of lump-sum financing, see the *New York Times,* June 3, 1934, p. 1.

32. We can trace Roosevelt's vacillations on the CWA cuts in successive articles in the *New York Times:* see December 14, 1933, p. 7; January 23, 1934, p. 1; and January 28, 1934, p. 1.

33. Leff, *Limits of Symbolic Reform,* 27, 50, 232–34.

34. Office of Management and Budget, *Budget of the U.S. Government, FY 2000, Historical Tables,* 21.

35. Leff, *Limits of Symbolic Reform,* 93–94.

36. Ibid., 96.

37. Ibid.

38. Ibid., 106.

39. Ibid., 112–13.

40. Ibid., 104–5.

41. Harold Groves, "Low American Taxes," *New Republic,* January 24, 1934, pp. 298–99.

42. Alan Brinkley, *Voices of Protest: Huey Long, Father Coughlin, and the Great Depression* (New York: Random House, 1982), 8–81.

43. Leff, *Limits of Symbolic Reform,* 287–93.

44. Robert Sherwood, *Roosevelt and Hopkins: An Intimate History* (New York: Harper and Row, 1948), 61ff. For examples of Republicans' attacks, see the *New York Times,* June 25, 1933, p. 1, and December 18, 1933, p. 1.

45. For example, see the *New York Times,* January 13, 1935, p. 1.

46. See James Patterson, *Congressional Conservatism and the New Deal* (Lexington: University of Kentucky Press, 1967).

47. Ibid.

48. Richard Lowitt and Maurine Beasley, eds., *One Third of a Nation* (Urbana: University of Illinois Press, 1981).

49. "Income Tax Cut for 99 Percent Since '32, Roosevelt Says," *New York Times*, October 22, 1936, p. 14; and "No Tax Increase Will Be Sought in 1937 Congress," *New York Times*, August 14, 1936, p. 1.

3. ROOSEVELT'S DILEMMA

1. Frank Freidel, *Franklin D. Roosevelt: A Rendezvous with Destiny* (Boston: Little, Brown, 1990), 402.

2. Robert Dallek, *Franklin D. Roosevelt and American Foreign Policy, 1932–1945* (New York: Oxford University Press, 1979), 7.

3. Ibid., 9–10.

4. Robert Herzstein, *Roosevelt and Hitler: Prelude to War* (New York: Paragon, 1989), 46.

5. Ibid., 19–20.

6. Ibid., 78–79.

7. Frances Perkins, *The Roosevelt I Knew* (New York: Viking, 1946), 349.

8. See, for example, the dispatch from William Dodd, ambassador to Germany, to Roosevelt of October 19, 1936, in Edgar Nixon, ed., *Franklin D. Roosevelt and Foreign Affairs*, vol. 3 (Cambridge, Mass.: Harvard University Press, 1969), 455–58.

9. *New York Times*, May 30, 1933, p. 1.

10. Franklin Roosevelt, *The Public Papers and Addresses of Franklin D. Roosevelt, 1933*, comp. Samuel Rosenman (New York: Random House, 1938–[ca. 1950]), June 16, 1933, pp. 249–51.

11. *New York Times*, June 5, 1934, p. 17.

12. Robert Sherwood, *Roosevelt and Hopkins: An Intimate History* (New York: Harper and Row, 1948), 66.

13. Ibid., 67.

14. Wayne Cole, *Roosevelt and the Isolationists, 1932–1945* (Lincoln: University of Nebraska Press, 1983), 163–186.

15. Roosevelt, *Public Papers, 1936*, 9.

16. Ibid., 236.

17. Ibid., vol. 7, pp. 66ff.

18. *New York Times*, December 5, 1937, p. 1.

19. Sherwood, *Roosevelt and Hopkins*, 75.

20. Roosevelt, *Public Papers, 1938,* 221ff.

21. Ibid., 252.

22. B. Mitchell Simpson, *Admiral Harold R. Stark: Architect of Victory* (Columbia: University of South Carolina Press, 1989), 13.

23. Ibid.

24. Eric Larrabee, *Commander in Chief* (New York: Norton, 1971), 14.

25. Ed Cray, *General of the Army: George C. Marshall* (New York: Norton, 1990), 126–40.

26. Ibid., 135.

27. Herzstein, *Roosevelt and Hitler*, 412.

28. Ibid.

29. Sherwood, *Roosevelt and Hopkins*, 101.

30. Mitchell, *Admiral Harold Stark*, 20.

31. Roosevelt, *Public Papers, 1939*, 3.

32. John Jeffries, "The 'New' New Deal: FDR and American Liberalism, 1937–1945," *Political Science Quarterly* 105 (winter 1990–1991): 387–418.

33. John Morton Blum, *Roosevelt and Morgenthau* (Boston: Houghton Mifflin, 1970), 1.

34. Harold Smith, "Daily Memoranda," June 13, 1939, Harold Smith Papers, Franklin D. Roosevelt Library, Hyde Park, New York.

35. Ibid., May 12, 1939.

36. Blum, *Roosevelt and Morgenthau*, 265.

37. Harold Smith, "Daily Memoranda," May 12, 1939, Smith Papers.

38. Richard Chapman, "Contours of Public Policy, 1939–1945." Ph.D. diss., Yale University, 1976, 82–85.

39. Harold Smith, "Memoranda of Conferences with the President," November 30, 1939, Smith Papers.

40. Chapman, "Contours of Public Policy," 85.

41. Ibid., 97.

42. Marriner Eccles, *Beckoning Frontiers: Public and Personal Recollections* (New York: Knopf, 1951), 333–34.

43. Cray, *General of the Army*, 153–55.

44. Ibid.

45. Roosevelt, *Public Papers, 1941*, 144.

46. George Gallup, *The Gallup Poll: Public Opinion, 1935–1948*, vol. 1 (New York: Random House, 1972), March 24, 1941, 270.

47. Larrabee, *Commander in Chief*, 8ff.

48. James Reston, "Put Victory Plan at $120 Billion," *New York Times*, December 5, 1941, p. 1.

49. *New York Times*, January 20, 1941, p. 1.

50. *New York Times*, March 14, 1940, p. 1.

51. Sherwood, *Roosevelt and Hopkins*, 102–4.

52. Samuel Rosenman, *Working with Roosevelt* (New York: Harper, 1952), 699.

53. Roosevelt, *Public Papers, 1940*, 293.

54. Ibid., vol. 10, p. 233.

55. Harold Smith, "Conferences with the President," September 24, 1940, Smith Papers.

56. Harold Smith, "Memorandum of Conference with the President," June 3, 1940, and "Daily Memoranda," June 25, 1940, both in Smith Papers.

57. Sherwood, *Roosevelt and Hopkins*, 280.

58. U.S. Congress, Joint Committee on Reduction of Nonessential Federal Expenditures, *Hearings*, 77th Cong., 1st sess., 1941, pt. 1, pp. 319–20.

4. THE CONSERVATIVES' REVENGE

1. Keith Eiler, ed., *Wedemeyer on War and Peace* (Palo Alto, Calif.: Hoover Institution Press, 1987), 232–33.

2. Ed Cray, *General of the Army: George C. Marshall* (New York: Norton, 1990), 262, 320–36.

3. Ibid.

4. Ibid., 267–300.

5. Franklin D. Roosevelt, *The Public Papers and Addresses of Franklin D. Roosevelt, 1943*, comp. Samuel Rosenman (New York: Random House, 1950), 97.

6. John Salmond, *The Civilian Conservation Corps, 1933–1942* (Durham: Duke University Press, 1967), 200–22.

7. For discussion of the OCD, see Joseph Lash, *Eleanor and Franklin* (New York: Norton, 1973), 731–46.

8. Richard Norman Chapman, "Contours of Public Policy" (Ph.D. diss., Yale University, 1976), 243–44.

9. Ibid., 257.

10. Roosevelt, *Public Papers, 1943*, 31.

11. Ibid., 16–17.

12. *Congressional Record*, 78th Cong., 1st sess., p. 618.

13. Harold Smith, "Memorandum of Conference with the President," March 17, 1943, Harold Smith Papers, Franklin D. Roosevelt Library, Hyde Park, New York.

14. Chapman, "Contours of Public Policy," 365.

15. *New York Times*, May 29, 1944, p. 29.

16. Roosevelt, *Public Papers, 1943*, 41–42.

17. Less than a week after Pearl Harbor, Rep. Robert Doughton, the North Carolina Democrat who chaired the House Appropriations Committee, balked even at raising $4 to $5 billion in new taxes, saying this would be politically infeasible (*New York Times*, December 13, 1941, p. 11).

18. Roosevelt, *Public Papers, 1942*, 6–20.

19. John Morton Blum, *Roosevelt and Morgenthau* (Boston: Houghton Mifflin, 1970), 431–40.

20. William O'Neill, *A Democracy at War: : America's Fight at Home and Abroad in World War II* (New York: Free Press, 1993), 95, and *New Republic,* January 19, 1942, pp. 69–70.

21. For a discussion of Roosevelt's vacillation and excessive timidity on taxation, see Harold Smith, "Conferences with the President," March 4, 1942, Smith Papers.

22. Keith Hutchison, "Wall Street's Tax Program," *Nation*, March 21, 1942, p. 396.

23. John MacCormac, "President Drafts Inflation Clamp on Wide Fronts," *New York Times*, April 14, 1942, p. 1. The British were more willing than the Americans to shoulder a heavy wartime taxes to fund the war; for a discussion of this see Raymond Daniell, "British Budget Raises Taxes Versus Luxuries, Tobacco, and Drinks," *New York Times*, April 15, 1942, p. 1.

24. Editorial, "Wages and Inflation," *Nation*, May 9, 1942, p. 532.

25. Thomas Hamilton, "Senators Criticize Withholding Tax as Cut in Bond Sale," *New York Times*, July 25, 1942, p. 1.

26. Henry Dorris, "90 Percent Profits Tax Is Voted by House: Surtax Rate Kept," *New York Times,* July 21, 1942, p. 1.

27. "New Tax Bill off Until Next March," *New York Times*, October 28, 1942, p. 17.

28. John Witte, *The Politics and Development of the Federal Income Tax* (Madison: University of Wisconsin Press, 1985), 120.

29. Roy Blough, *The Federal Taxing Process* (New York: Prentice Hall, 1952), 233.

30. Witte, *Politics and Development*, 120.

31. Ibid., 121.

32. Roosevelt, *Public Papers, 1944–1945,*, 80.

33. *Nation*, April 8, 1944, p. 107.

34. Witte, *Politics and Development*, 122.

35. Mark Leff, *The Limits of Symbolic Reform: The New Deal and Taxation, 1933–1939* (Cambridge: Cambridge University Press, 1984), 287.

36. Ibid., 11.

37. Jack Raymond, *Power at the Pentagon* (New York: Harper and Row, 1964), 51–53.

38. Ibid., 51–52.

39. Donald Nelson, *Arsenal of Democracy: The Story of American War Production* (New York: Harcourt Brace, 1946), 194–211.

40. Gregory Hooks, *Forging the Military-Industrial Complex: World War II's Battle of the Potomac* (Urbana: University of Illinois Press, 1991), 148.

41. *New York Times*, February 28, 1946, p. 17.

42. Robert Ferrell, *Harry S. Truman: A Life* (Columbia: University of Missouri, 1994), 156.

43. Ed Cray, *General of the Army: George C. Marshall* (New York: Norton, 1990), 186.

44. O'Neill, *Democracy at War*, 395–96, and Cray, *General of the Army*, 186–87, 536.

45. Frank Kofsky, *Harry S. Truman and the War Scare of 1948: A Successful Campaign to Deceive the Nation* (New York: St. Martin's, 1993), 13.

46. Cray, *General of the Army*, 536.

47. Hooks, *Forging the Military-Industrial Complex*, 145–48.

48. Arthur Hadley, *The Straw Hat: Triumph and Failure, America's Armed Forces* (New York: Random House, 1986), 29–73, and C. Kenneth Allard, *Command, Control, and the Common Defense* (New Haven: Yale University Press, 1990), 88–98.

49. Cray, *General of the Army*, 404.

50. Ibid., 192.

51. Ibid., 438–50.

52. Davis Ross, *Preparing for Ulysses: Politics and Veterans During World War II* (New York: Columbia University Press, 1969), 9–11, 283–86.

53. Ibid., 107–17.

54. Ibid., 89–124.

55. See data in figures 4.1 and 5.1 for domestic spending at the end of the war and in the postwar period, 64, 87.

56. Robert Caro, *The Path to Power*, vol. 1 of *The Years of Lyndon Johnson* (New York: Knopf, 1982), 458, 468, 473–74, 577, 627–28, and Robert Caro, *Means of Ascent*, vol. 2 of *The Years of Lyndon Johnson* (New York: Knopf, 1990), 232–33, 273–75, 268–69, 278–90.

5. TRUMAN'S NIGHTMARE

1. Truman's fixed shares approach can be seen in his discussions with Harold Smith of the postwar budgets. See Harold Smith, Diaries, entries of September 13–14 and December 19, 1945, January 4, 1946, Harold Smith Papers, Franklin D. Roosevelt Library, Hyde Park, New York. It is also evident in his many budget messages to Congress.

2. *New York Times*, August 11, 1945, p. 1. For the uncertainties Truman faced, see Charlie Ross, memo to President Truman, January 21, 1946, PSF-SF, Bureau of the Budget/Budget, Miscellaneous 1945–53, Harry S. Truman Library, Independence, Missouri.

3. Craufurd Goodwin and R. Stanley Herren, "The Truman Administration: Problems and Policies Unfold," in Craufurd Goodwin, ed., *Exhortation and Con-*

trols: The Search for a Wage-Price Policy, 1945–1975 (Washington, D.C.: Brookings Institution, 1975), 25; David McCullough, *Truman* (New York: Simon and Schuster, 1992), 167; and Harold Smith, Diary, April 18, 1945, Smith Papers.

4. "Reconversion Tied to Length of War in Vinson Report," *New York Times*, July 1, 1945, p. 1.

5. John Crider, "$18 Billion Tax Cut Predicted in Peace," *New York Times*, July 28, 1945, p. 1.

6. Associated Press, "House Republicans to Fight for a 20 Percent Income Tax Cut," *New York Times*, October 1, 1945, p. 1.

7. "Vinson Says Taxes Must Remain High," *New York Times*, September 4, 1945, p. 1, and "Tax Bill Shaping Begins Tomorrow," *New York Times*, September 30, 1945, p. 48.

8. *New York Times*, October 15, 1945, p. 1.

9. Clark Clifford, oral history interview, vol. 1, p. 67, Truman Library.

10. McCullough, *Truman*, 96.

11. Richard Haynes, *The Awesome Power: Harry S. Truman as Commander in Chief* (Baton Rouge: Louisiana State University Press, 1973), 14–16.

12. Joseph Feeney, oral history interview, Truman Library.

13. Arthur Krock, "The President: A Portrait," *New York Times Magazine*, April 7, 1946, p. 7.

14. McCullough, *Truman*, 234.

15. Ibid., 402.

16. Haynes, *Awesome Power*, 26–33.

17. John Sullivan, Daily Record, May 28, 1946, John Sullivan Papers, Truman Library, and Harold Smith, memo to Truman, May 22, 1946, PSF/SF, Bureau of the Budget, box 150, Truman Library.

18. John Gaddis, *We Now Know: Rethinking Cold War History* (New York: Oxford University Press, 1997), chaps. 1 and 2.

19. Harold Smith, Diary, February 28, 1946, Smith Papers.

20. Robert Manning, *Postwar Tax Plans for the Federal Government: A Description of the Various Possibilities* (Washington, D.C.: Government Printing Office, 1945), and John Coulter, *Postwar Fiscal Problems and Policies* (New York: Committee of the Americans, 1945). Most estimates predicted a modest budget of roughly $18 to $25 billion, as did Republicans like Wendell Willkie and Robert Taft (see *New York Times*, February 3, 1944, p. 3, and March 1, 1944, p. 23).

21. Elias Huzar, *The Purse and the Sword: Control of the Army by Congress Through Military Appropriations, 1933–1950* (New York: Greenwood, 1971), 319–373.

22. *New York Times*, February 28, 1946, p. 17.

23. Michael Sherry, *Preparing for the Next War: America Plans for the Next War* (New Haven: Yale University Press, 1977), 220–29.

24. Cabinet minutes, November 30, 1945, PSF/SF/Cab, box 156, Truman Library.

25. *New York Times*, December 3, 1945, p. 15.

26. Sherry, *Preparing for the Next War*, 220–29.

27. Davis Ross, *Preparing for Ulysses: Politics and Veterans During World War II* (New York: Columbia University Press, 1969), 187.

28. Huzar, *Purse and the Sword*, 319–73.

29. Sullivan, Daily Record, March 12, 1946, Sullivan Papers.

30. Lynn Rachele Eden, "The Diplomacy of Force: Interests, the State, and the Making of American Military Policy in 1948" (Ph.D. diss., University of Michigan, Ann Arbor, 1985).

31. McGeorge Bundy, *Danger and Survival: Choices About the Bomb in the First Years* (New York: Random House, 1988), 3.

32. *New York Times*, August 14, 1947, p. 1.

33. Sullivan, Daily Record, January 24, 1947, Sullivan Papers.

34. Melvyn Leffler, *A Preponderance of Power: National Security, the Truman Administration, and the Cold War* (Palo Alto: Stanford University Press, 1992), 55–99.

35. Edward Kolodziej, *Uncommon Defense and Congress, 1945–1953* (Columbus: Ohio State University Press, 1966), 38, and Haynes, *Awesome Power*, 120.

36. Alonzo Hamby, *Beyond the New Deal: Harry S. Truman and American Liberalism* (New York: Columbia University Press, 1973).

37. Leon Keyserling, "Harry S. Truman: The Man and the President," in William Levantrosser, ed., *Harry S. Truman: The Man from Independence* (New York: Greenwood, 1986), 235–36.

38. Harold Smith, Diary, January 4, 1946, Smith Papers.

39. Paul Douglas, *In the Fullness of Time: The Memoirs of Paul H. Douglas* (New York: Harcourt Brace Jovanovich, 1971), 132–34.

40. McCullough, *Truman*, 234.

41. Ibid., 192.

42. Harry S. Truman, *The Public Papers of the Presidents of the United States: Harry S. Truman, 1948* (Washington, D.C.: U.S. Government Printing Office, 1964), 777–79.

43. Charles Murphy, Richard Neustadt, David Stowe, and James Webb, joint oral history interview.

44. Clifford, oral history interview, vol. 1, p. 67.

45. David U. Shepard, "Reconversion, 1939–1946: Images, Plans, and Realities" (Ph.D. diss., University of Wisconsin–Madison, 1981), 215.

46. Ibid., 216.

47. Cabinet minutes, October 11, 1945, PSF/SF/Cab (State-2), Treas/box 160, October 11, 1945, Truman Library.

48. Harold Smith, Daily Record, November 20, 1945, Smith Papers.

49. *New York Times*, December 5, 1945, p. 1.

50. Mary Hedge Hinchey, "The Frustration of the New Deal Revival: 1944–1946" (Ph.D. diss., University of Missouri, 1965), 156–62.

51. Seymour Harris, "Targets for Tomorrow's Economy," *New Republic*, March 19, 1945, pp. 383–85.

52. Stephen Bailey, *Congress Makes a Law: The Story Behind the Full Employment Act of 1946* (New York: Columbia University Press, 1950), 23–24.

53. Ibid., 59–60.

54. Ibid., 128–49.

55. Ibid., 162–63.

56. Ibid., 164.

57. Ibid., 179–82.

58. Ibid., 227–32.

59. John Gaddis, *Strategies of Containment: A Critical Appraisal of Postwar American National Security Policy* (New York: Oxford University Press, 1982), and Leffler, *Preponderance of Power*, 108.

60. Clark Clifford, "Serving the President: The Truman Years," part 2, *New Yorker*, April 1, 1991, p. 55, and Leffler, *Preponderance of Power*, 109.

61. Clark Clifford, *Counsel to the President* (New York: Random House, 1991), 123–29.

62. Wayne Cole, *Roosevelt and the Isolationists, 1932–1945* (Lincoln: University of Nebraska Press, 1983).

63. George Gallup, *The Gallup Poll: Public Opinion, 1935–1971*, vol. 1 (New York: Random House, 1972), March 31, 1941, p. 567, and June 7, 1946, pp. 581–82.

64. Frederic Mosher and Poland Orwille, *The Costs of American Governments: Facts, Trends, and Myths* (New York: Dodd, Mead, 1964), 103, 117.

65. "Federal Aid and Catholic Schools," *Nation*, May 24, 1947, pp. 618–19.

66. *New York Times*, May 6, 1946, p. 27.

67. Ruth Moore, "Building Tomorrow's Slums," *New Republic*, January 6, 1947, pp. 17–20.

68. Homer Jack, "Chicago Has One More Chance," *Nation*, September 13, 1947, pp. 250–52.

69. Charles Abrams, "A Plan in a Platform," *Nation* (February 15, 1948), p. 548.

70. Moore, "Building Tomorrow's Slums," 18.

71. Ibid., 19.

72. Bernard Posner, "What'll We Use for Dough?" *New Republic*, June 3, 1946, pp. 828–29.

73. "Housing: Challenge and Failure," editorial, *New Republic*, July 7, 1947, pp. 14–15.

74. Henry Wallace, "One Course to Save the Democratic Party," *New Repub-*

lic, July 7, 1947, pp. 14–15, and Leonard Engel, "The Best Buys in Medical Care," *New Republic*, June 30, 1947, pp. 14–17.

75. Engel, "Best Buys in Medical Care," 16.

6. TRUMAN'S BOMBSHELLS

1. *New York Times*, November 10, 1946, p. 5.

2. *New York Times*, December 29, 1946, pt. 4, p. 7.

3. A. E. Holmans, *U.S. Fiscal Policy, 1945–1949* (New York: Oxford University Press, 1961), 56–85.

4. Ibid.; Harry S. Truman, *Public Papers of the Presidents of the United States: Harry S. Truman, 1947* (Washington, D.C.: Government Printing Office, 1964), 55–97.

5. Harold Smith, Diary, April 2, 1946, Harold Smith Papers, Franklin D. Roosevelt Library, Hyde Park, New York.

6. Antispending sentiment is detailed in George Gallup, *The Gallup Poll: Public Opinion, 1935–1948*, vol. 1 (New York: Random House, 1972), March 5, 1947, 632, whereas strong sentiment not to cut military spending appears in Gallup, February 28, 1947, p. 635.

7. *New York Times*, February 4, 1947, p. 1.

8. Ibid.

9. David McCullough, *Truman* (New York: Simon and Schuster, 1992), 541.

10. Arthur Krock, "In the Nation: A Slight Undercurrent of Politics," *New York Times*, March 25, 1947, p. 24.

11. Ibid.

12. For contemporary criticisms of Truman's assertion of communist insurgency, see Henry Wallace, "The Fight for Peace Begins," *New Republic*, March 24, 1947, pp. 12ff. See John Gaddis, *Strategies of Containment: A Critical Appraisal of Postwar American National Security Policy* (New York: Oxford University Press, 1982), for a scholarly critique of Truman's assertions.

13. *New York Times*, March 14, 1947, p. 1.

14. *New York Times*, May 30, 1947, p. 20.

15. McCullough, *Truman*, 562.

16. David Mayers, *George Kennan and the Dilemmas of U.S. Foreign Policy* (New York: Oxford University Press, 1988), 138–41, and Ed Cray, *General of the Army: George C. Marshall* (New York: Norton, 1990), 607–26.

17. Melvyn Leffler, *A Preponderance of Power: National Security, the Truman Administration, and the Cold War* (Palo Alto: Stanford University Press, 1992), 200.

18. McCullough, *Truman*, 564.

19. Truman, *Public Papers, 1948*, p. 21.

20. *New York Times*, June 17, 1947, p. 1.

21. Ibid.

22. Frank Kofsky, *Harry S. Truman and the War Scare of 1948* (New York: St. Martin's, 1993), 160–62, 165–66.

23. Ibid., 145.

24. Ibid., 104–22.

25. John Gaddis, *We Now Know: Rethinking Cold War History* (New York: Oxford University Press, 1997), chap. 2.

26. David Mayers, *George Kennan and the Dilemmas*, 114–19.

27. Ibid., 38–160.

28. Gilbert Smith, *The Limits of Reform: Politics and Federal Aid to Education, 1937–1950* (New York: Garland, 1982), 165–67.

29. Alonzo Hamby, *Beyond the New Deal: Harry S. Truman and American Liberalism* (New York: Columbia University Press, 1973), 209ff; Harvey Sitcoff, "Years of the Locust: Interpretations of the Truman Presidency," in Richard Kirkendall, ed., *The Truman Presidency as a Research Field: A Reappraisal, 1972* (Columbia: University of Missouri Press, 1974).

30. Truman, *Public Papers, 1948*, 35–41.

31. Helen Fuller, "Stalled in the Lobby," *New Republic* March 1, 1948, pp. 11–14.

32. Monte Poen, *Harry S. Truman Versus the Medical Lobby* (Columbia: University of Missouri Press, 1979), 222–30.

33. Russell Weigley, *History of the United States Army* (New York: Macmillan, 1967), 485–95; A. A. Vandegrift, "Vicious In-fighting," in Peter Karsten, ed., *The Military in America* (New York: Free Press, 1980), 363–69; and Clark Clifford, *Counsel to the President* (New York: Random House, 1991), 147–58.

34. Arthur Hadley, *The Straw Hat: Triumph and Failure, America's Armed Forces* (New York: Random House, 1986), 74–99.

35. Weigley, *History of the U.S. Army*, 492.

36. Ibid., 490–95.

37. Hadley, *Straw Hat*, 90–99.

38. David Hackworth, *Hazardous Duty* (New York: Morrow 1996), 315–26.

39. Henry Brandon, *Special Relationships: A Foreign Correspondent's Memoirs from Roosevelt to Reagan* (New York: Atheneum, 1988), 78.

40. Harold Lasswell warns of a garrison state with a bloated budget and loss of freedoms "under the influence of soldiers and police" in "How to Preserve Our Freedom While Rearming," November 10, 1948, Bureau of the Budget: Defense, box 9, James Webb Papers, Truman Library.

41. Leffler, *Preponderance of Power*, 355–56.

42. Ibid., 356.

43. Ibid.

44. Warner Schilling, "The Politics of National Defense: FY 1950," in Warner

Schilling, Paul Hammond, and Glen Snyder, eds., *Strategy, Politics, and Defense Budgets* (New York: Columbia University Press, 1962), 51.

45. Ibid.

46. Michael Hogan, *A Cross of Iron: Harry Truman and the Origins of the National Security State, 1945–1954* (Cambridge: Cambridge University Press, 1998), 266.

47. Paul Hammond, *Organizing for Defense: The American Military Establishment in the Twentieth Century* (Princeton: Princeton University Press, 1961), 251.

48. H. W. Brands, *Cold Warriors: Eisenhower's Generation and American Foreign Policy* (New York: Columbia University Press, 1988), 32.

49. Paul Hammond, "NSC-68: Prologue to Rearmament," in Schilling, Hammond, and Snyder, *Strategy*, 345.

50. Ibid., 340, 344.

51. Truman, *Public Papers, 1950*, 447.

52. McCullough, *Truman*, 775.

53. Truman, *Public Papers, 1950*, 518.

54. Ibid., 626.

55. Hogan, *Iron Cross*, 305.

56. Ibid., 322.

57. Ibid., 187.

58. Edward A. Kolodziej, *Uncommon Defense and Congress, 1945–1953* (Columbus: Ohio State University Press, 1966), 456.

59. Jack Snyder, *Myths of Empire: Domestic Politics and International Ambition* (Ithaca: Cornell University Press, 1991), 261.

60. Kolodziej, *Uncommon Defense and Congress*, 144.

61. Ibid., 147–50.

62. Ibid., 150.

63. David Halberstam, *The Fifties* (New York: Villard, 1993), 82.

64. Barton Bernstein, "The Truman Administration and the Korean War," in Michael Lacey, ed., *The Truman Presidency* (Cambridge: Cambridge University Press, 1989), 427–44. For an estimate of the cost of the war when narrow military and veterans' expenditures are combined, see Robert Stevens, *Vain Hopes, Grim Realities: The Economic Consequences of the Vietnam War* (New York: New Viewpoints, 1976), 83.

65. Paul Douglas, *Economy in the National Government* (Chicago: University of Chicago Press, 1952), 38–39.

66. W. H. Lawrence, "Stevenson Asserts Republicans Rule by 'Postponement,'" *New York Times*, September 15, 1953, p. 1, and Russell Porter, "Humphrey Sees Budget Cut of Five Billion More Next Year," *New York Times*, May 26, 1954, p. 1.

67. Stanley Levey, "Congress Assailed by AFL Council," *New York Times*,

August 11, 1954, p. 1, and A. H. Raskin, "AFL-CIO Maps Higher Pay Drive," *New York Times*, February 9, 1958, p. 1.

68. "Educator Assails 'Fear of Russia,'" *New York Times*, March 20, 1953, p. 28.

69. Stephen Ambrose, *Eisenhower: The President*, vol. 2 (New York: Simon and Schuster, 1984), 55–57.

70. See James Webb, Addresses, November 1948 and December 2, 1948, box 6, Webb Papers.

71. Frank Pace, memo to Harry Truman, July 8, 1949, PSF/SF/Bureau of the Budget, box 150, Budget Misc 45–53, Truman Library.

7. EISENHOWER'S AMBIVALENCE AND KENNEDY'S OBSESSION

1. John Newhouse, *War and Peace in the Nuclear Age* (New York: Knopf, 1989), 89, 91.

2. Stephen Ambrose, *Eisenhower: The President* (New York: Simon and Schuster, 1984), 248, 291.

3. Iwan Morgan, *Eisenhower Versus the "Spenders": The Eisenhower Administration, the Democrats, and the Budget, 1953–1960.* (New York: St. Martin's, 1990), 1–23.

4. Newhouse, *War and Peace*, 94.

5. Ambrose, *Eisenhower: The President*, 224.

6. Newhouse, *War and Peace*, 90.

7. Morgan, *Eisenhower Versus the "Spenders"*, 49–73.

8. Warner Schilling, "The Politics of National Defense: FY 1950," in Warner Schilling, Paul Hammond, and Glenn Snyder, eds., *Strategy, Politics, and Defense Budgets* (New York: Columbia University Press, 1962), 40–53; and Samuel Huntington, *The Common Defense: Strategic Programs in National Politics* (New York: Columbia University Press, 1961), 42, 75, 221, 466.

9. Ambrose, *Eisenhower: The President*, 90.

10. David Halberstam, *The Fifties* (New York: Villard, 1993), 406.

11. H. W. Brands, *The Devil We Knew* (New York: Oxford University Press, 1993), 41–46.

12. Ambrose, *Eisenhower: The President*, 133, 224–25.

13. Ibid., 193–96, 462–69, 584, 608.

14. Halberstam, *The Fifties*, 410.

15. Newhouse, *War and Peace*, 100.

16. Paul Johnson, "NATO's Vanishing Armies," *Nation*, April 13, 1957, pp. 310–12.

17. Brands, *The Devil We Knew*, 46–50.

18. Robert Norris, Steven Kosiak, and Stephen Schwartz, "Deploying the Bomb," in Stephen Schwartz, ed., *Atomic Audit: The Costs and Consequences of*

U.S. Nuclear Weapons Since 1940 (Washington, D.C.: Brookings Institution, 1998), 111–17.

19. John Gaddis, *We Now Know: Rethinking Cold War History* (New York: Oxford University Press, 1997), 221–22, 258–59.

20. Kevin O'Neill, "Building the Bomb," in Schwartz, *Atomic Audit*, 77.

21. Norris, Kosiak, and Schwartz, "Deploying the Bomb," 187.

22. Bruce Blair, John Pike, and Stephen Schwartz, "Targeting and Controlling the Bomb," in Schwartz, *Atomic Audit*, 206.

23. Newhouse, *War and Peace*, 110.

24. Ibid.

25. Ibid., 117–24, 143–46.

26. Blair, Pike, and Schwartz, "Targeting and Controlling the Bomb," 206.

27. For minutes of meetings of the National Security Council in which Eisenhower and his aides discussed the military budget, see National Security Council Series, Ann Whitman file, Dwight D. Eisenhower Library, Abilene, Kansas.

28. Ambrose, *Eisenhower: The President*, 118.

29. Huntington, *Common Defense*, 234–48.

30. Ibid., 251–64.

31. Mary Kaldor, *The Baroque Arsenal* (New York: Hill *and* Wang, 1981), 26.

32. Ibid.

33. Vern Haugland, "Bull Market for Missiles," *Nation*, June 1, 1957, p. 472.

34. Ibid., 472–75.

35. Ibid., 473–75.

36. Gregory Hooks, *Forging the Military-Industrial Complex: World War II's Battle of the Potomac* (Urbana: University of Illinois Press, 1991), 125–62, 225–66.

37. Haugland, "Bull Market for Missiles," 473.

38. Norris, Kosiak, and Schwartz, "Deploying the Bomb," 151.

39. Huntington, *Common Defense*, 251–77.

40. William Hill, "The Business Community and National Defense: Corporate Leaders and the Military" (Ph.D. diss. Stanford University, 1980), 416–35.

41. Blair, Pike, and Schwartz, "Targeting and Controlling the Bomb," 206.

42. Kaldor, *Baroque Arsenal*, 95.

43. Christopher S. Raj, *The American Military in Europe: Controversy over NATO Burden Sharing* (New Delhi: ABC Publishing, 1983), 63.

44. Huntington, *Common Defense*, 236–48.

45. Newhouse, *War and Peace*, 114.

46. Richard Hewlett and Jack Holl, *Atoms for Peace and War, 1953–1961* (Berkeley: University of California Press, 1989), 34–72. The scorpions quote is on p. 54.

47. Ibid.

48. Newhouse, *War and Peace*, 109–11.

49. Ibid., 123–25; and Norris, Kosiak, and Schwartz, "Deploying the Bomb," 187.

50. Ambrose, *Eisenhower: The President*, 561–64.

51. See "HEW—How Much Welfare?" *New York Times*, August 28, 1955, p. 26; Edwin Dale, "Eisenhower Proposes Expanded Welfare," *New York Times*, January 1, 1956, p. 1; Russell Baker, "Vote-Seeking Congress Turns to Social Issues," *New York Times*, May 6, 1956, p. B7; and John Morris, "An Evaluation of Welfare Programs as Carried out by the New Department," *New York Times*, July 28, 1956, p. 1.

52. Baker, "Vote-Seeking Congress," B7.

53. Gross domestic product measures the value of goods and services produced within a country's physical borders in a specific period, usually a year. Gross national product is the GDP plus income earned from work or investment broad.

54. Morgan, *Eisenhower Versus the "Spenders,"* 19.

55. Ibid.

56. Wilbur Cohen, oral history interview, Wilbur Cohen Papers, box 476, Lyndon B. Johnson Library, Austin, Texas.

57. Nicholas Lemann, The Promised Land: The Great Black Migration and How It Changed America (New York: Knopf, 1991), 70.

58. Edward Berkowitz, *Mr. Social Security: The Life of Wilbur J. Cohen* (Lawrence: University of Kansas Press, 1995), 49–70.

59. Ibid.

60. Martha Derthick, *Policy Making for Social Security* (Washington, D.C.: Brookings Institution, 1979), 254–70.

61. Ibid., 245.

62. Berkowitz, *Mr. Social Security*, 72–76.

63. Ibid., 93.

64. Administration Series, Ann Whitman file, Dodge: 1955 Budget (2), box 12, Eisenhower Library.

65. Morgan, *Eisenhower Versus the "Spenders,"* 1–23.

66. Richard O. Davies, *Age of Asphalt: The Automobile, the Freeway, and the Condition of Metropolitan America* (Philadelphia: Lippincott, 1975), 11–18.

67. Ibid., 18–24.

68. "Williams Urges U.S. School Plan," *New York Times*, October 21, 1955, p. 20; Harrison Salisbury, "Stevenson Gives School Aid Plan," *New York Times*, October 2, 1956, p. 1.

69. William Leuchtenberg, *In the Shadow of Franklin Roosevelt: From Harry Truman to Ronald Reagan* (Ithaca: Cornell University Press, 1983), 107–15.

70. Ibid., 84–88.

71. *New York Times*, February 1, 1961, p. 17.

72. James Reston, "Kennedy's Domestic Record," *New York Times*, July 19, 1961, p. 17.

73. Lemann, *Promised Land*, 123–34.

74. *New York Times*, April 9, 1961, p. 1.

75. *New York Times*, May 11, 1961, p. 1.

76. Joseph Pechman, oral history interview, Johnson Library.

77. Newhouse, *War and Peace*, 148.

78. Richard Reeves, *President Kennedy: Profile of Power* (New York: Simon and Schuster, 1994), 238.

79. Ibid., 38.

80. Fred Kaplan, *Wizards of Armageddon* (New York: Simon and Schuster, 1983), 63–66, 78–81.

81. Ibid., 63–66.

82. See, for example, Herman Kahn, *On Thermonuclear War* (Princeton: Princeton University Press, 1960).

83. Reeves, *President Kennedy*, 38, 231.

84. Kaplan, *Wizards of Armageddon*, 180–81.

85. Ibid., 283–85.

86. Schwartz, *Atomic Audit*, 10.

87. Arthur J. Art, *The TFX Decision: McNamara and the Military* (Boston: Little, Brown, 1968).

88. Paul Douglas, *Economy in the National Government* (Chicago: University of Chicago Press, 1952).

89. Ibid., 259–66.

90. For discussion of the lack of public comment on tax matters, see John Witte, *The Politics and Development of the Federal Income Tax* (Madison: University of Wisconsin Press, 1985), 331.

91. Norris, Kosiak, and Schwartz, "Deploying the Bomb," 166.

92. Ambrose, *Eisenhower: The President*, 86–87.

93. Raj, *American Military in Europe*, 5.

94. Huntington, *Common Defense*, 127–35.

95. Edward A. Kolodziej, *Uncommon Defense and Congress, 1945–1953* (Columbus: Ohio State University Press, 1966), 419–29 .

96. Huntington, *Common Defense*, 127–35.

97. Ibid., 153–54.

98. United Press International, "GOP Economy Call Assailed by Bailey," *New York Times*, July 30, 1961, p. 44.

99. Data on social investments appear in Office of Management and Budget, *Budget of the U.S. Government, FY 2000, Historical Tables*, table 3.1, pp. 43–44.

100. Tax data appear in Office of Management and Budget, *Budget of the U.S. Government, FY 2000, Historical Tables*, table 2.3, p. 31.

8. JOHNSON'S POLICY GLUTTONY

1. Joseph Pechman, oral history interview, Lyndon B. Johnson Library, Austin, Texas.

2. Robert Dallek, *Lone Star Rising: Lyndon Johnson and His Times, 1908–1960* (New York: Oxford University Press, 1991), 468–69.

3. *New York Times*, December 24, 1963, p. 1.

4. *New York Times*, November 30, 1963, p. 1.

5. *New York Times*, September 7, 1964, p. 1.

6. Ronnie Dugger, *The Politician: The Life and Times of Lyndon Johnson—The Drive for Power from the Frontier to the Master of the Senate* (New York: Norton, 1982), 26–27, 44–45, 136, 154, 297, 306. The Stalin quote appears p. 297.

7. Ibid., 307, 350, 362, 365, 370. See p. 370 for the tyrant quote.

8. Ibid., 371.

9. Robert Caro, *The Path to Power*, vol. 1 of *The Years of Lyndon Johnson* (New York: Knopf, 1982), 273–85, 312–13.

10. Joseph Califano, *The Triumph and Tragedy of Lyndon Johnson* (New York: Simon and Schuster, 1991). For a sympathetic view of Johnson's domestic accomplishments, see Irving Bernstein, *Guns or Butter: the Presidency of Lyndon Johnson* (New York: Oxford University Press, 1996), 117–306.

11. Dugger, *Politician*, 52–53, 91, 196–203, 210.

12. Dallek, *Lone Star Rising*, 403, 404, 427, 437, 445, 481, 495–96, 518, 535.

13. Ibid., 430; Dugger, *Politician*, 92–93.

14. Dugger, *Politician*, 343.

15. Ibid., 391.

16. Ibid., 344, 391; Vincent Burke and Vee Burke, *Nixon's Good Deed: Welfare Reform* (New York: Columbia University Press, 1974), 20–24, 36–39.

17. Lyndon B. Johnson, *Public Papers of the Presidents of the United States: Lyndon Johnson, 1963–1964* (Washington, D.C.: U.S. Government Printing Office, 1965), 76.

18. *New York Times*, January 22, 1964, p. 1.

19. Carl Brauer, *John F. Kennedy and the Second Reconstruction* (New York: Columbia University Press, 1967), 16–17, 112–13, 204.

20. Charles Schultze, oral history interview, Johnson Library.

21. Kermit Gordon, Charles Schultze, and William Cannon, oral history interviews, Johnson Library.

22. *New York Times*, December 29, 1963, p. 21.

23. Schultze, oral history interview.

24. Bernstein, *Guns or Butter*, 105.

25. Wilbur Cohen, oral history interview, series II, box 478, Johnson Library; and Cannon, oral history interview. Also see Christopher Jencks, "Johnson Versus Poverty," *New Republic*, March 28, 1964, pp. 15–18.

26. Henry Brandon, *Special Relationships: A Foreign Correspondent's Memoirs from Roosevelt to Reagan* (New York: Atheneum, 1988), 244; Dugger, *Politician*, 446; Dallek, *Lone Star Rising*, 444.

27. Dugger, *Politician*, 32.

28. Robert Scheer, "LBJ's Viet Words Return to Haunt Him," *Los Angeles Times*, March 25, 1997, p. B7.

29. Johnson, *Public Papers, 1963–1964*, 185–86.

30. William Gibbons, *The U.S. Government and the Vietnam War: Executive and Legislative Roles and Relationships*, part 2: *1961–1964* (Princeton: Princeton University Press, 1986), 209–50; Lyndon Johnson, *Public Papers, 1963–1964*, 45.

31. Gibbons, *U.S. Government and the Vietnam War*, pt. 2, 241.

32. Ibid., 230–40, 262–78.

33. David Kaiser, *American Tragedy: Kennedy, Johnson, and the Origins of the Vietnam War* (Cambridge, Mass.: Harvard University Press, 2000), 333–34.

34. Bernstein, *Guns or Butter*, 338, 564.

35. Kaiser, *American Tragedy*, 335.

36. Thomas O'Neill, *Man of the House: The Life and Political Memoirs of Speaker Tip O'Neill* (New York: Random House, 1987), 189–206.

37. Doris Kearns, *Lyndon Johnson and the American Dream* (New York: Harper and Row, 1976), 216–17, 252, and Robert Dallek, *Flawed Giant: Lyndon Johnson and His Times* (New York: Oxford University Press, 1998), 242–57.

38. Lyndon Johnson, *Public Papers, 1965*, 700.

39. *New York Times*, January 19, 1965, p. 1.

40. William Gibbons, *The U.S. Government and the Vietnam War*, part 3: *January–July 1965* (Princeton: Princeton University Press, 1989), 156.

41. James Bill, *George Ball: Behind the Scenes in U.S. Foreign Policy* (New Haven: Yale University Press, 1997), 162–63; and Deborah Shapley, *Promise and Power: The Life and Times of Robert McNamara* (Boston: Little, Brown, 1993), 312–15, 329–33.

42. Gibbons, *U.S. Government and the Vietnam War*, pt. 3, 127–29.

43. Hanson Baldwin, "Military's Needs Expected to Rise," *New York Times*, May 23, 1965, p. 1.

44. Robert Shogan, *The Riddle of Power: Presidential Power from Truman to Bush* (New York: Dutton, 1991), 101–29.

45. Michael Harrington, *The Other America: Poverty in the United States* (New York: Macmillan, 1962).

46. Sargent Shriver, memo to Lyndon Johnson, October 20, 1965, WHCF, container 26, Johnson Library.

47. Gibbons, *U.S. Government and the Vietnam War*, pt. 3, 69.

48. "Our Way of Life," editorial, *Nation*, August 16, 1965, pp. 69–70.

49. Joseph Pechman, oral history interview, Johnson Library.

50. Tom Wicker, "Guns or Butter: Republicans Pressing the Issue," *New York Times*, August 14, 1965, p. E9.

51. *New York Times*, December 17, 1965, p. 25.

52. Wicker, "Guns or Butter."

53. Califano, *Triumph and Tragedy*, 111.

54. Gibbons, *U.S. Government and the Vietnam War*, pt. 3, 389.

55. Schultze, oral history interview.

56. Henry Fowler, Report, Central Files, BE5, National/Ec, container 3, Johnson Library.

57. Joseph Barr, oral history interview, Johnson Library.

58. Joseph Califano, memo to President Johnson, July 7, 1966, CF/FG795, container 41, Johnson Library.

59. Charles Schultze, memo to President Johnson, July 7, 1966, CF/FG795, container 41, Johnson Library.

60. Charles Schultze, memo to President Johnson, "Great Expectations Vs. Disappointments," November 7, 1966, WHCF, Welfare/Ex We9, container 28, Johnson Library.

61. Schultze, oral history interview.

62. Robert Kinfer, memo to Charles Schultze, September 27, 1966, CF/FG1–1/FG11–1BOB, box 17, Johnson Library.

63. Gardner Ackley, memo to President Johnson, September 6, 1966, Johnson Library, CF/FG105–4, box 25, Johnson Library.

64. Califano, memo to President Johnson, September 1, 1966, CF/FI9, container 44, Johnson Library.

65. Johnson, *Public Papers, 1966*, 1449.

66. Donald Radler, memo to Marvin Watson, January 6, 1967, CF/OEO, box 21, Johnson Library,

67. Carey McWilliams, "High Noon in the Cow Palace," *Nation*, July 13, 1964, p. 25.

68. Johnson, *Public Papers, 1968–1969*, 83–111. The quotes appear on p. 83.

69. Arthur Okun, memo to President Johnson, March 15, 1968, CF/FI9/FI 11–4, container 44, Johnson Library.

70. Robert Norris, Steven Kosiak, and Stephen Schwartz, "Deploying the Bomb," in Stephen Schwartz, ed., *Atomic Audit: The Costs and Consequences of U.S. Nuclear Weapons Since 1940* (Washington, D.C.: Brookings Institution, 1998), 187.

71. Ibid.

72. John Newhouse, *War and Peace in the Nuclear Age* (New York: Knopf, 1989), 201–2.

73. Ibid., 200–203.

74. Ibid., 197.

75. Ibid., 202.

76. For differences between the Joint Chiefs of Staff and the administration on military spending, see Tom Johnson, Minutes, December 4, 1967, Johnson Meeting Notes, box 1, Johnson Library. Also see Tom Johnson, Johnson Meeting Notes, August 19, 1967, box 1.

77. Tom Johnson, Johnson Meeting Notes, August 19, 1967.

78. Bruce Blair, John Pike, and Stephen Schwartz, "Targeting and Controlling the Bomb," in Schwartz, *Atomic Audit,* 206.

79. Fred Kaplan, *Dubious Specter: A Skeptical Look at the Soviet Nuclear Threat* (Washington, D.C.: Institute for Policy Studies, 1980), 28–33.

80. Ibid., 89–90.

81. Newhouse, *War and Peace,* 198.

82. Ibid., 197.

83. Robert McNamara, *Blundering into Disaster* (New York: Pantheon, 1986), 57.

84. Recent research puts severe limits on the extent to which either the Soviet Union or China acted as the prime mover in North Vietnam's war with South Vietnam. See Lloyd Gardner and Ted Gittinger, eds., *International Perspectives on Vietnam* (College Station: Texas A&M University Press, 2000). In particular, see Robert Brigham, "Vietnam at the Center: Patterns of Diplomacy and Resistance," 98–107; Ilya Gaiduck, "Containing the Warriors: Soviet Policy Toward the Indochina Conflict, 1960–1965," 58–76; and Xiaoming Zhang, "Communist Powers Divided: China, the Soviet Union, and the Vietnam War," 77–97.

85. Newhouse, *War and Peace,* 208.

86. William Kaufmann, *Planning Conventional Forces, 1950–1980* (Washington, D.C.: Brookings Institution, 1982), 15.

87. Christopher S. Raj, *The American Military in Europe: Controversy over NATO Burden Sharing* (New Delhi: ABC Publishing, 1983), 269–71.85. Ibid., 260–69.

88. McNamara, *Blundering into Disaster,* 64–68.

89. Califano, *Triumph and Tragedy,* 284.

90. Edwin Dale, "U.S. Aides Concede Budget Gimmicks," *New York Times,* September 12, 1968, p. 1.

91. See Califano, memo to President Johnson, June 20, 1968, WHCF/Aides/Califano, box 57, Johnson Library.

92. George Gallup, *The Gallup Poll: Public Opinion, 1959–1971,* vol. 3 (New York: Random House, 1972), December 6, 1964, p. 1910.

9. NIXON'S MEGALOMANIA

1. John Ehrlichman, oral history interview, Nixon Presidential Materials, National Archives at College Park, Maryland.

2. John Ehrlichman, memo to President Nixon, October 21, 1970, WHSF, box 23, Nixon Presidential Materials.

3. Tom Wicker, *One of Us: Richard Nixon and the American Dream* (New York: Random House, 1991), 100–103, 105, 106, 197, 199.

4. Stephen Ambrose, *The Triumph of a Politician, 1962–1972,* vol. 2 of *Nixon* (New York: Simon and Schuster, 1989), 302.

5. Joan Hoff-Wilson, *Nixon Reconsidered* (New York: Basic, 1994), 18.

6. Wicker, *One of Us*, 422–23.

7. Henry Kissinger, *White House Years* (Boston: Little, Brown, 1979), 134ff.

8. Ibid., 204.

9. Wicker, *One of Us*, 246.

10. Leonard Silk, *Nixonomics: How the Dismal Science of Free Enterprise Became the Black Art of Controls* (New York: Praeger, 1972), 3–19.

11. James Reichley, *Conservatives in an Age of Change: The Nixon and Ford Presidencies* (Washington, D.C.: Brookings Institution, 1981), 232–42.

12. Kevin Phillips, *The Emerging Republican Majority* (New Rochelle, N.Y.: Arlington House, 1969), 461–74.

13. Richard Nixon, POF, Presidential Handwriting, boxes 2 and 3, Nixon Presidential Materials: see Nixon's repeated annotations on press stories, for example, on May 25, 1969; May 26, 1969; October 20, 1969; and November 10, 1969, that suggest his political uses of demonstrations.

14. Nixon's annotations on a speech by Richard Whalen, attached to a memo from Pat Buchanan on May 27, 1969, show Nixon's hawkish views with respect to the Soviets. See Nixon, POF, Presidential Handwriting, box 2.

15. Seymour M. Hersh, *The Price of Power: Kissinger in the White House* (New York: Summit, 1983), 66.

16. Kissinger, *White House Years*, 1049–96.

17. John Newhouse, *War and Peace in the Nuclear Age* (New York: Knopf, 1989), 214–15.

18. Ambrose, *Nixon*, vol. 2, 287, 309, 319, 401.

19. Ibid. 198.

20. Hersh, *Price of Power*, 46–53.

21. Ibid., 83–97.

22. Newhouse, *War and Peace*, 23–214.

23. Robert McNamara, *Blundering into Disaster* (New York: Pantheon, 1986), 64–68.

24. Newhouse, *War and Peace*, 216–17.

25. Various materials on post-Vietnam planning can be found in WHCF, Presidential Aides, Califano, box 57, Lyndon B. Johnson Library, Austin, Texas. Also Johnson, "Memo to Cabinet Secretaries, March 1, 1967, CF-FG1-FG11 (BOB 67), box 17, Johnson Library.

26. Charles Schultze, Edward Fried, Alice Rivlin, and Nancy Teeter, *Setting National Priorities: The 1973 Budget* (Washington, D.C.: Brookings Institution, 1972), 73–76.

27. Walter Reuther hints at the more radical version in U.S. Congress, Joint Economic Committee, Subcommittee on Economy in Government, *The Military Budget and National Economic Priorities*, 91st Cong., 1st sess., December 23, 1969, pt. 1, pp. 410–61.

28. "Federal Spending Cuts Now in the Works," *U.S. News and World Report*, April 28, 1969, pp. 94–96; *New York Times*, May 17, 1969, p. 26.

29. *New York Times*, June 13, 1969, p. 18.

30. See how Lyndon Johnson's budget message for his 1969 proposed budget emphasizes entitlements in *Congressional Quarterly Almanac, 1969* (Washington, D.C.: Congressional Quarterly, 1970), 9-A. Barry Blechman, Edward M. Gramlich, and Robert W. Hartman discuss how Democrats focused on entitlements during Nixon's first term in *Setting National Priorities: The 1975 Budget* (Washington, D.C.: Brookings Institution, 1974), 12.

31. *New York Times*, April 15, 1969, p. 1.

32. Walter Heller, memo to President Johnson, July 26, 1965, CF, box 14, Johnson Library.

33. Sargent Shriver, memo to President Johnson, October 20, 1965, WHCF/ExWe9, container 26, Johnson Library.

34. Unsigned memo to President Nixon on the Coleman Report, October 2, 1969, WHCF/SF/FG–61, box 55. See also Chester Finn, memo to President Nixon on Westinghouse Report, October 2, 1969, both in Nixon Presidential Materials.

35. Nixon, annotation on news report, February 17, 1969, POF, Presidential Handwriting Series, box 1.

36. Richard Arum, "Do Private Schools Force Public Schools to Compete?" *American Sociological Review* 61 (1996): 29–46.

37. Richard Nixon, memo on value-added tax, December 4, 1969, WHCF/CF/BE 69–70, box 2, Nixon Presidential Materials.

38. Ibid.

39. Elmo Zumwalt, *On Watch: A Memoir* (New York: Quadrangle, 1976), 281–82, 313–14.

40. Lawrence Korb, *The Fall and Rise of the Pentagon: American Defense Policies in the 1970s* (Westport, Conn.: Greenwood, 1979), 3–23.

41. Kissinger, *White House Years*, 32–33.

42. Richard Nixon, notes to Sen. Henry Jackson and others, September 25, 1969, POF, Presidential Handwriting Series, box 2.

43. Daniel Moynihan, memo to Richard Nixon, November 25, 1969, POF, Presidential Handwriting Series, box 3.

44. U.S. Congress, Joint Economic Committee, Subcommittee on Subcommittee on Economy in Government, *Hearings on the Military Budget and National Economic Priorities*, 91st Cong., 1st sess., June 1969, pp. 95–113.

45. Melvin Small, *Johnson, Nixon, and the Doves* (New Brunswick: Rutgers University Press, 1988), 193.

46. Richard Nixon, *The Public Papers of the Presidents of the United States: Richard Nixon, 1970* (Washington, D.C.: U.S. Government Printing Office, 1971), January 22, 1970, p. 12.

47. Ehrlichman, memo to John Campbell, January 30, 1970, WHCF/SP/ FI-FI14, box 24, Nixon Presidential Materials.

48. Ehrlichman, memo to President Nixon, October 21, 1970.

49. See Nixon's discussion of his budget message as discussed in the *New York Times*, February 3, 1970, p. 1.

50. Ibid.

51. Moynihan, memo to President Nixon, January 16, 1970, POF, Presidential Handwriting Series, box 5,

52. Moynihan, memo to Bob Haldeman, October 15, 1970, WHSF, Staff, Haldeman, box 48, Nixon Presidential Materials.

53. Zumwalt, *On Watch*, 304.

54. Editorial, *New York Times*, February 3, 1970, p. 42.

55. "Impact of Deep Cuts in Defense," *U.S. News and World Report*, February 16, 1970, pp. 31ff.

56. Pat Buchanan, memo to President Nixon, August 24, 1970. WHCF, Staff, Haldeman, box 48, Nixon Presidential Materials.

57. Ehrlichman, memo to President Nixon, October 21, 1970.

58. Timothy J. Conlan, "The Politics of Federal Block Grants from Nixon to Reagan," *Political Science Quarterly* 99, no. 2 (summer 1984): 247–70.

59. Joseph Califano, *The Triumph and Tragedy of Lyndon Johnson* (New York: Simon and Schuster, 1991), 10–12, 52.

60. Richard Nathan, *The Plot That Failed: Nixon and the Administrative Presidency* (New York: Wiley, 1975).

61. The Nixon quotes appear in Nixon, memo to Defense Program Review Committee, March 3, 1970, WHCF/SF/FI-FI14, box 24, Nixon Presidential Materials. Also see *Business Week*, February 21, 1970, p. 34.

62. *New York Times*, April 14, 1971, p. 28.

63. Korb, *Fall and Rise of the Pentagon*, 28–34.

64. Ambrose, *Nixon*, vol. 2, 500.

65. Buchanan, memo to President Nixon, June 8, 1972, WHSF, Buchanan, box 10, Nixon Presidential Materials.

66. Buchanan, memo to John Mitchell and Bob Haldeman, April 27, 1972, WHSF, Buchanan, box 9, Nixon Presidential Materials.

67. Buchanan, "Assault Strategy," June 8, 1972, WHSF, Buchanan, box 10, Nixon Presidential Materials.

68. *New York Times*, August 9, 1972, p. 19.

69. Gordon Strachan, "Memo to Pat Buchanan Containing Estimates from Weinberger," September 7, 1972, WHSF, Buchanan, box 8, Nixon Presidential Materials.

70. Buchanan, "Assault Strategy." Also see Buchanan, memo to Bob Haldeman, John Ehrlichman, and Charles Colson, September 13, 1972, WHSF, Buchanan, box 10, Nixon Presidential Materials.

71. Bill Baroody, memo to Charles Colson, August 30, 1972, WHSF, Buchanan, box 8, Nixon Presidential Materials. Also see Buchanan, memo to Haldeman, Ehrlichman, and Colson, September 13, 1972.

72. See McGovern's testimony in U.S. Congress, Joint Economic Committee, *Hearings: National Priorities, the Next Five Years,* 92 Cong., 2d sess., May 30 and 31 and June 1, 16, and 27, 1972.

73. Ambrose, *Nixon,* vol. 2, 453.

74. Hersh, *Price of Power,* 334–39.

75. Stephen Schwartz, ed., *Atomic Audit: The Costs and Consequences of U.S. Nuclear Weapons Since 1940* (Washington, D.C.: Brookings Institution, 1998), 187.

76. Newhouse, *War and Peace,* 234.

77. Ambrose, *Nixon,* vol. 2, 551.

78. Wicker, *One of Us,* 612.

79. *New York Times,* July 19, 1973, p. 21.

80. Nixon, *Public Papers, 1973,* March 1, 1973, p. 135.

81. Tom Geoghegan, "The New Federalism," *New Republic* (March 10, 1073), p. 21.

82. Ibid.

83. *New York Times,* October 5, 1973, p. 12.

84. March 19, 1973, WHCF/CF-F14, box 28, Nixon Presidential Materials.

85. *New York Times,* March 30, 1973, p. 1.

86. *New York Times,* June 15, 1973, p. 74.

87. *New York Times,* June 23, 1973, p. 26, and July 19, 1973, p. 21.

88. Bill Timmons, memo to President Nixon, September 15, 1973, WHCF/SF/CF-F1–4, box 28, Nixon Presidential Materials.

89. John Green, *The Limits of Power: The Nixon and Ford Administrations* (Bloomington: University of Indiana Press, 1992), 206.

90. To obtain these figures, I added funding for education, training, employment, and social programs from table 3.1 of Office of Management and Budget, *Budget of the U.S. Government, FY 2000, Historical Tables* (Washington, D.C.: U.S. Government Printing Office, 1999) to the annual expenditures for "health" in table 8.7 of the *Historical Tables.* (I deducted expenditures for "health-NIH research" and "health-other" research in table 9.8 because I focused on public health expenditures.)

91. Hoff-Wilson, *Nixon Reconsidered,* 123.

10. REAGAN'S FANTASIES

1. Lou Cannon, *President Reagan: The Role of a Lifetime* (New York: Simon and Schuster, 1991), 88–89; Ronnie Dugger, *On Reagan: The Man and His Presidency* (New York: McGraw Hill, 1983), 1–24; and Haynes Johnson, *Sleepwalking Through History: America in the Reagan Years* (New York: Norton, 1991), 67.

2. Laurence Barrett, *Gambling with History: Reagan in the White House* (New York: Penguin, 1983), 46–54.

3. Ronald Reagan, *An American Life* (New York: Simon and Schuster, 1990), 66–69.

4. Ibid., 132–33.

5. Ibid., 116–20.

6. Ibid., 120, 127.

7. Cannon, *President Reagan*, 88–89.

8. Dugger, *On Reagan*, 17.

9. Ibid., 117.

10. Paul Craig Roberts, *The Supply-Side Revolution: An Insider's Account of Policy Making in Washington* (Cambridge, Mass.: Harvard University Press, 1984), 27–30.

11. Ibid., 66–88.

12. Martin Anderson, *Revolution: The Reagan Legacy* (Palo Alto, Calif.: Hoover Institution Press, 1988), 150.

13. David Callahan, *Dangerous Capabilities: Paul Nitze and the Cold War* (New York: HarperCollins, 1990), 350–95.

14. Ibid., 402.

15. Andy Pasztor, *When the Pentagon Was for Sale* (New York: Scribner, 1995), 43–47.

16. Fred Kaplan, *Dubious Specter: A Skeptical Look at the Soviet Nuclear Threat* (Washington, D.C.: Institute for Policy Studies, 1980), 1–12, 55–58.

17. Fred Kaplan, *Wizards of Armageddon* (New York: Simon and Schuster, 1983), 382–84.

18. See, for example, Kaplan, *Dubious Specter*, and Tom Gervasi, *Arsenal of Democracy II: American Military Power in the 1980s and the Origins of the New Cold War* (New York: Grove, 1981), and *The Myth of Soviet Military Supremacy* (New York: Harper and Row, 1986).

19. Kaplan, *Dubious Specter*, 13–54.

20. Gervasi, *Arsenal of Democracy II*, 16–18.

21. Ibid., 18–30.

22. Ibid., 18–20.

23. Bruce Blair, John Pike, and Stephen Schwartz, "Targeting and Controlling the Bomb," in Stephen Schwartz, ed., *Atomic Audit: : The Costs and Consequences of U.S. Nuclear Weapons Since 1940* (Washington, D.C.: Brookings Institution, 1998), 206.

24. Gervasi, *Arsenal of Democracy II*, 6.

25. Callahan, *Dangerous Capabilities*, 378.

26. Kaplan, *Wizards of Armageddon*, 385–91.

27. Callahan, *Dangerous Capabilities*, 389–93.

28. Anderson, *Revolution*, 77, 94–96.

29. Pasztor, *When the Pentagon Was for Sale*, 64.

30. Ibid., 69.

31. Gregory Vistica, *Fall from Glory: The Men Who Sank the U.S. Navy* (New York: Simon and Schuster, 1995), 30–38.

32. Ibid., 53–56.

33. Ibid., 66–67.

34. Anderson, *Revolution*, 161–62.

35. Stockman, *The Triumph of Politics: Why the Reagan Revolution Failed* (New York: Harper and Row, 1986), 58.

36. Cannon, *President Reagan*, 243.

37. Stockman, *Triumph of Politics*, 355–64.

38. Cannon, *President Reagan*, 209–11.

39. Anderson, *Revolution*, 151–63; Reagan, *American Life*, 231–32.

40. Dugger, *On Reagan*, 25–42.

41. David Zucchino, *Myth of the Welfare Queen* (New York: Scribner, 1997), 65.

42. See Martin Anderson's emphasis on cutting programs for the working poor in *Welfare: The Political Economy of Welfare Reform in the United States* (Palo Alto, Calif.: Hoover Institution Press, 1978).

43. Dugger, *On Reagan*, 20–21.

44. Shields made this comment on several occasions during his appearances on the *Newshour with Jim Lehrer* of the Public Broadcasting Service in 1998 and 1999.

45. Samuel Hill and Dennis Owen, *The New Religious Political Right in America* (Nashville, Tenn.: Abingdon, 1982).

46. Anderson, *Revolution*, 234–53.

47. Dugger, *On Reagan*, 287.

48. Ibid., 289.

49. Anderson, *Revolution*, 236–37, and Edwin Meese, *With Reagan* (Washington, D.C.: Regenery Gateway, 1992), 135–39.

50. Dugger, *On Reagan*, 289.

51. Stockman, *Triumph of Politics*, 171.

52. Ibid. 92.

53. Ibid. 109.

54. Ibid. 106–8.

55. Meese, *With Reagan*, 135–44.

56. *New York Times*, April 3, 1981, p. 26.

57. Anderson, *Revolution*, 122–39.

58. Stockman, *Triumph of Politics*, 160.

59. Ibid.

60. Timothy Clark, "Want to Know Where the Budget Ax Will Fall? Read Stockman's Big Black Book," *National Journal*, February 14, 1981, pp. 274–81.

61. Stockman, *Triumph of Politics*, 159–62.

62. Ibid., 161–62.

63. Ibid., 167.

64. Ibid., 168.

65. Ibid. 121–22.

66. Thomas O'Neill, *Man of the House: The Life and Political Memoirs of Speaker Tip O'Neill* (New York: Random House, 1987), 344–46, 356.

67. Stockman, *Triumph of Politics*, 170–75.

68. *New York Times*, July 20, 1981, p. 4.

II. REAGAN'S GORDIAN KNOT

1. David Stockman, *The Triumph of Politics: Why the Reagan Revolution Failed* (New York: Harper and Row, 1986), 287–93.

2. George Hager and Eric Pianin, *Mirage: Why Neither Democrats Nor Republicans Can Balance the Budget* (New York: Random House, 1997), 122.

3. Ibid.

4. Martin Tolchin, "Support Grows for Alternatives to Reagan Budget," *New York Times*, March 1, 1982, p. A13.

5. Martin Tolchin, "House Democrats Back Bid for Quick Budget Vote," *New York Times*, March 18, 1982, p. B18.

6. Steven Weisman, "Reagan Vows to Go 'Extra Mile' to Get Accord on Budget," *New York Times*, April 21, 1982, p. A1.

7. Stockman, *Triumph of Politics*, 353–54.

8. Edwin Meese, *With Reagan: The Inside Story* (Washington, D.C.: Regenery Gateway, 1992), 138–42. Meese quotes himself on p. 138.

9. Hager and Pianin, *Mirage*, 132, 139, 140.

10. Ibid., 141–43.

11. Richard Darman, *Who's in Control? Polar Politics and the Sensible Center* (New York: Simon and Schuster, 1996), 112–19.

12. Ibid.

13. Stockman, *Triumph of Politics*, 376–94. See p. 373 for "willful act of ignorance" quote.

14. Jonathan Fuerbringer, "Reagan Reported Ready to Transfer Federal Program," *New York Times*, January 19, 1982, p. 1.

15. Daniel Moynihan, "The Trade Isn't a Bargain," *New York Times*, February 7, 1982, sec. 4, p. 19.

16. Timothy J. Conlan, "The Politics of Federal Block Grants from Nixon to Reagan," *Political Science Quarterly* 99, no. 2 (summer 1984): 269–70.

17. Steven Weisman, "Reagan Appeals for Freeze on Spending to Curb Deficit; Seeks Standby Tax for 1985," *New York Times*, January 26, 1983, p. 1.

18. William Schneider, "After Years of Change, the Consensus Holds," *National Journal,* January 12, 1985, p. 64.

19. John Pike, Bruce Blair, and Stephen Schwartz, "Defending Against the Bomb," in Stephen Schwartz, ed., *Atomic Audit: The Costs and Consequences of U.S. Nuclear Weapons Since 1940* (Washington, D.C.: Brookings Institution, 1998), 297.

20. Stephen Cohen, *Rethinking the Soviet Experience* (New York: Oxford University Press, 1985), 128–57.

21. John Newhouse, *War and Peace in the Nuclear Age* (New York: Knopf, 1989), 336.

22. Ronald Powaski, *The Cold War: The United States and the Soviet Union, 1917–1991* (New York: Oxford University Press, 1998), 249; and Don Oberdorfer, *The Turn: From the Cold War to a New Era* (New York: Poseidon, 1991), 66–67.

23. Daniel Moynihan, *Miles to Go: A Personal History of Social Policy* (Cambridge, Mass.: Harvard University Press, 1996), 66.

24. Robert Gates, *From the Shadows* (New York: Simon and Schuster, 1996), 508–9.

25. Ibid., 166.

26. Gregory L. Vistica, *Fall from Glory: The Men Who Sank the U.S. Navy* (New York: Simon and Schuster, 1995), 57–60.

27. Ibid., 168.

28. Vistica, *Fall from Glory,* 176.

29. Ibid., 163.

30. Ibid., 171.

31. Andy Pasztor, *When the Pentagon Was for Sale* (New York: Scribner, 1995), 123.

32. Vistica, *Fall from Glory,* 207–10.

33. Pasztor, *When the Pentagon Was for Sale,* 329.

34. Ibid., 151–55.

35. Ibid., 84.

36. Ibid., 133.

37. Ibid., 32.

38. Ibid., 122–25.

39. Ibid., 139.

40. Ibid.

41. Stockman, *Triumph of Politics,* 345–46.

42. Hager and Pianin, *Mirage,* 131–35.

43. Ibid., 142–45.

44. Ibid., 145–49.

45. Ibid., 147–48.

46. Ronald Reagan, *An American Life* (New York: Simon and Schuster, 1990), 338.

47. Hager and Pianin, *Mirage*, 148.

48. John Barry, *The Ambition and the Power* (New York: Viking, 1989), 448–78.

49. Stephen Engelberg, "Moynihan Asserts Stockman Said Reagan Doubted Tax-Cut Theory," *New York Times*, July 11, 1985, p. A 14.

50. See how Reagan used the word *linkage* in *New York Times*, February 5, 1981, p. 1. Also see Reagan's insistence that tax cuts and spending cuts be passed together in *New York Times*, February 20, 1981, p. 1.

51. Meese, *With Reagan*, 158.

52. Ibid., 148–62.

53. Donald Barlett and James Steele, *America: What Went Wrong?* (Kansas City, Mo.: Andrews and McMeel, 1992), 6.

54. See Tim Weiner, "Military Accused of Lies Over Arms," *New York Times*, June 28, 1993, p. 10; Pasztor, *When the Pentagon Was for Sale*, 57–58; and Schwartz, *Atomic Audit*, 17.

55. For rates of corporate taxation and revenues from corporate taxes, see Office of Management and Budget, *Budget of the U.S. Government, FY 2000, Historical Tables* (Washington, D.C.: U.S. Government Printing Office, 1999), table 2.1, pp. 27–28, and table 2.3, pp. 31–32.

12. BUSH'S MYOPIA

1. Michael Duffy and Dan Goodgame, *Marching in Place* (New York: Simon and Schuster, 1992), 12.

2. Herbert Parmet, *George Bush* (New York: Simon and Schuster, 1997), 220.

3. Michael Beschloss and Strobe Talbott, *At the Highest Levels: The Inside Story of the End of the Cold War* (Boston: Little, Brown, 1993), 3–4.

4. Ibid., 443–48, 471–73.

5. Duffy and Goodgame, *Marching in Place*, 12.

6. Don Oberdorfer, *The Turn: From the Cold War to a New Era* (New York: Poseidon, 1991), 328–34.

7. Duffy and Goodgame, *Marching in Place*, 136.

8. Mikhail Gorbachev, *Memoirs* (New York: Doubleday, 1996), 215–36.

9. Robert Gates, *From the Shadows* (New York: Simon and Schuster, 1996), 404–19.

10. Daniel Moynihan, *Miles to Go: A Personal History of Social Policy* (Cambridge, Mass.: Harvard University Press, 1996), 168. Also see Gates, *From the Shadows*, where he predicts the Soviet Union's demise, 68.

11. Ibid., 99.

12. Ibid., 122.

13. Ibid., 57–60.

14. Ibid., 57.

15. George Bush and Brent Scowcroft, *A World Transformed* (New York: Knopf, 1998), 74.

16. Ibid., 60.

17. Ibid., 215, 222, 229, and 293.

18. Beschloss and Talbott, *At the Highest Levels*, 134–39.

19. Richard Darman, *Who's in Control: Polar Politics and the Sensible Center* (New York: Simon and Schuster, 1996), 222–29.

20. Bush and Scowcroft, *World Transformed*, 139.

21. Ibid., 54.

22. Ibid., 53.

23. Duffy and Goodgame, *Marching in Place*, 20.

24. Mann is quoted in George Hager and Eric Pianin, *Mirage: Why Neither Democrats Nor Republicans Can Balance the Budget* (New York: Random House, 1997), 186.

25. Charles Kolb, *White House Daze: The Unmaking of Domestic Policy in the Bush Years* (New York: Free Press, 1994), 16–20.

26. Ibid., 93–94.

27. Duffy and Goodgame, *Marching in Place*, 27–28.

28. *Congressional Quarterly Almanac, 1989* (Washington, D.C., Congressional Quarterly, 1990), 79.

29. Hager and Pianin, *Mirage*, 171–72.

30. Duffy and Goodgame, *Marching in Place*, 56–62.

31. Kolb, *White House Daze*, 217–29.

32. Bush and Scowcroft, *World Transformed*, 238–40.

33. Ibid., 78.

34. Ibid., 215–29.

35. Ibid., 229.

36. Editorial, *New York Times*, January 30, 1990, p. A22.

37. Beschloss and Talbott, *At the Highest Levels*, 353.

38. Bush and Scowcroft, *World Transformed*, 280.

39. Ibid., 180–81.

40. Oberdorfer, *The Turn*, 395–96.

41. Thomas Friedman, *Lexus and the Olive Tree: Understanding Globalization* (New York: Farrar, Straus, Giroux, 1999), 338.

42. *New York Times*, March 17, 1990, p. 20.

43. *New York Times*, March 8, 1990, p. 24.

44. Carol Matlack, "Domestic Lobbies Try to Cash In," *National Journal*, April 14, 1990, pp. 884, 890–92.

45. Michael Oreskes, "Poll Finds U.S. Expects Peace Dividend," *New York Times*, January 25, 1990, p. B9.

46. Andrew Rosenthal, "Congress Is Warned by Bush Not to Cut Pentagon Budget," *New York Times*, January 13, 1990, p. A11.

47. Andrew Rosenthal, "Pentagon Freezing Construction as Bush Reviews Arms Priorities," *New York Times*, January 25, 1990, p. A1.

48. Andrew Rosenthal, "A 'War' Is Fought as Bush Looks On," *New York Times*, February 7, 1990, p. A13.

49. Budget authority is like a government checking account that contains sums that can be drawn upon (in this case, that were not spent during the Reagan administration).

50. Darman, *Who's in Control?* 191–92.

51. Ibid.

52. Hager and Pianin, *Mirage*, 158.

53. Ibid., 160.

54. Darman, *Who's in Control?* 227.

55. Hager and Pianin, *Mirage*, 160.

56. Richard Cohen, "Settling on a Number for Defense Cuts," *National Journal*, May 5, 1990, p. 1101.

57. Roger Hilsman, *George Bush Versus Saddam Hussein* (Novota, Calif.: Lyford Books, 1992), 41–42.

58. Bush and Scowcroft, *World Transformed*, 307–11.

59. Hilsman, *George Bush Versus Saddam Hussein*, 42–44.

60. Ibid., 248.

61. Ibid., 51–52.

62. Ibid., 49.

63. Duffy and Goodgame, *Marching in Place*, 135–36.

64. Ibid., 445.

65. Bush and Scowcroft, *World Transformed*, 327–29, 431–32.

66. Ibid., 425.

67. Ibid., 323.

68. Hager and Pianin, *Mirage*, 168–70, 178–79.

69. Ibid., 176–177.

70. Darman, *Who's in Control?* 177.

71. Hager and Pianin, *Mirage*, 178–79.

72. Darman, *Who's in Control?* 181.

73. Jeffrey Faux, "Back to the Peace Dividend: The Budget Pact Protects a Bloated Pentagon," *New York Times*, September 13, 1991, p. A15.

74. Richard Cohen, "Rumblings in the Ranks in the Budget Deal," *National Journal*, October 6, 1990, p. 2416.

75. Bush and Scowcroft, *World Transformed*, 418.

76. Hilsman, *George Bush Versus Saddam Hussein*, 205–9.

77. Jean Edward Smith, *George Bush's War* (New York: Holt 1992), 5.

78. Hilsman, *George Bush Versus Saddam Hussein*, 53–69.

79. Bush and Scowcroft, *World Transformed*, 491–92.

80. Patrick Tyler, "Pentagon Besieged," *New York Times*, September 5, 1991, p. 1.

81. Faux, "Back to the Peace Dividend."

82. Ibid.

83. Michael Ross, "Surprised Democrats Scramble for Credit, Seek Spending Cuts," *Los Angeles Times*, September 28, 1991, p. A12.

84. James Risen, "Deep Divisions Seen on Peace Dividend," *Los Angeles Times*, January 12, 1992, p. 1.

85. Patrick Tyler, "Top Congressman Seeks Deeper Cuts," *New York Times*, February 23, 1992, p. 1.

86. Elaine Sciolino, "$30 Billion in Excess Equipment Stored by Military, Panel Asserts," *New York Times*, February 4, 1992, p. 1.

87. Patrick Tyler, "Pentagon Imagines New Enemies," *New York Times*, February 17, 1992, p. 1.

88. Douglas Jehl, "Democrats Would Cripple Defense," *Los Angeles Times*, February 26, 1992, p. A10.

89. Patrick Tyler, "U.S. Strategic Plan," *New York Times*, February 8, 1992, p. 1.

90. Art Pine, "Cheney Issues Warning on Defense Cuts," *Los Angeles Times*, February 1, 1992, p. A15.

91. Elaine Sciolino, "CIA Chief Says Threat by Ex-Soviets Is Small," *New York Times*, January 23, 1992, p. A8.

92. Editorial, *New York Times*, May 13, 1992, p. A29.

93. The source of the data is Office of Management and Budget, *U.S. Budget, FY 2000, Historical Tables* (Washington, D.C.: Government Printing Office, 1999), table 3.1.

94. Robert Norris, Steven Kosiak, and Stephen Schwartz, "Deploying the Bomb," in Stephen Schwartz, ed., *Atomic Audit: The Costs and Consequences of U.S. Nuclear Weapons Since 1940* (Washington, D.C.: Brookings Institution, 1998), 187, and Blair, Pike, and Schwartz, "Targeting and Controlling the Bomb," in Schwartz, *Atomic Audit*, 206.

95. Blair, Pike, and Schwartz, "Targeting and Controlling the Bomb," 206.

96. Michael Sherraden, *Assets and the Poor* (Armonk, N.Y.: Sharpe, 1991).

97. Kolb, *White House Daze*, 207–8.

98. Burt Solomon, "Power to the People?" *National Journal*, January 26, 1991, p. 208.

99. Kolb, *White House Daze*, 213–17.

100. Lawrence Haas, "Stalled Rescues," *National Journal*, January 19, 1991, pp. 162–64.

101. Ed Rollins, *Bare Knuckles and Back Rooms* (New York: Broadway Books, 1996), 216.

102. Burt Solomon, "Will Bush Tee Off in 1992 with Bold Policy Strokes? *National Journal,* November 16, 1991, pp. 2818–19.

103. Rollins, *Bare Knuckles,* 264.

13. CLINTON AS BACKPEDALER AND COUNTERPUNCHER

1. Bob Woodward, *The Agenda: Inside the Clinton White House* (New York: Simon and Schuster, 1994), 211.

2. Ibid., 380–81.

3. Richard Cohen, "Democratic Leadership Council Sees Party Void and Is Ready to Fill It," *National Journal,* February 1, 1986, pp. 267–70.

4. Robert Reich, *The Work of Nations: Preparing Ourselves for Twenty-first-Century Capitalism* (New York: Knopf, 1991).

5. Woodward, *Agenda,* 24.

6. George Hager and Eric Pianin, *Mirage: Why Neither Democrats Nor Republicans Can Balance the Budget* (New York: Random House, 1997), 196–98.

7. Ed Rollins, *Bare Knuckles and Back Rooms* (New York: Broadway Books, 1996), 217–28.

8. William Kaufmann, *Assessing the Base Force: How Much Is Too Much?* (Washington, D.C.: Brookings Institution, 1992), 1.

9. *Los Angeles Times,* July 20, 1993, p. A1.

10. Kaufmann, *Assessing the Base Force,* 73–93.

11. Ibid., 48.

12. Ibid., 74. Kaufmann's Force 3 adds up to $139.1 billion, not $135 billion, perhaps as a result of rounding.

13. Ibid., 48–62.

14. Ibid., 75.

15. Ibid., 91.

16. Leslie Gelb, "$1.5 Trillion 'Defense,'" *New York Times,* April 17, 1992, p. A27.

17. Hager and Pianin, *Mirage,* 195.

18. Eric Schmitt, "Clinton and Bush Agree on Trimming Armed Forces, But Their Paths Vary," *New York Times,* October 21, 1992, p. A20.

19. *Los Angeles Times,* February 2, 1993, p. A9.

20. *Congressional Quarterly Almanac, 1993* (Washington, D.C.: Congressional Quarterly, 1994), 571.

21. Douglas Jehl, "Campaign Is Begun to Protect Money for Spy Agencies," *New York Times,* March 14, 1993, p. 1.

22. See, for example, Jane Gross, "Sparing Two Base Closings, Californians Lobby on," *New York Times,* March 14, 1993, p. 30.

23. *New York Times,* March 7, 1993, p. 1.

24. Editorial, *New York Times,* March 9, 1993, p. A14.

25. Lawrence Korb, "Our Overstuffed Military," *Foreign Affairs* 74 (November–December 1995): 26–27.

26. David Hackworth, *Hazardous Duty* (New York: Morrow 1996), 320.

27. David Hoffman, "Rotting Nuclear Subs Pose Threat in Russia," *Washington Post*, November 16, 1998, pp. A1, A22.

28. Jim Mann, "A Grim Diagnosis: Russia's a Sick and Dying Country," *Los Angeles Times*, May 19, 1999, p. A5.

29. Hager and Pianin, *Mirage*, 190–91.

30. Ibid., 205.

31. Linda Killian, *The Freshmen: What Happened to the Republican Revolution?* (Boulder, Colo.: Westview, 1998), 6.

32. Woodward, *Agenda*, 95–102, 113–24.

33. Ibid., 224.

34. Hager and Pianin, *Mirage*, 209–10.

35. Ibid.

36. Robert Reich, *Locked in the Cabinet* (New York: Vintage, 1998), 106.

37. Ibid.

38. Ibid., 107.

39. Hager and Pianin, *Mirage*, 221.

40. Dan Balz and Ronald Brownstein, *Storming the Gates: Protest Politics and the Republican Revival* (Boston: Little, Brown, 1996), 106–9.

41. Paul Starr, *The Social Transformation of American Medicine* (New York: Basic, 1984), 310–19.

42. John Witte, *The Politics and Development of the Federal Income Tax* (Madison: University of Wisconsin Press, 1985), 280.

43. Rosemary Stevens, *Welfare Medicine in America: The Case of Medicaid* (New York: Free Press, 1974), 131.

44. Joseph Califano, *The American Health-Care Revolution: Who Lives? Who Dies? Who Pays?* (New York: Random House, 1986), 4, 30–31.

45. Elizabeth Drew, *On the Edge: The Clinton Presidency* (New York: Simon and Schuster, 1994), 193.

46. Woodward, *Agenda*, 134.

47. Ibid., 190.

48. Balz and Brownstein, *Storming the Gates*, 105.

49. Drew, *On the Edge*, 287.

50. Stephen Engelberg and Katharine Seelye, "Gingrich: Man in Spotlight," *New York Times*, December 18, 1994, pp. 1, 20.

51. Newt Gingrich, Richard K. Armey, et al., *Contract with America*, ed. Ed Gillespie and Bob Schellhas (New York: Random House, 1994).

52. Dick Morris, *Behind the Oval Office* (Los Angeles: Renaissance Books, 1999), 389–417.

53. Hager and Pianin, *Mirage*, 244–50.

54. Ibid., 14–19.

55. Ibid., 27–29.

56. Ibid., 241–42.

57. Ibid., 255–58.

58. Ibid., 267–68.

59. Reich, *Locked in the Cabinet*, 295.

60. *Congressional Quarterly Almanac, 1996* 2–2.

61. W. Norton Grubb, *Learning to Work: The Case for Reintegrating Job Training and Education* (New York: Russell Sage Foundation, 1996).

62. Woodward, *Agenda*, 144.

63. Reich, *Locked in the Cabinet*, 150, 180–81.

64. David Ellwood, "Welfare Reform as I Knew It," *American Prospect*, no. 26 (May–June 1996): 27.

65. Steven Teles, *Whose Welfare? Aid to Families with Dependent Children and Elite Politics* (Lawrence: University Press of Kansas, 1996), 150–57.

66. *Congressional Quarterly Almanac, 1996*, 6–5.

67. Michael Meeropol, *Surrender: How the Clinton Administration Completed the Reagan Revolution* (Ann Arbor: University of Michigan Press, 1998), 236.

68. "From Social Security to the Environment, the Candidates' Positions," *New York Times*, November 5, 2000, p. 34.

14. CLINTON BOXES WITH REAGAN'S SHADOW

1. Richard Holbrooke, *To End a War* (New York: Modern Library, 1999), 24.

2. Elizabeth Drew, *On the Edge: The Clinton Presidency* (New York: Simon and Schuster, 1994), 147.

3. Holbrooke, *To End a War*, 173.

4. Ibid., 216.

5. Ibid., 261.

6. Paul Starobin, "Milosevic and Martyrdom," *National Journal*, April 3, 1999, pp. 873–79.

7. Elaine Sciolino and Ethan Bronner, "How a President, Distracted by Scandal, Entered Balkan War," *New York Times*, April 18, 1999, pp. 1, 12, 13.

8. Ibid., 12.

9. Ibid., 13.

10. William Kaufmann, *Decisions for Defense: Prospects for a New Order* (Washington, D.C.: Brookings Institution, 1991), and Lawrence Korb, "Our Overstuffed Military," *Foreign Affairs* 74 (November–December, 1995): 26–27.

11. Thomas Ricks, "Why the U.S. Army Is Ill-Equipped to Move into Kosovo Quickly," *Wall Street Journal*, April 16, 1999, pp. A1, A6.

12. Ibid., A13.

13. Ibid.

14. James Kitfield, "High-Tech Hegemony," *National Journal,* April 3, 1999, pp. 886–88.

15. Jimmy Carter, "Have We Forgotten the Path to Peace?" *New York Times,* May 27, 1999, p. A31.

16. Ibid.

17. Carter, "Have We Forgotten?"

18. Starobin, "Milosevic and Martrydom," 878–79.

19. Robert Scheer, "Cold War's End Leaves Danger of Nuclear War," *Los Angeles Times,* April 13, 1999, p. B7.

20. Thomas Friedman, "The Four Questions," *New York Times,* September 15, 1999, p. A31 .

21. Thomas Friedman, "Deadheads and Warheads," *New York Times*m February 16, 1999, p. A19.

22. Walter Pincus, "Kerrey: U.S. Should Cut Nuclear Arms Unilaterally," *Washington Post,* November 17, 1998, p. A13; and Walter Pincus, "Re-Read His Lips: Reduce Arms Now," *Washington Post,* October 11, 1998, pp. C1, C5.

23. Stansfield Turner, "Post–Cold War World Demands New Ways to Deal with Warheads," *Los Angeles Times,* January 11, 1999, p. B5.

24. *Congressional Quarterly Weekly,* May 16, 1998, pp. 1267–68.

25. *Congressional Quarterly Weekly,* July 11, 1998, p. 1892.

26. *Congressional Quarterly Weekly,* March 14, 1998, p. 655.

27. Guy Gugliotta, "Veto Is Making 'Pork Barrel' a Shell Game," *Washington Post,* October 18, 1997, pp. A1, A6.

28. Ibid., A6.

29. *Congressional Quarterly Weekly,* March 28, 1998, p. 810.

30. *Congressional Quarterly Weekly,* July 11, 1998, p. 1892.

31. George Will, "Like a Garbage Pail," *Washington Post,* October 25, 1998, p. C7.

32. Charles Lewis, *The Buying of the President 2000* (New York: Avon, 2000), 291.

33. Citizens for Tax Justice, *Hidden Entitlements* (Washington, D.C.: Citizens for Tax Justice, 1995), and Citizens for Tax Justice, *The Corporate Welfare Guidebook* (Washington, D.C.: Citizens for Tax Justice, 1995).

34. Aaron Zitner and Charles Sennott, "Business Breaks Defy Budget Ax," *Boston Globe,* August 24, 1997, p. 1.

35. Ibid.

36. Ibid.

37. Ibid.

38. Carl Cannon, "What We Did in China," *National Journal,* July 18, 1998, p. 167.

39. Caspar Weinberger, *The Next War* (Washington, D.C.: Regnery, 1996).

40. Jim Mann, "Fears of Chinese Spying Only Deepen U.S. Mistrust," *Los Angeles Times*, May 20, 1999, p. A16.

41. Warren Christopher, *In the Stream of History: Shaping Foreign Policy for a New Era* (Palo Alto: Stanford University Press, 1998), 152–64.

42. Mann, "Fears of Chinese Spying."

43. "Missiles and Chinese Fears," editorial, *Los Angeles Times*, March 23, 1999, p. B6, and Bob Drogin, "Defense Project Strains U.S.-China Ties," *Los Angeles Times*, March 22, 1999, pp. A1, A8.

44. Robert Scheer, "Our Secrets Are of No Use to Them," *Los Angeles Times*, May 11, 1999, p. B7.

45. Frank Gibney, "China Wants to Be a World Power," *Time*, June 7, 1999, p. 40.

46. Robert Pear, "Chief of Panel Seeks Increase in Medicare," *New York Times*, June 3, 1999, p. A16.

47. Ibid.

48. "A Mixed Budget Message," editorial, *Washington Post*, January 4, 1999, p. A18.

49. Andrew Taylor, "Clinton's Fancy Budget Work Upstages Skeptical GOP," *Congressional Quarterly Weekly*, February 7, 1998, p. 288.

50. Ibid.

51. Richard Stevenson, "After '97 Deal, New Showdown over the Budget," *New York Times*, July 21, 1998, p. A1.

52. George Hager and Helen Dewar, "GOP Scrambles as Clinton Vetoes $60 Billion Agriculture Bill," *Washington Post*, October 9, 1998, p. A4.

53. George Hager and Stephen Barr, "Budget Deal Is Reached," *Washington Post*, October 16, 1998, pp. A1, A16.

54. *Congressional Quarterly Almanac, 1998* (Washington, D.C.: Congressional Quarterly, 1999), 6–22.

55. Ibid., 8–14.

56. John Broder, "Clinton Offers His Budget, and the Battle Begins," *New York Times*, February 2, 1999, p. A16.

57. James Kitfield, "Defense," *National Journal*, February 6, 1999, p. 327.

58. Paul Starobin, "The Liberal Hawk Soars," *National Journal*, May 15, 1999, p. 1311.

59. Ibid., 1312.

60. David Baumann, "A Spending Bonanza, Thanks to Kosovo," *National Journal*, April 24, 1999, p. 1110.

61. Pat Towell, "Defense Bill Back on the Table," *Congressional Quarterly Weekly*, October 23, 1999, p. 2536.

62. David Baumann, "Black Ink Brawl," *National Journal*, February 6, 1999, p. 326.

63. Michael Weinstein, "No Comfort in New Solvency Figures," *New York Times*, April 1, 1999, p. A22.

64. Ibid.

65. Dan Balz and Ronald Brownstein, *Storming the Gates: Protest Politics and the Republican Revival* (Boston: Little, Brown, 1996), 59–84.

66. Molly Ivins, comments during C-SPAN interview, 1998.

67. George Stephanopoulos, *All Too Human* (Boston: Little, Brown, 1999), 328–41.

15. ON THE MAGNITUDE OF FAILED NATIONAL PRIORITIES

1. Data on discretionary and mandatory programs from 1962 through 2004 come from Office of Management and Budget, *Budget of the U.S. Government, FY 2000, Historical Tables* (Washington, D.C.: Government Printing Office, 1999), tables 8.6 and 8.7.

2. Costs of the Korean War, as well as associated costs for veterans' benefits, are provided by Robert Stevens, *Vain Hopes, Grim Realities: The Economic Consequences of the Vietnam War* (New York: New Viewpoints, 1976), 83.

3. Ibid.

4. Fred Kaplan, *Dubious Specter: A Skeptical Look at the Soviet Nuclear Threat* (Washington, D.C.: Institute for Policy Studies, 1980); Tom Gervasi, *Arsenal of Democracy II: American Military Power in the 1980s and the Origins of the New Cold War* (New York: Grove, 1981); and Richard Stubbing, *The Defense Game: An Insider Explores the Astonishing Realities of America's Defense Establishment* (New York: Harper and Row, 1986), 3–28.

5. Andy Pasztor, *When the Pentagon Was for Sale* (New York: Scribner, 1995), 57–58.

6. Data on military spending are found Office of Management and Budget, *Budget of the U.S. Government, FY 2000, Historical Tables*, table 3.1.

7. Military spending data are derived from Office of Management and Budget, *Budget of the U.S. Government, FY 2000, Historical Tables*, table 3.1.

8. David Stockman, *The Triumph of Politics: Why the Reagan Revolution Failed* (New York: Harper and Row, 1986), 283–84.

9. Stephen Schwartz, Introduction to Stephen Schwartz, ed., *Atomic Audit: The Costs and Consequences of U.S. Nuclear Weapons Since 1940* (Washington, D.C.: Brookings Institution, 1998), 27–30.

10. Steven Kosiak of the Center for Strategic and Budgetary Assessments, a think tank, kindly made portions of the database used in fig. 15.4 available to me. Various support and administrative functions are allocated to strategic forces, general purpose forces, and intelligence/communications in proportion to their relative size.

11. Schwartz, Introduction, 24.

12. Robert Norris, Steven Kosiak, and Stephen Schwartz, "Deploying the Bomb," in Schwartz, *Atomic Audit*, 166–67.

13. Schwartz, Introduction, 26.

14. Ibid., 23.

15. Ibid.

16. Norris, Kosiak, and Schwartz, "Deploying the Bomb," 167–68.

17. Ibid., 143–68.

18. For the best discussion of the Soviet disinclination to invade Western Europe, see Robert Jervis, *The Illogic of American Nuclear Strategy* (Ithaca: Cornell University Press, 1984).

19. For discussion of the tactical disagreements among experts regarding a Soviet invasion, see Stubbing, *Defense Game* 124–30.

20. Michael Gordon, "The Army's 'Air-Land Battle' Doctrine Worries, Upsets the Air Force," *National Journal*, June 18, 1979, 1274–77.

21. Stubbing, *Defense Game*, 129.

22. I estimate that costs for general purpose forces rose roughly $1.1 trillion during the Korean War, the Vietnam War, and the Reagan military buildup.

23. Kaufmann made his estimates in budget authority—monies Congress establishes as the pool from which appropriated funds can be drawn—so savings the United States could have realized had Congress followed his middle option are stated in budget authority rather than outlays (see Kaufmann, *Decisions for Defense* [Washington, D.C.: Brookings Institution, 1991], 74). (Because Kaufmann made his estimates only through 2002, I extend them to 2004 by increasing spending under his budget by the likely rate of inflation for the final two years.) For actual military budget authority for FYs 1992 through 2004, see Office of Management and Budget, *Budget of the U.S. Government, FY 2000, Historical Tables*, table 5.1.

24. To estimate expenditures for operations and maintenance and procurement for the years 1940 through 1961, which are not estimated in the *Historical Tables* put out by the Office of Management and Budget, I computed the average percentage of the narrow military budget spent on these two items from 1962 through 2004 and multiplied these averages by total narrow military spending from 1940 through 1961.

25. Stubbing, *Defense Game*.

26. A. Ernest Fitzgerald, *The High Priests of Waste* (New York: Norton, 1972), and Stubbing, *Defense Game*.

27. Gregory Hooks, *Forging the Military-Industrial Complex: World War II's Battle of the Potomac* (Urbana: University of Illinois, 1991), 148, and Fitzgerald, *High Priests of Waste*, 59–68. Seymour Melman cites a 1946 memorandum by General Eisenhower in which he cautions, "The possibility of utilizing some of our

industrial and technological resources as organic parts of our military structure should be carefully examined." See Melman, *Pentagon Capitalism: the Political Economy of War* (New York: McGraw-Hill, 1970), 233.

28. Fitzgerald, *High Priests of Waste*, 3–20.

29. Ibid., 21–58.

30. Stubbing, *Defense Game*, 228–31.

31. Ibid., 191–218; Fitzgerald, *High Priests of Waste*, 59–108.

32. Pasztor, *When the Pentagon Was for Sale*, 151–55.

33. Fitzgerald, *High Priests of Waste*, 109–72, 59–93.

34. These figures exclude the costs for benefits for veterans of the Vietnam and Korean wars.

35. Stubbing, *Defense Game*, 221–31.

36. U.S. Department of Defense, *Achieving an Innovative Support Structure for Twenty-first-Century Military Superiority: Report of the Defense Science Board 1996 Summer Study* (Washington, D.C.: U.S. Government Printing Office, November 1996), ES-2.

37. Stubbing, *Defense Game*, 242.

38. See, for example, Paul Kennedy, *The Rise and Fall of Great Powers: Economic Change and Military Conflict from 1500 to 2000* (New York: Random House, 1987). He incorrectly predicts the economic demise of both the Soviet Union and the United States because of their high military spending.

39. Fitzgerald, *High Priests of Waste*, 210, quotes Rowan's comments as they appeared in the *Washington Star*, October 2, 1968.

40. The data on interest payments appear in table 3.1, pp. 42–49, of OMB, *Budget of the U.S. Government, FY 2000, Historical Tables.*

41. Data on deficits are found in OMB, *Budget of the U.S. Government, FY 2000, Historical Tables*, table 1.3, pp. 23–24. Data on interest payments and interest payments as a percentage of GDP come from table 3.1, pp. 42–49, and table 6.1, pp. 103–9.

42. Data on the magnitude of corporate tax expenditures for fiscal years 1975 and 1982 appear in John Witte, *The Politics and Development of the Federal Income Tax* (Madison: University of Wisconsin Press, 1985), 276–82; for fiscal years 1998 through 1992, see U.S. Congress, Joint Committee on Taxation, *Estimates of Federal Tax Expenditures for FYs 1988 through 1992*, 103d Cong., 1st sess., 1993, and for FYs 1998 through 2004 from Office of Management and Budget, *Budget of the U.S. Government, FY 2000, Analytic Perspectives* (Washington, D.C.: Government Printing Office, 1999), 110–13. (I approximated data for intervening years to reach cumulative totals.)

43. "Eliminating 'Corporate Welfare' Tax Breaks," *Public Citizen*, November 14, 1996, pp. 3–4.

44. See Stephen Moore and Dean Stansel, "How Corporate Welfare Won:

Clinton and Congress Retreat from Cutting Business Subsidies," *Policy Analysis*, no. 254 (May 15, 1996): 1–25.

45. U.S. Congressional Budget Office, *Reducing the Deficit: Spending and Revenue Options, A Report to the Senate and House Committees on the Budget* (Washington, D.C.: Government Printing Office, March 1997), 392–94.

46. Ibid., 397–99.

47. Ibid., 395–96.

48. Ibid., 402–5.

49. Lawrence Haas, "Full Disclosure," *National Journal,* September 22, 1990, pp. 2252–54.

50. Arjun Makhijani, Stephen Schwartz, and William Weida, "Nuclear Waste Management and Environmental Remediation," in Schwartz, *Atomic Audit,* 353–56.

51. Iris Lav, associate director of the Center on Budget and Policy Priorities, interview by author, 1998, Washington, D.C.

52. David Cay Johnston, "Senate Committee Staff Proposes Limits on Corporate Tax Shelters," *New York Times,* May 25, 2000, pp. C1, C8.

53. Data on individuals' tax expenditures for fiscal years 1975 and 1982 come from Witte, *Politics and Development of the Federal Income Tax,* pp. 272–82; for fiscal years 1988 through 1992, see U.S. Congress, Joint Committee on Taxation, *Estimates of Federal Tax Expenditures for FYs 1988 Through 1992,* 103d Cong., 1st sess., 1993; and for fiscal years 1998 through 2004, see Office of Management and Budget, *Budget of the U.S. Government, FY 2000, Analytic Perspectives.* I approximated data for 1976–1981, 1983–1984, and 1993–1997 to reach cumulative totals.

54. Witte, *Politics and Development,* 299–310.

55. Ibid., 276–82.

56. For data on home mortgage expenditures, see Witte, *Politics and Development,* 276–82; U.S. Congress, Joint Committee on Taxation, *Estimates of Federal Tax Expenditures;* and OMB, *Budget of the U.S. Government, FY 2000, Analytic Perspectives,* 110–13.

57. U.S. Congress, Joint Committee on Taxation, *Estimates of Federal Tax Expenditures,* table 3.

58. U.S. Congressional Budget Office, *Reducing the Deficit,* 338–49.

59. Ibid., 357–58.

60. Ibid., 353, 370, 372.

61. Stockman, *Triumph of Politics,* 408.

62. Bruce Jansson, *The Reluctant Welfare State* (Pacific Grove, Calif.: Brooks/Cole, 1997), 38.

COLLECTIONS, ORAL HISTORIES, INTERVIEWS

Presidential Libraries

Dwight D. Eisenhower Library, Abilene, Kansas
Lyndon B. Johnson Library, Austin, Texas
Nixon Presidential Materials, National Archives at College Park, Md.
Franklin D. Roosevelt Library, Hyde Park, N.Y.
Harry S. Truman Library, Independence, Mo.

Collections

Roy Blough Papers, Truman Library
Arthur Burns Papers, Eisenhower Library
Joseph Califano Papers, Johnson Library
John Clark Papers, Truman Library
Wilbur Cohen Papers, Johnson Library
Gerhard Colm Papers, Truman Library
Matthew Connelly Papers, Truman Library
John Dodge Papers, Eisenhower Library

L. Laszlo Ecker-Racz Papers, Truman Library
Dwight Eisenhower Papers, Eisenhower Library
Arthur Flemming Papers, Eisenhower Library
Marion Folsom Papers, Eisenhower Library
Bryce Harlow Papers, Eisenhower Library
Gabriel Hauge Papers, Eisenhower Library
Lyndon Johnson Papers, Johnson Library
Leon Keyserling Papers, Truman Library
Richard Neustadt Papers, Truman Library
Matthew Nimetz Papers, Johnson Library
Richard Nixon Papers, Nixon Presidential Materials
Edwin Nourse Papers, Truman Library
Franklin Roosevelt Papers, Roosevelt Library
Harold Smith Papers, Roosevelt and Truman Libraries
John Sullivan Papers, Truman Library
Harry Truman Papers, Truman Library
James Webb Papers, Truman Library

Oral Histories

Gardner Ackley, Johnson Library
Joseph Barr, Johnson Library
David Bell, Truman Library
Percival Brundage, Eisenhower Library
Randolph Burgess, Eisenhower Library
William Cannon, Johnson Library
Douglass Cater, Johnson Library
Clark Clifford, Truman Library
Wilbur Cohen, Johnson Library
John Ehrlichman, Nixon Presidential Materials
Joseph Feeny, Truman Library
Arthur Flemming, Eisenhower Library
Kermit Gordon, Johnson Library
David Hansen, Truman Library
Walter Heller, Johnson Library
Roger Jones, Eisenhower Library
Leon Keyserling, Truman Library and Johnson Library

Charles Murphy, Richard Neustadt, David Stowe, and
  James Webb (joint oral history), Eisenhower Library
Arthur Okun, Johnson Library
Frank Pace, Truman Library
Joseph Pechman, Johnson Library
Charles Schultze, Johnson Library
David Stowe, Truman Library
Charles Thomas, Eisenhower Library

Interviews by Author (1998)

Robert Greenstein, Washington, D.C.
Robert McNamara, Washington, D.C.
Robert Jervis, New York City
Steven Kosiak, Washington, D.C.
Lawrence Korb, New York City
Iris Lav, Washington, D.C.
Seymour Melman, New York City
Martha Phillips, Washington, D.C.
Wendall Primus, Washington, D.C.
Robert Reischauer, Washington, D.C.
Isabel Sawhill, Washington, D.C.
Paul Warnke, Washington, D.C.

BIBLIOGRAPHY

I found it invaluable in this research to make extensive use of the *New York Times* where I have read widely under the headings of "budget," "military," "social spending," and "presidential" from 1933 to 1996. (Because biographies of presidents and most overviews of presidencies do not emphasize budget matters, I found these articles to be particularly useful.) Although news accounts must be read with caution, the articles are especially useful for their insights into the perspectives of protagonists in budget disputes in the executive branch, Congress, and special interest groups (such as the U.S. Chamber of Congress and labor groups).

To obtain liberal perspectives, I photocopied many articles from the *Nation* and from the *New Republic* from 1932 to 1969. These articles are invaluable because of their important insights about liberal perspectives on national priorities during each presidency.

I also made extensive use of *Congressional Quarterly Weekly, Fortune, U.S. News and World Report,* the *Los Angeles Times, National Journal,* and *Washington Post.* Specific articles from all these sources are cited throughout the notes but are not listed again here.

Aaron, Henry J. *Politics and the Professors: The Great Society in Perspective.* Washington, D.C.: Brookings Institution, 1978.

Acheson, Dean. *Present at the Creation: My Years in the State Department.* New York: Norton, 1969.

Adams, Henry. *Harry Hopkins: A Biography.* New York: Putnam, 1977.

Allard, C. Kenneth. *Command, Control, and the Common Defense.* New Haven: Yale University Press, 1990.

Ambrose, Stephen. *Eisenhower: Soldier, General of the Army, President-Elect, 1890–1952.* Vol. 1. New York: Simon and Schuster, 1983.

——. *Eisenhower: The President.* Vol. 2. New York: Simon and Schuster, 1984.

——. *Nixon.* 3 vols. New York: Simon and Schuster, 1987–1991.

Anderson, David L. "No More Koreas." In Krieg, *Dwight D. Eisenhower.*

Anderson, Martin. "The Objectives of the Reagan Administration's Social Welfare Policy." In Bawden, *The Social Contract Revisited.*

——. *Revolution: The Reagan Legacy.* Palo Alto, Calif.: Hoover Institution Press, 1988.

——. *Welfare: The Political Economy of Welfare Reform in the United States.* Palo Alto, Calif.: Hoover Institution Press, 1978.

Appleton, Sheldon. "Public Perceptions of Truman." In Levantrosser, *Harry S. Truman.*

Arnold, R. Douglas. *The Logic of Congressional Action.* New Haven: Yale University Press, 1990.

Art, Arthur J. *The TFX Decision: McNamara and the Military.* Boston: Little, Brown, 1968.

Arum, Richard. "Do Private Schools Force Public Schools to Compete?" *American Sociological Review* 61 (1996): 29–46.

Asbell, Bernard. *The Senate Nobody Knows.* New York: Doubleday, 1978.

Axinn, June and Michael Stern. *Dependency and Poverty.* Lexington, Mass.: Lexington Books, 1988.

Bailey, Stephen. *Congress Makes a Law: The Story Behind the Full Employment Act of 1946.* New York: Columbia University Press, 1950.

Balz, Dan and Ronald Brownstein. *Storming the Gates: Protest Politics and the Republican Revival.* Boston: Little, Brown, 1996.

Barlett, Donald and James Steele. *America: What Went Wrong?* Kansas City, Mo.: Andrews and McMeel, 1992.

Barrett, Laurence I. *Gambling with History: Reagan in the White House.* New York: Penguin, 1983.

Barry, John. *The Ambition and the Power.* New York: Viking, 1989.

Bawden, D. Lee, ed. *The Social Contract Revisited: Aims and Outcomes of President Reagan's Social Welfare Policy.* Washington, D.C.: Urban Institute, 1984.

Beito, David. *Taxpayers in Revolt*. Chapel Hill: University of North Carolina Press, 1989.

Berkowitz, Edward. *Mr. Social Security: The Life of Wilbur J. Cohen*. Lawrence: University of Kansas Press, 1995.

Berman, Larry. *Lyndon Johnson's War: The Road to Stalemate in Vietnam*. New York: Norton, 1989.

Berman, William C. *William Fulbright and the Vietnam War: The Dissent of a Political Realist*. Kent, Ohio: Kent State University Press, 1988.

Bernstein, Barton J. "America in War and Peace: The Test of Liberalism." In Hamby, *Harry S. Truman and the Fair Deal*.

——. "Commentary." In Kirkendall, *The Truman Period as a Research Field*.

——. "The Truman Administration and the Korean War." In Lacey, *The Truman Presidency*.

Bernstein, Barton J., ed. *Politics and Policies of the Truman Administration*. Chicago: Quadrangle, 1970.

Bernstein, Irving. *Guns or Butter: The Presidency of Lyndon Johnson*. New York: Oxford University Press, 1996.

Beschloss, Michael and Strobe Talbott. *At the Highest Levels: The Inside Story of the End of the Cold War*. Boston: Little, Brown, 1993.

Bill, James. *George Ball: Behind the Scenes in U.S. Foreign Policy* (New Haven: Yale University Press, 1997).

Bird, Richard M. "Tax Structure and the Growth of Government." In Eden, *Retrospectives on Public Finance*.

Birnbaum, Jeffrey H. and Alan S. Murray. *Showdown at Gucci Gulch: Lawmakers, Lobbyists, and the Unlikely Triumph of Tax Reform*. New York: Vintage, 1987.

Bixby, Ann Kallman. "Public Social Welfare Expenditures, Fiscal Years 1965–1987." *Social Security Bulletin* 53, no. 2 (February 1990): 10–16.

Blair, Bruce, John Pike, and Stephen Schwartz. "Targeting and Controlling the Bomb." In Schwartz, *Atomic Audit*.

Blechman, Barry M., Edward M. Gramlich, and Robert W. Hartman. *Setting National Priorities: The 1975 Budget*. Washington, D.C.: Brookings Institution, 1974.

Blough, Roy. *The Federal Taxing Process*. New York: Prentice Hall, 1952.

Blum, John Morton. *From the Morgenthau Diaries*. Boston: Houghton Mifflin, 1959.

——. *Roosevelt and Morgenthau*. Boston: Houghton Mifflin, 1970.

——. *United Against: American Culture and Society During World War II*. Colorado Springs, Colo.: U.S. Air Force Academy, 1983.

——. *V Was for Victory: Politics and American Culture During World War II*. New York: Harcourt Brace Jovanovich, 1976.

——. *Years of Urgency, 1938–1941*. Boston: Houghton Mifflin, 1965.

Boll, Michael M. *National Security Planning: Roosevelt Through Reagan.* Lexington: University of Kentucky Press, 1988.

Bornet, Vaughn. *The Presidency of Lyndon B. Johnson.* Lawrence: University of Kansas, 1983.

Boylan, James. "Reconversion in Politics: The New Deal Coalition in the Election of the Eightieth Congress." Ph.D. diss. Columbia University, 1971.

Brandon, Henry. *Special Relationships: A Foreign Correspondent's Memoirs from Roosevelt to Reagan.* New York: Atheneum, 1988.

Brands, H. W. *Cold Warriors: Eisenhower's Generation and American Foreign Policy.* New York: Columbia University Press, 1988.

———. *The Devil We Knew.* New York: Oxford University Press, 1993.

Brauer, Carl. *John F. Kennedy and the Second Reconstruction.* New York: Columbia University Press, 1967.

Bremer, William. *Depression Winters: New York Social Workers and the New Deal.* Philadelphia: Temple University Press, 1984.

Brigham, Robert. "Vietnam at the Center: Patterns of Diplomacy and Resistance." In Gardner and Gittinger, *Vietnam at the Center.*

Brinkley, Alan. "The New Deal and the Idea of the State." In Fraser and Gerstle, *Rise and Fall of the New Deal Order.*

———. *Voices of Protest: Huey Long, Father Coughlin, and the Great Depression.* New York: Random House, 1982.

Broad, William J. *Teller's War: The Top-Secret Story Behind the Star Wars Deception.* New York: Simon and Schuster, 1992.

Buchanan, James and Marilyn Flower. *The Public Finances: An Introductory Textbook.* 6th ed. Homewood, Ill.: Irwin, 1987.

Bundy, McGeorge. *Danger and Survival: Choices About the Bomb in the First Years.* New York: Random House, 1988.

Burk, Robert F. "Dwight D. Eisenhower and Civil Rights Conservatism." In Krieg, *Dwight D. Eisenhower.*

Burke, Vincent J. and Vee Burke. *Nixon's Good Deed: Welfare Reform.* New York: Columbia University Press, 1974.

Burns, James McGregor. *The Lion and the Fox.* New York: Harcourt, Brace, 1956.

Burt, Martha and Karen Pittman. *Testing the Social Safety Net: The Impact of Changes in Support Programs During the Reagan Administration.* Washington, D.C.: Urban Institute, 1985.

Bush, George and Brent Scowcroft. *A World Transformed.* New York: Knopf, 1998.

Califano, Joseph. *The American Health-Care Revolution: Who Lives? Who Dies? Who Pays?* New York: Random House, 1986.

———. *The Triumph and Tragedy of Lyndon Johnson.* New York: Simon and Schuster, 1991.

Callahan, David. *Dangerous Capabilities: Paul Nitze and the Cold War*. New York: HarperCollins, 1990.

Calleo, David P. *Beyond American Hegemony: The Future of the Western Alliance*. New York: Basic, 1987.

———. "SDI, Europe, and the American Strategic Dilemma." In Robert Tucker, George Liska, Robert Osgood, and David Calleo, *SDI and U.S. Foreign Policy*. Boulder, Colo.: Westview, 1987.

Campbell, Greg. *The Road to Kosovo: A Balkan Diary*. Boulder, Colo.: Westview, 1999.

Cannon, Lou. *President Reagan: The Role of a Lifetime*. New York: Simon and Schuster, 1991.

———. *Reagan*. New York: Putnam, 1982.

Caro, Robert. *The Path to Power*. Vol. 1 of *The Years of Lyndon Johnson*. New York: Knopf, 1982.

———. *Means of Ascent*. Vol. 2 of *The Years of Lyndon Johnson*. New York: Knopf, 1990.

Carron, Andrew. *The Plight of Thrift Institutions*. Washington, D.C.: Brookings Institution, 1982.

Catton, Bruce. *The War Lords of Washington*. New York: Harcourt Brace, 1948.

Chafe, William H. "Postwar American Society." In Lacey, *The Truman Presidency*.

Chandler, Lester. *Inflation in the United States, 1940–1948*. New York: Harper, 1951.

Chapman, Richard Norman. "Contours of Public Policy." Ph.D. diss., Yale University, 1976.

Chase, Stuart. *Goals for America: A Budget of Our Needs and Resources*. New York: Twentieth Century Fund, 1942.

———. *The Road We Are Traveling, 1914–1942*. New York: Twentieth Century Fund, 1942.

Christopher, Warren. *In the Stream of History: Shaping Foreign Policy for a New Era*. Palo Alto: Stanford University Press, 1998.

Chubb, John E. and Paul E. Peterson, eds. *The New Direction in American Politics*. Washington, D.C.: Brookings Institution, 1985.

Citizens for Tax Justice. *The Corporate Welfare Guidebook*. Washington, D.C.: Citizens for Tax Justice, 1995.

———. *Hidden Entitlements*. Washington, D.C.: Citizens for Tax Justice, 1995.

Clifford, Clark. "Serving the President: The Truman Years," part 1. *New Yorker*, March 25, 1991, pp. 40–68.

———. "Serving the President: The Truman Years," part 2. *New Yorker*, April 1, 1991, pp. 36–74.

———. "Serving the President: The Vietnam Years," part 3. *New Yorker*, May 20, 1991, pp. 59–68.

———. *Counsel to the President*. New York: Random House, 1991.

Clive, Alan. *State of War: Michigan in World War II.* Ann Arbor: University of Michigan Press, 1979.

Cochrane, James L. "The Johnson Administration: Moral Suasion Goes to War." In Craufurd Goodwin, ed., *Exhortation and Controls: The Search for a Wage-Price Policy, 1945–1971.* Washington, D.C.: Brookings Institution, 1975.

Cohen, Stephen. *Rethinking the Soviet Experience.* New York: Oxford University Press, 1985.

Cole, Wayne. *Roosevelt and the Isolationists, 1932–1945.* Lincoln: University of Nebraska Press, 1983.

Coleman, James. *Equality of Educational Opportunity.* Washington, D.C.: U.S. Government Printing Office, 1966.

Colm, Gerhard. *Essays in Public Finance and Fiscal Policy.* New York: Oxford University Press, 1955.

Committee for Economic Development. *An Emergency Tax Program for 1951.* New York: March 1951.

———. *A Postwar Federal Tax Plan for High Employment.* New York: 1944.

———. *Taxes and the Budget: A Program for Prosperity in a Free Economy.* New York: November 1947.

Condit, Doris M. *The Test of War, 1950–1953.* Vol. 2 of *History of the Secretary of Defense.* Washington, D.C.: U.S. Government Printing Office, 1988.

Congressional Quarterly Almanac, vols. for 1969, 1989, 1993, 1996, 1998. Washington, D.C.: Congressional Quarterly.

Conkin, Paul K. *Big Daddy from the Pedernales.* Boston: Twayne, 1986.

Conlan, Timothy J. "The Politics of Federal Block Grants from Nixon to Reagan." *Political Science Quarterly* 99, no. 2 (summer 1984): 247–70.

Cooling, Benjamin F. "The Military-Industrial Complex: Update for an Old American Issue." In Peter Karsten, ed., *The Military in America.* New York: Free Press, 1980.

Cooling, Benjamin F., ed. *War, Business, and American Society.* Port Washington, N.Y.: Kennikat, 1977.

Coulter, John. *Postwar Fiscal Problems and Policies.* New York: Committee of the Americans, 1945.

Cray, Ed. *General of the Army: George C. Marshall.* New York: Norton, 1990.

Crockett, Richard. *The Fifty Years' War.* London: Routledge, 1995.

Crowe, William J. *The Line of Fire.* New York: Simon and Schuster, 1993.

Crum, William. *From Fiscal Planning for Total War.* New York: National Bureau of Economic Research, 1942.

Dallek, Robert. *Flawed Giant: Lyndon Johnson and His Times.* New York: Oxford University Press, 1998.

———. *Franklin D. Roosevelt and American Foreign Policy, 1932–1945.* New York: Oxford University Press, 1979.

——. *Lone Star Rising: Lyndon Johnson and His Times, 1908–1960.* New York: Oxford University Press, 1991.

Darman, Richard. *Who's in Control? Polar Politics and the Sensible Center.* New York: Simon and Schuster, 1996.

David, Sheri I. "Eisenhower and the American Medical Association." In Krieg, *Dwight D. Eisenhower.*

Davies, Richard O. *Age of Asphalt: The Automobile, the Freeway, and the Condition of Metropolitan America.* Philadelphia: Lippincott, 1975.

Davis, Karen and Cathy Schoen. *Health and the War on Poverty.* Washington, D.C.: Brookings Institution, 1978.

Day, Kathleen. *S&L Hell.* New York: Norton, 1993.

De Marchi, Neil. "The First Nixon Administration: Prelude to Controls." In Craufurd Goodwin, ed., *Exhortation and Controls: The Search for a Wage-Price Policy, 1945–1971.* Washington, D.C.: Brookings Institution, 1975.

Derthick, Martha. *Policy Making for Social Security.* Washington, D.C.: Brookings Institution, 1979.

——. *Uncontrollable Spending for Social Service Grants.* Washington, D.C.: Brookings Institution, 1975.

Devine, Robert. *Illusion of Neutrality.* Chicago: University of Chicago Press, 1962.

Devine, Robert, ed. *Vietnam, the Environment, and Science.* Vol. 2 of *The Johnson Years.* Lawrence: University Press of Kansas, 1987.

Dobbs, Michael. *Madeleine Albright: A Twentieth-Century Odyssey.* New York: Holt, 1999.

Donovan, Robert J. *Conflict and Crisis: The Presidency of Harry S. Truman, 1945–1948.* New York: Norton, 1977.

——. *Tumultuous Years: The Presidency of Harry S. Truman, 1949–1953.* New York: Norton, 1982.

Dorwart, Jeffery. *Eberstadt and Forrestal: A National Security Partnership: 1909–1949.* College Station: Texas A&M University Press, 1991.

Douglas, Paul. *Economy in the National Government.* Chicago: University of Chicago Press, 1952.

——. *In the Fullness of Time: The Memoirs of Paul H. Douglas.* New York: Harcourt Brace Jovanovich, 1971.

Drew, Elizabeth. *On the Edge: The Clinton Presidency.* New York: Simon and Schuster, 1994.

Drukman, Mason. *Wayne Morse: A Political Biography.* Portland: Oregon Historical Society, 1997.

Duffy, Michael and Dan Goodgame. *Marching in Place.* New York: Simon and Schuster, 1992.

Dugger, Ronnie. *On Reagan: The Man and His Presidency.* New York: McGraw Hill, 1983.

——. *The Politician: The Life and Times of Lyndon Johnson—The Drive for Power from the Frontier to the Master of the Senate.* New York: Norton, 1982.

Eccles, Marriner. *Beckoning Frontiers: Public and Personal Recollections.* New York: Knopf, 1951.

Eden, Lorraine, ed. *Retrospectives on Public Finance.* Durham: Duke University Press, 1991.

Eden, Lynn Rachele. "The Diplomacy of Force: Interests, the State, and the Making of American Military Policy in 1948." Ph.D. diss, University of Michigan, Ann Arbor, 1985.

Edsall, Thomas. *Chain Reaction: The Impact of Race, Rights, and Taxes on American Politics.* New York: Norton, 1991.

——. *The New Politics of Inequality.* New York: Norton, 1984.

Ehrlichman, John D. *Witness to Power: The Nixon Years.* New York: Simon and Schuster, 1982.

Eiler, Keith, ed. *Wedemeyer on War and Peace.* Palo Alto, Calif.: Hoover Institution Press, 1987.

"Eliminating 'Corporate Welfare' Tax Breaks," *Public Citizen,* November 14, 1996, pp. 1–3.

Ellwood, David "Welfare Reform as I Knew It." *American Prospect,* no. 26 (May–June 1996): 22–29.

Enthoven, Alain C. *How Much Is Enough? Shaping the Defense Program, 1961–1969.* New York: Harper and Row, 1971.

Evangelista, Matthew. *Innovation and the Arms Race.* Ithaca: Cornell University Press, 1988.

Evans, Rowland and Robert Novak. *The Reagan Revolution.* New York: Dutton, 1981.

Fallows, James. *National Defense.* New York: Random House, 1981.

Fanton, Jonathan. "Robert A. Lovett: The War Years." Ph.D. diss, Yale University, 1978.

Fehrenback, T. R. *FDR's Undeclared War, 1939–1941.* New York: David McKay, 1967.

Fenno, Richard F. Jr. *The Power of the Purse.* Boston: Little, Brown, 1966.

Ferguson, Thomas. *Right Turn: The Decline of the Democrats and the Future of American Politics.* New York: Hill and Wang, 1986.

Ferrell, Robert H. *Eisenhower's Diaries.* New York: Norton, 1981.

——. *Harry S. Truman: A Life.* Columbia, Mo., University of Missouri, 1994.

Fite, Gilbert. *Richard Russell.* Chapel Hill: University of North Carolina Press, 1991.

Fitzgerald, A. Ernest. *The High Priests of Waste.* New York: Norton, 1972.

Fraser, Steve and Gary Gerstle. *The Rise and Fall of the New Deal Order, 1930–1980.* Princeton: Princeton University Press, 1989.

Freedman, Lawrence and Efraim Karsh. *The Gulf Conflict, 1990–1991.* Princeton: Princeton University Press, 1993.

Freidel, Frank. *Franklin D. Roosevelt: A Rendezvous with Destiny.* Boston: Little, Brown, 1990.

Friedberg, Aaron. "The Political Economy of American Strategy." *World Politics* 41, no. 1 (October 1988): 381–406.

Friedman, Thomas. *Lexus and the Olive Tree: Understanding Globalization.* New York: Farrar, Straus, Giroux, 1999.

Friedrich, Otto. "Freed from Greed?" *Time,* January 1, 1990, pp. 76–78.

Gaddis, John Lewis. "The Insecurities of Victory: The U.S. and the Perception of the Soviet Threat After World War II." In Lacey, *The Truman Presidency.*

———. *Strategies of Containment: A Critical Appraisal of Postwar American National Security Policy.* New York: Oxford University Press, 1982.

———. *We Now Know: Rethinking Cold War History.* New York: Oxford University Press, 1997.

Gaiduck, Ilya. "Containing the Warriors: Soviet Policy Toward the Indochina Conflict, 1960–1965." In Gardner and Gittinger, *Vietnam at the Center.*

Galbraith, John Kenneth. *Economics in Perspective: A Critical History.* Boston: Houghton Mifflin, 1987.

Gallup, George. *The Gallup Poll: Public Opinion, 1935–1971.* New York: Random House, 1972.

Gardner, Lloyd. "Freedom's Demands: Lyndon Johnson and the Costs of the Vietnam War." Paper presented at the America, Vietnam, and the War: Policy, Culture, Consequences Conference, Miami University, Oxford, Ohio, March 2–3, 1990, and filed in the Vertical File of Papers, Theses, and Dissertations, Lyndon B. Johnson Library, Austin, Texas.

———. "Harry Hopkins with Hand Grenades? McGeorge Bundy in the Kennedy and Johnson Years." Paper presented at Vietnam Symposium, Columbia University, New York, November 16, 1990, and filed in the Vertical File of Papers, Theses, and Dissertations, Lyndon B. Johnson Library, Austin, Texas.

———. "Isolation and Appeasement: An American View of Taylor's Origins of World War II." In Martel, *The Origins of the Second World War Reconsidered.*

Gardner, Lloyd and Ted Gittinger, eds. *International Perspectives on Vietnam.* College Station: Texas A&M University Press, 2000.

Gates, Robert. *From the Shadows.* New York: Simon and Schuster, 1996.

Geitsch, Darrell. "The Strategic Air Offensive and the Mutation of American Values, 1937–1945." In Peter Karsten, ed., *The Military in America.* New York: Free Press, 1980.

Gertoff, Raymond. *Assessing the Adversary.* Washington, D.C.: Brookings Institution, 1991.

Gervasi, Tom. *Arsenal of Democracy II: American Military Power in the 1980s and the Origins of the New Cold War.* New York: Grove, 1981.

——. *The Myth of Soviet Military Supremacy.* New York: Harper and Row, 1986.

——. *Soviet Military Power.* New York: Vintage, 1987.

Gibbons, William Conrad. "Lyndon Johnson, Vietnam, and the American Home Front." Paper presented at the Military History Symposium, Colorado Springs, Colorado, October 18, 1990, and filed in the Vertical File of Papers, Theses, and Dissertations, Lyndon B. Johnson Library, Austin, Texas.

——. *The U.S. Government and the Vietnam War: Executive and Legislative Roles and Relationships.* Part 2: *1961–1964.* Princeton: Princeton University Press, 1986.

——. *The U.S. Government and the Vietnam War: Executive and Legislative Roles and Relationships.* Part 3: *January–July 1965.* Princeton: Princeton University Press, 1990.

Gibney, Frank. "China Wants to Be a World Power." *Time,* June 7, 1999, p. 40.

Gingrich, Newt, Richard K. Armey, et al. *Contract with America.* Ed. Ed Gillespie and Bob Schellhas. New York: Random House, 1994.

Goldman, Peter and Tony Fuller. *The Quest for the Presidency, 1984.* New York: Bantam, 1985.

Goodchild, Peter. *J. Robert Oppenheimer.* New York: Fromm International, 1985.

Goodwin, Craufurd D. and R. Stanley Herren. "The Truman Administration: Problems and Policies Unfold." In Craufurd Goodwin, ed., *Exhortation and Controls: The Search for a Wage- Price Policy, 1945–1971.* Washington, D.C.: Brookings Institution, 1975.

Goodwin, Richard. *Remembering America: A Voice from the Sixties.* Boston: Little, Brown, 1988.

Gorbachev, Mikhail. *Memoirs.* New York: Doubleday, 1996.

Gordon, H. Scott. "The Eisenhower Administration: The Doctrine of Shared Responsibility." In Craufurd Goodwin, ed., *Exhortation and Controls: the Search for a Wage-Price Policy, 1945–1971.* Washington, D.C.: Brookings Institutions, 1975.

Gordon, Michael and Bernard Trainer. *The Generals' War.* Boston: Little, Brown, 1995.

Gosnell, Harold F. *Truman's Crises: A Political Biography of Harry S. Truman.* Westport, Conn.: Greenwood, 1980.

Graebner, Norman, ed. *National Security: Its Theory and Practice, 1945–1960.* New York: Oxford University Press, 1986.

Graham, Hugh Davis. *The Civil Rights Era: Origins and Development of National Policy, 1960–1972.* New York: Oxford University Press, 1990.

Green, John. *The Limits of Power: The Nixon and Ford Administrations.* Bloomington: University of Indiana Press, 1992.

Greenstein, Fred. *The Hidden-Hand Presidency: Eisenhower as Leader.* New York: Basic, 1982.

Greenstein, Robert and Paul Leonard. *An Analysis of the Budget Summit Agreement.* Washington, D.C.: Center on Budget and Policy Priorities, 1990.

———. *The Bush Administration Budget: Rhetoric and Reality.* Washington, D.C.: Center on Budget and Policy Priorities, 1990.

———. *Unchanged Priorities: The Fiscal Year 1992 Budget.* Washington, D.C.: Center on Budget and Policy Priorities, 1991.

———. *Who Will Bear the Pain? The Budget-Cutting Plans Take Shape.* Washington, D.C.: Center on Budget and Policy Priorities, 1990.

Greider, William. "The Education of David Stockman." *Atlantic Monthly,* December 1981, pp. 27–54.

Griffith, Robert. "Forging America's Postwar Order." In Lacey, *The Truman Presidency.*

Groves, Harold. *Postwar Taxation and Economic Progress.* New York: McGraw-Hill, 1946.

Grubb, W. Norton. *Learning to Work: The Case for Reintegrating Job Training and Education.* New York: Russell Sage Foundation, 1996.

Hackworth, David. *Hazardous Duty.* New York: Morrow, 1996.

Hadley, Arthur. *The Straw Hat: Triumph and Failure, America's Armed Forces.* New York: Random House, 1986.

Haffa, Robert P. *The Half War: Planning U.S. Rapid Deployment Forces to Meet a Limited Contingency, 1960–1983.* Boulder, Colo.: Westview, 1984.

Hager, George and Eric Pianin. *Mirage: Why Neither Democrats Nor Republicans Can Balance the Budget.* New York: Random House, 1997.

Haig, Alexander. *Caveat: Realism, Reagan, and Foreign Policy.* New York: Macmillan, 1984.

Halberstam, David. *The Best and the Brightest.* New York: Random House, 1972.

———. *The Fifties.* New York: Villard, 1993.

Hall, Brian. *The Impossible Country: A Journey Through the Last Days of Yugoslavia.* New York: Penguin, 1995.

Hamby, Alonzo. *Beyond the New Deal: Harry S. Truman and American Liberalism.* New York: Columbia University Press, 1973.

———. "The Clash of Perspectives and the Need for a New Synthesis." In Kirkendall, *Truman Period as a Research Field.*

———. "The Mind and Character of Harry S. Truman." In Lacey, *The Truman Presidency.*

Hamby, Alonzo, ed. *Harry S. Truman and the Fair Deal.* Lexington, Mass.: Heath, 1974.

Hamill, Pete. "The Revolt of the White Lower-Middle Class." In Louise Howe, ed., *The White Majority: Between Poverty and Affluence.* New York: Random House, 1970.

Hammond, Paul Y. "NSC-68: Prologue to Rearmament." In Schilling, Hammond, and Snyder, *Strategy, Politics, and Defense Budgets.*

——. *Organizing for Defense: The American Military Establishment in the Twentieth Century.* Princeton: Princeton University Press, 1961.

Hampson, Fen. *Unguided Missiles: How America Buys Its Weapons.* New York: Norton, 1989.

Hansen, Alvin. "The Postwar Economy." In Harris, *Postwar Economic Problems.*

Hardeman, D. B. *Rayburn: A Biography.* Austin: Texas Monthly Press, 1987.

Harrington, Michael. *The Other America: Poverty in the United States.* New York: Macmillan, 1962.

Harris, Seymour. *Academic Activist, 1920–1970.* San Diego, Calif.: S. E. Harris, 1972.

——. *Economics of Mobilization and Inflation.* New York: Norton, 1951.

——. *National Debt and the New Economics.* New York: McGraw-Hill, 1947.

——. "New Economics Versus New Deal." *Challenge,* September–October 1966.

Harris, Seymour, ed. *Postwar Economic Problems.* New York: McGraw-Hill, 1943.

——. *Saving American Capitalism: A Liberal Economic Program.* New York: Knopf, 1948.

Harrison, Cynthia E. "Stalemate: Federal Legislation for Women in the Truman Era." In Levantrosser, *Harry S. Truman.*

Hart, Albert G. and E. Cary Brown. *Financing Defense: Federal Tax and Expenditure Policies.* New York: Twentieth Century Fund, 1951.

Hart, Gary. *Right from the Start.* New York: Quadrangle, 1973.

Hartmann, Susan M. *Truman and the Eightieth Congress.* Columbia: University of Missouri Press, 1971.

Harwood, Richard, ed. *The Pursuit of the Presidency, 1980.* New York: Berkeley Books, 1980.

Haynes, Richard F. *The Awesome Power: Harry S. Truman as Commander in Chief.* Baton Rouge: Louisiana State University Press, 1973.

Heclo, Hugh. "Executive Budget Making." In Mills and Palmer, *Federal Budget Policy in the 1980s.*

Heller, Francis, H., ed. *The Truman White House: The Administration of the Presidency, 1945–1953.* Lawrence: Regents Press of Kansas, 1980.

Herring, George C. "The Strange 'Dissent' of Robert McNamara." Paper presented at Vietnam Symposium at Columbia University, New York City, November 16, 1990, and filed in the Vertical File of Papers, Theses, and Dissertations, Lyndon B. Johnson Library, Austin, Texas.

Hersh, Seymour M. *The Price of Power: Kissinger in the White House.* New York: Summit, 1983.

Herzstein, Robert. *Roosevelt and Hitler: Prelude to War.* New York: Paragon, 1989.

Hewlett, Richard and Jack Holl. *Atoms for Peace and War, 1953–1961.* Berkeley: University of California Press, 1989.

Higgs, Robert. *Crisis and Leviathan: Critical Episodes in the Growth of American Government.* New York: Oxford University Press, 1987.

Hill, Samuel and Dennis Owen. *The New Religious Political Right in America.* Nashville, Tenn.: Abingdon, 1982.

Hill, William. "The Business Community and National Defense: Corporate Leaders and the Military." Ph.D. diss., Stanford University, 1980.

Hilsman, Roger, *George Bush Versus Saddam Hussein.* Novota, Calif.: Lyford Books, 1992.

Hinchey, Mary Hedge. "The Frustration of the New Deal Revival: 1944–1946." Ph.D. diss., University of Missouri, Columbia, 1965.

Hodgson, Godfrey. *America in Our Time.* Garden City, N.Y.: Doubleday, 1976.

———. *The Colonel: The Life and Wars of Henry Stimson.* New York: Knopf, 1990.

Hoff-Wilson, Joan. *Nixon Reconsidered.* New York: Basic, 1994.

Hogan, Michael. *A Cross of Iron: Harry S. Truman and the Origins of the National Security State, 1945–1954.* New York: Cambridge University Press, 1998.

Holbrooke, Richard. *To End a War.* New York: Modern Library, 1999.

Holland, Lauren and Robert Hoover. *The MX Decision.* Boulder, Colo.: Westview, 1985.

Holmans, A. E. *U.S. Fiscal Policy, 1945–1949.* New York: Oxford University Press, 1961.

Hooks, Gregory. *Forging the Military-Industrial Complex: World War II's Battle of the Potomac.* Urbana: University of Illinois Press, 1991.

Huntington, Samuel. *The Common Defense: Strategic Programs in National Politics.* New York: Columbia University Press, 1961.

Huzar, Elias. *The Purse and the Sword: Control of the Army by Congress Through Military Appropriations, 1933–1950.* New York: Greenwood, 1971.

Hyman, Sidney, ed. *Beckoning Frontiers: Public and Personal Recollections.* New York: Knopf, 1951.

Janeway, Eliot. *Struggle for Survival: A Chronicle of Economic Mobilization.* New Haven: Yale University Press, 1951.

Janowitz, Morris. *Social Control of the Welfare State.* New York: Elsevier, 1976.

Jansson, Bruce. "The History and Politics of Selected Children's Programs and Related Legislation in the Context of Four Models of Political Behavior." Ph.D. diss., University of Chicago, 1975.

———. *The Reluctant Welfare State: A History of American Social Welfare Policies.* Pacific Grove, Calif.: Brooks/Cole, 1997.

Jeffries, John. "The 'New' New Deal: FDR and American Liberalism, 1937–1945." *Political Science Quarterly* 105 (winter 1990–1991): 387–418.

Jervis, Robert. *The Illogic of American Nuclear Strategy.* Ithaca: Cornell University Press, 1984.

Johnson, Haynes. *In the Absence of Power.* New York: Viking, 1980.

———. *Sleepwalking Through History: America in the Reagan Years*. New York: Norton, 1991.

Johnson, Lyndon Baynes. *The Public Papers of the Presidents of the United States: Lyndon B. Johnson, 1963–1969*. Washington, D.C.: U.S. Government Printing Office, 1965–1970.

Kahn, Herman. *On Thermonuclear War*. Princeton: Princeton University Press, 1960.

Kaiser, David. *American Tragedy: Kennedy, Johnson, and the Origins of the Vietnam War*. Cambridge, Mass.: Harvard University Press, 2000.

Kaldor, Mary. *The Baroque Arsenal*. New York: Hill and Wang, 1981.

Kane, Edward. *The S&L Insurance Mess: How Did It Happen?* Washington, D.C.: Urban Institute Press, 1989.

Kaplan, Fred M. *Dubious Specter: A Skeptical Look at the Soviet Nuclear Threat*. Washington, D.C.: Institute for Policy Studies, 1980.

———. *Wizards of Armageddon*. New York: Simon and Schuster, 1983.

Karsten, Peter. "Armed Progressives: The Military Reorganizes for the American Century." In Peter Karsten, ed., *The Military in America*. New York: Free Press, 1980.

Kaufmann, William. *Assessing the Base Force: How Much Is Too Much?* Washington, D.C.: Brookings Institution, 1992.

———. *Decisions for Defense: Prospects for a New Order*. Washington, D.C.: Brookings Institution, 1991.

———. *Glasnost, Perestroika, and U.S. Defense Spending*. Washington, D.C.: Brookings Institution, 1990.

———. *The McNamara Strategy*. New York: Harper and Row, 1964.

———. *Planning Conventional Forces, 1950–1960*. Washington, D.C.: Brookings Institution, 1982.

Kaufmann, William and Lawrence Korb. *The 1990 Defense Budget*. Washington, D.C.: Brookings Institution, 1989.

Kearns, Doris. *Lyndon Johnson and the American Dream*. New York: Harper and Row, 1976.

Kennan, George. *Memoirs, 1925–1950*. Boston: Little, Brown, 1967.

Kennedy, Paul. *The Rise and Fall of Great Powers: Economic Change and Military Conflict from 1500 to 2000*. New York: Random House, 1987.

Kettl, Donald F. "The Economic Education of Lyndon Johnson: Guns, Butter, and Taxes." In Devine, *The Johnson Years*, vol 2.

Keyserling, Leon H. "Harry S. Truman: The Man and the President." In Levantrosser, *Harry S. Truman*.

———. "Leon H. Keyserling." In Heller, *The Truman White House*.

———. "Old Economics on the New Frontier." *Progressive*, September 1961, pp. 21–24.

———. "Planning for a $300 Billion Economy." *New York Times Magazine*, June 18, 1950, pp. 9, 24–27.

Killian, Linda. *The Freshmen: What Happened to the Republican Revolution?* Boulder, Colo.: Westview, 1998.

Kimmel, Lewis. *Federal Budget and Fiscal Policy, 1789–1958.* Washington, D.C.: Brookings Institution, 1959.

Kinnard, Douglas. *Secretary of Defense.* Lexington: University of Kentucky Press, 1980.

Kirkendall, Richard, ed. *The Truman Period as a Research Field: A Reappraisal, 1972.* Columbia: University of Missouri Press, 1974.

Kissinger, Henry. *White House Years.* Boston: Little, Brown, 1979.

Kofsky, Frank. *Harry S. Truman and the War Scare of 1948.* New York: St. Martin's, 1993.

Kolb, Charles. *White House Daze: The Unmaking of Domestic Policy in the Bush Years.* New York: Free Press, 1994.

Kolodziej, Edward A. *Uncommon Defense and Congress, 1945–1953.* Columbus: Ohio State University Press, 1966.

Korb, Lawrence J. *The Fall and Rise of the Pentagon: American Defense Policies in the 1970s.* Westport, Conn.: Greenwood, 1979.

——. "Our Overstuffed Armed Forces." *Foreign Affairs* 74 (November–December 1995): 22–35.

Kotz, Nick. *Wild Blue Yonder.* New York: Pantheon, 1988.

Krieg, Joann, ed. *Dwight D. Eisenhower.* New York: Greenwood, 1987.

Kutler, Stanley L. *The Wars of Watergate: The Last Crisis of Richard Nixon.* New York: Knopf, 1990.

Kuttner, Robert. *Everything for Sale.* New York: Knopf, 1998.

——. *Revolt of the Haves: Tax Rebellions and Hard Times.* New York: Simon and Schuster, 1980.

Lacey, Michael J. "Introduction and Summary: The Truman Era in Retrospect." In Lacey, *The Truman Presidency.*

Lacey, Michael J., ed. *The Truman Presidency.* Cambridge: Cambridge University Press, 1989.

Ladd, Everett Carroll. "The Reagan Phenomenon and Public Attitudes Toward Government." In Salamon and Lund, *The Reagan Presidency.*

Larrabee, Eric. *Commander in Chief.* New York: Harper and Row, 1971.

Lash, Joseph P. *Eleanor and Franklin.* New York: Norton, 1971.

Leff, Mark. *The Limits of Symbolic Reform: The New Deal and Taxation, 1933–1939.* Cambridge: Cambridge University Press, 1984.

——. "The Politics of Sacrifice on the American Home Front in World War II." *Journal of American History* 77 (March 1991): 1296–1318.

Leffler, Melvyn. *A Preponderance of Power: National Security, the Truman Administration, and the Cold War.* Palo Alto: Stanford University Press, 1992.

Lemann, Nicholas. *The Promised Land: The Great Black Migration and How It Changed America.* New York: Knopf, 1991.

Leuchtenberg, William. *A Troubled Feast.* Boston: Little, Brown, 1979.

——. *Franklin D. Roosevelt and the New Deal.* New York: Harper and Row, 1963.

——. *In the Shadow of Franklin Roosevelt: From Harry Truman to Ronald Reagan.* Ithaca: Cornell University Press, 1983.

Levantrosser, William, ed. *Harry S. Truman: The Man from Independence.* New York: Greenwood, 1986.

Levitan, Sar A. and Clifford M. Johnson. *Beyond the Safety Net: Reviving the Promise of Opportunity in America.* Cambridge, Mass.: Ballinger, 1984.

Lewis, Charles. *The Buying of the President 2000.* New York: Avon, 2000.

Lichtenstein, Nelson. "From Cooperation to Collective Bargaining: Organized Labor and the Eclipse of Social Democracy in the Postwar Era." In Fraser and Gerstle, *Rise and Fall of the New Deal Order.*

——. "Labor in the Truman Era: Origins of the 'Private Welfare State.'" In Lacey, *The Truman Presidency.*

Lieberman, Carl. "The Eisenhower Administration and Intergovernmental Relations." In Krieg, *Dwight D. Eisenhower.*

Lo, Clarence Yin-Hsieh. "The Truman Administration's Military Budget." Ph.D. diss., University of California, Berkeley, 1978.

Lowi, Theodore. "Ronald Reagan—Revolutionary?" In Salamon and Lund, *The Reagan Presidency.*

Lowitt, Richard and Maurine Beasley, eds. *One Third of a Nation.* Urbana: University of Illinois Press, 1981.

Lutz, Harley. *Committee on Postwar Tax Policy.* New York: 1945.

MacNeil, Neil. *Dirksen: Portrait of a Public Man.* New York: World, 1970.

McBundy, George. *Danger and Survival: Choices About the Bomb in the First Fifty Years.* New York: Random House, 1988.

McClellan, David S. "Commentary." In Kirkendall, *Truman Presidency as a Research Field.*

McCullough, David. *Truman.* New York: Simon and Schuster, 1992.

McGovern, George. *Grassroots: Autobiography of George McGovern.* New York: Random House, 1976.

McJimsey, George. *Harry Hopkins: Ally of the Poor and Defender of Democracy.* Cambridge, Mass.: Harvard University Press, 1987.

McMurrer, Daniel and Isabel Sawhill. *Getting Ahead: Economic and Social Mobility in America.* Washington, D.C.: Urban Institute, 1998.

McNamara, Robert. *Blundering into Disaster.* New York: Pantheon, 1986.

——. *Essence of Security: Reflections in Office.* London: Hodder and Stoughton, 1968.

McNeil, Neil. *Dirksen: Portrait of a Public Man.* New York: World Publishing, 1970.

Makhijani, Arjun, Stephen Schwartz, and William Weida. "Nuclear Waste Management and Environmental Remediation." In Schwartz, *Atomic Audit.*

Mallin, Maurice A. *Tanks, Fighters, and Ships: U.S. Conventional Force Planning Since World War II.* Washington, D.C.: Brassey's, 1990.

Manley, John F. *The Politics of Finance: the House Committee on Ways and Means.* Boston: Little, Brown, 1970.

Manning, Robert. *Postwar Tax Plans for the Federal Government: A Description of the Various Possibilities.* Washington, D.C.: U.S. Government Printing Office, 1945.

Maraniss, David. *First in His Class: A Biography of Bill Clinton.* New York: Simon and Schuster, 1995.

Marcus, Isabel. *Dollars for Reform.* Lexington, Mass.: Lexington Books, 1981.

Markusen, Ann. "How We Lost the Peace Dividend." *American Prospect,* no. 13 (July–August 1997): 86–95.

Marmor, Theodore. *The Politics of Medicare.* Chicago: Aldine, 1975.

Martel, Gordon, ed. *The Origins of the Second World War Reconsidered: The A.J.P. Taylor Debate After Twenty-five Years.* Boston: Allen and Unwin, 1986.

Matusow, Allen J. *The Unraveling of America: A History of Liberalism in the 1960s.* New York: Harper and Row, 1984.

Mayer, Jane and Doyle McManus. *Landslide: The Unmaking of the President, 1984–1988.* Boston: Houghton Mifflin, 1988.

Mayer, Michael. "Eisenhower and Race." In Krieg, *Dwight D. Eisenhower.*

Mayers, David. *George Kennan and the Dilemmas of U.S. Foreign Policy.* New York: Oxford University Press, 1988.

Meeropol, Michael. *Surrender: How the Clinton Administration Completed the Reagan Revolution.* Ann Arbor: University of Michigan Press, 1998.

Meese, Edwin. *With Reagan: The Inside Story.* Washington, D.C.: Regnery Gateway, 1992.

Melanson, Richard A. "The Foundations of Eisenhower's Foreign Policy." In Melanson and Mayers, *Reevaluating Eisenhower's American Foreign Policy.*

Melanson, Richard A. and David Mayers, eds. *Reevaluating Eisenhower's American Foreign Policy.* Chicago: University of Illinois Press, 1987.

Melman, Seymour. *Pentagon Capitalism: The Political Economy of War.* New York: McGraw-Hill, 1970.

Meranto, Philip. *The Politics of Federal Aid to Education in 1965.* Syracuse: Syracuse University Press, 1967.

Meyer, Jack A. "Budget Cuts in the Reagan Administration: A Question of Fairness." In Bawden, *The Social Contract Revisited.*

Miller, Roger and Raburn Williams. *The New Economics of Richard Nixon: Freezes, Floats, and Fiscal Policy.* New York: Harper Magazine Press, 1972.

Millis, Walter. *Arms and the State: Civil-Military Elements in National Policy.* New York: Twentieth Century Fund, 1958.

Millis, Walter, ed. *Forrestal Diaries.* New York: Viking, 1951.

Mills, Gregory B. and John L. Palmer, eds. *Federal Budget Policy in the 1980s.* Washington, D.C.: Urban Institute, 1984.

Minarik, Joseph. "Tax Policy." In Mills and Palmer, *Federal Budget Policy in the 1980s.*

Molander, Earl A. "Historical Antecedents of Military-Industrial Criticism." In Cooling, *War, Business, and American Society.*

Moore, Stephen and Dean Stansel. "How Corporate Welfare Won: Clinton and Congress Retreat from Cutting Business Subsidies." *Policy Analysis,* no. 254 (May 15, 1996): 1–25.

Morgan, Iwan. *Eisenhower Versus the "Spenders": The Eisenhower Administration, the Democrats, and the Budget, 1953–1960.* New York: St. Martin's, 1990.

Morris, Dick. *Behind the Oval Office.* Los Angeles: Renaissance Books, 1999.

Mosher, Frederic and Poland Orwille. *The Costs of American Governments: Facts, Trends, and Myths.* New York: Dodd, Mead, 1964.

Moynihan, Daniel. *Maximum Feasible Misunderstanding: Community Action in the War on Poverty.* New York: Free Press, 1969.

——. *Miles to Go: A Personal History of Social Policy.* Cambridge, Mass.: Harvard University Press, 1996.

——. *The Politics of a Guaranteed Income.* New York: Random House, 1973.

Muller, Herbert J. *Adlai Stevenson: A Study in Values.* New York: Harper and Row, 1967.

Murray, Charles. *Losing Ground: American Social Policy, 1950–1980.* New York: Basic, 1981.

Musgrave, Richard A. "Tableau Fiscale." In Eden, *Retrospectives on Public Finance.*

Nash, George H. *The Conservative Intellectual Movement in the America Since 1945.* New York: Basic, 1976.

Nathan, Richard P. *The Plot That Failed: Nixon and the Administrative Presidency.* New York: Wiley, 1975.

National Urban Coalition. *Counterbudget.* Washington, D.C.: May 1971.

Nelson, Donald. *Arsenal of Democracy: The Story of American War Production.* New York: Harcourt Brace, 1946.

Neustadt, Richard E. "Congress and the Fair Deal: A Legislative Balance Sheet." In Hamby, *Harry S. Truman and the Fair Deal.*

Newhouse, John. *War and Peace in the Nuclear Age.* New York: Knopf, 1989.

Nitze, Paul H. *From Hiroshima to Glasnost: At the Center of Decision, A Memoir.* New York: Grove Weidenfeld, 1989.

Nixon, Edgar, ed. *Franklin D. Roosevelt and Foreign Affairs.* Vol. 3. Cambridge, Mass.: Harvard University Press, 1969.

Nixon, Richard. *The Public Papers of the Presidents of the United States: Richard Nixon, 1969–1974.* Washington, D.C.: U.S. Government Printing Office, 1971–1975.

Nordlinger, Eric. *Isolationism Reconfigured*. Princeton: Princeton University Press, 1995.

Norris, Robert, Steven Kosiak, and Stephen Schwartz. "Deploying the Bomb." In Schwartz, *Atomic Audit*.

Oberdorfer, Don. *The Turn: From the Cold War to a New Era*. New York: Poseidon, 1991.

Office of Management and Budget. *Budget of the U.S. Government, FY 2000, A Citizens' Guide to the Federal Budget*. Washington, D.C.: U.S. Government Printing Office, 1999.

——. *Budget of the U.S. Government, FY 2000, Analytic Perspectives*. Washington, D.C.: U.S. Government Printing Office, 1999.

——. *Budget of the U.S. Government, FY 2000, Historical Tables*. Washington, D.C.: U.S. Government Printing Office, 1999.

O'Neill, Kevin. "Building the Bomb." In Schwartz, *Atomic Audit*.

O'Neill, Thomas. *Man of the House: The Life and Political Memoirs of Speaker Tip O'Neill*. New York: Random House, 1987.

O'Neill, William. *A Democracy at War: America's Fight at Home and Abroad in World War II*. New York: Free Press, 1993.

Ott, David J. et al. *Nixon, McGovern, and the Federal Budget*. Washington, D.C.: American Enterprise Institute, 1972.

Palmer, John L. and Isabel V. Sawhill, eds. *The Legacy of Reaganomics: Prospects for Long-Term Growth*. Washington, D.C.: Urban Institute Press, 1984.

Parish, Thomas. *Roosevelt and Marshall*. New York: Morrow, 1989.

Parmet, Herbert. *George Bush*. New York: Simon and Schuster, 1997.

Pasztor, Andy. *When the Pentagon Was for Sale*. New York: Scribner, 1995.

Paterson, Thomas. *Kennedy's American Foreign Policy, 1961–1963*. New York: Oxford University Press, 1989.

——. *Meeting the Communist Threat: America's Cold War History*. New York: Oxford University Press, 1988.

——. *On Every Front: The Making of the Cold War*. New York: Norton, 1979.

Patterson, James T. *America's Struggle Against Poverty*. Cambridge, Mass.: Harvard University Press, 1981.

——. *Congressional Conservatism and the New Deal*. Lexington: University of Kentucky Press, 1967.

——. *Mr. Republican: A Biography of Robert A. Taft*. Boston: Houghton Mifflin, 1972.

Paul, Randolph E. *Taxation in the United States*. Boston: Little, Brown, 1954.

Pepper, Claude. *Pepper: Eyewitness to a Century*. New York: Harcourt Brace Jovanovich, 1987.

Perkins, Frances. *The Roosevelt I Knew*. New York: Viking, 1946.

Peterson, Paul E. "The New Politics of Deficits." In Chubb and Peterson, *New Direction in American Politics*.

———. "The Rise and Fall of Special Interest Politics." *Political Science Quarterly* 105, no. 4 (winter 1990–91): 539–56.

Phillips, Kevin. *The Emerging Republican Majority.* New Rochelle, N.Y.: Arlington House, 1969.

———. *Post-Conservative America: People, Politics, and Ideology in a Time of Crisis.* New York: Vintage, 1983.

Pickens, Donald K. "Truman's Council of Economic Advisers and the Legacy of New Deal Liberalism." In Levantrosser, *Harry S. Truman.*

Pike, John, Bruce Blair, and Stephen Schwartz. "Defending Against the Bomb." In Schwartz, *Atomic Audit.* :

Poen, Monte M. *Harry S. Truman Versus the Medical Lobby.* Columbia: University of Missouri Press, 1979.

———. "Rose, File It: What Harry Truman's Unmailed Letters Tell Us About the Thirty-Third President." In Levantrosser, *Harry S. Truman.*

Pollard, Robert. *Economic Security and the Origins of the Cold War.* New York: Columbia University Press, 1985.

———. "The National Security State Reconsidered: Truman and Economic Containment, 1945–1950." In Lacey, *The Truman Presidency.*

Poole, Walter J. *The Joint Chiefs of Staff and National Policy, 1950–1952.* Vol. 4 of *History of the Joint Chiefs of Staff.* Wilmington, Del.: Michael Glazier, 1980.

Porter, David. *The Seventy-sixth Congress and World War II.* Columbia: University of Missouri Press, 1979.

Powaski, Ronald. *The Cold War: The United States and the Soviet Union, 1917–1991.* New York: Oxford University Press, 1998.

Price, Ray. *With Nixon.* New York: Viking, 1977.

Quill, J. Michael. *Lyndon Johnson and the Southern Military Tradition.* Washington, D.C.: University Press of America, 1977.

Rabinowitch, Eugene, ed. *Minutes to Midnight: The International Control of Atomic Energy.* Chicago: Bulletin of the Atomic Scientists, 1950.

Raj, Christopher S. *The American Military in Europe: Controversy over NATO Burden Sharing.* New Delhi: ABC Publishing, 1983.

Raymond, Jack. *Power at the Pentagon.* New York: Harper and Row, 1964.

Reagan, Ronald. *An American Life.* New York: Simon and Schuster, 1990.

Reardon, Steven L. *History of the Office of the Secretary of Defense: The Formative Years, 1947–1950.* Washington, D.C.: U.S. Government Printing Office, 1984.

Reese, Thomas J. *The Politics of Taxation.* Westport, Conn.: Quorum Books, 1980.

Reeves, Richard. *President Kennedy: Profile of Power.* New York: Simon and Schuster, 1994.

Reeves, Thomas. *A Question of Character: A Life of John F. Kennedy.* New York: Free Press, 1991.

Reich, Robert. *Locked in the Cabinet.* New York: Vintage, 1998.

———. *The Work of Nations: Preparing Ourselves for Twenty-first-Century Capitalism.* New York: Knopf, 1991.

Reichard, Gary. *Reaffirmation of Republicanism: Eisenhower and the Eighty-third Congress.* Knoxville: University of Tennessee Press, 1975.

Reichley, A. James. *Conservatives in an Age of Change: The Nixon and Ford Presidencies.* Washington, D.C: Brookings Institution, 1981.

Reiss, Edward. *The Strategic Defense Initiative.* Cambridge: Cambridge University Press, 1992.

Roberts, Paul Craig. *The Supply-Side Revolution: An Insider's Account of Policy Making in Washington.* Cambridge, Mass.: Harvard University Press, 1984.

Rollins, Ed. *Bare Knuckles and Back Rooms.* New York: Broadway Books, 1996.

Roosevelt, Franklin Delano. *The Public Papers and Addresses of Franklin D. Roosevelt, 1928–1944/45,* comp. Samuel Rosenman. Vols. 1–13. New York: Random House, 1938-[ca. 1950].

Rosenberg, David Alan. "Origins of Overkill: Nuclear Weapons and American Strategy." In Graebner, *National Security.*

———. "Toward Armageddon: The Foundation of U.S. Nuclear Strategy." Ph.D. diss., University of Chicago, 1983.

Rosenman, Samuel. *Working with Roosevelt.* New York: Harper, 1952.

Ross, Davis. *Preparing for Ulysses: Politics and Veterans During World War II.* New York: Columbia University Press, 1969.

Rostow, W. W. *Europe After Stalin: Eisenhower's Three Decisions of March 11, 1953.* Austin: University of Texas Press, 1982.

Ruml, Beardsley. *The Pay-as-You-Go Income Tax Plan.* New York: Charles Young, 1942.

Ruml, Beardsley and H. Christian Sonne. *Fiscal and Monetary Policy.* Washington, D.C.: National Planning Association, 1944.

Safire, William. *Before the Fall: the Inside View of the Pre-Watergate White House.* New York: Doubleday, 1975.

Salamon, Lester M. and Michael S. Lund. "Governance in the Reagan Era: An Overview." In Salamon and Lund, *The Reagan Presidency.*

Salamon, Lester M. and Michael S. Lund, eds. *The Reagan Presidency and the Governing of America.* Washington, D.C.; Urban Institute, 1985.

Salmond, John. *The Civilian Conservation Corps, 1933–1942.* Durham: Duke University Press, 1967.

———. *A Southern Rebel: The Life and Times of Aubrey Willis Williams.* Chapel Hill: University of North Carolina Press, 1983.

Saulnier, Raymond J. "The Philosophy Underlying Eisenhower's Economic Policies." In Krieg, *Dwight D. Eisenhower.*

Savage, James D. *Balanced Budgets and American Politics.* Ithaca: Cornell University Press, 1988.

Schapsmeir, Edward L. and Frederick H. Schapsmeir. "Henry A. Wallace: The New Deal Philosopher." *Historian* 32, no. 2 (February 1970): 177–90.

Schilling, Warner R. "The Politics of National Defense: FY 1950." In Schilling, Hammond, and Snyder, *Strategy, Politics, and Defense Budgets.*

Schilling, Warner R., Paul Y. Hammond, and Glenn H. Snyder, eds. *Strategy, Politics, and Defense Budgets.* New York: Columbia University Press, 1962.

Schultze, Charles, Edward Fried, Alice Rivlin, and Nancy Teeter. *Setting National Priorities: The 1973 Budget.* Washington, D.C.: Brookings Institution, 1972.

Schulzinger, Robert D. *The Wise Men of Foreign Affairs: The History of the Council on Foreign Relations.* New York: Columbia University Press, 1984.

Schwartz, Stephen, ed. *Atomic Audit: The Costs and Consequences of U.S. Nuclear Weapons Since 1940.* Washington, D.C.: Brookings Institution, 1998.

Shapley, Deborah. *Promise and Power: The Life and Times of Robert McNamara.* Boston: Little, Brown, 1993.

Sherraden, Michael. *Assets and the Poor.* Armonk, N.Y.: Sharpe, 1991.

Sherry, Michael. *Preparing for the Next War: American Plans for the Next War.* New Haven: Yale University Press, 1977.

Sherwood, Robert E. *Roosevelt and Hopkins: An Intimate History.* New York: Harper, 1948.

Shogan, Robert. *The Riddle of Power: Presidential Leadership from Truman to Bush.* New York: Dutton, 1991.

Shoup, Carl. *Facing the Tax Problem.* New York: Twentieth Century Fund, 1937.

Silk, Leonard. *Nixonomics: How the Dismal Science of Free Enterprise Became the Black Art of Controls.* New York: Praeger, 1972.

Simons, Henry C. *Federal Tax Reform.* Chicago: University of Chicago, 1950.

Simpson, B. Mitchell. *Admiral Harold R. Stark: Architect of Victory.* Columbia: University of South Carolina Press, 1989.

Sitkoff, Harvey. "Years of the Locust: Interpretations of the Truman Presidency." In Kirkendall, *Truman Presidency as a Research Field.*

Sloan, John. "The Management and Decision-Making Style of President Eisenhower." *Presidential Studies Quarterly* 20, No. 2 (spring 1990): 295–313.

Small, Melvin. *Johnson, Nixon, and the Doves.* New Brunswick: Rutgers University Press, 1988.

Smeeding, Timothy. "Is the Safety Net Still Intact?" In Bawden, *The Social Contract Revisited.*

Smith, Gilbert. *The Limits of Reform: Politics and Federal Aid to Education, 1937–1950* .New York: Garland, 1982.

Smith, Hedrick. *Rethinking America: Innovative Strategies and Partnerships in Business and Education.* New York: Random House, 1995.

Smith, Jean Edward. *George Bush's War.* New York: Holt, 1992.

Snyder, Glenn. "The 'New Look' of 1953." In Schiller, Hammond, and Snyder, *Strategy, Politics, and the Defense Budget.*

Snyder, Jack. *Myths of Empire: Domestic Politics and International Ambition.* Ithaca: Cornell University Press, 1991.

Starr, Paul. *The Social Transformation of American Medicine.* New York: Basic, 1984.

Steel, Ronald. *Walter Lippmann and the American Century.* Boston: Little, Brown, 1980.

Stein, Herbert. *Governing the $5 Trillion Economy.* New York: Oxford University Press, 1989.

——. "The Organization of Economic Policy Making." In Thompson, *The Nixon Presidency.*

——. *Presidential Economics: The Making of Economic Policy from Roosevelt to Reagan.* New York: Touchstone, 1984.

Steiner, Gilbert. *The Children's Cause.* Washington, D.C.: Brookings Institution, 1976.

——. *State of Welfare.* Washington, D.C.: Brookings Institution, 1971.

Steinfels, Peter. *The Neoconservatives: The Men Who Are Changing America's Politics.* New York: Simon and Schuster, 1979.

Stephanopoulos, George. *All Too Human.* Boston: Little, Brown, 1999.

Steuerle, C. Eugene and Susan Wiener. *Spending the Peace Dividend: Lessons from History.* Washington, D.C.: Urban Institute, 1990.

Stevens, Robert Warren. *Vain Hopes, Grim Realities: The Economic Consequences of the Vietnam War.* New York: New Viewpoints, 1976.

Stevens, Rosemary. *Welfare Medicine in America: The Case of Medicaid.* New York: Free Press, 1974.

Stiglitz, Joseph. *Economics.* New York: Norton, 1993.

Stine, Harry. *ICBM: The Making of the Weapon That Changed the World.* New York: Orion, 1991.

Stockman, David. *The Triumph of Politics: Why the Reagan Revolution Failed.* New York: Harper and Row, 1986.

Stone, I. F. *The Haunted Fifties, 1953–1963.* Boston: Little, Brown, 1963.

——. *The War Years, 1939–1945.* Boston: Little, Brown, 1988.

Stromseth, Jane. *Origins of Flexible Response: NATO's Debate over Strategy in the 1960s.* New York: St. Martin's, 1988.

Stubbing, Richard. *The Defense Game: An Insider Explores the Astonishing Realities of America's Defense Establishment.* New York: Harper and Row, 1986.

Sundquist, James. *Politics and Policy: The Eisenhower, Kennedy, and Johnson Years.* Washington, D.C.: Brookings Institution, 1968.

Sunseri, Alvin R. "The Military-Industrial Complex in Iowa." In Cooling, *War, Business, and American Society.*

Teles, Steven. *Whose Welfare? Aid to Families with Dependent Children and Elite Politics*. Lawrence: University of Kansas Press, 1996.

Thirsk, Wayne. "Intellectual Foundations of the VAT in North America and Japan." In Eden, *Retrospectives on Public Finance*.

Thompson, Kenneth, ed. *The Nixon Presidency*. Washington, D.C.: University Press of America, 1987.

———. "The Strengths and Weaknessess of Eisenhower's Leadership." In Melanson and Mayers, *Reevaluating Eisenhower's American Foreign Policy*.

Timberg, Robert. *The Nightingale's Song*. New York: Simon and Schuster, 1995.

Trewhitt, Henry. *McNamara*. New York: Harper and Row, 1971.

Truman, Harry S. *Memoirs*. 2 Vols. New York: Doubleday, 1955.

———. *Mr. Citizen*. New York: Popular Library, 1953.

———. *The Public Papers of the Presidents of the United States: Harry S. Truman, 1945–1952/53*. 8 vols. Washington, D.C.: U.S. Government Printing Office, 1961–1966.

Tull, Charles J. "The State of Art in Truman Research." In Levantrosser, *Harry S. Truman*.

U.S. Bureau of the Budget. *Budgets of the U.S. Government, FYs 1933 Through 1939*. Ann Arbor, Mich.: University Microfilms, 1968.

U.S. Congress. Joint Committee on Reduction of Nonessential Federal Expenditures. *Hearings*, 77th Cong., 1st sess. 1941,

U.S. Congress. Joint Committee on Taxation. *Estimates of Federal Tax Expenditures for FYs 1988 Through 1992*. 103d Cong., 1st sess., 1993.

———. Joint Economic Committee. *Hearings*. 92d Cong., 1st sess. Part 2, August 9, 10, 11, 1971.

———. Joint Economic Committee. *Hearings: Economic Analysis and the Efficiency of Government*. 91st Cong., 2d sess., February 9, 1970.

———. Joint Economic Committee. *Hearings: National Priorities, the Next Five Years*, 92 Cong., 2d sess., May 30 and 31 and June 1, 16, and 27, 1972.

———. Joint Economic Committee. Subcommittee on Economy in Government. *The Military Budget and National Economic Priorities*. 91st Cong., 1st sess., December 23, 1969.

———. Joint Economic Committee. Subcommittee on Economy in Government. *Hearings on the Military Budget and National Economic Priorities*. 91st Cong., 1st sess., June 4–13, 17, 23–24, 1969.

———. Joint Economic Committee. Subcommittee on Priorities and Economy in Government. *Hearings: Five-Year Budget Projections*. 94th Cong., 1st sess., April 3, 4, 1975.

———. Joint Economic Committee. Subcommittee on Priorities and Economy in Government. *Hearings: National Priorities—The Next Five Years*. 92d Cong., 2d sess., May 30, 31, and June 1, 16, 27, 1972.

——. Joint Economic Committee. Subcommittee on Priorities and Economy. *Hearings: National Priorities and the Budgetary Process*. 93d Cong., 1st sess., April 25–27, 1973.

U.S. Congressional Budget Office. *Reducing the Deficit: Spending and Revenue Options, a Report to the Senate and House Committees on the Budget*. Washington, D.C.: U.S. Government Printing Office, March 1997.

U.S. Department of Defense. *Achieving an Innovative Support Structure for Twenty-first-Century Military Superiority: Report of the Defense Science Board 1996 Summer Study*. Washington, D.C.: U.S. Government Printing Office, November 1996.

Vandegrift, A. A. "Vicious Infighting." In Peter Karsten, ed., *The Military in America*. New York: Free Press, 1980.

Vatter, Harold G. *The U.S. Economy in the 1950s: An Economic History*. Chicago: University of Chicago Press, 1963.

——. *The United States Economy in World War II*. New York: Columbia University Press, 1985.

Vistica, Gregory L. *Fall from Glory: The Men Who Sank the U.S. Navy*. New York: Simon and Schuster, 1995.

Waltman, Jerold L. *Political Origins of the U.S. Income Tax*. Jackson: University Press of Mississippi, 1985.

Watson, Robert J. *History of the Joint Chiefs of Staff: The Joint Chiefs of Staff National Policy, 1953–1954*. Washington, D.C.: U.S. Government Printing Office, 1986.

Weaver, R. Kent. "Controlling Entitlements." In Chubb and Peterson, *New Direction in American Politics*.

Weida, William J. and Frank L. Gertcher. *The Political Economy of National Defense*. Boulder, Colo.: Westview, 1987.

Weigley, Russell F. *History of the U.S. Army*. New York: Macmillan, 1967.

Weinberger, Caspar. *The Next War*. Washington, D.C.: Regnery, 1996.

Weiner, Tim. *Blank Check: The Pentagon's Black Budget*. New York: Warner, 1990.

Westinghouse Learning Corp. and Ohio University. *The Impact of Head Start: An Evaluation of the Effects of Head Start on Children's Cognitive and Affective Development*. N.p., 1969.

White, Theodore H. *America in Search of Itself: The Making of a President, 1956–1980*. New York: Harper and Row, 1982.

Wicker, Tom. *JFK and LBJ: The Influence of Personality upon Politics*. New York: Morrow, 1968.

——. *One of Us: Richard Nixon and the American Dream*. New York: Random House, 1991.

Wildavsky, Aaron. *A History of Taxation and Expenditure in the Western World*. New York: Simon and Schuster, 1986.

———. *The New Politics of the Budgetary Process*. Glenview, Ill.: Scott, Foresman, 1988.

Williams, Phil. *The Senate and the U.S. Troops in Europe*. New York: St. Martin's, 1985.

Wills, Garry. *Nixon Agonistes: The Crisis of the Self-Made Man*. Boston: Houghton Mifflin, 1970.

Windsor, Duane. "Eisenhower's New Look Reexamined: The View of Three Decades." In Krieg, *Dwight D. Eisenhower.*

Witte, Edwin E. "Postwar Social Security." In Harris, *Postwar Economic Problems.*

Witte, John F. *The Politics and Development of the Federal Income Tax*. Madison: University of Wisconsin Press, 1985.

Wolfskill, George. *The Revolt of the Conservatives: A History of the American Liberty League, 1934–1940*. Boston: Houghton, Mifflin, 1962.

Wolfskill, George and John Hudson. *All but the People: Franklin Roosevelt and his Critics, 1933–1939*. London: Macmillan, 1969.

Wolman, Harold and Fred Teitelbaum. "Interest Groups and the Reagan Presidency." In Salamon and Lund, *The Reagan Presidency.*

Woods, Patricia D. *The Defense Budget Process in the Washington Community*. Washington, D.C.: Woods Institute, 1985.

Woods, Randall. *J. William Fulbright, Vietnam, and the Search for a Cold War Foreign Policy*. London: Cambridge University Press, 1998.

Woodward, Bob. *The Agenda: Inside the Clinton White House*. New York: Simon and Schuster, 1994.

———. *The Commander*. New York: Simon and Schuster, 1991.

Yarmolinsky, Adam. *The Military Establishment: Its Impacts on American Society*. New York: Harper and Row, 1971.

Young, Roland. *Congressional Politics in the Second World War*. New York: Columbia University Press, 1956.

Zhang, Xiaoming. "Communist Powers Divided: China, the Soviet Union, and the Vietnam War." In Gardner and Gittinger, *Vietnam at the Center.*

Zieger, Robert. *John L. Lewis, Labor Leader*. Boston: Twayne, 1988.

Zucchino, David. *Myth of the Welfare Queen* (New York: Scribner, 1997), 65.

Zumwalt, Elmo. *On Watch: A Memoir*. New York: Quadrangle, 1976.

INDEX

Bush's refusal of economic assistance to, 272–73; decision not to participate in development of Marshall Plan, 94; demonization of, 96–97, 105; disintegration of (1991), 285; fear of U.S. first strike from Reagan, 256; Gorbachev racing against time (1988), 263–66; invasion of Czechoslovakia (1968), 169; involvement in Afghanistan, 222, 223, 245, 264; launch of Sputnik (1957), 127; Nixon's detente with, 180; no evidence on increased spending in response to Reagan buildup, 245; as paper tiger (Part I), 117–20; as paper tiger (Part II), 166–71; politicians' continual magnification of threat to U.S. interests, 384; powerlessness over Ho Chi Minh, 184; primitive economy, 115; questionable naval force, 224; ripe for upheaval and dissolution in 1980s, 246–47; seeing themselves as nuclear underdog, 169; suffering successive invasions from Europe, 361; throwing in the towel., 263–68; unlikelihood of first strike against U.S., 356; unlikelihood of invasion of Europe, 118–19, 221, 356, 360–62; Warsaw Pact, 168, 264, 265; see also Cold war
Space program, 160
Sperling, Gene, 305
Spinney, Frank, 328
Stagflation, 181
Stalin, Josef: hope for rise of communism in Europe, 93; legitimate interests and grievances, 72; need for European buffer against invasion, 72–73; as pragmatist, 73; view of, as reincarnation of Hitler,

71–73, 97; willingness to test waters over Berlin, 98
Starobin, Paul, 341
START talks, 272, 289, 292, 329–30
Star Wars, 258, 330
Stennis, John, 159
Stephanopoulos, George, 296, 297
Steuerle, Eugene, 342
Stevenson, Adlai, 111, 133, 178
Stimson, Henry, 38
Stockman, David: astonishment at cumulative derivation of military budgets, 357; astonishment at Democrats' lack of opposition to domestic cuts, 235; complete discussion of pork barrel spending, 382; maneuvering for House vote on budget, 236; as powerless quarterback for massive cuts in social programs, 228–34; proposing large cuts in domestic budget, 225; on Reagan's deficit as "willful act of ignorance and grotesque irresponsibility," 243; as Reagan's director of OMB, 225; warning of deficits, 241
Strauss, Lewis, 127
Stubbing, Richard, 356, 364
Supplementary Security Income, actual and projected expenditures for, 352t
Supply-side theory, 218, 226, 385
Symington, Stuart, 101, 121, 127

Taber, John "Meataxe," 89, 90
Tables. See Charts
Taft, Robert A.: demanding cuts in Truman's military budget, 76; as Eisenhower's hope to mollify Old Guard Republicans, 121; fear of institutionalized national security state, 105; his initiatives on educa